W·I·S·H
The International
Handbook of
Women's Studies

W·I·S·H
The International Handbook of Women's Studies

Edited by

Loulou Brown (Freelance Editor and Writer)
Helen Collins (Consultant and Writer)
Pat Green (University of Wolverhampton)
Maggie Humm (University of East London)
Mel Landells (University of Plymouth)

HARVESTER
WHEATSHEAF

New York London Toronto Sydney Tokyo Singapore

First published 1993 by
Harvester Wheatsheaf
Campus 400, Maylands Avenue
Hemel Hempstead
Hertfordshire, HP2 7EZ
A division of
Simon & Schuster International Group

Typeset in 8½/9 pt Ehrhardt
by The Midlands Book Typesetting Company

Printed and bound in Great Britain by
Redwood Books, Trowbridge, Wiltshire

British Library Cataloguing in Publication Data

A catalogue record for this book is available from
the British Library

ISBN 0–7450–1413–5 (pbk)

1 2 3 4 5   97 96 95 94 93

Contents

Contents

Preface

WISH is the first reference guide to women's organisations and to women's studies courses, centres, training and resources world-wide. The information in this guide has not been published before on an international basis in this easy-to-use format.

Alphabetically arranged, WISH gives instant access to work and study opportunities internationally – including libraries, women's resource centres, bookshops and bookclubs. We hope WISH will also help networking between academics and activists and introduce you to a wide range of organisations concerned with women's issues.

The Editors are all members of the Women's Studies Network (UK) Association.* The Association initiated the project with Harvester Wheatsheaf to respond to a huge increase in requests, both from Britain and abroad, for a comprehensive guide to women's studies, training and research. The Editors of each section are as follows:

Introduction: Maggie Humm
International women's studies courses and research centres: Pat Green
Training: Helen Collins
Research resources: Mel Landells
Publications: Loulou Brown

The Editors wish to thank the many women who took the time to answer our letters and questionnaires, and particularly Jackie Jones of Harvester for her inspirational editing.

*Women's Studies Network (UK) Association. Membership: Pauline Brier, WYCROW, University of Bradford, Bradford BD7 1DP

List of Abbreviations

Courses	C
Training	
Arts and Media	AM
Assertiveness Training	AT
Equal Opportunities	EO
Health and Therapy	HT
Management	M
Self-employment	SE
Science, Technology and Computing	STC
Research Resources	
Libraries, Archives, Resource Centres and Information	L
Bookshops	B
Women's Organisations	O
Publications	
Journals	JO
Magazines	MA
Dictionaries	D
Handbooks	HA

Country Codes

Albania	ALB	Brazil	BRA	Dominican	
Algeria	ALG	Bulgaria	BUL	Republic	DOM
Antigua	AN	Cameroon	CAM	Ecuador	ECU
Argentina	AR	Canada	CAN	Egypt	EG
Australia	AUS	Chile	CHI	El Salvador	ELS
Austria	AU	China	CH	Estonia	EST
Bahamas	BA	Colombia	COL	Ethiopia	ETH
Bangladesh	BAN	Costa Rica	CR	Faroe Islands	FAR
Barbados	BAR	Croatia	CRO	Fiji	FIJ
Belgium	BEL	Cuba	CUB	Finland	FIN
Bolivia	BOL	Czech Republic	CZ	France	FR
Botswana	BOT	Denmark	DEN	Gambia	GAM

Germany	GER	Luxembourg	LUX	South Korea	SK
Ghana	GHA	Malaysia	MAL	Spain	SP
Great Britain		Mauritius	MAU	Sri Lanka	SL
and Northern		Mexico	MEX	Sudan	SUD
Ireland	GB	Namibia	NAM	Sweden	SWE
Greece	GRE	Netherlands	NET	Switzerland	SWI
Guatemala	GUA	New Caledonia	NC	Taiwan	TAI
Guyana	GUY	New Zealand	NZ	Tanzania	TAN
Haiti	HAI	Nicaragua	NIC	Thailand	THA
Honduras	HON	Nigeria	NIG	Togo	TOG
Hong Kong	HK	North Korea	NK	Trinidad and	
Hungary	HUN	Norway	NOR	Tobago	TT
Iceland	ICE	Pakistan	PAK	Tunisia	TUN
India	IND	Panama	PAN	Turkey	TUR
Indonesia	IN	Papua		Uganda	UGA
International	INT	New Guinea	PNG	Ukraine	UKR
Iran	IRA	Paraguay	PAR	United Arab	
Ireland	IRE	Peru	PER	Emirates	UAE
Israel	ISR	Philippines	PHI	United States	
Italy	IT	Poland	POL	of America	USA
Ivory Coast	IV	Portugal	POR	Uruguay	URU
Jamaica	JAM	Puerto Rico	PR	Venezuela	VEN
Japan	JAP	Romania	ROM	Vietnam	VIE
Kenya	KEN	Russia	RUS	Zaire	ZAI
Lebanon	LEB	Senegal	SEN	Zambia	ZAM
Liberia	LIB	Singapore	SIN	Zimbabwe	ZIM
Lithuania	LIT	South Africa	SA		

Introduction

This Handbook is a guide to international women's studies courses and centres, feminist organisations, libraries and publications and training for women.

Throughout the world, access to training, education and knowledge is the main means of access to social life. Since the 1970s feminist work has increased rapidly. This growth has changed not only women's thinking, but also educational and organisational structures, and has contributed to a new vision of social change.

By the year 2000 women will dominate the workforce. By the year 2000 women will probably still be earning half as much as men. Economic literacy, as much as language literacy, depends on access to training, support organisations and the kind of educational equity that women's studies teaching and research provides.

Purpose of WISH

The aim of the Handbook, then, is to empower women to participate fully in economic and educational life. The title of the Handbook recognises the fact that women's studies involves both feminist practice and feminist study. We feel it is crucial to acknowledge organisations outside as well as inside the academy, and the enrichment that links between the two bring about.

Each of the book's four sections lists major areas of activity under the general umbrella, 'women's studies'. The information in *WISH* was compiled by the five editors from a huge range of disparate listings and organisations throughout the world. The majority of the information has been collected very quickly during 1992. We do not pretend, therefore, that this is an exhaustive listing of information relevant to women's studies. Classifying feminisms into neat categories is itself very difficult; for example, women's training and research centres often overlap.

We know, however, that despite these limitations, the Handbook is the first international guide to women's organisations, research and studies in one handy volume, and that it will be useful to any intending student, professional or employment-seeking woman. The field is developing rapidly, and *WISH* has been created in a format to enable us to update it when readers send us information. There is a questionnaire to complete at the end of *WISH*.

The purpose of *WISH* is fourfold. First, it is intended as a clear guide to women's studies courses, identifying focuses and offering background information.

1

Second, it lists women's organisations and training possibilities. Third, *WISH* charts the range of women's academic work, listing key libraries, bookshops, publications and research centres. Finally, *WISH* as a whole acts as a guide to the achievement of women over the last two decades and looks forward to the work that is to come.

Although a few guides exist, these are often confined either to research or to training. *WISH* is the first general guide of its kind, and it aims to make visible women's creativity, organisational skills and new fields of knowledge throughout the world.

Women's studies – past, present and future

The past

The history of women's studies is connected with the development of the feminist movement in the USA and Europe at the end of the 1960s. Women's liberation asked new questions about knowledge and subjectivity, and inspired teachers and researchers to criticise existing disciplines and the assumptions on which these were based.

In America, women's studies was inspired by the free-university and civil rights movements, and in its early years included political subdivisions such as liberal and radical or cultural feminism. Similarly, in Britain women's studies appeared first in consciousness-raising groups with a political purpose; this can be seen in the titles of early publications: *Women's Struggle, The Big Flame* and so on. These groups were not created initially by academics but gelled around women's campaigns. One of the first British women's rights groups was formed in Hull to support the campaign led by Lil Bilocca and the fishermen's wives to improve the safety of trawlers. Another campaign supported the sewing machinists' strike for equal pay at Ford's of Dagenham in 1968. Together the two groups provoked a national trade union organisation for women's equal pay and rights.

In the early years, then, British women's studies related to specific issues such as health and the media, and often explored women's history in order to provide ammunition for campaigns: notably the National Abortion Campaign and Women's Aid. From such groups and action came some of the material which forms current women's studies. Educational endorsement of grassroots action started with Juliet Mitchell's women's studies classes (the first to be so called) at the Anti-University in London in 1968–9 and at Ruskin College, Oxford. Ruskin organised the first national women's conference in 1970. Both, again, were institutions on the fringes of British higher education.

The present

Women's studies is a young but broad academic field. Before 1970 it was difficult to find academic research which centred on women's contributions to culture and economics. Yet women's studies now exists throughout the world in one form or another. In Britain the first survey of women's studies courses (1981) listed 34 undergraduate courses, but most were options or one semester long. In 1992, the Women's Studies Network (UK) courses guide lists 66 institutions in higher education alone offering several qualifying courses. The first named Women's Studies MA was founded at Kent University (1981), and London University Adult Education classes grew from 6 to 29 between 1975 and 1988. One clear indication of the growing importance of women's studies across Europe is its inclusion in the European Community's Third Action Programme for Equal Opportunities. In America, 150 women's studies programmes were founded between 1970 and 1975, and there are now over 30,000 courses.

Structures
What constitutes women's studies varies from country to country, not only in numbers but also in relation to national characteristics such as the take-up of higher education. For example, it may well be that British women's studies has been more radical and has been concentrated in adult education until recently because Britain has such an élitist education structure. In other ways, women's studies is empowered by the lack of national organisations. Women's studies relies on the kinds of communication network – on journals and bookshops – which are listed in *WISH*. Drude Dahlerup in *The New Women's Movement*, describing Denmark's vibrant women's studies, points to the impact of feminist publishing, galleries and the lack of central organisations. In Britain, women's community organisations have often needed women's studies to sustain coalitions – for example, the Miners' Wives Strike Association.

Europe
Out of the Margins, a recent women's studies publication, contains a survey article by Christine Zmroczek and Claire Duchen drawn from the 1988–9 EC-sponsored women's studies survey. They argue that women's studies is shaped by the different national and political frameworks in which it grows.

Women's Studies – Europe (1991) shows Germany with 14 university women's studies centres followed by Sweden and Norway with 9 and 5 respectively. In France, with its strong focus on philosophy, women's research centres predominate (there are 10). Finland and Denmark allocate a state budget for women's studies, and Denmark therefore has women's studies research centres in all of its 5 universities. In Italy, with its radical, anti-institutional politics, women's studies has 12 libraries and 8 journals but no university centres.

The first western European meeting on women's studies was held in Brussels in 1988, and there are currently two women's studies organisations – WISE (Women's International Studies Europe) and ENWS (European Network of Women's Studies), both with ambitious long-term aims to enlarge the whole field of women's studies in Europe.

In 1990 the first women's studies conference with participants from eastern Europe was organised by the European Network. (The term 'higher education' in eastern Europe generally includes a wider range of professional training.) The same year saw the founding of the Hungarian Feminist Network and Szegedi; there are women's studies courses in Prague and Bratislava; and before the civil war there were centres in Ljublijana, Beograd and Zagreb. There are many European mobility programmes (ERASMUS, TEMPUS) and networking schemes like the British Council-funded Academic Links schemes in eastern Europe.

America

The NWSA (National Women's Studies Association) *Directory of Women's Studies Programs, Women's Centers, and Women's Research Centers for 1990* shows a 20 per cent increase in undergraduate women's studies courses between 1988 and 1990 alone with over 1,045 entries. The *Directory* lists 818 higher education institutions in the USA offering 621 programmes, compared to 78 listed by *Women's Studies Quarterly* in 1973. These represent 28 per cent of all accredited institutions in the USA. And while in 1986 only 23 institutions offered women's studies graduate work, by 1990 the figure had risen to 102.

International

Women's studies is a global movement. Korea has had courses since 1978; Japan currently has 280 women's studies courses, and women's studies is recognised throughout Asia and Central and Latin America. For example, from the first national conference in women's studies in India (Bombay, 1981) women's studies has been a catalyst for social change and India has over 22 women's studies centres funded directly by the University Grants Commission and an Association of over 500 members. Similarly, China has over 20 centres and 33 periodicals and newspapers devoted to women's issues (see Shanping, 1988).

Women's organisations

Empowering women is the key aim of women's organisations. Diversity and innovation are the main characteristics of feminist movements throughout the world. One obvious but clear feature is that women organise differently in different cultures. The transformations which have taken place since the 1970s are immense. In the 1970s many groups organised in a classic radical way – in part consciousness-raising, in part campaign-focused, these groups were often leaderless and without structure. New social movements raise new questions, and the next step of many groups was often the publication of a key manifesto: for example, the Combahee River Collective's *Statement* (1982) and the manifesto of the Irish Women's Movement, *Chains or Change? The civil wrongs of Irish women*. Such statements activated spaces in which Rape Crisis Centres and Women's Aid could flourish.

One good example is the Indian women's group Vimochana, founded in Bangalore in 1979 to express concern about personal and institutional violence to women. Vimochana gave public shape to these concerns in poster workshops, street theatre, and women's films and songs. The DAWN organisation (Development Alternatives with Women for a New Era), also founded in Bangalore (in 1984) by a group of researchers and activists, now numbers over 4,500 women. Rajasthan is the centre of the Women's Development Programme which administers all-women programmes of trainers. A national project on the Status of the Girl Child was undertaken in Rajasthan when trainers were sent to 800 villages (Menon, 1991).

In India women's studies grew out of a need to assess the impact of development on women. Training is at the centre of development work. For example, Video

SEWA, the video co-operative of the Self-Employed Women's Association India, shows the importance of media training as a tool for political organising for women's rights. The ESAMI (Eastern and Southern African Management Institute) in Tanzania is creating management and training courses for women. There is also WAND (Women and Development Unit) in Barbados and the Research Centre for Women's Studies, Bombay, among many others. This creation of training and organisations is an essential element for developing women's access to resources.

Similar innovative work has been undertaken in Mauritius by the Muvman Liberasyon Fam (MLF), founded in 1976. Like many women's groups, the MLF contributed to other struggles (the return of Diego Garcia Island) but also created new traditions for women such as Solidarite Fam – celebrations for International Women's Day (8 March).

A new momentum in women's organisations is happening in the European Community. The first General Assembly of the European Women's Lobby (EWL) was held in Brussels in 1990, and its agenda includes demands for a Council of Members for Equal Opportunities which would monitor migrant and atypical work issues as well as promoting women into decision-making positions.

International networks provide rich interchanges. For example, the Hawaiian Wa'anae Women's Support Group devised joint strategies with the Baqwis Women's Drop-in Centre, Manila. World-wide international networks flourish: for example, ISIS (Women's International Information and Communication Service, Geneva) and IUS (International Lesbian Information Service). The last decade has seen the growth of a number of international consortia. For example, the Institutional Linkage Program (ILP) was founded by Thai and Canadian universities in 1985 to award scholarships, launch training programmes and develop women's studies curriculae.

Another significant sign of women's organising ability and networking is women's challenges to public events. For example, the group African American Women in Defense of Ourselves formed one month after the Clarence Thomas–Anita Hill hearings to oppose the nomination and confirmation of Clarence Thomas as Associate Justice of the US Supreme Court. An advertisement placed in the *New York Times* by the organisation carried 1,603 signatures of women of African descent. This grassroots effort which united hundreds of African-American women is a milestone in the development of anti-racist and feminist groups.

Of equal significance are women's challenges to governments. For example, the Women in Nigeria group and the Equity Policy Center in Washington carry out research on policy changes in order to offer challenges to government policy.

International networking is an essential feminist practice given recent changes in global politics, such as the rise of fundamentalism, the dissolution of communism and the solidifying of Europe in 1992. It is not insignificant that the idea to found a Latin American Feminist Encounter was proposed by Venezuelan feminists in Copenhagen (1980) midway through the International Women's Decade (1975–85) (see Vargas, 1991). The United Nations Decade for Women encouraged the publication of international work about women's issues. Since 1981 there have been five Latin American and Caribbean Encounters exploring differences and similarities between activist and academic feminists in what are now arguably the largest feminist meetings world-wide. In 1981, in Colombia, 150 women were expected and 230 arrived. In 1985, 1,000 women came to Brazil. In 1987, Mexico welcomed 1,500 participants and produced the now famous collective document 'From Love to Necessity'. In 1989, 3,500 women with differing nationalisms, ethnicities and sexual preferences met in Argentina. This Encounter indicates the tendency of all feminist organisations towards pluralism and diversity, towards concrete and specific situations.

Research, libraries and scholarship: recent changes

If it is widely accepted that 'woman' is not a unitary category in women's organisations, the question remains whether it is a unifying category in women's studies scholarship. Feminist research includes research centres, libraries and resources, and research on women is the single most important instrument in changing social awareness. Feminist research has changed remarkably in the past few decades if book titles are an indication of change. *Sisterhood is Powerful, Revolutionary Feminism* and *Scum* have given way to *Patterns of Dissonance, Conflicts in Feminism* and *Feminisms*.

The most obvious and visible change is the new isms growing like mushroom spores as structuralism gives way to post-structuralism and post-modernism. In the West, feminist theory has grown to become an activity in itself. Another notable change is the commercial success of feminist work and the interest of university and general commercial publishers – as well as feminist publishers – in women's studies (most publishers have a separate women's studies catalogue). Also strategic financial support from national fellowship programmes (Mellon, Rockefeller and others) is being awarded for research on women.

Current research in women's studies is marked by two aims: to consolidate the expertise gained over the past several decades and to offer a critique of social representations, ethics and the academic disciplines. In the early 1970s, feminist research created the framework for a women's tradition. In the 1990s, feminist researchers are reshaping the framework of knowledge itself. Feminist scholars in a number of disciplines have undermined confidence in traditional ways of knowing. Feminist research has breached disciplinary boundaries as well as validating women's traditional arts. It has led to more interdisciplinary and open-ended ways of working. For example, in sociology, psychology and other disciplines, feminists have done more than provide information about women to tack on to existing information about men; they have challenged the dominant theories and concepts of mainstream disciplines. Feminist critiques of science, in particular the work of Evelyn Fox Keller, Sandra Harding and Donna Haraway, show that the role played by gender in science is both complex and variable. The use of different research models (the researcher being an integral part of the research) and the exposure of academic practices and structures that routinely disadvantage women have led to more adequate representations of women. Challenges to an ahistorical feminism, made, for example, by *Women in the World Atlas*, are informing academic work.

Like the structure of women's studies, feminist research is also shaped by national and political contexts. For example, the less industrialised nations of Europe such as Portugal and Greece are less able to introduce feminist research into national education. In Latin America, research on women is more extensive than women's studies. Research is an important contributor to development planning for women. For example, the Thailand Development Research Institute (TDRI) created its Women in Development project (WID) in 1988 in order to remedy the dearth of information on women's roles in domestic and non-domestic production. But there are key signs of growth. The most obvious is an increasing interdisciplinary focus to research. Another is an increase in academic and community links: for example, the *NWSA Directory* shows that many more of its 360 women's centres and 63 research centres are located in the community than in the educational sector.

The importance of libraries and archives must not be underestimated. Traditionally viewed as holders rather than as enablers of information, librarians have contributed significantly to resources for women's studies, including *Studies on Women Abstracts*, and the invaluable work of the University of Wisconsin women's studies librarians. The Fawcett Library based in London holds material ranging from an early autobiography, *The Book of Margery Kempe*, and documents of the domestic arts – the herbal remedies of Hannah Wolley (1678), for instance – to Emily Wilding Davison's trunk, which contained the return ticket from Epsom used to disprove her suicide attempt under the King's horse at Epsom. Libraries are also part of international networks. Links exist, for example, between the Fawcett and the International Archive for the Women's Movement in Amsterdam, and key publications have been issued by groups like the Women's International Resource Exchange and the American National Council for Research on Women.

The most dramatic intellectual development of the last decade has been the growing visibility of Black feminist scholarship. Barbara Smith's pioneering work *Toward a Black Feminist Criticism*, which interweaves the politics of race with the politics of sex, has been followed by a reformation of feminist knowledge. In literary criticism, for example, new areas undreamt of before the 1980s have been created: Chicano, African-American, Native American, Post-Colonial and Black Lesbian criticisms. The 1990s promise a new decade of feminist and womanist scholarship.

The future

As a result of the research, education and politics begun during the Women's Decade, a great deal has changed. The gap between theory and practice dissolves when we understand that this gap is much more a characteristic of Eurocentric thinking than it is of Afrocentric thought. The 1990s are making a firm commitment to global feminism. Women of colour world-wide are organising around common experiences of sexism, colonialism and economic exploitation. For example, DAWN addresses the concerns of women of differing classes, nationalities and regions and yet is not monolithic in its feminism. This integration of research and politics provides women's studies with an endless supply of questions to research and courses to develop.

In 'Resisting amnesia' Adrienne Rich claims that feminist history is history charged with meaning. It shows us images we have not seen before and throws new elements into relief. So what are the new elements of women's studies for the 1990s?

We have entered a new understanding of feminism by putting difference at the centre: for example, by focusing on the historical and cultural meanings of race. Women's studies is represented in all the disciplines, including sports, as well as being a discipline in its own right. Women's studies is pioneering in new technology. The American National Council for Research on Women has created a huge databank. Simon and Schuster are to publish the *International Encyclopaedia of Women's Studies*, edited by Cheris Kramarae and Dale Spender, which will be issued in electronic form as well as in print. There is the Women on Line Database and many others too numerous to mention. Adrienne Rich also says in her essay 'Resisting amnesia' that the educated guess is essential to feminist history, which is exactly why women's studies is so crucial. It is in some ways the public recognition of feminism as the critique of society and culture. Women's studies recognises and legitimates women's world-wide knowledge and practice.

References

Aaron, J., and Walby, S. (1991) *Out of the Margins*, Brighton: Falmer.

Combahee River Collective (1982) 'A Black feminist statement', in G. T. Hull *et al.* (eds), *All the Women Are White, All the Blacks Are Men But Some of Us Are Brave: Black Women's Studies*, New York: The Feminist Press.

Dahlerup, D. (1986) *The New Women's Movement*, London: Sage.

European Network of Women's Studies (1991) *Women's Studies – Europe Mailing List*, Ministry of Education and Science, PO Box 25000, NL-2700 LZ Zoetermeer.

Menon, R. (1991) 'Out of the ivory tower', *The Women's Review of Books*, vol. VIII, no. 5, February, pp. 31–2.

Rich, A. (1986) 'Resisting amnesia', in A. Rich (ed.), *Blood, Bread and Poetry*, New York: W. W. Norton.

Seager, J., and Olson, A. A. (1986) *Women in the World Atlas*, New York: Simon and Schuster.

Shanping, W. (1988) 'The emergence of women's studies in China', *Women's Studies International Forum*, vol. 11, no. 5, pp. 455–65.

Vargas, V. (1991) 'The Women's Movement in Peru: streams, spaces and knots', *European Review of Latin American and Caribbean Studies*, no. 50.

How to use this Handbook

We have designed *WISH* to be used for a variety of purposes. Precise 'how-to' introductions preface each section. Material in each section is arranged alphabetically by country and alphabetically within countries. In the 'Training', 'Research resources' and 'Publications' sections each country's listings are further subdivided into thematic categories such as 'Health', 'Equal opportunities' or 'Handbooks', 'Journals' and other self-explanatory categories. The coverage of the various sections is as follows:

- International women's studies courses and research centres: covers courses and centres dealing broadly with gender issues.
- Training: covers both work skills (employment/self-employment) and personal/interpersonal skills.
- Research resources: includes bookshops and bookclubs, libraries, archives, information and resource centres and women's organisations with a strong focus on women's issues.
- Publications: This section includes handbooks, guides and directories as well as general works on women's studies.

In selecting entries for *WISH* we have tried to give a clear picture of the whole field of women's studies in the 1990s. The development of resource materials is critical for the future of women's studies, with the help of *WISH* we can all find out more about women's studies, inform ourselves about women's research, continue to train ourselves, and develop our professional and personal lives.

1 | *International Women's Studies Courses and Research Centres*

Introduction

There is much feminist teaching and research being carried out in the 1990s. This guide is an attempt to collect information together in an international context. Inevitably there are gaps; what I have produced is a record of information collected and collated so far. Contacts and links are being made and new information continues to reach me, but I would still welcome further news from users of this Handbook, about teaching and research that has not been documented here.

The criterion for inclusion of material has been whether courses, or the focus of research, can be defined as 'women's studies' or as 'feminist' in orientation. The attempt to make this, the empowerment of women, the distinction as opposed to 'women orientated' is an important one.

This project has been revelatory; the extent of women's studies teaching and feminist research goes far beyond what I had expected, and reaches far more geographical points on the map, and many more students, than I had ever imagined. I am also aware of work that I have not been able to document: in the Nordic Countries, Canada, India and China for example, and in particular, teaching and research in the countries of the former USSR. Under the old Soviet system, research was carried out separately from educational institutes, and as yet very few centres for women's studies teaching and research have been established, although there is work being undertaken by individual scholars. One entry in particular that I am delighted to record is the Women's Studies Centre newly founded in 1992 at Vilnius University, Lithuania. The recent political changes are now opening up possibilities for important academic changes too, and I wish to applaud the work that Dr Giedre Purvanerchiene and her colleagues have begun; it is an exciting time for women's studies, and it is a reminder that there is still much to do.

How to use this section

The information in this section has been recorded by country, alphabetically, and then by state or by city. Addresses, telephone numbers and contact names are listed where possible, together with details about courses, qualifications gained (if known) and, where applicable, the research work being undertaken in women's

11

studies research centres in those institutions or organisations. Research centres are identified, where appropriate, immediately after the course and qualification details in each entry. Independent research organisations have also been included.

Addresses, and titles of courses, centres and organisations have been given in the spelling and language provided. I have indicated, when this is known, where courses are taught in English. Where the same university runs programmes in different faculties, these have been entered under a single entry reference number; where a university operates from a number of cities (as in the USA, for example), these have been referenced separately.

Acknowledgements

I would particularly like to thank the following, and acknowledge their generous help in providing me with encouragement, support, guidance and valuable information for this work.

Lisa Adkins, for giving me such a generous start by enabling me to use her work in the *Women's Studies Network UK Course Listings*, 1992–3.

Barbara Milech and her colleagues in the Gender Theory Group at the Curtin University of Technology, Perth, Western Australia, for their assistance and permission to use information drawn from *A Directory of Women's Studies in Australian Universities*, Kingswood, NSW: Women's Research Centre (University of Western Sydney, Nepean), 1992.

Sumiko Yoshida of the National Women's Education Centre in Japan for allowing me to use their *Survey of Courses on Women's Studies and Related Subjects in Institutions in Higher Education in Japan* (Fiscal, 1990) for most of the entries for Japan.

The Committee of Feminist Research: Danish Council for Research Policy, *Women's Studies and Feminist Research in Denmark* (1992).

GRIF, for the Equal Opportunities Units of the Commission of the European Communities, *GRACE – Student Guide to Women's Studies in the European Community* (1991).

National Women's Studies Association (USA), *Directory of Women's Studies Programs, Women's Centers, and Women's Research Centers* (1990).

Nordic Women's Studies, Reference Group, *Women's Studies and Research on Women in the Nordic Countries* (1991).

To all strong women everywhere, and to three strong women in particular: Phyllis, my mother, and Joanne and Sarah, my daughters.

Pat Green
University of Wolverhampton
1993

Argentina

Buenos Aires

ARC1

The Alicia Moreau De Justo Foundation
Corrientes 1485
1st 'A'
1042 BUENOS AIRES
☎ 40 5077/40 1805
Contact: Elana Tchalidy
☐ The foundation works to preserve the history of women, and carrying out social research on women's problems. Research on the life of Dr Alicia Moreau de Justo is also being carried out. Conferences, short courses and seminars are offered, and the Foundation publishes its work.

ARC2

Centre for the Study of Women
Olleros 2554 PB
1426 BUENOS AIRES
Contact: Gloria Bonder

ARC3

GT Condicion Femenina CLACSLO
(The Feminine Condition)
Consejo Latinoamericano de Ciencias Sociales
(Latin American Council of Social Science)
Avda. Pueyrredon 510–70
1032 BUENOS AIRES
Contact: Maria del Carme Feijo

ARC4

Women and Family, Argentinian Society of Family Therapy
Julian Alvarez 239
BUENOS AIRES
☎ 854 2147
Contact: Maria Christina Ravazzola
Courses: Women and Health; Women and Stereotypes; Women and Family; Women and Sexuality
☐ Founded in 1988, work involves teaching, publications, compiling bibliographical material as well as research projects. Work has included a study of the relationship between gender stereotypes and mental illness in a sample of Argentinian families. Clinical case studies are conducted to examine the practices in medical and psychological therapy.

Cordoba

ARC5

Multinational Women's Centre for Research and Training of the Inter-American Commission on Women
Av Velez Sarsfield 153
CORDOBA
☎ 45750
Contact: A. M. de Rodrigez Rojas
☐ The Women's Centre provides teaching, training courses, publications, an art gallery and a library, as well as supporting research projects. Recent research has focused on aboriginal women in Argentina, Bolivia and Paraguay, and on the careers of sociocultural workers.

Australia

Australian Capital Territory

AUSC1

Faculty of Arts
Australian National University
GPO Box 4
CANBERRA, ACT 2601
☎ 06 249 5090
Contact: J. J. Matthews
Course: Women's Studies
☐ Can be taken as a major on the undergraduate programme. Some units are also available through the University of Canberra.
Qualification: Degree
Course: Women's Studies
☐ Postgraduate-level work offered through coursework and research.
Qualifications: Graduate diploma, Master's degree, Doctorate

New South Wales

AUSC2

School of History, Philosophy and Politics
Macquarie University
NSW 2109
☎ 02 805 8857
Contact: Judy Lattas
Course: Women's Studies
☐ Can be taken as part of an undergraduate programme, with the Honours degree having been revised in 1991 to consist of 50 per cent coursework and 50 per cent research.
Qualifications: Degree, Honours degree
Course: Women's Studies

□ Postgraduate-level study is currently available by research, full or part-time, but a master's degree by coursework is planned for 1995. A Women's Studies Centre is currently being established.
Qualifications: Master's degree, Doctorate

AUSC3

University of New England, Armidale
ARMIDALE, NSW 2351
☎ 067 73 2580
Contact: Bronwyn Davies
Course: Women's Studies
□ Postgraduate-level coursework can be taken in one year full-time or two years part-time. Other post-graduate work is by research. Inter-institutional study is available through Deakin University, Murdoch Universities and the University of Queensland.
Qualifications: Postgraduate diploma, Master's degree, Doctorate

AUSC4

School of English
University of New South Wales
PO Box 1
KENSINGTON, NSW 2033
☎ 02 697 2303
Contact: Brigitta Olubas
Course: Women's Studies
□ Postgraduate level work, by course or by research, full or part-time. An undergraduate major in Women's Studies is proposed for 1994 onwards.
Qualifications: Master's degree, Master's degree (Hons)

AUSC5

Faculty of Arts
University of Sydney
127 Darlington Road
SYDNEY, NSW 2006
☎ 02 692 3638
Contact: Carole Adams
Course: Women's Studies
□ Can be taken as a major on the undergraduate programme, in the second and third year.
Qualifications: Degree, Honours degree, Master of Arts, Master of Letters, Master of Philosophy (by research), Doctorate
Course: Women's Studies
□ Postgraduate work available by course and by research.
Qualifications: Master of Arts, Master of Letters, Master of Philosophy (by research), Doctorate

Women's Studies Centre and Research Unit
□ Established in 1990 to promote both research and teaching. Gretchen Poiner is the Senior Research Officer, and the Director is Dr Barbara Caine.

AUSC6

Faculty of Humanities of Social Sciences
University of Western Sydney, Nepean
PO Box 10
KINGSWOOD, NSW 2747
☎ 02 678 7352
Contact: Deborah Chambers
Course: Women's Studies
□ Postgraduate-level work, full or part-time.
Undergraduate-level programmes are planned for 1994.
Qualifications: Master's degree, Doctorate

Women's Research Centre
□ Based on the Nepean campus to support Women's Studies research students.

AUSC7

University of Wollongong
Northfields Avenue
WOLLONGONG, NSW 2500
☎ 042 21 3630
Contact: Rebecca Albury
Course: Women's Studies
□ Available as part of the undergraduate programme.
Qualifications: Degree, Honours degree
Course: Women's Studies
□ Postgraduate level of study. Gender Studies units also available within the Master of Education programme.
Qualifications: Master's degree, Doctorate

Queensland

AUSC8

Faculty of Humanities
Griffith University
Kessels Road
NATHAN, Qld 4111
☎ 07 875 7573
Contact: Karen Fentie
Course: Women's Studies
□ Undergraduate programme available, can be taken full or part-time.
Qualification: Degree
Course: Women's Studies
Qualifications: Master's degree, Doctorate

Australian Institute for Women's Research and Policy (AIWRAP).
□ Established in 1991 in order to support access of Australian women to higher education and research; to strengthen links between researchers and policy practitioners; and to raise the profile of research on women and gender issues. The Director is Dr Chilla Bulbeck.

AUSC9
James Cook University of North Queensland
TOWNSVILLE, Qld 4811
☎ 077 81 4266
Contact: Cheryl Taylor
Course: Women's Studies
☐ Can be taken on the undergraduate programme, full or part-time.
Qualification: Degree
Course: Women's Studies
☐ Postgraduate level of study.
Qualifications: Graduate diploma, Master's degree, Doctorate

AUSC10
Queensland University of Technology
Carseldine Campus
PO Box 284
ZILLMERE, Qld 4034
☎ 07 864 4730
Contact: Jane Williamson-Fien
Courses: Women's Studies; Feminist Studies
☐ Interdisciplinary undergraduate work available, from 1993, within the School of Humanities and the School of Social Science.
Qualification: Degree
Course: Equity and Educational Management: Issues and Strategies
☐ Postgraduate level work within the Master's degree in Leadership in the Faculty of Education, Kelvin Grove campus.
Qualification: Master's degree

AUSC11
Department of English
University of Queensland
Qld 4072
☎ 07 365 2743
Contact: Barbara Garlick
Course: Women's Studies
☐ Can be taken as a major or a double major on the undergraduate programme. Inter-institutional study arrangements are available through Deakin University and Murdoch University (entries AUSC15 and AUSC24 respectively)
Qualification: Degree
Course: Women's Studies
☐ Individually created postgraduate-level work is available by research, or by combining coursework with research.
Qualifications: Postgraduate diploma, Master's degree, Doctorate

Women, Culture and Ideology Unit
☐ Housed in the English Department, serves to promote research and to publish *Hecate* and *Cauldron*. Associate Professor Carole Ferrier is the Director of the Unit.

South Australia

AUSC12
Women's Studies Discipline
Flinders University
GPO Box 2100
ADELAIDE, SA 5001
☎ 08 201 2404
Contact: Susan Sheridan
Course: Women's Studies
☐ Can be taken as a major on the undergraduate programme, full or part-time.
Qualifications: Degree, Honours degree
Course: Women's Studies
☐ Postgraduate-level work carried out by coursework and research.
Qualifications: Postgraduate diploma, Master's degree, Doctorate

AUSC13
Women's Studies Department
University of Adelaide
GPO Box 498
ADELAIDE, SA 5001
☎ 08 228 5267
Contact: Margaret Allen
Course: Women's Studies
☐ Available as part of the undergraduate programme, from the Department of Women's Studies, and from the Politics and English Departments.
Qualifications: Degree, Honours degree
Course: Women's Studies
☐ Postgraduate-level work, taken full or part-time.
Qualifications: Graduate Diploma, Master's degree, Doctorate

Research Centre for Women's Studies
☐ Established in 1983, the Centre's research enquiry is in the areas of feminist history, political study, feminist theory and cultural studies. Involved in teaching, supervision of research and publications. The Centre produces *Australian Feminist Studies*. The Director is Dr Susan Margarey.

AUSC14
University of South Australia
North Terrace
ADELAIDE, SA 5000
☎ 08 302 2603
Contact: Alison Mackinnon
Course: Women's Studies

Courses

☐ Available as a major on an undergraduate programme.
Qualification: Degree

Centre for Gender Studies
☐ A network for women researchers, the Centre is aiming to formalise its activities within the institution, and to work towards offering higher degrees in Women's Studies. Research in Gender Studies is supported, and the Centre organises submissions for research grants.

Victoria

AUSC15
Deakin University
Geelong Campus
GEELONG, Vic. 3217
☎ 052 27 1271
Contact: Alison Parker
Course: Women's Studies
☐ Can be taken as a major on the undergraduate programme. Inter-institutional study arrangements are available through University of Queensland and Murdoch University (entries AUSC11 and AUSC24 respectively).
Qualifications: Degree, Honours degree
Course: Women's Studies
☐ Postgraduate-level work, taken full or part-time.
Qualifications: Master's degree, Doctorate

Australian Women's Research Centre
☐ Newly established, the Centre supports students undertaking Women's Studies research. A bi-annual Women's Studies Summer Institute runs for fee-paying students (next one will be for two weeks in January 1994).

AUSC16
Department of Teacher Education
Deakin University
Rusden Campus
622 Blackburn Road
CLAYTON, Vic. 3168
☎ 03 542 7421
Contact: Marilyn Poole
Course: Women's Studies
Qualification: Graduate diploma

AUSC17
La Trobe University
Plenty Road
BUNDOORA, Vic. 3083
☎ 03 479 2430
Contact: Marilyn Lake
Course: Women's Studies

☐ Can be taken as a major on the undergraduate programme, full or part-time. Programmes in Education, Humanities and Social Science.
Qualifications: Degree, Honours degree
Course: Women's Studies
☐ Postgraduate-level work available in Humanities, Education, or by research. Can be taken full or part-time.
Qualifications: Master's degree, Doctorate

AUSC18
Monash University
CLAYTON, Vic. 3168
☎ 03 565 2996
Contact: Katherine Gibson
Course: Women's Studies
☐ Can be taken as a major on the undergraduate programme, full or part-time.
Qualifications: Degree, Honours degree
Course: Women's Studies
☐ Postgraduate-level work, by coursework and research. Can be taken full or part-time.
Qualifications: Master's degree, Doctorate

Centre for Women's Studies
☐ Established in 1987 within the Faculty of Arts, the Centre aims to encourage, support and supervise graduate research, as well as teach and run seminars, conferences and workshops.

AUSC19
Arts Faculty
Swinburne University of Technology
PO Box 218
HAWTHORN, Vic. 3122
☎ 03 819 8466
Contact: Tanya Castleman
Course: Women's Studies
☐ Postgraduate-level study available.
Qualifications: Graduate Diploma in Equal Opportunity Administration, Master's degree, Doctorate

Women's Studies College
☐ Research activities aim to address the roles of women in society generally, but specific focus is on women in the workforce; women in the fields of technology; organisation and management; and women and the family.

AUSC20
Faculty of Arts
University of Melbourne
PARKVILLE, Vic. 3052
☎ 03 344 5959
Contact: Maila Stivens
Course: Women's Studies

☐ Women's Studies can be taken in an inter-departmental undergraduate programme, at second and third-year levels.
Qualification: Degree, Combined Honours degree
Courses: Women's Health; Women's Studies
Qualification: Graduate diploma
Courses: Women's Health; Women's Studies
☐ Master of Medicine degree in Women's Health is available to medically qualified graduates. A research component is required in addition to coursework available through the Graduate Diploma in Women's Health. Master of Arts in Women's Studies is available by coursework or research.
Qualifications: Master's degree, Doctorate

Key Centre for Women's Health in Society
☐ Established within the Faculty of Medicine, Dentistry and Health Sciences, to promote both teaching and research in women's health.

AUSC21

Faculty of Arts
Victoria University of Technology
    PO Box 14428
    MMC MELBOURNE, Vic. 3000
☎   03 365 2305
Contact: Katie Hughes
Course: Women's Studies
☐ Available as a major within an interdisciplinary undergraduate programme.
Qualification: Degree
Course: Women's Studies
☐ Postgraduate study available part-time only in 1993.
Qualifications: Graduate certificate, Graduate diploma, Master's degree

Western Australia

AUSC22

Curtin University of Technology
    GPO Box U1987
    PERTH, WA 6001
☎   09 351 7621
Contact: Barbara H. Milech
Course: Women's Studies
☐ While Women's Studies is not offered as a specific major, feminist theory forms an important component on many units within the School of Communications and Cultural Studies. Units are also available within Social Sciences and Anthropology.
Qualifications: Degree, Honours degree
Course: Women's Studies
☐ Postgraduate studies, offered through coursework or research, or by combining both of these.
Qualifications: Postgraduate Diploma in English, Master's degree, Doctorate

Western Australian Inter-University Centre for Research on Women
☐ Curtin University is a partner in this collective enterprise for research.

AUSC23

Edith Cowan University
    2 Bradford Street
    MOUNT LAWLEY, WA 6050
☎   09 370 6323
Contact: Lekkie Hopkins
Course: Applied Women's Studies
☐ Currently available on the undergraduate programme as an interdisciplinary minor through the Department of Humanities. A major is planned for 1994.
Qualifications: Associate diploma, degree
Course: Women's Studies
☐ Postgraduate-level work with a professional orientation. Can be taken full or part-time.
Qualification: Graduate diploma (Applied)
Course: Women's Studies
Qualifications: Master's degree, Doctorate

Western Australian Inter-University Centre for Research on Women
☐ Edith Cowan University is a partner in this collective enterprise for research.

AUSC24

School of Humanities
Murdoch University
    South Street
    MURDOCH, WA 6150
☎   09 360 6234
Contact: Ien Ang
Course: Women's Studies
☐ Major undergraduate programme available at Murdoch University and as part of inter-institutional study arrangements through University of Queensland and Deakin University (entries AUSC11 and AUSC15 respectively).
Qualifications: Degree, Honours degree
Course: Women's Studies
☐ Interdisciplinary postgraduate-level work taken either full or part-time.
Qualifications: Graduate diploma, Master's degree, Doctorate

Western Australian Inter-University Centre for Research on Women
☐ Murdoch University is a partner in this collective, which is based at Murdoch for 1993 and 1994 where the contact is Bev Thiele in the School of Social Sciences.

AUSC25

Faculty of Arts
University of Western Australia
    NEDLANDS, WA 6009
☎   09 380 2063

Courses

Contact: Delys M. Bird
Course: Women's Studies
☐ Postgraduate-level study by coursework.
Qualification: Master's degree

Western Australian Inter-University Centre for Research on Women
☐ The University of Western Australia is a partner in this collective enterprise for research.

Bangladesh

BANC1

Women for Women: A Research and Study Group
> 15 Green Square
> Green Road
> DHAKA
☎ 50 46 97
Contact: Nazma Chawdhury
Courses: Research Methodology and Women's Issues; Women and Development
☐ Courses provided to promote research on women.
☐ The Group was founded in 1973 as a registered voluntary organisation, to research, and publish on, the lives of Bangladeshi women. Seminars are offered to disseminate research and information. Video production on the life and activities of rural Bangladeshi women is also an important activity. Work and research for the Group is done on a part-time voluntary basis.

Barbados

BARC1

DAWN (The Development Alternative with Women for a New Era)
> School of Continuing Studies
> University of the West Indies
> Pinelands,
> ST MICHAEL
☎ 426 9288
Contact: Peggy Antrobus
☐ Part of an expanding network of Third World feminists working for development change. Research programme includes alternative economic framework; reproductive rights and population; and the environment. Publications are available in English, Portuguese and Spanish.

BARC2

Extramural Department
University of the West Indies
> Pinelands,
> ST MICHAEL

☎ 436 6312
Contact: Peggy Antrobus

WAND (The Women and Development Unit)
☐ Work carried out by WAND aims to uncover women's role in history, and support the growth of a women's movement in the Caribbean. Outreach work and a publication programme supports this work and complements the Women and Development Studies programme in the University.

Belgium

Antwerp

BELC1

Centrum Vrouwenstudies
Universitaire Instelling Antwerpen
> Universiteitsplein
> 1 Wilrijk
> 2610 ANTWERP
☎ 03 820 28 50 ext. 2862
Contact: Nicole Derijckere
Courses: Vrouw en Management; Vrouw en Literatuur; Vrouw en Beeld; Beeld van de Vrouw in Theater en Film
☐ Interdisciplinary courses at degree level. Taught in Dutch and open to those without a degree.
Qualification: Certificate
Course: Steunpunt Women's Studies
☐ Three interdisciplinary postgraduate courses, taught in Dutch. Antwerp University is one of the eight European universities which participates in the Erasmus exchange programme in Women's Studies.

Brussels

BELC2

CREW (Centre for Research on European Women)
> 38 Rue Stevin
> 1040 BRUSSELS
☎ 02 230 51 58
☐ Established in 1980, CREW specialises in women and employment issues with a European focus. Comparative research on women's co-operatives and other collective self-managed businesses is carried out throughout the European Community. A monthly magazine is issued in English and French.

BELC3

Université des Femmes
> 1a place Quetelet
> 1030 BRUSSELS
☎ 02 219 61 07

Contact: Laurence Broze
Course: Seminaires Interdisciplinaires
□ Series of seminars aimed at adult education level.

BELC4

Groupe Interdisciplinaire d'Etudes sur les
Femmes-Gief
Université Libre de Bruxelles
50 avenue Fr. Roosevelt
CP 142
1050 BRUSSELS
☎ 02 650 39 56
Contact: Eliane Gubin
Course: Histoire des Femmes
□ A course of free public lectures, the Suzanne Tassier
Memorial Lectures.
Course: Biographies et Histoire des Femmes
□ Postgraduate interdisciplinary studies.
Qualification: Doctorate

BELC5

Faculty of Social Science
The Open University
Ave. van der Meerschen 26
1150 BRUSSELS
☎ 02 762 57 88
Contact: Monica Woodall
Course: Issues in Women's Studies
□ Interdisciplinary, distance learning courses taught
in English. Includes gender and education; girls into
mathematics; women, writing and culture; and women
into management.
Qualifications: Degree, Certificate

BELC6

Independent Feminist Group
Rosa-Rol en Samenleving
78 rue Gallait
1210 BRUSSELS
☎ 02 216 23 23
Contact: Renee Van Mechalen
Course: Vrouwenmythes en Vrouwenwerkelijkheid
□ A series of themes aimed at adult education level

BELC7

Centrum Voor Vrouwenstudies
Vrije Universiteit Brussel
Pleinklaan 2
1050 BRUSSELS
☎ 02 641 28 21
Contact: Micheline Scheys
Course: Sociology – Special Issues on the Gender
Perspective
□ Designed for American students as part of the BA
degree.

Qualification: Certificate, available for faculty students
who take the course on a part-time basis.

Gent

BELC8

Centrum Voor Historische Pedagogiek
Rijksuniversiteit Gent
Baertsoenkaai 3
9000 GENT
☎ 091 24 02 24 ext. 274
Contact: K. De Clerck
Course: Interdisciplinary Studies
□ The Women's Studies group has already published
research.

Brazil

BRAC1

Nucleo de Estudios Sobre a Mulher
(Centre for the Study of Women)
The Pontifal Catholic University
Rua Marques de Sao Vicente, 225 Gavea
RIO DE JANIERO 22453
☎ 529 9288
Contact: Fanny Tabak
Course: Women's Studies
□ The Centre for the Study of Women was founded
in 1981 as part of the Department of Sociology and
Politics. The Centre works to develop Women's
Studies courses and to publish work on women.
A monthly newsletter, *Boletim*, is published, as well
as books, articles and essays based on the Centre's
research.

Canada

Nova Scotia

CANC1

Mount Saint Vincent University
166 Bedford Highway
Halifax
NOVA SCOTIA B3M 2J6
Contact: Susan Clark

Institute for the Study of Women

Ontario

CANC2

Women in Development Consortium
Thai Studies Project
York University
4700 Keele Street
North York
ONTARIO M3J 1P3
Contact: Penny Van Esterik
☐ The Women in Development Consortium has links with the Women in Development Consortium at Thammasat University, Thailand (see entry THAC1).

CANC3

The Canadian Advisory Council
on the Status of Women (CACSW)
110 O'Connor St, 9th Floor
PO Box 1541, Sta. 'B'
Ottawa
ONTARIO K1P 5R5
☎ 613 992 4975
Contact: Sylvia Gold
☐ CACSW was established in 1973. It is an independent body funded by federal government, set up to advise government on issues concerning women. Research on women in agriculture; pay equity; child care; pornography; and the impact of free trade on women in manufacturing has been carried out. CACSW publishes research findings in both English and French.

CANC4

Canadian Research Institute for
the Advancement of Women (CRIAW)
151 Slater Street, Suite 408
Ottawa
ONTARIO K1P 5H3
☎ 613 563 0681
Contact: Linda Chippingdale
☐ Funded predominantly by the federal government through the Women's Programme, CRIAW uses both English and French languages. Projects have included 'Family Violence: Women's Solutions Across the North', and resources about reproductive technologies for use in women's and community groups. CRIAW awards research grants annually, as well as the Marta Danylewycz Memorial Award for research in women's history. These are available to Canadians or for Canadian research content. Research is published in *The CRIAW Papers*.

CANC5

Women's Bureau
Department of Labour
Ottawa
ONTARIO K1A 0J2

☎ 819 997 1550
Contact: Linda Geller-Schwartz
☐ Part of the federal department of Labour, the Women's Bureau was established in 1954. Research is carried out on issues relating to women's employment: maternity and child care leave; leave for workers with family responsibilities; equal pay for work of equal value; technological change; part-time work; job sharing; sexual harassment; reproductive health hazards in the workplace; and statistical analyses of women's employment situation. The Bureau regularly publishes statistical information in *Women in the Labour Force*.

CANC6

Centre for Women's Studies in Education
Ontario Institute for Studies Education
252 Bloor St West, Room S630
Toronto
ONTARIO M5S 1V6
Contact: Ruth Pierson

Quebec

CANC7

Simone de Beauvoir Institute
1455 de Maidonneuve Blvd West
Concordia University
Montreal
QUEBEC H3G 1M8
☎ 514 848 2370
Contact: Arpi Hamalian
Course: Women's Studies programme
☐ Available as a minor or major on the undergraduate programme. Postgraduate studies are available by special arrangement, and a master's degree is planned.
Qualifications: Certificate, Degree, Master's degree
☐ Established in 1978 in the Faculty of Arts and Science to promote both teaching and research in Women's Studies, the Institute houses collectives for research purposes: The Centre for Feminist Studies on Peace; Le Centre de Rechercher et d'Enseignement sur la Francophonie des Femmes; the Centre for Research and Teaching on Women and Work. Individual researchers have also carried out work on immigrant women, women and science, and women and power in organisations. The Institute also has a documentation centre.

Saskatchewan

CANC8
Women's Studies Research Unit
University of Saskatchewan
  Education Building
  Saskatoon
  SASKATCHEWAN S7N 0W0
Contact: Dawn Currie

China

CHC1
The Women's Committee of the United Nations
  Association of the Republic of China
  101 Ning Po West Street
  Taipei
  TAIWAN
Contact: Helen H. C. Yeh Lee
□ The Committee draws together women from all professions in order to conduct studies on women, and to research women's activities both in China and elsewhere, notably the United States, the Middle East and Asia. Community outreach programmes work on women's development. Scholarships and grants are offered to women graduates, school teachers, and women workers in other fields who wish to research abroad. The Committee's publications include *Women's Status in the Past Seven Decades* and *Women's Involvement in the Economic Development of the Republic of China*, both in Chinese. *Women's Achievements during the mid-Decade of the 1980s, The Chinese Family* and *Asian Women and World Peace* have all been published in English and are available free.

CHC2
Populations Studies Centre
National Taiwan University
  Taipei
  TAIWAN
☎ 3930097/3510241 ext. 2595
Contact: Elaine Tsui

Women's Research Programme
□ Founded in 1985 it aims to promote research on women and gender, to create public awareness about the changing status of women, and to network with other women's organisations in Taiwan. Research has included women workers; women's health; women's social supports and life satisfaction; and social roles, stress and depression in urban communities. A library houses books in English, Chinese, Japanese and Korean. Publications include a quarterly bulletin and conference reports, some of which are in English, or with English abstracts. The annual *Journal of Women and Gender Studies* is published in Chinese and English.

Czech Republic

CZC1
Charles University in Prague
  Box 695
  111 21 PRAGUE 1
☎ 232 71 06
Contact: Jana Hradilkova

Curriculum Centre and Library for Gender Studies
□ Established in 1991, with the assistance and support of the network of East–West Women. The Centre aims to develop Gender Studies and Women's Studies across both curricula and research programmes, and is establishing a data-base in Women's Studies. It has an interdisciplinary library resource centre.

The Research and Co-ordination Centre for Gender Studies East/West
Charles University in Prague
  PO Box 188
  111 21 PRAGUE 1
☎ 42 2 297541
Contact: Olga Kucerova
□ The Centre was established in 1991 with the aim of stimulating research, education and co-ordination in the field of gender studies.

Denmark

Aalborg

DENC1
FREIA – Centre for Feminist Research
University of Aalborg
  Fibigerstraede 2
  9220 AALBORG O
☎ 98 15 85 22
Contact: Ruth Emerek
Course: Women's Studies
□ A year-long interdisciplinary undergraduate Women's Studies programme offered within the Department of Social Sciences. Courses can be credited in other departments.
Qualification: Degree

□ Women researchers in FREIA are drawn primarily from the fields of anthropology, history, sociology, politics, economics and development studies. 'Changes in gender relations, power and identity' is the title of the current feminist programme of the Centre, which forms a framework for research projects.

Courses

Aarhus

DENC2

Cekvina – Women's Research Centre
University of Aarhus
　　Finlandsgade 26B
　　8210 AARHUS V
☎　86 16 58 55
Contact: Kirsten Gomard
Course: Gender, Communication and Culture
☐ Interdisciplinary postgraduate-level work, this is a one-year programme, taken after two years study for the Master's degree. Includes courses on abortion as a political issue; gender and communication; motherhood and sexuality; and communication training.
Qualification: Master's degree
☐ Founded ten years ago, the Centre is involved in teaching, research and publications. Cekvina also has a large reference library and documentation centre. The Centre also receives NORDPLUS and ERASMUS students as part of the WING exchange programme in Women's Studies.

Copenhagen

DENC3

Samkvind – Centre for Women's Studies in the Social Studies
University of Copenhagen
　　St Kannikestraede 11
　　1169 COPENHAGEN K
☎　33 91 21 66 ext. 251
Contact: Sanne Ipsen
Course: Women's Studies
☐ Both degree and postgraduate lectures and conferences in the Social Sciences.
☐ Founded in 1987, the Centre is a university department involved in teaching, research and publications, in order to initiate, co-ordinate and support women's studies within the faculty of Social Science.

Institute of Social Medicine
University of Copenhagen
　　Panum Institute
　　Blegdamsvej 3
　　2200 COPENHAGEN N
☎　31 35 79 00 ext. 2400
Contact: Birgit Petersson
Course: Feminist Research in Medicine
☐ First degree and postgraduate level. Interdisciplinary work that focuses on the physical, psychological and social situation of women.

Feminist Research Centre in Medicine
☐ Includes teaching, research, publications and documentation. The group of researchers arrange inter-Nordic and local courses, and meet regularly to discuss current research.

Danish Association for Women's and Gender Studies
☐ Founded in 1990, the Association's work is on a national and international level, initiating networking with international women's studies organisations. Acting as a scientific forum for all feminist scholars in Denmark, the association is currently working to establish a Danish journal for feminist studies and research.

DENC4

Centre for Development Research
　　Kongensgade 9
　　1472 COPENHAGEN K
☎　14 57 00
Contact: Kirsten Westergaard
☐ One of the Centre's priority research areas is on Third World women. Projects include: women in production and reproduction; gender and socioeconomic differentiation in Kericho, Kenya; and women's utilisation rates of primary health care and family planning services in Kenya.

DENC5

Institut for Klinisk Pskologi
　　Njalsgade 90
　　2300 COPENHAGEN S
☎　31 54 22 11
Contact: Libby-Tata Arcel
Course: Clinical Psychology
☐ Feminist studies about female identity, this course forms part of the clinical psychology degree programme. The courses are available to external students.

DENC6

Centre for Feminist Research and Studies
Copenhagen University – Amager
　　Njalsgade 106
　　2300 COPENHAGEN S
☎　31 54 22 11
Contact: Bente Rosenbeck
Courses: Marriage in Medieval Western Europe; Gender in Literary Research; Myths about Women; Jane Austen's Novels; Modernism, Postmodernism and Feminism seminar; Theorising Reproduction seminar.
☐ One-year programmes at both undergraduate and postgraduate-level work, in history, literature and feminist theory.
Qualifications: Degree, Master's degree, Doctorate
☐ The Centre is involved in teaching, research, publications and ERASMUS exchanges, and is part of the Faculty of Arts. Current research includes both

medieval and modern history and literature, the history of medicine and science, sexuality and nature, culture and gender.

DENC7

Kvindedaghojskolen 'Vera'
Halmtorvet 13
1700 COPENHAGEN V
☎ 31 24 36 30
Contact: Ellen Geske Lilsio
Course: General course for personal development with practical work
☐ An independent feminist group providing adult education-level courses aimed at young unemployed women without formal qualifications.

DENC8

Forum for Feminist Research
Denmarks Laererhojskole
Emdrupvej 101
2400 COPENHAGEN NV
☎ 39 69 66 33
Contact: Karen Borgnakke
Course: Educational Studies
☐ Degree-level work with an informal group in higher education.
☐ The Forum is established within the Royal Danish School of Educational Studies, which is an educational university with branches in different parts of the country. Gender perspectives have been introduced into research related to educational and teaching subjects through the work of the group.

DENC9

Center for Samfundsvidenskabelig Kvindeforskning
Nansensgade 1
1366 COPENHAGEN K
☎ 33 12 23 14
Contact: Else Christensen
☐ The Women's Research Centre in Social Science was founded in 1980 and is an independent organisation which is non-profit-making. Working papers are published, some in English.

Odense

DENC10

Center for Kvinde-Og Kønsstudier
Odense University
Campusvej 55
5230 ODENSE M
☎ 66 15 86 00 ext. 3388
Contact: Nina Lykke
Course: Gender and Culture

☐ Forms part of both the undergraduate and postgraduate programmes of study.
Course: Women's Culture and the Culture of Technology
☐ Postgraduate-level work, this is part of an Open University degree to which foreign students are welcome.
Qualifications: Degree, Master's degree
☐ The Centre for Feminist Studies is funded by the Faculty of Arts. Current research fields are feminist epistemology, feminist cultural analysis, feminist psychoanalysis, women's literature and feminist pedagogy.

Gruppen for Medicinsk Kvindeforskning på Fyn
The Institute of Community Health
Department of Social Medicine
Odense University
J.B. Winslowsvej 17
5000 ODENSE C
☎ 66 15 86 00 ext. 4930
Contact: Inger Schaumburg
☐ The Forum for Feminist Research in Medicine is open to women physicians and to women employed in Health and Social Services. Feminist perspectives are considered with regard to health and disease.

Roskilde

DENC11

Kvinde Pa Tvaers – Feminist Research Centre
Roskilde University Centre House 03.2.5
PO Box 260
4000 ROSKILDE
☎ 46 75 77 11 ext. 2555
Contact: Karen Sjørup
Course: Women's Studies
☐ Interdisciplinary courses and seminars at degree level.
☐ The focus of the Centre is work on theory and methodology in feminist research.

Dominican Republic

DOMC1

Centro de Investigacion para la Action Femenina (CIPAF)
Benigno Filomena Rojas no. 307
Aparado 1744
SANTO DOMINGO
Contact: Magaly Pineda

DOMC2

International Research and Training Institute for the Advancement of Women
Calle Cesar Nicolas Penson 102 A
Apartado Postal 21747
SANTO DOMINGO

☎ 685 2111
Contact: Eleni Stamiris
☐ Now a worldwide organisation with headquarters in Santo Domingo, the Institute's activities include training, and information and communication for and about women, as well as research. An important research focus is to develop methodology which ensures statistics and other information include and measure the work and condition of women. Research projects have included the position of women in the international economy; women and technology; access to credit for women; and women and co-operatives. INSTRAW publishes *INSTRAW News*, a biannual journal, in English, French and Spanish. A book, *Woman in the World Economy*, has also been published in Spanish, English and Japanese.

Ethiopia

Addis Ababa

ETHC1

African Training and Research Centre for Women
United Nations Economics Commission for Africa
Box 3001
ADDIS ABABA
Contact: Mary Tadesse

Faroe Islands

FARC1

Department of Faroese
University of the Faroe Islands
Debesartrod
100 TORSHAVN
☎ 298 15 304
Contact: Malan Simonsen
The Women's Studies Liaison Centre
☐ An interdisciplinary forum for Women's Studies researchers. The Centre registers women researchers and offers support, discussion and dissemination of research.

Finland

Helsinki

FINC1

The Christina Institute for Women's Studies
University of Helsinki
PO Box 4
00014 HELSINKI
☎ 0 191 3395/191 3387
Contact: Pia Purra
Course: Women's Studies
☐ Interdisciplinary and multidisciplinary courses across: art history, biblical exegetics, church history, communications, comparative culture studies, comparative literature, development studies, economic and social history, economics, education, Finnish literature, general linguistics, geography, history, philosophy, political history, political science, practical theology, psychology, social psychology, sociology, study of religions, systematic theology, and theatre research.
☐ The Institute is involved in teaching, research and publications. Reference Library available. Offers facilities for researchers. Chairperson of the Institute's Board is Auli Hakulinen.

Tampere

FINC2

Centre for Women's Studies and Gender Research
University of Tampere
Research Centre for Social Science
PO Box 607
33101 TAMPERE
☎ 31 15 68 95
Contact: Ulla Vuorela
☐ Associated with the Research Centre for Social Sciences, the Centre is active in research, the development of postgraduate studies in the field, and publications.

Turku/ABO

FINC3

Institute of Women's Studies
Abo Akademi University
20500 ABO (TURKU)
☎ 21 654 311
Contact: Maria Grönroos
☐ A national documentation centre and library in women's studies. The Institute co-ordinates and initiates women's studies and feminist research at Abo Akademi University, the swedish-language university of Finland. Courses are offered both in swedish and english.

FINC4

Naistutkimuksen Ohjausverkosto
Women's Studies Guidance Network
University of Turku
20500 TURKU
☎ 21 633 3245
Contact: Aili Nenola
☐ The activities of the Network cover a wide range of postgraduate research: women in the labour market; sexuality, socialisation and identity development; the welfare state; history of home technology; women in art, literature, sport, media, folklore, etc. Research activities are co-ordinated throughout the country.

☐ Women's studies courses are taught at most finnish universities. Information from Ms Liisa Husu, Coordinator for Finnish Women's Studies, Council for Equality between Men and Women, PO Box 267, 00171 Helsinki, Finland, tel. +358-0-160-5705.

France

Bron

FRC1

Centre Lyonnais d'Etudes Féministes
Irish Université Lyon II
  Av. Pierre Mendes France Case 11
  69676 BRON
☎ 78 77 23 23 ext. 484
Contact: Annik Houel
Course: Etude sur les Femmes et les Rapports de Sex
☐ Interdisciplinary studies at degree level.
Qualification: 2 UV DEUG
☐ The Centre d'Etudes Féministes is an informal group in higher education.

Nancy

FRC2

Department d'Etudes Britanniques et Nord-Americaines
Université de Nancy II
  23 Boulevard Albert ler
  BP 33–97
  54015 NANCY
Course: Histoire des Femmes Americaines du XIXe au XXe siècle
☐ Postgraduate level work.
Qualifications: Degree, Master's degree

Nanterre

FRC3

Section d'Anglais UFR Langues
Université de Paris X
  200 ave. de la République
  92001 NANTERRE
Contact: Judith Ezekial
Course: Histoire des Femmes Americaines en 19ème et 20ème Siècles
☐ Taught within the discipline of Modern Languages.
Qualifications: Degree, Master's degree

Paris

FRC4

Centre Parisien d'Etudes Critiques
  1 place de l'Odeon
  75006 PARIS
☎ 46 33 85 33
Contact: Deborah Elassman
Courses: Théorie Féministe; La Femme Palmpseste
☐ This programme is part of a course for American students at postgraduate level. Also taught in New York, USA.

FRC5

Dialogues de Femmes
  12 rue Georges Berger
  75017 PARIS
☎ 46 22 29 70
Contact: Alice Colanis
Courses: History discipline covering the issues of: France during the Occupation; Rights and Law; the Scientific Construction of Gender; the Situation of Algerian Women; Women's Organisations and the Catholic Church.
☐ Organised by an independent feminist group, and aimed at adult education level.

FRC6

Faculty of Social Science
The Open University
  28 rue du Fur
  75006 PARIS
☎ 45 44 77 03
Contact: Rosemary Pearson
Course: Issues in Women's Studies
☐ Interdisciplinary, distance learning courses taught in English. Includes gender and education; girls into mathematics; women, writing and culture; and women into management.
Qualifications: Degree, Certificate

FRC7

Institut d'Anglais
Université Paris VII
  10 rue Charles V
  75004 PARIS
☎ 42 74 27 54
Contact: Sully Morland
Courses: Femmes et Féminismes; Femmes, Famille, Folie; Histoire des Femmes en Grande Bretagne du XIXe et XXe Siècles.
☐ At postgraduate level, with teaching in English.
Qualifications: Degree, Master's degree, DEA

FRC8

Centre d'Enseignement, de Documentation & de Recherches pour les Etudes Féministes
CEDREF – Université Paris VII
  2 place Jussieu
  75251 PARIS
☎ 44 27 56 23
Contact: Liliane Kandel
Courses: Etudes Féministes; Femmes et Institutions; Femmes, Féminisme et Pouvoirs

Courses

☐ The Women's Studies programme is offered by CEDREF. Paris is one of the eight European universities which participates in the ERASMUS exchange programme in Women's Studies.
Qualifications: Degree, DEA, Master's degree

FRC9

Group for the Study of Sex Roles, Family, and Human Development
National Centre for Scientific Research
    87 Rue Carchinet
    PARIS 75017
Contact: Andrée Michel

St Denis

FRC10

Centre de Recherches & d'Etudes Feminines
Université Paris VIII
    2 rue de la Liberté
    93526 ST DENIS
☎ 49 40 65 03
Contact: Marguerite Sandre
Courses: Différence Sexuelle; Etudes Féministes Pluridisciplinaires; Ecriture, Appartenance et Exil; Seminaires Interdisciplinaires
Qualifications: Master's degree, Doctorate

Toulouse

FRC11

Simone, Conceptualisation et Communication de la Recherche/Femmes
Université de Toulouse-Le Mirail
    UFR d'Histoire
    5 allées Antonio Machado
    31058 TOULOUSE
☎ 61 50 43 94
Contact: Marie-France Brive
Courses: Femmes, Histoire, Sociétés, Culture; Etudes Féministes, Histoire-Sociologie-uv en Economie et Anglais
☐ These courses are offered within the History discipline.
Qualifications: Degree, DEUG, Master's degree

Centre for Feminist Research
☐ Activities include teaching, publications, documentation and ERASMUS exchanges, as well as research.

FRC12

UFR Sciences Sociales
Université Toulouse le Mirail
    5 allées Antonio Machado
    31058 TOULOUSE

☎ 61 50 42 50
Contact: Monique Haicault
Course: Sociologie du Travail des Femmes (Sociology of Women's Work)
☐ Assessment is by written and oral work.
Qualification: uv de DEUG

FRC13

UPR414
CNRS
    La Rotonde
    7 rue Guy Moquet
    94802 VILLEJUIF
☎ 47 26 46 58 ext. 647
Contact: Dominique Lhuillier
Courses: Ethnologie du Maghrebm; Jeunes Femmes de Parents Maghrebins; Immigrés en France
☐ Postgraduate-level work in ethnology.
Qualification: Doctorate

Germany

Berlin

GERC1

Feministiches Frauen-Gesundheits Zentrum EV
    Bambergerstrasse 51
    1000 BERLIN 30
☎ 030 213 9557
Contact: Sylvia Groth
Course: Women's Health
☐ Self-help courses aimed at adult education level

Independent Feminist Group
☐ Has a small library and documentation centre.

GERC2

Institute of Latin American Studies
Free University Berlin
    Abteilung Sociologie
    Rudesheimerstrasse 54–56
    1000 BERLIN 33
☎ 030 853 5855
Contact: Dr Renate Rott
Course: Latin American Studies
☐ Postgraduate-level feminist orientation about women.

GERC3

Dozentinnengruppe
Fuchberich Politische Wissenschaft der FU Berlin
    Ihnestrasse 321
    1000 BERLIN
☎ 030 838 6534
Contact: Birgit Sauer

Course: Grundkurse Politik und Geschichte
□ Series of courses within the Political Science discipline.

GERC4

Institut für Geschichtswissenschaft
Technische Universität Berlin
   Ernst-Reuter Platz 7
   1000 BERLIN 10
☎   030 314 25844
Contact: Karin Hansen
Course: Feminist Women's History
□ A minimum of one course is offered each semester, at degree level.

Bielefeld

GERC5

Fakultät Pädagogik
Universität Bielefeld
   Postfach 8604
   4800 BIELEFELD 1
☎   49 521 1604550
Contact: Juliane Jacobi
Course: Frauenstudien
□ A series of seminars and lectures aimed at degree level. Bielefeld is one of the eight European universities which participates in the ERASMUS exchange programme in Women's Studies.
Qualification: Certificate

GERC6

Frauenstudien – Fakultät für Geschichte und Philosophie
Universität Bielefeld
   Postfach 8640
   4800 BIELEFELD 1
☎   49 521 3219
Contact: Gisela Bock
Courses: Politsche und Indeengeschichte de Frauenbewegung in Europa und den USA 19/20JH; Industrielle Revolution und Frauenarbeit
□ Degree-level courses within the discipline of History. ERASMUS exchanges.
Qualification: Certificate

Dortmund

GERC7

Hochschuldidaktisches Zentrum
Hdz der Universität Dortmund
   Rheinlanddamm 199
   4600 DORTMUND 1
☎   0231 7551
Contact: Sigrid Metz-Gockel

Courses: Girls and School; The Private and Working Lives of Men and Women; Power and Sex
□ Postgraduate level, these courses form part of the teacher training programme.
Qualification: Master's degree

Essen

GERC8

Bereich Frauenstudies/Frauenforschung
Hochschuldidaktischen Zentrum-Universität Essen
   Universitätstrasse 12
   4300 ESSEN
☎   0201 183 3244 ext. 3309
Contact: Ingeborg Stahr
Courses: Female Socialisation; Women's Health; Women's Language; Women and Computer Technology; Feminist Research
□ Interdisciplinary studies aimed at adult education level.
Qualification: Certificate

Frankfurt

GERC9

Frankfurter Frauenschule
   SFBF Hohensaufenstrasse 8
   6000 FRANKFURT 4
☎   069 745674
Contact: Monika Gutheil
Courses: Fortbildungen; Bildungsurlaub
□ Gender Studies courses specific to professionals such as teachers and nurses.

Hamburg

GERC10

Frauenbildungszentrum-Denkträume
Archib Bibliothek Kurse
   Grindelallee 43
   2000 HAMBURG 13
☎   040 450644
Contact: Helga Braun
Courses: Lesben und Heteras; Feministische Theorie; Bildungsurlaub
□ Lesbian Studies based on weekend seminars. All courses aimed at adult education level.

Courses

GERC11

Frauen Technikzentrum – Deutscher Frauenring EV
WEDV-Weiterbildung für Frauen von Frauen
Normannenweg 2
2000 HAMBURG 26
☎ 040 251 4399
Contact: Ellen Sessar-Karpp
Course: Computer course and relevant economic topic
☐ New technology courses open to women who wish to improve their skills or carry out a specific project.
☐ The Women's Studies Centre has a co-operative partnership with other new technology training centres in Berlin, Cottbus, Dresden, Erfurt, Leipzig, Potsdam, Rostock and Schwerin.

Hanover

GERC12

Weiterbildungsstudium Arbeitswissenschaft
Universität Hannover
Lange Lambe 32
3000 HANOVER 1
☎ 0511 762 4847
Contact: Elisabeth Wienemann
Course: The Politics of Equal Opportunities and Positive Action
☐ Aimed at adult education level, the courses are available to those with two years' work experience.
Qualification: Certificate

Kiel

GERC13

Pädagogische Hochschule Kiel
Olshausenstrasse 75
2300 KIEL 1
☎ 49 431 880 1237
Contact: Renate Haas
Course: English Literature
☐ This course teaches English Literature with a feminist perspective.

München

GERC14

Verein Zur Förderung des Bayerischen Archiv der Frauenbewegung
Lilienstrasse 4
8000 MUNCHEN 80
☎ 089 714 9187
Contact: Hannelore Mabry

Course: Feminist History
☐ Taught at adult education level.

Osnabrück

GERC15

FB Sprach und Literaturwissenschaft
Universität Osnabrück
Neuer Graben 4-
Postfach 4469
4500 OSNABRUCK
☎ 0541 125232
Contact: Magdalene Heuter
Courses: Women in Literature; Literature of Women
☐ Postgraduate-level work.
Qualifications: Master's degree/Lehramter

GERC16

Frauenarchiv Natalie Barney EV
Langestrasse 76
4500 OSNABRUCK
☎ 0541 87599
Contact: Nathalie Crombee
Course: Feminist Seminars
☐ Interdisciplinary studies on feminist themes including literature, art, music, psychology, etc. Aimed at adult education.

Wachtverg-Berkum

GERC17

Faculty of Social Science
The Open University
Im Saufgang 1
5307 WACHTVERG-BERKUM
Contact: Julia Robertson
Course: Issues in Women's Studies
☐ Interdisciplinary, distance learning courses taught in English. Includes gender and education; girls into mathematics; women, writing and culture; and women into management.
Qualifications: Certificate, degree

Winzer

GERC18

Akademie für Kritische Matriarchale Forschung & Erfahrung-Hagia EV
Waghof 2
8351 WINZER
☎ 08545 1245
Contact: Heide Gottnre-Abendroth
Course: Matriarchy

☐ Short courses (4 weekends) within the Cultural Studies discipline.

Women's Studies Centre
☐ Independent feminist group.

Great Britain and Northern Ireland

Aberystwyth

GBC1

University College, Aberystwyth
    Hugh Owen Building
    ABERYSTWYTH SY23 3DY
☎   0970 62311
Contact: Jane Aaron
Courses: Extra-mural courses and courses in Departments of History and English

Bath

GBC2

University of Bath
    Claverton Down
    BATH BA2 7AY
☎   0225 826826 ext. 5664
Contact: Claire Duchen
Courses: Options in the School of Modern Languages and International Studies

Belfast

GBC3

Faculty of Social Science
The Open University in Northern Ireland
    40 University Road
    BELFAST BT7 1SU
☎   0232 230565
Course: Issues in Women's Studies
☐ Distance learning courses which can form part of a degree. Themes include gender and education; girls into mathematics; women, writing and culture; and women into management.
Qualifications: Diploma, certificate, degree

GBC4

Queens University of Belfast
    BELFAST BT7 1NN
☎   0232 245133 ext. 3712
Contact: Eithne McLaughlin
Courses: Women's Studies module options in Interdisciplinary Studies

☐ Minor honours or combined honours on the undergraduate programme.
Qualification: Degree

Birmingham

GBC5

Fircroft College of Adult Education
    1018 Bristol Road
    Selly Oak
    BIRMINGHAM B29 6LH
☎   021 472 0116
Contact: Hilary Hinds
Courses: Return to Study; Women's Studies
☐ One-year full-time (or two-year part-time) course for adult students who want to return to study. Women's Studies module available from 1992–3; modules in Literature, Politics and Sociology cover women's/gender issues.

GBC6

University of Birmingham
    Edgbaston
    BIRMINGHAM B15 2TT
☎   021 414 6060
Contact: Maureen McNeil
Courses: Women's Studies
☐ Options in the Departments of Cultural Studies; Economic and Social History; Social Policy and Social Work; French Studies. Women and Education Management.
Qualifications: Degree, Master's degree

GBC7

University of Central England in Birmingham
    Franchise Street
    Perry Barr
    BIRMINGHAM B42 5U
☎   021 331 5476
Courses: Courses in Schools of English and Sociology
Qualifications: Degree, Postgraduate diploma (equal opportunities)

Bradford

GBC8

University of Bradford
    BRADFORD BD7 1DP
☎   0274 383515/733466
Contact: Jalna Hanmer
Course: Women's Studies

Courses

□ Available in the Departments of Applied Social Studies; Social & Economic Studies; Peace Studies; European Studies; Modern Languages; Development & Project Planning; and Department of Industrial Technology.
Qualifications: Diploma, Master's degree Women's Studies (Applied)

West Yorkshire Centre for Research on Women (WYCROW); Violence, Abuse and Gender Relations Research Unit; Work and Gender Research Unit; Employment group; Women and Development group; Feminist Archive
□ Seminars on women and society, current research and issues.

Brighton

GBC9

University of Brighton
Falmer
BRIGHTON
☎ 0273 600900
Contact: Sally Munt
Course: Women's Studies
□ Part of the Humanities degree. There is a Master's degree planned.
Qualifications: Degree, Master's degree (in planning)

GBC10

University of Sussex
Falmer
BRIGHTON BN1 9QN
☎ 0273 606755 ext. 2433
Contact: Sybil Oldfield
Courses: Women's Studies options, including Sociology of Gender
Qualification: Degree
Courses: Gay and Lesbian Studies; Gender and Development; Women and Education
Qualifications: Master's degree, Doctorate

Research Centre in Women's Studies
Women and Technology Research Programme
University of Sussex
Science Policy Research Unit
Mantell Building, Falmer
BRIGHTON BN1 9RF
Contact: Felicity Henwood

Bristol

GBC11

University of Bristol
BRISTOL BS8 1TH
☎ 0272 303619

Contact: Liz Bird
Course: Women's Studies
□ Available in Continuing Education, with an undergraduate option in Department of Politics.
Qualifications: Degree, Master's degree
Course: Gender and Social Policy
□ Postgraduate-level work.
Qualification: Master's degree

GBC12

University of the West of England, Bristol
Coldharbour Lane
Frenchay
BRISTOL BS16 1QY
☎ 0272 656261
Contact: Carolyn Britton
Course: Women's Studies
□ Available in the Social Sciences and Humanities.
Qualifications: Diploma, Master's degree

Cambridge

GBC13

Anglia Polytechnic University
East Road
CAMBRIDGE CB1 7PT
☎ 0223 63721 ext. 2264
Contact: Penelope Kenrick
Courses: One-term Return to Study course; Women's Studies field in Joint Honours
□ Undergraduate programme to start 1993; part-time postgraduate-level work available (two years, with one-year diploma option)
Qualifications: Degree, Postgraduate diploma, Master's degree

Canterbury

GBC14

The University of Kent
CANTERBURY CT2 7NY
☎ 0227 764000 ext. 7534
Contact: Mary Evans
Courses: Seminar series in Women's Studies
□ Options on undergraduate programme as well as postgraduate study. (ESRC recognised)
Qualifications: Diploma, Degree, Master's degree, M.Phil., Doctorate

Cardiff

GBC15

University College, Cardiff
School of Social and Administrative Studies
62 Park Place
CARDIFF CF1 3AS
☎ 0222 874000 ext. 4175
Contact: Teresa Rees
Courses: Courses in School of Social and Administrative Studies
Qualification: Master's degree (M.Sc. Econ.)

Cheltenham

GBC16

Cheltenham and Gloucester College of Higher Education
PO Box 220
The Park
CHELTENHAM GL50 2QF
☎ 0242 532794
Contact: Melanie Ilic
Courses: Women's Studies modules
☐ Women's Studies can be taken as a major, minor or joint field of study within modular degree programme. Hoping to develop Master's degree.
Qualification: Degree

Chichester

GBC17

West Sussex Institute of Higher Education
Bishop Otter College
CHICHESTER PO19 4PE
☎ 0243 787911 ext. 285
Contact: Valerie Briginshaw
Courses: Women's/gender issues on Combined Studies and B.Ed. programme
☐ Developing a Women's Studies course/module for the BA Combined Studies degree.
Qualifications: B.Ed. degree, Combined Studies degree

Women's Studies/Feminist Research Group; Staff and Students Women's Group

Colchester

GBC18

University of Essex
Wivenhoe Park
COLCHESTER CO4 3SQ
☎ 0206 2628
Contact: Elaine Jordan

Courses: Sociology, History, Literature
Qualification: Degree
Courses: Women Writing; Sociology; Doctoral Programme in Feminist Theory
Qualifications: Master's degree, Doctorate

Coleraine

GBC19

University of Ulster
COLERAINE BT52 1SA
☎ 0265 44141 ext. 4393
Contact: Celia Davies
Courses: Information Technology for Women; Working with Women; Training for Tutoring; Training Assertiveness Trainers; Access course
☐ Short courses available from Department of Adult and Continuing Education
Qualifications: Certificate, Access certificate, Master's degree
Centre for Research on Women; Women's Studies Forum.

Coventry

GBC20

Coventry University
Priory Street
COVENTRY CV1 5FB
☎ 0203 838336
Contact: Susanne Haselgrove
Courses: Pre-access course and undergraduate options (freestanding)
Qualifications: Certificate, Degree

Women's Studies Centre
☐ Co-ordinates Women's Studies activities and feminist research group. Regular programme of seminars on women's studies/feminist issues.

GBC21

School of Women's Studies
University of Warwick
COVENTRY CV4 7AL
☎ 0203 523600
Contact: Terry Lovell
Course: Women's Studies
☐ Postgraduate training and research; plus variety of courses in Departments of English, Sociology, Law, Philosophy, Education.
Qualifications: Master's degree, Doctorate

Courses

Crawley

GBC22

Crawley College of Further Education
　College Road
　CRAWLEY RH10 1NR
☎ 0293 612686
Contact: Chris Silvester
Courses: Women's/gender issues in blocks on particular courses: Access; Social Care; Sociology; Health Care

Edinburgh

GBC23

University of Edinburgh
　EDINBURGH EH8 9XP
☎ 031 667 1011 ext. 4311
Contact: Liz Bondi
Course: Women's Studies
☐ Undergraduate option in Politics.
Qualification: Degree
Courses: Geography with Gender Studies; Social Policy with Gender Studies; Sociology with Gender Studies; Option on MAc/Diploma in Social Sciences, 'Gender in Society'
Qualification: Master's degree (Scotland), MAc/Diploma

Exeter

GBC24

Faculty of Arts
University of Exeter
　Cotley
　Streatham Rise
　EXETER EX4 4PE
☎ 0392 411907
Contact: Jo McDonagh
Course: Women's Studies
☐ Postgraduate-level work.
Qualification: Master's degree

Glasgow

GBC25

University of Strathclyde
　GLASGOW G1 1XH
☎ 041 552 4400 ext. 3604
Contact: Stevi Jackson
Course: Women's Studies
☐ M. Litt, Certificate, variety of courses.
Qualification: Master's degree

☐ There is a research group focusing on women at work, training, etc. Seminars and feminist theory day schools.

Hull

GBC26

University of Hull
　Cottingham
　HULL
Contact: Norma Butterworth
Course: Gender option in the Department of Sociology

Lancaster

GBC27

University of Lancaster
　LANCASTER LA1 4YL
☎ 0524 65201 ext. 2879
Contact: Janet Hartley
Courses: Women's Studies and options within programmes
☐ Undergraduate and postgraduate taught courses, together with postgraduate work by research.
Qualifications: Degree, Master's degree, M.Phil., Doctorate

Centre for Women's Studies, Feminist Reading Group, Language and Gender in the Classroom Group.
☐ Seminar series in Women's Studies. Research supervision is available in women and history, sexuality, feminist cultural studies, feminist issues in science, feminist literary studies, gender issues in education, social policy issues and 'race' and 'ethnicity' (ESRC recognised).

Leicester

GBC28

De Montfort University
　School of Arts
　PO Box 143
　LEICESTER LE1 9BH
☎ 0533 551551
Contact: Imelda Whelehan
Course: Women's Studies
☐ Available as options in Arts and Humanities; also as modules in postgraduate study in Historical and Cultural Studies.
Qualifications: Degree, Master's degree

GBC29
University of Leicester
   University Road
   LEICESTER
☎ 0533 522459
Contact: Sallie Westwood
Courses: Options in English and Sociology; Extra-mural Women's Studies
Qualifications: Degree, Master's degree

Liverpool and metropolitan area

GBC30
Edge Hill College of Higher Education
   St Helens Road
   ORMSKIRK L39 4QP
☎ 0695 575171
Contact: Juliet Cook
Courses: Women's Studies options on programmes
Qualifications: Degree, Master's degree

GBC31
University of Liverpool
   Eleanor Rathbone Building
   PO Box 147
   Myrtle Street
   LIVERPOOL L69 3BX
☎ 051 794 3011
Contact: Sylvia Bailey
Courses: Gender Issues in Social Work; Women's Studies in Sociology; Social Work; Continuing Education
Qualifications: Social work diploma, Master's degree

GBC32
Wirral Metropolitan College
   Carlett Park
   Eastham
   WIRRAL L62 OAY
☎ 051 327 6271
Contact: Lynne Curtis
Course: Women's Studies option on Access to Higher Education Course
☐ Variety of access courses for women – including Women's Studies.

London and Greater London

GBC33
Akina Mama wa Afrika (AMWA)
   Solidarity among African Women
   London Women's Centre
   Wesley House
   4 Wild Court
   LONDON WC2B 5AU
☎ 071 405 0678

Contact: Mabel Ikpoh
☐ AMWA is an autonomous organisation whose full membership is restricted to African women, although others can subscribe as friends. The focus is research on African women, publication and dissemination of findings, and co-ordinating with grassroots women to act as a pressure group for matters concerning African women. Particular research has been on the condition of African women in shelters and prisons, and on the status of educational opportunities and welfare rights. Other work includes sponsoring community activities, and AMWA has published *Focus on African Women*.

GBC34
Birkbeck College
University of London
   26 Russell Square
   LONDON WC1B 5DQ
☎ 071 631 6642
Contact: Mary Kennedy
Courses: Women's Studies; courses on gender; Lesbian Studies; Black Women's Studies
☐ Adult Education courses.
Course: Gender, Society and Culture
☐ Postgraduate-level work.
Qualification: Master's degree

GBC35
CHANGE
   PO Box 824
   LONDON SE24 9JS
☎ 071 277 6187
Contact: Georgina Ashworth
☐ CHANGE: International Reports, Women and Society is registered as an educational charitable trust. The aims are primarily to research and publish reports on women's condition and status worldwide, having resource facilities and consultancies for research, documentation and publications.

GBC36
Feminist International Network of Resistance to Reproductive and Genetic Engineering
   PO Box 583
   LONDON NW3 1RQ
☎ 44 532 681109
Contact: Debbie Steinberg
☐ FINRRAGE was established in order to provide a network for researchers on an international basis. Women from 26 countries are now part of this network. Research has been concerned with in vitro techniques, embryo transfer, sex predetermination, cloning, genetic engineering, contraception and population control, surrogacy, and infertility management. Activities include conferences and publications. *Reproductive and Genetic Engineering: Journal of International Feminist Analysis* is available in English, German, Dutch and French. FINRRAGE is working towards a firm base

to fund and resource the International Feminist Centre on Reproductive and Genetic Engineering.

GBC37

Goldsmiths' College
    LONDON SE14 6NW
☎   081 692 7171 ext. 2138/2046
Contact: Caroline Ramozanoglu
Courses: Women's Studies
☐ Available within the Departments of Education, Sociology, Anthropology and Social Administration. Postgraduate-level study in Gender Studies currently being developed.

GBC38

University of Greenwich
    Wellington Street
    LONDON SE18 6PF
☎   081 316 8000
Contact: Denise Leggett
Courses: Women's Studies options in Sociology and History
☐ Undergraduate and postgraduate courses within the School of Humanities.
Qualifications: Degree, Master's degree
Course: Gender and Ethnic Studies
☐ Taught within the School of Social Sciences.
Qualification: Master's Degree

GBC39

Hillcroft College
    South Bank
    SURBITON
    Surrey
☎   081 399 2688
Courses: Courses on women/gender; Introduction to Women's Studies; Women's Lives and Women's Roles

GBC40

Institute of Education
University of London
    20 Bedford Way
    LONDON WC1H OAH
☎   071 612 6322/6313
Contact: Diana Leonard
Courses: Women and Management; Gender, Society and Culture; Women's Studies and Education; Human Rights; courses in Departments of Curriculum Studies, Rights in Education, and English and Media Studies
Qualifications: Diploma, Master's degree

Centre for Research on Education and Gender
☐ Postgraduate training and research offered in both Women's Studies and Gender Studies.

GBC41

Kingston University
    Penrhyn Road
    KINGSTON UPON THAMES KT1 2EE
☎   081 549 1366
Contact: Anne Showstack Sassoon or Anita Walsh
Course: Women's Studies
☐ Half field on Combined Studies, and option area on Applied Social Science; also options on Languages, Economics and Politics.
Qualification: Degree

GBC42

London School of Economics
    Houghton Street
    LONDON WC2A 2AE
☎   071 405 7686
Contact: Sylvia Walby
Course: Women's Studies
☐ Available in the Sociology Department.

Centre for Research on Gender
☐ Seminar series on gender.

GBC43

University of East London
    Longbridge Road
    DAGENHAM
    Essex RM8 2AS
☎   081 590 7722
Contact: Maggie Humm
Course: Women's Studies
☐ Undergraduate and Postgraduate students can register topics in Women's Studies.
Qualifications: Degree, Master's degree, Doctorate

Women's Studies and Feminist Research Group
☐ Seminar series.

GBC44

University of North London
    1 Prince of Wales Road
    LONDON NW5 3LB
☎   071 607 2789 ext. 4086
Contact: Sue Lees
Course: Women's Studies
☐ Can be taken as part of the Access to Higher Education course. Available also as a major, joint or minor component of the Humanities Degree. Postgraduate work in MA on Representation.
Qualifications: Degree, Master's degree

Women's Studies Centre
☐ Programme of seminars on women's studies/feminist issues.

Abuse of Women and Children Studies and Resources Unit
University of North London
    Ladbroke House
    62–66 Highbury Grove
    LONDON N5 2AD
☎   071 607 2789 ext. 5014
Contact: Liz Kelly
☐ Independent research unit, also provide training, consultancy and resources on research, policy and practice. Has yearly training and conference programme and provides trainers/speakers to academic, practitioner and community groups.

GBC45

Faculty of Social Science
Southlands College
    Parkside
    Wimbledon
    LONDON SW19
☎   081 946 2234
Contact: Beryl Madoc-Jones
Course: Women's Studies
☐ Can be taken as part of a joint undergraduate programme. There are 16 subjects with which Women's Studies may combine.
Qualification: Degree

Women's Studies and Feminist Research Group
☐ Holds regular seminars.

GBC46

West London Institute
    Gordon House Campus
    TWICKENHAM
    Middlesex
☎   081 568 8741
Contact: Deborah Philips
Course: Women's Studies
☐ Options within the Department of English and American Studies.
Qualification: Degree

GBC47

Woolwich College
    Villas Road
    Plumstead
    LONDON SE18 2PN
☎   081 855 1216
Contact: Carole Green
Course: Course provisionally entitled Women's Issues and Biology based in Science Department.
☐ Accredited to LOCF (London Open College Federation); women's/gender issues on other courses.

Loughborough

GBC48

Department of Social Sciences
Loughborough University
    LOUGHBOROUGH LE11 3TU
☎   0509 263171
Contact: Barbara Bagilhole
Course: Women's Studies
☐ Postgraduate-level work.
Qualifications: Diploma, Master's degree

Manchester and Greater Manchester

GBC49

Manchester Metropolitan University
    All Saints
    MANCHESTER M15 6BH
☎   061 247 2000
Contact: Margaret Beetham
Course: Adult Education courses for Women at Work
Qualification: Diploma
Courses: Equal Opportunities; Politics of Women and Disability; Psychological Theory and Feminist Practice; Feminist Criticism and 19th Century Writing; Women and Philosophy; Lesbian Writing; Women and Stress; Women, Race and Class; Work in Women's Lives
☐ Postgraduate-level work which can be undertaken part-time.
Qualification: Master's degree

GBC50

University of Manchester
    Coupland Street
    MANCHESTER M13 9PL
☎   061 275 2496
Contact: Liz Stanley
Courses: Women's Studies courses in Department of Sociology; Feminist Studies
☐ Postgraduate studies in Feminist Thought available from 1992/3.
Qualification: Master's degree

Feminist and Gender Studies Centre; Feminist Research Group
☐ Seminars on feminist issues.

GBC51

University of Salford
    SALFORD M5 4WT
☎   061 745 5000
Contact: Georgina Waylen
Course: Women's Studies

Courses

□ Postgraduate-level work.
Qualification: Master's degree

Milton Keynes

GBC52

Open University
    Walton Hall
    MILTON KEYNES MK7 6AA
☎ 0908 652440
Contact: Linda Jones
Course: Women's Studies
□ Second-level course, taken as part of the under-graduate programme.
Qualification: Degree

Northampton

GBC53

Nene College
    Moulton Park
    NORTHAMPTON NN2 7AL
☎ 0604 715000 ext. 224
Contact: Gabriele Griffin
Course: Women's Studies
□ Options on Combined Studies in Drama, English, History, Sociology.
Qualifications: Degree, Master's degree (part-time and full-time), Doctorate

Oxford

GBC54

Oxford Brookes University
    Gypsy Lane
    Headington
    OXFORD OX3 OBP
☎ 0865 819762
Contact: Anne Digby
Course: Women's Studies
□ Undergraduate courses in Humanities, Planning, Sociology and Health Care. Postgraduate courses in Humanities.
Qualifications: Degree, Master's degree

GBC55

University of Oxford
    Queen Elizabeth House
    OXFORD
Contact: Shirley Ardener

Centre for Cross-Cultural Research on Women
□ Women's Studies Committee produces a termly listing of relevant lecture and seminar series.

Plymouth

GBC56

University of Plymouth
    PLYMOUTH PL4 8AA
☎ 0752 600600/233230
Contact: Pamela Abbott
Course: Women's Studies in Sociology; Social Policy and Administration; and Psychology
□ Postgraduate course is taken part-time.
Qualifications: Degree (B.Sc. Sociology, BA Social Policy and Administration, B.Sc. Psychology), Master's degree

Pontypridd

GBC57

University of Glamorgan
    PONTYPRIDD OF37 1DL
☎ 0443 480480 ext. 2692
Contact: Pauline Young
Course: Women's Studies
□ Various in Humanities; options in B.Sc. Behavioural Studies and BA Communications.
Qualification: Degree

Portsmouth

GBC58

University of Portsmouth
    Milldam Site
    Burnaby Road
    PORTSMOUTH PO1 3AS
☎ 0705 842234/842238
Contact: C. Lupton
Course: Women's Studies
□ Modules in range of undergraduate degrees; Gender Studies stream offered on MA in State, Policy & Social Change.
Qualifications: Degree, Master's degree

Women's Studies/ Feminist Research Group

Preston

GBC59

University of Central Lancashire
    Corporation Street
    PRESTON PR1 2TQ
☎ 0772 201201
Contact: Cathy Lubelska
Course: Women's Studies programme

□ Can be taken as a major, joint or minor on first degree. Postgraduate-level courses available. Seminars on women's studies/feminist issues held fortnightly.
Qualifications: Degree, Master's degree

Rotherham

GBC60

Rotherham College of Arts and Technology
Eastwood Lane
ROTHERHAM
☎ 0709 362111
Contact: Hilary Eadson
Course: Women's Studies programme
Qualifications: Sheffield University Certificate – equivalent to 1st year of degree; Women's Studies as part of Access into HE.

St Andrews

GBC61

University of St Andrews
St Andrews
FIFE KY16 9JU
☎ 0334 76161 ext. 7249
Contact: Daphne Hampson
Course: Women's Studies
□ Option in Department of Divinity.

Sheffield

GBC62

Sheffield Hallam University
Psalter Lane
SHEFFIELD S7 8UZ
☎ 0742 532601
Contact: Sue Hall
Course: Women's Studies
□ Units in Critical Studies Programme; Applied Social Science; Communication Studies; Fine Art; Historical Studies; English; short courses run by Women's Studies Centre.
Qualifications: Degree, Master's degree

GBC63

University of Sheffield
85 Wilkinson Street
SHEFFIELD S10 2GJ
☎ 0742 768555 ext. 4920
Contact: Victoria Robinson
Course: Women's Studies
□ Available in the Departments of Sociology, Social Policy, Literature, Law, Education, History.
Qualifications: Undergraduate certificate, Diploma

Periodic research group within Continuing Education
□ Seminars on feminist issues.

Southend

GBC64

Southend College of Technology
Carnarvon Road
SOUTHEND ON SEA SS2 6LS
☎ 0702 432205
Contact: Sue Sibley
Course: Women's Studies
□ Module on NOW (New Opportunities for Women) courses; women's/gender issues on other courses.

Stoke

GBC65

Staffordshire University
Brindley Building
Leek Road
STOKE ON TRENT
☎ 0782 412515
Contact: Ruth Waterhouse
Course: Women's Studies
□ Options in Modern Studies, Sociology, Psychology. Half degree with Modern Studies; postgraduate-level work proposed for 1992.
Qualifications: Degree, Master's degree (proposed)

Women's Research Group
□ Occasional seminars on women's studies/feminist issues.

Sunderland

GBC66

WEA/Durham University Adult and Continuing Education
270 Hylton Road
SUNDERLAND SR4 7XJ
Contact: Viv Shelley
Course: Women's Studies
□ Variety of short 'pre-Access' New Opportunities for Women courses in several centres.

Swansea

GBC67

University College, Swansea
Singleton Park
SWANSEA SA2 8PPP

☎ 0792 295499
Contact: Jane Elliot
Course: Women's Studies
☐ Postgraduate course within the Economics discipline, available from October 1992.
Qualification: Master's degree

Walsall

GBC68

Walsall College of Technology
St Pauls
WALSALL
☎ 0922 720824 ext. 289
Contact: Jane Collins
Course: Women's Studies option on Access to Higher Education course
☐ Accredited to BCAF (Black Country Access Federation).
Qualification: Access to Higher Education
Course: Women in Society
☐ A module available on the first year of an undergraduate Social Science course. Franchised through Coventry University.
Qualification: Degree

Winchester

GBC69

King Alfred's College
Sparkford Lane
WINCHESTER
Contact: Sarah Robinson
Courses: Women's/gender issues on several courses.

Wolverhampton

GBC70

Wulfrun College of Further Education
Paget Road
WOLVERHAMPTON WV6 0DU
☎ 0902 312062
Contact: Jeannie Millichamp
Courses: Assertiveness Training; Media Technology Training for Women; Women's Technician Training Scheme; Information Technology for Women
☐ The technician engineering and technology training is funded by Wolverhampton MBC and the European Social Fund.
Qualifications: City and Guilds; BTEC National Certificate
Course: Women's Studies option on Access to Higher Education course

☐ Access course accredited to BCAF (Black Country Access Federation).
Qualification: Access to Higher Education

GBC71

University of Wolverhampton
Dudley Campus
Castle View
DUDLEY DY1 3HR
☎ 0902 321000
Contact: Jenny Williams
Course: Women's Studies
☐ Modules include: Women's Words, Women's Lives; Women's Writing; Education and Work; Women as Citizens; Feminist Theory and the Contemporary Women's Movement; Women and Representation; Women and Social Science; Public Policy and Political Change. Women's Studies can be studied as a minor, joint or major on the undergraduate modular degree programme. Postgraduate-level work currently available as part-time study, and full-time study mode is being planned.
Qualifications: Degree, Postgraduate certificate, Diploma, Master's degree

Worcester

GBC72

Worcester College of Higher Education
Henwick Grove
WORCESTER WR2 6AJ
Contact: Vienna Duff
Course: Women's Studies
☐ Two-year Women Studies component course planned – hope to have first cohort of students in 1993.

York

GBC73

College of Ripon and St John
Lord Mayor's Walk
YORK
☎ 0904 656771
Contact: Lesley Forrest
Course: Women's Studies
☐ Part I and Part II courses in three-year degrees.

GBC74

University of York
Heslington
YORK YO1 5DD
☎ 0904 433671
Contact: Mary Maynard
Course: Women's Studies

□ Postgraduate-level work, includes contemporary feminist thought; poor relations, women and money; is there such a thing as feminine writing?; women and development; feminist utopias; 19th century feminism. *Qualifications*: Master's degree, Doctorate

Postgraduate Teaching & Research Centre; Centre for Women's studies/Feminist Research Group
□ Seminar programme run by Centre for Women's Studies; conferences and public lectures organised. York is one of the eight European universities which participate in the ERASMUS exchange programme in Women's Studies.

Greece

Athens

GREC1

Workshop on the Anthropology of Sex and Gender
University of the Aegean
　　Kanari 9 (DE)
　　10671 ATHENS
☎　01 362840
Course: Anthropology of Sex and Gender
□ This course is part of the programme of studies for social anthropology at undergraduate level.

GREC2

Diotima
Centre for Research in Women's Issues
　　2 Krekropos Street
　　10558 ATHENS
☎　32 28 791
Contact: Maria Repoussi
Course: Vocational Training Programme for Equality Counsellors
□ Programme of seminars in equal opportunities training, covering employment of women; gender in development; history and social analysis and politics of the women's emancipation movement; equal opportunities legislation; European studies; new technology; women at work; and practical training for women in specific working conditions.
□ The Centre for Research in Women's Issues is subsidised by the Foundation for Education Science 'Cyclades' and the ESF, and includes Women's Studies teaching and publications.

GREC3

General Secretariat for Youth
Direction of Employment
　　Acharon 417
　　11143 ATHENS
☎　0253 24 65
Contact: Vassiliki Vallianou
Course: Training for Unemployed Women

□ Adult education courses in: politics for women, politics of women; new directions in the development of the labour market; modern accounting for young women; gender and schooling – the link with future jobs.

GREC4

Kegme-Mediterranean Institute for Women's Studies
　　Harilaou Trikoupi St 115
　　11473 ATHENS
☎　01 3615660
Contact: Ketty Lazaris
Courses: Summer courses and seminars
□ Organised by an independent feminist group.
□ KEGME involves teaching, publications and documentation as well as research. Founded in 1982, the Institute conducts social science research from a feminist perspective with the aim of changing women's lives. Publications include a twice yearly newsletter; research reports; *Immigrant Women on the Move; The Employment, Health and Education of Migrant Women* in English (1987); and *Readings on Women's Studies in the Mediterranean* (1987).

GREC5

Department of Political Science
Panteion Academy of Political Science
　　Sygrou Ave 136
　　17176 ATHENS
Course: Gender and State Policy
□ Part of the undergraduate programme of studies in the Department of Political Science.

GREC6

Faculty of Architecture
Polytechnic School of Athens
　　28es Octobrion 42
　　10682 ATHENS
☎　3600170
Course: Women and Housing
□ This is part of the undergraduate programme of studies in the Faculty of Architecture.

Ioannina

GREC7

Department of Education
University of Ioannina
　　Daboli 30
　　45110 IOANNINA
☎　0651 21920
Course: Sociology of Education

☐ The course covers issues of sex and gender and is offered at undergraduate level.

Thessaloniki

GREC8

Architecture
Aristotle University of Thessaloniki
University Campus
54006 THESSALONIKI
☎ 031 0991580
Contact: Vana Tentokali
Courses: Introduction to the Human Sciences; Housing within the City
☐ The social construction of gender is introduced into the compulsory course in the first year, and the second is a design course for 2nd and 3rd year students, examining the relationship between housing design and family structure.
Qualification: Degree

GREC9

Department of English
Aristotle University Thessaloniki
54006 THESSALONIKI
☎ 031 99 1688
Contact: Ruth Parkin-Gourelas
Courses: Postmodernism in Women's Fiction; British Women's Theatre; A Theatre of Difference; Women Writers of the English Renaissance
☐ Available in the 3rd and 4th year of undergraduate studies. These courses are taught in English and take place in the winter term.
Qualification: Degree

Guyana

GUYC1

Faculty of Social Sciences
University of Guyana
PO Box 10 11 10
GEORGETOWN
☎ 63691
Contact: Janice M. Jackson
Course: Women's Studies in Literature and Sociology

Women's Studies Unit
☐ Established in 1987 for the purpose of both teaching and researching Women's Studies. Research has been carried out on women and work; violence against women; women and health; and women in higher education. Publication aims include newsletters and journals, and the Unit is establishing a documentation and resource centre.

Honduras

HONC1

Association of University Women in Honduras
El Centro
Tegucigalpa, DC
Casa No. 1241 y 7a Ave
HONDURAS
☎ 37 0294
Contact: M. L. de Betrand Anduray
☐ The Association of University Women in Honduras was founded in 1950 with the aim of obtaining equal employment opportunities and salaries. Research has been carried out on development and women in the Honduras. Publications include a history of feminism in Honduras and a monograph on Honduran women.

Hungary

HUNC1

Budapest University of Economics
1093 BUDAPEST
Fovam ter 8
☎ 361 1186 855/177
Contact: Katalin Koncz

Women's Studies Centre
☐ Established as recently as October 1992, the first of its kind in Hungary. The Centre focuses on research, networking and Women's Studies courses. Two international research projects are current. One is 'The Mechanisms of Promotion of Women to Top Leadership Positions in Public Life' (21 universities are participating). The second is 'The Position of Women in the Transitional Period'.

Iceland

ICEC1

Rannsoknastofa i kvennafraedum vio Haskola Island
Centre for Women's Studies
Iceland's University
Oddi IS101
REYKJAVIK
☎ 1 69 45 95
Contact: Gudrun Olafsdottir
☐ The Centre for Women's Studies was founded in 1990 in order to promote and co-ordinate women's studies and feminist research in Iceland.

India

Bombay

INDC1

SNDT Women's University
Sir Vithaldas Vidyavihar
Santa Cruz (West)
Juhu Road
BOMBAY 400049
Contact: M. Krishna Raj

Research Centre for Women's Studies

INDC2

Tata Institute of Social Sciences
PO Box 8313 Sion-Trombay Road
Deonar
BOMBAY 400088
☎ 5510400
Contact: Suma Chitnis
Course: Women's Studies programme
☐ Teaching at postgraduate level includes the areas of women and work; women and the law; and women and health.
Qualifications: Master's degree, Doctorate

Women's Studies Unit
☐ The Unit is involved in both teaching and research; and offers financial as well as intellectual support to researchers. Research has been carried out into the historical writings of the reform period in Maharashtra, identifying the transforming identity of women. State development policies for underprivileged groups are another area of research.

Hyderabad

INDC3

Osmania University Campus
HYDERABAD 500007
Contact: Shanta Ramershwar Rao

Anveshi Research Centre for Women's Studies

New Delhi

INDC4

Centre for Women's Development Studies (CWDS)
B–43 Panchshila Enclave
NEW DELHI 110017
☎ 6438428
Contact: Vina Mazumdar

☐ The CWDS was established in 1980 to research the socioeconomic and political status of women. The Centre also participates in publishing, teaching, training and policy debates on women's issues. The gender dimension of migrant labour, women's development and child care have been recent research activities of the Centre.

INDC5

Institute of Social Studies Trust (ISST)
M–1 Kanchenjunga
18 Barakhamba Road
NEW DELHI 110001
☎ 3323850/3312861
Contact: Devaki Jain
☐ The ISST was founded in 1964, and granted consultative status with the United Nations Economic and Social Council in 1985. Research into women's issues focuses on their economic roles, and the integration of women in development projects. The Institute houses a reference library containing material relevant to women, the poor and action agencies.

Pune

INDC6

Streevani
c/o Ishvani Kendra
Off Nagar Road
PUNE 411014
☎ 661820
Contact: Augustine Kanjamale
☐ Streevani (Voice of Women) was founded in 1982. Streevani's feminist research projects have included oral history with four groups in Maharashtra; the production of the film *Baj* ('Women'); case studies on women activists; and a reinterpretation of Hindu and Islamic myths about women.

Varanasi

INDC7

Indian Association for Women's Studies
Banras Hindu University
228 Faculty of Social Sciences
VARANASI 221005
Contact: Surinder Jetley

Centre for Women's Studies and Development
☐ Founded in 1987 to strengthen and develop Women's Studies in higher education. The Centre offers research fellowships for interdisciplinary work on women's studies. A diploma course in Women's Studies is being developed. The Centre publishes the *Newsletter of the Indian Association for Women's Studies*.

Ireland

Cork

IREC1

University College Cork
CORK
☎ 010 3521 276871
Contact: Aveen Henry
Course: Women's Studies
☐ Postgraduate-level study.
Qualification: Master's degree

Dublin

IREC2

Council for the Status of Women
54 Lower Mount Street
DUBLIN
☎ 607731/611791
Course: Assertiveness Training and Sexuality
☐ The Council was founded in 1973 through women's organisations joining together for the purpose of liaising between government departments, the European Economic Community, and themselves. The Council offers educational programmes for women's development, and facilitates the participation of women at policy-making level through the National Women's Talent Bank, which it also funds.

IREC3

Trinity College
DUBLIN 2
☎ 010 3531 7021975
Contact: Margaret Fine-Davis
Course: Women's Studies
☐ Postgraduate-level study.
Qualification: Master's degree

IREC4

University College Dublin
525 Library Building
University College
Belfield
DUBLIN 4
☎ 0 1 269 3244 ext. 7302
Contact: Ailbhe Smyth
Course: Women's Studies
☐ Interdisciplinary studies aimed at adult education level; open to students with no academic qualifications.
Qualifications: Diploma, Certificate
Courses: Feminism, Theories and Practice; Women's Studies, Perspectives and Methods; Women in Ireland 1848–1990

☐ Postgraduate-level work, with more emphasis on course work at diploma level. Research supervision for doctoral theses.
Qualifications: Diploma, Master's degree, Doctorate

Women's Education Research and Resource Centre (WERRC)
☐ Includes teaching, research, publications and documentation. Holds fortnightly feminist issues research seminars; regular workshops; public lectures and conferences. WERRC has its own library. Dublin is one of the eight European universities which participates in the ERASMUS exchange programme in Women's Studies.

Women's Studies Forum (WSF)
☐ Founded in 1983 across academic, administrative and library staff as well as undergraduate and postgraduate students. The aim of the WSF is to share and disseminate research and resources, particularly the development of research on Irish women, and to ensure its availability to women in the community. Seminars are therefore open to all women, with funding from the Arts Council for poetry readings and talks by women writers, artists and composers. Interdisciplinary research is encouraged, particularly in relation to collectively challenging patriarchal knowledge making.

IREC5

Women's Network
Trinity College
DUBLIN 2
☎ 3531 772941
Contact: Eileen Drew
Course: Women's Studies programme
☐ Postgraduate-level work in the Philosophy discipline.
Qualification: Master's degree

Galway

IREC6

Women's Studies Centre
Dept of Political Science and Sociology
University College Galway
GALWAY
☎ 353 91 24411
Contact: Anne Byrne
Courses: Gender, Culture and Irish Society; Women and Literature; Feminist Theory; Women and the Family; Women in History
☐ Interdisciplinary studies at undergraduate level. Women's Studies courses also available on the Continuing Education Programme. Postgraduate-level work is planned.
Qualification: Degree
☐ The Women's Studies Centre includes research as well as teaching.

Limerick

IREC7

Centre for Women's Studies
University of Limerick
    Plassey Technological Park
    LIMERICK
☎   061 333 644
Contact: Evelyn Mahon
Courses: A Cross Cultural Study of Women; Women's Rights in History; Technology, Innovation and Social Change; Sociology of Education; Philosophical Approaches to Gender; Sociology of Women and Work; Sociology of the Family; Women and the Law; Theories of Management.
□ Postgraduate-level work with an interdisciplinary focus.
Qualification: Graduate Diploma in Women's Studies
□ The Women's Studies Centre includes research as well as teaching.

Israel

Haifa

ISRC1

Women's Studies Programme
University of Haifa
    Mt Carmel
    HAIFA 31999
☎   240 111
Contact: Marilyn P. Safir
Courses: Women's Studies
□ A multidisciplinary undergraduate programme, drawing on the Humanities, Social Sciences, Education, Social Work and Religion.
□ The programme's wide-ranging profile research includes the following: feminization of education; sex differences in intellectual functioning; and the status of women faculty and staff at the University of Haifa. The KIDMA project is a programme to develop access to Women's Studies to women in the wider community. Publications include *The Struggle for Equality: Urban Workers in Prestate Israeli Society*; and *Women in Politics*.

Raanana

ISRC2

International Network for Sex Equity in Education (INSEE)
    22 Yehuda Halevi Street
    RAANANA 43556
☎   052 445795
Contact: Judith Abrahami-Einat

□ INSEE was founded in 1987 to work towards sex equity in education. Activities include the exchange of teaching materials, research projects and reports, and working towards joint publications with similar groups on an international basis. *INSEE Newsletter* is published to provide conference and study programme information.

Italy

Bologna

ITC1

Dipartimento Di Lingue E Letterature – Straniere Moderne
Universita Degli Studi di Bologna
    Via Zamboni 16
    40126 BOLOGNA
☎   39 51 227253
Contact: Vita Fortunati
Courses: Women and Theatre; Researching Women's Studies: Disciplines and Methodologies
□ Taught in Italian, these courses may form part of a degree. Students are encouraged to make contact with other women's groups. Bologna is one of the eight European universities which participate in the ERASMUS exchange programme in Women's Studies.
Qualification: Degree

City Women's Research and Resource Centre
□ Involves teaching and Erasmus exchanges as well as research. Tutorials can be made available for specific research topics.

Ferrara

ITC2

Gruppo Onda
    Via Savonarola 27
    44100 FERRARA
☎   40219
Contact: Gabriella Rosetti
Courses: Training Programmes for Women; Research Methodology and Gender Issues
□ Research activities include women and work; women in school; and women's training programmes. Funding for research projects can come from regional government and the European Community. A documentation and training centre is planned. Publications include *Foemina Faber: immaginini e conldizione del lavoro delle donne* (Milan, Angeli, 1989).

Courses

Florence

ITC3

Interdisciplinary Working Group on Women's Studies
European University Institute
Villa Schifanoia
Via Boccaccio 121
50133 FLORENCE
☎ 055 509 25 38
Contact: Heinz-Gerhard Haupt
Course: Private, Public, Citizenship
☐ At postgraduate level, the course looks at the following issues: is the legal individual male?; women at war; images of women soldiers; Italian immigrant women in Australia; ethnic identities and social rights; economics, the individual and politics affecting women; what is at stake in the conceptual debate among Italian feminism?; women, transnational politics and European Community law; is sex to gender as race is to ethnicity?

Milan

ITC4

GRIFF (Group for Research on Family and Feminism)
University of Milan
Department of Political Science
Via Conservatorio 7
MILAN
Contact: Laura Balbo

Pavia

ITC5

Sezione di Teorie dell'Educazione e Della Personalita
Universita di Pavia
Bordoni 12
27100 PAVIA
☎ 0 382 22123
Contact: Silvia Vegetti
Courses: Psicoanalisi della Maternita Psicologia Dinamica; Le Isteriche e Il Transfert Psicologia Dinamica
☐ These courses are available to students in the third year of university studies.

Rome

ITC6

Isis International
Via San Saba 5
00153 ROME
☎ 06 574 6479

Contact: Marilee Karl
☐ Established in 1974, Isis now has centres in Rome, Santiago and Geneva. It is a non-profit-making organisation which brings together researchers and grassroots women activities worldwide (a network of 15,000 contacts in over 100 countries). It maintains a collection of materials on women and provides an information service for researchers. Publications include *Women in Action*, a quarterly magazine; *Women in Development: A Resource Guide for Organisation and Action*. See also entry SWC1.

Verona

ITC7

Filo di Arianna
c/o Societa Lettreraria
Piazzetta Scalette Rubiani 1
37121 VERONA
☎ 0 45 83 45 96
Contact: Anna Tantini-Tomezzoli
Courses: Abitare il Corpo; Basta la Parola; Poetesse: Gertrud Kolmar/Emily Dickinson/Elizabeth Barrett-Browning; 'Liaisons Dangereuses', Love, Rivalry, Seduction and Envy Amongst Women
☐ All courses are at adult education level, and are drawn from the disciplines of Reproduction and Sexuality Studies, Communication Studies, Literature and Feminist Thought.

Japan

For further information about any of the following courses, please make initial contact with:

Information and International Exchange Division
National Women's Education Centre
728 Sugaya
Ranzan-machi
Hiki-gun
SAITAMA-KEN 355-02
☎ 0493 62 6711

Aichi

JAPC1

Aichi Shukutoku University
9 Aza Katahira
Oaza-Nagakute
Nagakute-cho
Aichi-gun
AICHI-KEN
Course: Women and Society
☐ Course within the Department of Literature.

JAPC2
Chukyo Women's University
    Myokozan
    Yokone-machi
    Oobu-shi
    AICHI-KEN
Courses: Women's History; Japanese Women's History; Living in a Women's World
□ Courses within General Education.

JAPC3
Nagoya University of Economics
    61–1 Uchikubo
    Inuyama-shi
    AICHI-KEN
Course: Women's Studies
□ Course within the Faculty of Economics.

JAPC4
Nagoya Women's University
    3–4 Shioji-cho
    Mizuho-ku
    Nagoya-shi
    AICHI-KEN
Course: Women's Studies
□ Course within the Faculty of Literature.

JAPC5
Nanzan University
    18 Yamazato-machi
    Showa-ku
    Nagoya-shi
    AICHI-KEN
Courses: Theory of Human Science; Life and Logic
□ Courses within General Education.

JAPC6
Nihon Fukushi University
    35–6 Aza Egemae
    Oaza Okuda
    Mihama-cho
    Chita-gun
    AICHI-KEN
Courses: Contemporary Social Problems; Development in Asia and Women's Role
□ Courses within the Faculty of Social Welfare.

JAPC7
Sugiyama Jogakuen University
    17–3 Motomachi
    Hoshigaoka
    Chikusa-ku
    Nagoya-shi
    AICHI-KEN
Courses: Women's Theory; Women's Labour Theory

Aomori

JAPC8
Hirosaki Gakuin University
    13–1 Minori-machi
    Hirosaki-shi
    AOMORI-KEN
Course: Women's Studies in the English Language
□ Course within the Department of Literature.

Chiba

JAPC9
Chiba University
    1–33 Yayoi-cho
    Chiba-shi
    CHIBA-KEN
Courses: Oriental History: Pre-Modern; History of the Family and Women in Korea; Sociology: Education, Family and Labour; Feminist Law; Considering Women; Women's Images written in the Literature of the World
□ Courses within the Faculties of Literature; Law and Economics and Arts and Education.

JAPC10
Kawamura Gakuen Women's University
    1133 Shimogato
    Abiko-shi
    CHIBA-KEN
Courses: Women's History; Educational History for Women; History of Women's Culture
□ Courses within the Faculty of Liberal Arts.

JAPC11
Tokyo Christian University
    3–301 Uchino
    Insei-machi
    Inba-gun
    CHIBA-KEN
Course: Women and Society
□ Course within the Faculty of Theology.

Ehime

JAPC12
Matsuyama University
    4–2 Bunkyo-cho
    Matsuyama-shi
    EHIME-KEN
Courses: Introduction to Women's Theory; Contemporary Law and the Change of the Women's Labor-Future Theme
□ Courses within the College of Economics, College of Management, College of Humanities and College of Law.

Courses

JAPC13

St Catherine Women's College
    660 Hojo
    Hojo-shi
    EHIME-KEN
Course: Women's Theory
☐ Course within the Faculty of Social Welfare.

Fukuoka

JAPC14

Chikushi Jogakuen University
    2–12–1 Ishizaka
    Dazaifu-shi
    FUKUOKA-KEN
Courses: Western Women's History: History of Emancipation of Women; Women and Culture; Japanese Women's History
☐ Courses within the Faculty of Arts.

JAPC15

Fukuoka Women's College
    1–1–1 Kasugaoka
    Higashi-ku
    Fukuoka-shi
    FUKUOKA-KEN
Course: Women's Studies
☐ Course within the Faculties of Literature and Life Science.

JAPC16

Kyushu University
    2–1 Ropponmatsu
    Chuo-ku
    Fukuoka-shi
    FUKUOKA-KEN
Course: Women's History Course
☐ Course within the College of General Education.

JAPC17

Kyushu Women's University
    1 Jiyugaoka
    Yahata Nishi-ku
    Kitakyushu-shi
    FUKUOKA-KEN
Course: Sociology: Women and the Occupations
☐ Course within the Faculties of Home Economics and Literature.

Fukushima

JAPC18

Koriyama Women's College
    3–25–2 Kaisei
    Koriyama-shi
    FUKUSHIMA-KEN
Course: Women and Labour Issues
☐ Course within the School of Home Economics.

Gifu

JAPC19

Gifu Women's University
    80 Taromaru
    Gifu-shi
    GIFU-KEN
Course: Women's Studies
☐ Course within the Faculty of Home Economics.

Gunma

JAPC20

Gunma Prefectural Women's University
    1395–1 Kaminote
    Tamamura-machi
    Sawa-gun
    GUNMA-KEN
Course: Issues on Higher Education for Women and Their Occupations
☐ Course within the Faculty of Arts.

JAPC21

Takasaki City University of Economics
    1300 Kaminamie-machi
    Takasaki-shi
    GUNMA-KEN
Course: Japanese Economics and Equal Opportunity for Employment
☐ Course within the Department of Economics.

Hiroshima

JAPC22

Hiroshima Jogakuin College
    4–13–1 Ushida Higashi
    Higashi-ku
    Hiroshima-shi
    HIROSHIMA-KEN
Course: Contemporary Society and Women
☐ Course within the Department of Literature.

JAPC23

Yasuda Women's University
6–13–1 Ando
Asaminami-ku
Hiroshima-shi
HIROSHIMA-KEN
Course: Women's Studies
☐ Course within the Faculty of Letters.

Hokkaido

JAPC24

Hokkaido University
Nishi 5 Kita 8
Kita-ku
Sapporo-shi
HOKKAIDO
Courses: Feminist Criticism; Men Dominated Society and Women
☐ Courses within the Faculty of General Education.

JAPC25

Hokkaido University of Education
Sapporo Campus
5–3–1 Ainosato
Kita-ku
Sapporo-shi
HOKKAIDO
Courses: Women's Theory: Our Family; Is Sex Role Stereotyping Possible to Create Love and Independence Between Men and Women?
☐ Courses within the Faculty of Education.

JAPC26

Sapporo Gakuin University
11 Bunkyo-dai
Ebetsu-shi
HOKKAIDO
Course: Women's Issues: Perspectives to Consider Women and Men
☐ Course within the Faculty of Humanities.

Hyogo

JAPC27

Hyogo University of Education
924–1 Shimokume
Yashio-machi
Kato-gun
HYOGO-KEN
Course: Human Rights and Education: The Dowa Minority, the Handicapped and Women
☐ Course within the Graduate School.

JAPC28

Kobe City University of Foreign Studies
9–1 Gakuen Higashi-machi
Nishi-ku
Kobe-shi
HYOGO-KEN
Courses: Reading Books Written in Foreign Languages; Sexual Harassment in America
☐ Courses within the Faculty of Foreign Studies.

JAPC29

Kobe University
1–1 Rokkadai-machi
Naka-ku
Kobe-shi
HYOGO-KEN
Courses: Human Rights (Emancipation of Women); Women and Men (Family, Home and Life Cycle); Japanese Women's History
☐ Courses within the College of Liberal Arts.

JAPC30

Kwansei Gakuin University
1–15–5 Ichiban-cho
Kamigahara
Nishinomiya-shi
HYOGO-KEN
Course: Men Dominated Society and Women
☐ Course within the Faculties of Theology, Literature, Sociology, Law, Economics, Commerce and Science.

JAPC31

Mukogawa Women's College
6–4–6 Ikegai-cho
Nishinomiya-shi
HYOGO-KEN
Courses: Women's Studies; The Change of Labour Circumstances and the Choice of Occupations by Women: Considering Working Style of Women After the Enactment of the Equal Opportunity Law
☐ Courses within the Faculty of Letters.

JAPC32

Shinwa Women's College
7–13–1 Kita-Machi
Suzurandai
Kita-ku
Kobe-shi
HYOGO-KEN
Course: Women's Issues: Theory of Marriage – Marriage History in Japan
☐ Course within the Faculty of Literature.

Courses

JAPC33

Sonoda Women's College
   7–29–1 Minamizuka-machi
   Amagasaki-shi
   HYOGO-KEN
Course: Women's Theory
☐ Course within the Department of Literature.

Ibaraki

JAPC34

Ibaraki University
   2–1 Bunkyo
   Mito-shi
   IBARAKI-KEN
Courses: Home Management: Household Work, House-wives' Work and Women's Labour; Family Relations: Introduction to Women's Studies
☐ Courses within the Faculty of Education.

JAPC35

Ryutsu Keizai University
   120 Hirahata
   Ryugasaki-shi
   IBARAKI-KEN
Course: Contemporary Women's Theory
☐ Course within the Faculty of Sociology.

Ishikawa

JAPC36

Kanazawa University
   1–1 Marunouchi
   Kanazawa-shi
   ISHIKAWA-KEN
Course: Japanese Women's History
☐ Course within the College of Liberal Arts.

Kanagawa

JAPC37

Kanto Gakuin University
   4834 Mutsuura-cho
   Kanazawa-ku
   Yohohama-shi
   KANAGAWA-KEN
Course: Gender Theory: Women and Contemporary Society
☐ Course within the Faculty of Literature.

JAPC38

Toyo Eiwa Women's University
   31–1 Mihocho
   Midori-ku
   Yokohama-shi
   KANAGAWA-KEN
Courses: Women's History and Women's Theory; Women's Sociology: Sex, Gender, Feminism
☐ Courses within the Faculty of Humanities.

JAPC39

Senshu University
   2–1–1 Higashi Mita
   Tama-ku
   Kawasaki-shi
   KANAGAWA-KEN
Courses: Education: Women, Men and Children; Human Relations Concerning Sex; Women's History
☐ Courses within the Faculties of Economics and Literature.

JAPC40

Tokai University
   1,117 Kitakaname
   Hiratsuka-shi
   KANAGAWA-KEN
Course: Theory of Women's Physical Activities
☐ Course within the Faculty of Physical Education.

Kumamoto

JAPC41

Kumamoto University
   2–40–1 Kurokami
   Kumamoto-shi
   KUMAMOTO-KEN
Course: Women and Literature
☐ Course within the Faculty of Letters.

JAPC42

Kumamoto Women's College
   2432-1 Mizuarai
   Kengun-machi
   Kumamoto-shi
   KUMAMOTO-KEN
Course: Women's Studies
☐ Course within the Faculties of Literature and Living Science.

Kyoto

JAPC43

Doshisha University
601 Genbu-cho
Higashi-iru
Karasuma
Imadegawa-dori
Kamigyo-ku
Kyoto-shi
KYOTO-FU
Course: World of Women and Men
☐ Course within the Faculties of Theology, Letters, Economics, Commerce and Technology.

JAPC44

Doshisha Women's College of Liberal Arts
602 Genbucho
Nishi-iru
Tera-machi
Imadegawa-dori
Ukyo-ku
Kyoto-shi
KYOTO-FU
Courses: Images of Women Presented in Mass Communication; Women and Culture
☐ Courses within General Education.

JAPC45

Hanazono University
8–1 Tsubonouchi-machi
Nishinokyo
Nakagyo-ku
Kyoto-shi
KYOTO-FU
Course: Special Course on Social Welfare: Concerning Men and Women
☐ Course within the Faculty of Literature.

JAPC46

Koka Women's College
38 Kuzunomachi
Nishi-kyogoku
Ukyo-ku
Kyoto-shi
KYOTO-FU
Course: Women in Japanese Medieval Era
☐ Course within the Faculty of Literature.

JAPC47

Kyoto Sangyo University
Motoyama
Kamigamo
Kita-ku
Kyoto-shi
KYOTO-FU
Course: Human Rights and Discrimination
☐ Course in the College of Liberal Arts.

JAPC48

Kyoto Seika University
137 Kinocho
Iwakura
Sakyo-ku
Kyoto-shi
KYOTO-FU
Courses: Women's Literature; Considering Sex Discrimination; Apartheid and Feminism; English Linguistics: Reading Feminism Written in English
☐ All courses within the Department of Humanities.

JAPC49

Kyoto Tachibana Women's University
34 Tamachi
Ohtakuyama
Yamashina-ku
Kyoto-shi
KYOTO-FU
Course: Theory of Women's Issues
☐ Course within the Faculty of Liberal Arts.

JAPC50

Kyoto University
Yoshida Honcho
Sakyo-ku
Kyoto-shi
KYOTO-FU
Courses: Gender and Social Education; Cultural Anthropology; Women's Studies
☐ Courses within the Faculty of Education and the College of Liberal Arts.

JAPC51

Kyoto University of Foreign Studies
6 Kasamecho
Nichinoin
Ukyo-ku
Kyoto-shi
KYOTO-FU
Course: American Literature and Women
☐ Course in the Faculty of English and American Literature.

JAPC52

Otani University
Kazusa-cho
Oyama
Kita-ku
Kyoto-shi
KYOTO-FU
Course: Reading English Works on Gender
☐ Course in the Faculty of Letters.

Courses

JAPC53

Ritsumeikan University
    56–1 Kita-machi
    Tojiin
    Kita-ku
    Kyoto-shi
    KYOTO-FU
Courses: Contemporary Women's Theory; Women's Issues
☐ Courses within the Faculties of Economics, Management, Industrial Sociology, Literature, Science, Engineering and International Relations.

JAPC54

Ryukoku University
    67 Honcho
    Hukakusazuka
    Fushimi-ku
    Kyoto-shi
    KYOTO-FU
Course: Women's Studies: Self-Reliance of Women and Men, and the Solution for it
☐ Course within the Faculties of Letters, Economics, Management and Law.

JAPC55

Women's Studies Society of Japan (WSSJ)
    Shokadou Women's Book Store
    Nishinotouinn-Nishiiru, Shimodachiuri
    Kamigyou-ku
    Kyoto-shi
    KYOTO
☎   075 441 6905
Contact: Toyoko Nakanishi
☐ The WSSJ was established in 1978 with the aim of conducting interdisciplinary studies on Japanese and foreign women in the areas of literature, history, sociology, psychology, economics and the politics of women's liberation. Funding for research comes from city governments and private enterprise. Publishes a monthly newsletter, *Voice of Women*, and an Annual Report on Women's Studies.

Mie

JAPC56

Mie University
    1515 Kamihama-cho
    Tsu-shi
    MIE-KEN
Course: Women's Theory
☐ Course within General Education.

Miyagi

JAPC57

Miyagi Gakuin College for Women
    9–1–1 Sakuragaoka
    Aoba-ku
    Sendai-shi
    MIYAGI-KEN
Course: Women and the Family
☐ Course within the Faculty of Arts and Sciences.

JAPC58

Tohoku Fukushi University
    1–8–1 Kunimi
    Aoba-ku
    Sendai-shi
    MIYAGI-KEN
Course: Women's Issues and Social Education
☐ Course within the Department of Social Welfare.

Nara

JAPC59

Nara Women's University
    Higashi-machi
    Kita Uoya
    Nara-shi
    NARA-KEN
Courses: Women's Issues and Social Education; History of Education for Women
☐ Courses within the Faculty of Letters.

Okayama

JAPC60

Notre Dame Sacred Heart Women's College
    2–16–9 Ifuku-cho
    Okayama-shi
    OKAYAMA-KEN
Course: Human Relations: Women's Issues
☐ Course within the Faculty of Home Economics.

JAPC61

Okayama University
    2–1–1 Tsushima Naka
    Okayama-shi
    OKAYAMA-KEN
Course: Women's Theory and Men's Theory
☐ Course within the School of Liberal Arts and Sciences.

Osaka

JAPC62

Hannan University
    5–4–33 Amami Higashi
    Matsubara-shi
    OSAKA-FU
Course: General Education on Women's Studies: Sex Difference, Sex Discrimination and Sex Role
☐ Course within the Faculties of Business and Economics.

JAPC63

Kinki University
    3–4–1 Kowakae
    Higashi Osaka-shi
    OSAKA-FU
Course: Women's Theory
☐ Course within the School of Literature, Arts and Cultural Studies.

JAPC64

Momoyama Gakuin University (St Andrew's University)
    237–1 Nishino
    Sakai-shi
    OSAKA-FU
Course: Issues on Human Rights: Future Studies on Men and Women
☐ Course within the Faculties of Economics, Sociology, Management and Literature.

JAPC65

Osaka City University
    3–3–138 Sugimoto
    Sumiyoshi-Ku
    Osaka-shi
    OSAKA-FU
Course: Theory of Women's Issues
☐ Course within General Education.

JAPC66

Osaka Kyoiku University
    4–88 Minami Kawabori-cho
    Tennoji-ku
    Osaka-shi
    OSAKA-FU
Courses: Anthropology of Men and Women; Emancipation of Women; Theory of Women's Issues
☐ Courses within the Faculties of Education and Liberal Arts.

JAPC67

Osaka University of Economics and Law
    2–2–8 Osumi
    Higashi Yodogawa-ku
    Osaka-shi
    OSAKA-FU
Course: International Law: Law for International Organisations
☐ Course within the Faculty of Law.

JAPC68

Osaka University of Foreign Studies
    8–1–1 Aomadani Higashi
    Minoo-shi
    OSAKA-FU
Course: Culture and Women in Medieval Era in Japan
☐ Course within the Faculty of Education.

JAPC69

Osaka Shoin Women's College
    4–2–26 Hishiya Nishi
    Osaka-shi
    OSAKA-FU
Courses: Women's Studies; Theory from the Women's New Perspectives
☐ Courses within the Faculty of Liberal Arts.

JAPC70

Osaka Women's University
    2–1 Daisen-machi
    Sakai-shi
    OSAKA-FU
Courses: History of Western Thought: Politics on Women and Their Feature; Theory of Household Work from 19th Century; Women's Theory
☐ Courses within the College of Arts and Sciences.

JAPC71

Tezukayama Gakuin University
    2–1823 Imakuma
    Osaka Sayama-shi
    OSAKA-FU
Courses: Modern Women's History; Women's History; Historiography
☐ Courses within the Department of Literature.

Saitama

JAPC72

Atomi Gakuen Women's University
    1–6–9 Nakano
    Niiza-shi
    SAITAMA-KEN
Courses: Moral Development of Women; Considering Women's Issues
☐ Courses within the Faculty of Literature.

Courses

JAPC73

Surugadai University
698 Ichinoki
Asu
Hanno-shi
SAITAMA-KEN
Course: Men and Women
☐ Course within the Faculty of Law.

JAPC74

Tokyo Kasei University
2–15–1 Inariyama
Sayama-shi
SAITAMA-KEN
Course: Women's Studies
☐ Course within the Faculties of Home Economics and Literature.

Shizuoka

JAPC75

Shizuoka University
836 Ohya
Shizuoka-shi
SHIZUOKA-KEN
Course: Social Psychology: Study of the Relationship Between Wife and Husband from the Perspectives of Social Psychology
☐ Course within the Faculties of Humanities and Social Sciences.

Tokushima

JAPC76

Shikoku Women's University
Furukawa
Ojincho
Tokushima-shi
TOKUSHIMA-KEN
Course: Women's Studies
☐ Course within General Education.

Tokyo

JAPC77

Aoyama Gakuin University
4–4–25 Shibuya
Shibuya-ku
TOKYO
Courses: Tradition of Women's Novels in Great Britain; Study on Women Writers in America; Women's Issues
☐ Courses within the Faculty of Literature.

JAPC78

Daito Bunka University
1–9–1 Takashimadaira
Itabashi-ku
TOKYO
Courses: Society and Home – From the Perspectives of Women's Studies; Women's Literature
☐ Courses within the Faculties of Literature, Economics, Foreign Studies, Law, and International Relations.

JAPC79

Japan Women's College of Physical Education
8–19–1 Kita-karasuyama
Setagaya-ku
TOKYO
Course: Women's Theory
☐ Course within the Faculty of Physical Education.

JAPC80

Japan Women's University
2–8–1 Mejirodai
Bunkyo-ku
TOKYO
Courses: Women's Issues and Family Issues; Women's Cultural Theory
☐ Courses within the Faculty of Literature.

JAPC81

Jissen Women's University
4–1–1 Osakaue
Hino-shi
TOKYO
Course: Women Novelists in Great Britain
☐ Course within the Faculty of Literature.

JAPC82

Keisen Jogakuen College
2–10–1 Minamino
Tama-shi
TOKYO
Course: Women's Studies
☐ Course within the Faculty of Humanities.

JAPC83

Kokugakuin University
4–10–28 Higashi
Shibuya-ku
TOKYO
Course: Sociology of Gender
☐ Course within the Faculty of Law.

JAPC84

Komazawa University
1–23–1 Komazawa
Setagaya-ku
TOKYO

Course: Theory of Women's Welfare
☐ Course within the Faculty of Literature.

JAPC85

Kyoritsu Women's University
1–710 Motohachioji-machi
Hachioji-shi
TOKYO
Courses: Reading 'Japanese Women's History'; Women Poets in Modern Japan; Women in Literature and Arts
☐ Courses within the Department of Arts and Letters.
Course: Reading Books on Women's Studies Written in English
☐ Course within the Department of Home Economics.
Course: Women's Theory
☐ Course within the Faculty of International Culture.

JAPC86

Musashi University
1–26–1 Toyotama-kami
Nerima-ku
TOKYO
Courses: English Literature: Images of Women in 1890s; Sociology: Mass Communication Theory from the Perspectives of Women's Studies
☐ Courses within the Faculty of Humanities.

JAPC87

Musashino Women's College
1–1–20 Shin-machi
Hoya-shi
TOKYO
Course: Women, and English and American Literature: Women's Life Style
☐ Course within the Faculty of Letters.

JAPC88

Nihon Shakaijigyo University
(Japan College of Social Work)
3–1–30 Takeoka
Kiyose-shi
TOKYO
Course: Theory of Women's Welfare
☐ Course within the Faculty of Social Welfare.

JAPC89

Ochanomizu University
2–1–1 Otsuka
Bunkyo-ku
TOKYO
Courses: Women's Issues: Women and Politics; Labour Economics: Women's Labour
☐ Courses within the Faculty of Home Economics.

JAPC90

Rikkyo University (St Paul's University)
3–34–1 Nishi-Ikebukuro
Toshima-ku
TOKYO
Course: Women's Issues and Social Education: What is the Theme of the Women's Emancipation Movement Since International Women's Year?
☐ Course within the Faculty of Social Relations.

JAPC91

Rissho University
4–2–16 Osaki
Shinagawa-ku
TOKYO
Course: Contemporary Society and Social Education
☐ Course within the Faculty of Literature.

JAPC92

Seikei University
3–3–1 Kita-machi
Kichijoji
Musashino-shi
TOKYO
Course: Women's Studies
☐ Course within the Faculty of Humanities.

JAPC93

Seisen Women's College
3–16–21 Higashi Gotanda
Shinagawa-ku
TOKYO
Course: Women and Society
☐ Course within the Faculty of Letters.

JAPC94

Showa Women's University
1–7–57 Taishido
Setgaya-ku
TOKYO
Courses: Women's Studies: Studies on Femininity; History of Women's Theory in Western Countries; Women and Home Management
☐ Courses within the Literature and Domestic Science Departments.

JAPC95

Sophia University
7–1 Kioi-cho
Chiyoda-ku
TOKYO
Course: Japanese View Concerning the Relation Between Men and Women
☐ Course within the Faculty of Humanities.

Courses

JAPC96
Tokyo Gakugei University
  4–1–1 Kita-machi
  Nukui
  Koganei-shi
  TOKYO
Course: Women's Studies
□ Course within the Faculty of Education.

JAPC97
Tokyo Kasei Gakuin University
  2600 Aihara-cho
  Machida-shi
  TOKYO
Course: Studies on Women's Issues
□ Course within the Faculty of Home Economics.

JAPC98
Toyo University
  5–28–20 Hakusan
  Bunkyo-ku
  TOKYO
Course: Women's Issues and Their Studies
□ Course within the Faculty of Literature.
Course: Contemporary Women's Theory
□ Course within the Faculty of Sociology

JAPC99
Tokyo University of Foreign Studies
  4–51–21 Nishigahara
  Kita-Ku
  TOKYO
Course: Present Situation of Women's Studies
□ Course within the Faculty of Foreign Studies.

JAPC100
Tokyo Women's Christian University
  2–6–1 Zenpukuji
  Suginami-ku
  TOKYO
Courses: Women's Theory: Women as Reproductive Sex; Sociology of Women and the Family; Women's Status and Role in the Contemporary Society; Women and Literature; Reproductive Control for Whom
□ Courses within the College of Arts and Sciences, and the College of Culture and Communication.

JAPC101
Tsuda College
  2–1–1 Tsuda-machi
  Kodaira-shi
  TOKYO
Courses: Ideology on Emancipation of Women; Women's Studies
□ Course within the Faculty of Arts and Sciences.

JAPC102
University of Tokyo
  3–8–1 Komaba
  Meguru-ku
  TOKYO
Course: Creation of Culture and Women's Position
□ Course within the College of Liberal Arts and Sciences.

JAPC103
Wako University
  2160 Kanai-cho Machida-shi
  TOKYO
Course: Tentative Study on Women's Studies: To Respect Sex
□ Course within the School of Humanities.
Course: Economic Growth and Women's Labour
□ Course within the School of Economics.

JAPC104
Waseda University
  1–6–1 Nishi-Waseda
  Shinjuku-ku
  TOKYO
Course: General Education: Some Issues of Modern Women's History
□ Course within the School of Literature.
Course: Life Style of Women Written in English Novels
□ Course within the School of Literature.

Tottori

JAPC105
Tottori University
  4–101 Minami
  Shozan-machi
  Tottori-shi
  TOTTORI-KEN
Course: Theory of Women's Education: History of Women's Education and Women's Labour Issues
□ Course within the Faculty of Education.

Yamaguchi

JAPC106
Yamaguchi Women's University
  3–2–1 Sakurabatake
  Yamaguchi-shi
  YAMAGUCHI-KEN
Course: 'Family' and Life Style of Women
□ Course within General Education.

Lebanon

LEBC1

Beirut University College
   PO Box 13 5053
   BEIRUT
☎ 811968
Contact: Julinda Abu Nasir

Institute for Women's Studies in the Arab World (IWSAW)

Lithuania

LITC1

Women's Studies Centre
University of Vilnius
   Universiteto g. 3
   VILNIUS 2731
☎ 0122 76 27 63
Contact: Giedre Purvaneckiene
Courses: 19th and 20th Century Women Writers' Letters; Women and Gender in Western Culture; Women and Culture; Women and Society
☐ These are elective credit courses available during 1992–3. The Centre is developing further courses so that Women's Studies can be offered as a minor or a major on the undergraduate programme.
Qualification: Degree
☐ The Centre was established as an independent research and study institute in March 1992. It involves research, library documentation and publications. Monthly seminars are held for scholarly discussion. Research is concentrated in the disciplines of Social Sciences, Humanities, Law and Medicine. The Centre, together with the Lithuanian University Women's Association (LUWA) and the University of Madison, will host a conference in August 1993: 'Women's Paths – East and West'.

Luxembourg

Moutfort

LUXC1

Faculty of Social Science
The Open University
   93 Route de Remich
   5330 MOUTFORT
☎ 35 97 61
Contact: Liv-Ellen Kennedy
Course: Issues in Women's Studies

☐ Distance learning courses taught in English. Can form part of a degree. Themes include gender and education; girls into mathematics; women writing and culture; women into management.
Qualifications: Certificate, Degree

Malaysia

Kuala Lumpur

MALC1

Women in Development Programme
Asian and Pacific Development Centre
   Pesiaran Duta
   PO Box 12224
   50770 KUALA LUMPUR
☎ 03 2548088
Contact: Noeleen Heyzer
Course: Research and Training of Women and Development Management
☐ Part of a training programme for improving skills for women.
☐ The Women in Development Programme is concerned with research, publications and outreach community programmes for the poorest women in the region. Key development issues in policy and planning that concern women are an important focus, and projects include: agricultural change and rural women; women and development planning; and the participation of women in the industrial process. 'Women and Poverty' and 'International Migration and Women' have also been specific research projects. Research findings are published, such as *Women Farmers and Rural Change in Asia: Towards Equal Access and Participation* (1987) and *Daughters of Industry: Work, Skills and Consciousness of Women Workers in Asia* (1988).

Penang

MALC2

School of Sciences
University Sains Malaysia
   11800 PENANG
☎ 04 883822 ext. 436
Contact: Wazir-Jahan Karim

Project KANITA
☐ A research and consulting body, Project KANITA has been concerned with academic, action-oriented and evaluative research, and the development of appropriate research tools and strategies. Research focus has included health and medicine; patterns of female employment; female leadership; participation of women

in national planning; and evaluation of governmental programmes for women. Research material is disseminated through local, national and international networks, conferences, workshops and publications.

Netherlands

Amsterdam

NETC1

IIAV – International Information Centre and Archives for the Women's Movement
Keizersgracht 10
1015 CN AMSTERDAM
☎ 020 624 42 68
□ The IIAV is the national information service in the Netherlands for data bases, catalogues and collections, as well as consultancy, research and special projects concerning women and women's studies. It is also a focal point for international exchange. Expertise in obtaining, storing and disseminating information on women is on a national and international basis. The IIAV has recently completed a research study for the Commission of the European Community, and is developing in-house training programmes.

NETC2

Afdeling Vrouwenstudies Letteren
Universiteit Amsterdam
Faculty of Arts
Spuistraat 210-kamer 350/352
1012 VT AMSTERDAM
☎ 020 525 38 72
Contact: Jannie Poelstra
Courses: Introduction Programme in Women's Studies; Women's Studies in History, Art History, Literature and Feminist Linguistics
□ Second-year undergraduate level. Research in these areas also available.
Qualification: Degree

Faculty of Psychology
University of Amsterdam
Roetersstraat 15 A528
1018 WB AMSTERDAM
☎ 020 525 68 92
Contact: Tineke Willems
Course: Women's Studies in Psychology
□ Themes include advanced psychological Women's Studies; feminist methods in psychology; and gender identity.

NETC3

Vrouwen Overleg Centrale Interfaculteit-VUA
Vrije Universiteit Amsterdam
Philosophy Department
de Boelelaan 1105
1081 HV AMSTERDAM

☎ 020 548 49 38
Contact: L. D. Derksen
Course: Women's Studies in Philosophy
□ For second-year undergraduate philosophy students.
Course: De Dynamick van het Zelfde en het Andere L. Irigaray
□ Within the discipline of feminist thought, this course is intended for doctoral students.

Den Haag

NETC4

Women and Development
Institute of Social Studies – ISS
PO Box 90733
2509 LS DEN HAAG
☎ 070 351 01 00
Contact: S. Wieringa
Course: Women and Development Specialisation
□ Postgraduate-level work.
Qualification: Master's degree

Groningen

NETC5

Werkgroep Vrouwenstudies Letteren – RUG
Rijsuniversiteit Groningen
Internationalisering Fac. der Letteren
PO Box 716
9700 AS GRONINGEN
☎ 050 63 58 40
Contact: Elisabeth Brouwer
Course: Introduction to Women's Studies in Linguistics, Literature and History
□ Available to 2nd and 3rd-year undergraduate students, this course concentrates on the work of Arlette Jacobs and Virginia Woolf.
Qualification: Degree
Courses: Postmodernism and Women's Studies; Feminist Literary Theory; Rights, Law and Body (Women's History); Politics and Culture in Dutch Feminism 1789–1956
□ Within the disciplines of Feminist Thought and History. Available to 3rd and 4th-year undergraduate students.
Qualification: Degree
Courses: Seminar in Historiography, Linguistics and Literary Theory; Epistemological Women's Studies
□ Within the discipline of History. Available to 4th-year students.
Qualification: Degree
Course: Dutch Studies; Women's Studies in Holland
□ Undergraduate course within the discipline of Cultural Studies.

Leiden

NETC6

Afdeling Vrouw en Recht
Rijksuniversiteit Leiden
Hugo de Grootstraat 27 postbus 9520
2300 RA LEIDEN
☎ 071 27 77 33
Contact: R. Holfmaat
Course: Women and International Law
☐ At postgraduate level, some knowledge of Dutch law and international law is necessary.

NETC7

Vakgroep Franse Taal en Letterkunde
Rijksuniversiteit Leiden
Van Wijkplaats 2 PO Box 9515
2300 RA LEIDEN
☎ 071 27 21 69
Contact: Y. Klent-Daoust
Course: Correspondences Feministes Journal Intime, Autobiographie
☐ Postgraduate-level course.

Leidschendam

NETC8

Faculty of Social Science
The Open University
Postbus 3044
2260 DE LEIDSCHENDAM
☎ 071 61 80 32
Contact: Christine Finlow-Bates
Course: Issues in Women's Studies
☐ Taught in English, these courses can form part of a degree by distance learning. Themes include: gender and education; girls into mathematics; women, writing and culture; and women into management.
Qualifications: Certificate, degree

Maastricht

NETC9

Faculty of Health Sciences
University of Limburg
PO Box 616
6200 MD MAASTRICHT
☎ 043 88 87 80
Contact: K. Horstman
Course: Women's Studies in Health

Nijmegen

NETC10

Studiegroep Vrouwengeschiedenis van de Croegmoderne Tijd
Tweede Oude Heselaan 524
6543 VL NIJMEGEN
Contact: Marit Monteiro
Course: History of Women during the Republic (16th–19th Centuries)
☐ At adult education level, these courses are open to members of the Study Group.

Rotterdam

NETC11

Department of Women's Studies
Erasmus University Rotterdam
PO Box 1738
3000 DR ROTTERDAM
☎ 010 400 23 99
Contact: H. J. Groenendijk
Course: Pre-Graduate Public Administration
☐ Degree-level work in social policy. Themes include: emancipation, labour and public administration; power and the labour position of women; and childcare – an analysis of government policy.

Tilburg

NETC12

Interfacultaire Werkgroep Vrouwenstudies
Katholieke Universiteit Brabant
Hogeschoollaan 225 (Kamer S–171)
5000 LE TILBURG
☎ 013 66 25 44
Contact: Coosje Couprie
Courses: Socialisation, Power and Sex; Thinking Sexual Difference and Arts of Women; Sex and Culture; Work, Emancipation and Policy; and Psychology and Women's Studies
☐ All are three- month courses designed as background to students in the social sciences, literature, economics and law.

Utrecht

NETC13

Rijksuniversiteit Utrecht
Drift 13
3512 BR UTRECHT
☎ 030 39 21 52
Contact: Anneke Vander Meulen
Course: Interfacultaire Cursussen

☐ Postgraduate-level course organised through the Anna Maria Van Schguurman Centre for Women's Studies. Themes include: feminist theory; changing the subject; historiography of the feminist ideas; sex, citizenship and justice.

Qualification: Master's degree

☐ Utrecht is one of eight European universities which participates in ERASMUS exchanges in Women's Studies. Some courses are taught in English. It also has a large and flourishing Women's Studies programme, with teaching being undertaken across a number of different faculties. See entries below. Addresses, telephone numbers and contact name are the same as above unless indicated otherwise.

Anna Maria Van Schguurman Centre for Women's Studies

☐ The Centre's activities include teaching, publications and documentation as well as research.

Women's Studies – Arts Faculty
Rijksuniversiteit Utrecht
  Drift 13
  3512 BR UTRECHT
☎ 030 39 21 25
Contact: Rosie Braidotti
Course: Vrouwenstudies Letteren
☐ Postgraduate-level course taught in English, and open to students in their fourth year.
Qualification: Master's degree

Women's Studies in Natural Science
Rijksuniversiteit Utrecht
  Centrumgebouw Noord – Padualaan 14
  3512 BR UTRECHT
☎ 31 30 392 376
Contact: Ineke Van Wingerden
Course: Vrouw en Natuurwetenschappen

Vrouwenstudies Rechten
Rijksuniversiteit Utrecht
  Janskerkhof 3a
  UTRECHT
☎ 030 393 293
Contact: J. E. Goldschmidt
Course: Internatinal Law and Women
☐ Concerned with applications of protective legislation and equal opportunities in EC law, the Council of Europe, the UN and international labour organisations.

Women's Studies in Social Geography
Rijksuniversiteit Utrecht
  Padualaan 14
  UTRECHT
☎ 030 532 199
Contact: B. de Pater
Course: Vrouwenstudies Sociale Geografie

Vrouwenstudies Sociale Wetenschappen
Rijksuniversiteit Utrecht
  Trans II (Uithof)
  Heidelberglaan 2
  Kamer 1402
  3584 CS UTRECHT
☎ 030 531 77
Contact: Kathy Davis
Course: Vrouwenstudies Sociale Wetenschappen
☐ Postgraduate-level work.
Qualifications: Master's degree, Doctorate

Projekt Feminisme en Theologie
Rijksuniversiteit Utrecht
  Transitorium II
  Heidelberglaan 2 room 830
  3584 CS UTRECHT
☎ 030 535 199
Contact: A. M. Korte
Course: Vrouwenstudies Theologie
☐ Themes include: gender-specific readings of the Bible; the culture philosophy of Julia Kristeva; women's poetry in the Middle Ages; applying women's history; feminist theological hermeneutics.

The Hague

NETC14

Institute of Social Studies
  PO Box 90733
  2509 LS THE HAGUE
☎ 070 351 01 00
Contact: A. Chhachhi
Course: Women and Development programme
☐ Structured around the women's movement in the Netherlands and other countries, with particular emphasis on women from Third World countries.
Qualification: Master's degree

NETC15

Promotion Committee for Emancipation Research (STEO)
  Lutherse Burgwal 10, 2512 CB
  THE HAGUE
☎ 070 61 43 21
Contact: Ricky Van Og
☐ STEO was founded by the Dutch government in 1985, through which priority areas of research in Women's Studies are pursued. Priority areas for research in 1989 were health, justice and law; languages and signs were explored. STEO uses its networking in the Netherlands to identify and bring together researchers in the field of Women's Studies. The Committee publishes reports of its work.

Wageningen

NETC16

Department of Women's Studies
Agricultural University Wageningen
Hollandswewg 1
6706 KN WAGENINGEN
☎ 08370 83374
Contact: Joan Wollfensperger
Courses: Women's Studies in the Agricultural Sciences;
Feminist Methods and Methodology
☐ Rural development and gender in Third World and
European countries; gender and agricultural sciences;
together with gender theory have formed the focus of
recent research. The Department publishes research,
usually in Dutch, but some is available in English.
Examples are congress papers, *Engendered Structure*
by Joan Wollfensperger, and *The Gender of Power* by
M. Leijenaar.

New Zealand

NZC1

Centre for Women's Studies
University of Waikato
Private Bag
HAMILTON
☎ 071 62 889
Contact: Jane Ritchie
Course: Women's Studies
Qualifications: Degree, Postgraduate diploma, Master's
degree
☐ The Centre was established in 1986, formally
recognising the field of Women's Studies, and collabo-
rating with the Centre for Continuing Education
Women's Programme. Research issues include: women
and work; women and education; women and smoking;
women and trade unions; feminism and racism; and
women's health. The Centre's aim is to appoint Maori
staff to add a Maori dimension to their work.

Nigeria

Bendel State

NIGC1

Women in Nigeria
PO Box 253, Samaru, Zaria
Kaduna State
or PO Box 5600, Benin City
BENDEL STATE
Contact: Glory Kilanko

☐ Women in Nigeria was established in 1982 as a
national, independent, non-religious organisation, to
research and disseminate information on women.
Research issues include: women and the family;
women and education; women in rural areas; women's
involvement in Nigeria's political and social economic
system; and violence against women and children. A
Resource and Documentation Centre is being established. Women in Nigeria publishes proceedings of
work.

Ibadan

NIGC2

Women's Research and Documentation Centre
(WORDOC)
Institute of African Studies
University of Ibadan
IBADAN
☎ 22 400550 ext. 2345
Contact: Bolanle Awe
☐ WORDOC was established in 1986 to co-ordinate
research and promote new methodologies. Researched
projects, publications and seminars provide a basis for
women's networking through WORDOC. Research
issues include agriculture; politics; culture; history; the
legal system; health; family; education; literature; and
the urban economy. Publications include a WORDOC
Newsletter and a directory of Nigerian scholars active
in Women's Studies.

Norway

Alta

NORC1

Faggruppa for distriktskvinneforskning og-utvikling
Finnmark College
Follumsvei
9500 ALTA
☎ 84 37 600
Contact: Sissel Fredriksen
☐ Members of the Research Group for Women and
Regional Development work in several institutions,
and concentrate on interdisciplinary research which
will promote feminist-oriented development locally,
nationally and globally.

Bergen

NORC2

Senter for humanistisk kvinneforskning
University of Bergen
Hermann Fossgt. 12
5007 BERGEN

☎ 55 21 24 71
Contact: Lisbeth Mikaelsson
Courses: Comprehensive courses in the Arts Faculty
☐ Course and seminar programme available to students on theoretical issues and research.

Centre for Women's Studies in the Humanities
☐ Founded in 1985 in order to co-ordinate research and develop feminist theory. Research fields are gender ideology in Christianity, literary analysis and women's history.

NORC3

Senter for samfunnsvitenskapelik kvinneforskning
University of Bergen
    Hans Holmboesgt. 22–24
    5007 BERGEN
☎ 55 21 21 76
Contact: Kristin Tornes
Course: Women's Perspectives in Economics, Social Anthropology and Political Science
☐ Seminars and lecture courses offered each term to promote interdisciplinary activities within the Faculty of Social Science.
☐ The Centre for Women's Studies in Social Sciences was established in 1987 to encourage feminist research in the social science fields where feminist work needs to be developed. The Centre is important for linking the various social science departments both for staff and students. Seminars and lectures which underpin co-operation between these departments are being emphasised.

NORC4

The Gender and Development Group
Centre for Development Studies
    Stromgaten 54
    5007 BERGEN
☎ 55 21 33 05
Contact: Tone Bleie
☐ The Gender and Development Group was formed in 1986 to focus priority on multidisciplinary gender research. Research programme has included history, comparative religion, anthropology, geography and philosophy.

Dragvoll

NORC5

Senter for kvinneforskning
Den allmennvitenskapelige hogskolen
    (College of Arts and Science)
University of Trondheim
    Hakon Magnussons gate 1b (Lade)
    7055 DRAGVOLL

☎ 47 7 59 17 88
Contact: Kari Melby
☐ The Centre for Women's Research was established for a trial period of four years up to the end of 1993. Activities include seminars emphasising development of interdisciplinary links and scientific theory, and a publication programme of research. The Centre offers accommodation for researchers, and guest researchers from abroad are welcome to apply.

Institute of Social Research in Industry (IFIM)
☐ Affiliated to the Foundation for Scientific and Industrial Research at the University of Trondheim (SINTEF). Women's Studies research is concerned with Women and Technology and Women and Work.

Lillehammer

NORC6

ODA (Oppland Distriktshogskole)
Oppland Regional College
    PO Box 1104 Skurva
    2601 LILLEHAMMER
☎ 61 28 80 00
Contact: Beatrice Halsaa
☐ Women scholars at Oppland Regional College have worked with the Ostland Research Foundation (division at Lillehammer, see entry NORC7) to promote feminist theory and joint research projects.

NORC7

Kvinner i regional utvikling
Ostland Research Foundation
    PO Box 1066 Skurva
    2601 LILLEHAMMER
☎ 61 26 03 01
Contact: Janneke van der Ros
☐ Women in Regional Development offers a feminist perspective in research projects on the situation and living conditions of women in the context of regional development. Co-operative projects are undertaken with other Women's Studies centres, e.g. the Finnmark Research Foundation, ODA at Oppland Regional College.

Oslo

NORC8

Arbeidsforskninginstituttet
Work Research Institute
    Stensberg gate 29
    PO Box 8179
    0034 OSLO 1
☎ 22 46 16 70
Contact: Anne Marie Berg

☐ A publicly financed centre, the Institute carries out two main programmes of Women's Studies research: gender, work and equality; and design and method.

NORC9

NAVF's utredningsinstitutt
Institute for Studies in Research and Higher Education
> Munthes gate 29
> 0260 OSLO 2
☎ 22 55 67 00
Contact: Ellen Brandt
☐ Research projects in Women's Studies concern women and higher education, e.g. hindrances for female researchers in and after the period of recruitment; women in medical, scientific and technological research in the university and college sector, 1974–1978; salary progression for college graduates.

NORC10

Norges rad for anvendt samfunnsforskning (NORAS)
> PO Box 8195
> 0034 OSLO 1
☎ 22 33 57 60
Contact: Ottil Tharaldsen
☐ NORAS aims to encourage research on factors which influence gender roles and development opportunities for women and men; and to study the consequences of public policies. A major research programme 'Research for Equal Status' was carried out as part of the Norwegian Action Plan for Equal Status for Women (1986–90). Information is available in English from NORAS.

NORC11

Norsk institutt for by-og regionsforskning (NIBR)
> PO Box 15 Grefsen
> 0409 OSLO 4
☎ 22 15 53 10
Contact: An-Magritt Jensen
☐ Research for NIBR is organised in Oslo, Trondheim and Alta. Research has an interdisciplinary focus, and covers work on municipal administration, e.g. shelters for battered women; industrial and populations-related problems, divorce and changes in family patterns, standard of living and welfare-related issues.

NORC12

Senter for kvinneforskning
University of Oslo
> PO Box 1040
> Blindern
> 0315 OSLO 3
☎ 22 85 89 30
Contact: Fride Eeg-Henriksen

☐ The Centre for Women's Research is located in a villa within walking distance of the campus. The Centre provides a base for affiliated, externally financed researchers, research scholars and students in order to strengthen women's research and for the integration of women's perspectives in research and teaching within the University. The Centre publishes research and contributes to Women's Studies journals.

NORC13

Institutt for samfunnsforskning (ISF)
> Munthes gate 31
> 0260 OSLO 2
☎ 22 55 45 10
Contact: Arnlaug Leira
☐ The ISF has been an important centre for research on women in Norway, since the 1960s. Gender equality was the focus of research in the 1980s, and in 1990 projects on women's family and equal status studies were undertaken.

NORC14

Institutt for sosialforskning (INAS)
> Munthes gate 31
> 0260 OSLO 2
☎ 22 55 45 10
Contact: Kari Skrede
☐ INAS is an independent institute with a special responsibility for research on social problems and the effects of public assistance programmes. The living conditions of women; changes in their life course patterns; and their situation in the Norwegian welfare state, have been the focus of some of the Women's Studies research carried out.

NORC15

Secretariat for Women and Research
> PO Box 2700
> 0131 OSLO
☎ 22 03 70 00
Contact: Tove Beate Pedersen
☐ Founded in 1977, the Secretariat is part of the Norwegian Research Council for Science and the Humanities (NAVF) and has the aim of initiating, co-ordinating and promoting research on women. The Secretariat publishes results of research, and also a journal, *Nytt on Kvinneforskning* (*News of Women's Studies*) five times per year.

NORC16

Transportokonomisk Institutt (TOI)
Institute of Transport Economics
> PO Box 6110 Etterstad
> 0602 OSLO 6
☎ 22 57 24 00
Contact: Randi Hjorthol

☐ TOI applies research to public policy on transport. From 1987 researchers have been working on gender analysis in different parts of the transport system. Particular projects have been: transportation and every-day life; women's perspectives on big-city traffic; and women's business trips.

NORC17

Kvinneforskningsgruppa ved Institutt for sprak of litteratur
University of Tromsø
    Breivika
    9000 TROMSØ
☎ 83 44 264
Contact: Gerd Bjørhovde
☐ The Women's Studies Group is housed in the Department of Language and Literature within the university, and research is carried out by tenured researchers and junior research fellows. Seminars and other activities, including publications, form part of the activities.

Pakistan

PAKC1

Applied Socio-Economic Research (ASR)
    Flat No. 8, 2nd Floor Sheraz Plaza
    PO Box 3154
    Gulberg
    LAHORE
☎ 877613
Contact: Nighat Said Khan
☐ ASR was founded in 1983 to work on a range of activities, including research, publishing, training, film production and documentation. Research issues include women and land; oral histories of women; women and Islam; and feminist theory in South Asia. Workshops are organised both at a grassroots level (e.g., video production training for women) and on conceptual and theoretical work on women and development and feminism.

Panama

PANC1

Instituto de Investigaciones y Capacitacion para la Promocion de la Mujer en Panama
    (Institute for Research on and Promotion of Women in Panama)
      Apartado Postal 6–5950 'El Dorado'
      PANAMA CITY
Contact: Marcela F. de Rodriquez

Paraguay

PARC1

Grupo de Estudio de la Mujer Paraguaya
    (Group for the Study of Women in Paraguay)
      Eligio Ayala 973 C.C. 2157
      ASUNCION
☎ 443734
Contact: Graziella Corvalan
☐ The Group was founded in 1985 to develop research on women's issues. Recent research issues include: women and the labour market; women and education, women and politics; and images of women in the media. Publications include a journal, *Enfoques du Mujer* (*Focus on Women*) and *Bibliografic de la Mujer Paraguaya* (*Bibliography of Paraguayan Women*).

Peru

PERC1

Flora Tristan Peruvian Women's Centre
    Parque Hernan Verlade 42
    LIMA 1
☎ 248008, 240839
Contact: Virginia Vargas
☐ The Centre was founded in 1979 to record and publish on women in Peru. Current research issues include the formation of the women's movement in Peru, and Gender Studies in the university. Outreach work in the community includes working with women in marginal urban sectors; reproductive and sexual rights of women; legal services and labour training programmes for women.

PERC2

Labour Association for Development
    Leon Verlarde 890-Lince
    LIMA 14
☎ 705682, 705688, 701446
Contact: Maruja Barrig
☐ An emphasis on research on women and employment has produced work on the fish canning industry; pharmaceutical laboratories; manufacturing industries; the informal urban sector; and the relationship between economic activity and the domestic unit. The Association also runs a daily radio programme, as well as training courses for union leaders and union organisation.

Philippines

Manila

PHIC1

Institute of Women's Studies
St Scholastica's College
> PO Box 3153
> MANILA

☎ 50 77 86
Contact: Mary John Mananzan
Course: Women's Studies
☐ Programmes aimed both at adult education level and as a prerequisite to graduation.
☐ The Institute operates four components comprising curricular activities; research and publications; outreach work; and resource development.

PHIC2

Labor Information Desk (LID)
Ateneo Centre for Social Policy and Public Affairs
> Room 230 Faura Hall
> PO Box 154
> MANILA

☎ 99 87 21 ext. 325/326
Contact: Eleanor R. Dionisio
☐ University-based, LID operates to research on, and support, the labour movement and its participation in social reform. Research activities have included gender equality in development; women in the trade union movement; and trade union education for women. Community-based activities include seminars for female workers and union leaders.

Quezon City

PHIC3

Centre for Women's Resources
> 43 Roces Avenue, 2nd Floor
> Mar Santos Building
> QUEZON CITY

☎ 99 27 55
Contact: Carolyn M. Anonuevo
☐ The Centre is a private, non-profit-making organisation, established in 1982 to conduct research, educate and publish. Participatory research on the conditions of women in various sectors, such as workers, students, urban and rural poor, and the professions, have been carried out. A woman-specific data-base is also being developed. The Centre publishes *Piglas Diwa* (*Liberating the Spirit*), a quarterly journal, and *Marso 8* (*March 8*), which reports on research.

PHIC4

Mediawatch Collective
> 12 Pasaje Dela Paz, Project 4
> QUEZON CITY

☎ 77 53 41, 721 68 69
Contact: P. S. Azarcon de la Cruz
☐ The Collective was founded in 1987 to monitor images of women in the media. Research has focused on the treatment of women in media on issues such as rape; the placement of women's stories in the news; and the response of women to such media messages and images. Publications include a monthly newsletter and *From Virgin to Vamp: Images of Women in Philippine Media*.

PHIC5

Philipina, Inc.
> 12 Pasaje de la Paz Street, Project 4
> 1109 QUEZON CITY

☎ 77 53 41
Contact: D. de Quiros Castillo
☐ Established in 1981, Philipina, Inc. is a secretariat base for Legislative Advocates for Women, a coalition of women's organisations working to seek legislative improvements for women. Research activities include policies and laws affecting women; the portrayal of women in the media; and work support systems to promote the needs of mothers for child care support structures. Philipina, Inc. is also involved with community outreach work with and for women – such as training, social credit, legal resources and community health. Publications include a pamphlet series by the Philippine Women's Research Collective and *Kamalayan*, an anthology of feminist writings.

PHIC6

Women's Resource and Research Centre
> Katipunan Parkway
> Loyola Heights
> QUEZON CITY

☎ 97 28 60, 98 24 21
Contact: Lucia Ticzon
☐ The Centre was founded in 1987 with the main aims of working at grassroots level for the development of Philippine women; supporting national and international women's movements; and developing academic research on women. Research focus includes feminist education and training for poor women; feminist participation in health care; women's information needs; non-sexist learning in the educational system; and theoretical studies in Third World feminism. Publications include a news bulletin called *Flights*.

Poland

POLC1

University of Lodz
  Women's Studies Centre
  Kosciuszki 65
  90514 LODZ
☎ 366337
Contact: Elzbieta H. Oleksy
Course: Interdisciplinary Women's Studies
☐ Practical training in a variety of fields, but also focusing on the role of women in a post-communist society.
☐ The first Women's Studies Centre in Poland was established in 1992, and co-operates with the International Women's Foundation based in Lodz, and with the Women's Caucus at Parliament. A Women's Information Centre and professional training for women are planned.

Portugal

Faro

PORC1

Escola Superior dé Educacao
  Quinta de Penha
  8000 FARO
☎ 089 8035616
Contact: J. E. Fernandes Viergas
Course: Social and Gender Equalities
☐ Within the discipline of Gender Studies, this forms part of the teacher training course.

Lisbon

PORC2

Faculdade De Psicologia E Ciencias Da Educacao
Universidade De Lisboa
  A.v/ Pinheiro Chagas 17–1
  1000 LISBON
Courses: Psychological Counselling for Women; Psycho-analysis; History and Anthropology
☐ Part of a Psychology and Educational Science degree.
Qualification: Degree

PORC3

Faculdade De Ciencias Sociais E Humanas
Universidade Nova De Lisboa
  Av. de Berna 24
  1000 LISBON
Contact: I. Allegro de Magalhaes
Course: Literature

☐ This course is at undergraduate level, and can form part of the Science and Humanities degree. Covers women's writing.
Qualification: Degree

Porto

PORC4

Faculdade Psicologia E Ciencia Da Educacao
Universidade Do Porto
  Rus das Taipas 76
  4000 PORTO
☎ 235 510315007
Contact: H. Ananjo Costa
Course: Women's Education and Patriarchy
☐ Within the discipline of Psychology, this course can form part of the Psychology and Educational Science degree.
Qualification: Degree

Senegal

SENC1

Association of African Women for Research and Development (AAWORD)
  BP 3304
  DAKAR
☎ 23 02 11
Contact: Ivy Matsepe Casaburi
☐ Established in 1977, AAWORD has established active networking within a regional, national and international focus. Research work has involved AAWORD in the development of gender as a major tool of analysis within social science in Africa. Publications include *Echo*, a bilingual quarterly; *The AAWORD Journal*; *Women and Rural Development in Africa*; and *Research on African Women; What Type of Methodology?*

SENC2

ENDA Third World
  BP 3370
  DAKAR
☎ 21 60 27
Contact: Marie H. Mottin-Sylla
☐ The Environment Development Action in the Third World (ENDA) has an international focus with its headquarters in Dakar. Indigenous development work is carried out by ENDA with grassroots groups which provides research, documentation, publications and training courses. Research activities have focused on income-generating activities for women in rural and urban areas; health and sanitation; research and action on female circumcision and AIDS. Internships and fellowships are offered. Publications include *African Environment*, a series published in English and French; and ENDA Third World Documents, leaflets on health,

technology and communication, published in French, English and Spanish.

South Africa

SAC1

Centre for Women's Studies
University of South Africa
    PO Box 392
    PRETORIA 0001
Contact: Sylvia Viljoen

South Korea

Seoul

SKC1

Korean Women's Development Institute
(KWDI)
    San 42–4, Bulkwang-don
    Eunpyung-ku
    SEOUL 122–040
☎   356 0070
Contact: Hyung Deok Kim
☐ The KWDI was founded in 1983 in order to carry out research on women's issues; develop women's capacities through education and training; promote effective utilisation of women's resources; and collate and disseminate information and research findings. Research focus has included the issues of law, policy, development of women's skills, women's employment and vocational training, and home-based work. Joint projects with women's organisations are also carried out, and the Institution has a Women's Volunteer Bank and a vocational information and counselling centre. Internships are available for both undergraduate and postgraduate students majoring in Women's Studies, Social Welfare or Sociology. Publications include *Women's Development News*, issued monthly; *KWDI Annual Reports*, and *Research Activity Reports (Korean)*.

SKC2

Sookmyung Women's University
    No. 53–12, 2–Ka Chungpa-Dong
    Yongsan-Ku
    SEOUL
Contact: Young Hai Park

Research Centre for Asian Women

Spain

Barcelona

SPC1

Facultad Geografia E Historia – Dept Prehistoria
Arqueologia Universidad
    Baldiri Reixach s/m
    08028 BARCELONA
☎   93 333 34 66 ext. 3152
Contact: Dolors Molas Font
Course: Les Femmes dans L'Empire Roman
☐ Postgraduate-level work within the discipline of History.
Qualification: Doctorate

SPC2

Seminari d'Estudis de la Dona
Universitat Autonoma de Barcelona
    Faculty de Sociologia
    Edefici b
    08913 BARCELONA
☎   93 582 24 09
Contact: Judith Astelarra Bonomi
Course: Estudis de la Dona
☐ Postgraduate-level work in the discipline of Sociology.
Qualification: Master's degree

SPC3

Centre d'Investigacio Historica de la Dona
Universitat de Barcelona
    61 Brusi
    08006 BARCELONA
☎   93 200 45 67
Contact: Montserrat Carbonell
Course: Master 1, 2 & 3 Estudis Entorn les Dones
☐ Interdisciplinary, postgraduate studies. Women without a university degree may be considered for this course.
Qualification: Master's degree
☐ The Centre for Research on the History of Women was founded in 1982 to promote historical research in Women's Studies. Research focus is on women's history and the history of art and cinema. Activities include teaching, publications, documentation, ERASMUS exchanges as well as research. Publications include *Beyond Silence: Women in the History of Cataluna*; *Thesaurus of Women's Social History* and *The Modern Woman of the Twentieth Century: The New Woman in Cataluna* (all in Catalan).

SPC4

Departmento Historia Contemporanea
Universitat de Barcelona
    Baldiri I Reixaxh s/n
    08028 BARCELONA
☎   93 240 92 00 ext. 236

Courses

Contact: Cristina Borderias
Courses: Travail Feminin et Changement Social; Mon Privat/Public de la Dona
☐ Available to students in the second cycle of study at undergraduate level.
Qualification: Degree

SPC5

Department Historia de la Filosofia, Estetica Y Filosofia de la Cultura
Universitat de Barcelona
  Facultat de Filosofia
  Baldiri Reixac s/n
  08023 BARCELONA
☎ 93 240 92 00 ext. 3260
Contact: Fina Birules
Course: Gender and Philosophy
☐ Seminars within the Philosophy Department, available to both undergraduate and postgraduate students.

SPC6

Seminari Universitari d'Estudis de les Dones
Universitat de Barcelona
  Facultat de Pedagogia Baldiri Reixac s/m
  Torre D-IC pis
  08026 BARCELONA
☎ 93 333 33 58 ext. 3371
Contact: Nuria Perez de Lara
Course: Estudis de les Dones
☐ Interdisciplinary studies at degree level, run by an informal group in higher education.

SPC7

Faculty of Social Science
The Open University
  The British Council
  Amigo 83
  08021 BARCELONA
☎ 93 207 14 21
Contact: Jovanka Babic
Course: Issues in Women's Studies
☐ Distance learning courses taught in English which can form part of a degree. Themes include: gender and education; girls into mathematics; women, writing and culture; and women into management.
Qualifications: Degree, Certificate

Donostia

SPC8

University of the Basque Country
  Trifunfo
  4 Bajo
  20007 DONOSTIA
☎ 94 346 84 78
Contact: K. Vazquez

Seminar of Women's Studies
☐ Established in 1981 this organisation has carried out research on the roles of women; sexual hierarchy; and attitudes toward gender in Basque society. The Seminar runs a documentation service which is open to the public. A three-year scholarship in history is offered to support a doctoral thesis. Publications include *Basque Women: Image and Reality*; *Language Rituals in Space*; and *Women and Words*.

Granada

SPC9

Departmento Sociologia y Psicologia Social
Universidad de Granada
  Facultad Politicas, Sociologia
  Recot Lopen Argneta 1
  18001 GRANADA
☎ 58 24 30 79
Contact: J. Iglesias de Ussel
Courses: La Designaldad Social en Function del Sexo; Situacion Social de la Mujer en Andalucia
Qualifications: Postgraduate degree, Doctorate

Madrid

SPC10

Facultad de Ciencias de la Informacion
Universidad Complutense de Madrid
  Ciudad Universitaria
  28040 MADRID
☎ 1 243 48 09 ext. 263
Contact: Gloria Nielfa
Course: Female Stereotypes Transmitted by Mass Media
☐ Media studies offered at postgraduate level.

Facultad de Geografia E Historia
Universidad Complutense de Madrid
  Ciudad Universitaria
  28040 MADRID
☎ 1 243 48 09 ext. 263
Contact: Gloria Nielfa
Courses: Sources and Methodology for the History of Medieval Women; Feminism beyond the Enlightenment, The Problem of the Subject; and Women, not to be and Evil.
☐ Postgraduate-level work in the disciplinary themes of History, Political Science and Philosophy. Taught in Spanish, this Women's Studies programme is run by university departments and the Institute of Feminist Research (see entry SPC11).

Facultad de Sociologia
Universidad Complutense de Madrid
Campus de Domosagua
28023 MADRID
☎ 1 243 48 09 ext. 263
Contact: Gloria Nielfa
Courses: Male and Female, The Social Construction of Gender; Methodology and Construction of Social Indicators applied to the area of Women and Health
□ Postgraduate courses that are registered with the Institute of Feminist Research.

SPC11

Instituto de Investigaciones Feministas
Universidad Complutense – Edificio Escuela de Estadistica
Ciudad Universitaria
Despacho 209
28040 MADRID
☎ 1 243 48 09 ext. 263
Contact: Gloria Nielfa
Courses: Feminism and Enlightenment; Art History and Feminism; Women Painters and Women's Image in Art; Roots and Developments of Thought; Dynamics of Global Economy and Women's Work; Anthropology and Feminism; Writing and Subversion
□ Themes from the disciplines of Philosophy, Art, Economics, Feminist Thought, Anthropology and Literature.

Women's Studies Centre
□ Activities include teaching, publications and documentation as well as research. Complutense is one of the eight European universities which participates in the ERASMUS exchange programme in Women's Studies.

Tarragone

SPC12

Facultat de Lletres
Universitat de Tarragone
Palca Imperial Tarroca s/n
43071 TARRAGONE
☎ 977 22 52 54
Contact: Elisabeth Russell
Course: Women, Literature and Society
□ Literature course available in the fourth year of the undergraduate degree programme.
Qualification: Degree

Valencia

SPC13

Instituto Universitario de Estudios de la Mujer
Universidad de Valencia
Facultad de Psicologia Avda Blasco Ibanez 21
46010 VALENCIA
☎ 6 386 44 20
Contact: Ester Barbera
Course: Discriminacion Sexual en Teoria y Practicas Cientificas
□ A multidisciplinary approach to equal opportunities, offered at postgraduate level.
Qualification: Master's degree

Sri Lanka

SLC1

Sri Lanka Association for the Advancement of Science
120/10 Wijerama Mawatha
COLOMBO 7
☎ 502153
Contact: Swarna Jayaweera

Centre for Women's Research (CENWOR)
□ Founded in 1984 to work on research on policy and action on women's issues. CENWOR has worked on the contribution of women to industrial development in Sri Lanka; and women in the Free Trade Zone. These studies formed part of the United Nations University Women's Work and Family Strategies international project. Current research includes work on the economic needs of women in urban, low-income families. CENWOR also has a Documentation Centre and Library, and a reference centre for Women's Studies. CENWOR is the focal point for INSTRAW in Sri Lanka. Young researchers are supported by an internship programme. CENWOR has published *UN Decade for Women: Progress and Achievements of Women in Sri Lanka*; it also publishes a biannual newsletter and has produced a video, *Nimble Fingers: Image and Reality*.

Sudan

Khartoum

SUDC1

Sudan Women's Research and Development Organisation
PO Box 208 I
KHARTOUM
Contact: Awartif Khalifa

Courses

☐ This organisation acts as a resource centre, both with Sudan and on an international basis; and promotes the development of the status of women by research projects and the initiation of self-help projects in rural and urban areas. It disseminates information and research findings through seminars and publications.

Omdurman

SUDC2

Ahfad University for Women
    PO Box 167
    OMDURMAN
Contact: Amna Rahama
Courses: Undergraduate programme; short courses for female village leaders
☐ A four-year undergraduate programme is offered, as well as short courses (3 to 6 months) for female village leaders working in community outreach.
☐ The university was established in 1966 with four schools: Family Sciences; Psychology and Preschool Education; Organisation Management; and Rural Education and Development. Research projects have focused on women's development and family planning in rural Khartoum and Sennar; the role of women in water supply and sanitation in Aferi villages, Kordofan; women and energy development; and women farmers and credit facilities in the Darfur region. Internships are available for women of remote areas, and fellowships can be provided for disadvantaged students. Publications include the biannual *Ahfad Journal: Women and change*, and an annual issue of the *Babiker Bedri Scientific Association for Women's Studies*.

Sweden

Gothenburg

SWEC1

The Women's Studies Centre
Gothenburg University
    41298 GOTHENBURG
☎   031 77 31 944
Contact: Eva Borgstrom

Women in Development
☐ Housed within the Women's Studies Centre.

Luleå

SWEC2

Forum for kvinnor if forskning och arbetsliv
Hogskolan i Luleå
Luleå University
    95181 LULEÅ

☎   920 915 70
Contact: Ann-Christine Haupt

Centre for Women in Research and Working Life

Lund

SWEC3

Lund University
    PO Box 1703
    22101 LUND
☎   46 10 76 24
Contact: Martha Ullerstan

Forum for Women Scholars and Research on Women

Orebro

SWEC4

Department of Political Science
Örebro College
    PO Box 923
    70130 ÖREBRO
☎   19 30 10 00
Contact: Gun Hedlund

Centre for Women's Studies and Research
☐ Housed within the Department of Political Science.

Stockholm

SWEC5

Stockholm University
    10691 STOCKHOLM
☎   8 16 22 22
Contact: Anita Dahlberg

Centre for Women Scholars and Research on Women

Swedish Network for Research and Gender Relations in the Third World.
☐ Research unit within the Population Participation Programme of the Development Study Unit, in the Department of Social Anthropology.

SWEC6

Arbetslivscentrum
    PO Box 5606
    11486 STOCKHOLM
☎   8 790 95 00

Centre for the Study of Working Life, Women's Research Group

☐ Women in working life is the research focus for

the Centre. Foreign female scholars are encouraged to conduct research.

Uppsala

SWEC7

Uppsala University
    Ostra Agatan 19 3r
    75322 UPPSALA
☎   18 18 25 00
Contact: Mona Eliasson
Course: Feminist Theory in the Humanities and Social Sciences
☐ Offered at both undergraduate and postgraduate level.

Centre for Women's Studies
☐ Established to offer support to women researchers. Work includes research on women and literature; psychological aspects of women's reproductive cycles; feminist theory; and feminist theology. Affiliation for visiting scholars to assist research can be arranged. Publications include *Uppsala Women's Studies in the Humanities*, an international series, and a newsletter, *Sofia*.

Switzerland

Geneva

SWC1

Isis-wicce
    3 chemin des Campanules
    1219 Aire
    GENEVA
☎   022 796 44 37
☐ Isis-wicce – Women's International Action-Oriented Resource Centre is a non-profit-making organisation which brings together researchers and grassroots women's activities worldwide (a network of 15,000 contacts in over 100 countries). It maintains a collection of materials on women and provides an information service for researchers. The Centre offers an Exchange Programme for women activists, especially from developing countries, an Internship Programme giving practical training, and a Scholarship Programme which offers short courses for women activists from developing countries.

International Feminist Network (IFN)
☐ Operates from Isis-wicce to work with, and support, campaigns on issues of justice, peace, sex discrimination and violence.

Tanzania

TANC1

University of Dar es Salaam
    Box 35185
    DAR ES SALAAM
Contact: Betty Komba Malekala

Women's Research and Documentation Project

Thailand

Bangkok

THAC1

Thammasat University
    BANGKOK
Contact: Malee Pruekpongsawalee

Women in Development Consortium
☐ Has links with the Women in Development Consortium, York University, Canada (see entry CANC2).

Head Yai

THAC2

Prince of Songkla University
    Faculty of Management Science
    HEAD YAI 90112
Contact: Sirirat Taneerananon

Women's Research and Development Centre

Chiangmai

THAC3

Faculty of Social Sciences
Chiangmai University
    CHIANGMAI
☎   053 221 699 ext. 3572
Contact: Virada Somswasdi

Women's Studies Programme
☐ Established in 1986 in order to focus research on women and development in northern Thailand. Objectives are to work from a historical perspective; to develop a theoretical framework for women's subordination and exploitation; and to liaise with both government and non-governmental organisations. Activities include seminars, conferences, workshops and lectures. Undergraduate courses are being established within the Faculty of Social Sciences. Publications

include newsletters, occasional papers, and a bibliography, *An Annotated Bibliography on Documents in Women's Studies of Northern Thailand*.

Trinidad and Tobago

TTC1

Caribbean Association for Feminist Research and Action (CAFRA)
PO Bag 442
Tunapuna Post Office
TUNAPUNA
☎ 663 8670
Contact: Rawida Balesh Soodeen
☐ Established in 1985 in Barbados, the Association has its secretariat located in Trinidad and Tobago. Overall aims are to develop a feminist approach which takes into account issues of race and class as well as sex, to promote the links between feminist research and action, and to support the feminist movement in the Caribbean. Recent research projects have been 'Women in Caribbean Agriculture' (WIVA) and 'Women's Caribbean History'. The Association publishes its work in a quarterly newsletter, *CAFRA News*.

Ukraine

UKRC1

Institute of Literature
Ukrainian Academy of Sciences
Grushevskogo STR 4
252001 KIEV 1
Contact: Solomea Pavlychko

Ukrainian Centre of Women's Studies
☐ Inaugural meeting held in June 1992. The Centre aims to carry out research on women in the Ukraine as well as to establish contact with European and American centres of Women's Studies and to take part in joint projects and research. Translation and publication of feminist works will also be undertaken by the Centre.

United States of America

Alabama

USAC1

University of Alabama
Box 870272
TUSCALOOSA, AL 35487–0272
☎ 205 348 5782
Contact: Rhoda Johnson
Course: Women's Studies programme

☐ The undergraduate programme can be taken as a minor or an area of concentration; the postgraduate programme as a major, minor or area of concentration.
Qualifications: Degree, Master's degree

USAC2

University of Alabama at Birmingham
University Station
BIRMINGHAM, AL 35294
☎ 205 934 9680
Contact: Genie Stowers
Course: Women's Studies programme
☐ Can be taken as a minor on an undergraduate programme.
Qualification: Degree

USAC3

Department of Foreign Language
Auburn University
8030 Haley Center
AUBURN, AL 36849
☎ 205 844 4345
Contact: Louise Katainen
Course: Women's Studies programme

Arizona

USAC4

Women's Studies Program
Arizona State University
TEMPE, AZ 85281–1801
☎ 602 965 2358
Contact: Nancy Felipe Russo
Course: Women's Studies programme
Qualifications: Certificate, Degree, Master's degree, Doctorate

USAC5

University of Arizona
Douglass 102
TUCSON, AZ 85721
☎ 602 621 7338
Contact: Karen Anderson
Course: Women's Studies programme
☐ Minor in English and History; specialisation in Sociology.
Qualification: Degree

Southwest Institute for Research on Women
☐ Specialises in research on women in the Southwest; ageing and widowhood.

USAC6

Northern Arizona University
Box 5695
FLAGSTAFF, AZ 86011

☎ 602 523 3300
Contact: J. Bowles
Course: Women's Studies programme
☐ A minor or an area of concentration on the undergraduate programme.
Qualification: Degree

USAC7

University of Arkansas at Little Rock
2801 South University
LITTLE ROCK, AR 72204
☎ 501 569 3234
Contact: J. S. Miller
Course: Women's Studies programme
☐ A minor on the undergraduate programme.
Qualification: Degree

USAC8

Henderson State University
ARKADELPHIA, AR 71923
☎ 501 246 5511
Contact: Juanita D. Sandford
Course: Women's Studies programme

California

USAC9

Antioch University, West
50 Fell Street
SAN FRANCISCO, CA 94102
Contact: Ani Mander
Course: Women's Studies programme

USAC10

Cabrillo College
6500 Soquel Drive
APTOS, CA 95003
☎ 408 479 6249
Contact: Rosemary Brogan
Course: Women's Studies programme
☐ A major taken on the undergraduate programme
Qualification: Degree

USAC11

California Lutheran University
60 West Olsen Road
THOUSAND OAKS, CA 91360
☎ 805 493 3345
Contact: Kathryn Swanson
Course: Women's Studies programme
☐ Can be taken as a minor on the undergraduate programme, or as a specialisation major.
Qualification: Degree

USAC12

California Polytechnic State University
SAN LUIS OBISPO, CA 91768
☎ 805 756 2706
Contact: Willi Coleman
Course: Women's Studies programme
☐ A minor on the undergraduate programme.
Qualification: Degree

USAC13

California State Polytechnic University
Pomona
3801 Temple Avenue
POMONA, CA 91768
☎ 714 869 3593
Contact: Patricia Lin
Course: Women's Studies programme
☐ A minor on the undergraduate programme
Qualification: Degree

USAC14

California State University, Bakersfield
9001 Stockdale Highway
BAKERSFIELD, CA 93309
☎ 805 664 2011
Contact: Anita DuPratt
Course: Women's Studies programme

USAC15

Center for Ethnic Women's Studies
California State University, Chico
CHICO, CA 95929
☎ 916 345 8118
Contact: Gayle Kimball
Course: Women's Studies programme
☐ A minor at either undergraduate or postgraduate level.

USAC16

California State University, Dominguez Hills
1000 East Victoria Street
CARSON, CA 90747
☎ 213 516 3759
Contact: Linda Pomerantz
Course: Women's Studies programme
☐ A minor on the undergraduate programme.
Qualification: Degree

USAC17

California State University, Fresno
School of Social Science
FRESNO, CA 93740–0078
☎ 209 278 2858
Contact: Susan Arpad
Course: Women's Studies programme
☐ A minor on the undergraduate programme.
Qualification: Degree

USAC18

California State University, Fullerton
MH–103
FULLERTON, CA 92634
☎ 714 773 2594
Contact: Diane Ross
Course: Women's Studies programme
☐ A minor on the undergraduate programme.
Qualification: Degree

USAC19

California State University, Hayward
HAYWARD, CA 94542
☎ 415 881 3221
Contact: Emily Stoper
Course: Women's Studies programme
☐ A minor on the undergraduate programme.
Qualification: Degree

USAC20

California State University, Long Beach
FO2–226
LONG BEACH, CA 90840
☎ 213 985 4839
Contact: Norma Chinchilla
Course: Women's Studies programme, with American Studies
☐ A major or a minor at undergraduate level, a special major at postgraduate level.
Qualifications: Degree, Master's degree

USAC21

California State University, Los Angeles
5151 State University Drive
LOS ANGELES, CA 90032
☎ 213 343
Contact: Sharon Bassett
Course: Women's Studies programme
☐ A minor on the undergraduate programme.
Qualification: Degree

USAC22

California State University, Northridge
18111 Nordhoff Street
NORTHRIDGE, CA 91330
☎ 818 885 3110
Contact: Eloise Klein Healy
Course: Women's Studies programme
☐ Can be a major, a minor or an area of concentration on the undergraduate programme.
Qualifications: Certificate, Degree

USAC23

California State University, Sacremento
6000 J. Street
SACRAMENTO, CA 95819
☎ 916 278 6817

Contact: Filomina Steady
Course: Women's Studies programme
☐ Can be taken as a major or a minor on the undergraduate programme. At postgraduate level can be taken as a minor, or as a specialised Master's degree.
Qualifications: Degree, Master's degree

USAC24

Department of Anthropology
California State University, San Bernadino
5500 University Parkway
SAN BERNADINO 92407
☎ 714 880 5503
Contact: Ellen Gruenbaum
Course: Women's Studies programme
☐ A minor or an area of concentration on the undergraduate programme. A minor at postgraduate level.
Qualifications: Certificate, Degree, Postgraduate certificate

USAC25

Ethnic and Women's Studies Department
California State University, Stanislaus
801 Monte Vista Avenue
TURLOCK, CA 95380
☎ 415 642 4607
Contact: J. J. Hendriks
Course: Women's Studies programme
☐ A minor or an area of concentration on the undergraduate programme.
Qualification: Degree

USAC26

University of California, Berkeley
301 Campbell Hall
BERKELEY, CA 94720
☎ 415 642 2767
Contact: Mary P. Ryan
Course: Women's Studies programme
☐ A major or a minor on the undergraduate programme. Can be studied as an area of concentration at postgraduate level.
Qualification: Degree

Beatrice M. Bain Research Center
University of California, Berkeley
Room 206, Building T9
BERKELEY, CA 94720
☎ 415 642 4607
Contact: Elizabeth Abel
☐ Research specialisation of the Centre is on women and gender.

USAC27

University of California, Davis
307, Young Hill
DAVIS, CA 95616

☎ 916 752 4686
Contact: Judith Newton
Course: Women's Studies programme

Women's Research and Resource Center
☐ The contact name for the Women's Research and Resource Center is Linda Morris.

USAC28

University of California, Irvine
    240 Humanities Office Building
    IRVINE, CA 92717
☎ 714 856 4234
Contact: Jane O. Newman
Course: Gender and Women's Studies programme
☐ A major or a minor on the undergraduate programme.
Qualification: Degree

USAC29

University of California, Los Angeles
    240 Kinsey Hall, 405 Hilgard Avenue
    LOS ANGELES, CA 90024–1453
☎ 213 206 8101
Contact: Karen Brodkin Sacks
Course: Women's Studies programme
☐ Can be taken as a major, or as a specialisation (area of concentration) on the undergraduate programme.
Qualifications: Certificate, Degree

Center for the Study of Women
University of California, Los Angeles
    236 Kinsey Hall, 405 Hilgard Avenue
    LOS ANGELES, CA 90024–1504
☎ 213 825 0590
Contact: Helen S. Astin

USAC30

Women's Studies Committee
University of California, Riverside
    900 University Avenue
    RIVERSIDE, CA 92521
☎ 714 787 3625
Contact: Sarah Stage
Course: Departmental Emphasis in History
☐ A minor on both undergraduate and postgraduate programmes.

USAC31

University of California, San Diego
    LA JOLLA, CA 92093
☎ 619 534 7127
Contact: Kathryn Shevelow
Course: Women's Studies programme
☐ Can be taken as a minor or area of concentration on the undergraduate programme
Qualification: Degree

USAC32

University of California, Santa Barbara
    SANTA BARBARA, CA 93106
☎ 805 961 4330
Contact: Sarah Fenstermaker
Course: Women's Studies programme
☐ Can be taken as a major.
Qualification: Degree

USAC33

University of California, Santa Cruz
    186 Kresge College
    SANTA CRUZ, CA 95064
☎ 408 459 4324
Contact: Gloria Hull
Course: Women's Studies programme
☐ Can be taken as a major.
Qualification: Degree
Course: Women's Studies programme
☐ Postgraduate study through History of Consciousness, Subscription.
Qualification: Doctorate

Feminist Studies Focused Research Activity
    University of California, Santa Cruz
    188 Kresge College
    SANTA CRUZ, CA 95064
☎ 408 459 4052
Contact: Wendy Brown

USAC34

Institute for the Study of Women and Men in Society
University of Southern California
    734 West Adams Boulevard
    LOS ANGELES, CA 90007
☎ 213 743 3683
Contact: Judith Glass

USAC35

City College of San Francisco
    50 Phelan Avenue/Box L206
    SAN FRANCISCO, CA 94112
☎ 415 239 3442
Contact: Susan Evans
Course: Women's Studies programme
☐ Specialisation: AA in General Education

USAC36

Claremont Colleges Consortium
    Scripps College
    Benezet 229
    CLAREMONT, CA 91711
☎ 714 621 8000 ext. 3250
Contact: J'nan Morese Sellery
Course: Women's Studies programme

☐ Can be taken as a major, a minor or an area of concentration at both undergraduate and postgraduate level.

USAC37

Cosumnes River College
 8401 Center Parkway
 SACRAMENTO, CA 95823
☎ 916 688 7354
Contact: A. Christine Harris
Course: Women's Studies programme
☐ Interdisciplinary Studies, Women's Studies option. Can be taken as a major, a minor or an area of concentration.
Qualifications: Certificate, Degree

USAC38

DeAnza College
 21250 Stevens Creek Boulevard
 CUPERTINO, CA 95014
☎ 408 864 8554
Contact: Julie Nash
Course: Women's Studies programme
☐ Courses can lead on to undergraduate level of study at San José State University.

USAC39

Diablo Valley College
 321 Golf Club Road
 PLEASANT HILL, CA 94523
☎ 415 685 1230
Contact: Diane Scott-Summers
Course: Women's Studies programme
☐ An area of concentration on the undergraduate programme.
Qualification: Certificate

USAC40

Fresno City College
 1101 East University Avenue
 FRESNO, CA 93741
☎ 209 442 8210
Contact: J. Walsh
Course: Women's Studies programme
☐ Specialisation: AA in Women's Studies.

USAC41

Harvey Mudd College
 Kingston Hall
 CLAREMONT, CA 91711
☎ 714 621 8000 ext. 3250
Contact: J'nan Morse Sellery
Course: Women's Studies programme

USAC42

Humboldt State University
 House 55
 ARCATA, CA 95521
☎ 704 826 4925
Contact: Karen Foss
Course: Women's Studies programme
☐ A minor on the undergraduate programme. A Special Major is available where Women's Studies is one of three areas.
Qualification: Certificate

USAC43

Loyola Marymount University
 Loyola Boulevard at West 80th Street
 LOS ANGELES, CA 90045
☎ 213 338 2757
Contact: Joanne Fisher
Course: Women's Studies programme
☐ A minor on the undergraduate programme.

USAC44

Mills College
 OAKLAND, CA 94613
☎ 415 430 2233
Contact: Carol George
Course: Women's Studies programme
☐ A major, a minor, or an area of concentration on the undergraduate programme.
Qualification: Degree

USAC45

Monterey Peninsula College
 980 Fremont Street
 MONTEREY, CA 93940
☎ 408 646 4160
Contact: Phyllis Peet
Course: Women's Studies programme
☐ A major on the undergraduate programme.

USAC46

Moorpark College
 7075 Campus Road
 MOORPARK, CA 93021
☎ 805 378 1452
Contact: Carole Ginet
Course: Women's Studies programme

USAC47

Women's Leadership Program
Mount St Mary's College
 12001 Chalon Road
 LOS ANGELES, CA 90049
☎ 213 476 2237
Contact: Cheryl Mabey
Course: Women's Studies programme
☐ A minor on the undergraduate programme.

USAC48

New College
777 Valencia Street
SAN FRANCISCO, CA 94110
☎ 415 861 4168
Contact: Betsy Kassoff
Course: Feminist Psychology programme
☐ Postgraduate work levels.
Qualifications: Master's degree in Psychology; Feminist Psychology

USAC49

Occidental College
1600 Campus Road
LOS ANGELES, CA 90041
☎ 213 259 2787
Contact: Kern L. King
Course: Women's Studies programme
☐ A minor or an area of concentration on the undergraduate programme.

USAC50

Ohlone College
43600 Mission Boulevard
FREMONT, CA 94539
☎ 415 659 6134
Contact: E. J. Foster-Hillard
Course: Women's Studies programme

USAC51

Pitzer College
1050 North Mills Avenue
CLAREMONT, CA 94539
☎ 415 659 6134
Contact: Ann Stromberg
Course: Women's Studies programme
☐ A major on the undergraduate programme.
Qualification: Degree

USAC52

Pomona College
550 Harvard Avenue
CLAREMONT, CA 91711
☎ 714 621 8000 ext. 2227
Contact: Deborah Burke
Course: Women's Studies programme
☐ A major on the undergraduate programme.
Qualification: Degree

USAC53

Rancho Santiago Community College
17th at Bristol Street
SANTA ANA, CA 92706
☎ 714 667 3000
Contact: Sharon Wayland
Course: Women's Studies programme

USAC54

University of Redlands
PO Box 3080
REDLANDS, CA 92706
☎ 714 793 2121 ext. 3893
Contact: Emily Culpepper
Course: Women's Studies programme
☐ Individualised major, or minor part of the undergraduate programme.
Qualification: Degree

USAC55

Social Science Division
Sacremento City College
3835 Freeport Boulevard
SACRAMENTO, CA 95822
☎ 916 449 7511
Contact: Suzanne Nissen
Course: Women's Studies programme
☐ A major on the undergraduate programme.

USAC56

Saddleback College
28000 Marguerite Parkway
MISSION VIEJO, CA 92692
☎ 714 582 4388
Contact: Anne Clasby
Course: Women's Studies programme
☐ A major on the undergraduate programme.

USAC57

San Diego City College
1313 Twelfth Avenue
SAN DIEGO, CA 92107
☎ 619 230 2400
Course: Women's Studies programme

USAC58

Women's Studies Department
San Diego State University
SAN DIEGO, CA 92182
☎ 619 594 6524
Contact: Bonnie Zimmerman
Course: Women's Studies programme
☐ A major or minor on the undergraduate programme, and a specialisation on the postgraduate programme.
Qualifications: Degree, Master's degree

USAC59

San Francisco State University
1600 Holloway Avenue
SAN FRANCISCO, CA 94132
☎ 415 338 1388
Course: Women's Studies programme

Courses

☐ A major, a minor or an area of concentration on the undergraduate programme. Postgraduate study available from 1991.
Qualifications: Degree, Master's degree

USAC60

San José State University
1 Washington Square
SAN JOSE, CA 94132
☎ 408 924 5590 or 5591
Contact: Lois Rita Helmbold
Course: Women's Studies programme
☐ A major, a minor or an area of concentration on both undergraduate and postgraduate programme. The MA is in Social Sciences with a focus on Women's Studies.
Qualifications: Degree, Master's degree

USAC61

Sierra College
5000 Rocklin Road
ROCKLIN, CA 95677
☎ 916 624 3333 ext. 2478
Contact: Mary Moon
Course: Women's Studies programme

USAC62

Sonoma State University
ROHNERT PARK, CA 94928
☎ 707 664 2840
Contact: Ellen Kay Trimberger
Course: Women's Studies programme
☐ A minor on the undergraduate programme, or a specialisation programme which is an Interdisciplinary Independent major with an emphasis on women.
Qualification: Degree

USAC63

Stanford University
STANFORD, CA 94305
☎ 415 723 2412
Contact: Sylvia J. Yanagisako
Course: Women's Studies programme
☐ A major or a minor on the undergraduate programme. Specialisation available.
Qualification: Honors Certificate in Feminist Studies

Institute for Research on Women and Gender
Stanford University
Serra House
STANFORD, CA 94305–8640
☎ 415 723 1994
Contact: Deborah L. Rhode

USAC64

University of the Pacific
3601 North Pacific Avenue
STOCKTON, CA 95211
☎ 209 946 2928
Contact: Sally Miller
Course: Women's Studies programme
☐ A minor on the undergraduate programme.

USAC65

West Valley College
14000 Fruitvale Avenue
SARATOGA, CA 95070
☎ 408 867 2200
Contact: Pat Bennett
Course: Women's Studies
Qualification: Degree

Colorado

USAC66

Colorado College
14E Cache La Poudre, Room 132
Armstrong Hall
COLORADO SPRINGS, CO 80903
☎ 719 473 2233
Contact: Judith Genova
Course: Women's Studies programme
☐ A minor on the undergraduate programme.

USAC67

University of Colorado, Boulder
Campus Box 246
BOULDER, CO 80309
☎ 303 492 8923
Contact: Marcia Westcott
Course: Women's Studies programme
☐ Can be a major on the undergraduate programme.
Qualifications: Certificate, Degree

USAC68

University of Colorado, Colorado Springs
Austin Bluffs Parkway
COLORADO SPRINGS, CO 80933–7150
☎ 719 593 3538
Course: Women's Studies programme
☐ A major on the undergraduate programme.

USAC69

Colorado State University
112 Student Services
FORT COLLINS, CO 80523
☎ 303 491 6384
Contact: Karen J. Wedge
Course: Women's Programmes and Studies

☐ Available on both undergraduate and postgraduate programmes.
Qualification: Certificate

USAC70

Denver Seminary
Christian Education Department
3401 South University Boulevard
ENGLEWOOD, CO 80110
☎ 303 751 6150
Contact: D. Williams
Course: Women's Studies programme
☐ An area of concentration on the postgraduate programme.

USAC71

University of Denver
2121 East Asbury
DENVER, CO 80208
☎ 303 871 2846
Contact: M. E. Warlick
Course: Women's Studies programme
☐ A major or a minor on the undergraduate programme.
Qualification: Degree

USAC72

Metropolitan State College of Denver
1006 Eleventh Street, Box 36
DENVER, CO 80204
☎ 303 556 8441
Contact: Jodi Wetzel
Course: Women's Studies programme
☐ A major on the undergraduate programme, by contract.
Qualification: Degree

USAC73

University of Northern Colorado
GREELEY, CO 80639
☎ 303 351 2607
Contact: Marcia Willcoxon
Course: Women's Studies programme
☐ A major or a minor on the undergraduate programme; an individualised postgraduate programme.
Qualifications: Degree, Master's degree, Doctorate

USAC74

University of Southern Colorado
PUEBLO, CO 81001
☎ 719 549 2729
Contact: B. A. Bassein
Course: Women's Studies programme
☐ An area of concentration on the undergraduate programme.

Connecticut

USAC75

Central Connecticut State University
1615 Stanley Street
NEW BRITAIN, CT 06050
☎ 203 827 7000
Contact: June Higgins
Course: Women's Studies programme
☐ An area of concentration on the undergraduate programme.

USAC76

Connecticut College
PO Box 5542
NEW LONDON, CT 06320
☎ 203 447 4119
Contact: Jane W. Torrey
Course: Women's Studies programme
☐ A major or a minor on the undergraduate programme. A student-designed specialisation is also offered.

USAC77

University of Connecticut
417 Whitney Road
STORRS, CT 06269–1181
☎ 203 486 3970
Contact: Lucy Creevey
Course: Women's Studies programme
☐ A major on the undergraduate programme.
Qualification: Degree

Institute for the Study of Women and Gender
☎ 203 486 2186
Contact: Patricia Carter

USAC78

Eastern Connecticut State University
Knight House
WILLIMANTIC, CT 06226
☎ 203 456 5535
Contact: Marcia Phillips McGowan
Course: Women's Studies programme
☐ A minor on the undergraduate programme.

USAC79

Hartford College for Women
260 Girard Avenue
HARTFORD, CT 06105
☎ 203 233 5662
Contact: Sharon Toffey Shepela

Women's Research Institute

Courses

USAC80

University of Hartford
200 Bloomfield Avenue
WEST HARTFORD, CT 06117
☎ 203 243 4741
Contact: Sherry Buckberrough
Course: Women's Studies programme
☐ A minor on the undergraduate programme.

USAC81

Quinnipiac College
Box 119
HAMDEN, CT 06518
☎ 1203 281 8702
Contact: Michele Hoffnung
Course: Women's Studies programme
☐ A minor or an Independent major on the undergraduate programme.
Qualification: Degree

USAC82

Trinity College
HARTFORD, CT 06457
☎ 203 297 2131
Contact: Joan D. Hedrick
Course: Women's Studies programme
☐ A minor, or an individually designed major, on the undergraduate programme.
Qualification: Degree

USAC83

Wesleyan University
287 High Street
MIDDLETOWN, CT 06423
☎ 203 347 9411 ext 2660
Contact: Gertrude Hughes
Course: Women's Studies programme
☐ A major, a minor or an area of concentration on the undergraduate programme. An area of concentration at postgraduate level.
Qualification: Degree

USAC84

Western Connecticut State University
181 White Street
DANBURY, CT 06810
☎ 2032 797 4094
Contact: Jerry Bannister
Course: Women's Studies programme
☐ A minor on the undergraduate programme.
Qualification: Degree

USAC85

Yale University
PO Box 5046
Yale Station, 80 Wall Street
NEW HAVEN, CT 06520

☎ 203 432 0845
Contact: Emily Honig
Course: Women's Studies programme
☐ A major or an area of concentration on the undergraduate programme.
Qualification: Degree

Delaware

USAC86

University of Delaware
333 Smith Hall
NEWARK, DE 19716
☎ 302 451 8474
Contact: Sandra Harding
Course: Women's Studies programme
☐ A major or a minor on the undergraduate programme.
Qualification: Degree

Women's Research Center
University of Delaware
Political Science Department
NEWARK, DE 19716
☎ 302 451 2000
Contact: Marian Palley
☐ Research specialism in Politics, History and Education.

District of Columbia

USAC87

The American University
4400 Massachusetts Avenue
WASHINGTON, DC 20016
☎ 202 885 2485
Contact: Muriel Cantor
Course: Women's Studies programme
☐ A minor or an area of concentration on the undergraduate programme. An area of concentration at postgraduate level.
Qualification: Degree

USAC88

Georgetown University
Department of English
WASHINGTON, DC 20057
☎ 202 687 7558
Contact: Leona M. Fisher
Course: Women's Studies programme
☐ A minor on the undergraduate programme.
Qualification: Interdisciplinary degree

USAC89

George Washington University
2201 G. Street, NW/217 Funger Hall
WASHINGTON, DC 20052

☎ 202 994 6942
Contact: P. Madoo Lengermann
Course: Women's Studies programme
☐ A minor on the undergraduate programme. An area of concentration at postgraduate level.
Qualifications: Degree, Master's degree

USAC90

Institute for Women's Policy Research
1400 20th Street NW, Suite 104
WASHINGTON, DC 20036
☎ 202 785 5100
Contact: Heidi Hartmann

USAC91

International Center for Research on Women
1717 Massachusetts Avenue NW, Suite 501
WASHINGTON, DC 20036
☎ 202 797 0007
Contact: Mayra Buvinic

USAC92

Program of Policy Research on Women and Families
2100 M. Street, NW
WASHINGTON, DC 20037
☎ 202 833 7200
Contact: Elaine Sorenson

USAC93

The Women's Research and Education Institute
1700 18th Street NW, Suite 400
WASHINGTON, DC 20009
☎ 202 328 7070
Contact: Betty Parsons Dooley

USAC94

Trinity College
Michigan Avenue and Franklin Street NE
WASHINGTON, DC 20017
☎ 202 939 5000
Contact: P. Weitzel-O'Neill
Course: Women's Studies programme
☐ A minor or an area of concentration on the undergraduate programme.

Florida

USAC95

Barry University
11300 Northeast Second Avenue
MIAMI SHORES, FL 33161
☎ 305 758 3392 ext. 532
Contact: Lillian Schanfield
Course: Women's Studies programme

☐ A minor on the undergraduate programme.
Qualification: Certificate

USAC96

Eckerd College
4200 54th Avenue South
ST PETERSBURG, FL 33771
☎ 813 867 1166
Contact: Carolyn Johnston
Course: Women's Studies programme
☐ A major on the undergraduate programme.
Qualification: Degree

USAC97

Women's Studies Center
Florida Atlantic University
Humanities Building 243E
BOCA RATON, FL 33431
☎ 407 367 3865
Contact: Helen Bannan
Course: Women's Studies programme
Qualification: Certificate

USAC98

Women's Studies Center
Florida International University
University Park
MIAMI, FL 33199
☎ 305 348 2408
Contact: Marilyn Hoder-Salmon
Course: Women's Studies programme
☐ An area of concentration on the undergraduate programme.
Qualification: Certificate

USAC99

Florida State University
R–126A
TALLAHASSEE, FL 32306
☎ 904 644 9514
Contact: Jean G. Bryant
Course: Women's Studies programme
☐ A minor on the undergraduate programme. A minor or an area of concentration at postgraduate level.

USAC100

University of Florida
GAINESVILLE, FL 32611
☎ 904 392 3365
Contact: Linda D. Wolfe
Course: Women's Studies programme
Qualification: Certificate

Women in Agricultural Development
  Institute of Food and Agricultural Sciences
  University of Florida
  3028 McCarty Hall
  GAINESVILLE, FL 32611
☎ 904 392 1965
Contact: Marilyn M. Swisher

USAC101

University of North Florida
  College of Arts and Sciences
  4567 St John's Bluff Road
  JACKSONVILLE, FL 32216
☎ 904 646 2758
Contact: Christine E. Rasche
Course: Women's Studies programme
□ A minor on the undergraduate programme.

USAC102

Nova University
  3301 College Avenue
  FT LAUDERDALE, FL 33314
☎ 305 475 7343
Contact: Kathleen Waites Lamm
Course: Women's Studies programme
□ An area of concentration on the undergraduate programme.
Qualification: Certificate

USAC103

Rollins College
  Box 2604
  WINTER PARK, FL 32789
☎ 407 646 2666
Contact: Rosemary Curb
Course: Women's Studies programme
□ A minor or an area of concentration on the undergraduate programme.

USAC104

University of South Florida
  4202 East Fowler Avenue
  TAMPA, FL 33620
☎ 813 974 2668
Contact: Janice Snook
Course: Women's Studies programme
□ A major or a minor on the undergraduate programme.
Qualification: Degree

USAC105

University of Tampa
  Social Science Department
  401 West Kennedy Boulevard
  TAMPA, FL 33606
☎ 813 253 3333 ext. 226
Contact: R. Piper

Course: Women's Studies programme
□ A minor on the undergraduate programme.

USAC106

University of West Florida
  Department of Sociology
  11000 University Parkway
  PENSACOLA, FL 32514
☎ 904 474 2797
Contact: Mary F. Rogers
Course: Women's Studies programme
□ A minor on the undergraduate programme.

Georgia

USAC107

Agnes Scott College
  DECATUR, GA 30030
☎ 404 371 6221
Contact: Christine Cozens
Course: Women's Studies programme
□ A minor on the undergraduate programme.

USAC108

Brenau Women's College
  Humanities Department
  Washington & Boulevard
  GAINESVILLE, GA 30501
☎ 404 534 6100
Contact: Leslie Jones
Course: Women's Leadership Development programme

USAC109

Clark Atlanta University
  223 Chestnut Street SW
  ATLANTA, GA 30314
☎ 404 880 8733
Contact: Alma Vinyard
Course: Women's Studies programme
□ A major or a minor on the undergraduate programme.

USAC110

Emory University
  210 Physicsa Building
  ATLANTA, GA 30322
☎ 404 727 0096
Contact: Elizabeth Fox-Genovese
Course: Women's Studies programme
□ A major, a minor or an area of concentration on the undergraduate programme. Postgraduate work through the Institute for Liberal Arts.
Qualifications: Degree, Master's degree, Doctorate

USAC111

Georgia College
Box 486
MILLEDGEVILLE, GA 31060
☎ 404 453 4504
Contact: Rosemary Begemann
Course: Women's Studies programme
□ A minor on the undergraduate programme.

USAC112

Georgia State University
University Plaza
ATLANTA, GA 30303
☎ 404 651 3152
Contact: Diane Fowlkes
Course: Women's Studies programme
□ A minor on the undergraduate programme, or a minor at postgraduate level. (Cognate for Ph.D. in Education, as field in political science by petition.)
Qualifications: Degree, Doctorate

USAC113

University of Georgia, Athens
230–F Main Library
ATHENS, GA 30602
☎ 404 542 2846
Contact: Patricia Del Rey
Course: Women's Studies programme
□ Specialisation: College of Home Economics, Child and Family.
Qualification: Certificate

USAC114

Kennesaw State College
History Department
Box 444
MARIETTA, GA 30061
☎ 404 423 6245
Contact: Ann W. Ellis
Course: Women's Studies programme
□ A minor on the undergraduate programme.

USAC115

Spelman College
350 Spelman Lane
Box 115
ATLANTA, GA 30311
☎ 404 681 3643
Contact: Beverly Guy-Sheftall
Course: Women's Studies programme
□ A minor on the undergraduate programme.

Women's Research and Resource Center
Spelman College
Box 362
ATLANTA, GA 30314

☎ 404 681 3643
Contact: Beverly Guy-Sheftall

Hawaii

USAC116

University of Hawaii at Hilo
Chancellor's Office
HILO, HI 96720–4091
☎ 808 933 3422
Contact: Trina Nahm-Mijo
Course: Women's Studies programme
Qualification: Certificate

USAC117

University of Hawaii at Manoa
2424 Maile Way
Porteus 722
HONOLULU, HI 96822
☎ 808 956 7464
Contact: Ann M. Keppel
Course: Women's Studies programme
□ A major on the undergraduate programme.
Qualification: Certificate

Women's Studies Research Center
□ Specialisation: Asian, Pacific and Hawaiian women.

Illinois

USAC118

Augustana College
ROCK ISLAND, IL 61210
☎ 309 794 7384
Contact: Nancy Huse
Course: Women's Studies programme
□ A major, a minor or an area of concentration on the undergraduate programme.

USAC119

Bradley University
Bradley Avenue
PEORIA, IL 61625
☎ 800 447 6460
Contact: Bonnie Gorden
Course: Women's Studies programme
□ A minor on the undergraduate programme.

USAC120

De Paul University
802 West Beldon Avenue
McSaw Building, Room 27
CHICAGO, IL 60614–3214
☎ 312 341 8800
Contact: Carol Zyganowski

Course: Women's Studies programme
☐ A minor on the undergraduate programme.

USAC121

Eastern Illinois University
Room 209 MLK Union
CHARLESTON, IL 61920
☎ 217 581 5947
Contact: Genie Lenihan
Course: Women's Studies programme
☐ A minor on the undergraduate programme.

USAC122

Illinois State University
302 Normal Avenue, Suite 200
NORMAL, IL 61761–6901
☎ 309 438 7963
Contact: Cynthia Huff
Course: Women's Studies programme
☐ A minor on the undergraduate programme.

USAC123

University of Illinois at Chicago
Box 4348, MIC360
CHICAGO, IL 60680
☎ 312 996 2441
Contact: Peg Strobel
Course: Women's Studies programme
☐ A minor on the undergraduate programme.
Qualification: Degree
☐ A Women's Studies Research Center is planned.

USAC124

University of Illinois at Urbana-Champaign
708 South Mathews
URBANA, IL 61801
☎ 217 333 2990
Contact: Jean Peterson
Course: Women's Studies programme
☐ A minor on the undergraduate programme.

USAC125

University of Illinois at Urbana-Champaign
801 South Wright,
CHAMPAIGN, IL 61820
☎ 217 333 1977
Contact: Kathleen Cloud
Course: Women in International Development
☐ A major (Independent Basis) or an area of concentration on the undergraduate programme.

USAC126

Knox College
GALESBURG, IL 61401
☎ 309 343 0112
Contact: Penny Gold
Course: Women's Studies programme

☐ An area of concentration on the undergraduate programme.

USAC127

Lake Forest College
LAKE FOREST, IL 60045
☎ 708 234 3100
Contact: A. Eskilson
Course: Women's Studies programme
☐ A minor or an area of concentration on the undergraduate programme.

USAC128

Loyola University of Chicago
6525 North Sheridan Road
CHICAGO, IL 60626
☎ 312 508 2934
Contact: Judith Wittner
Course: Women's Studies programme
☐ A minor on the undergraduate programme.
Qualification: Certificate

USAC129

Monmouth College
700 East Broadway
MONMOUTH, IL 61462
☎ 309 457 2165
Contact: Carolyn Kirk
Course: Women's Studies programme
☐ A minor on the undergraduate programme.

USAC130

Mundelein College
6363 North Sheridan Road
CHICAGO, IL 60660
☎ 312 262 8100
Contact: Prudence Moylan
Course: Women's Studies programme
☐ A minor or an area of concentration on the undergraduate programme. An area of concentration at postgraduate level.
Qualification: Degree

USAC131

Northeastern Illinois University
5500 North St Louis Avenue
CHICAGO, IL 60625
☎ 312 583 4050 ext. 3308
Contact: Irene Campos Carr
Course: Women's Studies programme
☐ A major or a minor on the undergraduate programme.

USAC132

Northern Illinois University
107 Reavis Hall
DEKALB, IL 60115
☎ 815 753 1038

Contact: Lois Self
Course: Women's Studies programme
☐ A minor on the undergraduate programme.

USAC133

Northwestern University
2000 Sheridan Road
EVANSTON, IL 60208
☎ 708 491 5871
Contact: Rae Moses
Course: Women's Studies programme
☐ A minor on the undergraduate programme.

USAC134

Roosevelt University
430 South Michigan Avenue
CHICAGO, IL 60605
☎ 312 341 3860
Contact: Carol Traynor Williams
Course: Women's Studies programme
☐ Forms part of the General Studies undergraduate and postgraduate programmes.
Qualifications: Degree, Master's degree

USAC135

Sangamon State University
Shepherd Road
SPRINGFIELD, IL 62794-9243
☎ 217 786 6706
Contact: Pat Langley
Course: Women's Studies programme
☐ A major or a minor on the undergraduate programme, and an individualised postgraduate programme is offered.
Qualifications: Degree, Master's degree

USAC136

Southern Illinois University at Carbondale
806 Chautauqua
CARBONDALE, IL 62901
☎ 618 453 5741
Contact: Kathryn Ward
Course: Women's Studies programme
☐ A minor on both the undergraduate and post-graduate programmes.
Qualification: Degree

USAC137

Southern Illinois University at Edwardsville
Box 1350
EDWARDSVILLE, IL 62026
☎ 618 292 2003
Contact: Pamela Decoteau
Course: Women's Studies programme
☐ A minor on the undergraduate programme. Available at postgraduate level through the Department of Philosophical Studies.
Qualifications: Degree, Master's degree

USAC138

Western Illinois University
Department of English and Journalism
Simpkins Hall
MACOMB, IL 61455
☎ 309 298 1422
Contact: Janice Welsch
Course: Women's Studies programme
☐ A minor on the undergraduate programme.

Indiana

USAC139

Ball State University
MUNCIE, IN 47036
☎ 317 285 5451
Contact: M. Stevenson
Course: Women's Studies programme
☐ A minor on the undergraduate programme.

USAC140

DePauw University
10 Asbury Hall
GREENCASTLE, IN 46135
☎ 317 658 4359
Contact: Barbara Steinson
Course: Women's Studies Programme
☐ A minor or an area of concentration on the undergraduate programme.

USAC141

Earlham College
Box 62
RICHMOND, IN 47374
☎ 317 983 1505
Contact: Barbara Caruso
Courses: Women's Studies programme; Peace and Global Studies; Human Development and Social Relations
☐ A major or an area of concentration on the undergraduate programme.
Qualification: Degree

USAC142

Goshen College
GOSHEN, IN 46526
☎ 219 535 7000
Contact: Anna Bowman
Course: Women's Studies programme
☐ A minor on the undergraduate programme.

USAC143

Indiana State University
Department of English
TERRE HAUTE, IN 47809
☎ 812 237 3137
Contact: Myrna Handley

Course: Women's Studies programme
☐ A minor on the undergraduate programme.

USAC144

Indiana University Bloomington
Memorial Hall East 131
BLOOMINGTON, IN 47405
☎ 812 855 0101
Contact: Mary Ellen Brown
Course: Women's Studies programme
☐ A minor or an area of concentration on the undergraduate programme. A minor at postgraduate level.
Qualifications: Degree, Doctorate

USAC145

Indiana University-Purdue University at Fort Wayne
2101 Coliseum Boulevard Room CM272
FORT WAYNE, IN 46805–1499
☎ 219 481 6711
Contact: Judi Di Iorio
Course: Women's Studies programme
☐ A minor or an area of concentration on the undergraduate programme.

USAC146

Indiana University-Purdue University at Indianapolis
425 University Boulevard (CA 001E)
INDIANAPOLIS, IN 46202
☎ 317 274 2306
Contact: Ann Donchin
Course: Women's Studies programme
☐ A minor on the undergraduate programme.

USAC147

Indiana University at South Bend
PO Box 7111
SOUTH BEND, IN 46634
☎ 219 237 4308
Contact: Gloria Kaufman
Course: Women's Studies programme
☐ A minor or an area of concentration on the undergraduate programme.

USAC148

Indiana University Southeast
4201 Grant Line Road
NEW ALBANY, IN 47150
☎ 812 941 2412
Contact: Susan Moffett Matthias
Course: Women's Studies programme
☐ A minor on the undergraduate programme.
Qualification: Certificate

USAC149

Purdue University
170 Pierce Hall
WEST LAFAYETTE, IN 47907
☎ 317 494 7685
Contact: Berenice A. Carroll
Course: Women's Studies programme
☐ A minor on the undergraduate programme.

USAC150

Purdue University Calumet
2233 171st Street
HAMMOND, IN 46323
☎ 219 989 2489
Contact: Jane R. Shoup
Course: Women's Studies programme
☐ A minor on the undergraduate programme.
Qualification: Certificate

USAC151

St Mary's College
71 Madelva
NOTRE DAME, IN 46556
☎ 219 284 4716
Contact: Linnea Vacca
Course: Women's Studies programme
☐ A minor on the undergraduate programme.

Iowa

USAC152

Cornell College
600 First Street
MT VERNON, IA 52314
☎ 319 895 42690
Contact: T. Shaw
Course: Women's Studies programme
☐ A major or a minor on the undergraduate programme.
Qualification: Degree

USAC153

Committee on Gender and Women's Studies
Grinnell College
Harry Hopkins House
GRINNELL, IA 50112
☎ 516 236 2100
Course: Women's Studies programme
☐ A minor on the undergraduate programme. An independent major can be taken.

USAC154

University of Iowa
202 Jefferson Building
IOWA CITY, IA 52242
☎ 319 335 0322

Contact: Martha Chamallas
Course: Women's Studies programme
☐ A minor or an area of concentration on the undergraduate programme. Postgraduate-level work in Feminist Anthropology, or a Specialised Ph.D.
Qualifications: Degree, Master's degree, Doctorate

USAC155

Iowa State University
203 Ross Hall
AMES, IA 50011
☎ 515 294 3286
Contact: Kathleen K. Hickok
Course: Women's Studies programme
☐ A major, a minor or an area of concentration on the undergraduate programme. Can be taken as an area of concentration at postgraduate level.
Qualification: Degree

USAC156

University of Northern Iowa
CEDAR FALLS, IA 50614
☎ 319 273 3509
Contact: Martha Reineke
Course: Women's Studies programme
☐ A minor on the undergraduate programme.

USAC157

Wartburg College
PO Box 1003
222 9th Street NW
WAVERLY, IA 50677
☎ 319 352 8201
Contact: Cheryl Jacobsen
Course: Women's Studies programme
☐ A minor or an area of concentration on the undergraduate programme.

Kansas

USAC158

Kansas State University
22 Eisenhower Hall
MANHATTAN, KS 66506
☎ 913 532 5738
Contact: Sandra Coyner
Course: Women's Studies programme
☐ A major or an area of concentration on the undergraduate programme.

USAC159

University of Kansas
2120 Wescoe Hall
LAWRENCE, KS 66045–2107
☎ 913 864 4120
Contact: Ann Schofield

Course: Women's Studies programme
☐ A major on the undergraduate programme.

USAC160

Wichita State University
Campus Box 82
WICHITA, KS 67208
☎ 316 689 3358
Contact: Sally L. Kitch
Course: Women's Studies programme
☐ A major or a minor on the undergraduate programme. Postgraduate-level work offered in Liberal Arts.
Qualifications: Degree, Master's degree

Research Group on Women and Work
☐ Research specialisation on professional women in the Wichita area.

Kentucky

USAC161

Brescia College
717 Frederica Street
OWENSBORO, KY 42301
☎ 502 686 4275
Contact: Marita Greenwell
Course: Contemporary Woman programme
☐ A minor on the undergraduate programme.

USAC162

University of Kentucky
241 Patterson Office Tower
LEXINGTON, KY 40506–0027
☎ 606 257 1388
Contact: Bonnie Cox
Course: Women's Studies programme
☐ A minor on the undergraduate programme.

USAC163

University of Louisville
LOUISVILLE KY4
☎ 502 588 6531
Contact: Ann Adey
Course: Women's Studies programme
☐ A minor on the undergraduate programme.

USAC164

Northern Kentucky University
537 Laudrum
HIGHLAND HEIGHTS, KY 41076
☎ 606 572 5550
Contact: Judith Bechtel
Course: Women's Studies programme
☐ A minor on the undergraduate programme.

Louisiana

USAC165

Louisiana State University
Allen Hall
BATON ROUGE, LA 70803
☎ 504 388 2236
Contact: Emily Toth
Course: Women's Studies
☐ Postgraduate-level work with a Departmental emphasis in English.

USAC166

University of New Orleans
Department of Sociology
NEW ORLEANS, LA 70148
☎ 504 286 6301
Contact: Susan Archer Mann
Course: Women's Studies programme
☐ A minor on the undergraduate programme.

USAC167

Tulane University
1229 Broadway
NEW ORLEANS, LA 70118
☎ 504 865 5238
Contact: Beth Willinger
Course: Women's Studies programme
☐ A minor or a self-designed minor on the undergraduate programme.
Qualification: Degree

Newcomb College Center for Research on Women
☐ Research specialisation on Southern women, and women's education.

Maine

USAC168

College of the Atlantic
Eden Street
BAR HARBOR, ME 04609
☎ 207 288 5015
Contact: Susan Lerner
Course: Women's Studies programme
☐ Forms part of a degree in Human Ecology.
Qualification: Degree

USAC169

Bates College
LEWISTON, ME 04240
☎ 207 786 6071
Contact: Elizabeth Tobin
Course: Women's Studies programme
☐ A major on the undergraduate programme.
Qualification: Degree

USAC170

Bowdoin College
BRUNSWICK, ME 0411
☎ 207 725 3620
Contact: Martha May
Course: Women's Studies programme
☐ A minor on the undergraduate programme.

USAC171

Colby College
Mayflower Hill Drive
WATERVILLE, ME 04901
☎ 207 872 3566
Contact: Debra Cambeu
Course: Women's Studies programme
☐ A major on the undergraduate programme. Individualised major also available.

USAC172

University of Maine
330 Shibles Hall
ORONO, ME 04469
☎ 207 581 1228
Contact: Evelyn S. Newlyn
Course: Women's Studies programme
☐ A major or an area of concentration on the undergraduate programme.
Qualifications: Certificate, Degree

USAC173

University of Southern Maine
96 Falmouth Street
PORTLAND, ME 04103
☎ 207 780 4289
Contact: Diane Long
Course: Women's Studies programme
☐ A major or a minor on the undergraduate programme.
Qualification: Degree

Maryland

USAC174

Frostburg State University
FROSTBURG, MD 21532
☎ 301 689 4445
Contact: Joy Kroeger Mappes
Course: Women's Studies programme
☐ A minor on the undergraduate programme.

USAC175

Goucher College
TOWSON, MD 21204
☎ 301 337 6274
Contact: Marianne Githens
Course: Women's Studies programme

☐ A major on the undergraduate programme.
Qualification: Degree

USAC176

National Women's Studies Association
University of Maryland at College Park
　1115 Mill Building
　COLLEGE PARK, MD 20742
☎　301 405 6877
Contact: Evelyn T. Beck
Course: Women's Studies programme
☐ An individualised major on the undergraduate programme.
Qualification: Certificate

USAC177

University of Maryland, Baltimore County
　5401 Wilkens Avenue
　BALTIMORE, MD 221228
☎　301 455 2001
Contact: Joan Korenman
Course: Women's Studies programme
☐ A major or a minor on the undergraduate programme.
Qualification: Degree (Disciplinary Studies)

USAC178

Towson State University
　TOWSON, MD 21204
☎　301 296 8782
Contact: Jo-Ann Pilardi
Course: Women's Studies programme
☐ A minor or an area of concentration on the undergraduate programme.
Qualification: Degree

Center for the Study of Women and Education
☐ Research projects and specialisation on curriculum transformation.

USAC179

Western Maryland College
　WESTMINSTER, MD 21157
☎　301 857 2593
Contact: T. Weinfeld
Course: Women's Studies programme
☐ A minor on the undergraduate programme.

Massachusetts

USAC180

Amherst College
　14 Grosvenor House
　AMHERST, MA 01002
☎　403 542 5781
Contact: Michele Barale
Course: Women's Studies programme

☐ A major or a minor on the undergraduate programme.
Qualification: Degree

USAC181

Boston College
　Department of Sociology
　McGuinn Hall
　CHESTNUT HALL, MA 02167
☎　617 552 3705
Contact: Sharlene Hesse-Biber
Course: Women's Studies programme
☐ A minor on the undergraduate programme.

USAC182

Boston University
　American Studies
　226 Bay State Road
　BOSTON, MA 02215
☎　617 353 2948
Contact: Dorothy Kelly
Course: Women's Studies programme
☐ A minor on the undergraduate programme.
Qualification: Degree

USAC183

Brandeis University
　WALTHAM, MA 02254–9110
☎　617 736 3033
Contact: Joyce Antler
Course: Women's Studies programme
☐ A minor on the undergraduate programme.
Qualification: Certificate

USAC184

Bridgewater State College
　BRIDGEWATER, MA 02325
☎　508 697 1200 ext. 2439
Contact: Evelyn Pezzulich
Course: Women's Studies programme
☐ A minor on the undergraduate programme.

USAC185

Clark University
　950 Main Street
　WORCESTER, MA 01520
☎　508 793 7358
Contact: Rachel Joffe Falmagne
Course: Women's Studies programme
☐ An area of concentration on the undergraduate programme.

USAC186

Curry College
　1071 Blue Hill Avenue
　MILTON, MA 02186
☎　617 333 0500 ext. 2240
Contact: Marlene Samuelson
Course: Women's Studies programme

☐ An individually initiated major, or minor on the undergraduate programme.
Qualifications: Certificate, Degree

USAC187

Emerson College
100 Beacon Street
BOSTON, MA 02116
☎ 617 578 8600
Course: Women's Studies programme
☐ A minor on the undergraduate programme.

USAC188

Emmanuel College
400 The Fenway
BOSTON, MA 02115
☎ 617 735 9975
Contact: Mary Mason
Course: Women's Studies programme
☐ A minor on the undergraduate programme.

USAC189

Episcopal Divinity School
99 Brattle Street
CAMBRIDGE, MA 02138
☎ 617 868 3450
Contact: Alison Cheek
Course: Feminist Liberation Theology programme
Qualifications: Degree, Master's degree, Doctorate

USAC190

Fitchburg State College
FITCHBURG, MA 01420
☎ 617 345 2151
Course: Women's Studies programme
☐ A minor on the undergraduate programme.

USAC191

Hamshire College
Box 740
AMHERST, MA 01002
☎ 413 549 4600
Contact: Rhonda Blair
Course: Women's Studies programme
☐ A minor on the undergraduate programme.
Qualification: Degree

USAC192

Harvard University
34 Kirkland Street
CAMBRIDGE, MA 02138
☎ 517 495 0500
Contact: Olwen Hufton
Course: Women's Studies programme
☐ A major, a minor or an area of concentration on the undergraduate programme.
Qualification: Degree

Harvard Divinity School
Harvard University
45 Francis Avenue
CAMBRIDGE, MA 02138
☎ 617 495 5705
Contact: Constance Buchanan
Course: Women's Studies in Religion; Religion, Gender and Culture
☐ Postgraduate-level work.
Qualification: Doctorate

USAC193

Harvard Extension School
20 Garden Street
CAMBRIDGE, MA 02138
☎ 617 495 9413
Contact: Suzanne Spreadbury
Course: Women's Studies programme
☐ An area of concentration on the undergraduate programme.

☎ 617 495 9417
Contact: Delise Battenfield
Course: Women's Studies programme
☐ Postgraduate programme in Liberal Arts.
Qualification: Master's degree

USAC194

University of Lowell
1 University Avenue
LOWELL, MA 01854
☎ 508 934 4600
Contact: Karen M. Harbeck
Course: Women's Studies programme
☐ A minor on the undergraduate programme.

USAC195

Massachusetts Institute of Technology
14E–316
CAMBRIDGE, MA 02139
☎ 617 253 8844
Contact: Susan Carey
Course: Women's Studies programme
☐ A major, a minor or an area of concentration on the postgraduate programme. A major, minor or an area of concentration on the undergraduate programme.
Qualification: Degree

USAC196

University of Massachusetts at Amherst
208 Bartlett Hall
AMHERST, MA 01002
☎ 413 545 1922
Contact: Lee Edwards
Course: Women's Studies programme
☐ A major or a minor on the undergraduate programme. Specialisation with individual concentration on degree.
Qualification: Degree

USAC197

University of Massachusetts at Boston Harbor Campus
    BOSTON, MA 02125
☎   617 287 6780
Contact: Catherine Manton
Course: Women's Studies programme
☐ A major or a minor on the undergraduate programme.
Qualification: Degree

USAC198

Psychology/Education Building
Mount Holyoke College
    SOUTH HADLEY, MA 01040
☎   413 538 2844
Contact: Jean Grossholtz
Course: Women's Studies programme
☐ A major or a minor on the undergraduate programme.
Qualification: Degree

USAC199

Interdisciplinary Studies Department
North Adams State College
    Church Street
    NORTH ADAMS, MA 01247
☎   413 664 4511
Contact: Cohane/Colligan and Ethier
Course: Women's Studies programme
☐ A minor on the undergraduate programme.

USAC200

Northeastern University
    524 HO/360 Huntington Avenue
    BOSTON, MA 02115
☎   617 437 2942
Contact: Laura L. Frader
Course: Women's Studies programme
☐ A minor on the undergraduate programme.

USAC201

Northern Essex Community College
    100 Elliot Street
    HAVERHILL, MA 01830
☎   508 374 3900
Contact: Priscilla B. Bellairs
Course: Women's Studies programme
☐ An area of concentration on the undergraduate programme.

USAC202

Pine Manor College
    400 Heath Street
    CHESTNUT HILL, MA 02167
☎   617 731 7000
Contact: Melinda Ponder
Course: Women's Studies programme
☐ A minor on the undergraduate programme.

USAC203

Quinsigamond Community College
    670 West Boylston Street
    WORCESTER, MA 01606
☎   508 853 2300
Contact: Elaine Fallon
Course: Women's Studies programme
☐ A minor on the undergraduate programme.

USAC204

Simmons College
    300 The Fenway
    BOSTON, MA 02115
☎   617 738 2160
Contact: Laurie Crumpacker
Course: Women's Studies programme
☐ A major on the undergraduate programme. Post-graduate programme in Liberal Studies.

USAC205

Simon's Rock of Bard College
    Alford Road
    GREAT BARRINGTON, MA 01230
☎   413 528 0771
Contact: Fran Mascia-Less
Course: Women's Studies programme
☐ A major with an area of concentration on the undergraduate programme.
Qualification: Degree

USAC206

Smith College
    Hatfield Hall
    NORTHAMPTON, MA 01063
☎   413 585 3336
Contact: Susan Van Dyne
Course: Women's Studies programme
☐ A major or a minor on the undergraduate programme.
Qualification: Degree

USAC207

Smith College
    138 Elm Street
    NORTHAMPTON, MA 01063
☎   413 585 3591
Contact: Susan C. Bourque
Course: Women's Studies programme – Project on Women and Social Change.
☐ A specialisation in Social Science, Public Policy, Women in Leadership and Politics.

USAC208

Southeastern Massachusetts University
    Old Westport Road
    NORTH DARTMOUTH, MA 02747
☎   508 999 8000
Contact: Barbara Jacobskind

Course: Women's Studies programme
☐ A major with specialisation through Multidisciplinary Studies. A minor on the undergraduate programme.
Qualification: Degree

USAC209

College of Arts and Science
Suffolk University
BOSTON, MA 02108
☎ 617 573 8460
Contact: Agnes S. Bai
Course: Women's Studies programme
☐ A minor on the undergraduate programme.

USAC210

Tufts University
55 Talbot Avenue
MEDFORD, MA 02155
☎ 617 381 3184
Contact: Peggy Barrett
Course: Women's Studies programme
☐ A minor on the undergraduate programme.

USAC211

Wellesley College
828 Washington Street
WELLESLEY, MA 02181
☎ 617 235 0320
Contact: Susan Reverby
Course: Women's Studies programme
☐ A major on the undergraduate programme.
Qualification: Degree

Center for Research on Women
☎ 617 431 1453
Contact: Susan Bailey

USAC212

Westfield State College
Western Avenue
WESTFIELD, MA 01086
☎ 413 568 3311 ext. 362
Contact: John Loughney
Course: Women's Studies programme
☐ A minor with an area of concentration on the undergraduate programme.

USAC213

Wheaton College
NORTON, MA 02766
☎ 1 800 541 3629
Contact: Frances A. Maher
Course: Women's Studies programme
☐ A minor on the undergraduate programme.

USAC214

Department of English
Williams College
Stetson Hall
WILLIAMSTOWN, MA 01267
☎ 413 597 2564
Contact: Lynda Bundtzen
Course: Women's Studies programme
☐ A minor with an area of concentration on the undergraduate programme. A contract major is available as a specialisation.

USAC215

Women's Theological Center
400 The Fenway
BOSTON, MA 02115
☎ 617 277 1330
Course: Women's Studies programme
☐ A minor on the undergraduate programme. An Independent Programme is available as a specialisation.

Michigan

USAC216

Albion College
ALBION, MI 49224
☎ 517 629 5511
Contact: Judith Lockyear
Course: Women's Studies programme
☐ A major with an area of concentration on the undergraduate programme.

USAC217

Central Michigan University
118 Pearce Hall
MOUNT PLEASANT, MI 48859
☎ 517 774 3148
Contact: Merlyn Mowrey
Course: Women's Studies programme
☐ A minor on the undergraduate programme.

USAC218

Eastern Michigan University
719 Pray-Harrold
YPSILANTI, MI 48197
☎ 313 487 1177
Contact: Margaret Crouch
Course: Women's Studies programme
☐ An area of concentration on the postgraduate programme. A minor on the undergraduate programme.
Qualification: Degree, Master's degree

USAC219

Grand Valley State University
Campus Drive
ALLENDALE, MI 49401

☎ 616 895 3416
Contact: Doris Rucks
Course: Women's Studies programme
☐ A minor on the undergraduate programme.

USAC220

Kalamazoo College
1200 Academy Street
KALAMAZOO, MI 49007
☎ 616 383 8494
Contact: Gail Griffin
Course: Women's Studies programme
☐ An area of concentration on the undergraduate programme.

USAC221

Michigan State University
301 Linton Hall
EAST LANSING, MI 48824
☎ 517 355 4495
Contact: Joyce Ladenson
Course: Women's Studies programme
☐ A postgraduate programme with Departmental emphasis. An area of concentration on the undergraduate programme.

USAC222

University of Michigan
234 West Engineering
ANN ARBOR, MI 48109
☎ 313 763 2047
Contact: Domna Stanton
Course: Women's Studies programme
☐ A major on the undergraduate programme.
Qualification: Degree

USAC223

Oakland University
307 Wilson Hall
ROCHESTER, MI 48309–4401
☎ 313 370 3389
Contact: Janice G. Schimmelman
Course: Women's Studies programme
☐ An area of concentration on the undergraduate programme.

USAC224

Wayne State University
3121 FAC/ADM
656 West Kirby Avenue
DETROIT, MI 48202
☎ 313 577 4103
Contact: Effie Ambler
Course: Women's Studies programme
☐ A minor on the undergraduate programme.
Qualification: Degree

USAC225

Western Michigan University
KALAMAZOO, MI 49008–3899
☎ 616 387 4900
Contact: Sushi Datta-Sandahu
Course: Women's Studies programme
☐ A major or a minor on the undergraduate programme.

Minnesota

USAC226

Augsburg College
731 21st Avenue South
MINNEAPOLIS, MN 55454
☎ 612 330 1063
Contact: Beverly J. Stratton
Course: Women's Studies programme
☐ A major or a minor on the undergraduate programme.
Qualification: Degree

USAC227

Bemidji State University
1500 Birchmont Drive NE
BEMIDJI, MN 56601–2699
☎ 218 755 4048
Contact: Patricia A. Rosenbrock
Course: Women's Studies programme
☐ A minor on the undergraduate programme.

USAC228

Carleton College
NORTHFIELD, MN 55057
☎ 507 663 4000
Contact: Barbara Allen
Course: Women's Studies programme
☐ An area of concentration on the undergraduate programme.

USAC229

Gustavus Adolphus College
ST PETER, MN 56082
☎ 507 931 7397
Contact: Deborah Downs-Mier
Course: Women's Studies programme
☐ A minor on the undergraduate programme.

USAC230

Macalester College
ST PAUL, MN 55105
☎ 612 696 6318
Contact: J. Michele Edwards
Course: Women's Studies programme
☐ A minor, with an area of concentration on the undergraduate programme. An individually designed Interdepartmental Major available as a specialisation.

USAC231

Mankato State University
MSU Box 64, PO Box 8400
MANKATO, MN 56002–8400
☎ 506 389 2077
Contact: Janet Lee
Course: Women's Studies programme
□ A major or a minor, with an area of concentration on the undergraduate programme. MS in Continuing Studies available as a specialisation.
Qualification: Degree

USAC232

University of Minnesota, Duluth
10 University Drive
DULUTH, MN 55812
☎ 218 726 7953
Contact: Charlotte MacLeod
Course: Women's Studies programme
□ Departmental emphasis on the postgraduate programme. A major or a minor on the undergraduate programme.
Qualification: Degree

Center for Research, Women's Studies Program
□ Research centre for staff, independent scholars and faculty members.

USAC233

University of Minnesota, Morris
MORRIS, MN 56267
☎ 612 589 2116
Contact: Miriam Darce Frenier
Course: Women's Studies programme

USAC234

University of Minnesota, Twin Cities
224 Church Street SE
MINNEAPOLIS, MN 55455
☎ 612 624 6006
Contact: Susan Geiger
Course: Women's Studies programme
□ A minor on the postgraduate programme. A major or a minor with an area of concentration on the undergraduate programme.
Qualification: Degree

University of Minnesota, Twin Cities
192 Pillsbury Drive SE
5 Eddy Hall
MINNEAPOLIS, MN 55455
☎ 612 624 6310
Contact: Shirley Garner

Center for Advanced Feminist Studies
□ Research specialisation on women and public policy, and women in international development.

Center on Women and Public Policy
University of Minnesota
Humphrey Institute of Public Affairs
301 19th Avenue, South
MINNEAPOLIS, MN 55455
☎ 612 625 4685
Contact: Barbara I. Nelson

International Women's Rights Action Watch
University of Minnesota
Humphrey Institute of Public Affairs
301 19th Avenue, South
MINNEAPOLIS, MN 55455
☎ 612 625 2505
Contact: Arvonne S. Frazer

USAC235

Moorhead State University
South Eleventh Street
MOORHEAD, MN 56560
☎ 218 236 4685
Contact: Sheila Coghill
Course: Women's Studies programme
□ A minor on the undergraduate programme.
Qualification: Degree

USAC236

Rochester Community College
851 30th Avenue SE
ROCHESTER, MN 55904
☎ 507 285 7218
Contact: Arlouene Olson
Course: Women's Studies programme
□ An area of concentration on the undergraduate programme.

USAC237

College of St Catherine
2004 Randolph Avenue
ST PAUL, MN 55105
☎ 612 690 6783
Contact: Catherine Lupori
Course: Women's Studies programme
□ A minor on the undergraduate programme.
Qualification: Degree

Abigail Quigley McCarthy Center for Research on Women specialises in research on women from Catholic tradition.

USAC238

St Cloud State University
8th Street/Education Building B120
ST CLOUD, MN 56301/4498
☎ 612 255 0121
Contact: Pat A. Samuel
Course: Women's Studies programme

☐ A minor on the undergraduate programme.
Qualification: Degree

USAC239

St Olaf College
    NORTHFIELD, MN 55057
☎   507 663 3231
Contact: Mary Cisar
Course: Women's Studies programme
☐ A major with an area of concentration on the undergraduate programme.
Qualification: Degree

USAC240

College of St Scholastica
    1200 Kenwood Avenue
    DULUTH, MN 55811
☎   218 723 8105
Contact: E. Stich
Course: Women's Studies programme
☐ A minor on the undergraduate programme.

USAC241

Willmar Community College
    PO Box 797
    WILLMAR, MN 56201
☎   612 231 5102
Course: Women's Studies programme
☐ An area of concentration on the undergraduate programme.

Mississippi

USAC242

Millsaps College
    1701 North State Street
    JACKSON, MN 39210
☎   601 354 5201
Contact: Judith W. Page
Course: Women's Studies programme
☐ An area of concentration on the undergraduate programme.

USAC243

Mississippi State University
    PO Drawer E
    MISSISSIPPI STATE, MS 39762
☎   601 325 2224
Contact: Susan Shelly
Course: Women's Studies programme
☐ An area of concentration on the undergraduate programme.
Qualification: Certificate

Missouri

USAC244

Avila College
    11901 Wornall Road
    KANSAS CITY, MO 65145
☎   816 942 8400
Contact: Dona Neuman
Course: Women's Studies programme
☐ A minor on the undergraduate programme.

USAC245

Central Missouri State University
    Wood Building
    WARRENSBURG, MO 64093
☎   816 429 4404
Contact: Patricia Ashman
Course: Women's Studies programme
☐ A minor on the undergraduate programme.

USAC246

University of Missouri, Columbia
    309 Switzler Hall
    COLUMBIA, MO 65211
☎   314 882 2703
Contact: Mary Jo Neitz
Course: Women's Studies programme
☐ A major, a minor or an area of concentration on the undergraduate programme.
Qualification: Degree

USAC247

University of Missouri, Kansas City
    5204 Rockhill Road
    KANSAS CITY, MO 64110–2499
☎   816 276 1111
Contact: Gail Pat Parsons
Course: Women's Studies programme
☐ A minor on the undergraduate programme.

USAC248

University of Missouri, St Louis
    8001 Natural Bridge Road
    ST LOUIS, MO 63121
☎   314 553 5581
Contact: Suzanna Rose
Course: Women's Studies programme
☐ Part of both the undergraduate and postgraduate programmes.
Qualification: Certificate

USAC249

St Louis University
    221 North Grand Boulevard
    ST LOUIS, MO 63103
☎   314 658 2295
Contact: J. Gibbons

Courses

Course: Women's Studies programme
☐ Part of the undergraduate programme.
Qualification: Certificate

USAC250

Stephens College
Box 2013
COLOMBIA, MO 65215
☎ 314 876 7103
Contact: Carol Perkins
Course: Women's Studies programme
☐ A minor or an area of concentration on the undergraduate programme.

USAC251

Washington University
One Brookings Drive
Campus Box 1078
ST LOUIS, MO 63130
☎ 314 889 5102
Contact: Joyce Trebilcot
Course: Women's Studies programme
☐ A major or a minor on an undergraduate programme.
Qualification: Degree

USAC252

Webster University
470 East Lockwood
ST LOUIS, MO 63119
☎ 314 968 7074
Contact: Monica M. Moore
Course: Women's Studies programme
☐ A minor on both the undergraduate and post-graduate programmes.
Qualification: Certificate

Montana

USAC253

University of Montana
Philosophy Department
MISSOULA, MT 59812
☎ 406 243 2845
Contact: Maxine Van de Wetering
Course: Women's Studies programme
☐ An area of concentration on the undergraduate programme.

Nebraska

USAC254

Bellevue College
Galvin Road at Harvell Drive
BELLEVUE, NE 68005
☎ 402 293 3736

Contact: Roxanne Sullivan
Course: Women's Studies programme
☐ A minor on the undergraduate programme.

USAC255

Kearney State College
KEARNEY, NE 68849
☎ 308 234 8294
Contact: Kathryn N. Benzel
Course: Women's Studies programme
☐ A minor on the undergraduate programme.

USAC256

University of Nebraska, Lincoln
202 Andrews Hall
LINCOLN, NE 68588–0333
☎ 402 472 6357
Contact: Maureen Honey
Course: Women's Studies programme
☐ An area of concentration on the postgraduate programme. A major or a minor on the undergraduate programme.
Qualification: Degree

Nevada

USAC257

University of Nevada, Las Vegas
LAS VEGAS, NV 89154
☎ 702 739 3322
Contact: Catherine Bellver
Course: Women's Studies programme
☐ A major or a minor on the undergraduate programme.
Qualification: Degree

USAC258

University of Nevada, Reno
090 UNR
RENO, NV 89557
☎ 702 784 1560
Contact: Elaine Enarson
Course: Women's Studies programme
☐ A minor on the undergraduate programme.

New Hampshire

USAC259

Colby-Sawyer College
Main Street
NEW LONDON, NH 03257
☎ 603 526 2010 ext. 591
Contact: Nancy Jay Crumbine
Course: Women's Studies programme

□ A major or a minor on the undergraduate programme.
A specialised major available via Interdisciplinary Studies.
Qualification: Certificate

USAC260

Dartmouth College
2 Carpenter Hall
HANOVER, NH 03755
☎ 603 646 2722
Contact: Anne Brooks
Course: Women's Studies programme
□ A modified major, or a minor available on the undergraduate programme.
Qualification: Certificate

USAC261

Keene State College
229 Main Street
KEENE, NH 03431
☎ 603 352 1909
Contact: Elenor VanderHaegen
Course: Women's Studies programme
□ A minor on the undergraduate programme.

USAC262

University of New Hampshire
307 Diamond Library
DURHAM, NH 03824
☎ 603 862 2194
Contact: Cathryn Adamsky
Course: Women's Studies programme
□ A minor on the undergraduate programme.
Qualification: Degree

USAC263

Plymouth State College
Bagley House
PLYMOUTH, NH 03264
☎ 603 536 5000 ext. 2387
Contact: Bev Hart
Course: Women's Studies programme
□ A minor on the undergraduate programme.

USAC264

Rivier College
South Main Street
NASHUA, NH 03060
☎ 603 888 1311 ext. 508
Contact: Marjorie Marcous Faiia
Course: Women's Studies programme
□ A minor on the undergraduate programme.

New Jersey

USAC265

Caldwell College
Department of Psychology
Ryerson Avenue
CALDWELL, NJ 07006
☎ 201 228 4424 ext. 394
Contact: Marie Hudson
Course: Women's Studies programme
□ Can be part of the undergraduate programme.
Qualification: Certificate

USAC266

Centenary College
400 Jefferson Street
HACKETTSTOWN, NJ 07840
☎ 201 852 1400
Contact: N. Muir
Course: Women's Studies programme
□ A minor on the undergraduate programme.

USAC267

Drew University
MADISON, NJ 07940
☎ 201 408 3632
Contact: Wendy Kolmar
Course: Women's Studies programme
□ A minor on the undergraduate programme.

USAC268

Georgian Court College
LAKEWOOD, NJ 08701
☎ 908 364 2200 ext. 354
Contact: Judith Beck
Course: Women's Studies programme
□ A minor on the undergraduate programme.

USAC269

Glassboro State College
Triad Building
GLASSBORO, NJ 08028
☎ 609 863 5249
Contact: Corann Okorodudu
Course: Women's Studies programme
□ An area of concentration on the undergraduate programme.

USAC270

Jersey City State College
2039 Kennedy Memorial Boulevard
JERSEY CITY, NJ 07305
☎ 201 547 6000 ext. 3551
Contact: Barbara Rubin
Course: Women's Studies programme
□ A minor or an area of concentration on the undergraduate programme.

Courses

USAC271

Kean College of New Jersey
History Department
UNION, NJ 07083
☎ 201 522 2000 ext. 2039
Contact: Sylvia Strauss
Course: Women's Studies programme
☐ A minor on the undergraduate programme.

USAC272

Mercer County Community College
PO Box B
TRENTON, NJ 08690
☎ 609 586 4800 ext. 325
Contact: Angela McClym
Course: Women's Studies programme
☐ An area of concentration on the undergraduate programme.

USAC273

Monmouth College
WEST LONG BRANCH, NJ 07764
☎ 201 571 4424
Contact: Donna Dolphin
Course: Women's Studies programme
☐ A minor on the undergraduate programme.

USAC274

Montclair State College
UPPER MONTCLAIR, NJ 07043
☎ 201 893 7416
Contact: Adele McCollum
Course: Women's Studies programme
☐ A minor on the undergraduate programme; an area of concentration on the postgraduate programme.
Qualifications: Degree, Master's degree

USAC275

Princeton Theological Seminary
CN 821 PRINCETON, NJ 08542
☎ 609 497 7911
Contact: Freda A. Gardner
Course: Women's Studies programme
☐ A major or an area of concentration on the undergraduate programme; also available at postgraduate level.

USAC276

Princeton University
218 Palmer Hall
PRINCETON, NJ 08544
☎ 609 258 5430
Contact: Christine Stansell
Course: Women's Studies programme
Qualification: Certificate

USAC277

Ramapo College of New Jersey
MAHWAH, NJ 07430
☎ 201 529 7576
Contact: Donna Crawley
Course: Women's Studies programme
☐ A minor on the undergraduate programme.

USAC278

Rider College
2083 Lawrenceville Road
LAWRENCEVILLE, NJ 08648
☎ 609 896 5145
Contact: Virginia Cyrus
Course: Women's Studies programme
☐ A minor on the undergraduate programme.
Qualification: Certificate

USAC279

Rutgers, The State University of New Jersey
Camden College of Arts and Sciences
Psychology Department
CAMDEN, NJ 08102
☎ 609 757 6013
Contact: Sheila Cosminsky
Course: Women's Studies programme
☐ A minor on the undergraduate programme.

USAC280

Rutgers, The State University of New Jersey
Douglass College
Voorhees Chapel, Lower Level
NEW BRUNSWICK, NJ 08903
☎ 201 932 9331
Contact: Alice Kessler-Harris
Course: Women's Studies programme
☐ A major or a minor on the undergraduate programme. Postgraduate-level course also available.
Qualifications: Certificate, Degree, Master's degree, Doctorate

Center for the American Woman and Politics
Rutgers, The State University of New Jersey
Douglass College
Eagleton Institute
NEW BRUNSWICK, NJ 08901
☎ 201 932 9384
Contact: Ruth B. Mandel

Center for Global Issues and Women's Leadership
Rutgers, The State University of New Jersey
Douglass College
Box 270
NEW BRUNSWICK, NJ 08903–0270
☎ 908 932 8782
Contact: Charlotte Bunch

Institute for Research on Women
Rutgers, The State University of New Jersey
Douglass College
Voorhees Chapel, Lower Level
NEW BRUNSWICK, NJ 08903
☎ 201 932 9072
Contact: Carol H. Smith

USAC281

Rutgers, The State University of New Jersey
Newark
360 King Boulevard
NEWARK, NJ 07102
☎ 201 648 5817
Contact: Fran Bartkowski
Course: Women's Studies programme
☐ A minor or an area of concentration on the undergraduate programme.

USAC282

Stockton State College
Jim Leeds Road
POMONA, NJ 08240
☎ 609 652 1776
Course: Women's Studies programme
Qualification: Certificate

USAC283

Trenton State College
Hillwood Lakes/CN 4700
TRENTON, NJ 086450
☎ 609 771 2539
Contact: Ellen G. Friedman
Course: Women's Studies programme
☐ A minor on the undergraduate programme.

USAC284

William Paterson College of New Jersey
Political Science Department
WAYNE, NJ 07470
☎ 201 595 2508
Contact: Carole Sheffield
Course: Women's Studies programme
☐ A minor on the undergraduate programme.

New Mexico

USAC285

Eastern New Mexico University
Station 19
PORTALES, NM 88130
☎ 505 562 2421
Contact: Janet Owens Frost
Course: Women's Studies programme
☐ A minor on the undergraduate programme.
Qualification: Certificate

USAC286

New Mexico State University
Box 30001, 3WSP
LAS CRUCES, NM 88003–0001
☎ 505 646 3448
Contact: Joan Jensen
Course: Women's Studies programme
☐ A minor or an area of concentration on the undergraduate programme.

USAC287

University of New Mexico
2142 Mesa Vista Hall
ALBUQUERQUE, NM 87131
☎ 505 277 3854
Contact: Elizabeth Jameson
Course: Women's Studies programme
☐ A minor on the postgraduate programme.
Qualifications: Master's degree, Doctorate

New York

USAC288

Alfred University
PO Box 806
ALFRED, NY 14802
☎ 607 871 2256
Contact: Susan Mayberry
Course: Women's Studies programme
☐ A minor on the undergraduate programme.

USAC289

Bard College
Annandale on Hodson
NEW YORK, NY 12504
☎ 914 758 6822
Contact: Michele D. Domini
Course: Women's Studies programme
☐ An area of concentration on the undergraduate programme, with a concentration in Women's Studies.
Qualification: Degree

USAC290

Barnard College
3009 Broadway
NEW YORK, NY 10027
☎ 212 854 2108
Contact: Natalie Kampen
Course: Women's Studies programme
☐ A major undergraduate programme.
Qualification: Degree

Barnard Center for Research on Women
☎ 212 854 2067
Contact: Ruth Farmer

USAC291

Brooklyn College of the City University of New York
Bedford Avenue and H Avenue
BROOKLYN, NY 11210
☎ 718 780 5485
Contact: Nancy Romer
Course: Women's Studies programme
□ A co-major in Women's Studies on the undergraduate programme.

USAC292

Buffalo State College
HB 113
BUFFALO, NY 14222
☎ 716 878 6403
Contact: Marianne Ferguson
Course: Women's Studies programme
□ A minor on the undergraduate programme.

USAC293

The City College of the City University of New York
Convent Avenue at 138th Street
NEW YORK, NY 10031
☎ 212 650 8269
Contact: Mary Jackson
Course: Women's Studies programme
□ Undergraduate programme in Interdisciplinary Studies with concentration on Women's Studies.
Qualification: Degree

USAC294

City University of New York Graduate School
33 West 42nd Street, Room 4004 GB
NEW YORK, NY 10036
☎ 212 642 2416
Contact: Judith Lorber
Course: Women's Studies programme

Center for the Study of Women and Society
☎ 212 642 2954
Contact: Sue Rosenberg Zalk

USAC295

Colgate University
HAMILTON, NY 13346–1398
☎ 315 824 1000 ext. 292
Contact: Kay Johnston
Course: Women's Studies programme
□ A major or a minor on the undergraduate programme.
Qualification: Degree

USAC296

Columbia University
763 Schermerhorn Extension
NEW YORK, NY 10027
☎ 212 854 1754
Contact: Martha Howell
Course: Women's Studies programme
□ A major on the undergraduate programme.
Qualification: Degree

Institute for Research on Women and Gender

USAC297

Cornell University
332 Uris Hall
ITHACA, NY 14853
☎ 607 255 6480
Contact: Nelly Furman
Course: Women's Studies programme
□ A major with an area of concentration or a minor on the undergraduate programme.

USAC298

Cornell University
New York State School of Industrial and Labour Relations
15 E. 26 Street
NEW YORK, NY 10010
☎ 212 340 2800
Contact: Esta R. Bigler

Institute for Women and Work
□ Research institute housed within the School of Industrial and Labour Relations.

USAC299

Empire State College of the State University of New York College
West 42nd Street
NEW YORK, NY 10036–6901
☎ 607 255 6480
Contact: Susan Halgarth
Course: Women's Studies programme
□ An area of concentration on the undergraduate programme, with a specialisation in Labour Studies.

USAC300

Fordham University
Rose Hill Campus
BRONX, NY 10458
☎ 212 579 2000
Contact: Diane S. Isaacs
Course: Women's Studies programme
□ A major on the undergraduate programme.

Qualification: Degree

USAC301

Hamilton College
College Hill Road
CLINTON, NY 13323
☎ 315 859 4285
Contact: Margaret Gentry
Course: Women's Studies programme
☐ A major or a minor on the undergraduate programme.

USAC302

Herbert Lehman College
250 Bedford Park Boulevard West
BRONX, NY 10468
☎ 212 960 8847
Contact: Joan P. Mencher
Course: Women's Studies programme
☐ A minor with an area of concentration on the undergraduate programme.

USAC303

Hofstra University
New College
1000 Fulton Avenue
HEMPSTEAD, NY 11550
☎ 516 560 6600
Contact: Linda Longmierl
Course: Women's Studies programme
☐ A minor on the undergraduate programme.
Qualification: Degree

USAC304

Hunter College of the City University of New York
695 Park Avenue
NEW YORK, NY 10021
☎ 212 772 5680
Contact: Rosalind P. Petchesky
Course: Women's Studies programme
☐ A co-major or a minor on the undergraduate programme.
Qualification: Degree

USAC305

Iona College
NEW YORK, NY 10801
☎ 914 633 2328
Contact: Barbara Barnes
Course: Women's Studies programme
☐ A minor on the undergraduate programme.

USAC306

Long Island University
C.W. Post Campus
BROOKVILLE, NY 11548
☎ 516 299 2404
Contact: Alice Scourby

Course: Women's Studies programme
☐ A minor on the undergraduate programme.

USAC307

Manhattenville College
125 Purchase Street
PURCHASE, NY 10577
☎ 914 694 2200 ext. 508
Contact: Nancy S. Harris
Course: Women's Studies programme
☐ A minor on the postgraduate programme. A minor on the undergraduate programme.

USAC308

Marymount College
TARRYTOWN, NY 10591
☎ 914 332 8381
Contact: Bernice W. Liddie
Course: Women's Studies programme
☐ A minor on the undergraduate programme.

USAC309

Mercy College
555 Broadway
DOBBS FERRY, NY 10522
☎ 914 693 4500 ext. 356
Contact: Fay Greenwald
Course: Women's Studies programme
☐ A major or a minor on the undergraduate programme.

USAC310

Nazareth College of Rochester
4245 East Avenue
ROCHESTER, NY 14610
☎ 716 586 2525
Contact: Catherine G. Valentine
Course: Women's Studies programme
☐ A minor with an area of concentration on the undergraduate programme.

USAC311

College of New Rochelle
NEW ROCHELLE, NY 10801
☎ 914 654 5000
Contact: Kristen Wenzel
Course: Women's Studies
☐ A minor on the undergraduate programme with Interdisciplinary Studies as a specialisation.
Qualification: Degree

USAC312

New York University
10 Washington Place
NEW YORK, NY 10003
☎ 212 998 7999
Contact: Carol Sternhill
Course: Women's Studies programme

☐ An area of concentration on the postgraduate programme. A major or a minor or an area of concentration on the undergraduate programme. With an individually designed specialisation in Gallatin Division Curriculum Model.
Qualification: Degree

Women's Studies Commission
New York University
    32 Washington Place
    NEW YORK, NY 10003
☎ 212 998 1212
☐ Specialises in research on women in human service professions.

USAC313

Parsons School of Design New School for Social Research
    66 West Twelfth Street
    NEW YORK, NY 10011
☎ 212 741 5620
Contact: Sandra Farginis
Course: Women's Studies programme
☐ Part of an undergraduate programme with an individualised major or through Interdisciplinary Studies.
Qualification: Degree

USAC314

Queens College of the City University of New York
    Department of English
    FLUSHING, NY 11367
☎ 718 520 7651
Contact: Susan K. Harris
Course: Women's Studies programme
☐ A major or a minor on the undergraduate programme.
Qualification: Degree

USAC315

University of Rochester
    538 Lattimore Hall
    ROCHESTER, NY 14627
☎ 716 473 7625
Contact: Bonnie Smith
Course: Susan B. Anthony Centre for Women's Studies programme
☐ A major or a minor on the undergraduate programme.
Qualification: Degree

USAC316

Russell Sage College
    TROY, NY 12180
☎ 518 270 2282
Contact: Kris Anderson

Course: Women's Studies programme
☐ A minor on the undergraduate programme.

USAC317

Sarah Lawrence College
    BRONXVILLE, NY 10708
☎ 914 395 2510
Contact: Carole Nichols
Course: Women's Studies programme
☐ A master's degree in Women's History on the postgraduate programme. An area of concentration on the undergraduate programme.
Qualification: Master's degree

National Council for Research on Women
☎ 212 570 5001
Contact: Mariam Chamberlain

USAC318

Skidmore College
    SARATOGA SPRINGS, NY 12866
☎ 518 584 5000
Contact: Mary Stange
Course: Women's Studies programme
☐ A minor on the undergraduate programme.

USAC319

St Lawrence University
    15 Hepburn Hall
    CANTON, NY 13617
☎ 315 379 9335
Contact: Valarie Lehr
Course: Gender Studies
☐ A minor on the undergraduate programme.

USAC320

State University of New York College at Albany
    1400 Washington Avenue
    HUM 117
    ALBANY, NY 12222
☎ 518 442 4188
Contact: Bonnie Spanier
Course: Women's Studies programme
☐ Liberal Studies with an area of concentration on the postgraduate programme. A major or a minor on the undergraduate programme.
Qualification: Degree, Master's degree

Center for Women in Government
State University of New York College at Albany
    1400 Washington Avenue
    Draper Hall, Room 302
    ALBANY, NY 12222
☎ 514 442 3900
Contact: Florence B. Bonner

Institute for Research on Women
State University of New York College at Albany
1400 Washington Avenue
ALBANY, NY 12222
☎ 518 442 4670
Contact: Christine E. Bose

USAC321
State University of New York College at Binghamton
Vestal Parkway East
Library North 1105
BINGHAMTON, NY 13901
☎ 607 777 2815
Contact: Deborah Hertz
Course: Women's Studies programme
☐ A minor on the undergraduate programme.

Sojourner Center for Research on Women
State University of New York College at Binghamton
BINGHAMTON, NY 13901
☎ 607 777 2815
Contact: Jane Collins

USAC322
State University of New York College at Brockport
BROCKPORT, NY 14420
☎ 716 395 2751
Contact: Beth Vonfossen
Course: Women's Studies programme
☐ An area of concentration on the postgraduate programme. A major or a minor on the undergraduate programme.

Community Research Center
State University of New York College at Brockport
BROCKPORT, NY 14420
☎ 716 395 5597
Contact:' Margaret Blackman
☐ With a specialisation on gender and cultural diversity.

USAC323
State University of New York College at Buffalo
1010 Clemens Hall
BUFFALO, NY 14260
☎ 716 636 2810
Contact: Elizabeth Kennedy
Course: Women's Studies programme
☐ American Studies on the postgraduate programme. A major or a minor on the undergraduate programme.
Qualification: Degree, Master's degree, Doctorate

Graduate Group for Feminist Studies
State University of New York College at Buffalo
527 O'Brien Hall
BUFFALO, NY 14260

☎ 716 636 2361
Contact: Claudia Freidefsky

USAC324
State University of New York College at Cortland
Department of Philosophy
CORTLAND, NY 13045
☎ 607 753 2014
Contact: Kathryn Russell
Course: Women's Studies programme
☐ A minor on the undergraduate programme.

USAC325
State University of New York College at Fredonia
Thompson Hall
FREDONIA, NY 14063
☎ 716 673 3111
Contact: James Hurtgen
Course: Women's Studies programme
☐ A major or a minor on the undergraduate programme with an Individualised major as a specialisation.
Qualification: Degree

USAC326
State University of New York College at Geneseo
GENESEO, NY 14454
☎ 716 245 5209
Contact: Margaret Matlin
Course: Women's Studies programme
☐ A minor on the postgraduate programme. A minor on the undergraduate programme.

USAC327
State University of New York College at New Paltz
Hohmann House
NEW PALTZ, NY 12561
☎ 914 257 3009
Contact: Amy Kesselman
Course: Women's Studies programme
☐ A major or a minor with an area of concentration on the undergraduate programme.
Qualification: Degree

USAC328
State University of New York College at Old Westbury
Box 210
OLD WESTBURY, NY 11568
☎ 516 876 3103
Contact: Laura Anchor
Course: Women's Studies programme
☐ An area of concentration on the undergraduate programme, with an American Studies specialisation.
Qualification: Degree

USAC329

State University of New York College at Oswego
Mahar Hall
OSWEGO, NY 13126
☎ 315 341 3443
Contact: Karen Halbersleben
Course: Women's Studies programme
☐ A minor on the undergraduate programme.

USAC330

State University of New York College at Plattsburgh
Hawkins Hall
PLATTSBURGH, NY 12901
☎ 518 564 3301
Contact: Eleanor P. Stoller
Course: Women's Studies programme
☐ A minor on an undergraduate programme.

USAC331

State University of New York College at Stony Brook
STONY BROOK, NY 11794
☎ 516 632 7690
Contact: Barbara Weinstein
Course: Women's Studies programme
☐ A part of the postgraduate programme. A minor on the undergraduate programme.
Qualification: Degree, Graduate certificate

USAC332

College of Staten Island of the City University of New York
715 Ocean Terrace
STATEN ISLAND, NY 10301
☎ 718 390 7818
Contact: Florence C. Parkinson
Course: Women's Studies programme
☐ A major or a minor on the undergraduate programme with a specialisation in Independent Study.
Qualification: Degree
Note: Women's Center is being formed.

USAC333

Suffolk County Community College
533 College Road
SELDEN, NY 11784
☎ 516 451 4365
Contact: Alice Goode-Elman
Course: Women's Studies programme
☐ A major with an area of concentration on the undergraduate programme.
Qualification: Degree

USAC334

Syracuse University
Hall of Languages, Room 307
SYRACUSE, NY 13244
☎ 315 443 3707
Contact: Diane Murphy
Course: Women's Studies programme
☐ A part of the postgraduate programme. A minor with an area of concentration on the undergraduate programme.

USAC335

Tompkins Cortland Community College
170 North Street
DRYDEN, NY 13053
☎ 607 844 8211
Contact: Sandra Pollack
Course: Women's Studies programme
☐ A major on the undergraduate programme.

USAC336

Union College
Social Sciences Building
SCHENECTADY, NY 12308
☎ 518 370 6423
Contact: Sharon Gmelch
Course: Women's Studies programme
☐ A major with an area of concentration on the undergraduate programme.
Qualification: Degree

USAC337

Vassar College
POUGHKEEPSIE, NY 12601
☎ 914 437 7144
Contact: Eileen Leonard
Course: Women's Studies programme
☐ A major or a minor on the undergraduate programme.
Qualification: Degree

USAC338

Wells College
Route 90
AURORA, NY 13206
☎ 315 364 3240
Contact: Leslie Miller-Bernal
Course: Women's Studies programme
☐ A minor on the undergraduate programme.

USAC339

York College of the City University of New York
JAMAICA, NY 11457
☎ 718 262 2430
Contact: Gloria Waldman
Course: Women's Studies programme
☐ An area of concentration on the undergraduate programme.

North Carolina

USAC340

Appalachian State University
East Hall
BOONE, NC 28608
☎ 704 262 2144
Course: Women's Studies programme
□ A minor on the postgraduate programme. A major (Interdisciplinary Studies), a minor (only self-designed) or an area of concentration on the undergraduate programme.

USAC341

Duke University
207 East Duke Building
DURHAM, NC 27706
☎ 919 684 5683
Contact: Jean O'Barr
Course: Women's Studies programme
□ A part of the postgraduate programme. An area of concentration on the undergraduate programme with an Honours specialisation at undergraduate level available.

Center for Research on Women
Duke University of North Carolina
☎ 919 684 6641
Contact: Christina Greene

USAC342

East Carolina University
Tenth Street, Brewster A204
GREENVILLE, NC 27858
☎ 919 757 6268
Contact: Marie T. Farr
Course: Women's Studies programme
□ A minor on the undergraduate programme.

USAC343

Elon College
Campus Box 2219
ELON COLLEGE, NC 27244
☎ 919 584 2260
Contact: Martha Smith
Course: Women's Studies programme
□ A minor on the undergraduate programme.

USAC344

Guilford College
5800 West Friendly Avenue
GREENSBORO, NC 27410
☎ 919 292 5511
Contact: Carol Stoneburner
Course: Women's Studies programme
□ A minor on the undergraduate programme.

USAC345

University of North Carolina at Chapel Hill
207 Caldwell Hall/CB 3135
CHAPEL HILL, NC 27599–3135
☎ 919 962 3908
Contact: Barbara J. Harris
Course: Women's Studies programme
□ A part of the postgraduate programme. An area of concentration on the undergraduate programme.
Qualification: Degree

USAC346

University of North Carolina at Charlotte
CHARLOTTE, NC 28223
☎ 704 547 4312
Contact: Lorine M. Getz
Course: Women's Studies programme
□ A minor on the undergraduate programme.

USAC347

University of North Carolina at Greensboro
108 Foust
GREENSBORO, NC 27412
☎ 919 334 5673
Contact: Jodi Bilinkoff
Course: Women's Studies programme
□ A major or a minor on the undergraduate programme.
Qualification: Degree

USAC348

Salem College
Main Hall/Old Salem
WINSTON-SALEM, NC 27108
☎ 919 725 5411
Contact: Gary Ljungquist
Course: Women's Studies programme
□ A part of the undergraduate programme.

USAC349

Wake Forest University
PO Box 7365/Reynolds Station
WINSTON-SALEM, NC 27109
☎ 919 759 5139
Contact: Mary DeShazer
Course: Women's Studies programme
□ An area of concentration on the postgraduate programme. A minor on the undergraduate programme.

North Dakota

USAC350

North Dakota State University
English Department
FARGO, ND 58105
☎ 701 237 7156
Contact: Jean Strandness

Course: Women's Studies programme
☐ A minor on the undergraduate programme.

USAC351

University of North Dakota
    Box 42 University Station
    GRAND FORKS, ND 58202
☎ 701 777 4115
Contact: Sandra J. Parsons
Course: Women's Studies programme
☐ A minor on the undergraduate programme.

Ohio

USAC352

The University of Akron
    Spicer 120
    AKRON, OH 44325–6218
☎ 216 972 7396
Contact: C. Gozansky-Garrison
Course: Women's Studies programme
☐ A part of the postgraduate programme. A part of the undergraduate programme.

USAC353

Antioch College
    YELLOW SPRINGS, OH 45387
☎ 513 767 6364
Contact: Marianne Whelchel
Course: Women's Studies programme
☐ An area of concentration on the undergraduate programme, with a European term abroad in Women's Studies as a specialisation.
Qualification: Degree

USAC354

Bowling Green State University
    BOWLING GREEN, OH 43402
☎ 419 874 7133
Contact: Karen Gould
Course: Women's Studies programme
☐ A major or a minor on the undergraduate programme.
Qualification: Degree

USAC355

Center for Women's Studies
University of Cincinnati
    ML-164
    CINCINNATI, OH 45221
☎ 513 556 6776
Contact: Hilda Smith
Course: Women's Studies programme
☐ A minor on the postgraduate programme. A part of the undergraduate programme.

Women's Research and Resource Institute
Contact: M. Christine Anderson

USAC356

University of Dayton
    300 College Park
    DAYTON, OH 43023
☎ 513 229 4285
Contact: Judith Martin
Course: Women's Studies programme
☐ A minor on the undergraduate programme.

USAC357

Denison University
    GRANVILLE, OH 45469
☎ 614 587 6536
Contact: Annette Van Dyke
Course: Women's Studies programme
☐ A major or a minor on the undergraduate programme.
Qualification: Degree

USAC358

Kent State University
    308 Bowman Hall
    KENT, OH 44242
☎ 216 672 2060
Contact: Trudy Steuernagel
Course: Women's Studies programme
☐ A minor on the undergraduate programme.

Project on Study of Gender and Education
Kent State University
    405 White Hall
    KENT, OH 44242
☎ 216 672 2178
Contact: Averil McClelland

USAC359

Kent State University, Salem Regional Campus
    2491 State Route 45 South
    SALEM, OH 44460
☎ 216 332 0361
Contact: Stephane Elise Booth
Course: Women's Studies programme
☐ A part of the undergraduate programme.

USAC360

Kenyon College
    GAMBIER, OH 43022
☎ 614 427 5140
Contact: Cheryl Steele
Course: Women's Studies programme
☐ Synoptic Major – individually designed available as a specialisation.

USAC361

Marietta College
MARIETTA, OH 45750
☎ 614 373 4643
Contact: Sara Shute
Course: Women's Studies programme
☐ A minor on the undergraduate programme.

USAC362

Miami University
OXFORD, OH 45056
☎ 513 529 4616
Contact: Ann Fuehrer
Course: Women's Studies programme
☐ A minor on the undergraduate programme.

USAC363

College of Mount St Joseph
MOUNT ST JOSEPH, OH 45051
☎ 513 244 4939
Contact: K. Clifton, V. M. Vorde
Course: Women's Studies programme
☐ A major or a minor on an undergraduate programme.
Qualification: Degree

USAC364

Oberlin College
Rice Hall 16
OBERLIN, OH 44074
☎ 216 775 8409
Contact: Sandra Zagarell
Course: Women's Studies programme
☐ A major or a minor on the undergraduate programme.
Qualification: Degree

USAC365

The Ohio State University
207 Dulles Hall
230 West 17th Avenue
COLUMBUS, OH 43210
☎ 614 292 1021
Contact: Susan Hartmann
Course: Women's Studies programme
☐ An area of concentration on the postgraduate programme. A major or a minor on the undergraduate programme.
Qualification: Degree, Master's degree

USAC366

Ohio University
Scott 320
ATHENS, OH 45701
☎ 614 593 4686
Contact: Linda C. Hunt
Course: Women's Studies programme

☐ Available on both undergraduate and postgraduate programmes. Specialisation at postgraduate level available through Interdisciplinary Programme.

USAC367

Ohio Wesleyan University
215 Sturgis Hall
DELAWARE, OH 43015
☎ 614 368 3577
Contact: Laurie Churchill
Course: Women's Studies programme.
☐ A major or a minor on the undergraduate programme.
Qualification: Degree

USAC368

College of Wooster
WOOSTER, OH 44691
☎ 216 263 2575
Contact: Susan Figge
Course: Women's Studies programme
☐ A major or a minor on the undergraduate programme.
Qualification: Degree

USAC369

Xavier University
3800 Victory Parkway
CINCINNATI, OH 45207
☎ 513 745 2042
Contact: Billie J. Johnson
Course: Women's Studies programme
☐ A minor on the undergraduate programme.

USAC370

Youngstown State University
DeBartolo Hall 435
YOUNGSTOWN, OH 435
☎ 216 742 1687
Contact: Pat Gilmartin-Zena
Course: Women's Studies programme
☐ A minor on the undergraduate programme.

Oklahoma

USAC371

University of Oklahoma
530 Physical Science Center
NORMAN, OK 73019
☎ 405 325 3481
Contact: Judith S. Lewis
Course: Women's Studies programme
☐ An Interdisciplinary part of the postgraduate programme. A minor on the undergraduate programme.

Courses

USAC372

University of Tulsa
    600 South College Avenue
    TULSA, OK 74104
☎   918 631 2000
Contact: Shari Benstock
Course: Women's Studies programme
☐ A Departmental emphasis in English on the graduate programme.

Oregon

USAC373

Oregon State University
    Social Science 111
    CORVALLIS, OR 97331
☎   503 737 2826
Contact: Heather Emberson
Course: Women's Studies programme
☐ A major or a minor with an area of concentration on the postgraduate programme. A minor with an area of concentration on the undergraduate programme.
Qualification: Degree, Master's degree

Women in International Development Program
    Office of International Research and Development
    Oregon State University, Snell 400
    CORVALLIS, OR 97331–1641
☎   503 754 2228
Contact: Revathi Balakrishnan

USAC374

University of Oregon
    636 Prince Lucien Campbell Hall
    EUGENE, OR 97403
☎   503 346 5529
Contact: Barbara Corrado Pope
Course: Women's Studies programme
☐ A part of the postgraduate programme. A minor on the undergraduate programme with an Interdisciplinary Master's Degree available as a specialisation.
Qualifications: Degree, Postgraduate diploma, Master's degree

Center for the Study of Women in Society
☎   503 346 5015
Contact: Sandra Morgen

USAC375

Portland State University
    PO Box 751
    PORTLAND, OR 97207
☎   503 725 3516
Contact: Johanna Brenner
Course: Women's Studies programme

☐ A minor on the undergraduate programme.
Qualification: Certificate

USAC376

Southern Oregon State College
    Psychology Department
    ASHLAND, OR 97520
☎   503 482 6206
Contact: Karen L. Salley
Course: Women's Studies programme
☐ A concentration in Interdisciplinary Studies. A minor with an area of concentration on the undergraduate programme.
Qualifications: Degree, Master's degree

Pennsylvania

USAC377

Allegheny College
    MEADVILLE, PA 16335
☎   814 332 2395
Contact: Mary Hudak
Course: Women's Studies programme
☐ A minor with an area of concentration on the undergraduate programme.

USAC378

Community College of Allegheny County
    North Campus
    808 Ridge Avenue
    PITTSBURGH, PA 15212
☎   412 237 2627
Contact: Edna McKenzie
Course: Women's Studies programme
☐ A part of the undergraduate programme.
Qualification: Certificate

USAC379

Bryn Mawr College
    Department of History
    BRYN MAWR, PA 19010
☎   215 526 5066
Contact: Jane Caplan
Course: Women's Studies programme
☐ A minor with an area of concentration on the undergraduate programme, with an Independent major in Women's Studies.

USAC380

Bucknell University
    LEWISBURG, PA 17837
☎   717 524 1545
Contact: Catherine Blair
Course: Women's Studies programme
☐ A minor on the undergraduate programme.

USAC381

Cabrini College
King of Prussia and Eagle Roads
RADNOR, PA 19087
☎ 215 971 8356
Contact: Kathleen Daley
Course: Women's Studies programme
☐ An area of concentration on the undergraduate programme, with concentration under Sociology available as a specialisation.

USAC382

California University of Pennsylvania
CALIFORNIA, PA 15419
☎ 412 938 5788
Contact: Margaret Spratt
Course: Women's Studies programme

USAC383

Carlow College
3333 Fifth Avenue
PITTSBURGH, PA 15213
☎ 412 578 6208
Contact: Ellie Wymard
Course: Women's Studies programme
☐ A minor on the undergraduate programme.
Qualification: Degree

USAC384

Cedar Crest College
3404 Linden Street
ALLENTOWN, PA 18104
☎ 215 395 5580
Contact: Ann Hill-Beuf
Course: Women's Studies programme
☐ An Independent minor with an area of concentration on the undergraduate programme.
Qualification: Degree

USAC385

East Stroudsburg University of Pennsylvania
309 Stroud Hall
EAST STROUDSBURG, PA 18301
☎ 717 424 3542
Contact: Anne Berkman
Course: Women's Studies programme
☐ An area of concentration on the undergraduate programme.

USAC386

Franklin and Marshall College
LANCASTER, PA 17604
☎ 717 291 4193
Contact: Nancy McDowell
Course: Women's Studies programme
☐ A minor on the undergraduate programme with a specialisation in a Special Studies major.

USAC387

Gettysburg College
GETTYSBURG, PA 17325
☎ 717 337 6788
Contact: Jean Potuchek
Course: Women's Studies programme
☐ A minor on the undergraduate programme.

USAC388

Haverford College
HAVERFORD, PA 19004
☎ 215 896 1156
Contact: Elaine Tuttle Hansen
Course: Women's Studies programme
☐ An area of concentration on the undergraduate programme.

USAC389

Indiana University of Pennsylvania
352 Sutton Hall
INDIANA, PA 15705
☎ 412 357 4753
Contact: Maureen C. McHugh
Course: Women's Studies programme
☐ An area of concentration on the postgraduate programme. A minor on an undergraduate programme.

USAC390

Lafayette College
c/o Psychology Department
EASTON, PA 18042
☎ 215 250 5294
Contact: Susan A. Basow
Course: Women's Studies programme
☐ A minor on an undergraduate programme, with an individualised major.

USAC391

LaSalle University
20th and Olney Street
PHILADELPHIA, PA 19141
☎ 215 951 1161
Contact: Linda E. Merians
Course: Women's Studies programme
☐ A minor on the undergraduate programme.

USAC392

Lehigh University
Department of Philosophy #15
BETHLEHEM, PA 18103
☎ 215 758 3776
Contact: Robin S. Dillon
Course: Women's Studies programme
☐ A minor on the undergraduate programme.
Note: Women's Centre being planned.

USAC393

Lycoming University
Lycoming Village
WILLIAMSPORT, PA 17701
☎ 717 321 4000
Contact: Emily R. Jensen
Course: Women's Studies programme
□ A major or a minor on an undergraduate programme.

USAC394

Neumann College
ASTON, PA 19014–1297
☎ 215 558 5579
Contact: Martha Boston
Course: Women's Studies programme
□ A minor on the undergraduate programme.

USAC395

Pennsylvania State University, McKeesport
University Drive
McKEESPORT, PA 15132
☎ 412 675 9461
Contact: Margaret L. Signorella
Course: Women's Studies programme
□ A minor on an undergraduate programme.

USAC396

Pennsylvania State University, University Park
13 Sparks Building
UNIVERSITY PARK, PA 16802
☎ 814 863 4025
Contact: Lynne Goodstein
Course: Women's Studies programme
□ A Department minor on the postgraduate programme. A major or a minor on the undergraduate programme.
Qualification: Degree

USAC397

University of Pennsylvania
106 Logan Hall
PHILADELPHIA, PA 19104–6304
☎ 215 898 8740
Contact: Janice Madden
Course: Women's Studies programme
□ A major or a minor on the undergraduate programme.
Qualification: Degree

Alice Paul Center for the Study of Women

USAC398

University of Pittsburgh
2632 Cathedral of Learning
PITTSBURGH, PA 15260
☎ 412 624 6485
Contact: Susan Hansen
Course: Women's Studies programme

□ An area of concentration on the postgraduate programme. A part of the undergraduate programme.

Women's Studies Research Center
□ Research focuses on the impact of economic restructuring and social change on women and gender.

USAC399

Shippensburg University of Pennsylvania
SHIPPENSBURG, PA 17257
☎ 717 532 9121
Course: Women's Studies programme
□ A minor on the undergraduate programme.

USAC400

Slippery Rock University Pennsylvania
B106 Bailey Library
SLIPPERY ROCK, PA 16057
☎ 412 794 7451
Contact: Jace Condravy
Course: Women's Studies programme
□ A minor on the undergraduate programme.

USAC401

Swarthmore College
500 College Avenue
SWARTHMORE, PA 19081–1397
☎ 215 328 8135
Contact: Marjorie Murphy
Course: Women's Studies programme
□ An area of concentration on the postgraduate programme. An area of concentration on the undergraduate programme.

USAC402

Temple University
Broad Street and Columbia Avenue
PHILADELPHIA, PA 19122
☎ 215 787 6753
Contact: Sherri Grasmuck
Course: Women's Studies programme
□ A major or a minor on the undergraduate programme.

USAC403

Villanova University
201 Vasey Hall
VILLANOVA, PA 19085
☎ 215 645 4483
Contact: Barbara Wall
Course: Women's Studies programme
□ An area of concentration at postgraduate level, with a specialisation through Interdisciplinary Studies.
Qualification: Degree

USAC404

West Chester University of Pennsylvania
211 Main Hall
WEST CHESTER, PA 19383
☎ 215 436 2464
Contact: Stacey Schlau
Course: Women's Studies programme
☐ An area of concentration on the postgraduate programme. A minor with an area of concentration on the undergraduate programme.

USAC405

Wilkes University
Liberal Arts and Human Sciences
South River Street
WILKES-BARRE, PA 18766
☎ 717 824 4651
Contact: Patricia B. Heaman
Course: Women's Studies programme
☐ A minor on the undergraduate programme.

USAC406

Wilson College
1015 Philadelphia Avenue
CHAMBERSBURG, PA 17201
☎ 717 264 4141 ext. 285
Contact: B. Ayers-Nachamkin
Course: Women's Studies programme
☐ A part of the undergraduate programme.

Rhode Island

USAC407

Brown University
Pembroke Centre/Box 1958
PROVIDENCE, RI 02912
☎ 401 863 2643
Contact: Elizabeth Weed
Course: Women's Studies programme
Qualification: Degree

Pembroke Center for Teaching and Research and Women
Contact: Karen Newman

USAC408

Rhode Island College
600 Mt Pleasant Avenue
PROVIDENCE, RI 02908
☎ 401 456 8377
Contact: Maureen T. Reddy
Course: Women's Studies programme
☐ A major or a minor with an area of concentration on the undergraduate programme.
Qualification: Degree

USAC409

University of Rhode Island
315 Roosevelt Hall
KINGSTON, RI 02881–0806
☎ 401 792 2892
Contact: Mary Ellen Reilly
Course: Women's Studies programme
☐ Departmental emphasis on the postgraduate programme. A major or a minor with an area of concentration on the undergraduate programme.
Qualification: Degree

South Carolina

USAVC410

College of Charleston
Philosophy Department
66 George Street
CHARLESTON, SC 29424
☎ 803 792 5687
Contact: Cheshire Calhoun
Course: Women's Studies programme
☐ A minor on the undergraduate programme.

USAC411

University of South Carolina
1710 College Street
COLUMBIA, SC 29208
☎ 803 777 4007
Contact: Sue V. Rosser
Course: Women's Studies programme
☐ An area of concentration on the postgraduate programme. A major or a minor with an area of concentration on the undergraduate programme.
Qualification: Degree

USAC412

Winthorp College
Arts and Sciences
ROCK HILL, SC 29731
☎ 803 323 2181
Contact: April Gordon
Course: Women's Studies programme
☐ A minor on the undergraduate programme.

South Dakota

USAC413

South Dakota State University
Political Science Department
BROOKINGS, SD 57007
☎ 605 688 4914
Contact: Eleanor A. Schwab
Course: Women's Studies programme
☐ A minor on the undergraduate programme.

Courses

USAC414

University of South Dakota
414 East Clark Street
VERMILLION, SD 5229
☎ 605 677 5073
Contact: Alice T. Gasque
Course: Women's Studies programme
☐ Selected Studies on a graduate programme. A minor with an area of concentration on the undergraduate programme.
Qualification: Degree

Tennessee

USAC415

Memphis State University
MEMPHIS, TN 38152
☎ 901 454 2169
Contact: Allison Graham
Course: Women's Studies programme

Center for Research on Women
☎ 901 454 2770
Contact: Lynn Cannon

USAC416

Middle Tennessee State University
Box 498
MURFREESBORO, TN 37132
☎ 615 898 2645
Contact: Nancy Rupprecht
Course: Women's Studies programme
☐ A minor on the undergraduate programme.

USAC417

University of Tennessee, Knoxville
2012 Lake Avenue
KNOXVILLE, TN 37994–4102
☎ 615 974 2409
Contact: Martha Lee Osbourne
Course: Women's Studies programme
☐ An area of concentration on the undergraduate programme.

USAC418

Vanderbilt University
Box 86, Station B
NASHVILLE, TN 37235
☎ 615 343 7808
Contact: Nancy Walker
Course: Women's Studies programme
☐ A minor on the undergraduate programme.

Texas

USAC419

El Paso Community College
919 Hunter Road
EL PASO, TX 79915
☎ 915 594 2595
Contact: Jeanne Foskett
Course: Women's Studies programme
☐ An area of concentration on the undergraduate programme.

USAC420

University of Houston, Clear Lake
2700 Bay Area Boulevard
HOUSTON, TX 77058
☎ 713 283 3319
Contact: Cynthia Miller
Course: Women's Studies programme
☐ A concentration on the postgraduate programme. An area of concentration on the undergraduate programme.

USAC421

Center for Women in Development
Our Lady of the Lake University of Antonio
411 Southwest 24th Street
SAN ANTONIO, TX 78207
☎ 512 434 6711 ext. 446
Contact: Jane Shafer

USAC422

Rice University
PO Box 1892
HOUSTON, TX 77251
☎ 713 527 4994
Contact: Helen Longino
Course: Women's Studies programme
☐ A minor on the undergraduate programme.

USAC423

Southern Methodist University
Dallas Hall 227
DALLAS, TX 75275
☎ 214 692 3612
Contact: Caroline Brettell
Course: Women's Studies programme
☐ A minor on the undergraduate programme.

USAC424

Southwest Texas State University
Flowers Hall
SAN MARCOS, TX 78666
☎ 512 245 2361
Contact: Lydia Blanchard

Course: Women's Studies programme
☐ A minor on the undergraduate programme.

USAC425

Southwestern University
　PO Box 770
　GEORGETOWN, TX 78626-0770
☎　512 863 1302–1380
Contact: Mary Visser
Course: Women's Studies programme
☐ A major or a minor on the undergraduate programme.
Qualification: Degree

Center for Texas Women in the Arts
☐ Texas women in the visual and performing arts is available as a specialisation.

USAC426

Stephen F. Austin State University
　NACOGDOCHES, TX 759624
☎　409 568 4405
Contact: Joy B. Reeves
Course: Women's Studies programme
☐ A minor on the undergraduate programme.

USAC427

Texas A & M University
　217 CD Blocker Building
　COLLEGE STATION, TX 77843–4227
☎　4098 845 9670
Contact: Hariette Andreadis
Course: Women's Studies programme
☐ Departmental emphasis on the postgraduate programme. A minor on the undergraduate programme.

USAC428

Texas Tech University
　PO Box 4170
　LUBBOCK, TX 79409
☎　806 742 3001
Contact: Gwendolyn T. Sorell
Course: Women's Studies programme
☐ Concentration in Interdisciplinary Studies on the postgraduate programme. A minor on the undergraduate programme.

USAC429

University of Texas at Arlington
　Department of Psychology
　ARLINGTON, TX 76019–0529
☎　817 273 3392
Contact: Sheila Collins
Course: Women's Studies programme
☐ An area of concentration on the postgraduate programme. An area of concentration on the undergraduate programme, with Interdisciplinary Studies available as a specialisation.

Women and Minorities Research and Resource Center
Contact: Kathleen Underwood

USAC430

University of Texas at Austin
　SSb 3.106
　AUSTIN, TX 78712
☎　512 471 1288
Contact: Laura Lein
Course: Women's Studies programme
☐ A minor or an area of concentration on the undergraduate programme.

USAC431

University of Texas at Dallas
　Box 688
　RICHARDSON, TX 75080
Contact: Nancy Tawana
Course: Women's Studies programme
☐ An area of concentration on the postgraduate programme. An area of concentration on the undergraduate programme.

USAC432

University of El Paso
　130 Liberal Arts
　University Avenue
　EL PASO, TX 79968
☎　915 747 5200
Contact: Sandra Beyer
Course: Women's Studies programme
☐ An area of concentration on the undergraduate programme.

USAC433

Texas Women's University
　PO Box 23029
　DENTON, TX 23029
☎　817 898 2256
Contact: Jean Saul
Course: Women's Studies programme
☐ A minor or an area of concentration on the undergraduate programme.

USAC434

Brigham Young University
　946 SWKT
　PROVO, UT 84602
☎　801 378 5294
Contact: Marie Cornwall
Course: Women's Studies programme

Women's Research Institute

Courses

USAC435

Utah State University
LOGAN, UT 84322–0710
☎ 801 750 1240
Contact: Pamela Riley
Course: Women's Studies programme
☐ A minor on the undergraduate programme.

Women and Gender Research Institute
☎ 801 750 2580
Contact: Sharon Ohlhorst

USAC436

University of Utah
217 Building 44
SALT LAKE CITY, UT 84112
☎ 801 581 8094
Contact: Patty Reagan
Course: Women's Studies programme
☐ A concentration on the postgraduate programme. A major or a minor on the undergraduate programme, with Graduate Literary Criticism (English) available as a specialisation.
Qualification: Degree

Vermont

USAC437

Bennington College
BENNINGTON, VT 05201
☎ 802 442 5401 ext. 270
Contact: Joan Goodrich
Course: Women's Studies programme
☐ An individualised major on the undergraduate programme.

USAC438

Burlington College
95 North Avenue
BURLINGTON, VT 05448
☎ 802 862 9619
Contact: Anna Blackner
Course: Women's Studies programme
☐ A major or a minor on the undergraduate programme.
Qualification: Degree

USAC439

Goddard College
PLAINFIELD, VT 05667
☎ 802 454 8311
Contact: Shelley Smith
Course: Women's Studies programme
Qualification: Degree

USAC440

Middlebury College
Munroe Hall
MIDDLEBURY, VT 05753
☎ 802 388 3711
Contact: Margaret K. Nelson
Course: Women's Studies programme
☐ A major or an area of concentration on the undergraduate programme.
Qualification: Degree

USAC441

Trinity College of Vermont
Colchester Avenue
BURLINGTON, VT 05401
☎ 802 658 0332 ext. 356
Contact: Barbara Davis Cheng
Course: Women's Studies programme
☐ Special Studies available as a specialisation.
Qualification: Degree

USAC442

University of Vermont
Box 14
Living and Learning Center
BURLINGTON, VT 05405–0348
☎ 802 656 4282
Contact: Joan Smith
Course: Women's Studies programme
☐ A minor or an area of concentration on the undergraduate programme.

Virginia

USAC443

George Mason University
4400 University Drive
FAIRFAX, VA 22030
☎ 703 323 2921
Contact: Karen Rosenblum
Course: Women's Studies programme
☐ A minor on the undergraduate programme.

Women's Studies Research and Resource Center

USAC444

Mary Baldwin College
STAUNTON, VA 24401
☎ 703 887 7068
Contact: Martha Noel Evans
Course: Women's Studies programme
☐ A minor on the undergraduate programme.
Qualification: Degree

USAC445

Mary Washington College
FREDERICKSBURG, VA 22401
☎ 703 899 4373
Contact: Carole Corcoran
Course: Race and Gender project
☐ A special major on the undergraduate programme.

USAC446

Old Dominion University
Hampton Boulevard
NORFOLK, VA 23529–0161
☎ 804 683 3241
Contact: Anita Clair-Fellman
Course: Women's Studies programme
☐ A major and a minor on the undergraduate programme. Also available with a Departmental emphasis on the postgraduate programme.
Qualifications: Degree, Master's degree.

USAC447

Randolph Macon College
Henry Street
ASHLAND, VA 23005
☎ 804 798 8372
Contact: Charlotte Fitzgerald
Course: Women's Studies focus
☐ A minor on the undergraduate programme.

USAC448

Randolph Macon Women's College
Box 952
LYNCHBURG, VA 24503
☎ 804 845 9583
Contact: Pamela Quaggiotto
Course: Women's Studies programme
☐ A minor on the undergraduate programme.

USAC449

University of Richmond
RICHMOND, VA 23173
☎ 804 289 8307
Contact: Suzanne W. Jones
Course: Women's Studies programme
☐ A major and a minor on the undergraduate programme.

USAC450

Virginia Commonwealth University
Box 2040
RICHMOND, VA 23284
☎ 804 367 6641
Contact: Diana Scully
Course: Women's Studies programme
☐ A minor on the undergraduate programme.

USAC451

Virginia Polytechnic Institute and State University
10 Sandy Hall
BLACKSBURG, VA 24061–0338
☎ 703 231 7615
Contact: Patricia Tracy
Course: Women's Studies programme
☐ An area of concentration on the undergraduate programme.

Women's Research Institute
Contact: Carol J. Burger
☐ Specialisations in women's issues and mental health.

USAC452

University of Virginia
11 Miner Hall
CHARLOTTESVILLE, VA 22901
☎ 804 982 2962
Contact: Ann J. Lane
Course: Women's Studies programme
☐ An area of concentration on the undergraduate programme.
Qualification: Degree

Washington

USAC453

Central Washington University
ELLENSBURG, WA 98926
☎ 509 963 1858
Contact: Ann S. Denman
Course: Women's Studies programme
☐ A minor on the undergraduate programme.

USAC454

Eastern Washington University
MS 166
CHENEY, WA 99004
☎ 509 359 2409
Contact: Lee Swedberg
Course: Women's Studies programme
☐ A minor on the undergraduate programme. Also courses available on the postgraduate programme.

USAC455

The Evergreen State College
Library 2211
OLYMPIA, WA 98505
☎ 206 866 6000
Contact: Pris Bowerman
Course: Women's Studies programme
☐ An area of concentration on the undergraduate programme.

Courses

USAC456

Pacific Lutheran University
TACOMA, WA 98447
☎ 206 535 8744
Contact: Elizabeth Brusco
Course: Women's Studies programme
☐ A minor or an area of concentration on the undergraduate programme. Specialisation available as an individualised major for Special Honours. Also individualised study available at postgraduate level in Social Sciences.
Qualifications: Degree, Master's degree

USAC457

University of Puget Sound
TACOMA, WA 98416
☎ 206 756 3431
Contact: Florence Sandler
Course: Women's Studies programme
☐ A minor on the undergraduate programme.

USAC458

Washington State University
Wilson Hall 301
PULLMAN, WA 99164-4032
☎ 509 335 1794
Contact: Jo Hockenhull
Course: Women's Studies programme
☐ A minor available on both the undergraduate and the postgraduate programme.

Women's Resource and Research Center
Washington State University
PULLMAN, WA 99164–7204
☎ 509 335 6830
Contact: Beth Prinz
☐ Specialises in Northwest region development, and rural women.

USAC459

University of Washington
GN–45
SEATTLE, WA 98195
☎ 206 543 6900
Contact: Sydney Janet Kaplan
Course: Women's Studies programme
☐ A major on the undergraduate programme of General Studies.
Qualification: Degree

Northwest Center for Research on Women
University of Washington
AJ–50 Cunningham Hall
SEATTLE, WA 98195
☎ 206 543 9531

Contact: Angela Ginorio
☐ Research specialisations of the Center are curriculum transformation; and women, science and technology.

USAC460

Yakima Valley Community College
PO Box 1647
YAKIMA, WA 98907
☎ 509 575 2915
Contact: Mary Doherty Kowalsky
Course: Women's Studies programme
☐ An area of concentration on the undergraduate programme.

West Virginia

USAC461

West Virginia University
200 Clark Hall
MORGANTOWN, WV 26506
☎ 304 293 2339
Contact: Judith Stitzel
Course: Women's Studies programme
☐ Liberal Studies as part of the postgraduate programme. A part of the undergraduate programme, with concentration in Women's Studies available as a specialisation.

Wisconsin

USAC462

Research Center on Women
Alverno College
3401 South 39th Street
MILWAUKEE, WI 53215
☎ 414 382 6061
Contact: Lola Stuller

USAC463

Beloit College
700 College Street
BELOIT, WI 53511
☎ 608 363 2391
Contact: Diane Lichtenstein
Course: Women's Studies programme
☐ A minor on the undergraduate programme, with an individually constructed major available as a specialisation.

USAC464

Carroll College
WAUKESHA, WI 53186
☎ 414 524 7263
Contact: Lori Kelly
Course: Women's Studies programme
☐ A minor on the undergraduate programme.

USAC465

Edgewood College
855 Woodrow Street
MADISON, WI 53711
☎ 608 257 4861
Contact: Esther Heffernan
Course: Women's Studies programme
□ A minor on an undergraduate programme.

USAC466

Madison Area Technical College
3550 Anderson Street
MADISON, WI 53704
☎ 608 246 6250
Contact: Sara Sherkow
Course: Women's Studies programme
□ An area of concentration on the undergraduate programme.

USAC467

Marquette University
Marquette Hall
MILWAUKEE, WI 53233
☎ 414 288 1430
Contact: Rebecca Bardwell
Course: Women's Studies programme
□ A minor on the undergraduate programme.

USAC468

Ripon College
300 Seward Street
RIPON, WI 54971
☎ 414 748 8131
Contact: Vance Cope-Kasten
Course: Women's Studies programme
□ A minor on the undergraduate programme.

USAC469

Viterbo College
815 South Ninth Street
LA CROSSE, WI 54601
☎ 608 791 0271
Contact: Mary Loges
Course: Women's Studies programme
□ A minor on the undergraduate programme.

USAC470

University of Wisconsin-Eau Claire
EAU CLAIRE, WI 54701
☎ 715 836 5717
Contact: Sarah Harder
Course: Women's Studies programme
□ A minor on the undergraduate programme.

USAC471

University of Wisconsin-Green Bay
2420 Nicolet Drive
GREEN BAY, WI 54311-7001
☎ 414 465 2355
Contact: Julie Brickley
Course: Women's Studies programme
□ A minor with an area of concentration on the undergraduate programme.

USAC472

University of Wisconsin-La Crosse
336 North Hall
LA CROSSE, WI 54601
☎ 608 785 8753 or 8734
Contact: Sondra O'Neale
Course: Women's Studies programme
□ A minor on the undergraduate programme.

Women's Studies Research Center
☎ 608 263 2053
Contact: Cyrena Pondrom

USAC473

University of Wisconsin-Madison
209 North Brooks Street
MADISON, WI 53715
☎ 608 263 4703
Contact: Betsy Draine
Course: Women's Studies programme
□ A minor with a Departmental emphasis in Women's History on the postgraduate programme. A major with the undergraduate programme.
Qualifications: Degree, Master's degree, Doctorate

Women's Studies Research Center
☎ 608 263 2051
Contact: Janet Hyde

USAC474

Women's Studies Consortium
1616 Van Hise Hall
1220 Linden Drive
MADISON, WI 53706
☎ 608 262 3056
□ Established in 1975, the Consortium co-ordinates Women's Studies teaching, research, outreach, library resource development, and international programmes across University of Wisconsin campuses.

USAC475

University of Wisconsin-Oshkosh
OSHKOSH, WI 54901
☎ 414 424 0384
Contact: Eleanor Amico
Course: Women's Studies programme
□ A minor on the undergraduate programme.

Courses

USAC476

University of Wisconsin-Parkside
KENOSHA, WI 53141
☎ 414 553 2162
Contact: Anne Stathane
Course: Women's Studies programme
☐ A minor on the undergraduate programme.

USAC477

University of Wisconsin-Platteville
446 Gardner Hall
PLATTEVILLE, WI 53818
☎ 608 342 1750
Contact: Gloria Stephenson
Course: Women's Studies programme
☐ An individually constructed major or a minor on the undergraduate programme.
Qualification: Degree

USAC478

University of Wisconsin-River Falls
Cascade Avenue
RIVER FALLS, WI 54022
☎ 715 425 3115
Contact: Meg Swenson
Course: Women's Studies programme
☐ A minor on the undergraduate programme.

USAC479

University of Wisconsin-Stevens Point
English Department–WWSP
STEVENS POINT, WI 54481
☎ 715 346 4347
Contact: Katherine Ackley
Course: Women's Studies programme
☐ A minor on the undergraduate programme.

USAC480

University of Wisconsin-Stout
School of Liberal Studies
MENOMONIE, WI 54751
☎ 715 232 1511
Contact: Sharon Nero
Course: Women's Studies programme
☐ A minor on the undergraduate programme.

USAC481

University of Wisconsin-Superior
SUPERIOR, WI 54880
☎ 715 394 8151
Contact: Delores Harms
Course: Women's Studies programme
☐ A minor on the undergraduate programme.

USAC482

University of Wisconsin-Whitewater
423 Heide Hall
WHITEWATER, WI 53190
☎ 414 472 1042
Contact: Audrey Roberts
Course: Women's Studies programme
☐ A major or a minor on the undergraduate programme.
Qualification: Degree

Wyoming

USAC483

Casper College
125 College Drive
CASPER, WY 82601
☎ 307 268 2491
Contact: Carolyn Logan
Course: Women's Studies programme
☐ A two-year Major – Liberal Arts option is available as a specialisation.

USAC484

University of Wyoming
PO Box 4297
LARAMIE, WY 82071
☎ 307 766 3919
Contact: Janet Clark
Course: Women's Studies programme
☐ A minor on the undergraduate programme.

Uruguay

URUC1

Grupo Estudio la Condicion de la Mujer en Uruguay (GRECMU)
Juan Pamilier 1174
MONTEVIDEO
Contact: Isabel Miranda

Group for the Study of Women in Uruguay

Vietnam

VIEC1

Research Centre on Women
6 Quinh Cong Trang
HANOI
Contact: Le Thi Nham Tuyet

Zimbabwe

ZIMC1

Women in Development Research Unit
Centre for Inter-racial Studies
    Box MP 167
    Mount Pleasant
    SALISBURY
Contact: Olivia D. Muchena

2 | *Training*

Introduction

This section addresses training opportunities for women in the following alphabetically arranged subject areas, which have been coded into abbreviations for ease of use:

Arts and media   AM
Assertiveness training   AT
Equal opportunities   EO
Health and therapy   HT
Management   M
Self-employment   SE
Science, technology and computing   STC

The information presented was obtained from a whole range of sources, such as books, bookshops, journals, newsletters, women's groups, women's resource centres and word of mouth, to mention just a few. In no way is the information collected a fully comprehensive account of women's training worldwide. Readers would benefit most of all by regarding it as an access point to enable women's groups and individual women to communicate, share and build upon each other's experience and expertise, exchange information and collaborate on developments in the field of women's training.

The world of training is one of constant change. Indeed, the only certainty seems to be that of future changes brought about by financial or political constraints and upheavals, or positive changes through the introduction of new training programmes to reduce the discrimination faced by women in employment and education. Changes in a country's economic position have an immediate impact on its ability to provide free or subsidised training. In turn, this affects the ability of training organizations to grow or, for many, simply survive. In a recession, the training budget is often the first to be reduced. The effect of the recession on the training organisations included here seems to be one of double diversity: first, in order to continue many have diversified to provide a wider range of courses; second, for survival, many have made decisions to broaden their client base to cater for both sexes.

How to use this section

Countries are arranged alphabetically under each training category heading. If you were searching for equal opportunities training courses in Kenya, for example, EOKEN is the code under which the course entries would be located. In general, the first three letters of a country's full title have been used for the purpose of coding.

Helen Collins

Arts and Media

Australia

AUSAM1

National Women's Consultative Council
 3–5 National Circuit
 BARTON ACT 2600
☎ 06 271 5723
Course: Women in Art and Media
☐ Vocational training and practical workshops for women interested in arts and media.

AUSAM2

South Australian Film Corporation (SAFC)
 3 Butler Drive
 Westside Commerce Centre
 113 Tapleys Hill Road
 HENDON, SA 5014
☎ 081 348 9355
Course: Women in Art and Media
☐ Vocational training and practical workshops for women interested in arts and media.

AUSAM3

SWIFT
 66 Albion St.,
 SURREY HILLS, NSW 2010
Course: Women in Art and Media
☐ Vocational training and practical workshops for women interested in arts and media.

Belgium

BELAM1

Ministère de la Prévoyance Sociale
 Rue de la Vierge Noire
 1000 BRUSSELS
Contact: Monique Derche
Course: Women in Art and Media
☐ Vocational training for women interested in arts and media.

BELAM2

Ministère de l'Emploi et du Travail
 51 rue Belliard
 1040 BRUSSELS
Contact: Brigitte Van Meelsen
Course: Women in Art and Media
☐ Vocational training and practical workshops for women interested in arts and media.

BELAM3

Ministère de l'Emploi et du Travail
 51 rue Belliard
 1040 BRUSSELS
Contact: Martine Voets
Course: Women in Art and Media
☐ Vocational training and practical workshops for women interested in arts and media.

BELAM4

STD Aalst
 De Ridderstraat 15
 9300 AALST
Contact: Francine Depoortere
Course: Women in Art and Media
☐ Vocational training for women interested in arts and media.

BELAM5

VDAB Vilvoorde
 Rollewagenstrat 22
 1800 VILVOORDE
Contact: Harry Van Vaerenbergh
Course: Women in Art and Media
☐ Vocational training and practical workshops for women interested in arts and media.

BELAM6

VDAB – Vilvoorde
 Rollewagenstraat 22
 1801 VILVOORDE
Contact: Luc Van Waes
Course: Women in Art and Media
☐ Vocational training and practical workshops for women interested in arts and media.

Canada

CANAM1

The Canadian Advisory Council on the Status of Women
 666 Sherbrooke Street W
 Montreal
 QUEBEC H3A 1E7
☎ 514 283 8123
Course: Women in Art and Media
☐ Vocational training and practical workshops for women interested in arts and media.

CANAM2
Canadian Congress for Learning Opportunities for Women
   47 Main Street
   Toronto
   ONTARIO M4E 2U6
☎   416 699 1909
Course: Women in Art and Media
☐ Vocational training and practical workshops for women interested in arts and media.

Denmark

DENAM1
Aben Datastue for Kvinder
   Ostre Stationsvej 36
   5000 ODENSE C
Contact: Dorrit Munk Jensen
Course: Women in Art and Media
☐ Vocational training for women interested in arts and media.

DENAM2
Alborg Tekniske Skole
   Oster Uttrupvej 1
   Postbox 2339
   8260 VIBY J
Contact: Sven Age Suhr
Course: Women in Art and Media
☐ Vocational training for women interested in arts and media.

DENAM3
AMU – Alborg
   Rodslet 77
   9430 VADUM
Contact: Else Hvid Jensen
Course: Women in Art and Media
☐ Vocational training for women interested in arts and media.

DENAM4
Anne Dorte Faester
   Birkeholm Terrasserne 431
   3520 FARUM
Contact: Anne Dorte Faester
Course: Women in Art and Media
☐ Vocational training for women interested in arts and media.

DENAM5
AOF
   Rugardsvej 9
   5000 ODENSE
Contact: Connie Lyders
Course: Women in Art and Media

☐ Vocational training for women interested in arts and media.

DENAM6
Arbejdsmarkedsstyrelsen
   Hejrevej 43
   2400 COPENHAGEN NV
Contact: Benthe Stig
Course: Women in Art and Media
☐ Vocational training for women interested in arts and media.

DENAM7
Arhus Tekniske Skole
   Halmstadsgade 6
   8200 ARHUS N
Contact: Marianne Thorsager
Course: Women in Art and Media
☐ Vocational training for women interested in arts and media.

DENAM8
Bodil Husted
   Hasselager alle 2
   Postbox 2339
   8260 VIBY J
Contact: Bodil Husted
Course: Women in Art and Media
☐ Vocational training for women interested in arts and media.

DENAM9
Cekvina
   (Women's Research Centre in Aarhus)
   University of Aarhus
   Finlandsgade 26
   8200 AARHUS N
☎   06 16 58 55
Contact: Elisabeth Flensted-Jensen
Course: Women's Creative Writing
☐ The Centre contains a library and an archive of women's creative writing; conducts research and training in women's writing and women's aesthetics.

DENAM10
Center for Kvindestudier
   (Centre for Women's Studies)
   Odense University
   Campusvej 55
   5230 ODENSE M
☎   09 15 86 00 ext. 318
Contact: Nina Lykke
Course: Women's Literature
☐ Research projects and training in women's literature; courses are offered to graduate students.

DENAM11
Center for Samfunds-Videnskabelig Kvindeforskning
(Women's Research Centre in Social Science)
Adelgade 49 St.tv
1304 COPENHAGEN K
☎ 01 12 23 14
Contact: Else Christensen
Course: Women's Contribution to Art and Social Science
☐ Research, working groups and discussion on women's contribution to art and social science.

DENAM12
Dansk Teknologisk Institut
Postbox 141
2630 TASTRUP
Contact: Claudia Anker Nielsen
Course: Women in Art and Media
☐ Vocational training for women interested in arts and media.

DENAM13
Forum for Kvindeforskning ved Danmarks Laerer-Hojskole
(The Forum for Feminist Research)
Emdrupvej 101
2400 COPENHAGEN NV
☎ 01 69 66 33 ext. 244
Contact: Ingeborg Appel
Course: Women's Educational Artistic Contributions
☐ Research and training into women's artistic and educational work, past and present.

DENAM14
Holbaek Tekniske Skole
Absalonsgade 20
4300 HOLBAEK
Contact: Ruth Lange
Course: Women in Art and Media
☐ Vocational training for women interested in arts and media.

DENAM15
KIMADAN
Nordvestvej 4
9600 ARS
Contact: Nina Ostergard
Course: Women in Art and Media
☐ Vocational training for women interested in arts and media.

DENAM16
Koge Handelskole
Kogleaksvej 25
4600 KOGE
Contact: Leif Hugo Rasmussen

Course: Women in Art and Media
☐ Vocational training for women interested in arts and media.

DENAM17
KVIL – Kurser i Vejle
Borgvold 6
7100 VEJLE
Contact: Inge Skotte Henriksen
Course: Women in Art and Media
☐ Vocational training for women interested in arts and media.

DENAM18
Kvindehistorisk Samling
(Women's History Archive)
The State Library
Universitetsparken
8000 AARHUS C
☎ 06 12 20 22 ext. 319
Contact: Britta Skovgaard
Course : Women's History
☐ Research and training in women's history.

DENAM19
KVINFO
(The Centre for Information on Women's Studies)
Laederstraede 15, 2. sal
1201 COPENHAGEN K
☎ 01 13 94 73
Contact: Jytte Larsen
Course: Women in Art and Media
☐ Research and training on women involved and interested in arts and media, past and present.

DENAM20
Kvindemuseet i Danmark
(The Women's Museum in Denmark)
Domkirkeplads 5
8000 AARHUS C
☎ 06 13 69 79
Course: Women's Museum and Past
☐ Workshops and discussion groups arranged for women interested in women's lives in past centuries.

DENAM21
Ligestillingskonsulent
Arbejdsformidlingen
Kjellerupsgade 12
9000 ALBORG
Contact: Anette Kortsen
Course: Women in Art and Media
☐ Vocational training for women interested in arts and media.

DENAM22

Martin Krogh
Hornbaekvej 58
9270 KLARUP
Contact: Martin Krogh
Course: Women in Art and Media
☐ Vocational training for women interested and involved in arts and media.

DENAM23

Nomi Hartmann
Pallisvej 41
8220 BRABRAND
Contact: Nomi Hartmann
Course: Women in Art and Media
☐ Vocational training for women interested in arts and media.

DENAM24

Odense Universitet
Campusvej 55
5230 ODENSE M
Contact: Daniel Fischer
Course: Women in Art and Media
☐ Vocational training for women interested in arts and media.

DENAM25

Organisationskontoret
Skottenborg 26
8800 VIBORG
Contact: Birgitte Haahr
Course: Women in Art and Media
☐ Vocational training for women interested in arts and media.

DENAM26

Udviklingsleder
Indvirde
Stationsvej 46
3460 BIRKEROD
Contact: Lene Sondberg
Course: Women in Art and Media
☐ Vocational training for women interested in arts and media.

DENAM27

Vejle Amtskommune
Damhaven 12
7100 VEJLE
Contact: Jens Bertelsen
Course: Women in Art and Media
☐ Vocational training for women interested and involved in arts and media.

France

FRAM1

Asprocep
189 avenue Corot
13014 MARSEILLE
Contact: I. Guernigou
Course: Women in Art and Media
☐ Vocational training and practical workshops for women interested in arts and media.

FRAM2

Asprocep
189 avenue Corot
13014 MARSEILLE
Contact: Marie Christine Lafayette
Course: Women in Art and Media
☐ Vocational training and practical workshops for women interested in arts and media.

FRAM3

EDF-GDF
16 rue de Monceau
75008 PARIS
Contact: Beatrice Thiery
Course: Women in Art and Media
☐ Vocational training and practical workshops for women interested in arts and media.

FRAM4

Education Nationale DAFCO de Caen
168 rue Caponière
BP 6184
14034 CAEN
Contact: Nicole Rioult
Course: Women in Art and Media
☐ Vocational training and practical workshops for women interested in arts and media.

FRAM5

IRFA Lorraine
1 rue du Coetloquet
BP 795
57013 METZ
Contact: Michele Gadelle
Course: Women in Art and Media
☐ Vocational training and practical workshops for women interested in arts and media.

FRAM6

Racine
211 av. Jean Jaures
75019 PARIS
Contact: Fernanda Mora
Course: Women in Art and Media
☐ Vocational training and practical workshops for women interested in arts and media.

Germany

GERAM1

Frauen Neuphilologie
Wilhelmstrasse 50
7400 TUBINGEN
Course: Feminist Magazine Publishing and Exhibitions.
☐ Organises exhibitions, research and small group workshops on all aspects of feminist magazine publishing.

Great Britain and Northern Ireland

GBAM1

Acton Community Arts Workshop
Action Hill Church
1B Gunnersbury Lane
LONDON W3 8EA
☎ 081 993 3665
Course: Women's Art and Photography
☐ Small friendly workshop groups held to enable participants to identify their own artistic skills and improve upon areas they wish to specialise in.

GBAM2

Anna is a Zebra Performance Group
49 Stainton Road
SHEFFIELD S11 7AX
☎ 0742 669889
Course: Children and Young Women's Performance Group
☐ Performance workshops for young women and children; run by a co-operative.

GBAM3

Anna-Michele Hantler
48 Bonnington Square
LONDON SW8 1TQ
☎ 071 587 1890
Contact: Anna Hantler
Course: Integrative Arts
☐ One-to-one consultancy or small group therapy work using an integrated arts approach.

GBAM4

Arian Productions Ltd
21 Holmwood Drive
FORMBY L37 IPG
☎ 07048 78050
Course: Script to Screen Video Production
☐ Advice and expertise on all aspects of video production.

GBAM5

Asian Women Writers Collective
76 Hindle House
Arcola Street
LONDON E8 2DX
☎ 071 241 4205
Course: Development/Publicity of Asian Women's Writing
☐ Small workshops for Asian women to develop and improve writing skills and enhance creativity.

GBAM6

Audio Visual Enterprise Centre
5 Brown Street
SHEFFIELD S1 2BS
☎ 0742 667115
Contact: Vicki Usherwood
Course: Video Production: Medical, Educational and Documentary
☐ Workshops and small group sessions covering all aspects of video production.

GBAM7

Boxclever Presentation Training
25 Bewdley Street
LONDON N1 1HB
☎ 071 607 5766
Course: Presentation Skills
☐ Courses and one-to-one tuition for women interested in artistic presentations.

GBAM8

Boxclever Productions
25 Bewdley Street
LONDON N1 1HB
☎ 071 607 5766
Course: Film and Television Production
☐ Advice and expertise on all aspects of film and television production.

GBAM9

Cambridge Women's Resources Centre
Hooper Street
CAMBRIDGE CB1 2NZ
☎ 0223 321148
Course: Women in Art and Media
☐ Vocational training and practical workshops for women interested in arts and media.

GBAM10

Campaign for Women in the Arts
Great Georges Project
The Blackie
Great George Street
LIVERPOOL L1 5EW
☎ 051 709 5109
Course: Women in the Arts

☐ Workshops and groups for promoting women's art and enhancing creativity.

GBAM11

The Cholmondeleys
17 Dukes Road
LONDON WC1H 9AB
☎ 071 383 3231
Course: Contemporary Dance and Choreography
☐ Small classes; tuition covers all elements of contemporary dance.

GBAM12

Cinenova
113 Roman Road
LONDON E2 0HU
☎ 081 981 6828
Course: Women's Film and Video Distribution
☐ Advice and expertise on all aspects of women's film and video distribution.

GBAM13

Custom Designed Prints
60 Wheatlands
Heston
HOUNSLOW TW5 0SA
☎ 081 570 3828
Course: Textile Design
☐ Advice and expertise on all aspects of textile design.

GBAM14

Dee Voce and Nawal Gadalla
41 Watling Crescent
CHESTER CH4 7HD
☎ 0244 679100
Contact: Dee Voce
Course: Circle Dance
☐ A women's partnership teaching small classes the art of circle dancing.

GBAM15

Design for Change Ltd
Unit 5, East Block
Panther House
38 Mount Pleasant
LONDON WC1X 0AP
☎ 071 837 2109
Course: Design and Artwork
☐ Advice, support and hands-on assistance for individuals and organisations requiring expertise with their artistic requirements.

GBAM16

Design Forum Ltd
Unit 5
Zair Works
111 Bishop Street
BIRMINGHAM B5 6JL
☎ 021 622 2821
Course: Design and T-Shirt Printing Co-operative
☐ Hands-on assistance and expertise available for individuals and organisations wishing to enhance their image through better design.

GBAM17

Dramatherapy North West
41 Netheroyd Hill Road
Fixby
HUDDERSFIELD HD2 2LS
☎ 0484 515047
Course: Dramatherapy Workshops
☐ Training workshops and summer school covering all aspects of drama therapy.

GBAM18

Elizabeth Aylmer Pottery
Widgery House
20 Market Street
Hatherleigh
OKEHAMPTON
Devon
☎ 0837 810624
Contact: Elizabeth Aylmer
Course: Pottery
☐ Small workshops covering all aspects of pottery, from stoneware to tableware.

GBAM19

Eurosearch Ltd
Chestnut House
BITTESWELL LE17 4SG
☎ 0455 556378
Course: Educational Consultancy and Publishing
☐ A women's partnership providing advice and training on educational and publishing issues.

GBAM20

Filament Film and TV Production Co.
1 Biggins
DUNBLANE FK15 9NX
☎ 0786 823395
Course: Women's Crews, Campaign, Training Programmes
☐ Training programmes covering many aspects of the film and TV industry.

GBAM21

Format Partners
19 Arlington Way
LONDON EC1R 1UY
☎ 071 833 0292
Course: Photography
□ Women's partnership; advice and consultancy on all aspects of photography.

GBAM22

Fusion Fire Theatre
c/o Unit 21
56 Garden Street
SHEFFIELD S1
☎ 0742 731398
Course: Women's Firedance Performance Workshops
□ Training workshops for women interested in fire-dancing.

GBAM23

Image Business
Three Smyrna Mansions
LONDON NW6 4LU
☎ 071 372 5781
Course: Calligraphy Tuition
□ Small group workshops or one-to-one tuition covering all aspects of the art of calligraphy.

GBAM24

Jenni Stuart Anderson Rag Rugs
The Birches
MIDDLETON-ON-THE-HILL HR6 0HZ
☎ 056887 229
Course: Rag Rug Workshops
□ Small workshops teaching all the elements associated with the craft of rag rug making.

GBAM25

Jewish Women's Arts and Education
London Women's Centre
4 Wild Court
LONDON WC2B 5AU
☎ 071 272 8177
Course: Jewish Women's Arts and Education
□ Workshops and group work to promote Jewish women's art and educational opportunities through project-based work.

GBAM26

Karen Vine
32 Lincoln Street
WAKEFIELD WF2 0EB
☎ 0924 298563
Contact: Karen Vine
Course: Illustration Workshops
□ Small workshops designed to encourage participants to develop areas of artistic interest to themselves.

GBAM27

Kim Daniel Wordsmith and Therapist
2 Tom Brown Street
RUGBY CV21 3JT
☎ 0788 568585
Contact: Kim Daniel
Course: Editing
□ Advice and consultancy and one-to-one support with editing manuscripts.

GBAM28

Lasso Design and Typesetting
20 Sussex Way
LONDON N7 6RS
☎ 071 272 9141
Course: Design, Artwork and Print
□ One-to-one assistance and advice; small groups are also catered for.

GBAM29

Leah Thorn
14 Lind Street
St Johns
LONDON SE8 4JE
☎ 081 692 4104
Contact: Leah Thorn
Course: Creative Woman! Workshops
□ Courses are held as workshops for small groups of women. The aim is to enable women to develop their skills and talents to reach their full potential; or to identify new abilities.

GBAM30

Lupton Stellakis
Studio 5
31 Upper Park Road
LONDON NW3 2UL
☎ 071 722 7912
Course: Architectural Services
□ Full range of architectural services, advice and information for clients.

GBAM31

Masbro Centre Women's Group
Masbro Centre
87 Masbro Road
LONDON W14 0LR
☎ 071 603 1293
Course: Arts and Adult Education
□ Workshops and courses run by women for women to reflect the Group's interests and develop women's art and creativity.

GBAM32

Matrix Feminist Architectural Co-op Ltd
The Printhouse
18 Ashwin Street
LONDON E8 3DL
☎ 071 249 7603
Course: Architectural Services; building courses
□ A women's co-operative specialising in helping other women to design and build projects of interest to themselves.

GBAM33

Maxine Davies
34 Ash Road
Horfield
BRISTOL BS7 8RN
☎ 0272 244899
Contact: Maxine Davies
Course: Journal Writing
□ One-to-one tuition or small group workshops on the art of journal writing.

GBAM34

Michele Drees
Basement Flat
15a Belsize Road
LONDON NW6 4RX
☎ 071 483 4552
Contact: Michele Drees
Course: Drum Tuition
□ One-to-one tuition or small group workshops on all aspects of drum playing.

GBAM35

Mime Theatre Company
60 Hardbury Road
Edgbaston
BIRMINGHAM B12 9NQ
☎ 021 440 6880
Course: Physical Theatre Workshops
□ Workshops on all aspects of live theatre and performing arts.

GBAM36

Monocrone Women's Photography Collective
Clapham Pool
Clapham Manor Street
LONDON SW4 6DB
☎ 071 978 2458
Course: Darkroom Teaching
□ One-to-one tuition or small group workshops covering all aspects of photography.

GBAM37

Monstrous Regiment
190 Upper Street
LONDON N1 1RQ

☎ 071 359 9842
Course: Theatre: Women's Experiences
□ Workshops and tours with theatre and live performances.

GBAM38

Nina Finburgh
1 Buckingham Mansions
West End Lane
LONDON NW6 1LR
☎ 071 435 9484
Contact: Nina Finburgh
Course: Acting and Audition Coaching
□ Acting and audition training workshops; one-to-one or small groups.

GBAM39

Opportunity Index
Wren House
Sutton Court Road
SUTTON SM1 4TL
☎ 081 661 9181
Course: Effective Advertising for Business Opportunities
□ Assistance, training and advice for companies interested in maximising the return on their advertising budget.

GBAM40

Organizers
Promotions House
21 Holmwood Drive
FORMBY L37 1PG
☎ 07048 78050
Course: Research and Communications
□ Assistance and advice for companies and individuals interested in improving their communication skills and networks.

GBAM41

Ovatones
Highgate Newtown Community Centre
25 Bertram Street
LONDON N19 5DQ
☎ 071 281 2528
Course: Music and Recording
□ Workshops covering all aspects of the music and recording industry.

GBAM42

Pavic Publications
Sheffield City Polytechnic
36 Collegiate Crescent
SHEFFIELD S10 2BP
☎ 0742 532380
Course: Business Plans and Training Materials

☐ One-to-one consultancy and small workshops covering all aspects of business planning and the production of training materials.

GBAM43

Pavilion
    235 Woodhouse Lane
    LEEDS LS2 3AP
☎   0532 431749
Course: Women's Photography
☐ Small workshops or one-to-one tuition.

GBAM44

Phoenix
    36 Cobham Road
    KINGSTON-UPON-THAMES KT1 3AF
☎   081 549 3041
Course: Feminist Dramatherapy
☐ Small workshops which examine the subject of dramatherapy; feminist perspective.

GBAM45

Popular Productions
    Aizlewood's Mill
    Nursery Street
    SHEFFIELD S3 8GG
☎   0742 823223
Course: Live Acts, Comedy and Entertainments
☐ Workshops covering the art of comedy and entertainment.

GBAM46

Quarry Garden
    Farnah Green
    BELPER DE5 2UP
☎   0773 822732
Contact: Lorna Dexter
Course: Dreamworkshops
☐ Small group workshops covering all aspects of dream analysis.

GBAM47

Quill Power
    22 Manguerite Close
    Bradwell
    GREAT YARMOUTH NR31 8RL
☎   0493 661958
Course: Calligraphy
☐ A women's co-operative offering one-to-one or small group workshops covering all aspects of the art of calligraphy.

GBAM48

Quilters' Guild
    OP66 Dean Clough Business Park
    HALIFAX HX3 5AX
☎   0422 347669

Course: Promotion and Training of Quilting
☐ Workshops and one-to-one instruction and tuition for developing quilting skills.

GBAM49

Second Sight
    Zair Works
    111 Bishop Street
    Highgate
    BIRMINGHAM B5 6JL
☎   021 622 4223/5750
Course: Video Production and Training
☐ Workshops providing training in video production.

GBAM50

Sheila Miller
    114 Hazellville Road
    LONDON N19 3NA
☎   071 281 7700
Contact: Sheila Miller
Course: Writing Skills
☐ Short courses covering all aspects of writing and journalism.

GBAM51

Skin and Blisters
    225 Tufnell Park Road
    LONDON N19 5EP
☎   071 607 6852
Course: Women's Circus Theatre Company
☐ A women's partnership staging circus acts and workshops for those interested in this form of entertainment.

GBAM52

Society of Women Artists
    Briarwood House
    Church Hill
    TOTLAND
    Isle of Wight PO39 0EU
☎   0983 753882
Course: Women's Art
☐ Courses and workshops for women artists to meet, exchange ideas and learn from each other's work.

GBAM53

Sound Kitchen
    c/o WMRP
    89a Kingsland High Street
    LONDON E8 2PB
☎   071 254 6536
Course: Music Production
☐ Small workshops covering all aspects of music production.

GBAM54

South West Women's Arts Network
  The Salem Chapel
  Broadhempston
  TOTNES TQ9 6BD
☎ 0803 813 293
Course: Women's Art
☐ Workshops and courses held by women's groups; encouraged to network and exchange ideas; holds regular meetings.

GBAM55

Spare Tyre Theatre Company
  Ground Floor
  Instrumental House
  207–215 Kings Cross Road
  LONDON WC1X 9DB
☎ 071 278 3140
Course: Spare Tyre Theatre Training Company
☐ Women-only training in theatre and live performance.

GBAM56

The Sphinx
  Sadler's Wells
  Rosemary Avenue
  LONDON EC1R 4TN
☎ 071 713 0991/2
Course: National Touring Company: Women's Writing
☐ Workshops discovering and celebrating women's writing.

GBAM57

The Spinning Jennies
  Spats Nite Club
  37 Oxford Street
  LONDON W1
Course: Women's DJ Service
☐ Women's DJ service; assistance for all occasions.

GBAM58

Splinter Community Arts
  Unit 5
  Mayfield Workshops
  19 Wednesday Road
  WALSALL
☎ 0922 725440
Course: Workshops in Textile Arts
☐ Small workshops which encourage participants to develop their ability through hands on experience with a range of textiles. Women's co-operative.

GBAM59

Support Architects
  29 Gloucester Avenue
  LONDON NW1

☎ 071 267 8312
Course: Architectural Design
☐ Assistance, help and advice for women interested in developing their own ideas and putting them into practice.

GBAM60

Switch Video Productions Ltd
  228 Broomfield Road
  CHELMSFORD CM1 4DY
☎ 0860 770521
Course: Video Production Training
☐ Workshops providing training in video production; hands-on experience.

GBAM61

Vera Productions
  30–38 Dock Street
  LEEDS LS10 1JF
☎ 0532 428646
Course: Video Production
☐ A women's partnership; training in all aspects of video production.

GBAM62

Walter Gardiner Photography
  Southdownview Road
  WORTHING BN15 8RL
☎ 0903 200528
Course: Architecture, Advertising and PR
☐ One-to-one advice and consultancy.

GBAM63

WHAM – Women's Heritage and Museums
  Heritage Development Office
  Museum of Science and Industry
  Newhall Street
  BIRMINGHAM B3 1RZ
☎ 021 235 1676
Course: Positive Images of Women
☐ Workshops and group work to promote positive images of women, past and present.

GBAM64

Wilde Designs
  115 Manor Road
  LONDON N16 5PB
☎ 081 800 4382
Course: Business Design and Presentations
☐ Expertise and information available to individuals or groups on all aspects of business design and formal presentations.

GBAM65

Winifred Wright Ceramics
  The Pottery
  PINMORE BY GIRVAN KA26 0TR
☎ 0465 84 662

Course: Pottery Courses
□ Small courses providing hands-on tuition in all aspects of pottery.

GBAM66

Women in Action
    Redfield
    Buckingham Road
    WINSLOW MK18 3LZ
☎   0296 715202
Course: Women's arts, events, festivals and exhibitions
□ A women's co-operative; arranges and stages events celebrating women's achievements in the world of art.

GBAM67

Women in Arts Project
    The Arts Council of Great Britain
    14 Great Peter Street
    LONDON SW1P 3NQ
Course: Women in Arts
□ Workshops and groups to promote women's art and develop and publicise their major contribution to art.

GBAM68

Women in Profile
    50 Hill Street
    Garnethill
    GLASGOW G3 6RH
☎   041 353 3312
Course: Art, Music and Theatre
□ Workshops for women to develop artistic and creative skills in a women-only environment.

GBAM69

Information Officer
Women in Publishing
    c/o The Bookseller
    12 Dyott Street
    LONDON WC1A 1DF
Course: Women in Publishing
□ Network for women in publishing; organises occasional seminars covering topics of popular interest to members.

GBAM70

Women's Eye Artists Co-operative
    7 Fortismere Avenue
    LONDON N10 3BN
☎   081 883 7342
Course: Women's Visual Artwork
□ A women's co-operative which runs small workshops to promote and develop women's artwork.

GBAM71

Women's Playhouse Trust
    Garden Studios
    11–15 Betterton Street
    LONDON WC2H 9BP

☎   071 379 0344
Course: Productions and Workshops
□ Theatrical productions and performance workshops.

GBAM72

Women Print
    Unit 25
    Devonshire House
    High Street, Digbeth
    BIRMINGHAM B12 0LP
☎   021 773 9065
Course: Photography Training Courses
□ Small group workshops for women covering all aspects of photography.

GBAM73

Women's Theatre Workshop
    Interchange Studios
    15 Dalby Street
    LONDON NW5 3NQ
☎   071 267 7360
Course: Theatre and New Writing
□ Workshops and group work to develop women's theatrical journalistic and writing skills in an all-women environment.

Italy

ITAM1

Commissione Nazionale Parita
    Presidenza Consiglio Ministri
    Palazzo Chigi Piazza
    Colonna
    00187 ROME
Contact: Alba Dini Martino
Course: Women's Art and Education
□ Vocational training for women interested in arts, media and education.

ITAM2

Editrice Co-operativa
    Libera Stampa
    Via Trinita dei Pellgrini 12
    00186 ROME
☎   06 686 43 87
Course: Women's Publishing
□ Co-operative; runs small group workshops and provides one-to-one consultancy on all aspects of women's publishing.

Japan

JAPAM1

Japan Institute of Labour
Chutaikin Building
7-6 Shibakoen 1-chome
Minato-ku
TOKYO, 105 Japan
Course: Women in Art and Media
□ Vocational training and practical workshops for women interested in arts and media.

Netherlands

NETAM1

Alida de Jong School
Mariaplaats 4a
3511 LH UTRECHT
☎ 030 31 54 24
Course: Women's Printing
□ Workshops providing hands-on experience and practical vocational training for women interested in arts and media.

NETAM2

Lena de Graaf School
Kon. Emmakade 119
2518 JJ THE HAGUE
☎ 070 363 59 63
Course: Women into Printing
□ Short courses and discussion groups for women interested and involved in arts and media.

NETAM3

Opleidingscentrum Informatica voor Vrouwen
Pater Brugmanstraat 4
6501 BFD NIJMEGEN
☎ 080 60 20 40
Course: Women in the Media
□ Vocational training for women interested and involved in arts and media.

NETAM4

STEW
Weesperzijde 4
1091 EA AMSTERDAM
Contact: D. Wayer
Course: Women in Art and Media
□ Vocational training and practical workshops for women interested in arts and media.

NETAM5

Verbond van Nederlandse Ondernemingen
Postbus 93093
2509 AB GRAVENHAGE
Contact: J. Van de Bandt Stel

Course: Women in Art and Media
□ Vocational training and practical workshops for women interested in arts and media.

New Zealand

NZAM1

Jolisa
c/o UCSA
90 llam Road
CHRISTCHURCH
Course: Women in Art and Media
□ Vocational training and practical workshops for women interested in arts and media.

NZAM2

Ponsonby Community Centre
Ponsonby
AUCKLAND
Course: Women in Art and Media
□ Vocational training and practical workshops for women interested in arts and media.

NZAM3

The Print Centre
17 Union Street
PO Box 1236
AUCKLAND
☎ 379 6503
Course: Women in Art and Media
□ Vocational training and practical workshops for women interested in arts and media.

Spain

SPAM1

CEDEL
C/Conde Borrell
334–336 Bjs
08029 BARCELONA
Contact: Elia Arbaizer Vaquero
Course: Women in Art and Media
□ Vocational training and practical workshops for women interested in arts and media.

Switzerland

SWIAM1

BALance
Militarstrasse 83a
8004 ZURICH
☎ 01 291 23 31
Contact: Theresa Schiffers
Course: Women in Art and Media

☐ Vocational training and practical workshops for women interested in arts and media.

SWIAM2

Eidgenössisches Büro für die Gleichstellung von Frau und Mann
    Eigerplatz 5
    3007 BERN
Course: Women in Art and Media
☐ Vocational training and practical workshops for women interested in arts and media.

United States of America

USAAM1

Applied Potential
    Box 19
    HIGHLAND PARK, IL 60035
☎ 312 432 0620
Course: Women in Art and Media
☐ Vocational training and practical workshops for women interested in arts and media.

USAAM2

Career Development Center
Randolph-Macon Women's College
    2500 Rivermont Avenue
    LYNCHBURG, VA 24503
☎ 804 846 7392
Course: Women in Art and Media
☐ Vocational training and practical workshops for women interested in arts and media.

USAAM3

Center for Continuing Education for Women
Greenville Technical College
    GREENVILLE, SC 29606
☎ 803 242 3170
Course: Women in Art and Media
☐ Vocational training and practical workshops for women interested in arts and media.

USAAM4

Creative Alternatives for Women
    431 Old York Road
    JENKINTOWN, PA 19046
☎ 215 576 5533
Course: Women in Art and Media
☐ Vocational training and practical workshops for women interested in arts and media.

USAAM5

Denver Women's Career Center
    1650 Washington Street
    DENVER, CO 80203
☎ 303 861 7254

Course: Women in Art and Media
☐ Vocational training and practical workshops for women interested in arts and media.

USAAM6

Department of Public Information
    United Nations
    NEW YORK, NY 10017
Contact: Project Manager, Women Issues
Course: Women in Art and Media
☐ Vocational training and practical workshops for women interested in arts and media.

USAAM7

Everywoman Opportunity Center Inc.
    1407–20 Genesee Building
    1 West Genesee Street
    BUFFALO, NY 14202
☎ 716 847 8850
Course: Women in Art and Media
☐ Vocational training and practical workshops for women interested in arts and media.

USAAM8

Face Learning Center, Inc
    12945 Seminole Boulevard
    Building 2, Suite 8
    LARGO, FL 33540
☎ 813 586 1110
Course: Women in Art and Media
☐ Vocational training and practical workshops for women interested in arts and media.

USAAM9

Focus on Women Program
Henry Ford Community College
    5101 Evergreen Road
    DEARBORN, MI 48128
☎ 313 271 2750
Course: Women in Art and Media
☐ Vocational training and practical workshops for women interested in arts and media.

USAAM10

Indiana University/Purdue University
    1301 East 38th Street
    INDIANAPOLIS, IN 46205
☎ 317 923 1321
Course: Women in Art and Media
☐ Vocational training and practical workshops for women interested in arts and media.

USAAM11

Lifelong Learning Women's Programs
Cuyahoga Community College
    2900 Community College Avenue
    CLEVELAND, OH 44115

☎ 216 241 5966
Course: Women in Art and Media
☐ Vocational training and practical workshops for women interested in arts and media.

USAAM12

Mid-Career Counselling Center
Suny at Stony Brook
Sociology and Behavioral Science Building
Room N235
STONY BROOK, NY 11794
☎ 516 246 3304
Course: Women in Art and Media
☐ Vocational training and practical workshops for women interested in arts and media.

USAAM13

Middle River Center
1515 Martin Boulevard
MIDDLE RIVER, MD 21220
☎ 301 574 7878
Course: Women in Art and Media
☐ Vocational training and practical workshops for women interested in arts and media.

USAAM14

New Options
545 Madison Avenue
NEW YORK, NY 10022
☎ 212 752 9898
Course: Women in Art and Media
☐ Vocational training and practical workshops for women interested in arts and media.

USAAM15

New Ways to Work
149 Ninth Street
SAN FRANCISCO, CA 94103
☎ 415 552 1000
Course: Women in Art and Media
☐ Vocational training and practical workshops for women interested in arts and media.

USAAM16

Resource Center for Women
445 Sherman Avenue
PALO ALTO, CA 94306
☎ 415 324 1710
Course: Women in Art and Media
☐ Vocational training and practical workshops for women interested in arts and media.

USAAM17

Widening Opportunity Research Center
Middlesex Community College
Division of Continuing Education
PO Box T
BEDFORD, MA 01730
☎ 617 275 8910
Course: Women in Art and Media
☐ Vocational training and practical workshops for women interested in arts and media.

USAAM18

A Womanschool Affiliate
Placement 500
424 Madison Avenue
NEW YORK, NY 10017
☎ 212 688 4606
Course: Women in Art and Media
☐ Vocational training and practical workshops for women interested in arts and media.

USAAM19

Womanspace: Career
Columbia University
211 Lewisohn Hall
Broadway and 116th Street
NEW YORK, NY 10027
☎ 212 280 2820
Course: Women in Art and Media
☐ Vocational training and practical workshops for women interested in arts and media.

USAAM20

Women's Career Development Center
Wright State University
140 East Monument Avenue
DAYTON, OH 45402
☎ 513 223 6041
Course: Women in Art and Media
☐ Vocational training and practical workshops for women interested in arts and media.

USAAM21

Women's Career Program
New York University
11 West 42nd Street
NEW YORK, NY 10036
☎ 212 790 1330
Course: Women in Art and Media
☐ Vocational training and practical workshops for women interested in arts and media.

USAAM22

The Women's Center
Jersey City State College
70 Audubon
JERSEY CITY, NJ 07305

☎   201 547 3189
Course: Women in Art and Media
☐ Vocational training and practical workshops for women interested in arts and media.

USAAM23

Women's Center, Career Development Center
Enterprise State Junior College
  Highway 84 East
  PO Box 1300
  ENTERPRISE, AL 36330
☎   205 347 5431
Course: Women in Art and Media
☐ Vocational training and practical workshops for women interested in arts and media.

USAAM24

Women's Educational Center
Reading Area Community College
  Box 1706
  2nd and Penn Streets
  READING, PA 19603
☎   215 372 4721
Course: Women in Art and Media
☐ Vocational training and practical workshops for women interested in arts and media.

USAAM25

Women's Resource Agency
  Suite 309
  25 N. Spruce
  COLORADO SPRINGS, CO 80905
☎   303 471 3170
Course: Women in Art and Media
☐ Vocational training and practical workshops for women interested in arts and media.

USAAM26

Women's Services
University of Nebraska at Omaha
  MBSC-Room 312
  60th and Dodge Streets
  OMAHA, NB 68182
☎   402 554 2200
Course: Women in Art and Media
☐ Vocational training and practical workshops for women interested in arts and media.

USAAM27

Working Opportunities for Women
  Suite 340
  2233 University Ave
  ST PAUL, MN 55404
☎   612 647 9961
Course: Women in Art and Media
☐ Vocational training and practical workshops for women interested in arts and media.

USAAM28

YWCA
  802 N. Lafayette Boulevard
  SOUTH BEND, IN 46601
☎   219 233 9491
Course: Women in Art and Media
☐ Vocational training and practical workshops for women interested in arts and media.

135

Assertiveness Training

Australia

AUSAT1

Affirmative Action Agency
   1st Floor, The Denison
   65 Berry Street
   PO Box 974
   NORTH SYDNEY, NSW 2060
☎ 02 957 4333
Course: Assertiveness for Women
☐ Practical workshops and small group sessions for women interested in examining behaviour and methods of communication; aimed at developing assertiveness skills.

AUSAT2

National Women's Consultative Council
   3–5 National Circuit
   BARTON, ACT 2600
☎ 06 271 5723
Course: Assertiveness for Women
☐ Practical workshops and small group sessions for women interested in examining behaviour and methods of communication; aimed at developing assertiveness skills.

Belgium

BELAT1

Eurydice
   17 rue Archimede
   1040 BRUSSELS
Contact: M. Vanandruel
Course: Assertiveness for Women
☐ Practical workshops and small group sessions for women interested in examining behaviour and methods of communication; aimed at developing assertiveness skills.

BELAT2

FGTB Regionale Liège Huy – Waremme
   9–11 place St Paul
   4000 LIEGE
Contact: Laurette Witsel
Course: Assertiveness for Women
☐ Practical workshops and small group sessions for women interested in examining behaviour and methods of communication; aimed at developing assertiveness skills.

BELAT3

FOREM
   Rue de Wallonnie 21
   4460 GRACE HOLLOGNE
Contact: Anne Sokol
Course: Assertiveness for Women
☐ Practical workshops and small group sessions for women interested in examining behaviour and methods of communication; aimed at developing assertiveness skills.

BELAT4

Institut voor Voortdurende Vorming van de Middenstand
   Josef II straat 30
   1040 BRUSSELS
Contact: M. J. Van der Aa-Broos
Course: Assertiveness for Women
☐ Practical workshops and small group sessions for women interested in examining behaviour and methods of communication; aimed at developing assertiveness skills.

BELAT5

Ministère de la Prévoyance Sociale
   Rue de la Vierge Noire
   1000 BRUSSELS
Contact: Monique Derche
Course: Assertiveness for Women
☐ Training to develop women's assertiveness.

BELAT6

National Verbond K.
   Secondair Onderwijs
   Guimardstraat 1
   1040 BRUSSELS
Contact: Dorothen Van Hoyweghen
Course: Assertiveness for Women
☐ Practical workshops and small group sessions for women interested in examining behaviour and methods of communication; aimed at developing assertiveness skills.

BELAT7

Rien Van Meensel
   Van Eevenstraat 2
   3000 LEUVEN
Contact: Rien Van Meensel
Course: Assertiveness for Women
☐ Practical workshops and small group sessions for women interested in examining behaviour and methods of communication; aimed at developing assertiveness skills.

BELAT8

Samenwerkingsverband
Stategisch Plan Kempen
Grote Markt 23
2300 TURNHOUT
Contact: Linda Stynen
Course: Assertiveness for Women
☐ Practical workshops and small group sessions for women interested in examining behaviour and methods of communication; aimed at developing assertiveness skills.

BELAT9

STD Aalst
De Ridderstraat 15
9300 AALST
Contact: Francine Depoortere
Course: Assertiveness for Women
☐ Training to develop women's assertiveness.

BELAT10

STD Hasselt
Thonissenlaan 47
3500 HASSELT
Contact: M. Wastiels
Course: Assertiveness for Women
☐ Practical workshops and small group sessions for women interested in examining behaviour and methods of communication; aimed at developing assertiveness skills.

BELAT11

VDAB
Keizerslaan 11
1000 BRUSSELS
Contact: Johan Van Oost
Course: Assertiveness for Women
☐ Practical workshops and small group sessions for women interested in examining behaviour and methods of communication; aimed at developing assertiveness skills.

Canada

CANAT1

The Canadian Advisory Council on the Status of Women
666 Sherbrooke Street W
Montreal
QUEBEC H3A 1E7
☎ 514 283 8123
Course: Assertiveness for Women
☐ Practical workshops and small group sessions for women interested in examining behaviour and methods of communication; aimed at developing assertiveness skills.

CANAT2

Canadian Congress for Learning Opportunities for Women
47 Main Street
Toronto
ONTARIO M4E 2U6
☎ 416 699 1909
Course: Assertiveness for Women
☐ Practical workshops and small group sessions for women interested in examining behaviour and methods of communication; aimed at developing assertiveness skills.

CANAT3

Ontario Women's Directorate
480 University Ave
2nd Floor
Toronto
ONTARIO M5G 1V2
Course: Assertiveness for Women
☐ Practical workshops and small group sessions for women interested in examining behaviour and methods of communication; aimed at developing assertiveness skills.

Denmark

DENAT1

Afdelingsleder
Arbejdsformidlingen
Faelledvej 3
8800 VIBORG
Contact: Margit Bjerre
Course: Assertiveness for Women
☐ Training to develop women's assertiveness.

DENAT2

AMS
Hejrevej 43
2400 COPENHAGEN NV
Contact: Charlotte Netterstrom
Course: Assertiveness for Women
☐ Training to develop women's assertiveness.

DENAT3

Arbejdsformidlingen
Dannebrogsgade 3
5000 ODENSE
Contact: Anne Marie Jacobsen
Course: Assertiveness for Women
☐ Training to develop women's assertiveness.

DENAT4

Arhus Universitet
8000 ARHUS

Contact: Drude Dahlerup
Course: Assertiveness for Women
☐ Training to develop women's assertiveness.

DENAT5

Athene
Rosenborggade 2
1130 COPENHAGEN K
Contact: Lotte Valbjorn
Course: Assertiveness for Women
☐ Training to develop women's assertiveness.

DENAT6

Beskaeftigelseskonsulent
Aftensang 1
6040 EGTVED
Contact: Ruth Syshoj
Course: Assertiveness for Women
☐ Vocational training for women interested in developing assertiveness skills.

DENAT7

The Centre for Feminist Research and Women's Studies
The University of Copenhagen – Amager
Njalsgade 106
2300 COPENHAGEN S
☎ 01 54 22 11
Contact: Anne Margrete Berg
Course: Women's Empowerment
☐ Research and training aimed at increasing the status of women participants in society.

DENAT8

Else Hansen
Sanatorievej 25
7140 STOUBY
Contact: Else Hansen
Course: Assertiveness for Women
☐ Training to develop women's assertiveness.

DENAT9

Horsens EDB-Centre
Tobaksgarden 10
8700 HORSENS
Contact: Inger Lindhardt
Course: Assertiveness for Women
☐ Training to develop women's assertiveness.

DENAT10

KAD
Ewaldsgade 3–9
2200 COPENHAGEN N
Contact: Lillian Knudsen
Course: Women's Assertiveness
☐ Training in assertiveness for women.

DENAT11

KIMADAN
Nordvestvej 4
9600 ARS
Contact: Nina Ostergard
Course: Assertiveness for Women
☐ Training to develop women's assertiveness.

DENAT12

Kommunikations – og
Servicecenter
Vejlevej 18
7300 JELLING
Contact: Anders Hess
Course: Assertiveness for Women
☐ Training to develop women's assertiveness.

DENAT13

Kvindeforum
(The Centre of Feminist Research)
University of Aalborg
Fibigerstraede 2
9220 AALBORG 0
☎ 08 15 85 22
Contact: Anna-Dorte Christensen
Course: Women's Empowerment
☐ Research and training aimed at enhancing women's status in society.

DENAT14

Kvindeligt Arbejderforbund
Ewaldsgade 3–9
2200 COPENHAGEN
Contact: Birte Kaiser
Course: Assertiveness for Women
☐ Training to develop women's assertiveness.

DENAT15

Kvindeligt Arbejderforbund
Kirkestraede
3730 NEKS 0
Contact: Britta Bergh Jensen
Course: Assertiveness for Women
☐ Training to develop women's assertiveness.

DENAT16

Kvinder pa Tvaers
(The Feminist Research Centre)
House 03.2.5
Roskilde University Centre
PO Box 260
4000 ROSKILDE
☎ 02 75 77 11 ext. 255
Contact: Karen Sjorup
Course: Women's Empowerment
☐ Research and training aimed at empowering women.

DENAT17
KVINFO
  Drabaeksvej 18
  3450 ALLEROD
Contact: Leslie Larson
Course: Assertiveness for Women
☐ Training to develop women's assertiveness.

DENAT18
Ligestillingskonsulent
  Arbejdsformidlingen
  Klosterengen 105
  4000 ROSKILDE
Contact: Annelise Rasmussen
Course: Assertiveness for Women
☐ Training to develop women's assertiveness.

DENAT19
Ligestillingskonsulent
  Arbejdsformidlingen
  Sonderbrogade 34
  7100 VEJLE
Contact: Mette Heinze
Course: Assertiveness for Women
☐ Training to develop women's assertiveness.

DENAT20
Ligestillingskonsulent
  HK
  H. C. Andersens Boulevard 50
  1780 COPENHAGEN V
Contact: Vibeke Abel
Course: Assertiveness for Women
☐ Training to develop women's assertiveness.

DENAT21
Ligestillingskonsulent
  Arbejdsformidlingen
  Ostervoldgade 4
  3700 RONNE
Contact: Vivi Statager
Course: Assertiveness for Women
☐ Training to develop women's assertiveness.

DENAT22
Plan 2000
  Magnolievangen 56
  3450 ALLEROD
Contact: Anne Fogh
Course: Assertiveness for Women
☐ Training to develop women's assertiveness.

DENAT23
Plan-it APs
  Magnolivangen 56
  3450 ALLEROD

Contact: Anna Eckhoff
Course: Assertiveness for Women
☐ Training to develop women's assertiveness.

DENAT24
RACU
  Vejle Amtskommune
  Damhaven 12
  7100 VEJLE
Contact: Nete Svennekaer
Course: Assertiveness for Women
☐ Training to develop women's assertiveness.

DENAT25
SAMKVIND
  (The Forum for Feminist Social Studies)
  St Kannikestraede 18
  1169 COPENHAGEN K
☎ 01 91 21 66 ext. 242
Contact: Sanne Ipsen
Course: Women's Empowerment
☐ Training and research aimed at empowering women in education and the social sciences.

France

FRAT1
AFPA Limoges Batîment
  68 rue de Babylone
  87036 LIMOGES
Contact: Suzettz Potevin
Course: Assertiveness for Women
☐ Practical workshops and small group sessions for women interested in examining behaviour and methods of communication; aimed at developing assertiveness skills.

FRAT2
Association Retravailler Franche-Comte
  74 Grande Rue
  25000 BESANCON
Contact: Janine Pfauvadel
Course: Assertiveness for Women
☐ Practical workshops and small group sessions for women interested in examining behaviour and methods of communication; aimed at developing assertiveness skills.

FRAT3
CIDFF du Lot
  50 rue St Urcisse
  4600 CAHORS
Contact: Anne-Marie Gerschel
Course: Assertiveness for Women
☐ Practical workshops and small group sessions for women interested in examining behaviour and methods of communication; aimed at developing assertiveness skills.

FRAT4

ESSOR
  76 allées J. Jaures
  31071 TOULOUSE
Contact: Michel Roquelaine
Course: Assertiveness for Women
☐ Practical workshops and small group sessions for women interested in examining behaviour and methods of communication; aimed at developing assertiveness skills.

FRAT5

Racine
  211 av. Jean Jaures
  75019 PARIS
Contact: Fernanda Mora
Course: Assertiveness for Women
☐ Practical workshops and small group sessions for women interested in examining behaviour and methods of communication; aimed at developing assertiveness skills.

Germany

GERAT1

Institut für Sozialpädagogik
  Sekr ER 15
  Life
  Strasse des 17. Juni 112
  1000 BERLIN 12
Contact: Michaela Znava
Course: Women's Assertiveness
☐ Vocational training aimed at assisting women in developing assertiveness skills.

Great Britain and Northern Ireland

GBAT1

The Act Consultancy
  25 Broomwood Road
  LONDON SW11 6HU
☎ 071 223 5620
Contact: Fiona Adamson
Course: Assertiveness Training for Women
☐ Examines the difference in passive, aggressive and assertive behaviour. Encourages the development of appropriate communication skills.

GBAT2ⁱ

Arbee Marketing Communication Training
  31 Kilmorie Road
  Forest Hill
  LONDON SE23 2SS
☎ 081 291 0884
Contact: Ruffo Bravette

Course: Assertiveness Training
☐ Examines the differences in passive, aggressive and assertive behaviour; develops appropriate responses and skills.

GBAT3

Beck Associates
  185 Lord Street
  HODDESDON EN11 8NQ
☎ 0992 464966
Contact: Jane Beck
Course: Personal Effectiveness: Assertiveness Training
☐ Examines appropriate forms of assertive behaviour for a variety of workplace and domestic situations.

GBAT4

Bilston Community College
  Springvale House
  Millfields Road
  WOLVERHAMPTON WV14 0QR
☎ 0902 493065
Contact: Alan Leivesley
Course: Assertiveness for Women
☐ Course helps to develop assertiveness for women and enables participants to apply skills in a range of situations.

GBAT5

Boxclever Presentation Training
  25 Bewdley Street
  LONDON N1 1HB
☎ 071 607 5766
Course: Assertiveness Training
☐ Course examines different forms of communication and behaviour, and encourages participants to identify and alter their own behaviour to cope better with possible areas of conflict.

GBAT6

Bridge
  Sulgrave Hall Village Centre
  Manor Road
  WASHINGTON NE38 3BJ
☎ 091 417 2445
Course: Confidence Building
☐ Course examines a range of techniques for building confidence and handling difficult situations more effectively.

GBAT7

Cambridge Women's Resources Centre
  Hooper Street
  CAMBRIDGE CB1 2NZ
☎ 0223 321148
Course: Assertiveness for Women

☐ Practical workshops and small group sessions for women interested in examining behaviour and methods of communication; aimed at developing assertiveness skills.

GBAT8

Carol Baxter
126 Eccles Old Road
Salford
MANCHESTER M6 8QQ
☎ 061 736 2654
Contact: Carol Baxter
Course: Assertiveness for Women
☐ Examines different methods of communication, and aims to develop appropriate assertive responses to a variety of situations.

GBAT9

Change Management Consultancy
PO Box 28
KENILWORTH CV8 2UW
☎ 0926 52636
Contact: Mr. Harinda Bahra
Course: Assertiveness Training
☐ This course is part of Change Consultancy's Human Relations programme. It includes an analysis of behavioural forms and appropriate types of response for a range of workplace and domestic situations.

GBAT10

Cobar Group Training Consultancy
Hillcrest House
104 Erlanger Road, Telegraph Hill
LONDON SE14 5TH
☎ 071 639 8547
Contact: Kate Cobb
Course: Assertion
☐ Course examines all aspects of behaviour and encourages participants to apply assertive responses to appropriate workplace and domestic situations.

GBAT11

Coranberg Associates
Ardfern
ARGYLL PA31 8QN
☎ 08525 249
Contact: Tricia Bloomfield
Course: Assertiveness
☐ Course includes an analysis of appropriate assertive skills which can be applied in the workplace, with family and friends and in the community.

GBAT12

Cunningham Consultancy
40 St Johns Avenue
BRENTWOOD CM14 5DG
☎ 0277 220269

Contact: Lynne Cunningham
Course: Self-Exploration and Assertiveness Training
☐ Examines all aspects of behaviour to encourage participants to enhance their communication skills and self-esteem.

GBAT13

The Domino Consultancy Ltd
56 Charnwood Road
SHEPSHED LE12 9NP
☎ 0509 505404
Contact: Mrs Pauline Hicks
Course: Assertiveness at Work
☐ This course is held as part of the Women's Management Development workshops. It includes an analysis of the theory of assertiveness and methods of putting it into practice.

GBAT14

ETAS
Alfred Street
Aston
BIRMINGHAM B6 7NR
☎ 021 327 2761
Contact: Christine Brain
Course: Assertiveness Training
☐ Courses held at the Women's Job Change venue and at Bournville College. Aimed at non-waged women.

GBAT15

Excel International Ltd
Excel House
35 Lind Road
SUTTON SM1 4PP
☎ 081 770 0465
Contact: Nancy Paul
Course: Assertiveness Training
☐ Course covers assertive skills for women and men, and enables participants to apply skills acquired in workplace and domestic situations.

GBAT16

Genesis
15 Redriff Close
MAIDENHEAD SL6 4DJ
☎ 0628 776174
Course: Assertiveness
☐ A women's partnership company which provides training courses and consultancy to individual women or women's groups to develop enhanced communication abilities.

GBAT17

The Industrial Society
48 Bryanston Square
LONDON W1H 7LN
☎ 071 262 2401

Contact: Gina King
Course: Positive Action Training: Assertiveness
☐ Course covers the reasons for different forms of behaviour, and encourages participants to develop increased confidence and skills in dealing with difficult situations in workplace.

GBAT18

Jackie Summers
   44 Holdenby Road
   LONDON SE4 2DA
☎   081 692 4089
Contact: Jackie Summers
Course: Assertion Training and Voice Work
☐ Courses are designed to assist participants to increase self-confidence and the ability to cope with difficult situations and handle areas of conflict. All behavioural types examined.

GBAT19

Kim Pearl
   94 Fairfax Road
   TEDDINGTON TW11 9BX
☎   081 977 7116
Contact: Kim Pearl
Course: Assertiveness Training
☐ Course covers all the elements of passive, assertive and aggressive behaviour, and develops the ability of participants to improve their own responses to difficult situations.

GBAT20

Liz Fletcher Life Skills
   119 Meadow Lane
   Chaddesden
   DERBY DE21 6PA
☎   0332 666312
Contact: Liz Fletcher
Course: Assertiveness Training
☐ Course covers a range of subjects which focus on self-help for participants to identify and improve their communication with others in domestic and work situations.

GBAT21

L. Olufemi Hughes
   4 Westhill Street
   BRIGHTON BN1 3RR
☎   0273 23524
Contact: L. Olufemi Hughes
Course: Assertion and Negotiation
☐ Course covers the methods of improving communication and becoming increasingly effective in individual or group situations, and confidence building.

GBAT22

Myrtle Berman
   2 Hillside
   Highgate Road
   LONDON NW5 1QT
☎   071 485 7482
Contact: Myrtle Berman
Course: Assertiveness
☐ Develops assertiveness. Course is set within the context of promoting equality of opportunity.

GBAT23

Northern Assertion Trainers (NAT)
   28 Lucknow Drive
   SUTTON IN ASHFIELD NG17 4LS
☎   0623 558415
Course: Assertion Training
☐ Course covers the range of behaviours exhibited in people, and takes into full account the skills required to handle communication more effectively through assertive responses.

GBAT24

Nottingham Women's Centre
   30 Chaucer St
   NOTTINGHAM NG1 5LP
☎   0602 240041
Contact: Jo Fraser
Course: Assertiveness Training
☐ The Centre runs a series of five short courses: open to all women; lesbian only; black women only; for differently abled women; and for young women.

GBAT25

Pamela Brown Associates Ltd
   4 Foxhill Gardens
   Upper Norwood
   LONDON SE19 2XB
☎   081 768 0533
Contact: Pam Brown
Course: Assertion
☐ Course looks at understanding behaviour, building confidence and self-esteem and communicating better in everyday situations.

GBAT26

Positive Feedback
   Studio 5, Beech Hall Centre
   Nursery Road
   HIGH BEECH
   Essex
☎   0279 410313
Contact: Laura Mellor
Course: Assertiveness at Work
☐ Courses designed to client's specifications and run in-house. External and residential venues available.

GBAT27

Prism – Management and Skills Training
The Lodge
Hawthorne Way
CAMBRIDGE CB4 1BT
☎ 0223 67999
Course: Assertiveness
☐ Assertiveness training provided to groups of different sizes to enable participants to identify strengths and weaknesses in their own behaviour and the behaviour of others.

GBAT28

Rachel Snee
41 Vivian Road
SHEFFIELD S5 6WJ
☎ 0742 562252
Contact: Rachael Snee
Course: Assertiveness Training
☐ Courses examine all of the issues which prevent and create barriers to effective assertive two-way communication.

GBAT29

Redwood Women's Training Association
5 Spennithorne Road
Skellow
DONCASTER DN6 8PF
☎ 0302 337151
Course: Assertiveness Training
☐ Organises and conducts training in all aspects of assertiveness.

GBAT30

Reena Bhavnani
157 Brooke Road
LONDON E5 8AG
☎ 081 806 9267
Contact: Reena Bhavnani
Course: Assertion
☐ Examines the appropriate use of different types of behaviour in a whole range of workplace and domestic situations.

GBAT31

Sandra Benjamin
102 Kings Hall Road
BECKENHAM BR3 1LN
☎ 081 658 2211
Contact: Sandra Benjamin
Course: Assertiveness Training
☐ Looks at the methods of identifying and differentiating between passive, assertive and aggressive behaviour, to help to develop assertive skills for self-development.

GBAT32

Staff Development Consultant
5 Trefelin Cottages
Llandegai
BANGOR LL57 4LH
☎ 0248 364147
Contact: Jean Hodder
Course: Assertion Training
☐ Course is run as part of the organisation's positive action programme. Encourages participants to identify assertive behaviour and take control of their own responses in a variety of situations.

GBAT33

Sue Cordingley
'Old Lakenham'
Pickering Street
Loose
MAIDSTONE
Kent
☎ 0622 747232
Contact: Sue Cordingley
Course: Assertiveness in Meetings
☐ Emphasis on recognising and developing assertive behaviour.

GBAT34

Women's Education Project
129 University Street
BELFAST B17 1HP
☎ 0232 230212
Contact: Geraldine Burns
Course: Assertiveness Training
☐ Course held at Newhill Youth & Community Centre.

Israel

ISRAT1

Israel Women's Network
14 Hatibonim Street
JERUSALEM
Contact: Prof. Alice Shalvi
Course: Assertiveness for Women
☐ Practical workshops and small group sessions for women interested in examining behaviour and methods of communication; aimed at developing assertiveness skills.

Netherlands

NETAT1

Annie van Dieren School
Wilhelminapark 55
5041 ED TILBURG
☎ 013 36 26 95

Course: Women's Assertiveness
☐ Workshops covering all aspects of assertiveness training for women.

NETAT2

Emancipatieraad
Lutherse Burgwal 10
2512 CB THE HAGUE
Contact: Frank Boddendijk
Course: Assertiveness for Women
☐ Practical workshops and small group sessions for women interested in examining behaviour and methods of communication; aimed at developing assertiveness skills.

NETAT3

Lena de Graaf School
Kon. Emmakade 119
2518 JJ THE HAGUE
☎ 070 363 59 63
Course: Assertiveness Training for Women
☐ Short courses covering all aspects of assertiveness for women.

New Zealand

NZAT1

Jolisa
c/o UCSA
90 llam road
CHRISTCHURCH
Course: Assertiveness for Women
☐ Practical workshops and small group sessions for women interested in examining behaviour and methods of communication; aimed at developing assertiveness skills.

NZAT2

National Advisory Council on the Employment of Women (NACE)
c/o Dept of Labour
Private Bag
WELLINGTON
Course: Assertiveness for Women
☐ Practical workshops and small group sessions for women interested in examining behaviour and methods of communication; aimed at developing assertiveness skills.

South Korea

SKAT1

Korean Women's Development Institute
CPO Box 2267
SEOUL 100

Course: Assertiveness for Women
☐ Practical workshops and small group sessions for women interested in examining behaviour and methods of communication; aimed at developing assertiveness skills.

Switzerland

SWIAT1

Centre for Human Rights
United Nations Office
Palais des Nations
1211 GENEVA 10
Course: Assertiveness for Women
☐ Practical workshops and small group sessions for women interested in examining behaviour and methods of communication; aimed at developing assertiveness skills.

SWIAT2

Femmedia
Klosterberg 19
4051 BASEL
☎ 061 272 03 23
Contact: Anita Fetz
Course: Assertiveness for Women
☐ Practical workshops and small group sessions for women interested in examining behaviour and methods of communication; aimed at developing assertiveness skills.

SWIAT3

Swiss Federation for Adult Education
Oerlikonerstrasse 38
8057 ZURICH
Course: Assertiveness for Women
☐ Practical workshops and small group sessions for women interested in examining behaviour and methods of communication; aimed at developing assertiveness skills.

United States of America

USAAT1

Career Center
Hamilton College
CLINTON, NY 13323
☎ 315 859 7346
Course: Assertiveness for Women
☐ Practical workshops and small group sessions for women interested in examining behaviour and methods of communication; aimed at developing assertiveness skills.

USAAT2

Career Directions for Women
301 Crown Street
PO Box 5557
NEW HAVEN, CT 06520
☎ 203 436 8242
Course: Assertiveness for Women
☐ Practical workshops and small group sessions for women interested in examining behaviour and methods of communication; aimed at developing assertiveness skills.

USAAT3

Center for Career Planning
Mills College
OAKLAND, CA 94613
☎ 415 632 2700
Course: Assertiveness for Women
☐ Practical workshops and small group sessions for women interested in examining behaviour and methods of communication; aimed at developing assertiveness skills.

USAAT4

Center for Continuing Education for Women
Greenville Technical College
GREENVILLE, SC 29606
☎ 803 242 3170
Course: Assertiveness for Women
☐ Practical workshops and small group sessions for women interested in examining behaviour and methods of communication; aimed at developing assertiveness skills.

USAAT5

Creative Alternatives for Women
431 Old York Road
JENKINTOWN, PA 19046
☎ 215 576 5533
Course: Assertiveness for Women
☐ Practical workshops and small group sessions for women interested in examining behaviour and methods of communication; aimed at developing assertiveness skills.

USAAT6

Drake University
1158 27th Street
DES MOINES, IA 50311
☎ 515 271 2916
Course: Assertiveness for Women
☐ Practical workshops and small group sessions for women interested in examining behaviour and methods of communication; aimed at developing assertiveness skills.

USAAT7

Education Opportunity Center
University of Alaska, Anchorage
3211 Providence Avenue
Library Building, Room 103
ANCHORAGE, AK 99504
☎ 907 263 1525
Course: Assertiveness for Women
☐ Practical workshops and small group sessions for women interested in examining behaviour and methods of communication; aimed at developing assertiveness skills.

USAAT8

Everywoman Opportunity Center Inc.
1407–20 Genesee Building
1 West Genesee Street
BUFFALO, NY 14202
☎ 716 847 8850
Course: Assertiveness for Women
☐ Practical workshops and small group sessions for women interested in examining behaviour and methods of communication; aimed at developing assertiveness skills.

USAAT9

Flexible Careers
37 South Wabash Avenue, Suite 703
CHICAGO, IL 60603
☎ 312 236 6028
Course: Assertiveness for Women
☐ Practical workshops and small group sessions for women interested in examining behaviour and methods of communication; aimed at developing assertiveness skills.

USAAT10

The Next Step Career Guidance Center Inc.
PO Box 423
MANSFIELD, MA 02048
☎ 617 339 7498
Course: Assertiveness for Women
☐ Practical workshops and small group sessions for women interested in examining behaviour and methods of communication; aimed at developing assertiveness skills.

USAAT11

Options for Women
8419 Germantown Avenue
PHILADELPHIA, PA 19118
Course: Assertiveness for Women
☐ Practical workshops and small group sessions for women interested in examining behaviour and methods of communication; aimed at developing assertiveness skills.

USAAT12

Re-entry Advisory Program
San Jose State University
   Old Cafeteeria Building
   SAN JOSE, CA 95192
☎ 408 277 2188
Course: Assertiveness for Women
☐ Practical workshops and small group sessions for women interested in examining behaviour and methods of communication; aimed at developing assertiveness skills.

USAAT13

Valencia Community College
   PO Box 3028
   ORLANDO, FL 32802
☎ 305 423 4813
Course: Assertiveness for Women
☐ Practical workshops and small group sessions for women interested in examining behaviour and methods of communication; aimed at developing assertiveness skills.

USAAT14

Vistas for Women
   YWCA
   515 North Street
   WHITE PLAINS, NY 10605
☎ 914 949 6227
Course: Assertiveness for Women
☐ Practical workshops and small group sessions for women interested in examining behaviour and methods of communication; aimed at developing assertiveness skills.

USAAT15

Woman Alive! Inc.
   YWCA
   229 Ogden Street
   PO Box 1121
   HAMMOND, IN 46325
☎ 219 933 7168
Course: Assertiveness for Women
☐ Practical workshops and small group sessions for women interested in examining behaviour and methods of communication; aimed at developing assertiveness skills.

USAAT16

Women's Career Program
New York University
   11 West 42nd Street
   NEW YORK, NY 10036
☎ 212 790 1330
Course: Assertiveness for Women
☐ Practical workshops and small group sessions for women interested in examining behaviour and methods of communication; aimed at developing assertiveness skills.

USAAT17

Womanscope Inc.
   5355 Phelps Luck Drive
   COLUMBIA, MD 21045
☎ 301 997 2916
Course: Assertiveness for Women
☐ Practical workshops and small group sessions for women interested in examining behaviour and methods of communication; aimed at developing assertiveness skills.

USAAT18

Woman's Way
   710 C Street, Suite 1
   SAN RAFAEL, CA 94901
☎ 415 453 4490
Course: Assertiveness for Women
☐ Practical workshops and small group sessions for women interested in examining behaviour and methods of communication; aimed at developing assertiveness skills.

USAAT19

Women's Career Information Center
Middlesex County College
   Woodbridge Avenue, West Hall Annex
   EDISON, NJ 08817
☎ 201 548 6000
Course: Assertiveness for Women
☐ Practical workshops and small group sessions for women interested in examining behaviour and methods of communication; aimed at developing assertiveness skills.

USAAT20

Women's Center for Continuing Education
Northern Michigan University
   MARQUETTE, MI 49855
☎ 906 227 2219
Course: Assertiveness for Women
☐ Practical workshops and small group sessions for women interested in examining behaviour and methods of communication; aimed at developing assertiveness skills.

USAAT21

Women's Network Inc.
   Suite 502
   Peoples Federal Building
   39 E, Market St
   AKRON, OH 44308
☎ 216 376 7852
Course: Assertiveness for Women

☐ Practical workshops and small group sessions for women interested in examining behaviour and methods of communication; aimed at developing assertiveness skills.

USAAT22

Women's Programs
County College of Morris
Route 10 and Center Grove Road
RANDOLPH, NJ 07801
☎ 201 361 5000
Course: Assertiveness for Women
☐ Practical workshops and small group sessions for women interested in examining behaviour and methods of communication; aimed at developing assertiveness skills.

USAAT23

Women's Programs
Armarillo College
PO Box 447
ARMARILLO, TX 79178
☎ 806 376 5111
Course: Assertiveness for Women
☐ Practical workshops and small group sessions for women interested in examining behaviour and methods of communication; aimed at developing assertiveness skills.

USAAT24

Women's Resource Center
226 Bostick NE
GRAND RAPIDS, MI 49503
☎ 616 456 8571
Course: Assertiveness for Women
☐ Practical workshops and small group sessions for women interested in examining behaviour and methods of communication; aimed at developing assertiveness skills.

USAAT25

Women's Resource Center
University of Richmond
RICHMOND, VA 23173
☎ 804 285 6316
Course: Assertiveness for Women
☐ Practical workshops and small group sessions for women interested in examining behaviour and methods of communication; aimed at developing assertiveness skills.

USAAT26

The Women's Resource Service
University of Missouri, Kansas City
5325 Rockhill Road
KANSAS CITY, MO 64110
☎ 816 276 1442

Course: Assertiveness for Women
☐ Practical workshops and small group sessions for women interested in examining behaviour and methods of communication; aimed at developing assertiveness skills.

Uruguay

URUAT1

Ministerio de Education y Cultura
Instituto de la Mujer
Reconguista 535 P.8
MONTEVIDEO
Course: Assertiveness for Women
☐ Practical workshops and small group sessions for women interested in examining behaviour and methods of communication; aimed at developing assertiveness skills.

Equal Opportunities

Australia

AUSEO1

Affirmative Action Agency
1st Floor, The Denison
65 Berry Street
PO Box 974
NORTH SYDNEY, NSW 2060
☎ 02 957 4333
Course: Equal Opportunities for Women
☐ Research and training aimed at enhancing equality of opportunity for women.

AUSEO2

BIR
PO Box 659
CARLTON, Vic. 3053
☎ 03 342 1100
Course: Equal Opportunities for Women
☐ Research and training aimed at enhancing equality of opportunity for women.

AUSEO3

CAPERS
PO Box 567
NUNDAH, Qld 4012
☎ 07 266 9573
Contact: Jan Cornfoot
Course: Equal Opportunities for Women
☐ Research and training aimed at enhancing equality of opportunity for women.

AUSEO4

EEO Policy and Programs Unit
PSC
Edmund Barton Building
BARTON, ACT 2600
☎ 06 272 3562
Course: Equal Opportunities for Women
☐ Research and training aimed at enhancing equality of opportunity for women.

AUSEO5

Family Planning
100 Alfred St
FORTITUDE VALLEY, Qld 4006
☎ 07 252 5168
Course: Equal Opportunities for Women
☐ Research and training aimed at enhancing equality of opportunity for women.

AUSEO6

National Women's Consultative Council
3–5 National Circuit
BARTON, ACT 2600
☎ 06 271 5723
Course: Equal Opportunities for Women
☐ Research and training aimed at enhancing equality of opportunity for women.

AUSEO7

Shrill
PO Box 303
CAMPERDOWN, NSW 2050
☎ 02 557 1955
Course: Equal Opportunities for Women
☐ Research and training aimed at enhancing equality of opportunity for women.

AUSEO8

Zig Zag
575 Old Cleveland Road
CAMP HILL, Qld 4152
☎ 07 843 1823
Course: Equal Opportunities for Women
☐ Research and training aimed at enhancing equality of opportunity for women.

Austria

AUEO1

The Branch for the Advancement of Women
PO Box 500
1400 VIENNA
Course: Equal Opportunities for Women
☐ Research and training aimed at enhancing equality of opportunity for women.

AUEO2

Centre for Women's Research
Wahringerstrasse 59
1090 VIENNA
Course: Women's Issues and Equal Opportunities
☐ Courses and seminars arranged on topics of interest to women

Belgium

BELEO1
ARGO
Regentlaan 40
1000 BRUSSELS
Contact: G. Van De Velde
Course: Equal Opportunities for Women
☐ Research and training aimed at enhancing equality of opportunity for women.

BELEO2
Association rue Blanche
ASBL
29 rue Blanche
1050 BRUSSELS
Contact: Nicole Samyn
Course: Equal Opportunities for Women
☐ Research and training aimed at enhancing equality of opportunity for women.

BELEO3
Les Cahiers du Grif
29 rue Blanche
1050 BRUSSELS
Contact: Veronique Degraef
Course: Equal Opportunities for Women
☐ Research and training aimed at enhancing equality of opportunity for women.

BELEO4
CGSP
44 rue de la Buanderie
1000 BRUSSELS
Contact: Francie Dekoninck
Course: Equal Opportunities for Women
☐ Research and training aimed at enhancing equality of opportunity for women.

BELEO5
Comité de Liaison des Femmes
1/a Place Quételet
1030 BRUSSELS
☎ 02 219 28 02
Course: Equal Opportunities for Women
☐ Courses and seminars arranged on topics of interest to members.

BELEO6
Commissariat Royal à l'Immigration
Résidence Palace
155 rue de la Loi
1040 BRUSSELS
Contact: Godelieve Vandamme
Course: Equal Opportunities for Women
☐ Research and training aimed at enhancing equality of opportunity for women.

BELEO7
Commissie Vrouwenarbeid
Belliardstraat 51
1040 BRUSSELS
Contact: Annemie Pernot
Course: Equal Opportunities for Women
☐ Research and training aimed at enhancing equality of opportunity for women.

BELEO8
Commissie Vrouwenarbeid
Gom Limburg
Kunstlaan 18
3500 HASSELT
Contact: Nicole Schoefs
Course: Equal Opportunities for Women
☐ Research and training aimed at enhancing equality of opportunity for women.

BELEO9
Commission des Affaires Sociales
Kortrijkstraat 171
8520 KUURNE
Contact: Paul Vangansbeke
Course: Equal Opportunities for Women
☐ Research and training aimed at enhancing equality of opportunity for women.

BELEO10
Crew
21 rue de la Tourelle
1040 BRUSSELS
☎ 02 230 51 58
Course: Equal Opportunities in Employment and Training
☐ Arranges training and conducts research into equality for women in employment and training.

BELEO11
Documentatiecentrum Rosa
Gallaitstraat 78
1210 BRUSSELS
Contact: Renee Van Mecheelen
Course: Equal Opportunities for Women
☐ Research and training aimed at enhancing equality of opportunity for women.

BELEO12
Equal Opportunities Unit
European Commission
200 rue de la Loi
1049 BRUSSELS
Contact: Helle Jacobson
Course: Equal Opportunities for Women
☐ Research and training aimed at enhancing equality of opportunity for women.

BELEO13
Equal Opportunities Unit
European Commission
200, rue de la Loi
1049 BRUSSELS
Contact: Margarida Pinto
Course: Equal Opportunities and Positive Action for Women
☐ Research and training aimed at increasing equal opportunities for women.

BELEO14
European Women's Lobby
22 rue de Meridien
1030 BRUSSELS
☎ 02 217 90 20
Course: Equal Opportunities
☐ Courses and seminars on subjects of interest to women

BELEO15
Febelgra
Belliardstraat 20, bus 16
1040 BRUSSELS
Contact: D. Salens
Course: Equal Opportunities for Women
☐ Research and training aimed at enhancing equality of opportunity for women.

BELEO16
FEMB–OBMB
Rue Gachardstraat 88
1050 BRUSSELS
Contact: Jacques Verstraeten
Course: Equal Opportunities for Women
☐ Research and training aimed at enhancing equality of opportunity for women.

BELEO17
FGTB
42 rue Haute
1000 BRUSSELS
Contact: Anne Tricot
Course: Equal Opportunities for Women
☐ Research and training aimed at enhancing equality of opportunity for women.

BELEO18
FGTB Regionale Liège Huy – Waremme
9–11 place St Paul
4000 LIEGE
Contact: Laurette Witsel
Course: Equal Opportunities for Women
☐ Research and training aimed at enhancing equality of opportunity for women.

BELEO19
FOREM
5 boulevard de l'Empereur
1000 BRUSSELS
Contact: Raymond Delbrouck
Course: Equal Opportunities for Women
☐ Research and training aimed at enhancing equality of opportunity for women.

BELEO20
FOREM
21 rue de Wallonnie 21
4460 GRACE HOLLAGNE
Contact: Anne Sokol
Course: Equal Opportunities for Women
☐ Research and training aimed at enhancing equality of opportunity for women.

BELEO21
Frederique Deroure
47 rue Van Aa
1050 BRUSSELS
Contact: Frederique Deroure
Course: Equal Opportunities for Women
☐ Research and training aimed at enhancing equality of opportunity for women.

BELEO22
G. Desiront Febelgra
Belliardstraat 20, bus 16
1040 BRUSSELS
Contact: G. Desiront Febelgra
Course: Equal Opportunities for Women
☐ Research and training aimed at enhancing equality of opportunity for women.

BELEO23
Institut de Formation Professionnelle Alimentation
709 chaussée de Mons
1600 LEEUW SAINT-PIERRE
Contact: Sonia Tkac
Course: Equal Opportunities for Women
☐ Research and training aimed at enhancing equality of opportunity for women.

BELEO24
Institut Provincial des Classes Moyenne
Euro Info Centre
Bd d'Avroy 28/30
4000 LIEGE
Contact: Monique Roover
Course: Equal Opportunities for Women
☐ Research and training aimed at enhancing equality of opportunity for women.

BELEO25

IRFEC Europe
Avenue Winston Churchill
119/16
1180 BRUSSELS
Contact: Elisabeth Van Stalle
Course: Equal Opportunities for Women
☐ Research and training aimed at enhancing equality of opportunity for women.

BELEO26

Kabinet Onderwijs Cel.ESF
Arcadengebouw Blok F
6de Verdieping
1010 BRUSSELS
Contact: Ingrid Snel
Course: Equal Opportunities for Women
☐ Research and training aimed at enhancing equality of opportunity for women.

BELEO27

Ministère de l'Intérieur et de la Formation Publique
15 rue du Gouvernement
1000 BRUSSELS
Contact: M. Verhaegen
Course: Equal Opportunities for Women
☐ Research and training aimed at enhancing equality of opportunity for women.

BELEO28

Ministerie of Lewerkstelling & Arbeid
Belliardstraat 51
1040 BRUSSELS
Contact: Eddy Schelstraete
Course: Equal Opportunities for Women
☐ Research and training aimed at enhancing equality of opportunity for women.

BELEO29

National Vrouwen Raad
De Meeussquare 28
0140 BRUSSELS
☎ 02 511 82 43
Course: Equal Opportunities for Women
☐ Arranges courses and seminars on subjects of interest to members.

BELEO30

Omschakelen VZW
Mubreidmstraat 498
2600 BERCHEM
Contact: Rita Ruys
Course: Equal Opportunities for Women
☐ Research and training aimed at enhancing equality of opportunity for women.

BELEO31

Parti Féministe Humaniste
(Parti Féministe Unifié)
Avenue des Phalenes 35 bte 14
1050 IXELLES
☎ 02 648 87 38
Course: Equality for Women
☐ Political party; arranges seminars and discussion groups on subjects of interest to women.

BELEO32

PME
1 rue des Halles
1000 BRUSSELS
Contact: Eliane Puleston
Course: Equal Opportunities for Women
☐ Research and training aimed at enhancing equality of opportunity for women.

BELEO33

Porte Ouverte
16 rue Americaine
1050 BRUSSELS
Course: Equal Opportunities for Women
☐ Seminars and workshops arranged on subjects of interest to members.

BELEO34

Samenwerkingsverband
Strategisch Plan Kempen
Grote Markt 23
2300 TURNHOUT
Contact: Linda Stynen
Course: Equal Opportunities for Women
☐ Research and training aimed at enhancing equality of opportunity for women.

BELEO35

SETA-UITA
3 rue Fosse aux Loups Bte
1000 BRUSSELS
Contact: Betty Samola
Course: Equal Opportunities for Women
☐ Research and training aimed at enhancing equality of opportunity for women.

BELEO36

Socialistische Vrouwen
Keizerslaan 13
1000 BRUSSELS
☎ 02 513 28 78
Course: Equal Opportunities for Women
☐ Political group; arranges seminars and discussion groups on subjects of interest to members.

BELEO37
STD Hasselt
 Thonissenlaan 47
 3500 HASSELT
Contact: M. Wastiels
Course: Equal Opportunities for Women
☐ Research and training aimed at enhancing equality of opportunity for women.

BELEO38
ULB – INFODOC
 50 avenue F. Roosvelt CP 142
 1050 BRUSSELS
Contact: Josiane Roelants
Course: Equal Opportunities for Women
☐ Research and training aimed at enhancing equality of opportunity for women.

BELEO39
Unité pour l'Egalité des Chances CEE
 200 rue de la Loi
 1049 BRUSSELS
Contact: Michele Tierlinck
Course: Equal Opportunities for Women
☐ Research and training aimed at enhancing equality of opportunity for women.

BELEO40
VDAB
 Keizerslaan 11
 1000 BRUSSELS
Contact: Johan Van Oost
Course: Equal Opportunities for Women
☐ Research and training aimed at enhancing equality of opportunity for women.

BELEO41
VDAB
 Keizerslaan 11
 1000 BRUSSELS
Contact: Hilde Van Praet
Course: Equal Opportunities for Women
☐ Research and training aimed at enhancing equality of opportunity for women.

BELEO42
Vrouwen Overleg Komitee
 Gallaitsraat 78
 1210 BRUSSELS
Course: Equal Opportunities and Feminism
☐ Pressure group: organises seminars and debates on feminist issues.

BELEO43
Women's Information Service
 European Commission
 200 rue de la Loi
 1049 BRUSSELS
☎ 02 2346111
Course: Equal Opportunities and Information for Women
☐ European-based newsletter for women; collects and disseminates information on women's training events.

BELEO44
Wonen en Werken
 Valkery Gang 26
 3000 LEUVEN
Contact: Julia Rottiers
Course: Equal Opportunities for Women
☐ Research and training aimed at enhancing equality of opportunity for women.

Bulgaria

BULEO1
Democratic Union of Women in Bulgaria
 BD Patriarche Evtimi 82
 SOFIA 1463
Course: Equal Opportunities for Women
☐ Arranges courses and seminars on topics of interest to members.

Canada

CANEO1
The Canadian Advisory Council on the Status of Women
 151 Sparks Street, Box 1541, Station B
 OTTAWA K1P 5R5
☎ 613 992 4975
Course: Equal Opportunities for Women
☐ Research and training aimed at enhancing equality of opportunity for women.

CANEO2
The Canadian Advisory Council on the Status of Women
 269 Main Street, Suite 600
 Winnipeg
 MANITOBA R3C 1B2
☎ 204 949 3140
Course: Equal Opportunities for Women
☐ Research and training aimed at enhancing equality of opportunity for women.

CANEO3

Ontario Women's Directorate
480 University Ave
2nd Floor
Toronto
ONTARIO M5G 1V2
Course: Equal Opportunities for Women
☐ Research and training aimed at enhancing equality of opportunity for women.

CANEO4

OWD
107C Johnson Ave
Thunder Bay
ONTARIO P7B 2V9
Course: Equal Opportunities for Women
☐ Research and training aimed at enhancing equality of opportunity for women.

CANEO5

The Pay Equity Commission
150 Eglinton Avenue East
5th Floor
Toronto
ONTARIO M4P 1E8
Course: Equal Opportunities for Women
☐ Research and training aimed at enhancing equality of opportunity for women.

Denmark

DENEO1

Afdelingsleder
Arbejdsformidlingen
Faelledvej 3
8800 VIBORG
Contact: Margit Bjerre
Course: Equal Opportunities for Women
☐ Research and training to enhance equality of opportunity for women.

DENEO2

AMS
Hejrevej 43
2400 COPENHAGEN NV
Contact: Dorte Cohr Lutzen
Course: Equal Opportunities for Women
☐ Research and training aimed at enhancing equality of opportunity for women.

DENEO3

AMU-center
Brovangen 2
3720 AKIRKEBY
Contact: Britta Keler
Course: Equal Opportunities for Women

☐ Research and training aimed at enhancing equality of opportunity for women.

DENEO4

Arbejdsformidlingen
Dannebrogsgade 3
5000 ODENSE
Contact: Anne Marie Jacobsen
Course: Equal Opportunities for Women
☐ Research and training aimed at enhancing equality of opportunity for women.

DENEO5

Arhus Universitet
8000 ARHUS
Contact: Drude Dahlerup
Course: Equal Opportunities for Women
☐ Research and training aimed at enhancing equality of opportunity for women.

DENEO6

CEKVINA
(Women's Research Centre in Arhus)
University of Arhus
Finlandsgade 26
8200 ARHUS N
☎ 06 16 58 55
Contact: Elisabeth Flensted-Jensen
Course: Equality for Women
☐ Training and research aimed at increasing women's equality.

DENEO7

Center for Samfunds-Videnskabelig Kvindeforskning
(Women's Research Center in Social Science)
Adelgade 49 St.tv
1304 COPENHAGEN K
☎ 01 12 23 14
Contact: Else Christensen
Course: Equality for Women
☐ Research and training aimed at enhancing women's equality.

DENEO8

The Centre for Feminist Research and Women's Studies
The University of Copenhagen – Amager
Njalsgade 106
2300 COPENHAGEN S
☎ 01 54 22 11
Contact: Bente Rosenbeck
Course: Equal Opportunities for Women
☐ Feminist research and women's studies centre; training sessions aimed at maximising commitment to greater equality for women.

DENEO9

Centre for Feminist Research
University of Copenhagen
Njalsgade 106
2300 COPENHAGEN S
☎ 45 31 22 11
Course: Feminism and Equal Opportunities
□ Advice and training organisation.

DENEO10

Danske Kvinders Nationalrad
Niels Hemmingsensgade 10, 2
1153 COPENHAGEN K
☎ 33 12 80 87
Course: Equal Opportunities for Women
□ National Council of Women; arranges seminars and courses of interest to members.

DENEO11

Else Hansen
Sanatorievej 25
7140 STOUBY
Contact: Else Hansen
Course: Equal Opportunities for Women
□ Research and training aimed at enhancing equality of opportunity for women.

DENEO12

Forum for Kvindeforskning ved Danmarks Laerer-Hojskole
(The Forum for Feminist Research)
Emdrupvej 101
2400 COPENHAGEN NV
☎ 01 69 66 33 ext. 244
Contact: Ingeborg Appel
Course: Equality for Women
□ Research and training aimed at enhancing women's equality.

DENEO13

Gruppen for Medicinsk Kvindeforskning
(Feminist Research in Medicine)
Institute of Social Medicine
Panum Institute, Blegdamsvej 3
2200 COPENHAGEN N
☎ 01 35 79 00
Contact: Birgit Petersson
Course: Equality for Women
□ Research and training aimed at enhancing women's equality.

DENEO14

Gruppen for Medicinsk Kvindeforskning pa Fyn
(Feminist Research in Medicine)
The Institute of Community Health
Odense University, J. B. Winslowsvej 17
5000 ODENSE C

☎ 09 15 86 00 ext. 493
Contact: Inger Schaumburg
Course: Equality for Women in Medicine and Social Sciences
□ Research and training aimed at enhancing women's equality in health and social sciences.

DENEO15

Horsens EDB-Center
Tobaksgarden 10
8700 HORSENS
Contact: Inger Lindhardt
Course: Equal Opportunities for Women
□ Research and training aimed at enhancing equality of opportunity for women.

DENEO16

KIMADAN
Nordvestvej 4
9600 ARS
Contact: Nina Ostergard
Course: Equal Opportunities for Women
□ Research and training aimed at enhancing equality of opportunity for women.

DENEO17

Kommunikations-og
Servicecenter
Vejlevej 18
7300 JELLING
Contact: Anders Hess
Course: Equal Opportunities for Women
□ Research and training aimed at enhancing equality of opportunity for women.

DENEO18

KVIL – Kurser i Vejle
Borgvold 6
7100 VEJLE
Contact: Inge Skotte Henriksen
Course: Equal Opportunities for Women
□ Research and training to enhance equality of opportunity for women.

DENEO19

Kvindeforum
(The Centre of Feminist Research)
University of Aalborg
Fibigerstraede 2
9220 AALBORG 0
☎ 08 15 85 22
Course: Equality for Women
□ Research and training aimed at increasing support and commitment to women's equality.

DENEO20

Kvindegruppen ved Danmarks Forvaltningshojskolf
(The Women's Group of Public Administration)
Lindevangs Alle 6
2000 FREDERIKSBERG
☎ 01 86 18 70
Contact: Gitte Haslebo
Course: Equal Opportunities for Women
☐ Training and consultancy aimed at improving women's influence and career possibilities.

DENEO21

Kvindehistorisk Samling
(Women's History Archive)
The State Library
Universitetsparken
8000 AARHUS C
☎ 06 12 20 22 ext. 31
Contact: Britta Skovgaard
Course: Equality for Women
☐ Workshops and discussion groups arranged on subjects of interest to women involved in the women's history archive.

DENEO22

Kvindeligt Arbejderforbund
Ewaldsgade 3-9
2200 COPENHAGEN N
Contact: Birte Kaiser
Course: Equal Opportunities for Women
☐ Research and training aimed at enhancing equality of opportunity for women.

DENEO23

Kvindeligt Arbejderforbund
Kirkestraede
3730 NEKS 0
Contact: Britta Bergh Jensen
Course: Equal Opportunities for Women
☐ Research and training aimed at enhancing equality of opportunity for women.

DENEO24

Kvindeligt Arbejderforbund
Ewaldsgade 3-9
2200 COPENHAGEN N
☎ 31 39 31 15
Course: Equal Opportunities for Women
☐ Women's union; arranges courses and seminars on subjects of interest to members.

DENEO25

Kvindemuseet i Danmark
(The Women's Museum in Denmark)
Domkirkeplads 5
8000 AARHUS C

☎ 06 13 69 79
Course: Equality for Women
☐ Projects aimed at enhancing women's equality.

DENEO26

Kvinder pa Tvaers
(The Feminist Research Center)
House 03.2.5
Roskilde University Centre
P.O. Box 260
4000 ROSKILDE
☎ 02 75 77 11 ext. 255
Contact: Karen Sjorup
Course: Equality for Women
☐ Research and training aimed at enhancing women's equality.

DENEO27

Kvindeudvalgetved Danmarks Tekniske Hojskole
(The Women's Committee)
The Technical University of Denmark
Studiekontoret, Building 101
2800 LYNGBY
☎ 02 88 22 22 ext. 22
Contact: Lise Damkjaer
Course: Equality for Women: Positive Action
☐ Research and training into strategies for recruiting and involving more women in technical education and careers.

DENEO28

KVINFO
(The Centre for Information on Women's Studies)
Laederstraede 15, 2, sal
1201 COPENHAGEN K
☎ 01 13 94 73
Contact: Jytte Larsen
Course: Equality for Women
☐ Training and research aimed at enhancing women's equality.

DENEO29

KVINFO
Drabaeksvej 18
3450 ALLEROD
Contact: Leslie Larson
Course: Equal Opportunities for Women
☐ Research and training aimed at enhancing equality of opportunity for women.

DENEO30

Ligestillingskonsulent
Arbejdsformidlingen
Klosterengen 105
4000 ROSKILDE

Contact: Annelise Rasmussen
Course: Equal Opportunities for Women
☐ Research and training to enhance equality of opportunity for women.

DENEO31

Ligestillingskonsulent
  Arbejdsformidlingen
  Sonderbrogade 34
  7100 VEJLE
Contact: Mette Heinze
Course: Equal Opportunities for Women
☐ Research and training aimed at enhancing equality of opportunity for women.

DENEO32

Ligestillingskonsulent
  HK
  H. C. Andersens Boulevard 50
  1780 COPENHAGEN V
Contact: Vibeke Abel
Course: Equal Opportunities for Women
☐ Research and training to enhance equality of opportunity for women.

DENEO33

Ligestillingskonsulent
  Arbejdsformidlingen
  Ostervoldgade 4
  3700 RONNE
Contact: Vivi Statager
Course: Equal Opportunities for Women
☐ Research and training aimed at enhancing equality of opportunity for women.

DENEO34

Martin Krogh
  Hornbaekvej 58
  9270 KLARUP
Contact: Martin Krogh
Course: Equal Opportunities for Women
☐ Research and training aimed at enhancing equality of opportunity for women.

DENEO35

Plan-it APs
  Magnolivangen 56
  3450 ALLEROD
Contact: Anna Eckhoff
Course: Equal Opportunities for Women
☐ Research and training aimed at enhancing equality of opportunity for women.

DENEO36

RACU
  Vejle Amtskommune
  Damhaven 12
  7100 VEJLE
Contact: Nete Svennekaer
Course: Equal Opportunities for Women
☐ Research and training aimed at enhancing equality of opportunity for women.

DENEO37

SAMKVIND
  (The Forum for Feminist Social Studies)
  St Kannikestraede 18
  1169 COPENHAGEN K
☎ 01 91 21 66 ext. 242
Contact: Sanne Ipsen
Course: Equality for Women
☐ Training and research aimed at enhancing women's equality.

France

FREO1

AFPA Limoges Batîment
  68 rue de Babylone
  87036 LIMOGES
Contact: Lucette Chavent
Course: Equal Opportunities for Women
☐ Research and training aimed at enhancing equality of opportunity for women.

FREO2

Asprocep
  189 avenue Corot
  13014 MARSEILLE
Contact: Marie Christine Lafayette
Course: Equal Opportunities for Women
☐ Research and training aimed at enhancing equality of opportunity for women.

FREO3

Association Retravailler Franche-Comte
  74 Grand Rue
  25000 BESANCON
Contact: Janine Pfauvadel
Course: Equal Opportunities for Women
☐ Research and training aimed at enhancing equality of opportunity for women.

FREO4

CEFAP
  13 cheminement du Professeur
  Bouasse – Hameau des Violettes
  31100 TOULOUSE
Contact: M. Lambert

Course: Equal Opportunities for Women
□ Research and training aimed at enhancing equality of opportunity for women.

FREO5

Centre d'Expression Manuelle et de Créations Artistiques
Chevrey – Arcenant
21700 NUITS ST GEORGES
Contact: Marie Christine Grennerat
Course: Equal Opportunities for Women
□ Research and training aimed at enhancing equality of opportunity for women.

FREO6

CIDFF du Lot
50 rue Ste Urcisse
46000 CAHORS
Contact: Anne-Marie Gerschel
Course: Equal Opportunities for Women
□ Research and training aimed at enhancing equality of opportunity for women.

FREO7

Fédération Régionale des CIVAM Languedoc Roussillon
5 place des Docteurs Dox
30250 SOMMIERES
Contact: Roselyne Bessac
Course: Equal Opportunities for Women
□ Research and training aimed at enhancing equality of opportunity for women.

FREO8

FEN
48 rue la Bruyère
75009 PARIS
Contact: Jacqueline Laroche
Course: Equal Opportunities for Women
□ Research and training aimed at enhancing equality of opportunity for women.

FREO9

Greta du Bocage
Rue du Commandant
Charcot 37-39
61100 FLERS
Contact: Annie Rossi
Course: Equal Opportunities for Women
□ Research and training aimed at enhancing equality of opportunity for women.

FREO10

GRETA Sudisère
1 rue des Trembles
38100 GRENOBLE
Contact: A. Baloyan

Course: Equal Opportunities for Women
□ Research and training aimed at enhancing equality of opportunity for women.

FREO11

GRETA Sudisère
1 rue des Trembles
38100 GRENOBLE
Contact: M. F. Motte
Course: Equal Opportunities and Positive Action for Women
□ Research and training aimed at enhancing equality of opportunity for women.

FREO12

IFRIS
12 rue Ampère
38016 GRENOBLE
Contact: Evelyne Paye
Course: Equal Opportunities for Women
□ Research and training aimed at enhancing equality of opportunity for women.

FREO13

Retravailler
25 avenue de la Libération
45000 ORLEANS
Contact: Jocelyne Welker
Course: Equal Opportunities for Women
□ Research and training aimed at enhancing equality of opportunity for women.

FREO14

Union Féminine Civique et Sociale
6 rue Beranger
75003 PARIS
☎ 42 72 19 18
Course: Equal Opportunities for Women
□ Women's organisation; arranges discussion groups and training sessions on subjects of interest to members.

Germany

GEREO1

Deutscher Frauenrat
Simrockstrasse 5
5300 BONN 1
☎ 0228 223008
Course: Equal Opportunities for Women
□ Umbrella group; arranges courses on subjects of interest to member organisations.

GEREO2

Fraueninitiative 6 Oktober
Postfach 120 401
Kirschallee 6
5300 BONN 1
☎ 0228 216913
Course: Women's Politics and Networking
☐ Arranges courses and seminars on subjects of interest to women.

GEREO3

Terre des Femmes
PO Box 2531
7400 TUBINGEN
☎ 07071 24289
Course: Equal Opportunities and Human Rights for Women
☐ Workshops, seminars and discussion groups on subjects of interest to members.

Great Britain and Northern Ireland

GBEO1

The Act Consultancy
25 Broomwood Road
LONDON SW11 6HU
☎ 071 223 5620
Contact: Fiona Adamson
Course: Creating and Implementing an Equal Opportunities Policy
☐ Course can be run as part of a series on equal opportunities issues or as a one-off course.

GBEO2

The Act Consultancy
25 Broomwood Road
LONDON SW11 6HU
☎ 071 223 5620
Course: Counselling and Training for Equality
☐ Aims to generate commitment and stimulate greater interest in equality; emphasis on benefits of equality for majority of workforce.

GBEO3

Anti-Discrimination and Equal Opportunities Training
3 Hill Street
LEICESTER LE1 3PT
☎ ex-directory
Contact: Dr J. Owusa-Bempah
Course: Racism-Awareness
☐ Examines historical and contemporary race issues, and provides information and guidance to participants in combating racism.

GBEO4

Anti-Discrimination and Equal Opportunities Training
3 Hill Street
LEICESTER LE1 3PT
☎ ex-directory
Contact: Dr J. Owusa-Bempah
Course: Equal Opportunities
☐ Examines the law on equal opportunities and creating and implementing workplace policies and good practice.

GBEO5

Anti-Discrimination and Equal Opportunities Training
3 Hill Street
LEICESTER LE1 3PT
☎ ex-directory
Contact: Dr J. Owusu-Bempah
Course: Sexism-Awareness
☐ Examines the causes and effects of sexism, and develops methods of combating it in the workplace.

GBEO6

Arbee Marketing Communication Training
31 Kilmorie Road
Forest Hill
LONDON SE23 2SS
☎ 081 291 0884
Contact: Ruffo Bravette
Course: Equal Opportunities Programme
☐ Examines the law on equal opportunities, the duties and obligations it places on employers and employees, developing workplace policy and turning policy into practice.

GBEO7

Asian Young Women's Project
8 Manor Gardens
LONDON N7 6LZ
☎ 071 263 6270
Course: Counselling and Support
☐ One-to-one and small group workshops for young Asian women.

GBEO8

Barking College of Technology
Lymington Road
DAGENHAM
Essex
☎ 081 599 3977
Contact: Peter Evans
Course: Development of Equal Opportunities Policy
☐ Examines the methods of developing, implementing and monitoring an equal opportunities policy in large organisations.

GBEO9

Beck Associates
185 Lord Street
HODDESDON EN11 8NQ
☎ 0992 464966
Contact: Jane Beck
Course: Women and Men Working Together
☐ Brings together policy and good practice in the field of equal opportunities to encourage enhanced relationships between employees in keeping with good equality practice.

GBEO10

Bilston Community College
Springvale House
Millfields Road
WOLVERHAMPTON WV14 0QR
☎ 0902 493065
Contact: Alan Leivesley
Course: Equal Opportunities for Practice Teachers
☐ Course examines all the legislative and policy issues concerning equal opportunities which affect staff involved in education.

GBEO11

Biographic Management Ltd
High Banks
Dark Lane
Rodborough
STROUD GL5 3UF
☎ 0453 765142
Contact: Jenny Daisley
Course: Designing Training for Equality
☐ Looks at the design and implementation of a variety of training packages for developing equal opportunities in the workplace.

GBEO12

Brent Industrial Training Unit
Ashley Gardens
Preston Road
WEMBLEY HA9 8NP
☎ 081 908 1708
Contact: Tahira Khan
Course: Positive Action
☐ Examines the historical and contemporary developments within positive action measures in the UK, and considers the implementation of new programmes for different-sized organisations.

GBEO13

The Brettonwood Partnerships Ltd
Professional Management Consultants
1 Raleigh House
Admirals Way, South Quay
LONDON E14 9SN
☎ 071 538 4040

Contact: Christopher D. King
Course: Equal Opportunities and Access
☐ Course looks at issues of access to public buildings and employers' premises, and considers the importance of mobility for workers with disabilities.

GBEO14

BSD Resources Management and Training Centre
44 Himley Crescent
Goldthorn Park
WOLVERHAMPTON
WV5 5DE
☎ 0902 332827
Contact: Bhajan Davsi
Course: Anti-Racist Strategies
☐ Course is designed according to the needs of clients to create and manage change effectively in a progressive organisation.

GBEO15

Bullivant Associates
St John's Innovation Centre
Cowley Road
CAMBRIDGE CB4 4WS
☎ 0223 4211 68
Contact: Dr Susan Bullivant
Course: Sexism Awareness
☐ Course looks at the causes and effects of sexism, and enables participants to become more aware of their own behaviour and to challenge that of others.

GBEO16

Cambridge Women's Resources Centre
Hooper Street
CAMBRIDGE CB1 2NZ
☎ 0223 321148
Course: Training and Education
☐ Courses to enhance equal opportunities in employment and education for women.

GBEO17

Cambridge Women's Resources Centre
Hooper Street
CAMBRIDGE CB1 2NZ
☎ 0223 321148
Course: Equal Opportunities for Women
☐ Research and training aimed at enhancing equality of opportunity for women.

GBEO18

Cardiff Women's Centre
2 Coburn Street
Cathays
CARDIFF CF2 4BS
☎ 0222 383024
Course: Resource and Information for Women

☐ Small workshops and training sessions for women to reflect local women's interests and increase equality in the larger community.

GBEO19

Centre for Studies in Crime and Social Justice
Edge Hill College of Higher Education
St Helens Road
ORMSKIRK L39 4QP
☎ 0695 584269
Contact: Kathryn Chadwick
Course: MA in Equal Opportunities and Human Rights
☐ Part-time evening course which aims to introduce students to the historical and theoretical debates which underpin equal opportunities and the more critical theories of human rights and civil liberties.

GBEO20

Change Management Consultancy
PO Box 28
KENILWORTH CV8 2UW
☎ 0926 52636
Contact: Mr Harinder Bahra
Course: Equal Opportunities in Recruitment and Selection
☐ Examines all issues associated with good equality practice in interviewing, the design and development of application forms and selection procedures.

GBEO21

Change Management Consultancy
PO Box 28
KENILWORTH CV8 2UW
☎ 0926 52636
Contact: Mr Harinder Bahra
Course: Anti-Racist Strategies
☐ Examines the causes and effects of racism, and encourages participants to develop individual and collective methods of combating racism.

GBEO22

Change Management Consultancy
PO Box 28
KENILWORTH CV8 2UW
☎ 0926 52636
Contact: Mr Harinder Bahra
Course: Racial and Sexual Harassment Training
☐ Looks at the causes and effects of harassment in the workplace, and examines methods of combating it completely in all organisations.

GBEO23

Christopher Bull Associates
18 Berwick Road
SHREWSBURY SY1 2LN
☎ 0743 272345/6

Contact: Christopher Bull
Course: Development Programme for Policy Implementation
☐ Course is designed for all staff involved in policy development in the workplace, and examines the role of training, review and monitoring.

GBEO24

Christopher Bull Associates
18 Berwick Road
SHREWSBURY SY1 2LN
☎ 0743 272345/6
Contact: Christopher Bull
Course: Racism Awareness Programme
☐ Course develops a thorough knowledge of the historical and contemporary issues surrounding racism and race relations; it examines the cause and effects of racism in practice.

GBEO25

Civil Service College
Sunningdale Park
Larch Avenue
ASCOT SL5 0QE
☎ 0344 23444 ext. 4329
Contact: Jane Tatum
Course: Training for Trainers in Equal Opportunities
☐ Examines the issues of relevance to those involved in training and developing equal opportunities programmes for a variety of workplaces.

GBEO26

Consultant Disability Services
20 Calder Court
7 Britannia Road
SURBITON KT5 8TS
☎ 081 390 0234
Course: Disability Equality Training
☐ Examines all the issues surrounding society's prejudice against disability, and challenges disability as a charity rather than a fundamental disability rights issue.

GBEO27

Cullen, Scholefield Associates
15 Harwood Road
Fulham
LONDON SW6 4QP
☎ 071 736 6975
Contact: Carole Marshall
Course: Developing Equal Opportunities Policies
☐ Course provides assistance to organisations wanting to develop and implement effective equal opportunities policies.

GBEO28

Cunningham Consultancy
40 St Johns Avenue
BRENTWOOD CM14 5DG
☎ 0277 220269
Contact: Lynne Cunningham
Course: Equality Awareness
☐ Includes training for managers and for the development of positive action programmes.

GBEO29

Daycare Trust/National Childcare Campaign
Wesley House
4 Wild Court
LONDON WC2B 5AU
☎ 071 405 5617
Course: Affordability, Quality and Choice in Childcare
☐ Promotes the interests of parents keen to develop quality childcare services at affordable prices; occasionally runs workshops on subjects of popular interest.

GBEO30

Dept of Adult and Continuing Education
University of Ulster at Jordanstown
NEWTOWNABBEY
Co. Antrim BT37 0QB
Contact: Pauline Murphy
Course: Equal Opportunities for Women
☐ Research and training aimed at enhancing equality of opportunity for women.

GBEO31

Discovering Disability
17 Sir George's Road
Freemantle
SOUTHAMPTON SO1 3AU
☎ 0703 635490
Course: Disability Equality Training
☐ Examines all of the issues which relate to disability in the workplace: prejudice, discrimination, the law and policy on disability to esteem rather than demean disabled lives.

GBEO32

The Domino Consultancy Ltd
56 Charnwood Road
SHEPSHED LE12 9NP
☎ 0509 505404
Contact: Mrs Pauline Hicks
Course: Implementing Equal Opportunities
☐ Covers all aspects of putting the theory and policy associated with equal opportunities in the workplace into practice to benefit both employers and employees alike.

GBEO33

Douglas Management and Training Development Ltd
101 Ansell Road
Tooting
LONDON SW17 7LT
☎ 081 672 2431
Contact: Mr Carlis Douglas-Sanusi
Course: Implementation of Equal Opportunities
☐ Course is designed and run for managers at all levels to assist them in developing the skills and insights required to manage and create improvements.

GBEO34

Douglas Management and Training Development Ltd
101 Ansell Road
Tooting
LONDON SW17 7LT
☎ 081 672 2431
Contact: Mr Carlis Douglas-Sanusi
Course: Positive Action Training
☐ Courses are designed and run for black staff and women; to tackle the effects of racism for black staff and self-development groups for black women managers.

GBEO35

Edge Hill College of HE
ORMSKIRK L39 4QP
☎ 0695 575171
Contact: Dr A. R. Kaushal
Course: CRE Code of Practice
☐ Course examines the implications of the Commission for Racial Equality's Code of Practice for organisations interested in developing improved equal opportunities.

GBEO36

Edge Hill College of HE
ORMSKIRK L39 4QP
☎ 0695 575171
Contact: Dr A. R. Kaushal
Course: Legal Requirements
☐ Course covers the main legal requirements on race relations in the UK. Also examines how these can be incorporated most effectively into organisational policy.

GBEO37

Equal Access Training Ltd
40 Ermine Close
Chinchilla Drive
HOUNSLOW TW4 7PW
☎ 081 577 0727
Contact: Daniel Obiago
Course: From Policy to Practice

☐ Course examines the development of equal opportunities in the workplace, and how best to turn policy into practice and to incorporate long-term improvements and changes.

GBEO38

Equalities Associates, The Laws Hotel Management Training Centre
High Street
TURVEY MK43 8DB
☎ 023 064 213
Contact: Mr Jerome Mack
Course: Racism and Sexism: Similarities and Differences
☐ Examines the causes and effects of both types of behaviour and considers methods of tackling and combating them both independently and collectively.

GBEO39

Equality Associates
38 Shawclough Way
ROCHDALE OL12 7HF
☎ 0706 42745
Contact: Wilf Knowles
Course: Harassment Policies
☐ Looks at the reasons for and development of workplace policies to deal with and combat harassment on the grounds of sex and race.

GBEO40

Equality at Work
Blackburn College
Feildon Street
BLACKBURN BB2 1LH
☎ 0254 57155
Contact: Ann Simpson
Course: Equal Opportunity Policy Development
☐ Course covers the development and review of equal opportunities policies for a whole range of organisational settings and sizes.

GBEO41

Equality Services
Leeds City Council
Dept of Education
2 Woodhouse Square
LEEDS LS3 1AD
☎ 0532 449603
Contact: Ian Law
Course: Equal Opportunity Policy Development
☐ Courses cover all elements of policy development; tailor-made for variously sized organisations to include implementation, monitoring and review.

GBEO42

Equal Opportunities Commission
Overseas House
Quay Street
MANCHESTER M3 3HN
☎ 061 833 9244
Course: Equal Opportunities
☐ Government organisation providing advice, support and information to employers and individuals on equal opportunities.

GBEO43

Equal Opportunities Commission for Scotland
St Andrews House
141 West Nile Street
GLASGOW G1 2RN
☎ 041 332 8018
Course: Equal Opportunities
☐ Government organisation; arranges occasional training sessions for employers and individuals.

GBEO44

Equal Opportunities and Interpersonal Skills
36 Trossachs Road
LONDON SE22 8PY
☎ 081 693 4875
Course: Equal Opportunities Training
☐ Short courses covering all aspects of equal opportunities: law, policy, policy implementation.

GBEO45

Eurosearch
Chestnut House
BITTLESWELL LE17 4SG
☎ 0455 556378
Contact: Marguerite Dawson
Course: Making Equal Opportunities Happen
☐ Examines all aspects associated with turning policy and theory into everyday practice.

GBEO46

Faculty of Education
Birmingham Polytechnic
Westbourne Road
Edgbaston
BIRMINGHAM B15 3TN
☎ 021 331 6101
Contact: Keith Rowley
Course: Postgraduate Diploma and MA in Equal Opportunities
☐ Part-time evening course to equip students from a range of professional spheres with theoretical understanding and practical expertise in the field of equal opportunities.

GBEO47

Farrell Cadwell Consulting & Training
18 Dunstable Road
RICHMOND-ON-THAMES TW9 1UH
☎ 081 940 0957
Contact: Pauline Farrell
Course: Leadership Workshops
☐ Joint women/men, black/white, able-bodied/disabled workshops which are designed to relate leadership and service issues to prejudice reduction and attitude change.

GBEO48

Farrell Cadwell Consulting & Training
18 Dunstable Road
RICHMOND-ON-THAMES TW9 1UH
☎ 081 940 0957
Contact: Pauline Farrell
Course: Racism Workshops for White People
☐ Examines the causes and effects of racism and develops methods of reducing it in the workplace; workshops are designed to encourage a non-confrontational environment.

GBEO49

Farrell Cadwell Consulting & Training
18 Dunstable Road
RICHMOND-ON-THAMES TW9 1UH
☎ 081 940 0957
Contact: Pauline Farrell
Course: Employee Relations Development Programme
☐ Organisation-wide strategies for improving equal opportunities and increasing the effectiveness of services to clients.

GBEO50

Fawcett Society
46 Harleyford Road
LONDON SE11 5AY
☎ 071 587 1287
Course: Equality
☐ A campaign group which organises occasional seminars and training sessions covering issues associated with equality between the sexes.

GBEO51

Focus Consultancy Ltd
1A Park Close
Knightsbridge
LONDON SW1X 7PQ
☎ 071 581 4384
Contact: Tuku Mukherjee

Course: Anti-Racist Education and Action Programme
☐ Designs anti-racist strategies as a central element of good management practice, tailor-made for specific improvements to be made within organisational structure.

GBEO52

Focus Disability
37 Severn Way
Bletchley
MILTON KEYNES MK3 7QG
☎ 0908 378880
Contact: Alan Counsell
Course: Employment Equality Training
☐ Course aimed at recruitment personnel; explores the many issues surrounding disability and considers it in relation to recruitment and staff training.

GBEO53

Frances Perry
16 Farndale Street
YORK YO1 4BP
☎ 0904 645215
Contact: Frances Perry
Course: Disability Awareness
☐ Looks at all aspects of disability and the effect it has of increasing prejudice and discrimination against workers with disabilities; examines methods of challenging myths and stereotypes.

GBEO54

Gill Taylor
47 St Leonards Road
LEICESTER LE2 1WT
☎ 0533 705876
Contact: Gill Taylor
Course: Equal Opportunities
☐ Tailor-made courses to suit participants' needs; covers the law on equal opportunities and development of policy to nurture a complete equality ethos within organisations.

GBEO55

GLAD
336 Brixton Road
LONDON SW9 7AA
☎ 071 274 0107
Contact: Michael Brothers
Course: Disability Awareness
☐ Covers the barriers to equality for workers with disabilities, and examines the negative effects of prejudice and discrimination on the lives of disabled people.

GBEO56

GLAD
336 Brixton Road
LONDON SW9 7AA

☎ 071 274 0107
Contact: Michael Brothers
Course: Legal Requirements
☐ Considers the equality laws and the rights and obligations they place on employers and employees.

GBEO57

Graham Elliot
28 Marshal's Drive
ST ALBANS AL1 4RQ
☎ 0727 51547
Contact: Graham Elliot
Course: Work with White Groups on Racism
☐ Covers the white conditioning that causes racism and looks at the effects of racism on our lives. Includes the development of personal goals to combat racism.

GBEO58

Greater London Enterprise Ltd
Enterprise Training Centre
63–67 Newington Causeway
LONDON SE1 6BD
☎ 071 403 0300 ext. 236
Contact: Sally Wilson
Course: Sexual/Racial Harassment
☐ Covers the causes and effects of harassment and the development of workplace policy as the best tool to handle and combat harassment.

GBEO59

Hackney Women's Centre
20 Dalston Lane
LONDON E8 3AZ
☎ 071 254 2980
Course: Equal Opportunities: Advice, Classes and Information
☐ Workshops and classes for local women to reflect women's issues and enhance equality in the wider community.

GBEO60

Host Training and Consultancy Services
Unit 2
24 London Road
HORSHAM RH12 1AY
☎ 0403 211440
Contact: Dorothy Berry-Lound
Course: Attitudes and Behaviour
☐ Course covers the causes and effects of prejudice and discrimination, and how they combine to disadvantage many people.

GBEO61

Host Training and Consultancy Services
Unit 2
24 London Road
HORSHAM RH12 1AY

☎ 0403 211440
Contact: Dorothy Berry-Lound
Course: Recruitment and Selection
☐ Course covers the legal requirements associated with equal opportunities in employment, and examines the methods of putting fairer recruitment procedures into everyday practice.

GBEO62

IBP Consultants Ltd
Vale House
18 The Vale
COULSDON CR5 2AW
☎ 081 660 7954
Contact: Dr Kirsty Ross
Course: Equal Opportunities Workshops for Senior Managers
☐ Course covers the law on equal opportunities and examines methods of developing workplace policy and putting it into practice.

GBEO63

IKWE21
92C Agar Grove
LONDON NW1 9TL
☎ 071 267 1987
Contact: Bennie Bunsee
Course: Race Equality Issues: Community Based
☐ Course examines the law and best policy on equal opportunities for minority ethnic groups and how best to put rhetoric into practice.

GBEO64

Industrial Relations Services Training
18–20 Highbury Place
LONDON N5 8QP
☎ 071 354 5858
Contact: Tracy Conners
Course: Discrimination Law
☐ A half-day course which briefs members on the legislation in relation to equal opportunities in the workplace; includes employers' obligations and rights of employees.

GBEO65

Industrial Relations Services Training
18–20 Highbury Place
LONDON, N5 8QP
☎ 071 354 5858
Contact: Tracy Conners
Course: How to Devise and Administer a Sexual Harassment Policy
☐ Covers the causes and effects of harassment, and methods of combating it internally through the implementation of effective workplace policy.

GBEO66

The Industrial Society
48 Bryanston Square
LONDON W1H 7LN
☎ 071 262 2401
Contact: Gina King
Course: Topical Conferences on Equal Opportunities Issues
☐ Courses are tailor-made to suit the requests of participants; popular topics are maternity, paternity and family leave, the career break and balancing family and work.

GBEO67

The Industrial Society
Peter Runge House
3 Carlton House Terrace
LONDON SW1Y 5DG
☎ 071 839 4300
Contact: Godwin K. Lessey
Course: Positive Action to Avoid Race Discrimination in Recruitment
☐ The purpose of the course is to help employers understand their duties and responsibilities and to equip them with the knowledge to understand different cultures.

GBEO68

Institute for a New Leadership Initiative (INLI)
71 High Street
Saltford
BRISTOL BS18 3EW
☎ 0225 873377
Contact: Rosemary Brennan
Course: Leadership Development
☐ This course is about assisting women and black people who generally suffer discrimination in access to education and employment; practical focus and flexible learning environment.

GBEO69

Interact Training and Consultancy Services
57 Brecon Road
Handsworth
BIRMINGHAM B20 3RW
☎ 021 523 4264
Contact: Fazlun Khalid
Course: Prejudice and Stereotyping
☐ Examines the causes of prejudice and the formation of stereotypes; challenges the widely held beliefs and encourages participants to question their own ideas.

GBEO70

Interact Training and Consultancy Services
57 Brecon Road
Handsworth
BIRMINGHAM B20 3RW
☎ 021 523 4264
Contact: Fazlun Khalid
Course: Recruitment and Selection
☐ Examines issues of fair selection, effective use of the law and creative use of equal opportunities policy to bring about a reduction in discrimination in recruitment processes.

GBEO71

Intergrad Europe
Harthill Grange
Hewelsfield
LYDNEY GL15 6XA
☎ 0594 530223
Contact: Jackie Keeley
Course: Equal Opportunities
☐ Course is aimed at the provision of equal opportunities in graduate recruitment; examines pre-recruitment, selection and career development.

GBEO72

Irish Women's Perspectives
c/o 123 Lavender Sweep
LONDON SW11 1EA
☎ 071 228 2327
Course: Irish Dimension in Equal Opportunities
☐ Support and information group which organises occasional seminars covering topics within the field of equality.

GBEO73

Jacqueline Brett
Ffynnon Goch
Penuwch
TREGARON SY25 6QZ
☎ 097 423 636
Contact: Jacqueline Brett
Course: Assessment of Training Needs
☐ Examines the development of training material and evaluation strategies for the successful implementation of equal opportunities policies in the workplace.

GBEO74

Jacqueline Brett
Ffynnon Goch
Penuwch
TREGARON SY25 6QZ
☎ 097 423 636
Contact: Jacqueline Brett
Course: Strategic Role of Training
☐ Examines the importance of training for all staff in the principles of equality in order to encourage maximum commitment to workplace policy and to develop good practice.

GBEO75

Jean Hodder
5 Trefelin Cottages
Llandegai
BANGOR LL57 4LH
☎ 0248 364147
Contact: Jean Hodder
Course: Positive Action for Women Returners
☐ Covers all elements of employment practice relating to women returners; encourages participants to try out a variety of job-related skills; flexible in approach.

GBEO76

Judi Clarke
PO Box 1528
LONDON N1 2AR
☎ 071 704 0825
Contact: Judi Clarke
Course: Policy Development
☐ Examines the issues and methods of policy development, implementation, training, monitoring and review.

GBEO77

Judith Rose
22 Mount Road
Perin
WOLVERHAMPTON WV4 5SW
☎ 0902 331266
Contact: Judith Rose
Course: Promoting Equality for People with Disabilities
☐ Course examines issues of access and mobility, the law and policy on disability, barriers to equality and promotion of increased equal opportunities.

GBEO78

Lesley Abdela
The Lodge
CANOCK MANOR SN10 3QQ
☎ 0380 840594
Contact: Lesley Abdela
Course: Equal Opportunities
☐ Short courses covering all aspects of equal opportunities law, policy and good practice.

GBEO79

L. Olumfemi Hughes
4 Westhill Street
BRIGHTON BN1 3RR
☎ 0273 23524
Contact: L. Olumfemi Hughes
Course: Sexual Harassment at Work
☐ Covers the causes and effects of harassment, methods of handling it assertively, combating it through effective use of workplace policy.

GBEO80

Marion Codd and Associates
53 Gloucester Street
SHEFFIELD S10 2FS
☎ 0742 728653
Contact: Marion Codd
Course: Dealing with Sexual Harassment
☐ Includes an analysis of what constitutes sexual harassment, and examines methods of dealing with it assertively and combating it in the workplace.

GBEO81

Marion Codd and Associates
53 Gloucester Street
SHEFFIELD S10 2FS
☎ 0742 728653
Contact: Marion Codd
Course: Implementing Equal Opportunities Policies
☐ Covers all the contemporary issues associated with putting policy on equality into everyday practice; from policy design and implementation to training, monitoring and evaluation.

GBEO82

Maureen Parris
43 North Circular Road
LONDON NW10 0PJ
☎ 081 961 4201
Contact: Maureen Parris
Course: Equality Issues
☐ Concentrates on topical issues in the field of equal opportunities; covers equality law and policy development, as well as examining methods of putting policy into practice.

GBEO83

Maya
127a Albion Road
LONDON N16 9PL
☎ 071 241 6864
Course: Training and Research for Equalities
☐ Short courses and advice; workshops.

GBEO84

Myrtle Berman
2 Hillside
Highgate Road
LONDON NW5 1QT
☎ 071 485 7482
Contact: Myrtle Berman
Course: Men and Women Working Together as Colleagues
☐ Aims to promote better working relationships between men and women by examining the role of equality in practice.

GBEO85

Myrtle Berman
2 Hillside
Highgate Road
LONDON NW5 1QT
☎ 071 485 7482
Contact: Myrtle Berman
Course: Awareness Training for Women in Management
☐ Examines all of the issues which are likely to confront women managers, and develops techniques and methods of handling difficult situations.

GBEO86

National Coalition Building Association
75 Colby Road
LEICESTER LE4 8LG
☎ 0533 695910
Contact: Val Carpenter
Course: Policy Development and Implementation
☐ Course examines all of the issues involved in developing an equal opportunities policy, including training, monitoring, and review and evaluation methods.

GBEO87

National Coalition Building Association
75 Colby Road
LEICESTER LE4 8LG
☎ 0533 695910
Contact: Val Carpenter
Course: Assertion Training
☐ Looks at the skills required to develop an assertive approach to a range of domestic and workplace situations where conflict can arise.

GBEO88

Newham Women's Training and Education Centre
22 Deanery Road
LONDON E15 4LP
☎ 081 519 5843
Course: Women's Training and Education
☐ Workshops and courses of interest to women participants to develop skills and increase equality in education and training.

GBEO89

Northern Ireland Women's European Platform
127 Ormeau Road
BELFAST BT7 1SH
☎ 0232 321 224
Course: Equal Opportunities For Women
☐ Umbrella group; arranges courses and discussion groups on subjects of interest to members.

GBEO90

Older Women's Project
Manor Gardens Centre
6–9 Manor Gardens
LONDON N7 6LA
☎ 071 281 3485
Course: Advice on Older Women's Campaigning
☐ Advice and information for older women on issues such as access to education, leisure and health services.

GBEO91

Pamela Brown Associates Ltd
4 Foxhill Gardens
Upper Norwood
LONDON SE19 2XB
☎ 081 768 0533
Contact: Pam Brown
Course: Equal Opportunities
☐ Examines all aspects of equal opportunities in the workplace, including legislative issues and policy development.

GBEO92

Pamela Brown Associates Ltd
4 Foxhill Gardens
Upper Norwood
LONDON SE19 2XB
☎ 081 768 0533
Contact: Pam Brown
Course: Action for Black Staff
☐ Looks at employment rights of all staff, with special emphasis on management development of black employees within an equal opportunities framework.

GBEO93

Patrick George
Kings Farm
Edlesborough
DUNSTABLE LU6 2JN
☎ 0525 220974
Contact: Patrick George
Course: Recruitment Procedures
☐ Examines the legal and policy issues of incorporating good equal opportunities practices in recruitment methods.

GBEO94

P.O. Dathorne (Associates)
24 Dors Close
Kingsway
LONDON NW9 7NT
☎ 081 200 1997
Contact: P. O. Dathorne
Course: Management and Equal Opportunities
☐ An up-to-the-minute analysis of all equal opportunities issues.

GBEO95

Positive Action
    3 Milfoil Avenue
    Conniburrow
    MILTON KEYNES MK14 7DY
☎   0908 677387
Course: Equal Opportunities
□ Tailor-made courses or group/one-to-one consultancy on the law associated with equal opportunities and the development of effective policy to turn intention into reality.

GBEO96

Race Relations
Employment Advisory Service
    Dept of Employment
    11 Belgrave Road
    LONDON SW1V 1RB
☎   0742 761978
Contact: M. J. Pope
Course: The Influence of Race Discrimination in Employment
□ Training course aimed at managers and personnel staff on the influence of race discrimination in employment, the law and the Commission for Racial Equality's Code of Practice.

GBEO97

Race Relations
Employment Advisory Service
    Dept of Employment
    11 Belgrave Road
    LONDON SW1V 1RB
☎   0742 761978
Contact: M. J. Pope
Course: Policy Development and Implementation
□ Examines all aspects of developing an equal opportunities policy, including training, monitoring and evaluation, and the purposes and methods of policy review.

GBEO98

Redfield Training Group
    Redfield
    WINSLOW MK18 3LZ
☎   0296 715202
Course: Women's Social, Economic and Emotional Empowerment
□ Women's collective; short courses and one-to-one consultancy.

GBEO99

Reena Bhavnani
    157 Brooke Road
    LONDON E5 8AG
☎   081 806 9267
Contact: Reena Bhavnani

Course: Women's Employment Rights
□ Examines all legislation associated with women at work: sex, race, disability, social welfare, social security and pension rights.

GBEO100

Rosalind Dean
    9 The Fairway
    SHEFFIELD S10 4LX
☎   0742 308077
Contact: Rosalind Dean
Course: Designing Training for Equality
□ Includes a comprehensive guide to the development of training packages for a range of different organisations.

GBEO101

Rosalind Dean
    9 The Fairway
    SHEFFIELD S10 4LX
☎   0742 308077
Contact: Rosalind Dean
Course: Developing the Neglected Resource
□ Course is aimed at those for whom equal opportunities for women has recently become a major priority, and who are thinking about the different options for action.

GBEO102

Sandra Benjamin
    102 Kings Hall Road
    BECKENHAM BR3 1LN
☎   081 058 2211
Contact: Sandra Benjamin
Course: Positive Action in Employment
□ Examines the purpose, design, implementation and review of positive action programmes in employment to counteract the effects of past discrimination.

GBEO103

Sandra Benjamin
    102 Kings Hall Road
    BECKENHAM BR3 1LN
☎   081 658 2211
Contact: Sandra Benjamin
Course: Management and Trade Union Commitment on Positive Action
□ Looks at methods of increasing support and commitment to positive action programmes in order to reduce the effects of discrimination.

GBEO104

Southall Black Sisters
    52 Norwood Road
    SOUTHALL UB2 4DW
☎   081 571 9595
Course: Equal Opportunities

168

□ Workshops and group talks on subjects of interest to group members to increase skills and sisterhood, and stimulate greater commitment to equality in the wider community.

GBEO105

Sue Cordingley Associates
'Old Lakenham'
Pickering Street,
MAIDSTONE
Kent
☎ 0622 747232
Contact: Sue Cordingley
Course: Equal Opportunities
□ Policy design, implementation and training available. Formal training sessions based on legislation or general awareness training.

GBEO106

Swansea Women's Resource and Training Centre
228 The High Street
SWANSEA SA1 1NY
☎ 0792 467365
Course: Equal Opportunities
□ Workshops and discussions designed to increase awareness of equality, and to examine how to challenge inequality in wider society.

GBEO107

The Venue Women's Centre
The Basildon Centre
Pagel Mead
BASILDON SF14 1DL
☎ 0268 294265
Course: Equal Opportunities
□ Discussions and workshops designed to increase awareness of equality, develop assertiveness and stimulate increased equality in wider society.

GBEO108

Waltham Forest Women's Centre
109 Hoe Street
LONDON E17 4SA
☎ 081 520 5318
Course: Equal Opportunities
□ Workshops and group discussions on a range of subjects which involve hands-on experience of skills for employment. Increases equality of access to employment and training.

GBEO109

Wandsworth Project for Young Women
1 Plough Terrace
LONDON SW11
☎ 081 871 8526
Course: Equal Opportunities Activities and Workshops

□ Workshops and group discussions for young women to increase self-confidence and make them more aware of equal opportunities.

GBEO110

Wandsworth BC Staff Training Centre
150 Lavender Hill
Battersea
LONDON SW11
☎ 081 871 7463/4
Contact: Errol A. Carbon
Course: Race Equality and Equal Opportunities
□ Course looks at the development of legislation and policy to promote race equality; examines the role of training and awareness raising in order to reduce racism.

GBEO111

Wandsworth BC Staff Training Centre
150 Lavender Hill
Battersea
LONDON SW11
☎ 081 871 7463/4
Contact: Errol A. Carbon
Course: Team Building a Multiracial Workforce
□ Course looks at topical issues in the development of harmonious workplaces which take into full account the racial and cultural differences and similarities of all members.

Greece

GREEO1

League for Women's Rights
41 Solonos Street
10672 ATHENS
Course: Equal Opportunities for Women
□ Women's group; arranges courses and seminars on subjects of interest to members.

GREEO2

Women's Union of Greece
8 Enianos Street
ATHENS
Course: Equal Opportunities for Women
□ Women's organisation; arranges seminars and workshops on subjects of interest to members.

Hungary

HUNEO1

Women's Steering Committee of Trade Unions
Dozsa Gyorgy ut 84/b
1415 BUDAPEST V1

Course: Equal Opportunities for Women in Employment
☐ Women's trade union group; arranges debates and training sessions on women's employment issues.

Iceland

ICEEO1

Federation of Icelandic Women's Societies
Tungata 14
101 REYKJAVIK
Course: Equal Opportunities for Women
☐ Courses and seminars on subjects of interest to women.

ICEEO2

Women's Alliance
PO Box 836
101 REYKJAVIK
☎ 1 13725
Course: Equal Opportunities and Feminism
☐ A feminist political party; arranges seminars and debates on women's issues.

Ireland

IREEO1

County Westmeath Vocational Education Committee
Bridge House
Bellevue Rd
MULLINGAR
Co. Westmeath
Contact: Brendan Daly
Course: Equal Opportunities for Women
☐ Research and training aimed at enhancing equality of opportunity for women.

IREEO2

Trade Union Women's Forum
c/o SIPTU Liberty Hall
DUBLIN 2
Course: Equal Opportunities for Women in Employment
☐ Trade union women's organisation; arranges seminars and training on subjects of interest to women.

Israel

ISREO1

Israel Women's Network
14 Hatibonim Street
JERUSALEM
Contact: Prof. Alice Shalvi
Course: Equal Opportunities for Women

☐ Research and training aimed at enhancing equality of opportunity for women.

Italy

ITEO1

Women in Agricultural Production
Food and Agricultural Organization (FAO)
Via delle Terme di Caracalla
00100 ROME
Course: Equal Opportunities for Women
☐ Research and training aimed at enhancing equality of opportunity for women.

ITEO2

INTERSIND
98 via Christofero
Colombo
00147 ROME
Contact: Enzo Avanzi
Course: Equal Opportunities for Women
☐ Research and training aimed at enhancing equality of opportunity for women.

ITEO3

OSFIN
Via P. Traversari 2
48100 RAVENNA
Contact: Cecilia De Vito
Course: Equal Opportunities for Women
☐ Research and training aimed at enhancing equality of opportunity for women.

Japan

JAPEO1

Japan Institute of Labour
Chutaikin Building
7-6 Shibakoen 1-chome
Minato-ku
TOKYO, 105 Japan
Course: Equal Opportunities for Women
☐ Research and training aimed at enhancing equality of opportunity for women.

JAPEO2

National Women's Ed. Centre
728 Sugaya, Ranzan-Machi
Hiki-gun
SAITAMA-KEN 355-02 Japan
Course: Equal Opportunities for Women
☐ Research and training aimed at enhancing equality of opportunity for women.

Luxembourg

LUXEO1

CGT Luxembourg
  26 rue R. Schuman
  3566 DUDELANGE
Contact: Gilberte Kennerknecht
Course: Equal Opportunities for Women
☐ Research and training aimed at enhancing equality of opportunity for women.

LUXEO2

Fédération National des Femmes Luxembourgeoises
  1 rue de la Forge
  1535 LUXEMBOURG
Course: Equal Opportunities for Women
☐ Courses and seminars on subjects of interest to members.

Netherlands

NETEO1

Emancipatieraad
  Anna Van Hannoverstraat 4-6
  Postbus 90806
  2509 LV THE HAGUE
☎ 070 33 47 82
Course: Equal Opportunities for Women
☐ Arranges courses and seminars on subjects of interest to members.

NETEO2

Nederlandse Vrouwen Raad
  Groot Hertoginnelaan 41
  2517 EC THE HAGUE
Course: Equal Opportunities for Women
☐ Umbrella group; arranges courses and discussion groups on subjects of interest to member groups.

NETEO3

STEW
  Weesperzijde 4
  1091 EA AMSTERDAM
Contact: E. Hengeveld
Course: Equal Opportunities for Women
☐ Research and training aimed at enhancing equality of opportunity for women.

NETEO4

Stichting 0 + 0
  Postbus 407
  2260 AK LEIDSCHENDAM
Contact: Carin Van Laere
Course: Equal Opportunities for Women

☐ Research and training aimed at enhancing equality of opportunity for women.

NETEO5

Stichting, Vrouwenvakopleiding Vrouwenbond FNV Zeeland
  Oude Vlissingseweg 32a
  Postbus 7034
  4330 GA MIDDELBURG
Contact: N. Blomsbeel
Course: Equal Opportunities for Women
☐ Research and training aimed at enhancing equality of opportunity for women.

NETEO6

Verbond van Nederlandse Ondernemingen
  Postbus 93093
  2509 AB GRAVENHAGE
Contact: J. Van de Bandt Stel
Course: Equal Opportunities for Women
☐ Research and training aimed at enhancing equality of opportunity for women.

NETEO7

Vrouwenbelangen
  Noordeinde 2a
  2311 CD LEIDEN
☎ 071 12 06 03
Course: Equal Opportunities for Women
☐ Political lobby group; arranges seminars and debates on women's issues.

NETEO8

Women's Secretariat
  Netherlands Trade Union Confederation
  PO Box 8456
  1005 AL AMSTERDAM
☎ 020 581 63 00
Course: Equal Opportunities for Women in Employment
☐ Trade union women's organisation; arranges debates and seminars on women's issues.

New Zealand

NZEO1

National Advisory Council on the Employment of Women (NACEW)
  c/o Dept of Labour
  Private Bag
  WELLINGTON
Course: Equal Opportunities for Women
☐ Research and training aimed at enhancing equality of opportunity for women.

NZEO2

The Print Centre
17 Union Street
PO Box 1236
AUCKLAND
☎ 379 6503
Course: Equal Opportunities for Women
☐ Research and training aimed at enhancing equality of opportunity for women.

NZEO3 ·

Women's Electoral Lobby
WEL Waikato
PO Box 9581
HAMILTON
Course: Equal Opportunities for Women
☐ Research and training aimed at enhancing equality of opportunity for women.

Norway

NOREO1

Centre for International Women's Issues (CEWI)
Fr Nansenspl. 6
0160 OSLO
☎ 22 42 62 45
Course: Equal Opportunities and International Issues
☐ Advice and training organisation.

NOREO2

Juridisk Radgivning for Kvinner
Postboks 6756 St Olavs Plass
0130 OSLO 1
☎ 22 11 25 00
Course: Legal Advice for Women
☐ One-to-one consultancy or small group support on all legal issues of concern to women.

Romania

ROMEO1

National Woman's Council
Office of the Chairman
Council of Ministers Str Academei 34
BUCHAREST
Course: Equal Opportunities for Women
☐ Arranges courses and seminars on subjects of interest to women.

South Korea

SKEO1

Korean Women's Development Institute
CPO Box 2267
SEOUL 100
Course: Equal Opportunities for Women
☐ Research and training aimed at enhancing equality of opportunity for women.

Spain

SPEO1

Centre Tecnic per la Dona
SA
Ronda Sant Pere, 68 pral
08010 BARCELONA
Contact: Anna Mercade i Ferrando
Course: Equal Opportunities for Women
☐ Research and training aimed at enhancing equality of opportunity for women.

SPEO2

UCSTE
Tirso de Molina 5-5
28012 MADRID
Contact: Carmen Pino Villalba
Course: Equal Opportunities for Women
☐ Research and training aimed at enhancing equality of opportunity for women.

Sweden

SWEEO1

Jamo-Equal Opportunities Ombudsman
Birger Jarls Torg 7
Riddarholmen
10333 STOCKHOLM
Course: Equal Opportunities
☐ Advice and consultancy on all aspects of equal opportunities.

SWEEO2

Syeriges Socialdemokratische Kvinnoforbun
Box 11044
10061 STOCKHOLM 11
☎ 08 44 95 80
Course: Equal Opportunities for Women
☐ Political group; arranges courses and seminars on subjects of interest to women.

Switzerland

SWIEO1

BALance
>   Militarstrasse 83a
>   8004 ZURICH
☎   01 291 23 31
Contact: Theresa Schiffers
Course: Equal Opportunities for Women
☐ Research and training aimed at enhancing equality of opportunity for women.

SWIEO2

BIGA, Bundesamt für Industrie, Gewerbe und Arbeit
>   Abteilung Berufsbildung
>   Bundesgasse 8
>   3003 BERN
☎   031 61 28 17
Contact: Christoph Schmitter
Course: Equal Opportunities for Women
☐ Research and training aimed at enhancing equality of opportunity for women.

SWIEO3

Centre for Human Rights
>   United Nations Office
>   Palais des Nations
>   1211 GENEVA 10
Course: Equal Opportunities for Women
☐ Research and training aimed at enhancing equality of opportunity for women.

SWIEO4

Focal Point for Women
ECE
>   Palais des Nations
>   1211 GENEVA 10
Course: Equal Opportunities for Women
☐ Research and training aimed at enhancing equality of opportunity for women.

SWIEO5

Femmedia
>   Klosterberg 19
>   4051 BASLE
☎   061 272 03 23
Contact: Anita Fetz
Course: Equal Opportunities for Women
☐ Research and training aimed at enhancing equality of opportunity for women.

SWIEO6

Office for Women Workers Questions
International Labour Organisation (ILO)
>   4 route des Morillons
>   1211 GENEVA 22

Course: Equal Opportunities for Women
☐ Research and training aimed at enhancing equality of opportunity for women.

SWIEO7

Los/osl
>   c/o Libs
>   Postfach 355
>   4021 BASLE
Course: Lesbian Studies
☐ National lesbian organisation; arranges group discussions on subjects of interest to members.

SWIEO8

Swiss Federation for Adult Education
>   Oberlikonerstrasse 38
>   PO Box 7
>   8057 ZURICH
Course: Equal Opportunities for Women
☐ Research and training aimed at enhancing equality of opportunity for women.

Thailand

THAEO1

ESCAP
>   Social Development Division
>   UN Building
>   Rajdamnern Avenue
>   BANGKOK 10200 2
Course: Equal Opportunities for Women
☐ Research and training aimed at enhancing equality of opportunity for women.

Trinidad and Tobago

TTEO1

ECLAC – Caribbean Women in Development
>   PO Box 1113
>   PORT-OF-SPAIN
Course: Equal Opportunities for Women
☐ Research and training aimed at enhancing equality of opportunity for women.

United States of America

USAEO1

Applied Potential
>   Box 19
>   HIGHLAND PARK, IL 60035
☎   312 432 0620
Course: Equal Opportunities for Women
☐ Research and training aimed at enhancing equality of opportunity for women.

USAEO2
Baltimore New Directions for Women Inc.
Administrative Offices
2517 North Charles Street
BALTIMORE, MD 21218
☎ 301 336 8570
Course: Equal Opportunities for Women
☐ Research and training aimed at enhancing equality of opportunity for women.

USAEO3
Career Counselling and Placement
Hunter College
695 Park Avenue
NEW YORK, NY 10021
☎ 212 570 5254
Course: Equal Opportunities for Women
☐ Research and training aimed at enhancing equality of opportunity for women.

USAEO4
Career Development Office
Smith College
Pierce Hall
NORTHAMPTON, MA 01063
☎ 413 584 2700
Course: Equal Opportunities for Women
☐ Research and training aimed at enhancing equality of opportunity for women.

USAEO5
Career Directions for Women
301 Crown Street
PO Box 5557
NEW HAVEN, CT 06520
☎ 203 436 8242
Course: Equal Opportunities for Women
☐ Research and training aimed at enhancing equality of opportunity for women.

USAEO6
Career/Life Alternatives
100 Whitney Avenue
NEW HAVEN, CT 06510
☎ 203 865 7377
Course: Equal Opportunities for Women
☐ Research and training aimed at enhancing equality of opportunity for women.

USAEO7
Career Planning and Placement Center
Moraine Valley Community College
10900 South 88th Avenue
PALOS HILLS, IL 60465
☎ 312 974 4300
Course: Equal Opportunities for Women

☐ Research and training aimed at enhancing equality of opportunity for women.

USAEO8
Career Research Institute
455 West 44th Street
NEW YORK, NY 10036
☎ 212 247 5351
Course: Equal Opportunities for Women
☐ Research and training aimed at enhancing equality of opportunity for women.

USAEO9
Center for Continuing Education of Women
University of California, Berkeley
Room 100, T-9 Building
BERKELEY, CA 94720
☎ 415 642 4786
Course: Equal Opportunities for Women
☐ Research and training aimed at enhancing equality of opportunity for women.

USAEO10
Center for Women's Services
Western Michigan University
A-331 Ellsworth Hall
KALAMAZOO, MI 49008
☎ 313 377 3033
Course: Equal Opportunities for Women
☐ Research and training aimed at enhancing equality of opportunity for women.

USAEO11
Continuing Education for Women
Washington University
Box 1064
ST LOUIS, MO 63130
☎ 314 889 6759
Course: Equal Opportunities for Women
☐ Research and training aimed at enhancing equality of opportunity for women.

USAEO12
Council for Career Planning, Inc.
310 Madison Avenue
NEW YORK, NY 10017
☎ 212 687 9490
Course: Equal Opportunities for Women
☐ Research and training aimed at enhancing equality of opportunity for women.

USAEO13
Counselling Services for Women
Villa Maria College
2551 West Lake Road
ERIE, PA 16505
☎ 814 838 1966

Course: Equal Opportunities for Women
☐ Research and training aimed at enhancing equality of opportunity for women.

USAEO14

Division for Women's Programmes
United Nations Development Programme
  One UN Plaza
  NEW YORK, NY 10017
Course: Equal Opportunities for Women
☐ Research and training aimed at enhancing equality of opportunity for women.

USAEO15

Drake University
  1158 27th Street
  DES MOINES, IA 50311
☎ 515 271 2916
Course: Equal Opportunities for Women
☐ Research and training aimed at enhancing equality of opportunity for women.

USAEO16

Focus on Women Program
Henry Ford Community College
  5101 Evergreen Road
  DEARBORN, MI 48128
☎ 313 271 2750 ext. 33
Course: Equal Opportunities for Women
☐ Research and training aimed at enhancing equality of opportunity for women.

USAEO17

George Washington University
  Suite 621–624
  2130 H Street NW
  WASHINGTON, DC 20052
☎ 202 676 7036
Course: Equal Opportunities for Women
☐ Research and training aimed at enhancing equality of opportunity for women.

USAEO18

Indiana University
  Owen Hall 201
  BLOOMINGTON, IN 47405
☎ 812 337 8995
Course: Equal Opportunities for Women
☐ Research and training aimed at enhancing equality of opportunity for women.

USAEO19

Job Resource Center
  Suite 23
  2015 J Street
  SACRAMENTO, CA 95814
☎ 916 441 2850

Course: Equal Opportunities for Women
☐ Research and training aimed at enhancing equality of opportunity for women.

USAEO20

More for Women, Inc.
  1435 Lexington Avenue
  NEW YORK, NY 10028
☎ 212 534 0852
Course: Equal Opportunities for Women
☐ Research and training aimed at enhancing equality of opportunity for women.

USAEO21

Options for Women
  8419 Germantown Avenue
  PHILADELPHIA, PA 19118
Course: Equal Opportunities for Women
☐ Research and training aimed at enhancing equality of opportunity for women.

USAEO22

Personnel Sciences Center
  341 Madison Avenue
  NEW YORK, NY 10017
☎ 212 661 1870
Course: Equal Opportunities for Women
☐ Research and training aimed at enhancing equality of opportunity for women.

USAEO23

Student Counselling Service
University of Arizona
  Old Main
  TUCSON, AZ 85721
☎ 602 626 2316
Course: Equal Opportunities for Women
☐ Research and training aimed at enhancing equality of opportunity for women.

USAEO24

The United Nations Development Fund for Women (UNIFEM)
  Room 1106
  304 East 45th Street
  NEW YORK, NY 10017
Course: Equal Opportunities for Women
☐ Research and training aimed at enhancing equality of opportunity for women.

USAEO25

Womanspace: Career
Columbia University
  211 Lewisohn Hall
  Broadway and 116th Street
  NEW YORK, NY 10027
☎ 212 280 2820

Course: Equal Opportunities for Women
☐ Research and training aimed at enhancing equality of opportunity for women.

USAEO26

Women in the United Nations
Office of Human Resources Management
United Nations
NEW YORK, NY 10017
Contact: The Co-ordinator
Course: Equal Opportunities for Women
☐ Research and training aimed at enhancing equality of opportunity for women.

USAEO27

Women's Career Center Inc.
121 North Fitzhugh Street
ROCHESTER, NY 14614
☎ 716 325 2274
Course: Equal Opportunities for Women
☐ Research and training aimed at enhancing equality of opportunity for women.

USAEO28

Women's Center
University of California at Santa Barbara
SANTA BARBARA, CA 93106
☎ 805 961 3778
Course: Equal Opportunities for Women
☐ Research and training aimed at enhancing equality of opportunity for women.

USAEO29

The Women's Center
Jersey City State College
70 Audubon
JERSEY CITY, NJ 07305
☎ 201 547 3189
Course: Equal Opportunities for Women
☐ Research and training aimed at enhancing equality of opportunity for women.

USAEO30

Women's Center
Montclair State College
Valley Road
UPPER MONTCLAIR, NJ 07043
☎ 201 893 5106
Course: Equal Opportunities for Women
☐ Research and training aimed at enhancing equality of opportunity for women.

USAEO31

Women's Center of Dallas
Quadrangle Suite 197
2800 Routh
DALLAS, TX 75201

☎ 214 651 9795
Course: Equal Opportunities for Women
☐ Research and training aimed at enhancing equality of opportunity for women.

USAEO32

Women's Resource Center
Southwest State University
MARSHALL, MN 56258
☎ 507 537 7160
Course: Equal Opportunities for Women
☐ Research and training aimed at enhancing equality of opportunity for women.

USAEO33

The Women's Resource Service
University of Missouri, Kansas City
5325 Rockhill Road
KANSAS CITY, MO 64110
☎ 816 276 1442
Course: Equal Opportunities for Women
☐ Research and training aimed at enhancing equality of opportunity for women.

Uruguay

URUEO1

Ministerio de Education y Cultura
Instituto de la Mujer
Reconguista 535 P.8
MONTEVIDEO
Course: Equal Opportunities for Women.
☐ Research and training aimed at enhancing equality of opportunity for women.

Health and Therapy

Australia

AUSHT1

CAPERS
PO Box 567
NUNDAH, Qld 4012
☎ 07 266 9573
Contact: Jan Cornfoot
Course: Women's Health
☐ Training in issues surrounding women's health.

AUSHT2

Family Planning
100 Alfred St
FORTITUDE VALLEY, Qld 4006
☎ 07 252 5168
Course: Women's Health
☐ Training in issues surrounding women's health.

AUSHT3

National Women's Consultative Council
3–5 National Circuit
BARTON, ACT 2600
☎ 06 271 5723
Course: Women's Health
☐ Training in issues surrounding women's health.

AUSHT4

Canterbury Family Centre
PaNDa
19 Canterbury Road
CAMBERWELL, Vic. 3124
☎ 03 882 5396
Course: Women's Health
☐ Training in issues surrounding women's health.

AUSHT5

South Australian Film Corporation (SAFC)
3 Butler Drive
Westside Commerce Centre
113 Tapleys Hill Road
HENDON, SA 5014
☎ 08 348 9355
Course: Women's Health
☐ Training in issues surrounding woman's health.

AUSHT6

Zig Zag
575 Old Cleveland Road
CAMP HILL, Qld 4152
☎ 07 843 1823
Course: Women's Health
☐ Training in issues surrounding women's health.

Belgium

BELHT1

ARGO
Regentlaan 40
1000 BRUSSELS
Contact: G. Van De Velde
Course: Women's Health
☐ Training in issues surrounding women's health.

BELHT2

Association rue Blanche
ASBL
29 rue Blanche
1050 BRUSSELS
Contact: Nicole Samyn
Course: Women's Health
☐ Training in issues surrounding women's health.

BELHT3

FGTB
42 rue Haute
1000 BRUSSELS
Contact: Anne Tricot
Course: Women's Health
☐ Training in issues surrounding women's health.

BELHT4

FOREM Centre de Formation
8 rue Jean Gomme
4802 HENSY
Contact: M. Servais
Course: Women's Health
☐ Training in issues surrounding women's health.

BELHT5

IRIS Unit
CREW s.c.
21 rue de la Tourelle
1040 BRUSSELS
Contact: Audrey Van Tuyckom
Course: Women's Health
☐ Vocational training covering issues surrounding women's health and therapy.

BELHT6

Kabinet Onderwijs Cel.ESF
Arcadengebouw Blok F
6de Verdieping
1010 BRUSSELS
Contact: Ingrid Snel

Course: Women's Health
☐ Training in issues surrounding women's health.

BELHT7

Ministère de l'Emploi et du Travail
  51 rue Belliard
  1040 BRUSSELS
Contact: Martine Voets
Course: Women's Health
☐ Training in issues surrounding women's health.

BELHT8

Rien Van Meensel
  Van Eevenstraat 2
  3000 LEUVEN
Contact: Rien Van Meensel
Course: Women's Health
☐ Training in issues surrounding women's health.

BELHT9

VDAB Vilvoorde
  Rollewagenstrat 22
  1800 VILVOORDE
Contact: Harry Van Vaerenbergh
Course: Women's Health
☐ Training in issues surrounding women's health.

BELHT10

VDAB Vilvoorde
  Rollewagenstraat 22
  1800 VILVOORDE
Contact: Luc Van Waes
Course: Women's Health
☐ Training in issues surrounding women's health.

Denmark

DENHT1

AMU-center
  Brovangen 2
  3720 AKIRKEBY
Contact: Britta Keller
Course: Women's Health
☐ Training in issues surrounding women's health.

DENHT2

AMU – Centret Vendsyssel
  Knivholtvej 18
  9900 FREDERIKSHAVN

Contact: Susanne Andersen
Course: Women's Health
☐ Research and training on issues surrounding
women's health.

DENHT3

Arbejdsformidlingen
  Teglvaerksgade 4
  6701 ESBJERG
Contact: Dorte Ulldall
Course: Women's Health
☐ Training in issues surrounding women's health.

DENHT4

Arbejdsformidlingen
  Oster Voldgade 4
  3700 RONNE
Contact: Henny Kofoed
Course: Women's Health
☐ Training in issues surrounding women's health.

DENHT5

Arhus Tekniske Skole
  Halmstadgade 6
  8200 ARHUS N
Contact: Kirsten Tejsner
Course: Women's Health
☐ Training in issues surrounding women's health.

DENHT6

Center for Kvindestudier
  (Centre for Women's Studies)
  Odense University
  Campusvej 55
  5230 ODENSE M
  ☎   09 15 86 00 ext. 318
Contact: Nina Lykke
Course: Feminist Psychoanalysis
☐ Research projects and training in feminist psycho-
analysis.

DENHT7

EDB – Daghojskolen
  Aben Datastue
  Aboulevarden 7 st
  8000 ARHUS C
Contact: Kirsten Kristensen
Course: Women's Health
☐ Research and training in women's health issues.

DENHT8

Foreingen af Daghojskoler
  Willemoesgade 14 Kld
  2100 COPENHAGEN 0
Contact: Monica Munck
Course: Women's Health
☐ Training in issues surrounding women's health.

DENHT9

Holbaek Tekniske Skole
Absalonsgade 20
4300 HOLBAEK
Contact: Annelise Nerving
Course: Women's Health
☐ Training in issues surrounding women's health.

DENHT10

Koge Handelskole
Lyngbyvej 19
4600 KOGE
Contact: Mona Engberg
Course: Women's Health
☐ Training in issues surrounding women's health.

DENHT11

Kvindeforum
(The Centre of Feminist Research)
University of Aalborg
Fibigerstraede 2
9220 AALBORG 0
☎ 08 15 85 22 ext. 229
Contact: Anna-Birte Ravn
Course: Women's Health
☐ Research and training in women's health.

DENHT12

Ligestillingskonsulent
Arbejdsformidlingen
Tondergade 14
1752 COPENHAGEN V
Contact: Mette Iversen
Course: Women's Health
☐ Research and training on issues surrounding women's health.

DENHT13

RUE
Aebelogade 7
2100 COPENHAGEN 0
Contact: Lis Meier Carlsen
Course: Women's Health
☐ Training in issues surrounding women's health.

France

FRHT1

AFPA Limoges Batiment
68 rue de Babylone
87036 LIMOGES
Contact: Lucette Chavent
Course: Women's Health
☐ Training in issues surrounding women's health.

FRHT2

Centre d'Expression Manuelle et de Créations Artistiques
Chevrey – Arcenant
21700 NUITS ST GEORGES
Contact: Marie Christine Grennerat
Course: Women's Health
☐ Training in issues surrounding women's health.

FRHT3

ESSOR
76 allées J. Jaures
31071 TOULOUSE
Contact: Michel Roquelaine
Course: Women's Health
☐ Training in issues surrounding women's health.

FRHT4

IRFA Lorraine
1 rue du Coetloquet
BP 795
57013 METZ
Contact: Michele Gadelle
Course: Women's Health
☐ Training in issues surrounding women's health.

FRHT5

TUAC auprès de l'OCDE
26 avenue de la Grande Armée
75017 PARIS
Contact: Yolande Durand
Course: Women's Health
☐ Training in issues surrounding women's health.

Great Britain and Northern Ireland

GBHT1

Abertawe Hypnotherapy Centre
161 Belgrave Road
Gorseinon
SWANSEA SA4 2RB
☎ 0792 893091
Contact: Gaynor Rosier
Course: Hypnotherapy and Pyschology using Ericksonian Techniques
☐ One-to-one or small group therapy.

GBHT2

Aggie Jakubska
  37 Norwood Terrace
  Shipley
  BRADFORD BD18 2BD
☎ 0274 582044
Contact: Aggie Jakubska
Course: Reichian Bodywork Psychotherapy and Groupwork
☐ One-to-one or small group session therapy.

GBHT3

Alison Denham
  66 Victoria Gardens
  Horsforth
  LEEDS LS18 4PH
☎ 0532 583194
Contact: Alison Denham
Course: Medical Herbalist
☐ One-to-one consultancy or small groups.

GBHT4

Anne Ashley
  20 Connaught Avenue
  LONDON E4 7AA
☎ 081 529 0553
Contact: Anne Ashley
Course: Aromatherapy
☐ One-to-one consultancy or small workshops.

GBHT5

Arbee Marketing Communication Training
  31 Kilmorie Road
  Forest Hill
  LONDON SE23 2SS
☎ 081 291 0884
Contact: Ruffo Bravette
Course Stress Management
☐ Examines the causes and effects of stress, and develops methods of overcoming problems associated with it.

GBHT6

Association for Improvements in the Maternity Services
  40 Kingswood Avenue
  LONDON NW6 6LS
☎ 081 960 5585
Course: Advice and Information on Pregnancy and Childbirth
☐ One-to-one support or small workshops to provide personal assistance to clients on child-related issues.

GBHT7

Association for Post-Natal Illness
  7 Gowan Avenue
  LONDON SW6 6RH
☎ 071 731 4867
Course: For Sufferers of Post-Natal Depression
☐ One-to-one counselling, support and advice for women suffering from the effects of post-natal depression.

GBHT8

Association of Breastfeeding Mothers
  Sydenham Green Health Centre
  Holmshaw Close
  LONDON SE26 4TH
☎ 081 778 4769
Course: Education for Mothers on Breastfeeding
☐ One-to-one or small group sessions for mothers interested in breastfeeding their babies.

GBHT9

Avenue Community Nursing Home
  47 The Avenue
  Linthorpe
  MIDDLESBROUGH TS5 6PE
Course: Help for Long-Term Mentally Ill
☐ A women's collective group which provides support, information and advice to the mentally ill and to their carers.

GBHT10

Birth Control Campaign
  27–35 Mortimer Street
  LONDON WC1N 7RJ
☎ 071 580 9360
Course: Birth Control Education and Training
☐ Advice and consultancy, information and support on all aspects of birth control for women.

GBHT11

Bradford Women's Therapy Service
  c/o 108 Sunbridge Road
  BRADFORD BD1 2NE
☎ 0274 725794
Course: Subsidised Therapy Service for Women
☐ One-to-one or small group discounted therapy sessions.

GBHT12

Breast Care and Mastectomy Association
15–19 Britten Street
LONDON SW3 3TZ
☎ 071 867 8275
Course: Breast Care
☐ One-to-one emotional support and practical help.

GBHT13

Caesarean Support Group of Cambridge
81 Elizabeth Way
CAMBRIDGE CB4 1BQ
☎ 0223 314211
Course: Non-Medical Support for Caesarean Birth
☐ Small groups or one-to-one help and support for women who have undergone a caesarean section.

GBHT14

Cardiff Centre of the Alexander Technique
27 Pen-y-lan Road
Roath
CARDIFF CF2 3PG
☎ 0222 485521
Course: Personal Management
☐ Use of the Alexander Technique to increase personal effectiveness.

GBHT15

Care Alternatives Ltd
206 Worple Road
LONDON SW20 8PN
☎ 081 946 8202
Course: Help for Elderly and Disabled People to Live Independently
☐ A women's partnership which assists people to live independently and without institutionalisation; advice, training and information.

GBHT16

Carers' National Association
29 Chilworth Mews
LONDON W2 3RG
☎ 071 724 7776
Course: Carers' Interests
☐ Organisation representing the interests of full and part-time carers. Provides advice and sometimes runs workshops on issues of popular interest.

GBHT17

Catherine Barry
LONDON
☎ 081 963 0068
Contact: Catherine Barry

Course: Reflexology and Massage for Women
☐ Women only; reflexology and massage.

GBHT18

Choice Stress Defusion
89 High Street
DUDLEY DY1 1QP
☎ 0384 459924
Course: Stress Counselling
☐ One-to-one or small group workshops.

GBHT19

Christine Bowles
First Floor Flat
50 Woodstock Road
Redland
BRISTOL BS6 7EP
☎ 0272 245248
Contact: Christine Bowles
Course: Aromatherapy and Career Counselling
☐ One-to-one advice and expertise or group consultancy.

GBHT20

Cianne Longdon
LONDON SW16
☎ 0606 782924
Contact: Cianne Longdon
Course: Workshops, Therapy/Sexual Abuse
☐ One-to-one counselling and therapy workshops.

GBHT21

Claudia Jones Organisation
103 Stoke Newington Road
LONDON N16 8BX
☎ 071 241 1646
Contact: Claudia Jones
Course: Afro-Caribbean Health Education and Culture
☐ Women's group; small group workshops and one-to-one consultancy.

GBHT22

Coping with Change
58 Wix's Lane
LONDON SW4 0AQ
☎ 071 223 2917
Course: Remotivation, Reorientation and Holistic Support
☐ Small workshops or one-to-one support for individuals interested in regaining a healthy balance in their lifestyles and combining more effectively their different roles in life.

GBHT23

Cystitis and Candida
75 Mortimer Road
LONDON N1 5AR
☎ 071 249 8664
Course: Information and Counselling
☐ Information, counselling and lectures for women.

GBHT24

Cytoscreen Ltd
385 Station Road
HARROW HA1 2AW
☎ 081 861 3862
☐ Advice on screening; training in small groups.

GBHT25

Dalston Children Centre
76 Shacklewell Lane
LONDON E8 2EY
☎ 071 254 9661
Course: Helping Working Families
☐ One-to-one and group workshops for family support.

GBHT26

Delcia McNeil
Flat 2
56 Queens Avenue
LONDON N10 3NU
☎ 081 442 0391
Contact: Delcia McNeil
Course: Pyschotherapy, Counselling and Healing
☐ Advice and small group workshops on all aspects of
healing

GBHT27

Diane Hodgson
MAIDENHEAD SL6
☎ 0628 776174
Contact: Diane Hodgson
Course: Psychodynamic Counselling and Therapy
☐ Counselling and therapy provided for individuals
and small groups to assist with a variety of problems
and issues.

GBHT28

Ms Edit Bodis
The Laurels, Berry Hill Lane
Donnington Le Heath
LEICESTER LE6 2FB
☎ 05308 36780
Contact: Edit Bodis
Course: Stress Management Training
☐ Covers the causes and effects of stress, and examines
methods of stress reduction and relaxation.

GBHT29

Elizabeth Chew
Bow
LONDON E3
☎ 081 981 1553
Contact: Elizabeth Chew
Course: Counselling, Psychosynthesis
☐ Women-only counselling and psychosynthesis therapy.

GBHT30

Elizabeth Hendry
152 Park Street Lane
Park Street
ST ALBANS AL2 2AU
☎ 0727 872010
Contact: Elizabeth Hendry
Course: Counselling Using Transactional Analysis
☐ One-to-one or very small group counselling sessions
using transactional analysis.

GBHT31

FACT
BM Liberation
LONDON WC1N 3XX
Course: Feminist Aquarian Consciousness Tapes
☐ Advice and small group workshops on Aquarian
consciousness.

GBHT32

Fiona Aitken
28 Lucknow Drive
SUTTON IN ASHFIELD NG17 4LS
☎ 0623 558415
Contact: Fiona Aitken
Course: Therapeutic Massage and Reflexology
☐ One-to-one or small group workshops.

GBHT33

Gill Whisson, IPTI, ITEC
30 The Plaza
Jubilee Hall Sports Centre
Covent Garden
LONDON WC2
☎ 071 836 4007
Contact: Gill Whisson
Course: Therapeutic Healing with Oils
☐ Advice and guidance on all aspects of healing with oils.

GBHT34

Grosvenor Centre
16 Grosvenor Avenue
Handsworth
BIRMINGHAM B20 3NR
☎ 021 356 5886
Course: Massage and Reflexology
☐ Advice and small group workshops covering all
elements of the techniques of massage and reflexology.

GBHT35

Hastings and Rother District Women's Network
c/o Susan McGrath
Farleys, Udimore
RYE TN31 6BD
☎ 0424 882884
Course: Education and Counselling for Women
☐ Training, education, counselling and support for women; the Network encourages exchange of information and mutual assistance.

GBHT36

Islington Women's Counselling
Eastgate Building
131b St Johns Way
LONDON N19 3RQ
☎ 071 281 2673
Course: Analytic Counselling
☐ Counselling for women.

GBHT37

Joan Bevan, RPT
11 The Lee
Allesley Park
COVENTRY CV5 9HY
☎ 0203 670847
Contact: Joan Bevan
Course: Polarity and Cranio-Sacral Therapy
☐ Advice and small group workshops covering all aspects of polarity and cranio-sacral therapy.

GBHT38

Julie Anderson
Blackbirds
Little Bardfield
BRAINTREE CM7 4TU
☎ 0371 810983
Contact: Julie Anderson
Course: Psychotherapy, Hypnotherapy and Self-Development
☐ One-to-one or small group workshops.

GBHT39

Kim Daniel
2 Tom Brown Street
RUGBY CV21 3JT
☎ 0788 568585
Contact: Kim Daniel
Course: Women's Massage Therapy
☐ One-to-one consultancy, women's massage.

GBHT40

London Women's Therapy Network
3 Carysfort Road
LONDON N16 9AA
☎ 081 855 2510
Course: Feminist Psychotherapy and Counselling

☐ Psychotherapy and counselling sessions; one-to-one or small groups.

GBHT41

Luna Hawxwell
37 Norwood Terrace
Shipley
BRADFORD BD18 2BD
☎ 0274 582044
Contact: Luna Hawxwell
Course: Therapeutic/Relaxation Massage for Women
☐ Advice and small group workshops covering all elements of therapeutic and relaxation massage techniques for women.

GBHT42

Lynne Morgan
9 Hydepark Terrace
LEEDS LS6 1BJ
☎ 0532 754040
Contact: Lynne Morgan
Course: Feminist Psychotherapy Workshops
☐ Women's workshops; psychotherapy and spirituality.

GBHT43

Manya McClew
216 Grafton Road
LONDON NW5 4AX
☎ 071 267 7399
Contact: Manya McClew
Course: Feminist Gestalt Therapy
☐ One-to-one or small group Gestalt therapy workshops.

GBHT44

Maxine Davies
34 Ash Road
Horfield
BRISTOL BS7 8RN
☎ 0272 244899
Contact: Maxine Davies
Course: Therapy
☐ One-to-one or small group therapy sessions covering a variety of issues.

GBHT45

Meet-A-Mum Association (MAMA)
c/o 58 Maiden Avenue
LONDON SE25 4HS
☎ 081 656 7318
Course: Self-Help for New Mothers
☐ One-to-one or small group sessions for mothers to meet, socialise and provide mutual support.

GBHT46

Micheline Arcier Aromatherapy
7 William Street
LONDON SW1X 9HL

☎ 071 235 3545

Course: Aromatherapy Clinics

☐ Clinic-type workshops covering all aspects of aromatherapy, its uses and applications.

GBHT47

Miscarriage Association
c/o Clayton Hospital
Northgate
WAKEFIELD WF1 3JS
☎ 0924 200799

Course: Information and Support for Women

☐ One-to-one help and counselling for women and families who have experienced recent miscarriages.

GBHT48

National Association for Maternal and Child Welfare
1 South Audley Street
LONDON W1Y 6JS
☎ 071 493 2601

Course: Education in Childcare

☐ One-to-one support and small group sessions to support and improve mother and child welfare.

GBHT49

New Perspectives
1 Dutton Locks
Weaverham
NORTHWICH CW8 3QQ
☎ 0606 854035

Course: Counselling and Training for Health

☐ Looks at the range of barriers which exist against health, and examines methods of increased health and well-being.

GBHT50

North London Network for Counselling and Psychotherapy
216 Grafton Road
LONDON NW5 4AX
☎ 071 267 7399

Course: Feminist Gestalt Therapy

☐ Women only; one-to-one or small group Gestalt therapy workshops.

GBHT51

Nuala White
10 Alexander Road
LONDON N19 3PQ
☎ 071 263 2076

Contact: Nuala White

Course: Feminist Therapy and Group Consultancy

☐ Women only; one-to-one or group workshops.

GBHT52

Oxford Women's Centre
Community Education Centre
Union Street Complex
OXFORD
☎ 0865 245925

Course: Health and Leisure

☐ Information and workshops for women on health issues and leisure interests.

GBHT53

Pauline A. Henderson
51 Evering Road
LONDON N16 7PU
☎ 071 249 5118

Contact: Pauline Henderson

Course: Psychotherapy/Counselling

☐ One-to-one or small group workshops.

GBHT54

Pellin Centre
43 Killyon Road
LONDON SW8 2XS
☎ 071 622 0148

Course: Psychotherapy Training and Individual Therapy

☐ One-to-one therapy and support; also runs training courses in psychotherapy.

GBHT55

Positively Women
5 Sebastian Street
LONDON EC1V 0HE
☎ 071 490 2327

Course: Advice and Support for Women with HIV

☐ Advice, support and information on health issues for women with HIV.

GBHT56

Project for Advice, Counselling and Education
67–69 Cowcross Street
LONDON EC1M 6PB
☎ 071 251 2689

☐ Course held at Park Lane Family Centre, 3 Elwood St, London N5. Open to women and men. Costs: voluntary groups, £40 per person; statutory groups, £50; commercial organisations, £60.

GBHT57

Quest Cancer Test
Woodbury
Harlow Road
CROYDON CM19 5HF
☎ 0279 793671

Course: Cancer Testing and Research

☐ Clinics and one-to-one consultation and advice.

GBHT58

Quest Educational Developments
    Calf House Farm
    Abbot Brow, Mellor
    BLACKBURN BB2 7HU
☎ 0254 813209
Course: Stress Management
□ One-to-one or small group workshops examining the causes, effects and methods of handling and negating the effects of stress in our lives.

GBHT59

Reading Birth Centre
    c/o 10 Portrush Close
    Woodley
    READING RG5 3PB
☎ 0734 698275
Course: Women-Centred Childbirth
□ Workshops for local women who are interested in having their own wishes taken into account during pregnancy and at childbirth.

GBHT60

Salford Women's Centre
    89 Rowans Close
    Churchill Way
    Salford
    MANCHESTER M6 5AL
☎ 061 736 3844
Course: Counselling
□ Workshops and one-to-one counselling sessions to explore issues of interest to the group. Childcare available.

GBHT61

The Sanctuary
    PO Box 2615
    LONDON W14 0DW
☎ 071 371 4666
Course: Counselling for Sexually Abused Women
□ One-to-one counselling and support for sexually abused women; arranges discussion groups on subjects of interest to women involved.

GBHT62

Sequinpark Women's Health Club and Gym
    134 Stoke Newington Church Street
    LONDON N16 0JU
☎ 071 241 1449
□ Advice and activities on all aspects of women's health.

GBHT63

Sequinpark Women's Health Club and Gym
    17 Crouch Hill
    LONDON N4 4AP
☎ 071 272 6857

□ Advice and activities on all aspects of women's health.

GBHT64

Sequinpark Women's Health Club and Gym
    240 Upper Street
    LONDON N1 1RU
☎ 071 272 6857
□ Advice and activities on all aspects of women's health.

GBHT65

Sharon Lester and Rose Priest
    28 Asmuns Place
    LONDON NW11 7XG
☎ 081 458 4135
Contact: Sharon Lester
Course: Chiropractic
□ One-to-one or small group sessions; advice and information.

GBHT66

Society to Support Home Confinements
    Lydgate
    67 Lydgate Lane
    Wolsington
    BISHOP AUCKLAND DL13 3HA
☎ 0388 528044
Course: Women Wanting Home Confinements
□ One-to-one and workshop groups for women wanting to have their babies at home.

GBHT67

Soma
    c/o 37 Norwood Terrace
    Shipley
    BRADFORD BD18 2BD
☎ 0274 582044
Course: Body Awareness in Counselling Training
□ One-to-one consultancy and small group workshops.

GBHT68

South London Natural Health Centre
    7a Clapham Common Southside
    LONDON SW4 7AA
☎ 071 720 8817
Course: Natural Health
□ Advice and activities on all aspects of natural health.

GBHT69

Sparta Fitness Enterprises Ltd
    18 Harrisons Rise
    Waddon
    CROYDON CR0 4LA
☎ 081 688 7995
Course: Stress Counselling

□ Small courses covering all aspects of stress: causes, effects and methods of reducing its negative effect on health and well-being.

GBHT70

Springfield Centre
  4 Springfield Road
  ST LEONARDS-ON-SEA TN38 0TU
☎ 0424 428470
Course: Counselling and Healing with Reflexology
□ Takes into complete account the needs of the individual and group dynamics, and focuses the contents and style accordingly in a flexible learning environment.

GBHT71

Susan Jane Hale
  15A London Road
  Loughton
  MILTON KEYNES MK5 8AB
☎ 0908 691356
Contact: Susan Hale
Course: Stress Management
□ One-to-one or small group workshops examining the causes and effects of stress; explores ways of handling and negating its effects.

GBHT72

Training Office
Haringey Housing Service
  Alexandra House, 10 Station Road
  Wood Green
  LONDON N22 6UW
☎ 081 975 9700 ext. 3027
Contact: Veronika Harris
Course: Developing Strategies for HIV/AIDS Training
□ Covers all elements of employment practice as it relates to AIDS and HIV in the workplace.

GBHT73

Well Natural Health Centre
  87 Drayton Road
  Kings Heath
  BIRMINGHAM B14 7LP
☎ 021 443 1580
Course: Natural Therapies Workshops
□ Small workshops covering all elements of natural therapy and its effect on overall well-being.

GBHT74

Womankind
  76 Colston Street
  BRISTOL BS1 5BB
☎ 0272 252507
Course: Women and Mental Health

□ Arranges workshops and discussion groups on subjects of interest to women members.

GBHT75

Women Unlimited
  79 Pathfield Road
  LONDON SW16 5PA
☎ 081 677 7503
Course: Counselling Training and Consultancy
□ One-to-one support and small group workshops in counselling skills.

GBHT76

Women's Alternative Health Centre Project
  c/o 31 Manor Row
  BRADFORD BD1 4PS
Course: Alternative Health Therapies for Women
□ One-to-one or small group workshops.

GBHT77

Women's Counselling and Therapy Service
  Oxford Chambers
  Oxford Place
  LEEDS LS1 3AX
☎ 0532 455725
Course: Counselling and Therapy
□ One-to-one or small counselling and therapy groups; advice, training and support.

GBHT78

Women's Counselling Services
  NORTHWOOD
  Middlesex
☎ 0923 820306
Course: Depression, Sickness and Relationships
□ One-to-one or small group workshops exploring and examining the causes and effects of different types of behaviour, and developing positive responses.

GBHT79

Women's Health Information and Support Centre
  Junction 7
  3–7 Hazelwood Road
  NORTHAMPTON NN1 1LG
☎ 0604 397 23
Course: Women's Health
□ Education and information on all aspects of women's health.

GBHT80

Women's Health Information Mobile
  23 Mill Street
  ASHWELL SG7 5LY
☎ 046 274 2288
Course: Health Information for Women
□ Health information on all aspects of women's health.

GBHT81

Women's Midlife Experience Centre
   318 Summer Lane
   BIRMINGHAM B19 3RL
☎   021 359 3562
Course: Training and Encouragement for Women in Midlife
□ Training and support to encourage women during their middle years.

GBHT82

Women's Tapeover
   c/o 66 Oakfield Road
   LONDON N4 4LB
Course: Information for Blind and Partially Sighted
□ Support and practical help for blind and partially sighted women.

GBHT83

Women's Therapeutic Bodywork Collective
   c/o Flat 3
   371 High Road
   Wood Green
   LONDON N22 4JA
☎   081 888 1735
Course: Massage-Related Bodywork for Women
□ Small workshops covering all aspects of massage of interest to women.

GBHT84

Women's Therapy Centre
   6 Manor Gardens
   LONDON N7 6LA
☎   071 263 6200
Course: Feminist Psychotherapy for Women
□ Women only; one-to-one or small group workshops.

GBHT85

Women's Therapy Link
   16 Hazelmere Court
   26 Palace Road
   LONDON SW2 3NH
☎   081 671 2267
Course: Psychotherapy and Counselling
□ Women only; one-to-one or small group workshops.

Italy

ITHT1

Centro Simonetter Tosi
   c/o Centro Femminista Internazionale
   Via della Lungare 19
   00165 ROME
☎   06 6879775
Course: Women's Health

□ Arranges courses and seminars for members on women's health issues.

Netherlands

NETHT1

STEW
   Weesperzijde 4
   1091 EA AMSTERDAM
Contact: D. Wayer
Course: Women's Health
□ Training in issues surrounding women's health.

New Zealand

NZHT1

Harvest Clinic
   405 Richmond Road
   Grey Lym
   AUCKLAND
☎   09 378 9274
Contact: Kathleen Best
Course: Women's Health
□ Training in issues surrounding women's health.

Portugal

PORHT1

IEFP
   Rue de Xabregas 52
   1900 LISBON
Contact: Lucia Martins
Course: Women's Health
□ Workshops on aspects of women's health.

United States of America

USAHT1

Adult Career Resource Center
Oakton Community College
   1600 E. Golf Road
   DES PLAINES, IL 60016
☎   312 635 1672
Course: Women's Health
□ Training in issues surrounding women's health.

USAHT2

Advocates for Women, Inc.
   414 Mason St, 4th Floor
   SAN FRANCISCO, CA 94102
☎   415 391 4870
Course: Women's Health
□ Training in issues surrounding women's health.

USAHT3

Career Center
Hamilton College
CLINTON, NY 13323
☎ 315 859 7346
Course: Women's Health
☐ Training in issues surrounding women's health.

USAHT4

Career Development Center
Randolph-Macon Women's College
2500 Rivermont Avenue
LYNCHBURG, VA 24503
☎ 804 846 7392
Course: Women's Health
☐ Training in issues surrounding women's health.

USAHT5

Career Services
Women's Educational and Industrial Union
366 Boylston Street
BOSTON, MA 02116
☎ 617 536 5651
Course: Women's Health
☐ Training in issues surrounding women's health.

USAHT6

Center for Women's Services
Western Michigan University
A-331 Ellsworth Hall
KALAMAZOO, MI 49008
☎ 313 377 3033
Course: Women's Health
☐ Training in issues surrounding women's health.

USAHT7

Douglass Advisory Services for Women
Douglass College
132 George Street
NEW BRUNSWICK, NJ 08903
☎ 201 932 9603
Course: Women's Health
☐ Training in issues surrounding women's health.

USAHT8

Every Woman's Place
23 Strong Avenue
MUSKEGON, MI 49441
☎ 616 726 4493
Course: Women's Health
☐ Training in issues surrounding women's health.

USAHT9

Focus on Women
Montana State University
9 Hamilton Hall
BOZEMAN, MT 59717
☎ 406 994 2012
Course: Women's Health
☐ Training in issues surrounding women's health.

USAHT10

Frederick New Directions for Women
23 West 3rd Street
FREDERICK, MD 21701
☎ 301 694 6322
Course: Women's Health
☐ Training in issues surrounding women's health.

USAHT11

Lifelong Learning Women's Programs
Cuyahoga Community College
2900 Community College Avenue
CLEVELAND, OH 44115
☎ 216 241 5966
Course: Women's Health
☐ Training in issues surrounding women's health.

USAHT12

Office of Career Counselling and Placement
Kingsborough Community College
2001 Oriental Boulevard, Room C102
BROOKLYN, NY 11235
☎ 212 934 5115
Course: Women's Health
☐ Training in issues surrounding women's health.

USAHT13

Office of Career Planning
Wheaton College
NORTON, MA 02766
☎ 617 285 7722
Course: Women's Health
☐ Training in issues surrounding women's health.

USAHT14

Office of Career Services
Barnard College
606 West 120th Street
NEW YORK, NY 10027
☎ 212 280 2033
Course: Women's Health
☐ Training in issues surrounding women's health.

USAHT15

Placement 500
424 Madison Avenue
NEW YORK, NY 10017
☎ 212 688 4606

Course: Women's Health
☐ Training in issues surrounding women's health.

USAHT16

Resources for Women
University of Pennsylvania
Houston Hall
PHILADELPHIA, PA 19104
☎ 215 243 5537
Course: Women's Health
☐ Training in issues surrounding women's health.

USAHT17

Ruth Shapiro Associates
200 East 30th Street
NEW YORK, NY 10016
☎ 212 889 4284
Course: Women's Health
☐ Training in issues surrounding women's health.

USAHT18

The Women's Center
University of Delaware
NEWARK, DE 19711
☎ 302 738 8733
Course: Women's Health
☐ Training in issues surrounding women's health.

USAHT19

Women's Center
Converse College
SPARTANBURG, SC 29301
☎ 803 585 6421
Course: Women's Health
☐ Training in issues surrounding women's health.

USAHT20

The Women's Opportunities Center
University of California, Extension Irvine
Box AZ
Irvine, CA 92716
☎ 714 833 7128
Course: Women's Health
☐ Training in issues surrounding women's health.

USAHT21

Women's Resource Center
226 Bostick NE
GRAND RAPIDS, MI 49503
☎ 616 456 8571
Course: Women's Health
☐ Training in issues surrounding women's health.

USAHT22

Working Opportunities for Women
2233 University Ave
Suite 340
ST PAUL, MN 55114
☎ 612 647 9961
Course: Women's Health
☐ Training in issues surrounding women's health.

Management

Australia

AUSM1

Affirmative Action Agency
1st Floor, The Denison
65 Berry Street
PO Box 974
NORTH SYDNEY, NSW 2060
☎ 02 957 4333
Course: Management Development for Women
□ Vocational training for women interested in management development.

AUSM2

BIR
PO Box 659
CARLTON, Vic. 3053
☎ 03 342 1100
Course: Management Development for Women
□ Vocational training for women interested in management development.

AUSM3

EEO Policy and Programs Unit
PSC
Edmund Barton Building
BARTON, ACT 2600
☎ 06 272 3562
Course: Management Development for Women
Vocational training for woman interested in management development.

Austria

AUM1

The Branch for the Advancement of Women
PO Box 500
1400 VIENNA
Course: Management Development for Women
□ Vocational training for women interested in management development.

AUM2

Unit for the Integration of Women in Industrial Development
Department for Programmes Development
PO Box 300
1400 VIENNA
Course: Management Development for Women
□ Vocational training for women interested in management development.

Belgium

BELM1

ASBL CERA
BP 87 Etterbeek 1
1040 BRUSSELS
Contact: Dominique Ruelle-Charlez
Course: Management Development for Women
□ Vocational training aimed at developing women managers.

BELM2

Les Cahiers du Grif
29 rue Blanche
1050 BRUSSELS
Contact: Veronique Degraef
Course: Management Development for Women
□ Vocational training aimed at developing women managers.

BELM3

Commissariat Royal à l'Immigration
Residence Palace
155 rue de la Loi
1040 BRUSSELS
Contact: Godelieve Vandamme
Course: Management Development for Women
□ Vocational training for women interested in management development.

BELM4

CSC
121 rue de la Loi
1040 BRUSSELS
Contact: Anne-Françoise Theunissen
Course: Management Development for Women
□ Vocational training for women interested in management development.

BELM5

Documentatiecentrum Rosa
Gallaistraat 78
1210 BRUSSELS
Contact: Chris Zwaenepoel
Course: Management Development for Women
□ Vocational training for women interested in management development.

BELM6

Equal Opportunities Unit
European Commission
200 rue de la Loi
1049 BRUSSELS
Contact: Helle Jacobson

Course: Management Development for Women
☐ Research and training in women's management development.

BELM7

Equal Opportunities Unit
European Commission
   200 rue de la Loi
   1049 BRUSSELS
Contact: Margarida Pinto
Course: Management Development for Women
☐ Research and training aimed at enhancing women's status in society, improving women's career possibilities and access to management-level career opportunities.

BELM8

European Parliament
   Belliardstraat 97
   1040 BRUSSELS
Contact: Lode Van Outrive
Course: Management Development for Women
☐ Vocational training for women interested in management development.

BELM9

Eurydice
   17 rue Archimede
   1040 BRUSSELS
Contact: M. Vanandruel
Course: Management Development for Women
☐ Vocational training for women interested in management development.

BELM10

FEMB – OBMB
   88 rue Gachardstraat
   1050 BRUSSELS
Contact: Jacques Verstraeten
Course: Management Development for Women
☐ Vocational training for women interested in management development.

BELM11

FOREM
   5 boulevard de l'Empereur
   1000 BRUSSELS
Contact: Raymond Delbrouck
Course: Management Development for Women
☐ Vocational training aimed at developing women managers.

BELM12

FOREM Centre de Formation
   8 rue Jean Gome
   4802 HENSY
Contact: M. Servais
Course: Management Development for Women
☐ Vocational training for women interested in management development.

BELM13

Forem Service Ranst
   25 rue Montoyer
   1040 BRUSSELS
Contact: M. Van Ranst
Course: Management Development for Women
☐ Vocational training for women interested in management development.

BELM14

G. Desiront
   Belliardstraat 20, bus 16
   1040 BRUSSELS
Contact: G. Desiront
Course: Management Development for Women
☐ Vocational training aimed at developing women managers.

BELM15

GOM – ESA
   Desguinlei 102 bus 13
   2018 ANTWERP
Contact: Heidi Vanheusden
Course: Management Development for Women
☐ Vocational training for women interested in management development.

BELM16

Institut voor Voortdurende Vorming en Onderzoek in de Confectie
   Montoyerstraat 31
   1040 BRUSSELS
Contact: Jan Van Depoele
Course: Management Development for Women
☐ Vocational training for women interested in management development.

BELM17

Institut voor Voortdurende Vorming van de Middenstand
   Josef II straat 30
   1040 BRUSSELS
Contact: M. J. Van der Aa-Broos
Course: Management Development for Women
☐ Vocational training for women interested in management development.

BELM18
IRIS Unit
> CREW s.c.
> 21 rue de la Tourelle
> 1040 BRUSSELS

Contact: Audrey Van Tuyckom
Course: Management Development for Women
☐ Vocational training for women's management development.

BELM19
Maison de l'Europe de Courcelles
> 46 rue P. Monnoyer
> 6180 COURCELLES

Contact: Martine Denille
Course: Management Development for Women
☐ Vocational training aimed at developing women managers.

BELM20
Ministère de l'Emploi et du Travail
> 51 rue Belliard
> 1040 BRUSSELS

Contact: Brigitte Van Meelsen
Course: Management Development for Women
☐ Vocational training for women interested in management development.

BELM21
NCMV
> Spastraat 8
> 1040 BRUSSELS

Contact: Marianne Thyssen
Course: Management Development for Women
☐ Vocational training for women interested in management development.

BELM22
SETA-UITA
> Rue Fosse aux Loups Bte 3
> 1000 BRUSSELS

Contact: Betty Samola
Course: Management Development for Women
☐ Vocational training aimed at developing women managers.

BELM23
VDAB
> Keizerslaan 11
> 1000 BRUSSELS

Contact: Hilde Van Praet
Course: Management Development for Women
☐ Vocational training for women interested in management development.

Canada

CANM1
The Canadian Advisory Council on the Status of Women
> 151 Sparks Street, Box 1541, Station B
> OTTAWA K1P 5R5
> ☎ 613 992 4975

Course: Management Development for Women
☐ Vocational training for women interested in management development.

CANM2
The Canadian Advisory Council on the Status of Women
> 269 Main Street, Suite 600
> Winnipeg
> MANITOBA R3C 1B2
> ☎ 204 949 3140

Course: Management Development for Women
☐ Vocational training for women interested in management development.

CANM3
Canadian Congress for Learning Opportunities for Women
> 47 Main Street
> Toronto
> ONTARIO M4E 2U6
> ☎ 416 699 1909

Course: Management Development for Women
☐ Vocational training for women interested in management development.

CANM4
Ontario Women's Directorate
> 480 University Ave
> 2nd Floor
> Toronto
> ONTARIO M5G 1V2

Course: Management Development for Women
☐ Vocational training for women interested in management development.

CAMN5
OWD
> 107C Johnson Ave
> Thunder Bay
> ONTARIO P7B 2V9

Course: Management Development for Women
☐ Vocational training for women interested in management development.

CAMN6

The Pay Equity Commission
150 Eglington Avenue East
5th Floor
Toronto
ONTARIO M4P 1E8
Course: Management Development for Women
☐ Vocational training for women interested in management development.

Denmark

DENM1

Aben Datastue for Kvinder
Ostre Stationsvej 36
5000 ODENSE C
Contact: Dorrit Munk Jensen
Course: Management Development for Women
☐ Vocational training for women managers.

DENM2

Alborg Tekniske Skole
Oster Uttrupvej 1
Postbox 2339
8260 VIBY J
Contact: Sven Age Suhr
Course: Management Development for Women
☐ Vocational training aimed at developing women managers.

DENM3

Anne Dorte Faester
Birkeholm Terrasserne 431
3520 FARUM
Contact: Anne Dorte Faester
Course: Management Development for Women
☐ Vocational training aimed at developing women managers.

DENM4

AOF
Rugardsvej 9
5000 ODENSE
Contact: Connie Lyders
Course: Management Development for Women
☐ Vocational training for women interested in developing management skills.

DENM5

Arbejdsformidlingen
Norreport 15
8000 ARHUS
Contact: Jytte Petersen
Course: Management Development for Women
☐ Vocational training for women's management development.

DENM6

Arbejdsformiddingen
Vilhelmskildevej 1E
5700 SVENOBORG
Contact: Anne Marie Jacobsen
Course: Management Development for Women
☐ Vocational training for women interested in management development.

DENM7

Arbejdsmarkedsstyrelsen
Hejrevej 43
2400 COPENHAGEN NV
Contact: Benthe Stig
Course: Management Development for Women
☐ Vocational training to develop women managers.

DENM8

Arhus Tekniske Skole
Halmstadsgade 6
8200 ARHUS N
Contact: Marianne Thorsager
Course: Management Development for Women
☐ Vocational training aimed at developing women managers.

DENM9

Beskaeftigelseskonsulent
Ullasvej 23
3700 RONNE
Contact: Kirstine Jorgensen
Course: Management Development for Women
☐ Vocational training to develop women managers.

DENM10

Bjarne Grubbe Jensen
Petersmindevej 50
5000 ODENSE C
Contact: Bjarne Grubbe Jensen
Course: Management Development for Women
☐ Vocational training for women's management development.

DENM11

Bodil Husted
Hasselager alle 2
Postbox 2339
8260 VIBY J
Contact: Bodil Husted
Course: Management Development for Women
☐ Vocational training aimed at developing women managers.

DENM12
DA
Vester Voldgade 113
1552 COPENHAGEN
Contact: Margit Harup Grove
Course: Management Development for Women
☐ Research and training in women's management development.

DENM13
Dansk Teknologist Institut
Postbox 141
2630 TASTRUP
Contact: Claudia Anker Nielsen
Course: Management Development for Women
☐ Vocational training aimed at developing women managers.

DENM14
Handelshojskolens Kvindenetvaerk
(Women's Network of Business Admin)
Institute of Organisation and Industrial Sociology
Blaagaardsgade 23 B
2200 COPENHAGEN N
☎ 01 37 05 55
Contact: Jytte Bonde
Course: Women Executives in the Labour Market
☐ Research and training aimed at enhancing the position of women in the economy and particularly at management level.

DENM15
Holbaek Tekniske Skole
Absalonsgade 20
4300 HOLBAEK
Contact: Ruth Lange
Course: Management Development for Women
☐ Vocational training aimed at developing women managers.

DENM16
KIMADAN
Nordvestvej 4
9600 ARS
Contact: Nina Ostergard
Course: Management Development for Women
☐ Vocational training aimed at developing women managers.

DENM17
Koge Handelskole
Kogleaksvej 25
4600 KOGE
Contact: Leif Hugo Rasmussen
Course: Management Development for Women

☐ Vocational training for women interested in management.

DENM18
Kvindegruppen ved Danmarks Forvaltningshojskolf
(The Women's Group of Public Administration)
Lindevangs Alle 6
200 FREDERIKSBERG
☎ 01 86 18 70
Contact: Gitte Haselbo
Course: Management Development Training for Women
☐ Courses are offered in management training for female managers, and management development training for women.

DENM19
Ligestillingskonsulent
Arbejdsformidlingen
Kjellerupsgade 12
9000 ALBORG
Contact: Anette Kortsen
Course: Management Development for Women
☐ Vocational training aimed at developing women managers.

DENM20
Nomi Hartmann
Pallisvej 41
8220 BRABRAND
Contact: Nomi Hartmann
Course: Management Development for Women
☐ Vocational training aimed at developing women managers.

DENM21
Odense Universitet
Campusvej 55
5230 ODENSE M
Contact: Daniel Fischer
Course: Management Development for Women
☐ Vocational training aimed at developing women managers.

DENM22
Organisationskontoret
Skottenborg 26
8800 VIBORG
Contact: Birgitte Haahr
Course: Management Development for Women
☐ Vocational training for women interested in developing management skills.

DENM23

Udviklingsleder
Indvirke
Stationsvej 46
7100 BIRKEROD
Contact: Lene Sondberg
Course: Management Development for Women
□ Vocational training for women interested in management development.

DENM24

Vejle Amtskommune
Damhaven 12
7100 VEJLE
Contact: Jens Bertelsen
Course: Management Development for Women
□ Vocational training for women's management development.

Dominican Republic

DOMM1

International Research and Training Institute for the Advancement of Women (INSTRAW)
PO Box 21747
SANTO DOMINGO
Course: Management Development for Women
□ Vocational training for women interested in management development.

France

FRM1

Centre d'Information des Droits de la Femme
Centre Municipal Duguesclin
Place Chanzy
79000 NIORT
Contact: Christine Girard
Course: Management Development for Women
□ Vocational training for women interested in management development.

FRM2

CIDFF du Lot
50 rue Ste Urcisse
46000 CAHORS
Contact: Rosa Posa Guinea
Course: Management Development for Women
□ Vocational training for women interested in management development.

FRM3

EDF-GDF
16 rue de Monceau
75008 PARIS

Contact: Beatrice Thiery
Course: Management Development for Women
□ Vocational training for women interested in management development.

FRM4

Fédération Régionale des CIVAM Languedoc Roussillon
5 place des Docteurs Dox
30250 SOMMIERES
Contact: Roselyne Bessac
Course: Management Development for Women
□ Vocational training for women interested in management development.

FRM5

Greta du Bocage
Rue du Commandant
Charcot 37–39
61100 FLERS
Contact: Annie Rossi
Course: Management Development for Women
□ Vocational training for women interested in management development.

FRM6

GRETA Sudisere
1 rue des Trembles
38100 GRENOBLE
Contact: A. Baloyan
Course: Management Development for Women
□ Vocational training for women interested in management development.

FRM7

GRETA Sud Manche
2 rue de Verdun
50300 AVRANCHES
Contact: Armelle Brault
Course: Management Development for Women
□ Vocational training for women interested in management development.

FRM8

Mission d'Education Permanente
30 avenue de Fretilly
17000 LA ROCHELLE
Contact: Guy Roy
Course: Management Development for Women
□ Vocational training for women interested in management development.

FRM9

Secrétariat d'Etat chargé des Droits des Femmes
31 rue Le Pelletier
75009 PARIS
Contact: Françoise Divisia

Course: Management Development for Women
☐ Vocational training for women interested in management development.

Great Britain and Northern Ireland

GBM1

Amber Training
   6 Sutton Road
   GRANBY NG13 9PY
☎ 0949 51006
Course: Management: Women's Development
☐ Examines all the issues of interest to women as managers, and to those women who wish to develop management skills for a range of organisational settings.

GBM2

Arbee Marketing Communication Training
   31 Kilmorie Road
   Forest Road
   LONDON SE23 2SS
☎ 081 291 0884
Contact: Ruffo Bravette
Course: Management Development for Women
☐ Examines issues of relevance to women managers and to those who wish to become managers.

GBM3

Beck Associates
   185 Lord Street
   HODDESDON EN11 8NQ
☎ 0992 464966
Contact: Jane Beck
Course: Management Development for Women
☐ Designed for women who want to become managers or those who wish to improve their management skills.

GBM4

Bilston Community College
   Springvale House
   Millfields Road
   WOLVERHAMPTON WV14 0QR
☎ 0902 493065
Contact: Alan Leivesley
Course: Women into Management
☐ Examines issues relating to women as managers, and the barriers which prevent women breaking the glass ceiling.

GBM5

Biographic Management Ltd
   High Banks
   Dark Lane
   Rodborough
   STROUD GL5 3UF
☎ 0453 765142

Contact: Jenny Daisley
Course: Women in Management/Women as Leaders
☐ Two courses run parallel to develop women as employees and to enhance their chances of obtaining higher-grade positions.

GBM6

Boxclever Presentation Training
   25 Bewdley Street
   LONDON N1 1HB
☎ 071 607 5766
Course: Presentation and Personal Effectiveness
☐ Courses and one-to-one advice for women.

GBM7

Calderdale MBC
   Franus St
   HALIFAX HX1 3V2
☎ Contact: D. McAll
Course: Management Development for Women
☐ Vocational training for women interested in management development.

GBM8

Carol Baxter
   126 Eccles Old Road
   Salford
   MANCHESTER M6 8QQ
☎ 061 736 2654
Contact: Carol Baxter
Course: Management Skills for Women
☐ Examines a whole range of management issues for women managers and those who wish to pursue a management career.

GBM9

Cobar Group, Training Consultancy
   Hillcrest House
   104 Erlanger Road, Telegraph Hill
   LONDON SE14 5TH
☎ 071 639 8547
Contact: Kate Cobb
Course: Developing Women Managers
☐ Covers all issues of relevance to women as managers and to those women who wish to pursue management careers.

GBM10

Corranbeag Associates
   Ardfern
   ARGYLL PA31 8QN
☎ 085 25249
Course: Women: Human Resource Development
☐ Examines the issues which prevent women reaching their full potential, and looks at methods of enhancing women's status at work through human resource planning and development.

GBM11

Course Centre Ltd
13 Loraine Road
LONDON N7 6EZ
☎ 071 607 2197
Course: Management
□ Offered on a formal training or consultancy basis to assist managers and those women who wish to consolidate their career experience and develop management skills.

GBM12

Coventry Technical College
The Butts
COVENTRY CV1 3GD
Contact: Liz Yates
Course: Management Development for Women
□ Vocational training for women interested in management development.

GBM13

Cranford Training Group
High Street
CRANFORD TW5 9PD
☎ 081 897 2001
Contact: Kate Evans
Course: Women for Management
□ Courses are free and run part time only, leading to nationally recognised qualifications.

GBM14

Cullen, Scholefield Associates
Max Welton House
41 Boltro Road
HAYWARDS HEATH RH16 1BJ
☎ 0444 455052
Course: Management Development
□ Examines skills and methods of acquiring management attributes and putting them into practice.

GBM15

The Domino Consultancy Ltd
56 Charnwood Road
SHEPSHED LE12 9NP
☎ 0509 505404
Contact: Mrs Pauline Hicks
Course: Women's Management Development Workshops
□ Courses are run in-house for organisations, and include communicating as women, managing time, stress, conflict and creating a positive self-image.

GBM16

Douglas Management and Training Development Ltd
101 Ansell Road
Tooting
LONDON SW17 7LT
☎ 081 672 2431
Contact: Mr Carlis Douglas-Sanusi
Course: Women in Management
□ This course has been developed for black and white women in the UK and abroad; team work based on developing appropriate strategies for tackling barriers to equal opportunities.

GBM17

Dow-Stoker Ltd
The Mill
Stortford Road
Hatfield Heath
Nr BISHOP'S STORTFORD CM22 7DL
☎ 0279 730056
Contact: Linda Stoker
Course: Women in Management
□ Covers all of the issues related to women as managers and to those who wish to pursue careers as managers.

GBM18

Dunfermline Women's Training Centre
5/7 Comely Park
DUNFERMLINE KY12 7HU
Contact: Anne Barr
Course: Management Development for Women
□ Vocational training for women interested in management development.

GBM19

Elaine Green
19a Gabriel Street
LONDON SE23 1DW
☎ 081 699 4621
Contact: Elaine Green
Course: Management
□ Covers the range of skills which are necessary to succeed in management and to nuture those skills which already exist among participants to develop leadership skills.

GBM20

EM Courses Ltd
4 Mapledale Avenue
CROYDON CR0 5TA
☎ 081 654 4659
Contact: Dr Eleanor MacDonald
Course: Personal Effectiveness and Management Skills

☐ Covers all elements of management to increase personal effectiveness, enhance self-esteem, improve communication and build confidence.

GBM21

Equal Access Training Ltd
40 Ermine Close
Chinchilla Drive
HOUNSLOW TW4 7PW
☎ 081 577 0727
Contact: Daniel Obiago
Course: Management Development for Women
☐ Examines issues of importance to women managers and to those who wish to pursue management careers.

GBM22

Eurosearch
Chestnut House
BITTLESWELL LE17 4SG
☎ 0455 556378
Contact: Marguerite Dawson
Course: Management Development Programme
☐ Considers all the issues of importance to women managers and develops strategies for improved self-confidence, image, esteem and prospects.

GBM23

Excel International Ltd
Excel House
35 Lind House
SUTTON SM1 4PP
☎ 081 770 0465
Contact: Nancy Paul
Course: Development of Women in Management
☐ Looks at how women can become managers; and once they are, how they can make full use of their talents and reach their full potential.

GBM24

Handsworth College
Soho Road
Handsworth
BIRMINGHAM B21
☎ 021 551 6031
Contact: Liz Burkitt
Course: Women into Management
☐ Students have the opportunity to gain BTEC Certificate in Management Studies, BTEC Small Business Computer Systems, BTEC National French.

GBM25

IBP Consultants Ltd
Vale House
18 The Value
COULSDON CR5 2AW
☎ 081 660 7954
Contact: Dr Kirsty Ross

Course: Women: Breaking the Glass Ceiling
☐ A women-only programme which examines the issues women face when they want to climb the corporate ladder and reach higher-grade jobs.

GBM26

Pamela Brown Associates Ltd
4 Foxhill Gardens
Upper Norwood
LONDON SE19 2XB
☎ 081 768 0533
Contact: Pam Brown
Course: Women into Management
☐ Examines management development topics for women managers and women at other grades who wish to become managers.

GBM27

Patrick George
Kings Farm
Edlesborough
DUNSTABLE LU6 2JN
☎ 0525 220974
Contact: Patrick George
Course: Staff Development
☐ Staff development programmes with special emphasis on women's management development and career prospects.

GBM28

Positive Feedback
Studio 5, Beech Hall Centre
Nursery Road
HIGH BEECH
Essex
☎ 0279 410313
Contact: Laura Mellor
Course: Women in Management
☐ Courses designed to client's specifications and run in-house. External and residential venues available.

GBM29

Positive Feedback Training Consultancy
Studios 1-2, Beech Hall
Nursery Road
HIGH BEECH IG10 4AE
☎ 0279 410313
Course: Personal Effectiveness and Management Skills
☐ Covers all of the issues associated with increased personal effectiveness which lead to better management skills.

GBM30

Rachel Snee
41 Vivian Road
SHEFFIELD S5 6WJ

☎ 0742 562252
Contact: Rachel Snee
Course: Management Development
□ Courses tailor made to suit organisations or individuals, consider the whole range of management skills required to succeed.

GBM31

Rosemary Chapman Associates
31 Eland Road
LONDON SW11 5JX
☎ 071 223 2251
Course: Management Development
□ Short courses and one-to-one consultancy for women interested in management careers.

GBM32

South Glamorgan Women's Workshop
Edena House
East Canal Wharf
CARDIFF CF1 5AQ
Contact: Jean Golten
Course: Management Development for Women
□ Vocational training for women interested in management development.

GBM33

Staff Development Consultant
5 Trefelin Cottages
Llandegai
BANGOR LL57 4LH
☎ 0248 364147
Contact: Jean Hodder
Course: Management Development for Women using the Outdoors
□ Covers all the skills relating to good management practice, and develops the competence of all participants through outdoor interaction in an all-female environment.

GBM34

Sue Cordingley Associates
'Old Lakenham'
Pickering Street
MAIDSTONE
☎ 0622 747232
Contact: Sue Cordingley
Course: Management Training for Women
□ Designed to enable women to enter and succeed in managerial-level jobs.

GBM35

Training 2000: The Scottish Alliance for Women's Training
30 Rutland Square
EDINBURGH EH1 2BW

☎ 031 229 6775
Course: Training Promotion
□ Courses designed for small and large groups of women on a range of topics to reflect women's interests and career enhancement.

GBM36

Vida Pearson (Resource)
22 Main Street
Hoby
LEICESTER LE14 3DT
☎ 0664 434451
Contact: Vida Pearson
Course: Women and Power: Management Development
□ Looks at the reasons why few women are in positions of authority and how power is generally held by men; examines methods of enhancing women's management potential.

GBM37

WEDA
Aston Science Park
Love Lane
Aston Triangle
BIRMINGHAM B7 4BJ
Contact: Anne Douglas
Course: Management Development for Women
□ Vocational training for women interested in management development.

GBM38

Women in Management
64 Marryat Road
LONDON SW19 5BN
☎ 081 944 6332
Course: Women in Management
□ Support and advice network for women in management and for women interested in management careers; organises occasional training seminars.

GBM39

Women's Education Project
129 University Street
BELFAST BT7 1HP
☎ 0232 230212
Contact: Geraldine Burns
Course: Management Skills
□ Course held at North Belfast Community Development Centre. Examines aspects of management for women managers and for women interested in careers in management.

Greece

GREM1

OAED
 PO Box 70017
 16610 GLYFADA
Contact: Dimitri Hassomeri
Course: Management Development for Women
☐ Research and training aimed at enhancing women's management development.

Ireland

IREM 1

John Bowman
 59 Pembroke Lane
 Ballsbridge
 DUBLIN 4
Contact: John Bowman
Course: Management Development for Women
☐ Vocational training for women interested in management development.

Israel

ISRM1

Israel Women's Network
 14 Haltibonim Street
 JERUSALEM
Contact: Prof. Alice Shalvi
Course: Management Development for Women
☐ Vocational training for women interested in management development.

Japan

JAPM1

Japan Institute of Labour
 Chutaikin Building
 7-6 Shibakoen 1-chome
 Minato-ku
 TOKYO, 105 Japan
Course: Management Development for Women
☐ Vocational training for women interested in management development.

JAPM2

National Women's Ed. Centre
 728 Sugaya, Ranzan-Machi
 Hiki-gun
 SAITAMA-KEN, 355-02 Japan
Course: Management Development for Women
☐ Vocational training for women interested in management development.

Netherlands

NETM1

Annie van Dieren School
 Wilhelminapark 55
 5041 ED TILBURG
☎ 013 362 695
Course: Management Development for Women
☐ Workshops and discussion groups covering all aspects of management development for women.

NETM2

Janneke Dierx School
 Oude Vlissingseweg 32a
 4336 AD MIDDELBURG
☎ 011 802 35 18
Course: Women's Career Development
☐ Advice and assistance for women interested in enhancing their career possibilities; management development.

NETM3

Stichting, Vrouwenvakopleiding Vrouwenbond FNV Zeeland
 Oude Vlissingseweg 32a
 Postbus 7034
 4330 GA MIDDELBURG
Contact: N. Blomsbeel
Course: Management Development for Women
☐ Vocational training for women interested in management development.

NETM4

Vrouwenvakschool Informatica Amsterdam
 Wodanstraat 1–3
 1076 CC AMSTERDAM
☎ 020 662 70 96
Course: Management Development for Women
☐ Development workshops and vocational training for women interested in management.

New Zealand

NZM1

National Advisory Council on the Employment of Women (NACEN)
c/o Dept of Labour
Private Bag
WELLINGTON
Course: Management Development for Women
☐ Vocational training for women interested in management development.

NZM2

Women's Electoral Lobby
WEL Waikato
PO Box 9581
HAMILTON
Course: Management Development for Women
☐ Vocational training for women interested in management development.

Portugal

PORM1

Formedia
Av. Do Brasil 88 7 Esq
2700 LISBON
Contact: Isabel Baltazar
Course: Management Development for Women
☐ Vocational training for women interested in management development.

PORM2

IEFP
52 rue de Xabregas
1900 LISBON
Contact: Lucia Martins
Course: Management Development for Women
☐ Training covering all aspects of women's management development.

PORM3

Instituto do Emprego e Formacao Profissional
Av. José Malhoa 11–5
1000 LISBON
Contact: Maria Do Carmo Nunes
Course: Management Development for Women
☐ Vocational training for women interested in management development.

PORM4

Instituto do Emprego e Formacao Profissional
Av. José Malhoa 11-5
1000 LISBON
Contact: Maria Everilde
Course: Management Development for Women
☐ Vocational training for women interested in management development.

South Korea

SKM1

Korean Women's Development Institute
CPO Box 2267
SEOUL 100
Course: Management Development for Women
☐ Vocational training for women interested in management development.

Spain

SPM1

CEDEL (Centro de Estudios de Desarrollo Economico Local)
Conde de Borell
334–336 Bajos
08029 BARCELONA
Contact: Josefa Sanchez
Course: Management Development for Women
☐ Vocational training for women interested in management development.

SPM2

Centre Technic de la Dona
Ronda Sant Pere
08010 BARCELONA
☎ 317 46 50
Course: Management Development for Women
☐ Vocational training for women interested in management development.

SPM3

Centre Tecnic per la Dona
SA
Ronda Sant Pere, 68 pral
08010 BARCELONA
Contact: Anna Mercade i Ferrando
Course: Management Development for Women
☐ Vocational training for women interested in management development.

SPM4

UCSTE
Tirso de Molina 5–5
28012 MADRID

Contact: Carmen Pino Villalba
Course: Management Development for Women
☐ Vocational training for women interested in management development.

Switzerland

SWIM1

Focal Point for Women
ECE
    Palais des Nations
    1211 GENEVA 10
Course: Management Development for Women
☐ Vocational training for women interested in management development.

SWIM2

Femmedia
    Klosterberg 19
    4051 BASLE
☎   061 272 03 23
Contact: Anita Fetz
Course: Management Development for Women
☐ Vocational training for women interested in management development.

SWIM3

Office for Women Workers Questions
International Labour Organisation (ILO)
    4 route des Morillons
    1211 GENEVA 22
Course: Management Development for Women
☐ Vocational training for women interested in management development.

SWIM4

Swiss Federation for Adult Education
    Oerlikonerstrasse 38
    PO Box 7
    8057 ZURICH
Course: Management Development for Women
☐ Vocational training for women interested in management development.

United States of America

USAM1

Administrative Offices
Baltimore New Directions for Women Inc.
    2517 North Charles Street
    BALTIMORE, MD 21218
☎   301 336 8570
Course: Management Development for Women
☐ Vocational training for women interested in management development.

USAM2

A Better Way
    Suite 1030
    4000 Town Center
    SOUTHFIELD, MI 48075
☎   313 352 4320
Course: Management Development for Women
☐ Vocational training for women interested in management development.

USAM3

Career Counselling and Placement
Hunter College
    695 Park Avenue
    NEW YORK, NY 10021
☎   212 570 5254
Course: Management Development for Women
☐ Vocational training for women interested in management development.

USAM4

Career Development Office
Smith College
    Pierce Hall
    NORTHAMPTON, MA 01063
☎   413 584 2700
Course: Management Development for Women
☐ Vocational training for women interested in management development.

USAM5

Career Development Office
Marymount College
    TARRYTOWN, NY 10591
☎   914 631 3200
Course: Management Development for Women
☐ Vocational training for women interested in management development.

USAM6

Career Development and Self-Marketing Workshops
Ruth Shapiro Associates
    200 East 30th Street
    NEW YORK, NY 10016
☎   212 889 4284
Course: Management Development for Women
☐ Vocational training for women interested in management development.

USAM7

Career Planning and Placement Center
Moraine Valley Community College
    10900 South 88th Avenue
    Palos Hills, IL 60465
☎   312 974 4300
Course: Management Development for Women

☐ Vocational training for women interested in management development.

USAM8

Career Research Institute
455 West 44th Street
NEW YORK, NY 10036
☎ 212 247 5351
Course: Management Development for Women
☐ Vocational training for women interested in management development.

USAM9

Career Services
Women's Educational and Industrial Union
366 Boylston Street
BOSTON, MA 02116
☎ 617 536 5651
Course: Management Development for Women
☐ Vocational training for women interested in management development.

USAM10

Career Studies Center
Hamline University
1536 Hewitt Avenue
ST PAUL, MN 55104
☎ 612 641 2302
Course: Management Development for Women
☐ Vocational training for women interested in management development.

USAM11

Center for Continuing Education for Women
University of California, Berkeley
Room 100, T-9 Building
BERKELEY, CA 94720
☎ 415 642 4786
Course: Management Development for Women
☐ Vocational training for women interested in management development.

USAM12

Continuing Education for Women
Washington University
Box 1064
ST LOUIS, MO 63130
☎ 314 889 6759
Course: Management Development for Women
☐ Vocational training for women interested in management development.

USAM13

Continuum, Inc.
785 Center Street
NEWTON, MA 02158
☎ 617 964 3322

Course: Management Development for Women
☐ Vocational training for women interested in management development.

USAM14

Counselling Services for Women
Villa Maria College
2551 West Lake Road
ERIE, PA 16505
☎ 814 838 1966
Course: Management Development for Women
☐ Vocational training for women interested in management development.

USAM15

Counselling Women
14 East 60th Street
NEW YORK, NY 10022
☎ 212 486 9755
Course: Management Development for Women
☐ Vocational training for women interested in management development.

USAM16

George Washington University
Suite 621–624
2130 H Street NW
WASHINGTON, DC 20052
☎ 202 676 7036
Course: Management Development for Women
☐ Vocational training for women interested in management development.

USAM17

Indiana University
Owen Hall 201
BLOOMINGTON, IN 47405
☎ 812 337 8995
Course: Management Development for Women
☐ Vocational training for women interested in management development.

USAM18

Job Resource Center
Suite 23
2015 J Street
SACRAMENTO, CA 95814
☎ 916 441 2850
Course: Management Development for Women
☐ Vocational training for women interested in management development.

USAM19

Middle River Center
1515 Martin Boulevard
MIDDLE RIVER, MD 21220
☎ 301 574 7878

Course: Management Development for Women
☐ Vocational training for women interested in management development.

USAM20

Office of Career Services
Barnard College
606 West 120th Street
NEW YORK, NY 10027
☎ 212 280 2033
Course: Management Development for Women
☐ Vocational training for women interested in management development.

USAM21

Personnel Sciences Center
341 Madison Avenue
NEW YORK, NY 10017
☎ 212 661 1870
Course: Management Development for Women
☐ Vocational training for women interested in management development.

USAM22

Resource Women, The Untapped Resource, Inc.
Suite 200
1258 Euclid Avenue
CLEVELAND, OH 44115
☎ 216 579 1414
Course: Management Development for Women
☐ Vocational training for women interested in management development.

USAM23

Student Counselling Service
University of Arizona
Old Main
TUCSON, AZ 85721
☎ 602 626 2316
Course: Management Development for Women
☐ Vocational training for women interested in management development.

USAM24

Vistas for Women
YWCA
515 North Street
WHITE PLAINS, NY 10605
☎ 914 949 6227
Course: Management Development for Women
☐ Vocational training for women interested in management development.

USAM25

Women in the United Nations
Office of Human Resources Management
United Nations
NEW YORK, NY 10017
Contact: The Co-ordinator
Course: Management Development for Women
☐ Vocational training for women interested in management development.

USAM26

Women's Career Information Center
Middlesex County College
Woodbridge Avenue, West Hall Annex
EDISON, NJ 08817
☎ 201 548 6000
Course: Management Development for Women
☐ Vocational training for women interested in management development.

USAM27

Women's Center
University of California at Santa Barbara
SANTA BARBARA, CA 93106
☎ 805 961 3778
Course: Management Development for Women
☐ Vocational training for women interested in management development.

USAM28

Women's Indicators and Statistics
Department of Social Affairs
NEW YORK, NY 10017
Course: Management Development for Women
☐ Vocational training for women interested in management development.

USAM29

Women's Opportunities
YWCA
9th and Walnut Streets
CINCINNATI, OH 45202
☎ 513 241 7090
Course: Management Development for Women
☐ Vocational training for women interested in management development.

USAM30

Women's Resource Center for the Grand Traverse Area
918 West Front Street
TRAVERSE CITY, MI
☎ 616 941 1210
Course: Management Development for Women
☐ Vocational training for women interested in management development.

USAM31

Women's Resource Center
University of Richmond
UNIVERSITY COLLEGE, VA 23173
☎ 804 285 6316
Course: Management Development for Women
☐ Vocational training for women interested in management development.

USAM32

Women's Services
University of Nebraska at Omaha
MBSC-Room 312
60th and Dodge Streets
OMAHA, NB 68182
☎ 402 554 2200
Course: Management Development for Women
☐ Vocational training for women interested in management development.

USAM33

Workshops for Women
Janice LaRouche Assoc. Inc.
333 Central Park West
NEW YORK, NY 10025
☎ 212 MO3 0970
Course: Management Development for Women
☐ Vocational training for women interested in management development.

USAM34

YWCA
802 N. Lafayette Boulevard
SOUTH BEND, IN 46601
☎ 219 233 9491
Course: Management Development for Women
☐ Vocational training for women interested in management development.

Uruguay

URUM1

Ministerio de Education y Cultura
Instituto de la Mujer
Reconguista 535 P.8
MONTEVIDEO
Course: Management Development for Women
☐ Vocational training for women interested in management development.

Self-Employment

Australia

AUSSE1

Affirmative Action Agency
1st Floor, The Denison
65 Berry Street
PO Box 974
NORTH SYDNEY, NSW 2060
☎ 02 957 4333
Course: Business Start-ups for Women
□ Vocational training for women interested in developing self-employment projects.

AUSSE2

National Women's Consultative Council
3–5 National Circuit
BARTON, ACT 2600
☎ 06 271 5723
Course: Business Start-ups for Women
□ Vocational training for women interested in developing self-employment projects.

Austria

AUSE1

Department for Programme Development
Unit for the Integration of Women in Industrial Development
PO Box 300
1400 VIENNA
Course: Business Start-ups for Women
□ Vocational training for women interested in developing self-employment projects.

Belgium

BELSE1

CGSP
44 rue de la Baunderie
1000 BRUSSELS
Contact: Francie Dekoninck
Course: Business Start-ups for Women
□ Vocational training for women interested in developing self-employment projects.

BELSE2

Cognitech
11A avenue van Becelaere
1170 BRUSSELS
Contact: M. Van Remoortere
Course: Business Start-ups for Women
□ Vocational training for women interested in developing self-employment projects.

BELSE3

Commissie Vrouwenarbeid
Belliardstraat 51
1040 BRUSSELS
Contact: Annemie Pernot
Course: Business Start-ups for Women
□ Vocational training for women interested in developing self-employment projects.

BELSE4

Commisie Vrouwenarbeid
Gom Limburg
Kunstlaan 18
3500 HASSELT
Contact: Nicole Schoefs
Course: Business Start-ups for Women
□ Vocational training for women interested in developing self-employment projects.

BELSE5

Febelgra
Belliardstraat 20, bus 16
1040 BRUSSELS
Contact: D. Salens
Course: Business Start-ups for Women
□ Vocational training for women interested in developing self-employment projects.

BELSE6

FOREM
2 route de Bavay
7080 FRAMERIES
Contact: Christine Romanowicz
Course: Business Start-ups for Women
□ Vocational training for women interested in developing self-employment projects.

BELSE7

FOREM
36 rue de la Classiere
7100 LA LOUVIERE
Contact: Alexandre Forum
Course: Business Start-ups for Women
□ Vocational training for women interested in developing self-employment projects.

BELSE8

Forem Service Ranst
25 rue Montoyer
1040 BRUSSELS

Contact: M. Van Ranst
Course: Business Start-ups for Women
☐ Vocational training for women interested in developing self-employment projects.

BELSE9
Formation Professionnelle des Indépendants
WTC Tour II – 3ème étage
Bd Emile Jacquemain
162 – Bte 16
1210 BRUSSELS
Contact: Monique Prevot
Course: Business Start-ups for Women
☐ Vocational training for women interested in developing self-employment projects.

BELSE10
Institut de Formation Professionnelle Alimentation
709 chaussée de Mons
1600 LEEUW SAINT-PIERRE
Contact: Sonia Tkac
Course: Business Start-ups for Women
☐ Vocational training for women interested in developing self-employment projects.

BELSE11
IRIS Unit
CREW s.c
21 rue de la Tourelle
1040 BRUSSELS
Contact: Delma MacDevitt
Course: Business Start-ups for Women
☐ Vocational training for women interested in developing self-employment projects.

BELSE12
Ministère de l'Interieur et de la Formation Publique
15 rue du Gouvernement
1000 BRUSSELS
Contact: M. Verhaegen
Course: Business Start-ups for Women
☐ Vocational training for women interested in developing self-employment projects.

BELSE13
Ministerie van Onderwijs
Rijksadministratief Centrum
Arcadegebouw 5de
Verdieping
1000 BRUSSELS

Contact: Noelle Dendas
Course: Business Start-ups for Women
☐ Vocational training for women interested in developing self-employment projects.

BELSE14
Nationaal Verbond K.
Secondair Onderwijs
Guimardstraat 1
1040 BRUSSELS
Contact: Dorothen Van Hoyweghen
Course: Business Start-ups for Women
☐ Vocational training for women interested in developing self-employment projects.

BELSE15
Netwerk
'Diversificatie van de Beroepskeuse van meisjes en vrouwen'
Prinsenstraat 51
1850 GRIMBERGEN
Contact: Helma Verhulst
Course: Business Start-ups for Women
☐ Vocational training for women interested in developing self-employment projects.

BELSE16
PME
1 rue des Halles
1000 BRUSSELS
Contact: Eliane Puleston
Course: Business Start-ups for Women
☐ Vocational training for women interested in developing self-employment projects.

BELSE17
ULB – INFODOC
50 Avenue F. Roosevelt CP 142
1050 BRUSSELS
Contact: Josiane Roelants
Course: Business Start-ups for Women
☐ Vocational training for women interested in developing self-employment projects.

BELSE18
Unité pour l'Egalité des Chances CEE
200 rue de la Loi
1049 BRUSSELS
Contact: Michele Tierlinck
Course: Business Start-ups for Women
☐ Vocational training for women interested in developing self-employment projects.

BELSE19
VDAB
Keiserslaaan 11
1000 BRUSSELS
Contact: Gaston Deman
Course: Business Start-ups for Women
☐ Vocational training for women interested in developing self-employment projects.

BELSE20
Wonen en Werken
Valkery Gang 26
3000 LEUVEN
Contact: Julia Rottiers
Course: Business Start-ups for Women
☐ Vocational training for women interested in developing self-employment projects.

Canada

CANSE1
The Canadian Advisory Council on the Status of Women
666 Sherbrooke Street W
Montreal
QUEBEC H3A 1E7
☎ 514 283 8123
Course: Business Start-ups for Women
☐ Vocational training for women interested in developing self-employment projects.

CANSE2
The Canadian Advisory Council on the Status of Women
269 Main Street, Suite 600
Winnipeg
MANITOBA R3C 1B2
☎ 204 949 3140
Course: Business Start-ups for Women
☐ Vocational training for women interested in developing self-employment projects.

CANSE3
Canadian Congress for Learning Opportunities for Women
47 Main Street
Toronto
ONTARIO M4E 2U6
☎ 416 699 1909
Course: Business Start-ups for Women
☐ Vocational training for women interested in developing self-employment projects.

CANSE4
Student Counselling Services
University of Calgary
Calgary
ALBERTA T2N 1N4
☎ 403 284 5893
Course: Business Start-ups for Women
☐ Vocational training for women interested in developing self-employment projects.

Chile

CHISE1
ECLAC
Edificio Naciones Unidas
Avenida Dag Hammarskjold
Casilla 179–D
SANTIAGO
Course: Business Start-ups for Women
☐ Vocational training for women interested in developing self-employment projects.

Denmark

DENSE1
AMS
Hejrevej 43
2400 COPENHAGEN NV
Contact: Dorte Cohr Lutzen
Course: Business Start-ups for Women
☐ Vocational training for women interested in developing self-employment projects.

DENSE2
AMU – Alborg
Rodslet 77
9430 VADUM
Contact: Else Hvid Jensen
Course: Business Start-ups for Women
☐ Vocational training for women interested in developing self-employment projects.

DENSE3
AMU – Centret Vendsyssel
Knivholtvej 18
9900 FREDERIKSHAVN
Contact: Jytte Vibeke Jensen
Course: Business Start-ups for Women
☐ Vocational training for women interested in developing self-employment projects.

DENSE4

Anders Bang
Glaesersvej 21
Koge Handelskole
4600 KOGE
Contact: Anders Bang
Course: Business Start-ups for Women
☐ Vocational training for women interested in developing self-employment projects.

DENSE5

AOF
Rugardsvej 9
5000 ODENSE
Contact: Karin Jensen
Course: Business Start-ups for Women
☐ Vocational training for women interested in developing self-employment projects.

DENSE6

Arbejdsformidlingen
Ringgade 253
6400 SONDERBORG
Contact: Elin Lunding
Course: Business Start-ups for Women
☐ Vocational training for women interested in developing self-employment projects.

DENSE7

Arbejdsformidlingen
Norreport 15
8000 ARHUS
Contact: Jytte Petersen
Course: Business Start-ups for Women
☐ Vocational training for women interested in developing self-employment projects.

DENSE8

Arbejsformidlingen
Vilhelmskildevej 1E
5700 SVENOBORG
Contact: Anne Marie Jacobsen
Course: Business Start-ups for Women
☐ Vocational training for women interested in developing self-employment projects.

DENSE9

Athene
Rosenborggade 2
1130 COPENHAGEN
Contact: Lotte Valbjorn
Course: Business Start-ups for Women
☐ Vocational training for women interested in developing self-employment projects.

DENSE10

Beskaeftigelseskonsulent
Ullasvej 23
3700 RONNE
Contact: Kirstine Jorgensen
Course: Business Start-ups for Women
☐ Vocational training for women interested in developing self-employment projects.

DENSE11

DA
Vester Voldgade 113
1552 COPENHAGEN V
Contact: Margit Hurup Grove
Course: Business Start-ups for Women
☐ Vocational training for women interested in setting up their own employment projects.

DENSE12

Direktoratet for Folkeoplysning
Vestergade 29–31
1456 COPENHAGEN K
Contact: Inger Marie Dyrholm
Course: Business Start-ups for Women
☐ Vocational training for women interested in developing self-employment projects.

DENSE13

DSB
Solvgade 40
1307 COPENHAGEN K
Contact: Anette Wolters
Course: Business Start-ups for Women
☐ Vocational training for women interested in developing self-employment projects.

DENSE14

EDB – Daghojskolen
Aben Datastue
Aboulevarden 7 st
8000 ARHUS C
Contact: Kirsten Kristensen
Course: Business Start-ups for Women
☐ Vocational training for women interested in developing self-employment projects.

DENSE15

Erhvervs-og
Arbejdsmarkedsafdelingen
Skottenborg 26
8800 VIBORG
Contact: Jan Sorensen
Course: Business Start-ups for Women
☐ Vocational training for women interested in developing self-employment projects.

DENSE16
Erhvervsskoleafdelingen
Undervisningsministeriet
H. C. Andersens Bvd 43
1553 COPENHAGEN K
Contact: Birgitte Simonsen
Course: Business Start-ups for Women
☐ Vocational training for women interested in developing self-employment projects.

DENSE17
Ligestillingskonsulent
Arbejdsformidlingen
Helsingorsgade 10
3400 HILLEROD
Contact: Susanne Langer
Course: Business Start-ups for Women
☐ Vocational training for women interested in developing self-employment projects.

DENSE18
Plan 2000
Magnolievangen 56
3450 ALLEROD
Contact: Anne Fogh
Course: Business Start-ups for Women
☐ Vocational training for women interested in developing self-employment projects.

Ethiopia

ETHSE1
African Training and Research Centre for Women
PO Box 3001
ADDIS ABABA
Course: Business Start-ups for Women
☐ Vocational training for women interested in developing self-employment projects.

France

FRSE1
Bureau of Studies and Programming
UNESCO
7 place de Fontenoy
75700 PARIS
Contact: Co-ordinator of Programmes
Course: Business Start-ups for Women
☐ Vocational training for women interested in developing self-employment projects.

FRSE2
CEFAP
13 cheminement du Professeur
Bouasse – Hameau des Violettes
31100 TOULOUSE
Contact: M. Lambert
Course: Business Start-ups for Women
☐ Vocational training for women interested in developing self-employment projects.

FRSE3
Education Nationale DAFCO de Caen
168 rue Caponière
BP 6184
14034 CAEN
Contact: Nicole Rioult
Course: Business Start-ups for Women
☐ Vocational training for women interested in developing self-employment projects.

FRSE4
FEN
48 rue la Bruyère
75009 PARIS
Contact: Jacqueline Laroche
Course: Business Start-ups for Women
☐ Vocational training for women interested in developing self-employment projects.

FRSE5
GRETA Sudisere
1 rue des Trembles
38100 GRENOBLE
Contact: Joelle Bernard
Course: Business Start-ups for Women
☐ Vocational training for women interested in developing self-employment projects.

FRSE6
GRETA Sud Manche
2 rue de Verdun 2
50300 AVRANCHES
Contact: Armelle Brault
Course: Business Start-ups for Women
☐ Vocational training for women interested in developing self-employment projects.

FRSE7
Retravailler Franche-Comte
2 boulevard Carnot
90000 BELFORT
Contact: Jeanine Pfauvadel
Course: Business Start-ups for Women
☐ Vocational training for women interested in developing self-employment projects.

FRSE8

Women's Institute for Continuing Education
American College in Paris
    31 Avenue Bosquet
    75007 PARIS
☎   551 21 57
Course: Business Start-ups for Women
☐ Vocational training for women interested in developing self-employment projects.

Germany

GERSE1

Institut fur Sozialpädagogik
    Sekr ER 15
    Life
    Strasse des 17.Juni 112
    1000 BERLIN 12
Contact: Michaela Znava
Course: Business Start-ups for Women
☐ Vocational training for women interested in setting up their own employment projects.

Great Britain and Northern Ireland

GBSE1

Abbey Services
    Park House
    106 Park Road
    TEDDINGTON TW11 0AN
☎   081 943 9443
Course: Training for Self-builders
☐ Courses and one-to-one support for people interested in developing their own business projects.

GBSE2

Antur Teifi
    Teifi Valley Business Centre
    Aberarad, Newcastle
    EMLYN SA38 9BD
☎   0239 710238
Course: Training and Business Support
☐ Small courses tailor made for local groups and individuals to enable successful business start-ups and established businesses to gain local up-to-date support on grants and other forms of financial assistance.

GBSE3

Avon CDA
    49 Colston Street
    BRISTOL BS1 5AX
☎   0272 254711
Course: Business Advice and Support

☐ Individual and small group consultancy to local people on the availability of local and European assistance to small business start-ups.

GBSE4

Bedcoda
    Enterprise House
    7 Gordon Street
    LUTON LU1 2QP
☎   0582 400949
Course: Business Workshops
☐ Small workshops for groups or individuals on the issues surrounding self-employment.

GBSE5

Birmingham CDA
    Co-operative Enterprise Centre
    Zair Works, 111–119 Bishop Street
    Highgate
    BIRMINGHAM B5 6JL
☎   021 622 6973
Course: Business Workshops
☐ Small workshops for individuals or groups on the issues surrounding self-employment or co-operative development.

GBSE6

Birmingham Women's Enterprise Development Agency
    31 Frederick Street
    Hockley
    BIRMINGHAM B1 3HH
☎   021 200 2025
Course: Self-employment for Women
☐ Workshops and one-to-one support for women interested in setting up on their own.

GBSE7

Black Country CDA (Central Office)
    Lich Chambers
    Exchange Street
    WOLVERHAMPTON WV1 1TS
☎   0902 312736
Course: Business Advice and Support
☐ Small workshops and one-to-one support for local people interested in setting up small businesses as co-operatives.

GBSE8

Black Country CDA (Dudley)
    89 High Street
    DUDLEY DY1 1QP
☎   0384 239664
Course: Business Advice and Support
☐ Small workshops to groups and individuals who are interested in setting up small projects locally.

GBSE9

Black Country CDA (Sandwell)
  Sandwell Business Advice Centre
  Victoria Street
  WEST BROMWICH B70 8ET
☎ 021 525 2204
Course: Business Advice and Support
☐ Small workshops for groups or individuals who are interested in setting up projects locally.

GBSE10

Black Country CDA (Thread Project)
  2nd Floor, Smethwick Enterprise Centre
  Rolfe Street
  Smethwick
  SANDWELL B66 2AR
☎ 021 555 6071
Course: Asian Women's Clothing Training Centre
☐ Small workshops to enable participants to develop their textile and needlecraft skills; support for those interested in setting up small local projects.

GBSE11

Black Country CDA (Walsall)
  Walsall Enterprise Agency
  139/144 Lichfield Street
  WALSALL WS1 1SE
☎ 0922 616959
Course: Business Advice and Support
☐ Small workshops for groups or individuals to examine the issues associated with setting up small projects individually or co-operatively.

GBSE12

Bolton Neighbourhood Economic Development Agency
  Bolton Enterprise Centre
  Washington Street
  BOLTON BL3 5EY
☎ 0204 22213
Course: Business Advice and Training
☐ Small workshops for individuals or groups to examine the issues involved in setting up small projects locally.

GBSE13

Bootstrap Enterprises (Blackburn)
  Unit 1, Bootstrap Workshops
  Mill Lane
  BLACKBURN BB2 2AA
☎ 0254 680367
Course: Business Advice and Training
☐ Small workshops for individuals or groups to examine the issues involved in setting up projects locally.

GBSE14

Bootstrap Enterprises (Hackney)
  The Print House
  18 Ashwin Street
  LONDON E8 3DL
☎ 071 254 0775
Course: Business Advice and Support
☐ Small workshops for individuals or groups to examine the issues involved in setting up small projects locally.

GBSE15

Bradford CDA
  Unit 3–4
  Theatre Royal Workshops
  Snowdon Street
  BRADFORD BD1 3DT
☎ 0532 461737
Course: Business Advice and Support
☐ Small workshops for individuals or groups to examine the issues involved in setting up projects locally.

GBSE16

Bradford Women's Technology Centre
  1st Floor, Broomfield House
  Bolling Road
  BRADFORD BD4 7BG
Contact: Ann Pugh
Course: Business Start-ups for Women
☐ Vocational training for women interested in developing self-employment projects.

GBSE17

Brighton Area CDA
  42 Baker Street
  BRIGHTON BN1 4JN
☎ 0273 670815
Course: Business Advice and Support
☐ Small workshops for individuals or groups to examine the issues involved in setting up small projects locally.

GBSE18

Bristol Women's Workshop
  Totterdown Centre
  144 Wells Road
  Totterdown
  BRISTOL BS4 2AG
☎ 0272 711672
Course: Woodwork Courses for Women
☐ Covers the complete range of skills required for women to continue education and training, enter employment or develop skills acquired into self-employment projects.

GBSE19
Calderdale MBC
Franus St
HALIFAX HX1 3V2
Contact: D. McAll
Course: Business Start-ups for Women
☐ Vocational training for women interested in developing self-employment projects.

GBSE20
Cambridge CDA
The Business Centre
71a Lensfield Road
CAMBRIDGE CB2 1EN
☎ 0223 60977
Course: Business Advice and Support
☐ Small workshops for individuals or groups to examine the issues involved in setting up small projects locally.

GBSE21
Camden Enterprise Ltd
57 Pratt Street
LONDON NW1 0DP
☎ 071 482 2128
Course: Business Advice, Training and Consultancy
☐ Workshops and groups for individuals examining all of the issues associated with setting up projects locally.

GBSE22
Cardiff & Vale CDA
Enterprise House
127 Bute Street
CARDIFF CF1 5LE
☎ 0222 494411
Course: Co-operative Support
☐ Advice and training for local people interested in setting up co-operatives.

GBSE23
Cheshire CDA
Unit 7, Catherine Street
Bewsey Industrial Estate
WARRINGTON WA5 5LH
☎ 0925 35158
Course: Business Advice and Support
☐ Workshops for individuals and groups on all the issues involved in setting up a local project.

GBSE24
Community Enterprise Lothian Ltd
37 George Street
EDINBURGH EH2 2HN
☎ 031 220 2201
Course: Community Enterprises and Advice

☐ Workshops for individuals and groups on all aspects of setting up a local project.

GBSE25
Coventry Technical College
The Butts
COVENTRY CV1 3GD
Contact: Liz Yates
Course: Business Start-ups for Women
☐ Vocational training for women interested in developing self-employment projects.

GBSE26
Coventry WEDA
Enterprise House
Sheriff's Orchard
COVENTRY CV1 1QN
☎ 0203 633737
Course: Women's Enterprise Development
☐ Assistance and training for women wishing to set up their own employment projects.

GBSE27
Cutting Edge Workshop Ltd
Unit 3a, Central Trading Estate
Bath Road
BRISTOL BS4 3EH
Course: Woodwork for Women
☐ Courses are aimed at providing women with the work experience and skills required to enjoy and develop their expertise and, if desired, to start self-employment projects.

GBSE28
Devon CDA
138 North Road East
PLYMOUTH PL4 6AQ
☎ 0752 223481
Course: Start up Business Advice
☐ Small workshops aimed at local people who wish to set up their own businesses.

GBSE29
Dovetail Consultants Ltd
24 Trinity Avenue
Lenton
NOTTINGHAM NG7 2EU
☎ 0602 783627
Course: Business Start-ups
☐ Short courses, advice and information on setting up in business

GBSE30
Dow-Stoker Ltd
2nd Floor, The Mill
Stortford Road, Hatfield Heath
Nr BISHOP'S STORTFORD CM22 7DL

☎   0279 730056
Course: Training Small Business Start-up
□ A women's partnership which specialises in assisting women to set up their own businesses and nurture existing skills into self-employment projects.

GBSE31

Dunfermline Women's Training Centre
    5–7 Comely Park
    DUNFERMLINE KY12 7HU
Contact: Anne Barr
Course: Business Start-ups for Women
□ Vocational training for women interested in developing self-employment projects.

GBSE32

Durham Co-Operative Development Association
    New College
    Framwellgate Moor
    DURHAM DH1 5ES
☎   091 386 4404
Course: Co-operative Advice
□ Workshops and support for local people interested in setting up their own projects locally.

GBSE33

Ealing CDA
    Charles House
    Bridge Road
    SOUTHALL UB2 4BD
☎   081 574 4724
Course: Training Toward Co-operative Development
□ Workshops, training and advice for local people who are interested in setting up their own projects.

GBSE34

East Anglian CDA
    34 Exchange Street
    NORWICH NR2 1AX
☎   0603 765853
Course: Co-operative Development
□ Locally held workshops and training sessions for people interested in setting up their own projects.

GBSE35

European Commission Women's Local Employment Initiative Programme
    Scottish Enterprise Foundation
    University of Stirling
    STIRLING FK9 4LA
☎   0786 73171
Course: Business Start-ups
□ Advice and grants on self-employment projects for women.

GBSE36

Face Ltd
    17–18 Market Place
    GLASTONBURY BA6 9HL
☎   0458 833917
Course: Business Start-up Programme
□ Covers all the issues associated with starting a business: financial planning, marketing, purchasing, business planning, sources of advice and assistance.

GBSE37

Foleshill Women's Training Ltd
    70–72 Elmsdale Avenue
    Foleshill
    COVENTRY
☎   0203 637693
Course: Asian Women's Business Training/Start-up
□ Designed to encourage local Asian women to acquire business skills and, if desired, to set up their own self-employment projects.

GBSE38

Greater Manchester CDA
    23 New Mount Street
    MANCHESTER M4 4DE
☎   061 833 9496
Course: Business Advice and Support
□ Workshops for local groups and individuals on all of the issues involved in setting up projects locally.

GBSE39

Gwen Savage & Co.
    69 High Street
    BANGOR BT20 5BD
☎   0247 271489
Contact: Gwen Savage
Course: Business Training
□ Courses for local people interested in finding out about business activities and the issues involved in running a business, help and advice with book-keeping and accounts.

GBSE40

Lambeth Women's Workshop Ltd
    Unit C22, Park Hall Trading Estate
    Martell Road
    LONDON SE21 8EA
☎   081 670 0339
Course: Joinery Training for Disadvantaged Women
□ Courses are run by the workshop which is a voluntary organisation; includes hands-on experience of manufacturing products out of wood; self-employment projects encouraged.

GBSE41

Lancashire Enterprise PLC
    Enterprise House
    17 Ribblesdale Place
    Winkley Square
    PRESTON PR1 3NA
Contact: Carol Worrell
Course: Business Start-ups for Women
☐ Vocational training for women interested in developing self-employment projects.

GBSE42

Linda Scott
    21 Auld House
    Wyned
    PERTH PH1 1RG
☎ 0738 34745
Contact: Linda Scott
Course: Small Business and Workers Co-operatives
☐ Advice and start-up assistance on setting up local projects.

GBSE43

New Working Women
    3 St Peter's Buildings
    New York
    LEEDS LS9 8NJ
☎ 0532 432474
Course: Women's Business and Management Training
☐ A women's co-operative which specialises in assisting women to develop management skills, nurture talents and resources, and consider self-employment projects.

GBSE44

Northern Ireland CDA
    23–25 Ship Quay Street
    DERRY CITY BT48 6DL
☎ 0504 371733
Course: Business Assistance, Training and Advice
☐ Workshops and individual support for those interested in setting up their own projects.

GBSE45

Port Talbot CDA
    2nd Floor, Royal Buildings
    Talbot Road
    PORT TALBOT SA13 1BN
☎ 0639 895173
Course: Free Business Start-up Assistance
☐ Workshops for individuals and groups on all of the issues involved in setting up projects locally.

GBSE46

Redfield Centre
    Redfield
    WINSLOW MK18 3LZ
☎ 0296 714983
Course: Business Workshops
☐ Small group workshops to examine the issues involved in business in an environmentally friendly and non-threatening style.

GBSE47

Wales Co-operative Development and Training Centre
    Llandaff Court
    Fairwater Road
    CARDIFF CF5 2XP
☎ 0222 554955
Course: Advice and Training
☐ Workshops for individuals and groups on a range of issues concerning self-employment and the development of local project financing.

GBSE48

Women into Business
    Small Business Bureau, Suite 46
    Westminster Palace Gardens
    Artillery Row
    LONDON SW1P 1RR
☎ 071 976 7262
Course: Women into Business
☐ Network group which arranges seminars and events for women in business; support and assistance for women wishing to set up their own business projects.

GBSE49

Women's Economic Futures
    c/o CEI Consultants
    42 Frederick Street
    EDINBURGH EH2 1EX
☎ 031 225 3144
Course: Women's Economic Development
☐ Advice and consultancy for women on all aspects of business.

GBSE50

Women's Enterprise Development Agency
    Aston Science Park
    Love Lane
    Aston Triangle
    BIRMINGHAM B7 4BJ
☎ 021 236 2707
Course: Helping Women Set Up In Business
☐ Workshops and training sessions to individual women or groups on the range of issues involved in setting up in business.

GBSE51

Women's Enterprise Unit
Scottish Enterprise Foundation
    University of Stirling
    STIRLING FK9 4LA
☎ 0786 73171

Course: Training and Advice on Business Start-up Skills
☐ Workshops and training sessions on the range of issues involved in setting up businesses by women.

Greece

GRESE1

OAED
> PO Box 70017
> 16610 GLYFADA

Contact: Dimitri Hassomeri
Course: Business Start-ups for Women
☐ Vocational training for women interested in developing self-employment projects.

Israel

ISRSE1

Israel Women's Network
> 14 Hatibonim Street
> JERUSALEM

Contact: Prof. Alice Shalvi
Course: Business Start-ups for Women
☐ Vocational training for women interested in developing self-employment projects.

Italy

ITSE1

Commissione Nazionale Parita
> Presidenza Consiglio Ministri
> Palazzo Chigi Piazza
> Colonna
> 00187 ROME

Contact: Alba Dini Martino
Course: Business Start-ups for Women
☐ Vocational training for women interested in developing self-employment projects.

ITSE2

Women in Agricultural Production
Food and Agricultural Organization (FAO)
> Via delle Terme di Caracalla
> 00100 ROME

Course: Business Start-ups for Women
☐ Vocational training for women interested in developing self-employment projects.

Japan

JAPSE1

National Women's Ed. Centre
> 728 Sugaya, Ranzan-Machi
> Hiki-gun
> SAITAMA-KEN, 355-02

Course: Business Start-ups for Women
☐ Vocational training for women interested in developing self-employment projects.

Kenya

KENSE1

Focal Point for Women
United Nations Centre for Human Settlements (HABITAT)
> PO Box 30030
> NAIROBI

Course: Business Start-ups for Women
☐ Vocational training for women interested in developing self-employment projects.

KENSE2

United Nations Environment Programme
> PO Box 30552
> NAIROBI

Course: Business Start-ups for Women
☐ Vocational training for women interested in developing self-employment projects.

Netherlands

NETSE1

Anke Weidema School
> Vondellaan Ic
> 9402 NA ASSEN
> ☎ 059 20 419 99

Course: Businesss Development for Women
☐ Advice and assistance for women interested in setting up their own employment projects.

NETSE2

Anna Polak School
> H. Gerhardstraat 2
> 1502 CK ZAANDAM
> ☎ 075 17 41 15

Course: Business Start-ups for Women
☐ Workshops covering all aspects of business start-ups for women interested in self-employment projects.

NETSE3

Opleidingscentrum Informatica voor Vrouwen
Pater Brugmanstraat 4
6501 BN NIJMEGEN
☎ 080 60 20 40
Course: Business Start-ups for Women
☐ Vocational training workshops for women interested in developing their own employment projects.

NETSE4

Suze Baart School
Donizettilaan la
2324 BE LEIDEN
☎ 071 32 03 55
Course: Business Start-ups for Women
☐ Vocational training for women interested in developing self-employment projects.

New Zealand

NZSE1

National Advisory Council on the Employment of Women (NACEW)
c/o Dept of Labour
Private Bag
WELLINGTON
Course: Business Start-ups for Women
☐ Vocational training for women interested in developing self-employment projects.

NZSE2

Ponsonby Community Centre
Ponsonby
AUCKLAND
Course: Business Start-ups for Women
☐ Vocational training for women interested in developing self-employment projects.

NZSE3

The Print Centre
17 Union Street
PO Box 1236
AUCKLAND
☎ 379 6503
Course: Business Start-ups for Women
☐ Vocational training for women interested in developing self-employment projects.

South Korea

SKSE1

Korean Women's Development Institute
CPO Box 2267
SEOUL 100

Course: Business Start-ups for Women
☐ Vocational training for women interested in developing self-employment projects.

Spain

SPSE1

Centre Technic de la Dona
Ronda Sant Pere
08010 BARCELONA
☎ 317 46 50
Course: Business Start-ups for Women
☐ Vocational training for women interested in developing self-employment projects.

SPSE2

INEM
Condessa de Venadito
28027 MADRID
Contact: José Ramon Llorente Zamorano
Course: Business Start-ups for Women
☐ Vocational training for women interested in developing self-employment projects.

SPSE3

Instituto de la Mujer
Almagro 36
28010 MADRID
Contact: Maria Angeles Salle
Course: Business Start-ups for Women
☐ Vocational training for women interested in developing self-employment projects.

Switzerland

SWISE1

BALance
Militarstrasse 83a
8004 ZURICH
☎ 01 291 23 31
Contact: Theresa Schiffers
Course: Self-Employment Projects for Women
☐ Advice and one-to-one consultancy for women interested in setting up their own employment projects.

SWISE2

BIGA, Bundesamt für Industrie Gewerbe und Arbeit
Abteilung Berufsbildung
Bundesgasse 8
3003 BERN
☎ 031 61 28 17
Contact: Christoph Schmitter
Course: Business Start-ups for Women

☐ Vocational training for women interested in developing self-employment projects.

SWISE3

Eidgenössisches Büro für die
Gleichstellung von Frau und Mann
Eigerplatz 5
3007 BERN
Course: Business Start-ups for Women
☐ Vocational training for women interested in developing self-employment projects.

Thailand

THASE1

Social Development Division
ESCAP
UN Building
Rajdamnern Avenue
BANGKOK 10200 2
Course: Business Start-ups for Women
☐ Vocational training for women interested in developing self-employment projects.

Trinidad and Tobago

TTSE1

ECLAC – Caribbean Women in Development
PO Box 1113
PORT-OF-SPAIN
Course: Business Start-ups for Women
☐ Vocational training for women interested in developing self-employment projects.

United States of America

USASE1

Advocates for Women, Inc.
414 Mason St, 4th Floor
SAN FRANCISCO, CA 94102
☎ 415 391 4870
Course: Business Start-ups for Women
☐ Vocational training for women interested in developing self-employment projects.

USASE2

Continuum, Inc.
785 Centre Street
NEWTON, MA 02158
☎ 617 964 3322
Course: Business Start-ups for Women
☐ Vocational training for women interested in developing self-employment projects.

USASE3

Counselling Women
14 East 60th Street
NEW YORK, NY 10022
☎ 212 486 9755
Course: Business Start-ups for Women
☐ Vocational training for women interested in developing self-employment projects.

USASE4

Denver Women's Career Center
1650 Washington Street
DENVER, CO 80203
☎ 303 861 7254
Course: Business Start-ups for Women
☐ Vocational training for women interested in developing self-employment projects.

USASE5

Department of Public Information
United Nations
NEW YORK, NY 10017
Contact: Project Manager, Women's Issues
Course: Business Start-ups for Women
☐ Vocational training for women interested in developing self-employment projects.

USASE6

Division for Women's Programmes
United Nations Development Programme
One UN Plaza
NEW YORK, NY 10017
Course: Business Start-ups for Women
☐ Vocational training for women interested in developing self-employment projects.

USASE7

Douglass Advisory Services for Women
Douglass College
132 George Street
NEW BRUNSWICK, NJ 08903
☎ 201 932 9603
Course: Business Start-ups for Women
☐ Vocational training for women interested in developing self-employment projects.

USASE8

Education Opportunity Center
University of Alaska, Anchorage
3211 Providence Avenue
Library Building, Room 103
ANCHORAGE, AK 99504
☎ 907 263 1525
Course: Women in Science and Technology
☐ Vocational training for women interested in science and technology, for educational and employment contexts.

USASE9

Every Woman's Place
23 Strong Avenue
MUSKEGON, MI 49441
☎ 616 726 4493
Course: Business Start-ups for Women
☐ Vocational training for women interested in developing self-employment projects.

USASE10

Flexible Careers
Suite 703, 37 South Wabash Avenue
CHICAGO, IL 60603
☎ 312 236 6028
Course: Business Start-ups for Women
☐ Vocational training for women interested in developing self-employment projects.

USASE11

More for Women, Inc.
1435 Lexington Avenue
NEW YORK, NY 10028
☎ 212 534 0852
Course: Business Start-ups for Women
☐ Vocational training for women interested in developing self-employment projects.

USASE12

New Options
545 Madison Avenue
NEW YORK, NY 10022
☎ 212 752 9898
Course: Business Start-ups for Women
☐ Vocational training for women interested in developing self-employment projects.

USASE13

New Ways to Work
149 Ninth Street
SAN FRANCISCO, CA 94103
☎ 415 552 1000
Course: Business Start-ups for Women
☐ Vocational training for women interested in developing self-employment projects.

USASE14

The Next Step Career Guidance Center Inc.
PO Box 423
MANSFIELD, MA 02048
☎ 617 339 7498
Course: Business Start-ups for Women
☐ Vocational training for women interested in developing self-employment projects.

USASE15

Office of Career Planning
Vassar College
Raymond Avenue
POUGHKEEPSIE, NY 12601
☎ 914 452 7000
Course: Business Start-ups for Women
☐ Vocational training for women interested in developing self-employment projects.

USASE16

Resource Center for Women
445 Sherman Avenue
PALO ALTO, CA 94306
☎ 415 324 1710
Course: Business Start-ups for Women
☐ Vocational training for women interested in developing self-employment projects.

USASE17

The United Nations Development Fund for Women (UNIFEM)
Room 1106
304 East 45th Street
NEW YORK, NY 10017
Course: Business Start-ups for Women
☐ Vocational training for women interested in developing self-employment projects.

USASE18

Valencia Community College
PO Box 3028
ORLANDO, FL 32802
☎ 305 423 4813
Course: Business Start-ups for Women
☐ Vocational training for women interested in developing self-employment projects.

USASE19

Widening Opportunity Research Center
Division of Continuing Education
Middlesex Community College
PO Box T
BEDFORD, MA 01730
☎ 617 275 8910
Course: Business Start-ups for Women
☐ Vocational training for women interested in developing self-employment projects.

USASE20

Woman Alive! Inc
YWCA
229 Ogden Street
PO Box 1121
HAMMOND, IN 46325
☎ 219 933 7168
Course: Business Start-ups for Women

☐ Vocational training for women interested in developing self-employment projects.

USASE21

The Women's Center
The University of Delaware
McDowell Hall
NEWARK, DE 19711
☎ 302 738 8773
Course: Business Start-ups for Women
☐ Vocational training for women interested in developing self-employment projects.

USASE22

Women's Center
Converse College
SPARTANBURG, SC 29301
☎ 803 585 6421
Course: Business Start-ups for Women
☐ Vocational training for women interested in developing self-employment projects.

USASE23

Women's Center, Career Development Center
Enterprise State Junior College
Highway 84 East
PO Box 1300
ENTERPRISE, AL 36330
☎ 205 347 5431
Course: Business Start-ups for Women
☐ Vocational training for women interested in developing self-employment projects.

USASE24

Women's Center for Continuing Education
Northern Michigan University
MARQUETTE, MI 49855
☎ 906 227 2219
Course: Business Start-ups for Women
☐ Vocational training for women interested in developing self-employment projects.

USASE25

Women's Center of Dallas
Quadrangle Suite 197
28000 Routh
DALLAS, TX 75201
☎ 214 651 9795
Course: Business Start-ups for Women
☐ Vocational training for women interested in developing self-employment projects.

USASE26

Women's Indicators and Statistics
Department of Social Affairs
NEW YORK, NY 10017
Course: Business Start-ups for Women

☐ Vocational training for women interested in developing self-employment projects.

USASE27

Women's Opportunities
YWCA, 9th and Walnut Streets
CINCINNATI, OH 45202
☎ 513 241 7090
Course: Business Start-ups for Women
☐ Vocational training for women interested in developing self-employment projects.

USASE28

Women's Resource Agency
Suite 309 25 N. Spruce
COLORADO SPRINGS, CO 80905
☎ 303 471 3170
Course: Business Start-ups for Women
☐ Vocational training for women interested in developing self-employment projects.

USASE29

Women's Resource Center
Southwest State University
MARSHALL, MN 56258
☎ 507 537 7160
Course: Business Start-ups for Women
☐ Vocational training for women interested in developing self-employment projects.

USASE30

Workshops for Women
Janice LaRouche Assoc. Inc.
333 Central Park West
NEW YORK, NY 10025
Course: Business Start-ups for Women
☐ Vocational training for women interested in developing self-employment projects.

Science, Technology and Computing

Australia

AUSSTC1

Affirmative Action Agency
    1st Floor, The Denison
    65 Berry Street
    PO Box 974
    NORTH SYDNEY, NSW 2060
☎ 02 957 4333
Course: Women in Science and Technology
□ Vocational training for women interested in science and technology, for educational and employment contexts.

AUSSTC2

National Women's Consultative Council
    3–5 National Circuit
    BARTON, ACT 2600
☎ 06 271 5723
Course: Women in Science and Technology
□ Vocational training for women interested in science and technology, for educational and employment contexts.

AUSSTC3

Shrill
    PO Box 303
    CAMPERDOWN, NSW 2050
☎ 02 557 1955
Course: Women in Science and Technology
□ Vocational training for women interested in science and technology, for educational and employment contexts.

AUSSTC4

SWIFT
    66 Albion St
    SURREY HILLS, NSW 2010
Course: Women in Science and Technology
□ Vocational training for women interested in science and technology, for educational and employment contexts.

Belgium

BELSTC1

ASBL CERA
    BP 87 Etterbeek 1
    1040 BRUSSELS
Contact: Dominique Ruelle-Charlez
Course: Women in Science and Technology
□ Vocational training for women interested and involved in science and technology.

BELSTC2

Cognitech
    11A avenue van Becelaere
    1170 BRUSSELS
Contact: M. Van Remoortere
Course: Women in Science and Technology
□ Vocational training for women interested in science and technology, for educational and employment contexts.

BELSTC3

Commission des Affaires Sociales
    Kortrijkstraat 171
    8520 KUURNE
Contact: Paul Vangansbeke
Course: Women in Science and Technology
□ Vocational training for women interested in science and technology, for educational and employment contexts.

BELSTC4

CSC
    121 rue de la Loi
    1040 BRUSSELS
Contact: Anne-Francoise Theunissen
Course: Women in Science and Technology
□ Vocational training for women interested in science and technology, for educational and employment contexts.

BELSTC5

Documentatiecentrum Rosa
    Gallaitstraat 78
    1210 BRUSSELS
Contact: Renee Van Mecheelen
Course: Women in Science and Technology
□ Vocational training for women interested in science and technology, for educational and employment contexts.

BELSTC6

Documentatiecentrum Rosa
    Gallaistraat 78
    1210 BRUSSELS
Contact: Chris Zwaenepoel
Course: Women in Science and Technology
□ Vocational training for women interested in science and technology, for educational and employment contexts.

BELSTC7

European Parliament
    Belliardstraat 97
    1040 BRUSSELS
Contact: Lode Van Outrive
Course: Women in Science and Technology

☐ Vocational training for women interested in science and technology, for educational and employment contexts.

BELSTC8
Formation Professionelle des Independants
WTC Tour II – 3ème étage
Bd Emile Jacquemain
162 – Bte 16
1210 BRUSSELS
Contact: Monique Prevot
Course: Women in Science and Technology
☐ Vocational training for women interested and involved in science and technology.

BELSTC9
FOREM
5 boulevard de l'Empereur
1000 BRUSSELS
Contact: Murielle Sempoux
Course: Women in Science and Technology
☐ Vocational training for women interested in science and technology, for educational and employment contexts.

BELSTC10
FOREM
2 route de Bavay
7080 FRAMERIES
Contact: Christine Romanowicz
Course: Women in Science and Technology
☐ Vocational training for women interested and involved in science and technology.

BELSTC11
Forum
36 rue de la Classière
7100 LA LOUVIERE
Contact: Alexandre Rectem
Course: Women in Science and Technology
☐ Vocational training for women interested and involved in science and technology.

BELSTC12
Frederique Deroure
47 rue Van Aa
1050 BRUSSELS
Contact: Frederique Deroure
Course: Women in Science and Technology
☐ Vocational training for women interested and involved in science and technology.

BELSTC13
GOM – ESA
Desguinlei 102, bus 13
2018 ANTWERP
Contact: Heidi Vanheusden
Course: Women in Science and Technology

☐ Vocational training for women interested in science and technology, for educational and employment contexts.

BELSTC14
Institut Provincial des Classes Moyenne
Euro Info Centre
Bd d'Avroy 28/30
4000 LIEGE
Contact: Monique Roover
Course: Women in Science and Technology
☐ Vocational training for women interested and involved in science and technology.

BELSTC15
Institut voor Voortdurende Vorming en Onderzoek in de Confectie
Montoyerstraat 31
1040 BRUSSELS
Contact: Jan Van Depoele
Course: Women in Science and Technology
☐ Vocational training for women interested in science and technology, for educational and employment contexts.

BELSTC16
IRFEC Europe
Avenue Winston Churchill
119/16
1180 BRUSSELS
Contact: Elisabeth Van Stalle
Course: Women in Science and Technology
☐ Vocational training for women interested in science and technology, for educational and employment contexts.

BELSTC17
IRIS Unit
CREW s.c
21 rue de la Tourelle
1040 BRUSSELS
Contact: Delma MacDevitt
Course: Women in Science and Technology
☐ Vocational training for women interested and involved in science and technology.

BELSTC18
Maison de l'Europe de Courcelles
46 rue P. Monnoyer
6180 COURCELLES
Contact: Martine Denille
Course: Women in Science and Technology
☐ Vocational training for women interested and involved in science and technology.

BELSTC19
Ministerie of Lewerkstelling & Arbeid
Belliardstraat 51
1040 BRUSSELS
Contact: Eddy Schelstraete

Course: Women in Science and Technology
☐ Vocational training for women interested and involved in science and technology.

BELSTC20

Ministerie van Onderwijs
Rijksadministratief Centrum
Arcadegebouw 5de
Verdieping
1000 BRUSSELS
Contact: Noelle Dendas
Course: Women in Science and Technology
☐ Vocational training for women interested and involved in science and technology.

BELSTC21

NCMV
Spastraat 8
1040 BRUSSELS
Contact: Marianne Thyssen
Course: Women in Science and Technology
☐ Vocational training for women interested in science and technology, for educational and employment contexts.

BELSTC22

Netwerk
'Diversificatie van de Beroepskeuse van meisjes en vrouwen'
Prinsenstraat 51
1850 GRIMBERGEN
Contact: Helma Verhulst
Course: Women in Science and Technology
☐ Vocational training for women interested in science and technology, for educational and employment contexts.

BELSTC23

Omschakelen VZW
Mubreidmstraat 498
2600 BERCHEM
Contact: Rita Ruys
Course: Women in Science and Technology
☐ Vocational training for women interested and involved in science and technology.

BELSTC24

VDAB
Keiserslaaan 11
1000 BRUSSELS
Contact: Gaston Deman
Course: Women in Science and Technology
☐ Vocational training for women interested and involved in science and technology.

Canada

CANSTC1

The Canadian Advisory Council on the Status of Women
151 Sparks Street, Bow 1541, Station B
OTTAWA K1P 5R5
☎ 613 992 4975
Course: Women in Science and Technology
☐ Vocational training for women interested in science and technology, for educational and employment contexts.

CANSTC2

Canadian Congress for Learning Opportunities for Women
47 Main Street
Toronto
ONTARIO M4E 2U6
☎ 416 699 1909
Course: Women in Science and Technology
☐ Vocational training for women interested in science and technology, for educational and employment contexts.

CANSTC3

Ontario Women's Directorate
480 University Ave
2nd Floor
Toronto
ONTARIO M5G 1V2
Course: Women in Science and Technology
☐ Vocational training for women interested in science and technology, for educational and employment contexts.

CANSTC4

Student Counselling Services
University of Calgary
Calgary
ALBERTA T2N 1N4
☎ 403 284 5893
Course: Women in Science and Technology
☐ Vocational training for women interested in science and technology, for educational and employment contexts.

Denmark

DENSTC1

AMU-Center
Brovangen 2
3720 AKIRKEBY
Contact: Britta Keller
Course: Women in Science and Technology
☐ Vocational training for women interested and involved in science and technology.

DENSTC2

AMU – Centret Vendsyssel
Knivholtvej 18
9900 FREDERIKSHAVN
Contact: Jytte Vibeke Jensen
Course: Women in Science and Technology
☐ Vocational training for women interested in science and technology.

DENSTC3

AMU – Centret Vendsyssel
Knivholtvej 18
9900 FREDERIKSHAVN
Contact: Susanne Andersen
Course: Women in Science and Technology
☐ Vocational training for women interested in science and technology.

DENSTC4

Anders Bang
Glaesersvej 21
Koge Handelskole
4600 KOGE
Contact: Anders Bang
Course: Women in Science and Technology
☐ Vocational training for women interested and involved in science and technology.

DENSTC5

AOF
Rugardsvej 9
5000 ODENSE
Contact: Karin Jensen
Course: Women in Science and Technology
☐ Vocational training for women interested in science and technology.

DENSTC6

Arbejdsformidlingen
Teglvaerksgade 4
6701 ESBJERG
Contact: Dorte Ulldall
Course: Women in Science and Technology
☐ Vocational training for women interested and involved in science and technology.

DENSTC7

Arbejdsformidlingen
Ringgade 253
6400 SONDERBORG
Contact: Elin Lunding
Course: Women in Science and Technology
☐ Vocational training for women interested and involved in science and technology.

DENSTC8

Arbejdsformidlingen
Oster Voldgade 4
3700 RONNE
Contact: Henny Kofoed
Course: Women in Science and Technology
☐ Vocational training for women interested in science and technology.

DENSTC9

Arhus Tekniske Skole
Halmstadgade 6
8200 ARHUS N
Contact: Kirsten Tejsner
Course: Women in Science and Technology
☐ Vocational training for women interested and involved in science and technology.

DENSTC10

Beskaeftigelseskonsulent
Aftensang 1
6040 EGTVED
Contact: Ruth Syshoj
Course: Women in Science and Technology
☐ Vocational training for women interested and involved in science and technology.

DENSTC11

Bjarne Grubbe Jensen
Petersmindevej 50
5000 ODENSE C
Contact: Bjarne Grubbe Jensen
Course: Women in Science and Technology
☐ Vocational training for women interested in science and technology.

DENSTC12

Center for Kvindeforskning og Undervisning
(The Centre for Feminist Research and Women's Studies)
University of Copenhagen – Amager
Njalsgade 106
2300 COPENHAGEN S
☎ 01 54 22 11 ext. 23
Contact: Bente Rosenbeck
Course: Feminist Interpretation of Natural Science and Medicine
☐ Training and research into natural sciences from an entirely feminist perspective

DENSTC13

Direktoratet for Folkeoplysning
Vestergade 29–31
1456 COPENHAGEN K
Contact: Inger Marie Dyrholm
Course: Women in Science and Technology

☐ Vocational training for women interested and involved in science and technology.

DENSTC14

DSB
> Solvgade 40
> 1307 COPENHAGEN K

Contact: Anette Wolters
Course: Women in Science and Technology
☐ Vocational training for women interested and involved in science and technology.

DENSTC15

Erhvervs-og
> Arbejdsmarkedsafdelingen
> Skottenborg 26
> 8800 VIBORG

Contact: Jan Sorensen
Course: Women in Science and Technology
☐ Vocational training for women interested in science and technology.

DENSTC16

Erhvervsskoleafdelingen
> Undervisningsministeriet
> H. C. Andersens Bvd 43
> 1553 COPENHAGEN K

Contact: Birgitte Simonsen
Course: Women in Science and Technology
☐ Vocational training for women interested and involved in science and technology.

DENSTC17

Foreingen af Daghojskoler
> Willemoesgade 14 Kld
> 2100 COPENHAGEN O

Contact: Monica Munck
Course: Women in Science and Technology
☐ Vocational training for women interested in science and technology.

DENSTC18

Gruppen for Medicinsk Kvindeforskning
Pa Fyn
> (Feminist Research in Medicine)
> The Institute of Community Health
> Odense University, J. B. Winslowsvej 17
> 5000 ODENSE C

☎ 09 15 86 00 ext. 493
Contact: Inger Schaumburg
Course: Feminist Perspectives on Health and Disease
☐ Research and training concerned with considering health and disease in a feminist perspective.

DENSTC19

Handelshojskolens Kvindenetvaerk
> (Women's Network of Business Admin.)
> Institute of Organisation and Industrial
> Sociology
> Blaagaardsgade 23B
> 2200 COPENHAGEN N

☎ 01 37 05 55
Contact: Jytte Bonde
Course: Women and Technology
☐ Research and training aimed at improving women's access to and involvement in technology.

DENSTC20

Holbaek Tekniske Skole
> Absalongsgade 20
> 4300 HOLBAEK

Contact: Annelise Nerving
Course: Women in Science and Technology
☐ Vocational training for women interested and involved in science and technology.

DENSTC21

KAD
> Ewaldsgade 3–9
> 2200 COPENHAGEN N

Contact: Lillian Knudsen
Course: Women into Technology
☐ Research and training sessions for women interested and involved in technology and computing.

DENSTC22

Koge Handelskole
> Lyngbyvej 19
> 4600 KOGE

Contact: Mona Engberg
Course: Women in Science and Technology
☐ Vocational training for women interested and involved in science and technology.

DENSTC23

Kvindeforum
> (The Centre of Feminist Research)
> University of Aalborg
> Fibigerstraede 2
> 9220 AALBORG O

☎ 08 15 85 22 ext. 22
Contact: Anna-Birte Ravn
Course: Computer Technology for Women
☐ Computer technology projects for women interested and involved in computer technology.

DENSTC24

Kvindeudvalgerved Danmarks Tekniske Hojskole
(The Women's Committee)
The Technical University of Denmark
Studiekontoret, Building 101
2800 LYNGBY
☎ 02 88 22 22 ext. 221
Contact: Lise Damkjaer
Course: Women in Technology
☐ Research and training which examines women's attitudes to technology in education and employment.

DENSTC25

Ligestillingskonsulent
Arbejdsformidlingen
Tondergade 14
1752 COPENHAGEN V
Contact: Mette Iversen
Course: Women in Science and Technology
☐ Vocational training for women interested and involved in science and technology.

DENSTC26

Ligestillingskonsulent
Arbejdsformidlingen
Helsingorsgade 10
3400 HILLEROD
Contact: Susanne Langer
Course: Women in Science and Technology
☐ Vocational training for women interested and involved in science and technology.

DENSTC27

RUE
Aebelogade 7
2100 COPENHAGEN O
Contact: Lis Meier Carlsen
Course: Women in Science and Technology
☐ Vocational training for women interested and involved in science and technology.

France

FRSTC1

AFPA Limoges Batîment
68 rue de Babylone
87036 LIMOGES
Contact: Suzettz Potevin
Course: Women in Science and Technology
☐ Vocational training for women interested in science and technology, for educational and employment contexts.

FRSTC2

Asprocep
189 avenue Corot
13014 MARSEILLE
Contact: I. Guernigou
Course: Women in Science and Technology
☐ Vocational training for women interested in science and technology, for educational and employment contexts.

FRSTC3

Bureau of Studies and Programming
UNESCO
7 place de Fontenoy
75700 PARIS
Contact: Co-ordinator of Programmes
Course: Women in Science and Technology
☐ Vocational training for women interested in science and technology, for educational and employment contexts.

FRSTC4

Centre d'Information des Droits de la Femme
Centre Municipal Duguesclin
Place Chanzy
79000 NIORT
Contact: Christine Girard
Course: Women in Science and Technology
☐ Vocational training for women interested in science and technology, for educational and employment contexts.

FRSTC5

GRETA Sudisere
1 rue des Trembles
38100 GRENOBLE
Contact: Joelle Bernard
Course: Women in Science and Technology
☐ Vocational training for women interested in science and technology, for educational and employment contexts.

FRSTC6

IFRIS
12 rue Ampère
38016 GRENOBLE
Contact: Evelyne Paye
Course: Women in Science and Technology
☐ Vocational training for women interested in science and technology, for educational and employment contexts.

FRSTC7

Mission d'Education Permanente
30 avenue de Fretilly
17000 LA ROCHELLE
Contact: Guy Roy
Course: Women in Science and Technology
☐ Vocational training for women interested in science and technology, for educational and employment contexts.

FRSTC8

Retravailler
25 avenue de la Libération
45000 ORLEANS
Contact: Jocelyne Welker
Course: Women in Science and Technology
☐ Vocational training for women interested in science and technology, for educational and employment contexts.

FRSTC9

Secrétariat d'Etat chargé des Droits des Femmes
31 rue Le Pelletier
75009 PARIS
Contact: Françoise Divisia
Course: Women in Science and Technology
☐ Vocational training for women interested in science and technology, for educational and employment contexts.

FRSTC10

TUAC auprès de l'OCDE
26 avenue de la Grande Armée
75017 PARIS
Contact: Yolande Durand
Course: Women in Science and Technology
☐ Vocational training for women interested in science and technology, for educational and employment contexts.

FRSTC11

Women's Institute for Continuing Education
American College in Paris
31 avenue Bosquet
75007 PARIS
☎ 551 21 57
Course: Women in Science and Technology
☐ Vocational training for women interested in science and technology, for educational and employment contexts.

Germany

GERSTC1

Network of Women in Archaeology
c/o Sigrum M. Karlisch
Wildermuthstr. 40
7400 TUBINGEN
☎ 0251 862285
Course: Women in Archaeology
☐ Seminars and group workshops for women involved and interested in archaeology.

Great Britain and Northern Ireland

GBSTC1

Asset Computer Management
11 Foxes Dale
LONDON SE3 9BD
☎ 081 852 7501
Course: Computer Training

☐ Small workshops providing training in information technology.

GBSTC2

Belavia Ltd
253 Old Road
CLACTON ON SEA CO15 3LU
☎ 0255 435392
Course: Computer Training
☐ Pre- and post-sales advice, consultancy and training in the use of new technology.

GBSTC3

Birmingham Women's Workshop
Unit 9, Whitworth Industrial Park
Tilton Road
Small Heath
BIRMINGHAM
☎ 021 773 5511
Contact: Carol Machon
Course: Computing and Electronics
☐ Trainees have the opportunity to gain nationally recognised qualifications. All courses are for unemployed women.

GBSTC4

Birmingham Women's Workshop
Tilton Road
Small Heath
BIRMINGHAM
☎ 021 773 5511
Contact: Marilyn Mason
Course: Computing and Electronics
☐ Various-length courses available for non-waged women, leading to nationally recognised qualifications.

GBSTC5

Boxclever Presentation Training
25 Bewdley Street
LONDON N1 1HB
☎ 071 607 5766
Course: Radio and TV Skills
☐ Short courses designed for women who are interested in radio and TV technology.

GBSTC6

Bradford Women's Technology Centre
1st Floor, Broomfield House
Bolling Road
BRADFORD BD4 7BG
Contact: Ann Pugh
Course: Women in Science and Technology
☐ Vocational training for women interested in science and technology, for educational and employment contexts.

GBSTC7

Cambridge Women's Resources Centre
Hooper Street
CAMBRIDGE CB1 2NZ
☎ 0223 321148

Course: Women in Science and Technology
☐ Vocational training for women interested in science and technology, for educational and employment contexts.

GBSTC8

Camden Training Centre
   57 Pratt Street
   LONDON NW1 0DP
☎ 071 482 2103
Course: Information Technology
☐ A voluntary group which assists women trainees to develop and increase their skills and confidence in the use of information technology.

GBSTC9

CDS Training for Enterprise Ltd
   36 Slater Street
   LIVERPOOL L1 4BX
☎ 051 708 6213
Course: Technology
☐ Covers all aspects of technology and allows trainees to sample in detail areas in which they wish to specialise.

GBSTC10

CTS Training
   New Mansion House
   Wellington Road South
   STOCKPORT SK1 3UA
☎ 061 477 7979
Course: Professional Training for Computer Users
☐ Tailor-made courses designed for user's requirements.

GBSTC11

Cutting & Wear Resistant Development Ltd
   Greasbrough Road
   ROTHERHAM S60 1QG
☎ 0709 3619041
Course: Oil Drilling Equipment
☐ Advice and consultancy service; manufacturer.

GBSTC12

Dept of Adult and Continuing Education
University of Ulster at Jordanstown
   NEWTOWNABBEY BT37 0QB
Contact: Pauline Murphy
Course: Women in Science and Technology
☐ Vocational training for women interested in science and technology, for educational and employment contexts.

GBSTC13

Dove Workshop Ltd
   Roman Road
   Banwen
   NEATH SA10 9LW
☎ 0639 700024

Course: Computing and Desk Top Publishing
☐ Workshops and small group work to introduce participants to new technology and improve their skills for entry into higher-level courses or employment.

GBSTC14

Dunfermline Women's Training Centre
   Unit 10, Dickinson Street
   Elgin Street Industrial Estate
   DUNFERMLINE KY12 7SL
☎ 0383 621038
Course: Computing and Electronics
☐ Women-only training in computing and electronics; equips participants for further training or for employment.

GBSTC15

Edinburgh Women's Training Centre
   5 Hillside Crescent
   EDINBURGH EH7 5DY
☎ 031 557 1139
Course: Computing and Electronics
☐ Workshops for women to gain hands-on experience of new technology.

GBSTC16

Female Bytes
   21a Goldhurst Terrace
   LONDON NW6 3HD
☎ 071 625 8804
Course: Computer Training for Women
☐ A women's partnership which runs courses at various levels for women interested in learning about computers.

GBSTC17

Fullemploy Training
   County House
   190 Great Dover Street
   LONDON SE1 4YB
☎ 071 378 1774
Contact: Martin Boorer
Course: Training in Office Skills to Black Clients
☐ Aimed at increasing access rates of black people into modern office environments.

GBSTC18

Girls Workshop
   The Old Police Station
   Sommerville Road
   St Andrews
   BRISTOL
☎ 0272 232042
Course: Technical and Craft Education of Girls
☐ Female-only training courses which examine and provide hands-on experience of a whole range of craft and technical skills. Participants can specialise or 'taste' several.

GBSTC19

Greater London Enterprise
63–67 Newington Causeway
LONDON SE1 6BD
☎ 071 403 0300
Course: Technology
□ Courses aimed at assisting local people to acquire up-to-date skills in the field of new technology and information technology.

GBSTC20

Hall Green College
Floodgate Street
Digbeth
BIRMINGHAM
☎ 021 778 2311
Contact: Kate Mulleady
Course: Women's Technology Training Programme (WTTP)
□ Trainees will have the opportunity to gain RSA, CLAIT, Pitman Typing, Pitman Audio or Pitman Wordprocessing, and either go on to further training or gain employment.

GBSTC21

Handsworth College
Soho Road
Handsworth
BIRMINGHAM B21
☎ 021 551 6031
Contact: Liz Burkitt
Course: Women's Technology Training Programme (WTTP) Administration
□ Trainees have the opportunity to gain RSA, CLAIT, RSA Dip. in IT or RSA English, and either go on to further training or gain employment.

GBSTC22

Lancashire Enterprise PLC
Enterprise House
17 Ribblesdale Place
Winkley Square
PRESTON PR1 3NA
Contact: Carol Worrell
Course: Women in Science and Technology
□ Vocational training for women interested in science and technology, for educational and employment contexts.

GBSTC23

Lewisham Women's Training Centre
Unit 14, Blackheath Business Centre
78b Blackheath Hill
LONDON SE10 8BA
☎ 081 691 5071
Course: Women's Training Centre Skills Courses

□ Courses are run throughout the year; popular courses are in manual skills or in science and information technology. All courses are women-only.

GBSTC24

Linkom Financial Services
32 Hill Street
Totterdown
BRISTOL BS3 4TW
☎ 0272 717435
Course: Computer Training
□ Short courses to assist participants to develop the skills required to use new technology and software in a variety of situations.

GBSTC25

Liverpool Women's Technology Scheme
24 Hardman Street
LIVERPOOL L1 9AX
☎ 051 709 4356/9
Contact: Gill Moglione
Course: Foundation Course in New Technology
□ Women must be over 25 and there is positive action for black women and lone parents. Courses run from April to March each year. Nursery place or money for childcare provided.

GBSTC26

Louise Wadley
227 Glyn Road
LONDON E5 0JP
☎ 081 985 4805
Contact: Louise Wadley
Course: Electrical Work, Film and TV
□ One-to-one advice and expertise available, also small group workshops.

GBSTC27

Micro Connection
3 Bristol Way
Stoke Gardens
SLOUGH SL1 3QE
☎ 0753 528725
Course: Bespoke Software/Identity Card Systems
□ A women's partnership which specialises in providing advice, assistance and training for individuals and companies wishing to enhance their information technology.

GBSTC28

Microsyster
London Women's Centre
Wesley House, 4 Wild Court
Kingsway
LONDON WC2B 5AU
☎ 071 430 0655
Course: Women's Computer Training

□ Short courses at various levels run by women for women interested in learning about the computer industry.

GBSTC29

National Woman and Computing Network
  c/o Microsyster
  Wesley House, 4 Wild Court
  Kingsway
  LONDON WC2B 5AU
☎ 071 430 0655
Course: Network of Women Working with Computers
□ Network arranges occasional seminars and training events for members on topics of popular interest.

GBSTC30

Ovatones
  Highgate Newtown Community Centre
  25 Bertram Street
  LONDON N19 5DQ
☎ 071 281 2528
Course: Live Recording Workshops
□ Workshops covering all aspects of live recording.

GBSTC31

Reen Pilkington
  18 Richborne Terrace
  LONDON SW8 1AU
☎ 071 587 1655
Course: Desk Top Publishing
□ Small workshops and one-to-one advice and consultancy.

GBSTC32

Sound Kitchen c/o WMRP
  89a Kingsland High Street
  LONDON E8 2PB
☎ 071 254 6536
Course: Sound Engineering Training
□ Small workshops covering all aspects of sound engineering.

GBSTC33

South Glamorgan Women's Workshop
  Edena House
  East Canal Wharf
  CARDIF CF1 5AQ
Contact: Jean Golten
Course: Women in Science and Technology
□ Vocational training for women interested in science and technology, for educational and employment contexts.

GBSTC34

South Glamorgan Women's Workshop
  Edena House
  East Canal Wharf
  CARDIFF CF1 5AQ

☎ 0222 493351
Course: Training in Computing and Electronics
□ Short courses at various levels for women interested in learning about computing and electronics.

GBSTC35

Stirling Women's Technology Centre
  The Arcade
  Kings Street
  STIRLING
☎ 0786 50980
Course: Computing
□ Computing courses for women new to computers, or for women interested in improving their skills.

GBSTC36

Sutton Coldfield College
  Erdington Centre
  Edwards Road
  BIRMINGHAM B24
☎ 021 355 5671
Contact: Brenda Thorogood
Course: Women's Technology Training Programme (WTTP)
□ Trainees will have the opportunity to gain RSA, CLAIT or the NEBSMS qualification, and either go on to further education or gain employment.

GBSTC37

Third Feathers Club Women's Afternoon
  17 Bramham Gardens
  LONDON SW5 0JJ
☎ 071 373 2681
Course: Women's Workshops
□ Workshops on a range of subjects to reflect group's interests. Free childcare.

GBSTC38

Trade Union Studies Centre
Hall Green College
  Floodgate Street
  BIRMINGHAM B5
☎ 021 773 2311
Contact: Sue Morris
Course: Information Technology Trainers Course
□ Trainees have the opportunity to gain City & Guilds 726 Information Technology, and City & Guilds 926 Training Award.

GBSTC39

Tyseley Training Centre
  124 Amington Road
  Tyseley
  BIRMINGHAM
☎ 021 706 3040
Contact: Monica Brown

Course: Women's Technology Training Programme (WTTP) – electronics and computing
☐ Trainees have the opportunity to gain City & Guilds 726 Computing and Electronics, and City & Guilds in Computer Aided Design.

GBSTC40
WEDA
    Aston Science Park
    Love Lane
    Aston Triangle
    BIRMINGHAM B7 4BJ
Contact: Anne Douglas
Course: Women in Science and Technology
☐ Vocational training for women interested in science and technology, for educational and employment contexts.

GBSTC41
Women and Children Centre
Norton Hall
    Ralph Road
    BIRMINGHAM B8 1NA
☎ 021 328 3043
Contact: Louise Kilbride
Course: Wordprocessing
☐ Opportunity to study towards nationally recognised qualifications.

GBSTC42
Women in Computing
    Campaign Director
    Staffordshire Polytechnic
    College Road
    STOKE ON TRENT ST4 2DE
☎ 0782 744531 ext. 3438
Course: Women in Computing
☐ Organises and conducts training and small workshops for women interested in careers in computing and technology.

GBSTC43
Women in Construction Advisory Group
    Southbank House
    Black Prince Road
    LONDON SE1 7SJ
☎ 071 587 0028
Course: Construction Skills
☐ A voluntary organisation which runs courses and seminars for women in the construction industry, and for women interested in entering this type of occupation.

GBSTC44
Women in Engineering Centre
    c/o Electrical Engineering Department
    South Bank Polytechnic
    LONDON SE1 0AA

☎ 071 928 8989 ext. 2042
Course: Careers Advice: Engineering
☐ Organises seminars and liaises with training organisations to promote the interests of mature women in engineering.

GBSTC45
Women into Information Technology Foundation
    The Campaign Office, Concept 2000
    250 Farnborough Road
    FARNBOROUGH GU14 7LU
☎ 0252 528329
Course: Women into Information Technology
☐ Organises training seminars and events for women in information technology careers, and for women interested in entering careers involving information technology.

GBSTC46
Women into Science and Engineering
    Nottingham Polytechnic
    Burton Street
    NOTTINGHAM NG1 4BU
☎ 0602 418418
Course: Women's Science and Engineering Network
☐ Organises seminars, courses and training for women in science and engineering professions, and for women interested in entering this type of work.

GBSTC47
Women into Technology in the European Community (WITEC)
    Sheffield University
    65 Wilkinson Street
    SHEFFIELD S10 2GJ
☎ 0742 768653
Course: Technology Training
☐ Organises training, grants and placements for women in technology.

GBSTC48
Women's Computer Centre
    Wesley House, 4 Wild Court
    Kingsway
    LONDON WC2B 5AU
☎ 071 430 0112
Course: Courses in Computing for Women
☐ Women-only training: introductory courses for beginners or refresher courses for women wishing to improve their skills.

GBSTC49
Women's Media Resource Project
    89a Kingsland High Street
    LONDON E8 2PB
☎ 071 254 6536

Course: Sound Technologies, Film and Video
☐ Women-only project which runs workshops and training courses to develop women's skills in sound technology.

GBSTC50

Women's Technology Centre
    c/o Dalmarnock Initiative Base
    35 Springfield Road
    GLASGOW G40 3EL
☎   041 551 8822
Course: Computing and Technology for Women
☐ Workshops and one-to-one training for women interested in computing and technology.

GBSTC51

Women's Technology Scheme
    24 Hardman Street
    LIVERPOOL L1 9AX
☎   051 709 4356
Contact: Gill Moglione
Course: Foundation Course in New Technology
☐ Vocational training for women interested in technology, for educational and employment contexts. Women must be over 25 years old, and there is positive action for black women and lone parents.

GBSTC52

Women's Technology Scheme
    24 Hardman Street
    LIVERPOOL L1 9AX
☎   051 709 4359
Contact: Phil Godfrey
Course: BTEC National Certificate in Electronics (women only)
☐ Vocational training for women interested in electronics, for educational and employment contexts.

GBSTC53

Women's Technology Scheme
    24 Hardman Street
    LIVERPOOL L1 9AX
☎   051 709 4359
Contact: June Gilbert
Course: Telematics and Telecommunications Course
☐ Vocational training for women interested in telematics and telecommunications, for educational and employment contexts. General aptitude for computing and maths required.

GBSTC54

Women's Training Network
    Newton Hill House
    Newton Hill Road
    LEEDS LS7 4JE
☎   0532 374718

Course: Quality Women-Only Training
☐ Women-only courses in new technology, computing and electronics.

Ireland

IRESTC1

County Westmeath Vocational Education Committee
    Bridge House
    Bellevue Rd
    MULLINGAR
    Co. Westmeath
Contact: Brendan Daly
Course: Women in Science and Technology
☐ Vocational training for women interested in science and technology, for educational and employment contexts.

IRESTC2

John Bowman
    59 Pembroke Lane
    Ballsbridge
    DUBLIN 4
Contact: John Bowman
Course: Women in Science and Technology
☐ Vocational training for women interested in science and technology, for educational and employment contexts.

Italy

ITSTC1

INTERSIND
    98 via Christofero
    Colombo
    00147 ROME
Contact: Enzo Avanzi
Course: Women in Science and Technology
☐ Vocational training for women interested in science and technology, for educational and employment contexts.

ITSTC2

OSFIN
    2 via P. Traversari
    48100 RAVENNA
Contact: Cecilia De Vito
Course: Women in Science and Technology
☐ Vocational training for women interested in science and technology, for educational and employment contexts.

Japan

JAPSTC1

Japan Institute of Labour
　　Chutaikin Building
　　7–6 Shibakoen 1-chome
　　Minato-ku
　　TOKYO, 105 JAPAN
Course: Women in Science and Technology
☐ Vocational training for women interested in science and technology, for educational and employment contexts.

JAPSTC2

National Women's Education Centre
　　728 Sugaya Ranzan-Machi
　　Hiki-gun
　　SAITAMA-KEN,
　　355–02 JAPAN
Course: Women in Science and Technology
☐ Vocational training for women interested in science and technology, for educational and employment contexts.

Kenya

KENSTC1

Focal Point for Women
United Nations Centre for Human Settlements (HABITAT)
　　PO Box 30030
　　NAIROBI
Course: Women in Science and Technology
☐ Vocational training for women interested in science and technology, for educational and employment contexts.

KENSTC2

United Nations Environment Programme
　　PO Box 30552
　　NAIROBI
Course: Women in Science and Technology
☐ Vocational training for women interested in science and technology, for educational and employment contexts.

Luxembourg

LUXSTC1

CGT Luxembourg
　　26 rue R. Schuman
　　3566 DUDELANGE
Contact: Gilberte Kennerknecht
Course: Women in Science and Technology
☐ Vocational training for women interested in science and technology, for educational and employment contexts.

Netherlands

NETSTC1

Alida de Jong School
　　Mariaplaats 4a
　　3511 LH UTRECHT
☎　030 31 54 24
Course: Women's Technology
☐ Arranges vocational training for women interested and involved in technology.

NETSTC2

Anke Weidema School
　　Vondellaan Ic
　　9402 NA ASSEN
☎　059 20 419 99
Course: Women into Technology
☐ Vocational training for women interested and involved in technology.

NETSTC3

Anna Polak School
　　H. Gerhardstraat 2
　　1502 CK ZAANDAM
☎　075 17 41 15
Course: Women into Technology
☐ Vocational training for women interested and involved in technology.

NETSTC4

Emancipatieraad
　　Lutherse Burgwal 10
　　2512 CB DEN HAAG
Contact: Frank Boddendijk
Course: Women in Science and Technology
☐ Vocational training for women interested in science and technology, for educational and employment contexts.

NETSCT5

Janneke Dierx School
　　Oude Vlissingseweg 32a
　　4336 AD MIDDELBURG
☎　011 80 235 18
Course: Women into Technology
☐ Workshops and discussion groups for women interested and involved in technology.

NETSTC6

Stichting 0 + 0
　　Postbus 407
　　2260 AK LEIDSCHENDAM
Contact: Carin Van Laere
Course: Women in Science and Technology
☐ Vocational training for women interested in science and technology, for educational and employment contexts.

NETSTC7

Suze Baart School
Donizettilaan 1a
2324 BE LEIDEN
☎ 071 32 03 55
Course: Women into Technology
☐ Vocational training workshops for women interested and involved in technology.

NETSTC8

Vrouwenvakschool Informatica Amsterdam
Wodanstraat 1–3
1076 CC AMSTERDAM
☎ 020 66 270 96
Course: Women into Technology
☐ Vocational training for women interested and involved in technology.

New Zealand

NZSTC1

National Advisory Council on the Employment of Women (NACEW)
c/o Dept of Labour
Private Bag
WELLINGTON
Course: Women in Science and Technology
☐ Vocational training for women interested in science and technology, for educational and employment contexts.

NZSTC2

Ponsonby Community Centre
Ponsonby
AUCKLAND
Course: Women in Science and Technology
☐ Vocational training for women interested in science and technology, for educational and employment contexts.

Portugal

PORSTC1

Instituto do Emprego e Formacão Profissional (IEFP)
Av. José Malhoa 11–5
1000 LISBON
Contact: Maria Do Carmo Nunes
Course: Women in Science and Technology
☐ Vocational training for women interested in science and technology, for educational and employment contexts.

PORSTC2

Instituto do Emprego e Formacão Profissional (IEFP)
Av. José Malhoa 11–5
1000 LISBON

Contact: Maria Everilde
Course: Women in Science and Technology
☐ Vocational training for women interested in science and technology, for educational and employment contexts.

South Korea

SKSTC1

Korean Women's Development Institute
CPO Box 2267
SEOUL 100
Course: Women in Science and Technology
☐ Vocational training for women interested in science and technology, for educational and employment contexts.

Spain

SPSTC1

CEDEL
C/Conde Borrell
334–336 Bjs
08029 BARCELONA
Contact: Elia Arbaizer Vaquero
Course: Women in Science and Technology
☐ Vocational training for women interested in science and technology, for educational and employment contexts.

SPSTC2

Centre Technic de la Dona
Ronda Sant Pere
08010 BARCELONA
☎ 317 46 50
Course: Women in Science and Technology
☐ Vocational training for women interested in science and technology, for educational and employment contexts.

SPSTC3

INEM
Condessa de Venadito
28027 MADRID
Contact: José Ramon Llorente Zamorano
Course: Women in Science and Technology
☐ Vocational training for women interested in science and technology.

SPSTC4

Instituto de la Mujer
Almagro 36
28010 MADRID
Contact: Maria Angeles Salle
Course: Women in Science and Technology
☐ Vocational training for women interested in science and technology, for educational and employment contexts.

Switzerland

SWISTC1

BIGA, Bundesamt für Industrie
Gewerbe und Arbeit
    Abteilung Berufsbildung
    Bundesgasse 8
    3003 BERN
☎   031 61 28 17
Contact: Christoph Schmitter
Course: Women in Science and Technology
☐ Vocational training for women interested in science and technology, for educational and employment contexts.

United States of America

USASTC1

Adult Career Resource Center
Oakton Community College
    1600 E. Golf Road
    DES PLAINES, IL 60016
☎   312 635 1672
Course: Women in Science and Technology
☐ Vocational training for women interested in science and technology, for educational and employment contexts.

USASTC2

A Better Way
    4000 Town Center
    SOUTHFIELD, MI 48075
☎   313 352 4320
Course: Women in Science and Technology
☐ Vocational training for women interested in science and technology, for educational and employment contexts.

USASTC3

Career Development Office
Marymount College
    TARRYTOWN, NY 10591
☎   914 631 3200
Course: Women in Science and Technology
☐ Vocational training for women interested in science and technology, for educational and employment contexts.

USASTC4

Career/Life Alternatives
    100 Whitney Avenue
    NEW HAVEN, CT 06510
☎   203 865 7377
Course: Women in Science and Technology
☐ Vocational training for women interested in science and technology, for educational and employment contexts.

USASTC5

Career Studies Center
Hamline University
    1536 Hewitt Avenue
    ST PAUL, MN 55104
☎   612 641 2302
Course: Women in Science and Technology
☐ Vocational training for women interested in science and technology, for educational and employment contexts.

USASTC6

Center for Career Planning
Mills College
    OAKLAND, CA 94613
☎   415 632 2700 ext. 2
Course: Women in Science and Technology
☐ Vocational training for women interested in science and technology, for educational and employment contexts.

USASTC7

Council for Career Planning, Inc.
    310 Madison Avenue
    NEW YORK, NY 10017
☎   212 687 9490
Course: Women in Science and Technology
☐ Vocational training for women interested in science and technology, for educational and employment contexts.

USASTC8

Face Learning Center, Inc.
    12945 Seminole Boulevard
    Building 2, Suite 8
    LARGO, FL 33540
☎   813 586 1110
Course: Women in Science and Technology
☐ Vocational training for women interested in science and technology, for educational and employment contexts.

USASTC9

Focus on Women
Montana State University
    9 Hamilton Hall
    BOZEMAN, MT 59717
☎   406 994 2012
Course: Women in Science and Technology
☐ Vocational training for women interested in science and technology, for educational and employment contexts.

USASTC10

Frederick New Directions for Women
    23 West 3rd Street
    FREDERICK, MD 21701
☎   301 694 6322
Course: Women in Science and Technology
☐ Vocational training for women interested in science and technology, for educational and employment contexts.

USASTC11

Indiana University/Purdue University
1301 East 38th Street
INDIANAPOLIS, IN 46205
☎ 317 923 1321
Course: Women in Science and Technology
□ Vocational training for women interested in science and technology, for educational and employment contexts.

USASTC12

Mid-Career Counselling Center
Suny at Stony Brook
Room N235
Sociology and Behavioral Science Building
STONY BROOK, NY 11794
☎ 516 246 3304
Course: Women in Science and Technology
□ Vocational training for women interested in science and technology, for educational and employment contexts.

USASTC13

Office of Career Counselling and Placement
Kinsborough Community College
Room C102
2001 Oriental Boulevard
BROOKLYN, NY 11235
☎ 212 934 5115
Course: Women in Science and Technology
□ Vocational training for women interested in science and technology, for educational and employment contexts.

USASTC14

Office of Career Planning
Wheaton College
NORTON, MA 02766
☎ 617 285 7722
Course: Women in Science and Technology
□ Vocational training for women interested in science and technology, for educational and employment contexts.

USASTC15

Office of Career Planning
Vassar College
Raymond Avenue
POUGHKEEPSIE, NY 12601
☎ 914 452 7000
Course: Women in Science and Technology
□ Vocational training for women interested in science and technology, for educational and employment contexts.

USASTC16

Re-entry Advisory Program
San Jose State University
Old Cafeteria Building
SAN JOSE, CA 95192
☎ 408 277 2188
Course: Women in Science and Technology

□ Vocational training for women interested in science and technology, for educational and employment contexts.

USASTC17

Resources for Women
University of Pennsylvania
Houston Hall
PHILADELPHIA, PA 19104
☎ 215 243 5537
Course: Women in Science and Technology
□ Vocational training for women interested in science and technology, for educational and employment contexts.

USASTC18

Resource Women, The Untapped Resource Inc.
Suite 200
1258 Euclid Avenue
CLEVELAND, OH 44115
☎ 216 579 1414
Course: Women in Science and Technology
□ Vocational training for women interested in science and technology, for educational and employment contexts.

USASTC19

Womanscope, Inc.
5355 Phelps Luck Drive
COLUMBIA, MD 21045
☎ 301 997 2916
Course: Women in Science and Technology
□ Vocational training for women interested in science and technology, for educational and employment contexts.

USASTC20

Woman's Way
Suite 1
710 C Street
SAN RAFAEL, CA 94901
☎ 415 453 4490
Course: Women in Science and Technology
□ Vocational training for women interested in science and technology, for educational and employment contexts.

USASTC21

Women's Career Center Inc.
121 North Fitzhugh Street
ROCHESTER, NY 14614
☎ 716 325 2274
Course: Women in Science and Technology
□ Vocational training for women interested in science and technology, for educational and employment contexts.

USASTC22

Women's Career Development Center
Wright State University
140 East Monument Avenue
DAYTON, OH 45402

☎   513 223 6041
Course: Women in Science and Technology
☐ Vocational training for women interested in science and technology, for educational and employment contexts.

USASTC23

Women's Center
Montclair State College
Valley Road
UPPER MONTCLAIR, NJ 07043
☎   201 893 5106
Course: Women in Science and Technology
☐ Vocational training for women interested in science and technology, for educational and employment contexts.

USASTC24

Women's Educational Center
Reading Area Community College
Box 1706
2nd and Penn Streets
READING, PA 19603
☎   215 372 4721
Course: Women in Science and Technology
☐ Vocational training for women interested in science and technology, for educational and employment contexts.

USASTC25

Women's Network Inc.
Suite 502
People's Federal Building
39 East Market St
AKRON, OH 44308
☎   216 376 7852
Course: Women in Science and Technology
☐ Vocational training for women interested in science and technology, for educational and employment contexts.

USASTC26

The Women's Opportunities Center
University of California, Extension, Irvine
Box AZ
IRVINE, CA 92716
☎   714 833 7128
Course: Women in Science and Technology
☐ Vocational training for women interested in science and technology, for educational and employment contexts.

USASTC27

Women's Programs
County College of Morris
Route 10 and Center Grove Road
RANDOLPH, NJ 07801
☎   201 361 5000
Course: Women in Science and Technology
☐ Vocational training for women interested in science and technology, for educational and employment contexts.

USASTC28

Women's Programs
Armarillo College
PO Box 447
ARMARILLO, TX 79178
☎   806 376 5111
Course: Women in Science and Technology
☐ Vocational training for women interested in science and technology, for educational and employment contexts.

USASTC29

Women's Resource Center for the Grand Traverse Area
918 West Front Street
TRAVERSE CITY, MI
☎   616 941 1210
Course: Women in Science and Technology
☐ Vocational training for women interested in science and technology, for educational and employment contexts.

3 | *Research Resources*

Introduction

This section consists of four areas: bookshops; book clubs; libraries, archives, resource centres and information; and women's organisations.

I have included bookshops which specialise in feminist books and bookshops which have a feminist or women's studies section. In countries where there are such bookshops, they are often an important source of local information for women. Where possible I have indicated the type of bookshop.

The part listing libraries, archives, resource centres and information contains libraries and archives which have special collections of materials about women. Information and resource centres are largely run by women for women, but I have also included government, academic and international agencies which provide information on the status of women or research resources. Where possible I have indicated if the agency is a government body or funded by the government. Not all information and services are provided free, and it is best to enquire with a reply paid letter or international reply coupon when first approaching any agency or organisation.

There are an immense number of women's local, national and international networks and organisations, often acting informally, at grass roots and in response to immediate political campaigns or women's local needs. This, together with the inadequate funding and/or oppression with which many women's groups are forced to operate, creates an ever-changing movement. With this in mind, the list of women's organisations includes only national women's organisations and umbrella groupings, but using these networks it should be possible to make contact with groups not listed. For reasons of space the description of each entry is very limited and may not do justice to the full range of activities, services or information available. The entries are designed as an indicator of the range of services and organisations available and are by no means exhaustive. I would encourage readers to explore further by approaching information centres or organisations for specific contacts or information they need.

There is also a combined international list of women's organisations, resource centres and international agencies providing information about and for women. Where these organisations also provide a specific service to the country where they are situated, they are also included in the listing for that country.

How to Use This Section

This section is divided alphabetically by country and each resource area is then listed alphabetically. The resources for each area are listed alphabetically by their English-language name, where it was available. In the case of the United States, the bookshops section is organised alphabetically by state. An international section of organisations and agencies appears at the end.

Acknowledgements

I would like to thank the many women from all over the world who have sent me information. Without their help this section would not have been possible.

Mel Landells
1993

Antigua

Libraries, Archives, Resource Centres and Information

ANL1

Women's Desk
Ministry of Education, Culture, Youth.
Women's Affairs and Sports
ST JOHN'S
☐ Government agency which provides information on women in Antigua.

Argentina

Bookshops

ARB1

Saga
Hipolito Yrgoyen 2296
esq. Pichincha Loc 2
1089 BUENOS AIRES
☐ Feminist bookshop.

Libraries, Archives, Resource Centres and Information

ARL1

Centre of Women's Studies
Nicaragua 4908
1414 BUENOS AIRES
☐ Documents and researches women's problems. Organises courses, conferences and seminars.

ARL2

Multinational Women's Centre for Research and Training of the Inter-American Commission on Women
Avenue Velez Sarsfield 153
CORDOBA
☎ 45750
☐ Art gallery and specialised library.

ARL3

Women's Library Association
Marcelo T. de Alvear 1155
1058 BUENOS AIRES
☐ Catalogues work of women's movements and collects written material on women. Provides educational seminars and courses.

Women's Organisations

ARO1

Argentine Association of Women in Legal Careers
Corrientes 1958
3o piso E
BUENOS AIRES
☎ 49 1648
☐ Professional organisation which also offers advice to women suffering violence.

ARO2

Juana Manso Women's House
Dean Funes 1077
CORDOBA
☐ Legal advice for women suffering violence.

ARO3

Women's Council of the Republic of Argentina
Casilla de Correo 116
Sucursal 48
1060 BUENOS AIRES
☐ Umbrella organisation.

ARO4

Women's Union of Argentina (UMA)
Cassilla de Carreo no. 3901
del Correo Central
1000 BUENOS AIRES
☐ Umbrella organisation.

Australia

Bookshops

AUSB1

Abbey's Bookshop
131 York Street
SYDNEY, NSW
☐ Alternative bookshop with women's studies section.

AUSB2

Action Books
25 New Street
RINGWOOD, Vic.
☐ Alternative bookshop with women's studies section.

AUSB3

Arcane Bookshop
212 William Street
PERTH, WA 6000
☎ 09 328 5073
☐ Alternative bookshop with feminist section.

AUSB4

Ariel Booksellers
42 Oxford Street
PADDINGTON, NSW
☐ Alternative bookshop with women's studies section.

AUSB5

Bellbird Books
10 George Street
ARTARMON, NSW
☐ Alternative bookshop with women's studies section.

AUSB6

Book and Cranny
168 Belmore Road
RANDWICK, NSW
☐ Bookshop with women's studies section.

AUSB7

Books Etcetera
38 Oxford Street
DARLINGHURST, NSW
☐ Alternative bookshop with women's studies section.

AUSB8

The Bookshop
DARLINGHURST, NSW
☎ 02 331 1103
☐ Feminist bookshop.

AUSB9

The Bookshop
NEWTOWN, NSW
☎ 02 514 244
☐ Feminist bookshop.

AUSB10

Bray's Books
268 Darling Street
BALMAIN, NSW
☐ Alternative bookshop with women's studies section.

AUSB11

Constant Reader Bookshop
27 Willoughby Road
CROWS NEST, NSW
☐ Alternative bookshop with women's studies section.

AUSB12

Dymocks Bookstore
Level 5, Carousel Centre
BONDI JUNCTION, NSW
☐ Bookshop with women's studies section.

AUSB13

Elspeth Douglas Bookseller
36 Marmion Parade
TARINGA, Qld
☐ Alternative bookshop with women's studies section.

AUSB14

Emerald Hill Books
336 Clarendon Street
SOUTH MELBOURNE, Vic.
☐ Alternative bookshop with women's studies section.

AUSB15

The Feminist Bookstore
Shop 9, Orange Grove Plaza
Balmain Road
LILYFIELD, NSW 2040
☎ 02 810 2666
☐ Feminist bookshop.

AUSB16

Friends of the Earth
366 Smith Street
COLLINGWOOD, Vic, 3066
☐ Alternative bookshop with women's studies and feminist sections.

AUSB17

Friends of the Earth
222 Brunswick Street
FITZROY, Vic 3065
☎ 03 419 8700
☐ Alternative bookshop with women's section.

AUSB18

Gertrudes
39 Gertrude Street
FITZROY, Vic. 3065
☎ 03 417 4662
☐ Women's bookshop.

AUSB19

Gleebook
191 Glebe Point Road
GLEBE, NSW
☐ Alternative bookshop with women's studies section.

AUSB20

Greensleeves Bookshop
247 Sandy Bay Road
HOBART
Tasmania
☎ 238 839
☐ Alternative bookshop with feminist section.

AUSB21

Hartwigs
245 Brunswick Street
FITZROY, Vic. 3065
☎ 03 417 7147
☐ Alternative bookshop with feminist section.

AUSB22

Hartwigs
72A Acland Street
ST KILDA, Vic.
☎ 03 525 3952
☐ Alternative bookshop with feminist section.

AUSB23

International Bookshop
17 Elizabeth Street
MELBOURNE, Vic.
☎ 03 614 2859
☐ Alternative bookshop with women's section.

AUSB24

La Trobe University Bookshop
La Trobe University
BUNDOORA, Vic.
☐ Bookshop with women's studies section.

AUSB25

Lesley McKay's Bookshop
401 New South Head Road
DOUBLE BAY, NSW
☐ Bookshop with women's studies section.

AUSB26

Lincoln Bookshop
620 Swanston Street
CARLTON, Vic.
☐ Alternative bookshop with women's studies section.

AUSB27

The Lindfield Bookshop
352 Pacific Highway
LINDFIELD, NSW
☐ Alternative bookshop with women's section.

AUSB28

Melbourne Co-op Bookshop
330 Swanston Street
MELBOURNE, Vic.
☐ Alternative bookshop with women's studies section.

AUSB29

Moir's Bookshop
8/43 Burns Bay Road
LANE COVE, NSW
☐ Alternative bookshop with women's studies section.

AUSB30

Murphy Sisters Bookshop
240 The Parade
Norwood
ADELAIDE, SA 5067
☎ 332 7508
☐ Women's bookshop.

AUSB31

Open Leaves
71 Cardigan Street
CARLTON, Vic. 3053
☎ 03 347 2353
☐ Feminist bookshop with women's studies, lesbian and feminist mail order booklists.

AUSB32

Readings Bookshop
338 Lygon Street
CARLTON, Vic. 3053
☐ Alternative bookshop with women's section.

AUSB33

Readings Bookshop
710 Glenferrie Road
HAWTHORN, Vic.
☐ Alternative bookshop with women's studies section.

AUSB34

Readings Bookshop
269 Glenferrie Road
MALVERN, Vic.
☐ Alternative bookshop with women's studies section.

AUSB35

Readings Bookshop
153 Toorak Road
SOUTH YARRA, Vic.
☐ Alternative bookshop with women's studies section.

AUSB36

Shrew Women's Bookshop
37 Gertrude Street
FITZROY, Vic. 3065
☎ 03 419 5595
☐ Women's bookshop.

AUSB37

Smith's Bookshop
76 Alinga Street
CANBERRA, ACT
☐ Alternative bookshop with women's studies section.

AUSB38

Spiral Bookseller and Publisher
    269 Smith Street
    FITZROY, Vic. 3065
☎   03 417 2576
☐ Alternative bookshop with women's issues section.

AUSB39

University Bookshop
    University of Queensland
    ST LUCIA, Qld
☐ Bookshop with women's studies section.

AUSB40

University Co-op Bookshop
    Bay House
    Kettle Lane (Rear 80 Bay St)
    SYDNEY, NSW
☐ Bookshop with women's studies section.

AUSB41

The Women's Bookshop
    11 Gladstone Road
    Highgate Hill
    BRISBANE, Qld 4101
☎   07 844 6650
☐ Feminist bookshop.

Libraries, Archives. Resource Centres and Information

AUSL1

Office of Indigenous Women
Aboriginal and Torres Straight Islander Commission
    234 Sussex Street
    SYDNEY, NSW 2000
☎   02 283 4820
☐ Information on indigenous women.

AUSL2

Contrary Mary Co. Ltd
    PO Box 107
    MORUYA, NSW 2537
☐ Feminist library and information on women's welfare issues.

AUSL3

Women's Directorate
Department of Industrial Relations, Employment, Training and Further Education
    1 Oxford Street
    DARLINGHURST, NSW 2010
☎   02 266 8390

☐ Government agency providing information and advice on women's employment.

AUSL4

Sex Discrimination Commissioner
Human Rights and Equal Opportunities Commission
    24th Floor
    388 George Street
    SYDNEY, NSW 2000
☎   02 229 7600
☐ Commonwealth government agency providing information on the Sex Discrimination Act.

AUSL5

Immigrant Women's Health Information Project
    7/25 Barbara Street
    FAIRFIELD, NSW 2165
☎   02 726 4059
☐ Provides advice and information for immigrant women on health issues.

AUSL6

Leichhardt Women's Health Centre
    164 Flood Street
    LEICHHARDT, NSW
☐ Information on women's health.

AUSL7

New South Wales Women's Advisory Council
    Level 2
    4–10 Campbell Street
    HAYMARKET, NSW 2000
☎   02 561 8840
☐ Advises the state government on issues concerning women and consults with women in the community.

AUSL8

New South Wales Women's Refuge Referral Resource Centre
    PO Box 10
    PETERSHAM, NSW 2049
☎   02 560 1605
☐ Advice and referrals for women suffering violence.

AUSL9

Newcastle Women's Health Centre
    c/o Working Women's Centre
    Corner Industrial Drive and Avon Street
    MAYFIELD, NSW 2304
☎   049 68 2511
☐ Advice, information and counselling for women.

AUSL10

Office of the Status of Women
Department of Prime Minister and Cabinet
CANBERRA, ACT 2600
□ Government department providing information on women in Australia.

AUSL11

Vida Publications
GPO Box 889
CANBERRA, ACT 2601
□ Provides information for researchers on women's issues and monthly index of newspaper articles on women.

AUSL12

Women and Development Network of Australia
262 Pitt Street
3rd Floor
SYDNEY, NSW 2000
□ Works with Australian aid agencies to press for policies and aid programmes which are controlled by and benefit women. Provides speakers, research and consultancy services.

AUSL13

Women's Art Gallery
375 Brunswick Street
FITZROY, Vic. 3056
☎ 03 419 0718
□ Gallery of women artists.

AUSL14

Women's Health and Information Centre
Royal Women's Hospital
Gratton Street
CARLTON, Vic. 3053
☎ 03 344 2007
□ Women's information and drop-in centre.

AUSL15

Women's Information and Referral Exchange
3rd Floor
238 Flinders Lane
MELBOURNE, Vic. 3000
☎ 03 654 6844
□ Free information service to women and referrals to other women's groups.

AUSL16

Women's Information Service
280 Adelaide Street
BRISBANE, Qld
☎ 07 229 1264
□ Information for women.

AUSL17

Women's Information Switchboard
122 Kintore Avenue
ADELAIDE, SA
□ Advice, aid and information for women.

AUSL18

Women's Liberation Switchboard
☎ 03 416 0850
□ Information service for women on groups and social events for women. Melbourne based.

Women's Organisations

AUSO1

Australian Federation of Medical Women
5 Elaine Place
DURAL, NSW 2158
□ Organisation for women working in the medical profession.

AUSO2

Australian Federation of University Women
Suite 11, 6th Floor
Dymocks Building
George Street
SYDNEY, NSW 2000
☎ 02 232 5629
□ Organisation for women working in universities.

AUSO3

Black Women's Action in Education Foundation
PO Box 141
REDFERN, NSW 2016
□ Provides advice on education and limited sponsorship for black women.

AUSO4

Country Women's Association
PO Box 15
POTTS POINT, NSW 2011
☎ 02 358 2923
□ Central organisation with hundreds of branches throughout Australia.

AUSO5

Domestic Violence Advocacy Service
PO Box H154
HARRIS PARK, NSW 2150
☎ 02 637 3741
□ Provides legal advice and advocacy for women.

AUSO6

Feminist Network on Reproductive Technology
PO Box H154
HARRIS PARK, NSW 2150
☎ 02 637 5012
☐ Feminist group monitoring reproductive technology.

AUSO7

Lesbian Network
PO Box 215
ROZELLE, NSW 2039
☎ 02 660 1565
☐ Feminist lesbian network.

AUSO8

Lesbian Studies and Research Group
PO Box K396
HAYMARKET, NSW 2000
☐ Women researching lesbian issues.

AUSO9

Moruya Wimmins House
PO Box 107
MORUYA, NSW 2537
☐ Refuge, support and helpline for women suffering domestic violence. Lesbian support service.

AUSO10

National Council of Women of Australia
PO Box 161
STEPNEY, SA 5069
☐ Umbrella organisations with 500 affiliated women's groups.

AUSO11

National Foundation for Australian Women
PO Box 1465
CANBERRA, ACT 2601
☎ 06 247 2276
☐ Feminist organisation committed to protecting and advancing the interests of women.

AUSO12

Society of Women Writers NSW Inc.
PO Box 1388
SYDNEY, NSW 2000
☎ 02 528 9373
☐ Organisation for women writers.

AUSO13

South Sydney Women's Centre
231 Abercrombie Street
CHIPPENDALE, NSW 2008
☎ 02 319 2613
☐ Meeting place for women's groups.

AUSO14

United France Associations of Women
PO Box R15
Royal Exchange
SYDNEY, NSW 2000
☐ Umbrella group for women's organisations working for equal opportunities.

AUSO15

Women in Film and Television
PO Box 648
BROADWAY, NSW 2007
☎ 02 281 2058
☐ Women's networking and lobbying group.

AUSO16

Women in Publishing
PO Box 41
ARTARMON, NSW 2064
☐ Organisation for women in publishing.

AUSO17

Women in Science Enquiry Network
Science Faculty
Australian National University
PO Box 4
CANBERRA, ACT 2601
☎ 06 249 4726
☐ National network for women in science.

AUSO18

Women in Touch
42 Eastern Avenue
REVESBY, NSW 2212
☎ 02 77 7809
☐ Informal women's discussion group.

AUSO19

Women Lawyers Association of New South Wales
170 Phillip Street
SYDNEY, NSW 2000
☎ 02 223 8442
☐ Professional association of women lawyers.

AUSO20

Women's Abortion Action Campaign
PO Box E233
ST JAMES, NSW 2000
☎ 02 569 3819
☐ Campaigns for free abortion and contraception on demand and an end to enforced sterilisation.

AUSO21

Women's Electoral Lobby
> 3 Lobelia Street
> O'CONNOR, ACT 2601

☐ Electoral lobby organisation for women's liberation.

AUSO22

Women's International League for Peace and Freedom
> 156 Castlereagh Street
> 3rd Floor
> SYDNEY, NSW 2000
> ☎ 02 232 3406

☐ Branch of worldwide organisation working for peace and disarmament.

AUSO23

Women's Legal Resources Centre
> PO Box H154
> HARRIS PARK, NSW 2150
> ☎ 02 637 4597

☐ Aims to improve women's awareness of their legal rights and campaigns for legal reforms. Legal advice for women.

AUSO24

Women's Liberation House
> 63 Palace Street
> PETERSHAM, NSW 2059
> ☎ 02 569 3819

☐ Meeting place for women's groups.

AUSO25

Women's Media Research Group
> PO Box 675
> GLEBE, NSW 2037
> ☎ 02 552 1935

☐ Group for women researching women's issues in the media.

AUSO26

Women's Studies Association and Research Centre for Women's Studies
> University of Adelaide
> PO Box 498
> ADELAIDE, SA 5001

☐ National women's studies organisation.

Austria

Bookshops

AUB1

Frauenzimmer
> Langegasse 11
> 1080 VIENNA
> ☎ 0222 43 86 78

☐ Feminist bookshop.

Libraries, Archives, Resource Centres and Information

AUL1

Centre for Women's Research
> Vienna Communication Centre for Women in Austria
> Wahringerstrasse 59
> 1090 VIENNA

☐ Feminist reference library.

AUL2

Stichwort – Archive of the Women's and Lesbian Movement
> Bergasse 5/24
> 1090 VIENNA
> ☎ 0222 31 48 544

☐ Multi-media feminist library and documentation centre.

AUL3

Women's Centre
> Wahringerstrasse 59
> 1090 VIENNA
> ☎ 0222 48 50 57

☐ Women's information.

AUL4

Women's Research Documentation Centre
> Institut für Wissenschaft und Kunst
> Berggrasse 17/1
> 1090 VIENNA

☐ Research and documentation on Austrian women.

Women's Organisations

AUO1

Austrian Council of Women
> Wilhelm Exnergasse 34–36
> VIENNA
> ☎ 0222 348 4493

☐ Umbrella organisation for women's groups.

AUO2
Medical Women's International Association
(See International section)

AUO3
United Nations Branch for the Advancement of Women
(See International section)

AUO4
Working Group Against Traffic in Women and Sex Tourism
    Weyrgrasse 5/1
    1030 VIENNA
☎ 0222 7133594
☐ Investigating, providing information and campaigning on traffic in women, drawing attention to Austria's role in sex tourism.

Bahamas

Women's Organisations

BAO1
Council for Women in the Bahamas
    PO Box 1145
    NASSAU
☐ Umbrella organisation.

BAO2
National Women's Movement
    PO Box 4646
    NASSAU
☐ Campaigning group.

Bangladesh

Libraries, Archives, Resource Centres and Information

BANL1
Women for Women
    15 Green Square
    Green Road
    DHAKA
☎ 50 46 97
☐ Research library.

Women's Organisations

BANO1
Policy Research for Development Alternatives
    5/3 Barabo Mahanpur
    Ring Road
    Shaymoli
    DHAKA 7
☐ Devises alternative development policies for women.

Barbados

Libraries, Archives, Resource Centres and Information

BARL1
Women and Development Unit
    c/o Extra Mural Department
    University of the West Indies
    Pinelands
    ST MICHAEL
☎ 426 9288
☐ Library, research and consultancy services. Networking between individuals, women's groups and institutions in the Caribbean.

Women's Organisations

BARO1
Barbados Council of Women
    Lyrias
    CHRISTCHURCH
☐ Umbrella organisation.

Belgium

Bookshops

BELB1
Artemys
    Galerie Bortier
    8–10 rue St Jean
    BRUSSELS
☎ 02 512 03 47
☐ Feminist bookshop.

BELB2
Dulle Griet
    Tiensestraat 45
    3000 LOUVAIN
☐ Women's bookshop.

BELB3

Les Rabouilleuses
221 chaussée d'Ixelles
1050 BRUSSELS
☐ Women's bookshop.

Libraries, Archives, Resource Centres and Information

BELL1

Documentation Centre
21 rue de la Tourelle
1040 BRUSSELS
☎ 02 230 5158
☐ Information and documentation centre on women and employment. Research and consultancy services to international organisations.

BELL2

Feminist Library
78 rue Gallait
1210 BRUSSELS
☎ 02 216 23 23
☐ Women's library.

BELL3

Group for Feminist Research and Information
29 rue Blanche
1050 BRUSSELS
☎ 02 538 84 87
☐ Information and documentation centre.

BELL4

L'Une, L'Autre
99 boulevard de Waterloo
1000 BRUSSELS
☐ Library and resource centre.

BELL5

Lesbian Archives
BP 2024
1000 BRUSSELS
☎ 02 215 99 38
☐ Lesbian archive and newsletter.

BELL6

Maison des Femmes
29 rue Blanche
1050 BRUSSELS
☐ Major, multi-activity women's centre. Contact for women's groups.

BELL7

Secrétariat de la Commission du Travail des Femmes
Ministère de l'Emploi et du Travail
51–53 rue Belliard
1040 BRUSSELS
☐ Government agency providing information and advice on women at work.

BELL8

Women's University
1a place Quetelet
1030 BRUSSELS
☐ Documentation centre.

Women's Organisations

BELO1

Belgian Association of Female Jurists
Ringlaan 134
1180 BRUSSELS
☐ Submits suggestions for legal reforms which affect women, and networks between women in all areas of the legal profession.

BELO2

Belgian Federation of University Women
29 rue Blanche
1050 BRUSSELS
☐ Professional organisation for academic women.

BELO3

Collective for Battered Women
29 rue Blanche
1050 BRUSSELS
☎ 02 539 27 44
☐ Support and advice for women suffering violence.

BELO4

European Network of Women
38 rue Stevin
1040 BRUSSELS
☐ Researches and monitors EC legislation on women.

BELO5

National Belgian Women's Council (CNFB) (French speaking)
60 rue de la Prévoyance
1000 BRUSSELS
☎ 02 514 49 49
☐ Umbrella organisation.

BELO6

National Council of Women (Flemish speaking)
Louizalaan 183
1050 BRUSSELS
☐ Umbrella organisation.

BELO7

National Network on Women's Studies and Associations
c/o Micheline Scheys
University of Brussels
Pleinlaan 2
1050 BRUSSELS
☎ 02 641 21 11
☐ National women's studies organisation.

BELO8

National Women's Council
De Meeussquare 28
1040 BRUSSELS
☎ 02 511 82 43
☐ Umbrella organisation.

BELO9

Space for Women
P.A./Elcker-Ilk
Blyde Inkomstsraat 115
3000 LEUVEN
☐ Group of women architects who research on women's space in planning, architecture and housing.

BELO10

Women's Artistic and Cultural Union
80 boulevard Louis Schmidt
Be. no. 2
1040 BRUSSELS
☐ A worldwide federation of women artists which also organises exhibitions.

BELO11

Women's Consultative Committee
Leidtsstraat 27–29
1210 BRUSSELS
☎ 02 215 38 48
☐ Umbrella organisation for Flemish-speaking feminist groups.

BELO12

Women's Liaison Committee
1a place Quetelet
1030 BRUSSELS
☐ Umbrella organisation for groups and individuals working for equality for women.

BELO13

Women's Organisation for Equality
29 rue Blanche
off av. Louise
BRUSSELS
☎ 02 538 47 73
☐ English-speaking organisation.

Bolivia

Libraries. Archives, Resource Centres and Information

BOLL1

Women's Centre for Information and Development
Avda Villazon 1958
Oficina 3a
30 piso
Casilla 22433
LA PAZ
☐ Information centre.

Women's Organisations

BOLO1

National Confederation of Women's Institutions
Calle Batallon Colorados
Edificio El Condor
Piso-9-Oficina 907
Apartado 4471
LA PAZ
☎ 360653
☐ Umbrella group which co-ordinates voluntary groups, focusing on women's education.

BOLO2

National Women's Council of Bolivia
Casilla 2573
LA PAZ
☐ Umbrella organisation.

Botswana

Libraries, Archives, Resource Centres and Information

BOTL1

Women's Affairs Unit
Department of Culture
Registration and Social Welfare Matters
Private Bag 00185
GABORONE

☐ Government agency which carries out research and policy formulation for women. Co-ordinates women's activities nationally.

Women's Organisations

BOTO1

Botswana Council of Women
PO Box 339
GABORONE
☐ Umbrella organisation.

Brazil

Libraries, Archives, Resource Centres and Information

BRAL1

Women's Network
Rua Joao Ramalho 991
Bairro Perdizes
CP 1803
01051 SAO PAULO
☐ Documentation centre.

Women's Organisations

BRAO1

Cabo Women's Centre
Rua Pe. Antonio Alves 20
54.500 Cabo
PERNAMBUCO
☎ 521 0785
☐ Educational, training, medical and legal centre for women.

BRAO2

Centre for Brazilian Women
Rua Franklin Roosevelt 39/703
RIO DE JANEIRO
☐ Support, advice and information.

BRAO3

DAWN, Development Alternatives with women for a New Era
(See International section)

BRAO4

National Women's Council of Brazil
Rua Barata
Ribeiro 539, Apartado 201
Copacabana
72000 RIO DE JANEIRO

☎ 257 9043
☐ Umbrella organisation.

BRAO5

Sociadade Brasil Mulher
Rua Fidalga 548
sala 16
CEP 05432
SAO PAOLO
☐ Umbrella organisation for Brazilian women.

BRAO6

State Council of Women's Condition
Rua Estados Unidos 346
01427 SAO PAULO
☐ Promotes equality for women and supports women suffering violence.

BRAO7

Women's Network
Rua Joao Ramalho 991
Bairro Perdizes
CP 1803
01051 SAO PAULO
☐ Networks between women's groups in São Paulo city. Carries out research and runs courses and lectures.

Bulgaria

Women's Organisations

BULO1

Democratic Union of Women in Bulgaria
Bd Patriarche Evtimi 82
SOFIA 1463
☐ Umbrella organisation.

Canada

Bookshops

CANB1

Bold Print Inc.
478 River Avenue at Osborne
Winnipeg
MANITOBA
☎ 452 9682
☐ Bookshop with women's section.

CANB2

L'Essentielle
420 East rue Rachez
Montreal
QUEBEC H2J 2G7

☎ 514 844 3277
□ Feminist bookshop

CANB3

Octopus East
1146 Commercial
Vancouver
BRITISH COLUMBIA V5L 3X3
☎ 604 253 0913
□ Alternative bookshop with feminist section.

CANB4

Toronto Women's Bookstore
73 Harbord Street
Toronto
ONTARIO
☎ 416 922 8744
□ Feminist bookshop.

CANB5

Vancouver Women's Books
315 Cambie Street
Vancouver
BRITISH COLUMBIA
☎ 604 684 0523
□ Women's bookshop.

CANB6

Women's Bookstore
380 Elgin Street at Gladstone
Ottawa
ONTARIO
☎ 613 922 8744
□ Women's bookshop.

Libraries, Archives, Resource Centres and Information

CANL1

Canadian Advisory Council on the Status of Women
110 O'Connor Street
9th Floor, Box 1541
Station B
Ottawa
ONTARIO K1P 5R5
□ Government-funded autonomous information service.

CANL2

Canadian Research Institute for the Advancement of Women
151 Slater Street
Suite 408
Ottawa
ONTARIO K1P 5H3

☎ 613 563 0681
□ Resource centre open to the public.

CANL3

Canadian Women's Movement Archives
PO Box 128
Station P
Toronto
ONTARIO M5S 2S7
□ Collection of contemporary material from the Canadian women's movement.

CANL4

Resources for Feminist Research
252 Bloor Street West
Toronto
ONTARIO
□ Provides information for feminist researchers.

CANL5

Simone de Beauvoir Institute
1455 de Maisonneuve Boulevard West
Concordia University
Montreal
QUEBEC H3G 1M8
☎ 514 848 2370
□ Documentation centre and reading room.

CANL6

Status of Women in Canada
151 Sparks Street
10th Floor
Ottawa
ONTARIO K1A 1C3
□ Government agency concerned with policy development.

CANL7

Women's Bureau
Department of Labour
Ottawa
ONTARIO K1A 0J2
☎ 613 997 1550
□ Government agency providing information on women's equality status in the labour market.

Women's Organisations

CANO1

Amethyst Women's Addiction Centre
407 Queen Street
Ottawa
ONTARIO K1R 5A6
□ Treatment, preventive and educational centre.

CANO2

Canadian Association for the Advancement of Women and Sport
  323 Chapel Street
  Ottawa
  ONTARIO K1N 7Z2
□ Campaigns to improve the status and participation of women in sport.

CANO3

Canadian Association of Elizabeth Fry Societies
  Suite 600
  251 Slater Street
  Ottawa
  ONTARIO K2P 1X3
□ Works to help women in prison and women in conflict with the law.

CANO4

Canadian Association for Women in Science
  1087 Meyerside Drive
  Suite 5
  Mississauga
  ONTARIO L5T 1M5
□ Promotes equal opportunities for women in scientific professions.

CANO5

Canadian Coalition Against Media Pornography
  PO Box 1075
  Station B
  Ottawa
  ONTARIO K1P 5R1
□ Campaigns to persuade the government to enforce laws against pornography.

CANO6

Canadian Congress for Learning Opportunities for Women
  47 Main Street
  Toronto
  ONTARIO M4E 2V6
□ Promotes feminist education.

CANO7

Canadian Federation of University Women
  55 Parkdale Avenue
  Ottawa
  ONTARIO K1Y 1E5
□ Umbrella organisation for university women's clubs. Conducts research and awards grants to students and libraries.

CANO8

Canadian Research Institute for the Advancement of Women
  151 Slater Street
  Suite 408
  Ottawa
  ONTARIO K1P 5H3
□ Sponsors research and publishes papers on women's experience.

CANO9

Canadian Women's Studies Association
  Dept of Sociology
  University of Winnipeg
  Winnipeg
  MANITOBA R3B 2E9
□ National network of women's studies academics.

CANO10

Information and Action Network for Women
  CP 5, Sillery
  Quebec
  MONTREAL G1T 2P7
□ An informal network to inform women of their rights.

CANO11

International Organisation for Women in Mathematics Education
  Ontario Institute for Studies in Education
  252 Bloor Street West
  Toronto
  ONTARIO M5S 1V6
□ Aims to further research into gender and mathematics, and increase the participation of girls in mathematics. Worldwide membership.

CANO12

MATCH International Centre
  205 Elgin Street
  Ottawa
  ONTARIO K2P 1L5
□ Funds women's projects in Third World countries, and supports women's groups to organise supportive links with Third World women.

CANO13

National Action Committee on the Status of Women
  344 Bloor Street West
  Suite 505
  Toronto
  ONTARIO M58 1W9
□ Umbrella organisation for feminist groups throughout Canada. Lobbies for women's equality.

CANO14

National Association of Women and the Law
 Suite 400
 1 Nicholas Street
 Ottawa
 ONTARIO K1N 7B7
☐ Campaigns for improvement in women's legal status.

CANO15

National Council of Women of Canada
 270 MacClaren Street
 Room 20
 Ottawa
 ONTARIO K2P 0M3
☐ Umbrella organisation.

CANO16

National Farmers Union Women's Department
 250C–2nd Avenue South
 Saskatoon
 SASKATCHEWAN S7K 2M1
☐ Campaigns on a wide range of issues affecting rural women in particular.

CANO17

Native Women's Association of Canada
 195A Bank Street
 Suite 200
 Ottawa
 ONTARIO K2P 1W7
☐ Advocates an active role for Indian women in achieving equality for Indian peoples. Networks between native Indian women's organisations.

CANO18

Pauktuutit, Inuit Women's Association
 Suite 804
 200 Elgin Street
 Ottawa
 ONTARIO K2P 1L5
☐ Campaigns for the rights of Inuit women and Inuit people, and encourages links between Inuit women and Aboriginal peoples.

CANO19

Voice of Women
 736 Bathurst Street
 Toronto
 ONTARIO M5S 2R4
☐ Campaigns for a reallocation of resources away from military spending.

CANO20

West Coast Women and Words Society
 Box 65563
 Station F
 Vancouver
 BRITISH COLUMBIA V5N 5K5
☐ Network for women writers, critics and publishers.

CANO21

Women's Health Interaction
 55 Arthur Street
 Ottawa
 ONTARIO K1R 7B9
☐ Network of women concerned with women's health issues.

CANO22

Women's Legal Education and Action Fund
 344 Bloor Street West
 Suite 403
 Toronto
 ONTARIO M5S 1N9
☐ Supports women in equality cases through the courts and conducts research.

CANO23

World Association of Women Journalists and Writers
 3945 Boulevard St Martin Quest
 Chomedey
 Laval
 QUEBEC H7T 1B7
☐ World network of women journalists.

Chile

Libraries, Archives, Resource Centres and Information

CHIL1

Centre for Women's Studies
 Purisima 353
 SANTIAGO
☎ 771 194
☐ Information centre and archive.

CHIL2

Isis International
 Casilla 2067
 Correo Central
 SANTIAGO
☐ Aims to eliminate sex discrimination and to improve women's social, economic and political position. Worldwide information and communication service with offices in Italy and Chile.

CHIL3

National Women's Secretariat
Villavicencio 341
Oficina 21
SANTIAGO
☐ Documentation and information.

Women's Organisations

CHIO1

Committee for the Defence of Women's Rights
Abdon Cifuentes 66
SANTIAGO
☐ Organisation campaigning for women's rights and equality.

CHIO2

Latin-American Association for the Integration of Women
Aladim Casilla 9450
SANTIAGO
☐ Campaigns to integrate women into public life.

CHIO3

National Women's Secretariat
Villavicencio 341
Oficina 21
SANTIAGO
☐ Legal advice, education training and information for women.

CHIO4

Women's Alternative Media Unit
Casilla 16-637
Correo 9
SANTIAGO
☐ Women's radio network and news agency aiming to increase the information available on Latin American women.

CHIO5

Women's Organisation for Disarmament, Unification and Development in Latin America
Londres 88
2o piso
SANTIAGO
☐ Women's organisation working for women's rights, social and economic reforms, peace and disarmament.

China

Women's Organisations

CHO1

All-China Women's Federation
50 Deng Shikou
BEIJING
☐ Communist Party-led, all-women organisation.

Colombia

Libraries, Archives, Resource Centres and Information

COLL1

'Being a Woman' Documentation and Communication Centre
Apartado aereo 25922
BOGOTA
☐ Umbrella feminist organisation providing information and documentation on women.

COLL2

Centre for Information and Research on Women in Colombia
Carrera 13B no. 25/76
BOGOTA
☐ Information on women in Colombia.

COLL3

Centre for Women's Studies and Investigation
Apartado aereo 49105
MEDELLIN
☐ Information centre.

COLL4

National Association of Rural and Native Women of Colombia (ANMUCIC)
Apartado aereo
Carre 10, 20–30, OF 601
Ministerio de Agricultura
1041 BOGOTA
☐ Government agency for rural and native women.

Women's Organisations

COLO1

National Council for the Integration of Women in Development
Palacio de San Carlos
Calle 10, numero 5–51
BOGOTA

☐ Aims to increase women's participation in public life, and co-ordinates between government departments and industry.

COLO2

National Women's Council of Colombia
 Calle 82, 14A–17
 Oficinas 308/309
 BOGOTA
☐ Umbrella organisation.

Costa Rica

Libraries, Archives, Resource Centres and Information

CRL1

Feminist Centre for Information and Action
 Apartado 949
 SAN JOSE 1000
☐ Information for women.

CRL2

General Directorate for Women and the Family
 c/o Ministry of Culture, Youth and Sport
 Apartado 10 227
 SAN JOSE
☎ 227581
☐ Government agency assisting the creation of women's training centres. Also supports women's groups.

CRL3

Women's Information Programme
 National University
 Apartado 1009
 Centro Colon
 SAN JOSE
☎ 376363 ext. 2458
☐ Documentation centre and national network specialising in women and development.

CRL4

Women's Office, Social-Labour Promotion Division
 c/o Ministry of Labour and Social Security
 Apartado 10 133
 SAN JOSE
☐ Government agency encouraging self-employment for women and covering both industrial and rural areas.

Women's Organisations

CRO1

Servico Especial de la Mujer Latino-Americana
 Apartado 70 10001
 SAN JOSE
☐ Latin American network of women journalists.

CRO2

Women's International League for Peace and Freedom
 Apartado 287
 2100 Guadalupe
 SAN JOSE
☐ Branch of worldwide organisation working to improve the status of women and promote peace.

Cuba

Women's Organisations

CUBO1

Federation of Cuban Women
 Paseo 260
 Entre 11 y 13
 VEDADO LA HAVANA
☐ Seeks to enhance the political participation of women and to improve women's cultural and technical knowledge.

Czech Republic

Libraries, Archives, Resource Centres and Information

CZL1

Curriculum Centre and Library for Gender Studies
 Charles University in Prague
 Gender Studies
 Box 695
 111 21 PRAGUE 1
☎ 232 71 06
☐ Information and consultation services. Library, database, national and international network.

Denmark

Bookshops

DENB1

Aarhus Bogcafe
 Norregade 24
 8000 AARHUS C

☎ 86 13 32 68
☐ Bookshop with women's studies and feminist section.

DENB2

Atheneum Boghandel
Norregade 6
1165 COPENHAGEN K
☎ 33 12 69 70
☐ Bookshop with women's studies and feminist section.

DENB3

Humaniorabogladen
Njalsgade 80
2300 COPENHAGEN S
☎ 31 54 17 10
☐ Bookshop with women's studies and feminist section.

DENB4

Kobenhavne Bogcafe
Kultorvet 11
COPENHAGEN
☐ Women's bookshop.

DENB5

Samfundslitteratur RUC
Narbjergveg 35
PO Box 260
4000 ROSKILDE
☎ 46 75 77 11
☐ Bookshop with women's studies and feminist section.

DENB6

Sammenslutningen Kvideshuset Bogcafe
Gothersgade 37
COPENHAGEN
☐ Women's bookshop in women's centre selling books by women, for women and about women.

DENB7

Studenterboghandelen
Campusvej 55
5230 ODENSE M
☎ 66 15 87 47
☐ Bookshop with women's studies and feminist section.

DENB8

Studiebogladen
Sondergade 20
8000 AARHUS C
☎ 86 13 10 66
☐ Bookshop with women's studies and feminist section.

DENB9

Women's Bookshop
Gyldenlovesgade
COPENHAGEN
☎ 33 14 16 76
☐ Women's bookshop.

Libraries, Archives, Resource Centres and Information

DENL1

Centre for Feminist Research and Women's Studies
University of Copenhagen-Amagar
Njalslade 106
2300 COPENHAGEN
☐ Information on women's studies activities in Denmark.

DENL2

Centre for Interdisciplinary Information on Women's Studies
Nyhavn 22
1051 COPENHAGEN
☎ 33 13 50 88
☐ Reference library and index of women researchers. Includes the Danish Women's Photo Archive.

DENL3

Women's Art Gallery
Fredensgade 28 B
AARHUS
☐ Gallery of women artists.

DENL4

Women's Centre
Havenegade 22
AARHUS
☐ Information centre and meeting place.

DENL5

Women's Centre
Gyldenlovesgade
COPENHAGEN
☎ 33 14 16 76
☐ Women's information and bookshop.

DENL6

Women's History Archive
The State Library
Universitetsparken
8000 AARHUS C
☎ 86 12 20 22 ext. 319
☐ Women's studies documentation and information centre on the Danish women's movement.

DENL7
Women's Information Centre
Nyhavn 22
1051 COPENHAGEN
☎ 33 12 50 88
☐ Reference library and material on women. Quarterly bibliography, lectures and journal.

DENL8
Women's Library and Documentation Centre
University of Aarhus
Finlansgade 26
8200 AARHUS N
☎ 86 16 58 55
☐ Material on women.

DENL9
Women's Museum in Denmark
Domkirkeplads 5
8000 AARHUS C
☎ 86 13 69 79
☐ Women's museum and women's history.

Women's Organisations

DENO1
Co-ordinator for Danish Women's Studies
Kirsten Grønbaek-Hansen
Centre for Feminist Research
University of Copenhagen
Njalsgade 106
2300 COPENHAGEN
Denmark
☎ 31 54 22 11

DENO2
Feminist Research in Medicine
Institute of Social Medicine
Panum Institute
Blegdamsvej 3
2200 COPENHAGEN N
☎ 31 35 79 00 ext. 2400
☐ Feminist women working in medical research.

DENO3
Forum for Feminist Research in Medicine
The Institute of Community Health
Department of Social Medicine
Odense University
J. B. Winslowsvej 17
5000 ODENSE C
☎ 66 15 86 00
☐ Women's organisation for women working on feminist medical research.

DENO4
International Network of Women in the Arts
(See International section)

DENO5
National Association for Women and Gender Research in Denmark
Institute of Social Medicine
Panum Institute
Blegdamsvej 3
2200 COPENHAGEN N
☎ 31 35 79 00
☐ National organisation for researchers into women and gender.

DENO6
National Council of Danish Women
Niels Hemmingensgade 8
1153 COPENHAGEN
☎ 01 13 80 87
☐ Umbrella organisation.

DENO7
National Danish Women's Movement (DKN)
Niels Hemmingensgade 10, 2
1153 COPENHAGEN
☎ 33 12 80 87
☐ National campaigning organisation for women's rights and equality.

DENO8
National Forum for Feminist Scholars in Denmark
Centre for Feminist Research and Women's Studies
University of Copenhagen-Amager
Njalslade 106
2300 COPENHAGEN
☐ Network of Danish women's studies.

DENO9
Women for Peace
Postbox 314
5700 SVENDBORG
☐ Campaigns for disarmament and reallocation of military spending to food aid.

Dominican Republic

Libraries, Archives, Resource Centres and Information

DOML1

Camila Henriquez Urena Documentation Centre
Luis F. Thomen # 358
Ensanche Quisqueya
PO Box 1744
SANTO DOMINGO
☎ 563 5263
□ Feminist monographic, scientific and documental information.

DOML2

United Nations International Research and Training Institute for the Advancement of Women (INSTRAW)
(See International section)

DOML3

Women Technicians in Communication
Apartado 284–9
Los Rios
SANTO DOMINGO
□ Communication and information centre for women.

Women's Organisations

DOMO1

Feminist Study Circle
Calle Hostos esq. El Conde
Edificio Baquero
4ta planta
Apartado 430
Apartado 2793
SANTO DOMINGO
□ Group of feminist scholars who produce monthly publications on women's issues.

DOMO2

National Women's Council
El Conde St 23A
SANTO DOMINGO
□ Umbrella organisation.

DOMO3

Women in Development
Avda. Maximo Gomez No. 70
SANTO DOMINGO
□ Women's organisation offering training to rural women.

DOMO4

Women Technicians in Communication
Apartado 284–9
Los Rios
SANTO DOMINGO
□ Promotes women's integration in development through the media. Produces publications and supports research on women in the media.

Ecuador

Libraries, Archives, Resource Centres and Information

ECUL1

Front for Promoting and Integrating Women in Development
M. Casares 1164
QUITO
☎ 235 411
□ Library, training, education and legal advice centre.

ECUL2

National Office for Women
c/o Ministry of Social Welfare
850 Robles y 9 de Octubre
QUITO
☎ 545 434
□ Government agency providing information on women.

ECUL3

Women's Centre
Casilla 5733
GUAYAQUIL
□ Information centre.

Women's Organisations

ECUO1

Autonomous Group of Women
Calle Chile y Guayaquil
Edif
Guerrero Mosa
2o piso. Of. 207
QUITO
□ Campaigning group.

ECUO2

Co-ordinating Committee of Feminist Organisations
Manosca y Veracruz
QUITO

☎ 211 639
☐ Networking organisation.

ECUO3

Ecuadorean Centre for Women's Promotion and Action
Apartado 182-C
Sucursal 15
Los Rios y Gandara
QUITO
☎ 230 844
☐ Conducts research, offers legal advice and promotes the feminist movement.

ECUO4

Front for Promoting and Integrating Women in Development
M. Casares 1164
QUITO
☎ 235 411
☐ Campaigns to include women in development.

ECUO5

National Women's Union of Ecuador
Avda. Versalles 1103 y Carrion
QUITO
☎ 237 796
☐ Umbrella organisation.

ECUO6

Permanent Committee for Women's Rights
Pasaje Rossea 133
Esmereldas 854
QUITO
☎ 212 813
☐ Campaigns on women's equality and women's rights.

ECUO7

Union of Working Women
Flores 846 y Manabi
QUITO
☎ 514 013
☐ Network for women in paid work.

ECUO8

Women's Action Centre
Bogota 400 y Tegucigalpa
Casilla 10201
GUAYAQUIL
☎ 271 954
☐ Networks and co-ordinates women's groups. Publishes and raises awareness on women's issues.

ECUO9

Women's Liberation League
Calle Ilaquita
Urb
Cristobal Enriquez
Mena 2
QUITO
☐ Campaigns on women's issues and for women's equality.

Egypt

Libraries, Archives, Resource Centres and Information

EGL1

Regional Information Network on Arab Women
Social Research Centre
American University in Cairo
PO Box 2511
113 Sharia Kasr-el-Aini
CAIRO
☐ Information centre.

Women's Organisations

EGO1

Arab Women's Solidarity Association
(See International section)

EGO2

Hoda Cha'arawi Association
22 Kasr El Aini Street
CAIRO
☐ Feminist organisation campaigning for equal rights for women and better access to health and welfare.

EGO3

Society for the Economic Liberation of Women
8 Dareeh Saad
Kasrel Einy
CAIRO
☐ Campaigns to raise the standard of living of poor and uneducated women. Offers training for women.

El Salvador

Libraries, Archives, Resource Centres and Information

ELSL1

Instituto de Investigacion Capacitacion y des Arrollo de la Mujer
    Apartado Postal 1703
    SAN SALVADOR
☐ Documentation and information.

Women's Organisations

ELSO1

Women's Legal Aid Centre (CALMUS)
    Apartado Postal 1703
    SAN SALVADOR
☐ Legal aid and advocacy for women.

Estonia

Libraries, Archives, Resource Centres and Information

ESTL1

Family Research Institute
    c/o Anu Laas
    Tartu University
    2 Liivi St
    2400 TARTU
☎ 01434 35436
☐ Provides information on women's studies, research resources and women's organisations in Estonia.

Women's Organisations

ESTO1

Estonian Country Women's Union
    c/o Anu Laas
    67–46 Uus St
    2400 TARTU
☎ 01434 57284
☐ Affiliated to Associated Country Women of the World.

ESTO2

Estonian Women's Union
    c/o Krista Kilvet
    1A Lossi plats
    0106 TALLINN
☎ 0142 559601
☐ Union for Estonian women.

ESTO3

Tartu Women's Society
    c/o Tiiu Muursepp
    65 Kastani St
    2400 TARTU
☐ Organisation for Tartu women.

ESTO4

University Women of Estonia
    c/o Inge Orgo
    4 Hermanni St 1
    2400 TARTU
☐ Organisation for women graduates and academics.

Ethiopia

Libraries, Archives, Resource Centres and Information

ETHL1

African Training and Research Centre for Women
(See International section)

Faroe Islands

Women's Organisations

FARO1

The Women's Studies Liaison
    Department of Faroese
    Debesartroo
    100 TORSHAVN
☎ 298 15 304
☐ Faroese women's studies organisation.

Fiji

Women's Organisations

FIJO1

National Council of Women in Fiji
    PO Box 840
    SUVA
☐ Campaigning umbrella organisation.

Finland

Libraries, Archives, Resource Centres and Information

FINL1

Centre for Women's Studies and Gender Research
University of Tampere
PO Box 607
33101 TAMPERE
☎ 31 156 895
☐ Information and documentation centre.

FINL2

The Christina Institute for Women's Studies
University of Helsinki
Vuorikatu 4 a 10
5th Floor
00100 HELSINKI
☎ 0 191 3395
☐ Women's studies library.

FINL3

Institute for Women's Studies at Åbo Ahademi University
Gezelivsgaten 2A
20500 ÅBO (TURKU)
☎ 21 654 589
☐ Women's studies library. Information and documentation centre.

FINL4

UNIONI, The League of Finnish Feminists
Bulevard 11A
HELSINKI
☎ 0 643 158
☐ Women's information, library and café. Open University courses.

Women's Organisations

FINO1

Association for Women's Studies in Finland
University of Jyvaskyla
Dept of Social Policy
PO Box 35
40351 JYVASKYLA
☎ 41 603 081
☐ Promotes and supports women's studies in Finland. Participates in the development of national research policies.

FINO2

Co-ordinator for Finnish Women's Studies
Liisa Husu
Council for Equality Between Men and Women
PO Box 267
00171 HELSINKI
☎ 0 160 5705
☐ The Council for Equality Between Men and Women is the parliamentary body which promotes equality and co-ordinates research.

FINO3

Finnish Federation of University Women
Fredrikinkatu 41A8
00120 HELSINKI
☎ 0 608 432
☐ Networks between country-wide branches of university women.

FINO4

National Council of Women in Finland
Pohjoisranta 16A
00170 HELSINKI
☎ 0 631 226
☐ Umbrella organisation.

FINO5

NYTKIS, Finnish Women's Organisation for Joint Action
Pohjoisranta 16A
00170 HELSINKI
☎ 0 631 226
☐ Co-operative body between women's organisations.

FINO6

Women for Peace
Bulevardi 11A
00120 HELSINKI 12
☎ 0 649 382
☐ Campaigns against nuclear power and for disarmament.

France

Bookshops

FRB1

Autres Cultures
46 rue Sauffroy
75017 PARIS
☎ 42 63 56 71
☐ Lesbian and gay bookshop.

FRB2

Du Côté des Femmes
19 rue du Cirque
59800 LILLE
☎ 20 51 54 88
☐ Women's bookshop and meeting place.

FRB3

Les Dames
2 place des Celestins
LYONS
☐ Women's bookshop.

FRB4

Librairie Carabosses
58 rue de la Roquette
75001 PARIS
☐ Feminist bookshop.

FRB5

Librairie des Femmes
Rue Pavillion
MARSEILLES
☐ Women's bookshop.

FRB6

Librairie des Femmes
74 rue de Seine
75006 PARIS
☎ 43 29 50 75
☐ Feminist bookshop.

FRB7

Librairie Fourmi Ailes
8 rue du Fouarre
PARIS
☎ 43 29 40 99
☐ Alternative bookshop with feminist section.

FRB8

La Maison des Femmes
13 Cité de L'Ameublement
PARIS 11E
☐ Bookshop in women's centre.

FRB9

Les Mots à la Bouche
6 rue St Croix de la Bretonnière
75004 PARIS
☎ 42 78 88 30
☐ Lesbian and gay bookshop.

FRB10

Le Papivore
27 rue de la Madeline
NIMES
☐ Feminist bookshop.

FRB11

Shakespeare & Company
Quai de Montebello
PARIS 5
☐ English-language bookshop with women's section.

FRB12

L'Utopie
8 rue Joseph-Cadei
NICE
☐ Feminist bookshop and café.

FRB13

Village Voice
5 rue Princesse
75006 PARIS
☎ 46 33 36 47
☐ Alternative American bookshop with women's section.

Libraries, Archives, Resource Centres and Information

FRL1

Agency for Information for Women
21 rue de Jeuneurs
75002 PARIS
☐ Documentary material on feminist research.

FRL2

Centre for Feminist Research and Information (CRIF)
1 rue des Fosses-St-Jaques
75005 PARIS
☐ Centre for feminist research and communications.

FRL3

Delegation for Women's Status – Documentation Service
14 boulevard de la Madeleine
75008 PARIS
☐ Documents all material relevant to women and publishes information.

FRL4

Elles Tournent le Page
8 impasse des Trois-Soeurs
PARIS 11E
☐ Library, workshops and information centre.

FRL5

Femmes Avenir: Centre for Women's Studies and Information
6 Cité Martignac
75007 PARIS
☎ 45 51 02 68
□ Women's documentation centre.

FRL6

Femmes, Fichier Audiovisuel. ORAVEP (Observatory of Audiovisual Resources for Continuing Education)
Secrétariat d'Etat Chargé des Droits des Femmes
31 rue La Peletier
75009 PARIS
☎ 47 70 41 58
□ Videos and workbooks for sale and hire.

FRL7

The French Institute of Social History
11 rue des Quatre-Fils
75003 PARIS
□ Houses the archives of Helene Brion, author of a feminist encyclopaedia.

FRL8

International Library and Documentation Centre (BDIC)
Centre Universitaire
9200 NANTERRE
□ Houses material collected by Gabrielle Duchene on feminism and pacifism between the two World Wars.

FRL9

La Maison des Femmes
13 Cité de l'Ameublement
PARIS 11E
□ Information service.

FRL10

Lesbian Archives (ARCL)
BP 662
75531 PARIS 11
☎ 48 05 25 89
□ Lesbian archives, lending library and information service.

FRL11

Marguerite Durand Library
79 rue Nationale
75013 PARIS
☎ 45 70 80 30
□ The major feminist collection in France.

FRL12

Ministry for Women's Rights
53 Avenue d'Iena
PARIS 75700
□ Government agency information centre.

FRL13

National Women's Information and Documentation Centre (CNIDF)
7 rue de Jura
75013 PARIS
☎ 43 31 12 34
□ Documentation centre.

FRL14

Simone de Beauvoir Audio-Visual Centre
29 rue du Colisée
PARIS 18E
☎ 42 25 17 75
□ Archive of audio-visual material by and about women.

FRL15

Social Museum (CEDIAS)
5 rue Las Cases
75007 PARIS
□ Information on the history of women in the social services.

FRL16

State Secretariat for Women's Rights
31 rue Le Peletier
75009 PARIS
☎ 47 70 41 58
□ Government advisory body.

FRL17

Women and Christianity
Faculté de théologie
25 rue du Plat
69002 LYONS
□ Research and documentation centre.

FRL18

Women's Career Guidance and Information Centre
81 rue Sénac
MARSEILLE 13001
☎ 91 47 14 05
□ Information and advice centre.

FRL19

Women's Documentation and Information Centre
24 rue Mignet
AIX-EN-PROVENCE
□ Documentation and information for women.

FRL20

Women's Information Agency
  21 rue des Jeuneurs
  75002 PARIS
□ Press and information agency concerned only with information about women. Archives and documentation centre.

FRL21

Women's Resource Centre
  Centre Lyonnais D'Etudes Féministes
  Université de Lyon II
  Avenue Pierre Lendes
  69676 LYONS
☎ 78 77 23 23
□ Resource centre and lending library.

FRL22

Women's Rights Information Centre
  155 rue du Molinel
  59800 LILLE
☎ 20 54 27 66
□ Information on women's rights.

Women's Organisations

FRO1

Association National des Etudes Féministes (ANEF)
  2 ter Passage des Marais
  75010 PARIS
□ French women's studies association.

FRO2

Choisir
  30 rue Rambuteau
  75003 PARIS
□ Organisation working for abortion and contraceptive rights.

FRO3

European Association Against Sexual Harassment at Work
  71 rue St Jaques
  75005 PARIS
☎ 46 28 74 08
□ Campaigns against violence to women at work.

FRO4

Feminist Interdisciplinary Group
  Maison des Sciences de l'Homme
  54 boulevard Raspail
  75006 PARIS
□ Cross-disciplinary members concerned with a feminist critique of science.

FRO5

Flora Tristan Study Club
  22 avenue de Saint-Mande
  75012 PARIS
□ Studies the relationship between class struggle and feminism.

FRO6

French Association of Women Engineers
  10 rue Vauquelin
  75005 PARIS
□ Encourages girls to take up engineering, and promotes French women engineers nationally and internationally.

FRO7

Grief et Groupe Simone
  Université de Toulouse
  Le Mirail
  5 allée Antonio Machado
  31058 TOULOUSE
☎ 61 41 11 05
□ University women's group.

FRO8

Groupe d'Initiative Femmes et Developpement
  29 rue Saint-Armand
  75015 PARIS
□ Assists women working in Third World development.

FRO9

International Council of Women
(See International section)

FRO10

International Union of Women Architects
  14 rue Durmont d'Urville
  75116 PARIS
□ Professional association of women architects.

FRO11

La Maison des Femmes
  13 Cité de L'Ameublement
  PARIS 11E
□ Postal address and meeting place for many women's groups.

FRO12

The League for the Rights of Women
  54 Avenue de Choisy
  75013 PARIS
□ Campaigning group for women's rights.

FRO13

National Association for the Defence of Women Prostitutes
    6 rue Frochet
    75009 PARIS
☐ Organisation defending the rights of women prostitutes.

FRO14

The National Council of Women of France
    11 rue de Viarmes
    BP 115-01
    75022 PARIS
☎ 42 897 50 82
☐ Umbrella organisation.

FRO15

Psychanalyse et Politique
    12 rue de la Chaise
    75007 PARIS
☐ Lacanian group campaigning for women's liberation.

FRO16

Reseau Femmes et Developpement
    15–21 rue de l'Ecole de Médecine
    75005 PARIS
☐ Women's and development organisations network in France and the Third World.

FRO17

Seminar Limits Frontières
    Association LMF
    7 rue Boulle
    75001 PARIS
☐ Radical feminist group which holds monthly seminars.

FRO18

SOS Femmes Alternatives
    54 avenue de Choisy
    PARIS 13E
☎ 45 85 11 37
☐ Help for women suffering violence.

FRO19

Union of French Women
    146 rue du Faubourg Poissonnière
    75010 PARIS
☎ 45 26 03 33
☐ Umbrella organisation.

FRO20

Union of Women Painters and Sculptors
    22 rue Choron
    75009 PARIS
☐ Association for women painters and sculptors.

FRO21

Women and Development Network
    18 rue de Varenne
    75007 PARIS
☐ Network for women working in development.

Gambia

Libraries, Archives, Resource Centres and Information

GAML1

Women's Bureau
    1 Marina Parade
    c/o The President's Office
    State House
    BANJUL
☐ Government body advising and co-ordinating on matters relating to women. Provides income-producing projects, research and training.

Women's Organisations

GAMO1

Gambia Women's Federation
    PO Box 83
    BANJUL
☐ Umbrella organisation.

Germany

Bookshops

GERB1

Amazonas
    Schmidstrasse 12
    4630 BOCHUM
☎ 0234 683194
☐ Women's bookshop.

GERB2

Aradia
    Reginastrasse 14
    3500 KASSEL
☎ 0561 17210
☐ Women's bookshop.

GERB3

Bambuls
    August-Bebel Strasse 154
    4800 BIELEFELD
☎ 0521 68461
☐ Women's bookshop.

GERB4

Chrysalis
Buddenstrasse 22
4400 MUNSTER
☎ 0251 55505
☐ Women's bookshop.

GERB5

Droppel (f)emina
Am Brogel 1
5600 WUPPERTAL
☎ 0202 87707
☐ Women's bookshop.

GERB6

Elisara
Schmiedgasse 11
8900 AUGSBURG
☎ 0821 154303
☐ Women's bookshop.

GERB7

Frauen-Bücher-Zimmer
Becherstrasse 2
4000 DUSSELDORF
☎ 0211 464405
☐ Women's bookshop.

GERB8

Frauenbuchladen
Herforderstrasse 64
4800 BIELEFELD
☐ Women's bookshop.

GERB9

Frauenbuchladen
Magnikitchstrasse 4
3300 BRAUNSCHWEIG
☎ 0531 40744
☐ Women's bookshop.

GERB10

Frauenbuchladen
Rhainnon
Moltkestrasse 66
5000 COLOGNE
☎ 0221 523120
☐ Women's bookshop and women-only café.

GERB11

Frauenbuchladen
Kiesstrasse 27
6000 FRANKFURT
☎ 069 705295
☐ Women's bookshop.

GERB12

Frauenbuchladen
Bismark Str. 98
2000 HAMBURG
☎ 040 420 4748
☐ Feminist bookshop.

GERB13

Frauenbuchladen
Hartwigstrasse 7
3000 HANOVER
☐ Women's bookshop.

GERB14

Frauenbuchladen
Theaterstrasse 16
6900 HEIDELBERG
☎ 06221 22201
☐ Women's bookshop.

GERB15

Frauenbuchladen
Rathausplatz 9
8960 KEMPTEN
☎ 0831 18228
☐ Women's bookshop.

GERB16

Frauenbuchladen
Kleinreutherweg 28
8500 NUREMBERG
☎ 0911 352403
☐ Women's bookshop.

GERB17

Frauenbuchladen
Olgastrasse 75
7000 STUTTGART
☎ 0711 234649
☐ Women's bookshop.

GERB18

Frauenbuchladen Labrys
Hohenstaufenstrasse 64
BERLIN
☎ 030 215 2500
☐ Women-only lesbian and feminist bookshop.

GERB19

Frauenbuchladen Miranda
U-Bahnhof Leopaldplatz
Nazarethkirchstrasse 42
1000 BERLIN 65
☐ Women's bookshop.

GERB20

Frauenbuchladen Sappho
Luxemburgstrasse 2
6200 WIESBADEN
☎ 0611 371515
☐ Feminist bookshop.

GERB21

Hagazussa
Friensenstrasse 12
2800 BREMEN
☎ 0421 74140
☐ Women's bookshop.

GERB22

Hexenhaus
Obere Schrangenstrasse 17
2120 LUNEBURG
☎ 041 314 7893
☐ Women's bookshop.

GERB23

Inngrid Ewald
Brockhaustrasse 32
7031 LEIPZIG
☎ 0341 478 7713
☐ Women's bookshop.

GERB24

Laura
Burgstrasse 21
3400 GOTTINGEN
☎ 0551 47317
☐ Women's bookshop.

GERB25

Lesen und Schreiben
Albrechstrasse 10
2940 WILHELMSHAVEN
☎ 04421 53693
☐ Women's bookshop.

GERB26

Lillemor's Frauenbuchladen
Arcisstrasse 57
8000 MUNICH
☎ 089 272 1205
☐ Feminist bookshop.

GERB27

Lilth Frauenbuchladen und Verlag
Knesebeckstrasse 86/87
1000 BERLIN 12
☎ 030 312 3102
☐ Women's bookshop with feminist English and German titles.

GERB28

Marga-Schoeller Bücherstube
Knesebeckstrasse 33
1000 BERLIN 12
☎ 030 881 1122
☐ Large selection of feminist, lesbian and English-language books.

GERB29

Mitfahrzenstrale
Moltkestr. 66
COLOGNE
☎ 0221 523152
☐ Feminist bookshop.

GERB30

Mother Jones
Jahnstrasse 17
4500 OSNABRUCK
☎ 0541 43700
☐ Women's bookshop.

GERB31

Nora Frauenbuchladen
Breitestrasse 36
5300 BONN
☎ 0288 654767
☐ Women's bookshop.

GERB32

Prinz Eisenherz
Bleibtreustrasse 52
1000 BERLIN 12
☎ 030 313 9936
☐ Lesbian and gay bookshop.

GERB33

Thalestria
Bunnagasse 2
7400 TUBINGEN
☎ 07071 26590
☐ Women's bookshop.

GERB34

Violetta
Lindenstrasse 18
2900 OLDENBURG
☎ 0441 883039
☐ Women's bookshop.

GERB35

Zimpzicke
Adlerstrasse 45
4600 DORTMUND
☎ 0231 140821
☐ Women's bookshop.

Libraries, Archives, Resource Centres and Information

GERL1

Archive of the German Women's Movement
Sommerweg 1b
3500 KASSEL
☎ 0561 55600
☐ Archives and documentation on the women's movement in Germany.

GERL2

Archive of the Women's Research, Education and Information Centre
Dandelmannstrasse 15 & 47
1000 BERLIN 19
☎ 030 322 1035
☐ Archives, information and historians network.

GERL3

Autonomous Women's Archives of Wiesbaden
Postfach 2848
6200 WIESBADEN
☐ Women's archives.

GERL4

Feminist Archive
Ubierring 47
5000 COLOGNE 1
☎ 0221 317029
☐ Feminist archives by appointment.

GERL5

Feminist Archive and Documentation Centre
Arndtstrasse 18
6000 FRANKFURT 1
☎ 069 745044
☐ Collects and publishes documents relating to women's activities. In particular, the contemporary women's movement.

GERL6

Feminist Educational and Documentation Information
Wilhelm-Marx Strasse 58
8500 NUREMBERG
☐ Information and documentation centre for women.

GERL7

Fraueninfothek
Leibnizstrasse 57
1000 BERLIN
☎ 030 324 5078
☐ Detailed information on women's organisations and services for women.

GERL8

Frauenpress
Severinstrasse 92
5000 COLOGNE
☐ Women's news bureau, press agency and information service.

GERL9

Frauenzentrum Berlin
Stresemannstrasse 40
1000 BERLIN
☎ 030 251 0912
☐ Help, information, library and archive for women.

GERL10

Lesbian Information Service
Kulmer Strasse 20A
1000 BERLIN 30
☐ Information and therapy centre.

GERL11

University Centre for the Promotion of Women's Studies and Research on Women
Freie Universität Berlin
Königin-Luise-Strasse 34
1000 BERLIN 33
☐ Bibliographic and documentation services.

GERL12

Das Verborgene Museum
Schluterstrasse 70
1000 BERLIN
☎ 030 313 3656
☐ Women's gallery.

GERL13

Women's Centre
Hamburger Allee 45
FRANKFURT
☎ 069 772659
☐ Women's information.

GERL14

Women's Centre
Gullst. 3
MUNICH
☎ 089 725 4271
☐ Women's information.

GERL15

Women's Culture Centre
Die Begine
Postdamer Strasse 139
1000 BERLIN 30
☎ 030 215 4325

☐ Multi-cultural centre for women. Music, theatre and films for women.

GERL16

Women's Health and Therapy Centre
Bambergerstrasse 51
1000 BERLIN 30
☎ 030 213 9597
☐ Information on women's health and therapy centre.

GERL17

Women's Museum
Nerostrasse 16
6200 WIESBADEN
☎ 0611 528400
☐ Archives, seminars and debates.

GERL18

Women's Music Centre
Schwedenstrasse 14
1000 BERLIN 65
☎ 030 784 7297
☐ Archives and information on women in music.

Women's Organisations

GERO1

Berlin Women's Council
Bayreutherstrasse 41
1000 BERLIN 30
☎ 030 213 4383
☐ Umbrella organisation.

GERO2

Berlin Women's Federation of 1945
Ansbacherstrasse 63
1000 BERLIN 30
☐ Runs courses to assist women to improve their position in the labour market. Campaigns for equality in education, work and public life.

GERO3

Co-ordinating and Counselling Centre for Women's Continuing Education
Knesebeckstrasse 33/34
1000 BERLIN 12
☐ Promotes and supports women entering higher education.

GERO4

Deutscher Frauenrat
Simrockstrasse 5
5300 BONN 1
☎ 0228 223008
☐ Umbrella organisation.

GERO5

Equal Rights for Women in the Mass Media
Am Ehrenkamp 15
4800 BIELEFELD 12
☎ 0521 49777
☐ Campaigns to increase the number of women working in the media, and to improve the image of women in the mass media.

GERO6

Feminist Literature Group
c/o Inge Stefan
Literaturwissenschaftliches Seminar
Von-Melle-Park 6
2000 HAMBURG 13
☐ Group for the feminist study of literature.

GERO7

Foundation Group for the Building of a Feminist Party
Christrosenweg 5
8000 MUNICH 70
☐ Campaigns for a feminist society, holds seminars and demonstrations. Liaises with other feminist and anti-military groups in Germany and other countries.

GERO8

German Association of University Women
Werderstrasse 68
2000 HAMBURG 13
☎ 040 445880
☐ Networking group between university women, both nationally and internationally. Promotes women in research and offers fellowships to students.

GERO9

German Women Lawyers Association
Strasschensweg 28
5300 BONN 1
☐ Professional association of women lawyers working to improve the laws for women.

GERO10

German Women's Council
Simrockstrape 5
5300 BONN
☐ Umbrella group.

GERO11

German Women's Ring
Wall 42
23 KIEL
☎ 0431 97222
☐ Promotes civic education for women to enable them to take a more active role in public life.

GERO12

Marie-Schlei Association
Hadermannsweg 23
2000 HAMBURG 61
☐ Fundraising organisation to assist women's co-operatives in the Third World.

GERO13

Medical Women's International Association
Herbert-Lewin-strasse 5
5600 COLOGNE 41
☐ Network of national women's medical associations and individuals.

GERO14

National Council of German Women's Organisations
Augustastrasse 42
5300 BONN 2
☐ Networking group for women's organisations committed to legal and social equality for women.

GERO15

Network of Women in Archaeology
Wildermuthstrasse 40
7400 TUBINGEN
☎ 0251 862285
☐ Group for feminist archaeologists.

GERO16

University Centre for the Promotion of Women's Studies and Research on Women
Freie Universität Berlin
Königen-Luise-Strasse 34
1000 BERLIN 33
☐ Promotes women's studies and offers counselling and guidance throughout Germany.

GERO17

Women of the World – Office for Intercultural Education and Encounter
Warendoferstrasse 6
5000 COLOGNE 91
☐ Examines women's issues and international co-operation, mainly between Germany and the Third World.

GERO18

Women's Aid
Landesregierung Nordrhein-Westfallen
Mannesmannufer LA
4000 DUSSELDORF
☎ 0221 037 1226
☐ Centre to support women suffering violence.

GERO19

Women's History Research Group
c/o Gisela Bock
Faculty of Human Sciences and Philosophy
Bielefeld University
Postfach 8640
4800 BIELEFELD 1
☐ Group for women's history researchers.

GERO20

Women's Initiative 6th October
Kirschallee 6
Postfach 120 401
5300 BONN 1
☐ Campaigning and networking group working for equal social, sexual and political rights for women.

GERO21

Women's International Democratic Federation
Unter den Linden 13
1080 BERLIN
☐ Eastern European women's federation uniting women in Eastern Europe and the Third World.

GERO22

Women's International League for Peace and Freedom
Weseler Weg 2
4005 MEERBUSCH 1
☐ Works for worldwide peace and disarmament.

GERO23

Women's International Studies Europe
(See International section)

Ghana

Libraries, Archives, Resource Centres and Information

GHAL1

National Council on Women and Development
PO Box M53
ACCRA
☐ Government advisory body on matters relating to women and their integration into development.

Women's Organisations

GHAO1

Ghana Assembly of Women
PO Box 459
ACCRA

☎ Accra 25873
☐ Umbrella organisation.
☎ 091 386 1296
☐ Alteranative bookshop with women's section.

Great Britain and Northern Ireland
Channel Islands

Bookshops

GBB1

Modern Books and Advice Centre
3 St James Street
St Helier
JERSEY CI
☎ 0534 76371
☐ Alternative bookshop with feminist section.

England

Book Clubs

GBBC1

The Women's Book Club
45/46 Poland Street
LONDON WIV 4AU
☎ 071 437 1019

Bookshops

GBB1

Acorn Bookshop
17 Chatham Street
READING RG1 7JF
☎ 0734 584425
☐ Alternative bookshop with women's section.

GBB2

Africa Bookcentre Ltd
38 King Street
Covent Garden
LONDON WC2E 8JT
☎ 071 240 6649
☐ Specialist Africa bookshop with African women's studies section.

GBB3

Alleycat Bookshop
288 Sutton Street
DURHAM DH1 4BW
☎ 091 386 1296
☐ Alternative bookshop with women's section.

GBB4

Alternative Bookshop
15 Margarets Buildings
BATH BA1 2LP
☎ 0225 334299
☐ Alternative bookshop with women's studies section.

GBB5

Blackthorn Books
70 High Street
LEICESTER LE1 5YP
☎ 0533 21896
☐ Alternative bookshop with feminist and women's records sections. Feminist mail order booklist available.

GBB6

The Bookcase
29 Market Street
HASTINGS
E. Sussex
☎ 0424 845353
☐ Alternative bookshop with lesbian and women's studies sections.

GBB7

The Book Loft
160A Wellington Road
Withington
MANCHESTER M20 9FU
☎ 061 445 2772
☐ Alternative bookshop with women's studies section.

GBB8

Bookmarks
265 Seven Sisters Road
LONDON N4 2DE
☎ 081 802 6145
☐ Alternative bookshop with sexual politics section.

GBB9

Bookplace
13 Peckham High Street
LONDON SE15
☎ 071 701 1757
☐ Alternative bookshop with women's fiction section.

GBB10

The Brighton Peace Centre
28 Trafalgar Street
BRIGHTON BN1 4ED
☎ 0273 692880
☐ Alternative bookshop with women's rights and sexual politics sections.

GBB11

Browne's Bookshop
56 Mill Road
CAMBRIDGE CB1 2AS
☎ 0223 350968
☐ Alternative bookshop with women's section.

GBB12

Cactus Books
2B Hope Street
Hanley
STOKE ON TRENT
☎ 0782 204449
☐ Alternative bookshop with women's section.

GBB13

Central Books
37 Grays Inn Road
LONDON WC1X 8PS
☎ 071 242 6166
☐ Alternative bookshop with feminist section.

GBB14

Centreprise Bookshop
136 Kingsland High Street
Hackney
LONDON E8 2NS
☎ 071 254 9632
☐ Alternative bookshop with women's studies section.

GBB15

Changes Bookshop
242 Belsize Road
LONDON NW6 4BT
☎ 071 328 8242
☐ Alternative bookshop with women's psychology section. Women's psychology mail order booklist available.

GBB16

The Clock Bookshop
138 High Street
LOWESTOFT NR32 1HR
☐ Alternative bookshop with feminist section.

GBB17

Compendium Books
234 Camden High Street
LONDON NW1 8QS
☎ 071 485 8944
☐ Alternative bookshop with feminist section. Women's studies and gender mail order booklist available.

GBB18

Deptford Bookshop
55 Deptford High Street
LONDON SE8 4AA
☎ 081 691 8339
☐ Alternative bookshop with women's and lesbian sections.

GBB19

East End Bookshop
178 Whitechapel Road
LONDON E1 1BJ
☎ 071 247 0216
☐ Alternative bookshop with women's section.

GBB20

Frontline Books
1 Newton Street
Piccadilly
MANCHESTER M1 1HW
☎ 061 236 1101
☐ Alternative bookshop with feminist section.

GBB21

Gays The Word
66 Marchmont Street
LONDON WC1N 1AB
☎ 071 278 7654
☐ Specialist gay bookshop with lesbian and feminist sections.

GBB22

Grapevine Bookshop
Dales Brewery
Gwydir Street
CAMBRIDGE CB1 2LJ
☎ 0223 61808
☐ Alternative bookshop with feminist fiction and women's studies section.

GBB23

Green Ink Bookshop
8 Archway Mall
Junction Road
LONDON N19 5RG
☎ 071 263 4748
☐ Alternative bookshop with feminist section.

GBB24

Greenleaf Bookshop
82 Colston Street
BRISTOL BS1 5BB
☎ 0272 211369
☐ Alternative bookshop with feminist section. Women's mail order booklist available.

GBB25

Harriet Tibman Bookshop
27–29 Grove Lane
Handsworth
BIRMINGHAM B21 9ES
☎ 021 554 8479
☐ Alternative bookshop with women's section.

GBB26

Housemans Bookshop
5 Caledonian Road
Kings Cross
LONDON N1 9DX
☎ 071 837 4473
☐ Alternative bookshop with feminist section.

GBB27

Independent Bookshop
69 Surrey Street
SHEFFIELD S1 2LH
☎ 0742 737722
☐ Alternative bookshop with section on sexual politics.

GBB28

Index Bookcentre (Brixton)
10–12 Atlantic Road
LONDON SW9 8HY
☎ 071 274 8342
☐ Alternative bookshop with women writers section.

GBB29

Inner Bookshop
34 Cowley Road
OXFORD OX4 1HZ
☎ 0865 245301
☐ Alternative bookshop with women's section.

GBB30

In Other Words
72 Mutley Plain
PLYMOUTH PL4 6LF
☎ 0752 663889
☐ Alternative bookshop with feminist and lesbian sections.

GBB31

John Sheridan (1988) Ltd
19 Anlaby Road
HULL HU1 2PJ
☎ 0482 28759
☐ Alternative bookshop with feminist section.

GBB32

Key Books
14 St Martins House Parade
Bull Ring Centre
BIRMINGHAM B5 5DL
☎ 021 643 8081
☐ Alternative bookshop with feminist section.

GBB33

Kilburn Bookshop
8 Kilburn Bridge
Kilburn High Road
LONDON NW6
☎ 071 328 7071
☐ Alternative bookshop with feminist studies section.

GBB34

Labour Party Bookshop
150 Walworth Road
LONDON SE17 1JT
☎ 071 234 3339
☐ Socialist bookshop with feminist section. Feminist mail order booklist available.

GBB35

Lamp Bookshop
91 Bradshawgate
LEIGH WN7 4ND
☎ 0942 606667
☐ Alternative bookshop with women's writing section and mail order list on women's health.

GBB36

LUU Bookshop
PO Box 157
LEEDS LS1 1UH
☎ 0532 444974
☐ Alternative bookshop with feminist section.

GBB37

Mushroom Bookshop
10 Heathcote Street
NOTTINGHAM NG1 3AA
☎ 0602 582506
☐ Alternative bookshop with feminist and lesbian sections.

GBB38

New Beacon Books
76 Stroud Green Road
LONDON N4 3EN
☎ 071 272 4889
☐ Alternative bookshop with women's studies section.

GBB39

Newham Parents Centre
743–7 Barking Road
LONDON E13 9ER
☎ 081 552 9993
☐ Alternative bookshop with women's section.

GBB40

News From Nowhere Co-operative Ltd
112 Bold Street
LIVERPOOL L1 4HY
☎ 051 708 7270
☐ Feminist and radical bookshop. Lesbian and gay mail order booklist available.

GBB41

October Books
4 Onslow Road
SOUTHAMPTON SO2 0JB
☎ 0703 224489
☐ Alternative bookshop with feminist section. Women's mail order booklist available.

GBB42

121 Bookshop
121 Railton Road
Herne Hill
LONDON SE24
☎ 071 274 6655
☐ Alternative bookshop with feminist section.

GBB43

Page One Books
9 Princess Avenue
HULL
Humberside
☎ 0482 41925
☐ Alternative bookshop with women's studies section. Booklists available.

GBB44

Pathfinder Bookshop
47 The Cut
LONDON SE1 8LL
☎ 071 401 2409
☐ Alternative bookshop with feminist section.

GBB45

Porcupine Bookseller
Basement, 5 Caledonian Road
LONDON N1 9DX
☐ Alternative bookshop with women's studies and fiction sections. Second-hand section.

GBB46

Progressive Books
12 Berry Street
LIVERPOOL L1 4JQ
☎ 051 709 1905
☐ Alternative bookshop with feminist section.

GBB47

Public House Bookshop
21 Little Preston Street
BRIGHTON BN1 2HQ
☎ 0273 28357
☐ Alternative bookshop with women's studies section.

GBB48

Reading International Support Centre Bookshop
103 London Street
READING RG1 4QA
☎ 0734 586692
☐ Alternative bookshop with women's section.

GBB49

Reading Matters
10 Lymington Avenue
Wood Green
LONDON N22
☎ 081 881 3187
☐ Alternative bookshop with women's studies section.

GBB50

Silver Moon Women's Bookshop
64–68 Charing Cross Road
LONDON WC2H 0BB
☎ 071 836 7906
☐ Specialist women's bookshop with mail order and quarterly selection booklist.

GBB51

South Essex Bookshop
335 Ley Street
ILFORD
☎ 081 478 2948
☐ Alternative bookshop with feminist section.

GBB52

Stoke Newington Bookshop
153 Stoke Newington High Street
LONDON N16 0NY
☎ 071 249 2808
☐ Alternative bookshop with sexual politics section.

GBB53

Tall Storeys Bookshop
88 St James Street
BRIGHTON BN2 1TP
☎ 0273 697381
☐ Alternative bookshop with women's studies section.

GBB54

The Wedge
High Street
COVENTRY
☐ Alternative bookshop with feminist section.

GBB55

Well Read
University of Northumbria Students Union
2 Sandyford Road
NEWCASTLE NE1 8SB
☎ 091 261 7993
☐ Alternative bookshop with women's studies section
and women's studies mail order list.

GBB56

Workers Film Association Bookshop
9 Lucy Street
MANCHESTER M15 4BX
☎ 061 848 9785
☐ Alternative bookshop with women's section. Women's
mail order booklist available.

Libraries, Archives, Resource Centres and Information

GBL1

Christian Women's Information and Resources
Blackfriars
St Giles
OXFORD OX1 3LY
☎ 0865 516218
☐ Information for women.

GBL2

Equal Opportunities Commission
Overseas House
Quay Street
MANCHESTER M3 3HN
☎ 061 833 9244

☐ Government-funded body monitoring equal opportunities.

GBL3

Equal Opportunities Commission Information Centre
Overseas House
Quay Street
MANCHESTER M3 3HN
☐ Library containing books, periodicals and leaflets
mainly dealing with equal opportunities and sex
discrimination.

GBL4

Fawcett Library
City of London Polytechnic
Old Castle Street
LONDON E1 7NT
☎ 071 247 5826
☐ Britain's main historical research library. Also
contains current material.

GBL5

Feminist Archive
Trinity Road Library
St Phillips
BRISTOL BS2 0NW
☎ 0272 350025
☐ Library of women's lives in the twentieth century.

GBL6

Feminist Audio Books
52–54 Featherstone Street
LONDON EC1Y 8RT
☎ 071 251 2908
☐ Tape library of books by, for and about women for
blind and partially sighted women.

GBL7

Feminist Library and Information Centre
5 Westminster Bridge Road
LONDON SE1 7XW
☎ 071 928 7789
☐ Contemporary collection of books and periodicals,
worldwide. Research register.

GBL8

King's Cross Women's Centre
71 Tonbridge Street
LONDON WC1H 9DZ
☎ 071 837 7509
☐ Multi-racial information, advice and resource centre.
Meeting place for women's groups.

GBL9

Lesbian Archive
c/o BCM Box 7005
LONDON WC1N 3XX
☎ 071 405 6475
☐ Lesbian documentation and materials, past and present.

GBL10

Lesbian Information Centre
BM 7005
LONDON WC1N 3XX
☎ 071 405 6475
☐ Information service.

GBL11

Midwives Information and Resource Centre
Institute of Child Health
Royal Hospital for Sick Children
St Michael's Hill
BRISTOL BS2 8BJ
☎ 0272 251791
☐ Information service to enable midwives to keep up to date. Serves UK and overseas.

GBL12

The Pankhurst Centre
60–62 Nelson Street
Chorlton on Medlock
MANCHESTER M13 9WP
☎ 061 273 5673
☐ Resource and meeting centre for women.

GBL13

Rights of Women
52–54 Featherstone Street
LONDON EC1Y 8RT
☎ 071 251 6575
☐ Information, research and advice on the law and legal practices as they affect women in the UK.

GBL14

Women Artists' Slide Library
Economic History Department
Liverpool University
8 Abercromby Square
LIVERPOOL L69 3BX
☎ 051 794 2416
☐ 20,000 slides of women artists, past and present.

GBL15

Women's Audio Archive
45A Redchurch Street
LONDON E2 7DJ
☐ Audio archive for women.

GBL16

Women's Health and Reproductive Rights Information Centre
52–54 Featherstone Street
LONDON EC1Y 8RT
☎ 071 251 6580
☐ Information centre and library.

GBL17

Women's Health Information and Support Centre
Junction 7
Hazlewood Road
NORTHAMPTON NN1 1LG
☎ 0604 39723
☐ Support and information for women on health issues.

GBL18

Women's International Resource Centre
173 Archway Road
LONDON N6 5BL
☎ 081 341 4403
☐ Resource and information centre with worldwide links with women's groups.

GBL19

Women's Library
30 Chaucer Street
NOTTINGHAM NG1 5LP
☎ 0602 411 475
☐ Women's library.

GBL20

The Women's Resource Centre
The Saga Centre
326 Kensal Road
LONDON W10 5BZ
☎ 081 964 4656
☐ Resource centre for women.

Women's Organisations

GBO1

Academic Women's Achievement Group
University College
Gower Street
LONDON WC1E 6BT
☎ 071 380 7050 ext. 7232
☐ Association of women academics aiming to increase the representation of women in university work.

GBO2

Akina Mama wa Afrika
London Women's Centre
Wesley House
4 Wild Court
LONDON WC2B 5AU
☎ 071 430 1044
☐ Organisation of African women living in Britain addressing the particular problems faced by African women living in Britain.

GBO3

Associated Countrywomen of the World
(See International section)

GBO4

Association of Radical Midwives
62 Greetby Hill
ORMSKIRK L39 2DT
☎ 0695 572776
☐ Encourages midwives in their support of a woman's active participation in childbirth. Campaigns to keep choices in childbirth open to women.

GBO5

British Federation of University Women
Crosby Hall
Cheyne Walk
LONDON SW3 5BA
☎ 071 352 5354
☐ Association of women graduates.

GBO6

Centre for Research and Education on Gender
Institute of Education
University of London
20 Bedford Way
LONDON WC1H 0AL
☐ Network for researchers concerned with women's issues on sexuality and gender.

GBO7

Change
(See International section)

GBO8

Commonwealth Secretariat – Women and Development Programme
(See International section)

GBO9

English Collective of Prostitutes
PO Box 287
LONDON NW6 5QU
☐ Network of prostitute women.

GBO10

European Women in Mathematics
(See International section)

GBO11

Fawcett Society
46 Harleyford Road
LONDON SE11 5AY
☎ 071 587 1287
☐ Campaigns for the removal of inequalities based on gender.

GBO12

Feminist International Network of Resistance to Reproductive and Genetic Engineering
Box 38 LOP
52 Call Lane
LEEDS LS1 6DT
☐ International network monitoring developments in reproductive technology.

GBO13

Foundation for Women's Health Research and Development
Africa Centre
38 King Street
LONDON WC2E 8JT
☐ African women's health issues and campaign against female circumcision.

GBO14

Gender and Mathematics Association
c/o Department of Mathematical Sciences
Goldsmiths' College
LONDON SE14 6NW
☐ National network concerned with gender inequalities in mathematics.

GBO15

International Association of Women in Radio and Television
43 Gainsborough Street
SUDBURY CO10 6EU
☐ Holds conferences and networks between women. Index of women willing to work in Third World broadcasting projects.

GBO16

Medical Women's Federation
Tavistock House North
Tavistock Square
LONDON WC1H 9HX
☎ 071 387 7765
☐ Promotes study and practice of medicine among women.

GBO17

Microsyster
    c/o London Women's Centre
    Wesley House
    4 Wild Court
    LONDON WC2B 5AU
☐ Women's collective providing services to women's groups and individual women working in computing.

GBO18

National Abortion Campaign
    Wesley House
    4 Wild Court
    LONDON WC2B 5AU
☐ Campaigns to improve women's abortion rights.

GBO19

National Advisory Centre on Careers for Women
    Drayton House
    30 Gordon Street
    LONDON WC1H 0AX
☎   071 380 0177
☐ Educational charity which advises women and girls about careers.

GBO20

National Alliance of Women's Organisations
    279–281 Whitechapel Road
    LONDON E1 1BY
☎   071 247 7052
☐ Promotes charitable projects for the benefit of women. Membership open to women's organisations.

GBO21

National Council of Women
    34 Lower Sloane Street
    LONDON SW1W 8BP
☎   071 730 0619
☐ Umbrella organisation with individual members.

GBO22

National Women and Computing Network
    c/o London Women's Centre
    Wesley House
    4 Wild Court
    LONDON WC2B 5AU
☐ Holds meetings and a register of women interested in computing.

GBO23

Network of Women Writers Association
    8 The Broadway
    WOKING GU21 5AP
☎   09328 64377
☐ Women writers network.

GBO24

Rights of Women
    52–54 Featherstone Street
    LONDON EC1Y 8RT
☐ Information, research and advice on the law and legal practices as they affect women in the UK.

GBO25

Society of Women Artists
    34 South Molton Street
    LONDON W1Y 2BP
☐ Encourages the showing of work by women.

GBO26

300 Group
    9 Poland Street
    LONDON W1V 3DG
☎   071 734 3457
☐ Campaigning for equal representation for women in Parliament and public office.

GBO27

UK Asian Women's Centre
    1 Stamford Road
    Handsworth
    BIRMINGHAM B20 3PJ
☐ Provides range of services for Asian women, including education, advice, support, and cultural and social events.

GBO28

Womankind
(See International section)

GBO29

Women and Manual Trades
    52–54 Featherstone Street
    LONDON EC1Y 8RT
☎   071 251 9192
☐ Encourages girls and women to consider work in skilled trades and construction. Provides advice and information.

GBO30

Campaign Director
Women in Computing
    Staffordshire Polytechnic
    College Road
    STOKE ON TRENT ST4 2DE
☎   0782 744531

GBO31

Women in Economic and Social History
    Department of Economic History
    University of Liverpool
    PO Box 147
    LIVERPOOL L69 3BX
☎   051 794 2413

GBO32

Women in German Studies
School of Modern Languages
German Department
University of Salford
SALFORD M5 4WT
☎ 061 745 5000 ext. 4092

GBO33

Secretary
Women in Higher Education Network (WHEN)
Chemistry Department
University of Nottingham
NOTTINGHAM NG7 2RD
☐ Network for women working in higher education.

GBO34

Women in Libraries
c/o London Women's Centre
Wesley House
4 Wild Court
London WC2B 5AU
☐ Promotes the idea of feminist book collections, and aims to counter discrimination in the profession.

GBO35

Women in Medicine
15 Lyons Fold
SALE M33 1LF
☎ 081 986 1275
☐ Organisation providing support for women doctors and medical students which campaigns against racism and stereotyping of women in medicine.

GBO36

Women in Physics Committee
The Institute of Physics
47 Belgrave Square
LONDON SW1X 8QX
☎ 071 235 6111
☐ Professional organisation for women in physics.

GBO37

Women into Science and Engineering
Nottingham Polytechnic
Burton Street
NOTTINGHAM NG1 4BU
☎ 0602 418418

GBO38

Women's Aid Federation England
PO Box 391
BRISTOL BS99 7WS
☎ 0272 633494 (Admin.) 0272 633542 (Helpline)

GBO39

Women's Engineering Society
Department of Civil Engineering
Imperial College of Science and Technology
Imperial College Road
LONDON SW7 2BU
☎ 071 589 5111 ext. 4731
☐ Assists women and girls to train as engineers. Network of professional women engineers in the UK.

GBO40

Women's Environmental Network
287 City Road
LONDON EC1V 1LA
☎ 071 490 2511
☐ Network linking women concerned especially with environmental issues which affect women.

GBO41

Women's Film Television and Video Network
79 Wardour Street
LONDON W1V 3PH
☎ 071 434 2076
☐ Feminist networking and campaigning organisation.

GBO42

Women's History Network
Institute of Historical Research
Senate House
Malet Street
LONDON WC1E 7HU
☐ Networking for women working in women's history.

GBO43

Women's Legal Defence Fund
29 Great James Street
LONDON WC1N 3ES
☐ Free service to women to enable them to take sex discrimination cases to court.

GBO44

Women's Sports Foundation
c/o London Women's Centre
Wesley House
4 Wild Court
LONDON WC2B 5AU
☐ Promotes women's interests in sport, and equal opportunities for women in sport.

GBO45

Women's Studies Group 1500–1825
53 New Dover Road
CANTERBURY CT1 3DP
☎ 0227 462471

GBO46

Jenny Dale
Women's Studies Network (UK) Association
 University of North London
 1 Prince of Wales Road
 LONDON NW5 3LB
☎ 071 607 2789
☐ National women's studies association.

GBO47

Women's Therapy Centre
 6 Manor Gardens
 LONDON N7 6LA
☐ Runs courses and workshops, and promotes women's therapy in the UK.

GBO48

World Federation of Mental Health – Women's Network
 c/o Social Work Department
 St George's Hospital
 MORPETH NE61 2NU
☐ Campaigns around women's mental health needs worldwide.

Northern Ireland

Bookshops

GBB58

Bookworm Community Bookshop
 16 Bishop Street
 DERRY BT48 6PW
☎ 0504 261616
☐ Alternative bookshop with feminist section.

GBB59

Just Books
 7 Winetavern Street
 Smithfield
 BELFAST BT1 1JQ
☎ 0232 325426
☐ Alternative bookshop with feminist section.

GBB60

Newleaf Books
 c/o Viva Wholefoods
 21 Society Street
 COLERAINE
☎ 0265 58403
☐ Alternative bookshop with feminist section.

Libraries, Archives, Resource Centres and Information

GBL21

Equal Opportunities Commission of Northern Ireland
 Chamber of Commerce House
 22 Great Victoria Street
 BELFAST BT2 7LX
☎ 0232 242752
☐ Government-funded equality commission.

GBL22

Northern Ireland Women's Rights Movement Women's Centre
 19A North Street Arcade
 BELFAST BT1
☐ Information and networking centre.

GBL23

Women's Centre
 7 London Street
 DERRY CITY
☎ 0504 267672
☐ Women's information.

GBL24

Women's Information Group Drop-In Centre
 115A Ormeau Road
 BELFAST BT7
☎ 0232 246378
☐ Information and support centre.

Women's Organisations

GBO49

Belfast Rape Crisis Collective
 41 Waring Street
 BELFAST
☎ 0232 249 696
☐ Emotional and practical help for women and girls who have survived sexual abuse.

GBO50

Irish Federation of University Women
 8 Mount Pleasant
 BELFAST BT9 5DS
☐ Professional association of university women.

GBO51

Northern Ireland Women's Aid
 129 University Street
 BELFAST
☎ 0232 249041

☐ Federation of women's aid groups which offer shelter and counselling to women suffering violence.

GBO52

Northern Ireland Women's European Platform
127 Ormeau Road
BELFAST BT7 1SH
☎ 0232 321224
☐ Umbrella organisation for Northern Ireland's women's groups.

GBO53

Northern Ireland Women's Rights Movement
18 Donegal Street
BELFAST BT1 2GP
☎ 0232 243363
☐ Umbrella group providing support for women's groups in Northern Ireland. Campaigns, lobbies and conducts research on women's issues.

GBO54

Queen's University Women's Group
c/o Student Union
University Road
BELFAST BT7
☐ Student women's group.

GBO55

Women in Media
7 Winetavern Street
BELFAST BT1 1JQ
☐ Produces videos and publications about women, and campaigns for abolition of laws discriminating against women.

GBO56

Women's Law and Research Group
26 Mount Merrion Avenue
BELFAST BT6
☎ 0232 646949
☐ Group of women working in law and research.

GBO57

Women's News Collective
185 Donegal Street
BELFAST BT1 2FJ
☎ 0232 322823
☐ Women journalists' collective.

GBO58

Women's Support Network
c/o The Hummingbird
79 Shankill Road
BELFAST BT13 1FD
☎ 0232 240642
☐ Women's support network.

Scotland

Bookshops

GBB61

Boomtown Books
167 King Street
ABERDEEN AB2 3AE
☎ 0224 645433
☐ Alternative bookshop with women's section.

GBB62

Changes Bookshop
340 West Princes Street
Kelvinbridge
GLASGOW G4 9HF
☎ 041 357 3631
☐ Alternative bookshop with women's section.

GBB63

Clyde Books
15–19 Parnie Street
GLASGOW G1 5RJ
☎ 041 552 4699
☐ Alternative bookshop with women's studies section.

GBB64

West and Wilde Bookshop
25A Dundas Street
EDINBURGH EH3 6QQ
☎ 031 556 0079
☐ Alternative bookshop with feminist section. Lesbian and books for women mail order booklists available.

Libraries, Archives, Resource Centres and Information

GBL25

Equal Opportunities Commission for Scotland
St Andrew House
141 West Nile Street
GLASGOW G1 2RN
☎ 041 332 8018
☐ Government-funded agency providing information on equal opportunities.

Women's Organisations

GBO59

Scottish Convention of Women
YWCA Edinburgh Council Headquarters
7 Randolph Place
EDINBURGH EH3 7TE

□ Umbrella organisation for national and regional women's organisations. Aims to assist women to work together in Scotland.

GBO60

Scottish Women's Aid
13 North Bank Street
EDINBURGH EH1 2LN
☎ 031 225 8011
□ Provides information, support and a refuge for women suffering violence.

GBO61

Women in Scotland Bibliography Group
Open University in Scotland
EDINBURGH

Wales

Bookshops

GBB65

Emma's Community Book and Coffee Shop Ltd
19 Bryn-Y-Mor Road
Brynmill
SWANSEA SA1 4JH
☎ 0792 476901
□ Alternative bookshop with women's section.

GBB66

Peace Shop Ltd
56 Mackintosh Place
CARDIFF CF2 4RQ
☎ 0222 489260
□ Alternative bookshop with women's section.

GBB67

Quarry Bookshop
Lyngwern Quarry
MACHYNLLETH SY20 9AZ
☎ 0654 2400
□ Alternative bookshop with feminist section.

Libraries, Archives, Resource Centres and Information

GBL26

Equal Opportunities Commission
Caerwys House
Windsor Lane
CARDIFF CF1 1LB
□ Government-funded agency providing information on equal opportunities in Wales.

GBL27

Women's Centre
2 Coburn Street
Cathays
CARDIFF
□ Women's information centre.

Women's Organisations

GBO62

Welsh Women's Aid
38–48 Crwys Road
CARDIFF CF2 4NN
☎ 0222 390874
□ Supports and campaigns on behalf of women's refuges in Wales.

Greece

Bookshops

GREB1

To Vivlio to Pedi
Sina 38
10672 ATHENS
□ Bookshop with women's section.

GREB2

Women's Bookshop
Massalias 20
10680 KOLONAKI
☎ 361 1423
□ Feminist bookshop.

Libraries, Archives, Resource Centres and Information

GREL1

Centre for Documentation and Study of Women's Problems
Asklipiou 26
ATHENS
□ Documentation on women's issues.

GREL2

KEGME, Mediterranean Women's Studies Institute
192/B Leoforus Alexandras
11545 ATHENS
☎ 361 5660

☐ Information and documentation centre. (See International section)

Women's Organisations

GREO1

Federation of Greek Women (OGE)
Acadimas 52
10679 ATHENS
☐ Umbrella organisation.

GREO2

League for Women's Rights
41 Solonos Street
10672 ATHENS
☐ Group works for women's liberation and equality, organises conferences and studies, and provides legal assistance to women.

GREO3

National Council of Hellenic Women
38 Voulis Road
10557 ATHENS
☎ 322 7609
☐ Umbrella organisation.

GREO4

Union of Greek Women (EGE)
Ainianos 8
10678 ATHENS
☎ 823 4937
☐ Feminist socialist group campaigning for equal rights for women.

Guatemala

Libraries, Archives, Resource Centres and Information

GUAL1

National Women's Office
Sexta Avda 5-66
Nivel Tercero
Oficina 307
Zona 1
GUATEMALA CITY
☐ Government body researching women's involvement in economic and social development.

Women's Organisations

GUAO1

National Council of Guatemalan Women
13 Calle 3-15
Zona 10
GUATEMALA CITY
☐ Umbrella organisation.

Guyana

Libraries, Archives, Resource Centres and Information

GUYL1

Women's Studies Unit
Faculty of Social Sciences
University of Guyana
PO Box 10 11 10
GEORGETOWN
☎ 63691
☐ Documentation and resource centre.

Haiti

Women's Organisations

HAIO1

National Council of Women of Haiti
BP 1082
PORT-AU-PRINCE
☐ Umbrella organisation.

Hong Kong

Bookshops

HKB1

Hong Kong Book Centre
On Lok Yuen Building
25 Des Voeux Road C
HONG KONG
☎ 522 3669
☐ Bookshop with feminist titles.

HKB2

Swindon Book Co. Ltd
13–15 Lock Road
Tsimshatsui
KOWLOON
☎ 366 8001
☐ Bookshop with feminist titles.

Libraries, Archives, Resource Centres and Information

HKL1

Asia Monitor Resource Centre
444 Nathan Road 8-B
KOWLOON
☎ 332 1346
☐ Information centre.

Women's Organisations

HKO1

Association for the Advancement of Feminism
Room 1202
Yam Tze Commercial Building
17–23 Thomson Road
WANCHAI
☐ Feminist campaigning organisation.

HKO2

Committee for Asian Women
(See International section)

HKO3

Hong Kong Association of University Women
PO Box 11708
HONG KONG
☐ Federation of women graduates.

HKO4

Hong Kong Council of Women
PO Box 819
HONG KONG
☐ Umbrella organisation.

Hungary

Libraries, Archives, Resource Centres and Information

HUNL1

National Council of Hungarian Women
Nepkoztarsasag utja 124
1391 BUDAPEST
☐ Government advisory body on women's affairs.

Women's Organisations

HUNO1

Feminist Network
Szerb utca 8
1056 BUDAPEST
☐ National network for Hungarian feminists.

HUNO2

Szegedi Feminist Group
Jozeg Atila University
Egyetem utca 2
6722 SZEGEDI
☐ Feminist study group.

Iceland

Libraries, Archives, Resource Centres and Information

ICEL1

Centre for Women's Studies
Iceland's University
Oddi
101 REYKJAVIK
☎ 1 694595
☐ Information and database on women's studies.

ICEL2

Iceland's Library for Women's History
Hjaroarhaga 26
107 REYKJAVIK
☎ 1 12204
☐ Women's history library, archive and information centre.

Women's Organisations

ICEO1

Federation of Icelandic Women's Societies
Tungata 14
101 REYKJAVIK
☐ Umbrella organisation.

ICEO2

Network for Icelandic Women's Studies
Haskoli Islands
101 REYKJAVIK
☎ 1 69 43 00
☐ Network of women's studies scholars in Iceland.

ICEO3

Red Stocking Movement
Skolavordustig 12
101 REYKJAVIK
☐ Feminist campaigning group.

ICEO4

Women's Alliance
Hotel Vik
Vallarstroeti 4
101 REYKJAVIK

□ National women's group which publishes a newsletter and magazine.

ICEO5

Women's Rights Association of Iceland
Hallveigarstaoir
Tungata 14
101 REYKJAVIK
□ Women's organisation campaigning for women's equality of status and opportunity.

India

Bookshops

INDB1

Streelekha
67 – II Floor, Blumoon Complex
Mahatma Gandhi Road
BANGALORE 560011
□ Feminist bookshop and meeting place.

Libraries, Archives, Resource Centres and Information

INDL1

Centre for Women's Development Studies
B43 Panchshila Enclave
NEW DELHI 110 017
☎ Delhi 643428

INDL2

Institute of Social Studies Trust
M-1 Kanchenjunga
18 Barakhamba Road
NEW DELHI 110001
☎ 3323850
□ Library, research and consultancy services.

INDL3

Research Centre for Women's Studies
Women's University
Juhu Road
Santacruz
BOMBAY 400054
□ Collects and disseminates information and promotes women's studies.

INDL4

Women's Studies Unit
Tata Institute of Social Sciences
PO Box 8313 Sion-Trombay Road
Deonar
BOMBAY 400088

☎ 5510400
□ Specialised documentation centre.

Women's Organisations

INDO1

All India Women's Conference
Sarojini House
6 Bhagwan Dass Road
NEW DELHI
□ Campaigning organisation for women's social, economic and property rights. Organises crèches, nursery schools, family planning, training and cultural activities.

INDO2

Country Women's Association of India
6/1 Gurusaday Datta Road
CALCUTTA 700019
□ Networks between rural and urban organisations for women. Promotes social and cultural activities and income-generating projects for women.

INDO3

Dr Surinder Jetley
Indian Association for Women's Studies
New D/3 F.F.
Bhu Campus
VARANASI 5

INDO4

Inwan Federation of University Women's Associations
Devonshire House
3 Westfield Estate
Bhulabhai Desai Road
BOMBAY 400026
□ Campaigns to improve professional and educational conditions for university women.

INDO5

Kali for Women
N84 Panchshila Park
NEW DELHI 110017
□ Provides a forum for Third World women to speak for themselves. Campaigns, publishes and has books and literature for reference.

INDO6

Manushi
C1/202 Lajpat Nagar
NEW DELHI 110024
☎ 617022

□ Focuses on women in the Third World and the Indian sub-continent in particular. Researches and provides legal aid and speakers.

INDO7

National Council of Women in India
Poona Medical Foundation
Ruby Hall Clinic
40 Sassoon
PO Box No. 70
PUNE 411001
□ Umbrella organisation with individual members.

INDO8

Pacific and Asian Women's Forum
(See International section)

INDO9

Vimochana – Forum for Women's Rights
PO Box 4605
BANGALORE 560046
□ Socialist feminist group campaigning against violence to women.

INDO10

Women's Indian Association
Indian Council for World Affairs
43 Greenways
MADRAS 600028
☎ Madras 416607

INDO11

Young Women for Changes in the Social Status of Women
M-51 Shopping Complex
Greater Kailash Market
NEW DELHI 110048
□ Campaigns for women's economic and social equality.

Ireland

Bookshops

IREB1

Books Upstairs
36 College Green
DUBLIN 2
☎ 01 796 687
□ Alternative bookshop with women's studies section.

IREB2

Cody Books
Kieran Street
KILKENNY
□ Alternative bookshop with women's section.

IREB3

Education Resource Centre
5–7 Cathal Brugha Street
DUBLIN 1
☎ 01 364 533
□ Women's section in education bookshop.

IREB4

Hawkins House
Churchyard Lane
GALWAY
□ Irish and feminist bookshop.

IREB5

Hodges Figges
Kildare Street
DUBLIN
□ Bookshop with women's section.

IREB6

The Other Place Bookshop
6/7 Augustine Street
CORK
□ Alternative bookshop with women's studies section. Lesbian mail order booklist available.

IREB7

Quay Co-op Bookshop
24 Sullivan's Quay
CORK
☎ 021 317660
□ Alternative bookshop with women's and lesbian sections.

IREB8

Sheela-Na Gig
Cornstore Mall
Middle Street
GALWAY
☎ 091 66849
□ Feminist bookshop.

IREB9

Well Red Books
Dublin Resource Centre
6 Crow Street
DUBLIN 2
☎ 01 771 974
□ Alternative bookshop with feminist section.

Libraries, Archives, Resource Centres and Information

IREL1

Cork Women's Place
27A McCurtain Street
CORK
☎ 021 504491
□ Library relating to women's issues, advice and information centre.

IREL2

Employment Equality Agency
36 Upper Mount Street
DUBLIN 2
☎ 01 605966
□ Government body.

IREL3

Trinity College Library
Trinity Street
DUBLIN
□ Copy of all Irish and UK books.

IREL4

University College Dublin Women's Studies Forum
University College
DUBLIN 4
☎ 01 693 244 ext. 8129
□ Databank of resources on Irish women's studies.

IREL5

Women's Centre
53 Dame Street
DUBLIN 3
□ Women's information.

IREL6

Women's Education, Research and Resource Centre
Level 5, Library Building
University College
DUBLIN
☎ 01 269 3244
□ Library and information centre.

IREL7

Women's Information Network
☎ 01 679 4700
□ Telephone information service for women.

IREL8

Women's Place
Quay Co-op
Sullivans Quay
CORK
☎ 021 317 660
□ Women's space and library.

Women's Organisations

IREO1

Campaign Against Sexual Exploitation
PO Box 1207
DUBLIN 4
□ Campaigns to abolish pornography.

IREO2

Campaign Against Violence Against Women
107 Baggot Street
DUBLIN 2
□ Group campaigning against violence to women.

IREO3

Challenge
Beulah
The Hill
Lower Glengeary Road
DUN LAOGHAIRE
Co. Dublin
□ Campaigns to obtain tax equality for women.

IREO4

The Secretary
Cork Federation of Women's Organisations
Winnipeg
Ballea Road
CARRIGALINE
Co. Cork
□ Umbrella organisation for women's groups in the Cork area.

IREO5

Council for the Status of Women
64 Lower Mount Street
DUBLIN 2
☎ 01 615268
□ Umbrella organisation which promotes equality for women and provides speakers, information and referrals.

IREO6

Dublin Rape Crisis Centre
70 Lower Leeson Street
DUBLIN 2
□ Information and support centre.

IREO7

Dublin Well Woman Centre
73 Lower Leeson Street
DUBLIN 2
☐ Campaigns for improvement on women's health issues, and provides medical services and counselling for women.

IREO8

Irish Countrywomen's Association
58 Merrion Road
Ballsbridge
DUBLIN 4
☐ Networks between country-wide guilds, provides education and conducts research.

IREO9

Irish Federation of University Women
Kilconer
Bishopstown
CORK
☐ Group for university women in Ireland.

IREO10

Women in Learning
c/o Women's Room
Trinity College Students' Union
No. 6 Trinity College
DUBLIN 2
☐ Radical feminist group which aims to provide new courses and new ways of learning.

IREO11

Women in Publishing
39 Carnew Street
DUBLIN 7
☐ Group of women in publishing.

IREO12

Women's Political Association
6 Cross Avenue
BLACKROCK
Co. Dublin
☐ Encourages, supports and promotes women in public and political activities.

IREO13

Women's Studies Association
Centre for Women's Studies
NIHE
PLESSEY
Limerick
☐ Irish women's studies association.

Israel

Libraries, Archives, Resource Centres and Information

ISRL1

Women's Studies Program
University of Haifa
Mt Carmel
31999 HAIFA
☎ 240111
☐ Resource centre for information about the status of women.

Women's Organisations

ISRO1

Council of Women's Organisations in Israel
Wizo Club
1 Mapu Street
JERUSALEM
☎ 02 243899
☐ Umbrella organisation.

ISRO2

Israel Feminist Movement
PO Box 30441
TEL AVIV
☎ 03 234314
☐ Campaigns for increased participation by women in political and public activities, and for sexual, social and employment rights for women.

ISRO3

Israel Women's Network
PO Box 3171
91037 JERUSALEM
☐ Campaigns to improve the status of women in Israel.

ISRO4

LO Combat Violence Against Women
58 Sokolov Street
HERZLIA
☐ Shelter, women's aid centre, counselling and information for women suffering violence. Offers assistance to students researching domestic violence.

ISRO5

Palestinian Union of Women Workers' Committees
PO Box 20576
JERUSALEM

☐ Nationalist, socialist feminist organisation aiming to improve women's social, cultural and economic position. Runs local training, cultural and educational programmes.

ISRO6

Tel Aviv Rape Crisis Centre
PO Box 33401
TEL AVIV
☐ Support and information centre.

ISRO7

Woman to Woman – Haifa's Women's Centre
88 Arlosoroff Street
HAIFA
☐ Liaises with rape crisis centre, battered women's shelters and the Israel Feminist Movement. Works for equal rights and opportunities for women.

Italy

Bookshops

ITB1

Al Tempo Ritrovato
Piazza Farnese
ROME
☎ 06 654 37 49
☐ Feminist bookshop.

ITB2

La Tarantola
Via Lanusei 15/21
CAGLIARI
☎ 66 68 82
☐ Women's bookshop.

ITB3

Librellula
Strada Magiore 23-A
BOLOGNA
☎ 23 47 05
☐ Feminist bookshop.

ITB4

Libreria Delle Donne
Via Fiesolana 2/B
50122 CATANIA
☎ 24 03 24
☐ Feminist bookshop.

ITB5

Libreria Delle Donne
Via Fiesolana 2/B
FLORENCE

☎ 24 03 84
☐ Women's bookshop.

ITB6

Libreria Delle Donne
Via Dogana 2
MILAN
☐ Feminist bookshop.

Libraries, Archives, Resource Centres and Information

ITL1

Centre for Women's Documentation
Contrada della Rosa 14
44100 FERRARA
☐ Women's library.

ITL2

Centro di Studi Stirici sul Movimento di Liberazione Della Donna in Italia
Via Romagnosi 3
20121 MILAN
☎ 02 869 3911
☐ Information and contact for women's groups.

ITL3

Donnawomanfemme
Via S. Benedetto in Arenula 4–12
00186 ROME
☐ Library and information centre.

ITL4

Exist as a Woman
c/o Unione Femminile
Corso di Porta Nuova 32
20121 MILAN
☐ Provides information on the history of women.

ITL5

Historical Studies Centre on the Women's Liberation Movement in Italy
Via Romagnosi 3
20121 MILAN
☐ Conducts research and collects documentation on women and the women's movement.

ITL6

Institute for Information, Research and Action on Health
Via dei Sabelli 100
00185 ROME
☐ Provides information, counselling and seminars on women's health issues, in particular abortion and contraception.

ITL7

Isis International

Via San Saba 5
00153 ROME

☐ Aims to eliminate sex discrimination and to improve women's social, economic and political position. World-wide and national information and communication services with offices in Italy and Chile.

ITL8

National Commission for Implementation of Equality Between Men and Women

Presidenza del Consiglio dei Ministri
Palazzo Chigi
001 ROME

☐ Government agency collecting and distributing information on matters affecting the equality status of women.

ITL9

National Committee for Equality Between Men and Women

Ministero del Lavoro e Della Previdenza Sociale
Via Giulia 6
00100 ROME

☐ Government advisory body.

ITL10

Research Centre for Archives on Women

Orientale University
30 Piazza So Giovanni Maggiore
80134 NAPLES

☐ Women's archives.

ITL11

Union of Italian Women

Via Cairoli 14/7
GENOVA
☎ 298 703

☐ Reference library and legal advice for women.

ITL12

Virginia Woolf Centre

Via del Governo Vecchio 39
ROME

☐ Documentation centre and library.

ITL13

Women's Centre

Via San Francesco di Sales 1A
00165 ROME
☎ 06 68 64 201

☐ Women's information centre.

ITL14

Women's Centre of Documentation, Research and Initiative

Via Galliera no. 4
40121 BOLOGNA
☎ 23 38 63

☐ Documentation, research and publications on women.

ITL15

Women's Documentation Centre

Contrada della Rosa 14
44100 FERRARA

☐ Library of documents and books on women and the women's movement.

Women's Organisations

ITO1

Association for Women's Health

Viale Gorizia 52
00198 ROME

☐ Organisation campaigning to improve women's health care.

ITO2

Association of Women Against Violence to Women

Largo Arenula
26 ROME
☎ 06 654 4909

☐ Campaigns against violence to women.

ITO3

Casa delle Donne

Via Fiochetto 13
10152 TURIN

☐ Active women's centre and contacts for groups in the area.

ITO4

Italian Association for Women in Development

Via Tagliamento 14
int. 8
00198 ROME
☎ 06 852 252

☐ Concerned with women in development in the Third World. Runs a resource centre and holds conferences and exhibitions.

ITO5

Milanese Women's Action Centre

Viale Tibaldi 41
20316 MILAN
☎ 02 832 4067

☐ Campaigns on women's issues.

ITO6

Movement for the Liberation of Women
Via di Torre Argentina 18
001 ROME
☐ Feminist campaigning group.

ITO7

National Italian Women's Council
Piazza dei Quirti 3
00192 ROME
☐ Umbrella organisation.

ITO8

Turin Women's House
Via Vanchiglia 3
10124 TURIN
☎ 011 812 2519
☐ Base for local women's groups and runs courses for women.

ITO9

Union of Italian Women
Via Pieroni 27
57100 LIVORNO
☎ 0586 887009
☐ Umbrella organisation.

ITO10

Women for Peace and Disarmament
CP 713
36100 VICENZA
☎ 0444 500 457
☐ Campaigns for universal disarmament.

ITO11

Women in Careers
1 via Santa Maria alla Porta
20123 MILAN
☐ Aims to promote women's professional role in business.

ITO12

Women in Development Europe (WIDE)
Palazzo della Civilta del Lavoro
ROME
☎ 06 46 43 48
☐ Branch of European organisation concerned with development.

ITO13

Women's Aid
Casa Delle Donne
UDI di Milano
Via Bugutta 12
20121 MILAN

☎ 02 760 8212
☐ Advice and support for women suffering violence.

Ivory Coast

Libraries, Archives, Resource Centres and Information

IVL1

Ministry of Women's Affairs
BP 200
ABIDJAN
☐ Government agency providing information on the status of women.

Women's Organisations

IVO1

Association des Femmes Ivoriennes
BP 2005
ABIDJAN
☐ Umbrella organisation.

Japan

Bookshops

JAPB1

Matsukado
Nishi-iru
Nishinotoin
Shimodachiuri Dori
Kamigyo-ku
KYOTO
☎ 075 441 6905
☐ Feminist bookshop.

JAPB2

Ms Crayon House
3-8-15 Kita Aoyana
Minato-ku
TOKYO 106
☎ 03 3406 6492
☐ Feminist bookshop.

Libraries, Archives, Resource Centres and Information

JAPL1

Asian Women Workers Centre
2-3-18-34 Nishi-waseda
Shinjuku
TOKYO 169
☐ Information and support for Asian women workers.

JAPL2

National Women's Education Centre
728 Ranzan-cho Oaza Sugaya
Hiki-gun
SAITAMA-KEN 355-02
☎ 0493 62 6711
☐ National and international information and networking centre.

Women's Organisations

JAPO1

Federation of Japanese Women's Organisations
303, 4-11-9, Sendagaya
Shibuya
TOKYO
☐ Promotes international solidarity between women, and campaigns to improve and defend women's rights and welfare.

JAPO2

International Feminists of Japan
c/o Agora
Shinjuku 1-9-6
TOKYO 160
☐ Organisation for Japanese feminists.

JAPO3

Japanese Association of University Women
Toyama Mansion 241
Shinjuku 7-17-18
TOKYO
☐ Networks between university women and conducts research on women's issues.

JAPO4

Japanese Women
Fusen Kaikan (Women's Suffrage Centre)
21–11 Yoyogi 2-chome
Shibuya-ku
TOKYO 151

JAPO5

National Federation of Regional Women's Organisations
c/o Zenkoku Fujin Kaikan
Shibuya 1-17-7
TOKYO
☐ Networking organisation between women's groups.

JAPO6

The Women's Action Group
Nakazawa Building, 3rd Floor
23 Arakicho
Shinjuku-ku 164
TOKYO

☎ 03 357 9565
☐ Feminist action group with international network.

JAPO7

Women's Studies Society of Japan
c/o Matsukado Women's Bookstore
Nishi-iru
Nishinotoin
Shimodachiuri Dori
Kamigyo-ku
KYOTO
☎ 075 441 6905
☐ Wide variety of women concerned with the liberation of Japanese women.

Kenya

Libraries, Archives, Resource Centres and Information

KENL1

Women's Bureau
Ministry of Culture and Social Service
PO Box 30276
NAIROBI
☐ Government body co-ordinating women's organisations. Aims to integrate women into national development.

Women's Organisations

KENO1

African Women Link
(See International section)

KENO2

Kenya Medical Women's Association
PO Box 49877
NAIROBI
☐ Professional organisation for women in the medical profession which also encourages young women to enter medicine.

KENO3

National Council of Women of Kenya
PO Box 4371
NAIROBI
☎ 24634
☐ Umbrella organisation.

KENO4

Women's Progress
Maendalaeo House
PO Box 44412
NAIROBI

☐ Campaigns to improve the political, economic and social status of women in Kenya. Fund-raises for women's development projects.

Lebanon

Libraries, Archives, Resource Centres and Information

LEBL1

Institute for Women's Studies in the Arab World
Beirut University College
PO Box 13
5053 BEIRUT
☐ Research and resource centre.

Women's Organisations

LEBO1

Council of Lebanese Women
PO Box 16
5640 BEIRUT
☐ Umbrella organisation.

LEBO2

Institute for Women's Studies in the Arab World
Beirut University College
PO Box 13
5053 BEIRUT
☐ Networks between women's groups and organises conferences.

Liberia

Women's Organisations

LIBO1

The Liberian Federation of Women's Organisations
University of Liberia
MONROVIA
☐ Co-ordinates and networks between women's organisations. Encourages women's participation in development and social, economic and political life.

LIBO2

National Federation of Liberian Women
PO Box 2703
MONROVIA
☐ Umbrella organisation.

Luxembourg

Women's Organisations

LUXO1

Foyer de la Femme
BP 160
2011 LUXEMBOURG
☐ French-speaking women's centre.

LUXO2

Frauenzentrum
17 Avenue Monterey
LUXEMBOURG
☐ German-speaking women's centre.

LUXO3

Luxembourg Federation of University Women
10 rue de L'Abbe-Lemire
1927 LUXEMBOURG
☐ Organisation for women working in universities.

LUXO4

Movement for the Liberation of Women
BP 174
LUXEMBOURG
☐ Campaigning group for women's liberation.

LUXO5

National Federation of Women in Luxembourg
PO Box 172
LUXEMBOURG
☎ 44 48 64
☐ Umbrella organisation.

LUXO6

National Women's Council
BP 160
2011 LUXEMBOURG
☐ Umbrella organisation.

LUXO7

Women's Aid
Foyer Paula Bove
38–40 rue d'Anvers
1130 LUXEMBOURG
☐ Support for women suffering violence.

LUXO8

Women's Liberation Movement
66 route de Hollerich
1740 LUXEMBOURG
☎ 49 05 83
☐ Campaigns on a wide variety of women's issues.

Malaysia

Libraries, Archives, Resource Centres and Information

MALL1

National Advisory Council on the Inter-Action of Women in Development
Implementation and Co-ordination Unit
Prime Minister's Department
Jalan Dato Onn
KUALA LUMPUR
☐ Government advisory body promoting women's participation in political, social and economic life.

Women's Organisations

MALO1

Asian and Pacific Centre for Women and Development
(See International section)

Joint Action Committee on Violence Against Women
PO Box 89
36008 TELUK INTAN
☐ Supports women victims of violence.

MALO2

National Council of Women's Organisations
157 Jalan Tun
Razak
50400 KUALA LUMPUR
☎ 3 298 92 51
☐ Umbrella organisation.

MALO3

Women's Crisis Centre
57 Jalan Macalister
11400 PENANG
☐ Support and aid to women victims of physical or mental violence.

Mauritius

Libraries, Archives, Resource Centres and Information

MAUL1

Ministry of Women's Rights and Family Affairs
6th Floor
Government Centre
PORT LOUIS
☎ 01 2264

☐ Government body aiming to eliminate sexual discrimination and to promote women's participation in development.

Women's Organisations

MAUO1

Muvman Liberasyon Fam Collective
Celicourt Antelm Street
Lakaz Ros
FOREST SIDE
☐ Radical socialist organisation campaigning for women's rights and equality.

MAUO2

Women's International League for Peace and Freedom
PO Box 545
PORT LOUIS
☐ Campaigns for de-militarisation and disarmament.

Mexico

Women's Organisations

MEXO1

Autonomous Group of University Women
Av. Universidad 1815 A/201
Col. Oxtapulco Universidad
MEXICO DF
☐ Organisation for women in universities.

MEXO2

CIDHAL
Cuernavaca
Apartado Postal 579
MORELOS

MEXO3

National Women's Council
c/o M. Lavalle Urbina
Cuvier 45
MEXICO CITY 5
☐ Umbrella organisation.

Netherlands

Bookshops

NETB1

Antiquariat Loreli
Prinsengracht 495
1016 HR AMSTERDAM
☐ Women's bookshop.

NETB2

BoekenNel
Grote Berg 11
5611 KH EINDHOVEN
☎ 040 43 06 39
☐ Women's bookshop.

NETB3

De Feeks
v. Welderenstraat 34
6511 ML NIJMEGEN
☎ 080 23 93 81
☐ Women's bookshop.

NETB4

Helleveeg
Bentinckstraat 36
6811 EE ARNHEM
☐ Women's bookshop.

NETB5

Savannah Bay
Telingstraat 13
3512 GV UTRECHT
☐ Women's bookshop.

NETB6

Shikasta
Junusstraat 1-A
6701 AX WAGENINGEN
☐ Women's bookshop.

NETB7

Trix
Prinsestraat 122
2513 CH THE HAGUE
☐ Women's bookshop.

NETB8

Trui
Folkingestraat 14
9711 JW GRONINGEN
☐ Women's bookshop.

NETB9

Vrolijk
Paleisstraat 135
1012 ZL AMSTERDAM
☐ Gay and lesbian bookshop with specialist feminist section.

NETB10

Xantippe
Prinsengracht 290
1016 HJ AMSTERDAM
☐ Women's bookshop.

Libraries, Archives, Resource Centres and Information

NETL1

Amsterdam Women's House
95 Nieuwe Herengracht
RX AMSTERDAM
☐ Feminist information and action centre. Meeting place for numerous women's groups.

NETL2

Clara Wichmann Institute
Singel 373
1012 WL AMSTERDAM
☐ Documentation on women and the law.

NETL3

International Information and Archives Centre for the Women's Movement
Keizersgracht 10
1015 CN AMSTERDAM
☎ 020 24 42 68
☐ Large collections of books, archival material, periodicals and photographs on the women's movement.

NETL4

Lesbian Archives
Postbox 40 62
8901 EB LEEUWARDEN
☎ 6661 50
☐ Library of books and material on lesbians, single and young women. Conducts research programmes.

NETL5

Ministry for Social Affairs – Dept of Equal Opportunities
Anna van Hannoverstraat 42
595 BJ THE HAGUE
☐ Government agency providing information on equal opportunities in The Netherlands.

NETL6

National Resource Centre for Education Work with Women
Visschersplein 4-D4
3511 LX UTRECHT
☐ Information service for those working with women in education.

NETL7

Women's Centre
Landelijk, Steunpunt Zelfverdediging
Overtoom 270
1054 JB AMSTERDAM
☐ Information and support for women.

NETL8

Women's Emancipation Support Point
Westvest 139-2611
AZ DELFT
☎ 015 13 61 40
☐ State-subsidised advice, support and information centre.

NETL9

Women's Library
Karel du Jardinstraat 52
AMSTERDAM
☐ Women's library.

Women's Organisations

NETO1

Association for Women's Interests
Noordeinde 2A
2311 CD LEIDEN
☎ 071 12 06 03
☐ Working for women's equality in all areas.

NETO2

Dolle Mina
Postbus 6
1000 AA AMSTERDAM
☐ Women's action group.

NETO3

Dutch Women's Studies Association
University of Utrecht
Heidelberglaan 2
3584 CS UTRECHT
☎ 030 53 18 81
☐ Association for Dutch women working in women's studies.

NETO4

European Network of Women's Studies
(See International section)

NETO5

Foundation for Research Consultation on Sexual Violence
c/o Marian Grunel
University of Utrecht
Heidelberglaan 2
3584 CS UTRECHT
☐ Network for women researchers into sexual violence.

NETO6

Gender and New Information Technologies (GRANITE)
c/o Kitty Verrips – SISWO
PO Box 19079
1000 GB AMSTERDAM
☐ Aims to put new technology into gender courses and to make new technology courses aware of gender issues.

NETO7

International Lesbian Information Service
(See International section)

NETO8

International Working Group on Feminism and Theology
University of Utrecht
Heidelberglaan 2
Room 826A
3584 CS UTRECHT
☐ Network for women in theology.

NETO9

National Consultation for Women's Studies in Agriculture
c/o Ans Hobbelink
PO Box 101
6700 AC WAGENINGEN
☐ Network for women in agricultural studies.

NETO10

National Consultation for Women's Studies in Anthropology
c/o Dr Anna Aalten
Social Anthropology Centre
Oude Zijds Achterburgwal 185
1012 DK AMSTERDAM
☐ Network for women in anthropology.

NETO11

National Consultation for Women's Studies in Geography
c/o Lenie Scholten
University of Nijmegen
KNAG Department of Women's Studies
Thomas van Aquinostraat 6-0418
6522 BD NIJMEGEN
☐ Network for women in geography.

NETO12

National Foundation for Women and Housing
Weena 756
3014 DA ROTTERDAM
□ National organisation concerned with women's issues in housing.

NETO13

National Women's Council (NVR)
Laan van der Meerenvoort 30
2517 AL THE HAGUE
□ Umbrella group for women's organisations.

NETO14

National Women's History Organisation
Keizersgracht 10
1015 CN AMSTERDAM
□ Provides advice and information and promotes the study of women's history.

NETO15

Netherlands Association of University Women
PO Box 33
3155 ZG MAASLAND
□ Networking organisation between Dutch university women.

NETO16

Network of Women in Dutch Development Agencies
PO Box 11640
2502 AP THE HAGUE
☎ 070 62 41 91
□ Information and networking centre for women working in Third World development.

NETO17

RHEA (Women and Reproductive Technology)
c/o Linda Wilkens
PO Box 15105
3501 BC UTRECHT
□ Network and campaigning group on women and reproductive technology.

NETO18

Society of Women in the Fine Arts
Keizergracht 10
1015 CN AMSTERDAM
□ Organisation for women in fine arts.

NETO19

University Women of Europe
(See International section)

NETO20

Women Against Rape
Herengracht 65
AMSTERDAM
□ Women's campaigning group.

NETO21

Women and Politics Section of the Dutch Association for Science and Politics
c/o Monique Leijenaar
P. N. van Eyckhof 3
LEIDEN
□ Women's section of national organisation.

NETO22

Women in the Media
Jan van Eyckstraat 25
AMSTERDAM
□ Organisation concerned with women's representation in the media:

NETO23

Women's Aid
Landelijk Steunpunt Vrowen
Biltstraat 101C
3572 UTRECHT
☎ 030 31 41 43
□ Support and shelter for women suffering violence.

NETO24

Women's Global Network on Reproductive Rights
(See International section)

NETO25

Josine Spits, President
Women's History Association
Lokhorststraat 22d
3211 TA LEIDEN
□ Association for women in history.

NETO26

Women's International Studies Europe (WISE)
(See International section)

NETO27

Dutch Women's Studies Association
Heidelberglaan 2
3584 CS UTRECHT
☎ 030 53 18 81
□ Dutch section of European network.

New Zealand

Bookshops

NZB1

Bennett's Bookshop
36 Broadway
PALMERSTON N
□ Bookshop with women's studies section.

NZB2

Bennett's University Book Centre
PO Box 13066
Hillcrest
HAMILTON
□ Bookshop with women's studies section.

NZB3

Broadsheet Bookshop
228 Dominion Road
Balmoral
AUCKLAND
☎ 09 607 162
□ Women's bookshop.

NZB4

Dimensions
NZI Arcade
Garden Place
HAMILTON
☎ 7 80656
□ Women's bookshop.

NZB5

The Kate Sheppard Women's Bookshop
145 Manchester Street
CHRISTCHURCH
☎ 3 790 784
□ Feminist bookshop.

NZB6

Lesbian Bookshop
228 Dominion Road
AUCKLAND
☎ 09 607 162
□ Lesbian bookshop.

NZB7

Scorpio Books
Phoenix House
Corner Hereford Street and Oxford Terrace
CHRISTCHURCH
☎ 3 792 882
□ Alternative bookshop with lesbian and feminist sections.

NZB8

Unity Books
19 High Street
AUCKLAND
☎ 09 370 393
□ Lesbian and gay bookshop.

NZB9

Unity Books
119–125 Willis Street
WELLINGTON
☎ 04 738 438
□ Lesbian and feminist bookshop.

NZB10

University Bookshop
University Drive
CHRISTCHURCH
□ Bookshop with women's studies section.

NZB11

University Bookshop
378 Great King Street
DUNEDIN
□ Bookshop with women's studies section.

NZB12

Victoria Book Centre
15 Mount Street
WELLINGTON
☎ 04 729 585
□ Alternative bookshop with women's studies section.

NZB13

Whitcoulls Ltd
312 Lambton Quay
WELLINGTON
□ Bookshop with women's studies section.

NZB14

Women's Place Bookshop
58 Courtenay Place
WELLINGTON
☎ 04 851 802
□ Women's bookshop.

Libraries, Archives, Resource Centres and Information

NZL1

Lesbian and Gay Rights Resource Centre
PO Box 11-695
Manners Street
WELLINGTON
☎ 04 845 003
□ Archives and reference library.

NZL2

National Advisory Council on the Employment of Women
> Department of Labour
> Private Bag
> WELLINGTON

☐ Government advisory body on women and employment which publishes and distributes information on women and employment.

NZL3

Womanline
☎ 09 765 173
☐ Telephone information and referral service run from Auckland.

NZL4

The Women's Library
> 63 Ponsonby Road
> AUCKLAND

☐ Extensive women's and lesbian library.

Women's Organisations

NZO1

National Council of Women of New Zealand
> PO Box 12-117
> WELLINGTON

☐ Co-ordinates and unites women's organisations throughout New Zealand. Researches and campaigns on women's issues.

NZO2

Society for Research on Women in New Zealand
> PO Box 12-270
> WELLINGTON

☐ Sponsors and carries out research on women's issues.

NZO3

Wellington Lesbian Herstory Group
> PO Box 3623
> WELLINGTON

☐ Group documenting the lives of New Zealand lesbians.

NZO4

Women's International League for Peace and Freedom
> 2 Raumato Terrace
> Khandallah
> WELLINGTON 4

☐ Campaigns on a range of disarmament issues.

NZO5

Women's Studies Association (NZ)
> PO Box 5067
> AUCKLAND 1

☐ Network for women's studies.

Nicaragua

Women's Organisations

NICO1

Association of Nicaraguan Women Luisa Amanda Espinoza (AMNLAE)
> Apartado A238
> MANAGUA

☐ Campaigns for women's inclusion in social, political and cultural life.

Nigeria

Libraries, Archives, Resource Centres and Information

NIGL1

Women's Research and Documentation Unit
> University of Ibadan
> Institute of African Studies
> IBADAN

☐ Documentation centre. National and international network and focus for women's studies.

Women's Organisations

NIGO1

National Council of Women's Societies in Nigeria
> PO Box 3063
> Tafawa Balewa Square Complex
> LAGOS
☎ 63 16 37
☐ Umbrella organisation.

NIGO2

Nigerian Association of University Women
> Department of Home Economics
> Owerri
> IMO STATE

☐ Networks between university women and encourages women to go into higher education. Monitors legislation and provides financial assistance to young women at school.

Norway

Bookshops

NORB1

Oslo Bogcafe
 C. J. Jambross plass 2
 OSLO 1
☐ Alternative bookshop with women's section.

NORB2

Universitetsbokhandeln
 Postboks 307
 Blindern
 OSLO 1
☐ University bookshop with women's studies section.

Libraries, Archives, Resource Centres and Information

NORL1

Centre for Information on Women and Development
 Fr. Nansens Pl. 6
 0160 OSLO
☎ 22 42 62 45
☐ Information for women working in development.

NORL2

Centre for Women's Studies
 University of Oslo
 PO Box 1040 (Ullevalsveien 105)
 Blindern
 0315 OSLO 3
☎ 22 45 43 70
☐ Library open to visitors.

NORL3

Documentation Services for Literature About Women
 University Library
 University of Bergen
 5007 BERGEN
☎ 5 21 30 50
☐ Documentation on women.

NORL4

Equal Status Council
 Postboks 8004
 0111 OSLO
☐ Government organisation providing information on women's equality status in Norway.

NORL5

Information Office for Norwegian Literature Abroad
 Postboks 239
 Sentrum
 OSLO 1
☐ Government-funded organisation which compiles bibliographic material and provides reading lists on request from abroad.

NORL6

Legal Advice for Women
 Postboks 6898
 St Olavs Plass
 0130 OSLO 1
☐ Free legal advice for women. Provides speakers for schools and women's groups.

NORL7

Women's Centre
 Kvinnehuset
 Radhusgate 2
 OSLO
☎ 22 41 28 64
☐ Women's information and contact for women's groups in Norway.

Women's Organisations

NORO1

Co-ordinator for Norwegian Women's Studies
 Tove Beate Pedersen
 NAVF's Secretariat for Women and Research
 Sandakerveien 99
 0489 OSLO 4
☎ 22 22 55 71

NORO2

Crisis Centre for Abused and Raped Women
 Postboks 4649
 Sofienburg
 0506 OSLO 5
☎ 22 35 00 48
☐ Information, help and accommodation for women. Carries out research into the abuse of women.

NORO3

Joint Action Against Pornography and Prostitution
> Postboks 1280
> Vika
> 0111 OSLO

☐ Coalition of many groups working in this area.

NORO4

Norwegian Research Council for Science and the Humanities – Secretariat for Women and Research
> Sandakerveien 99
> 0489 OSLO 4
☎ 22 15 70 12

☐ Aims to increase the recruitment of women to all research disciplines. Promotes, co-ordinates and disseminates information on women's studies.

NORO5

Norwegian Women's National Council
> Fr. Nansensplass 6
> 0160 OSLO 1

☐ Umbrella organisation.

NORO6

The Research Group for Women and Regional Development
> Finnmark College
> Follumsvei
> 9500 ALTA
☎ 84 37 600

☐ Interdisciplinary group promoting feminist-orientated development locally, nationally and worldwide.

NORO7

Women in Men's Work
> Kvinnehuset
> Radhusgt 2
> 0151 OSLO 1

☐ Supports women in traditionally male occupations, and encourages girls to enter them.

NORO8

Women's Front
> Boks 53
> Bryn
> 0611 OSLO 6

☐ Organisation of 65 country-wide groups fighting the oppression of women.

Pakistan

Women's Organisations

PAKO1

All Pakistan Women's Association
> 67–B Garden Road
> KARACHI 3
☎ 71 29 91

☐ Aims to further the welfare of women in Pakistan. Consults with the government.

PAKO2

Asian Women's Institute
(See International section)

PAKO3

Pakistan Association for Women's Studies
> c/o Tahera Aftab
> C–12 Staff Town
> University of Karachi
> KARACHI 75270
☎ 47 18 28

☐ Organisation for women's studies scholars.

PAKO4

Simorgh
> PO Box 3328
> Gulberg 2
> LAHORE

☐ Feminist organisation aiming to promote alternative perspectives for solving women's problems.

Paraguay

Women's Organisations

PARO1

Group for the Study of Women in Paraguay
> Eligio Ayala 973 C.C. 2157
> ASUNCION
☎ 443734

☐ Promotes research and discussion on women's issues in Paraguay.

Peru

Libraries, Archives, Resource Centres and Information

PERL1

'Flora Tristan' Peruvian Women's Centre
> Parque Hernan Velarde 42
> LIMA 1
☎ 248008

☐ Researches women's problems and networks between women's groups. Information centre.

PERL2

Women's Documentation Centre
    CENDOC Mujer
    Avenue LaMar 170
    LIMA 18
☐ Documentation and information on women in Peru.

Women's Organisations

PERO1

'Creativity and Change' Cultural Promotion
    Jiron Quilca 431
    LIMA
☐ Educational and publishing activities on issues such as health, violence to women and women's rights.

PERO2

National Women Educators Association
    Maximo Abril 695
    Jesus Maria
    LIMA
☎   310562
Association for women in teaching.

PERO3

National Women's Council of Peru
    Francia 706
    Miraflores
    LIMA 6
☐ Umbrella organisation.

Philippines

Libraries, Archives, Resource Centres and Information

PHIL1

Association of the New Filipina
    25 S Pascual Street
    MALABON
    Metro Manila
☐ Research services for women.

PHIL2

Centre for Women's Resources
    2nd Floor Mar Santos Building
    43 A Roces Avenue
    QUEZON CITY
☎   99 27 55
☐ Feminist organisation providing a public library and audio-visual material.

PHIL3

ISIS – International Resource and Information Centre
    85–A East Maya Street
    Philamlife Homes
    QUEZON CITY
    1104
☎   99 32 92
☐ Extensive library and information centre.

PHIL4

Women's Resource and Research Centre
    Katipunun Parkway
    Loyola Heights
    QUEZON CITY
☎   97 28 60
☐ International communications network for groups and individuals concerned with women's issues.

Women's Organisations

PHIO1

Civic Assembly of Women of the Philippines
    Philippines Women's University
    1743 Taft Avenue
    MANILA
☎   58 82 01
☐ Umbrella organisation.

PHIO2

GABRIELA
    Santos Building
    2nd Floor General Malvar Ext.
    DALVEO CITY
☐ Umbrella organisation for over 100 women's groups, campaigning on equal rights.

PHIO3

Mediawatch Collective
    12 Pasaje Dela Paz. Proj. 4
    1109 QUEZON CITY
☎   77 53 41
☐ Monitors images of women in the media and campaigns for improved representation for women.

PHIO4

Metro Manila Council of Women Balikatan Movement
    82–A Midland 11
    Washington Street
    Greenhills West
    SAN JUAN
    Metro Manila
☐ Campaigns for an improvement in women's status and conditions. Provides training and initiates income-generating projects.

PHIO5

National Federation of Peasant Women
1 Mines Street
Corner Lands Street
Project 6
QUEZON CITY
Metro Manila
☐ Campaigns for land reform and distribution to widowed and separated women, for an end to discrimination against peasant women and for health and reproductive rights.

PHIO6

Pilipina Inc.
12 Pasaje Dela Paz. Proj. 4
1109 QUEZON CITY
☎ 77 53 41
☐ Promotes economic justice and equity for women.

PHIO7

Third World Movement Against the Exploitation of Women
PO Box 1434
MANILA
2800
☐ Network for women's organisations and individuals. Data bank on women's resources. (See International section)

Poland

Libraries, Archives, Resource Centres and Information

POLL1

Women's Studies Centre
University of Lodz
al. Kosciuski 65
90–514 LODZ
☐ Established in 1992 with plans for a women's information centre.

Portugal

Libraries, Archives, Resource Centres and Information

PORL1

Commission for Equality and Women's Rights
Av. da Republica
32–2o Esq.
1093 LISBON

☎ 1 797 29 65
Rua Ferreira Borges
62–1o E
4000 PORTO
☎ 2 200 38 48
☐ Government agency women's documentation and information centres.

PORL2

Commission of the Situation of Women
Av. da Republica 32. 1
1093 LISBON
☎ 1 797 60 81
☐ Government advisory body.

PORL3

Women's Information and Documentation Centre
Filipe de Mata 115–A
1600 LISBON
☐ Information and documentation centre.

PORL4

Women's Publishing House Co-operative
Filipe de Mata 115–A
1600 LISBON
☐ Feminist documentation centre and library.

Women's Organisations

PORO1

Association for Women's Studies
University Coimbra
c/o Faculdade de Economia
Avenue Dias da Silva 165
3000 COIMBRA
☐ Women's studies association of Portugal.

PORO2

Democratic Women's Movement
Av. Duque de Loule 111, 4
1000 LISBON
☎ 1 352 78 53
☐ Campaigns for women's rights and equality.

Puerto Rico

Libraries, Archives, Resource Centres and Information

PRL1

Commission for Women's Affairs
Apartado 11382
Estacion Fernandez Juncos
SANTURCE 00910

☎ 722 2907
□ Women's studies library. Also conducts conferences, workshops, training and research.

PRL2
Women's Information Centre
Centro Cultural
Calle José de Diego
Apartado 791
CIDRA 00639
□ Government training, advice and information.

Women's Organisations

PRO1
Association of Women Artists of Puerto Rico
Apartado 2280
Estacion UPR
RIO PIEDRAS 00931
☎ 792 1848
□ Promotes and supports the work of women artists.

PRO2
Co-ordinating Body of Feminist Organisations
Apartado 21936
Estacion UPR
RIO PIEDRAS 00931
□ Co-ordinates national feminist groups.

PRO3
Julia de Burgos Refuge
Apartado 2433
SAN JUAN 00936
□ Shelter, counselling and legal assistance for women suffering violence.

PRO4
Organisation for the Development of Women's Rights
Facultad de Direcho
Universidad Catolica de Puerto Rico
Estacion 6
PONCE 00732
□ Campaigns for legislation beneficial to women. Provides advice, conferences and workshops.

Russia

Libraries, Archives, Resource Centres and Information

RUSL1
Centre for Gender Studies
Institute of Socio-Economic Problems of Population
27 Krasitova Street
MOSCOW 117218
☎ 125 73 02
□ Library and resource centre.

Senegal

Libraries, Archives, Resource Centres and Information

SENL1
ENDA Third World
(See International section)
BP 3370
DAKAR
☎ 21 60 27

Women's Organisations

SENO1
Association of African Women for Research and Development
(See International section)

Singapore

Women's Organisations

SINO1
Association of Women for Action and Research
Tanglin PO Box 244
SINGAPORE 9124
□ Feminist organisation campaigning for women's equality and against sexist representations. Carries out research on women's problems.

SINO2
Baha'i Women's Committee
68 Lorong 16
04–03 Association Building
SINGAPORE 1439
□ Promotes welfare and rights for women. Arranges talks, seminars and educational programmes.

SINO3
National Council of Women of Singapore
9 Balmoral Road
SINGAPORE 1025
☐ Umbrella organisation.

South Africa

Women's Organisations

SAO1
Durban Women's Bibliography Group
Department of African Studies
University of Natal
DURBAN

SAO2
National Council of Women of South Africa
8 Linksfield Heights
Linksfield
JOHANNESBURG 2192
☐ Umbrella organisation promoting equal rights.
Campaigns and lobbies on welfare issues.

South Korea

Bookshops

SKB1
Chonno Book Centre
84–9 Chongro 1-Ga
Chongno-gu
SEOUL
☎ 02 733 2331
☐ Bookshop with feminist section.

SKB2
Kyobo Book Centre
1 Chongro 1-Ga
Chongno-gu
SEOUL
☎ 02 730 7891
☐ Bookshop with feminist section.

SKB3
Tarakbang
60–5 Daehyun-Dong
Seodaemun-gu
SEOUL
☎ 02 362 7132
☐ Bookshop with feminist section.

Libraries, Archives, Resource Centres and Information

SKL1
Korean Women's Development Institute
San 42–4, Bulkwang-don
Eunpyung-ku
SEOUL 122-040
☎ 02 356 0070
☐ Government-funded agency collecting and distributing information on women. Vocational information and counselling centre.

Spain

Bookshops

SPB1
Libreria des Mujeres
San Cristobal 17
28012 MADRID
☎ 221 70 43
☐ Feminist bookshop.

SPB2
Libreria des Mujeres
calle San Juan de la Cruz 4
ZARAGOZA
☎ 45 26 52
☐ Feminist bookshop.

SPB3
Libreria Donna
calle Emporador 7
VALENCIA
☎ 352 76 98
☐ Feminist bookshop.

SPB4
Libreria Fulmer
calle Zaragosa 36
SAVILLE
☎ 22 71 78
☐ Feminist bookshop

SPB5
Libreria Mujeres
calle San Augustine
MALAGA 11
☐ Feminist bookshop.

SPB6
La Sal Bar y Biblioteca Feminista
Carrer de la Riereta 8
BARCELONA
☐ Feminist bookshop.

Libraries, Archives, Resource Centres and Information

SPL1

Centre for Historical Research on Women
C. Brusi 61
08006 BARCELONA
☐ Library and documentation centre.

SPL2

Centre for the Study of Motherhood
Numancia
no 111–115, A3
08029 BARCELONA
☐ Collection of material on motherhood and a museum of motherhood.

SPL3

Documentation Centre of the Institute of Women
Almagro 36
28010 MADRID
☎ 410 51 12
☐ Documentation centre on women.

SPL4

Groups of the Feminist Movement
calle Barquillo 44
2 Izq.
MADRID
☎ 319 369
☐ Feminist library and meeting place for feminist groups.

SPL5

Women's Documentation Centre
Civic Centre 'La Sedeta'
Passatge Llavallol
08025 BARCELONA
☐ Documentation on women in Spain.

SPL6

Women's Information Centre
Menendez y Pelayo 11
28009 MADRID
☐ Information for women.

Women's Organisations

SPO1

Association of University Women
Miguel Angel 9
28010 MADRID
☐ Organisation for Spanish university women.

SPO2

Comision para la Investigacion de Malos tratos a Mujeres
☎ 900 100 009
☐ Helpline for women suffering domestic violence.

SPO3

Co-ordination of Feminist Organisations
Barquillo 44
28004 MADRID
☐ Umbrella organisations of Spanish women's groups.

SPO4

National Council of Women in Spain
Calle Diputacion
306 pral.
08009 BARCELONA
☎ 3179688
☐ Umbrella organisation which campaigns against discrimination.

SPO5

Women's Institute
Ministry of Culture
Almagro 36
28010 MADRID
☐ Autonomous advisory body to the government. Researches the position of women and makes recommendations on legislative reform.

Sweden

Bookshops

SWEB1

Bokhandeln Brod Rosor
Haga Osterg 26–28
41301 GOTHENBURG
☐ Women's bookshop.

SWEB2

Bokhandeln Halva Himlen
Engelbrektsgatan 11
70210 OREBRO
☐ Women's bookshop.

SWEB3

Kvinnobokhandeln Medusa
Wollmar Yxkullsgaten 33
12650 STOCKHOLM
☎ 08 84 50 07
☐ Feminist bookshop.

Research Resources

SWEB4
Rosa Rummet
Lilla Friskaregaten 12
LUND
☎ 046 15 71 34
☐ Gay and lesbian bookshop.

SWEB5
Rosa Rummet
Sveavagen 57
STOCKHOLM
☎ 08 736 02 15
☐ Gay and lesbian bookshop.

Libraries, Archives, Resource Centres and Information

SWEL1
Centre for Women in Research and Working Life
Lulea University
95181 LULEA
☎ 920 915 70
☐ Library and information service.

SWEL2
Centre for Women Scholars and Research on Women
Stockholm University
10691 STOCKHOLM
☎ 08 16 22 22
☐ Library and information service.

SWEL3
Centre for Women's Studies
Linkoping University
58183 LINKOPING
☎ 013 28 21 74
☐ Library and information service.

SWEL4
Centre for Women's Studies
University of Lund
Box 117
22100 LUND
☎ 046 10 76 24
☐ Women's studies library and support for women researchers.

SWEL5
Centre for Women's Studies
Umea University
90187 UMEA
☎ 090 16 60 43
☐ Library and information service.

SWEL6
Centre for Women's Studies
Uppsala University
Ostra Agatan 19
75322 UPPSALA
☎ 018 18 22 75
☐ Library and information service.

SWEL7
Unit for Gender Equality Statistics
Statistical Central Bureau
106991 STOCKHOLM
☎ 08 783 4000
☐ Statistical information on women in Sweden.

SWEL8
Women in Development
The Women's Studies Centre
Göteborg University
41298 GOTHENBURG
☎ 031 63 19 44
☐ Library and information.

SWEL9
Women's Centre
Gamlestadstorget 12
GOTHENBURG
☎ 031 21 12 65
☐ Information and meeting centre.

SWEL10
Women's History Collections
Göteborg University Library
PO Box 5096 (Renstromsgaten 4)
40222 GOTHENBURG
☎ 031 63 17 61
☐ National archive, library and documentation centre on women's history.

SWEL11
Women's Studies Centre
Göteborg University
41298 GOTHENBURG
☎ 031 63 19 44
☐ Library and information service.

Women's Organisations

SWEO1
All Women's House
Svartensgaten 3
11620 STOCKHOLM
☐ Legal aid, counselling and refuge for women suffering violence.

SWEO2

Centre for Women Scholars and Research on Women
 Uppsala University
 75237 UPPSALA
□ Co-ordinates work of women scholars in Sweden.

SWEO3

Forum for Women Scholars and Research on Women
 Lund University
 PO Box 1703
 22101 LUND
☎ 046 10 76 24
□ Information and network for women scholars.

SWEO4

Frederika Bremer Association
 Hornsgaten 52
 11721 STOCKHOLM
☎ 08 44 32 61
□ Umbrella organisation with 60 branches campaigning for equality for women.

SWEO5

Women's Front
 PO Box S
 16304 STOCKHOLM
☎ 08 39 51 03
□ Feminist organisation campaigning for equal rights, the abolition of nuclear weapons, the preservation of the environment and against pornography.

SWEO6

Women's International League for Peace and Freedom
 Packhusgrand 6
 11130 STOCKHOLM
☎ 08 21 17 20
□ Branch of worldwide organisation campaigning for peace and disarmament.

Switzerland

Bookshops

SWIB1

Frauenbuchladen
 Gerechtigkeitsgasse 6
 8000 ZURICH
☎ 01 202 62 74
□ Feminist bookshop.

SWIB2

Gnossenschaftsbuchladen
 Postfach 4410
 LIESTAL
☎ 061 91 56 70
□ Feminist bookshop.

SWIB3

L'Inédite
 Cardinal Mermillod 18
 1227 GENEVA
☎ 022 43 22 33
□ Feminist bookshop.

SWIB4

Librairie du Boulevard
 25 Boulevard du Pont d'Arve
 1205 GENEVA
☎ 022 28 70 54
□ Alternative bookshop with feminist section.

SWIB5

Point de Rencontre
 76 Avenue des Communautés Réunies
 1200 GENEVA
□ Women's bookshop.

Libraries, Archives, Resource Centres and Information

SWIL1

Bureau of Equality of Rights Between Men and Women
 2 rue Henri Fazay
 1211 GENEVA
☎ 022 27 20 65
□ Information on women's equality in Switzerland.

SWIL2

Isis Women's International Cross Cultural Exchange (ISIS-WICCE)
 3 chemin des Campanules
 1219 GENEVA
☎ 022 796 44 37
□ An international women's resource centre. Extensive network with annual cultural exchanges around changing themes.

SWIL3

Women's Archives
 Kanzleizentrum
 Kanzleistrasse 56
 8004 ZURICH
□ Swiss women's archives.

SWIL4

Women's Centre
Langmauerweg 1
3011 BERN
☎ 061 22 07 73
☐ Information and meeting place.

SWIL5

Women's Centre
La Maison
Association pour un Centre Femme
30 avenue Peschier
1206 GENEVA
☎ 022 789 26 00
☐ Library, video archives, workshops, exhibitions and meeting place.

SWIL6

Women's Centre
Maison des Femmes
Galerie l'Eglantine
1022 LAUSANNE
☐ Organisation providing free legal aid for women.

SWIL7

Women's Centre
Mattengasse 27
ZURICH
☎ 01 27 28 503
☐ Library and information.

SWIL8

Women's Health Centre
4 rue de Mole
GENEVA
☎ 022 738 66 66
☐ Information on women's health.

SWIL9

Women's Health Centre
Mattengasse 27
8005 ZURICH
☎ 01 272 77 50
☐ Information on women's health.

SWIL10

Women's Information Centre
Point de Rencontre
76 avenue des Communautés Réunies
1200 GENEVA
☐ Information centre.

SWIL11

Women's Library
Seltigenstrasse 11
7002 BERN

☎ 061 45 44 40
☐ Women's library

Women's Organisations

SWIO1

International Federation of University Women
(See International section)

SWIO2

National Council of Women in Switzerland
Altikofenstrasse 182
Postfach 101
3048 WORBLAUFEN
☎ 031 58 48 48
☐ Umbrella group with individual members.

SWIO3

Rape Crisis Line
Case Postale 459
1211 GENEVA
☎ 022 733 63 63
☐ Rape crisis phone line service.

SWIO4

Swiss Association for Women's Rights
1111 ROMANEL
Morges
☐ Campaigning for equal rights in all fields.

SWIO5

The Swiss Association of Women in Feminist Research
Sekretariat M. Marti
Klosterparkgassli 8
5430 WETTINGEN
☎ 056 26 06 18
☐ Organisation of more than 900 members interested in feminist research.

SWIO6

Swiss Women
Case Postale 323
1227 GENEVA
☐ Focuses on political and social issues for Swiss women.

SWIO7

Women Against Domestic Violence
Solidarité Femme
ccp 540–1211
GENEVA 13
☎ 022 797 10 10
☐ Organisation assisting women suffering domestic violence.

SWIO8
Women's International League for Peace and Freedom
(See International section)

Taiwan

Bookshops

TAIB1
Eslite
No. 429 Section 1
Tun-hua South Road
TAIPEI
☎ 02 775 5977
□ Bookshop with feminist titles.

Women's Organisations

TAIO1
Women's Research Programme
Population Studies Centre
National Taiwan University
TAIPEI
☎ 02 393 0097
□ Conducts and promotes interdisciplinary research on women in Taiwan. Large collection of books and papers on women from Taiwan, usually available only to university staff and students.

Tanzania

Libraries, Archives, Resource Centres and Information

TANL1
Women's Research and Documentation Centre
Box 35185
University of Dar es Salaam
DAR ES SALAAM
□ Documentation on women in Tanzania.

Thailand

Libraries, Archives, Resource Centres and Information

THAL1
Women's Information Centre and Foundation
PO Box 7–47
BANGKOK 10700
□ Information for women.

THAL2
Women's Studies Programme
Faculty of Social Sciences
Chiangmai University
CHIANGMAI
☎ 053 221 699 ext. 3572
□ Information and database on women's studies.

Women's Organisations

THAO1
Anjaree
PO Box 322
Rajdamnem
BANGKOK 10200
□ Feminist network.

THAO2
Foundation for Women
35/267 Charansanitwongse Road 62
Soi Wat Paorohit
BANGKOK 10700
□ Feminist organisation which runs training courses, counselling service and shelter for women suffering violence.

THAO3
National Council for Women of Thailand
Manangkasila Mansion
Lanluang Road
BANGKOK 10300
□ Umbrella organisation and discussion forum for women's organisations in Thailand.

THAO4
Thai Association of University Women
49/1 Sukhumvit 38
BANGKOK 10110
□ Organisation for graduate women. Runs training, community and income-generating projects.

THAO5
Women in Development Consortium (WIDCIT)
Office of the Rector
Thammasat University
BANGKOK
□ Network for women in development.

THAO6
Women Lawyers Association of Thailand
6 Sukhothai Road
BANGKOK 10300
□ Organisation for women working in the legal profession which promotes legal education and encourages women to enter the law.

Trinidad and Tobago

Women's Organisations

TTO1

Caribbean Association for Feminist Research and Action
(See International section)

TTO2

National Council of Women in Trinidad and Tobago
118 Saddle Road
Gor. Lynch Drive
MARAVAL
□ Umbrella organisation.

Tunisia

Libraries, Archives, Resource Centres and Information

TUNL1

All of Tunisia Women for Research and Information on Women
7 rue Sinan Pacha
TUNIS
□ Information on Tunisian women.

Turkey

Libraries, Archives, Resource Centres and Information

TURL1

Women's Library and Information Centre
Fener Mah
Fener P.T.T. yam (tarihi bina)
Halic
34220 ISTANBUL
☎ 1 523 74 08
□ Collection of visual, written and verbal documents concerning women from the Ottoman era to the present. Organises conferences, seminars, concerts and exhibitions by women authors and artists.

Ukraine

Libraries, Archives, Resource Centres and Information

UKRL1

Ukranian Centre for Women's Studies
c/o Svetlana Koupriashkina
Konstantinovskaya Str. 19, apt. 15
Kiev–71
253071 UKRAINE
☎ 044 417 56 43
□ Feminist library.

United States of America

Bookclubs

USABC1

Liberation Book Club
PO Box 453
SOUTH NAWALK, CT 06856
□ Lesbian and gay bookclub.

Bookshops (alphabetical by state)

USAB1

Lodestar Books
2020 B 11th Avenue
BIRMINGHAM, AL 35205
☎ 205 939 3356
□ Alternative bookshop with feminist and women's studies sections.

USAB2

Opening Books
303 Pratt Avenue
HUNTSVILLE, AL 35801
☎ 205 536 5880
□ Women's bookshop.

USAB3

Alaska Women's Bookstore
2470 East Tudor Road
ANCHORAGE, AK 99507
☎ 907 562 4716
□ Women's bookshop.

USAB4

Aradia Bookstore
116 West Cottage
FLAGSTAFF, AZ 86002
☎ 779 3817
□ Feminist bookshop.

USAB5

Humanspace Books
1617 North 32nd Street
PHOENIX, AZ 85008
☎ 220 4419
☐ Feminist bookshop.

USAB6

Antigone Books
403 East 5th Street
TUCSON, AZ 85705
☎ 792 3715
☐ Feminist bookshop.

USAB7

Enchanted Room Bookshop
808 East University
TUCSON, AZ 85719
☎ 622 8070
☐ Alternative bookshop with lesbian, feminist and women's studies sections.

USAB8

The Bookery
121 East Congress
TUCSON, AZ 85701
☐ Alternative bookshop with women's section.

USAB9

Wild Iris Bookstore
143A Harvard Avenue
CLAREMONT, CA 91711
☎ 714 626 8283
☐ Feminist bookshop.

USAB10

Valley Women
805 East Olive
FRESNO, CA 93728
☎ 209 233 3600
☐ Feminist bookshop.

USAB11

Gualala Books
PO Box 765
GUALALA, CA 95445
☐ Alternative bookshop with feminist section.

USAB12

Different Drummer Bookshop
1027 North Coast Highway
LAGUNA BEACH, CA 92651
☎ 714 497 6699
☐ Feminist bookshop.

USAB13

Fahrenheit 451
509 South Coast Highway
LAGUNA BEACH, CA
☎ 714 494 5151
☐ Alternative bookshop with feminist section.

USAB14

Chelsea Bookstore
2501 East Broadway
LONG BEACH, CA
☎ 213 434 2220
☐ Alternative bookshop with feminist, women's studies and women's music sections.

USAB15

Dodds Books
4818 East 2nd Street
LONG BEACH, CA
☎ 213 438 9948
☐ Alternative bookshop with feminist section.

USAB16

Bread and Roses
13812 Ventura Boulevard
Sherman Oaks
LOS ANGELES, CA
☎ 213 986 5376
☐ Alternative bookshop with women's section.

USAB17

Sisterhood Bookstore
1351 Westwood Boulevard
LOS ANGELES, CA 90024
☎ 213 477 7300
☐ Feminist bookshop.

USAB18

A Different Light
4014 Santa Monica Boulevard
Silverlake
LOS ANGELES, CA 90029
☎ 213 668 0629
☐ Gay and lesbian bookshop with women's studies and women's music sections.

USAB19

Two Sisters Bookshop
605 Cambridge Avenue
MENLO PARK, CA 94025
☎ 213 323 4778
☐ Feminist bookshop.

USAB20

Coalesce Books
845 Main Street
MORRO BAY, CA 93442
☎ 213 772 2880
☐ Feminist and alternative bookshop.

USAB21

Baybridge Books
901 Broadway
OAKLAND, CA 94607
☎ 415 835 5845
☐ Alternative bookshop with women's studies section.

USAB22

Mama Bear's
3536 Telegraph Avenue
OAKLAND, CA
☎ 415 428 9684
☐ Feminist bookshop.

USAB23

Page One
966 North Lake Avenue
PASADENA, CA 91104
☎ 818 798 8694
☐ Feminist bookshop.

USAB24

Lioness Bookstore
2224 'J' Street
SACRAMENTO, CA 95816
☎ 916 442 4657
☐ Feminist bookshop.

USAB25

Paradigm
1302 Kettner Boulevard
SAN DIEGO, CA 92101
☎ 619 232 5909
☐ Feminist bookshop.

USAB26

Modern Times Bookstore
968 Valencia Street
SAN FRANCISCO, CA 94110
☎ 510 282 9246
☐ Feminist bookshop.

USAB27

Old Wives Tales
1009 Valencia Street
SAN FRANCISCO, CA 94110
☎ 510 821 4676
☐ Women's bookshop.

USAB28

Sisterspirit
175 Stochton Avenue
SAN JOSE, CA 95126
☎ 408 293 9372
☐ Feminist bookshop.

USAB29

Choices Books
906 Garden Street
SANTA ANA, CA 93101
☎ 805 965 5477
☐ Feminist bookshop.

USAB30

Earthling Bookshop
1236 State Side
SANTA ANA, CA 93101
☎ 714 965 0926
☐ Alternative bookshop with women's studies section.

USAB31

Claire Light
1110 Petaluma Hill Road
SANTA ROSA, CA 95404
☎ 707 575 8879
☐ Feminist bookshop.

USAB32

The Book Loft
1207 Soquel Avenue
SANTA CRUZ, CA 95062
☎ 408 429 1812
☐ Alternative bookshop with women's section.

USAB33

Vacaville Book Company
315 Main Street
VACAVILLE, CA 95688
☎ 707 449 0550
☐ Alternative bookshop with lesbian and women's sections.

USAB34

Storytellers
379 East Main Street
VENTURA, CA 93001
☎ 805 648 4651
☐ Feminist bookshop.

USAB35

Explorer Booksellers
221 East Main
ASPEN, CO 81611
☎ 303 925 5336
☐ Alternative bookshop with feminist section.

USAB36

Book Garden
2625 East 12th Avenue
DENVER, CO 80206
☎ 303 399 2004
☐ Feminist bookshop.

USAB37

Bloodroot
85 Ferris Street
Black Rock
BRIDGEPORT, CT 06605
☎ 203 576 9165
☐ Feminist bookshop.

USAB38

Reader's Feast
529 Farmington Avenue
HARTFORD, CT 06105
☎ 203 232 3710
☐ Feminist bookshop.

USAB39

Lammas
1426 21st Street NW
WASHINGTON, DC
☎ 202 755 8218
☐ Feminist and lesbian bookshop.

USAB40

Lamda Rising
39 Baltimore Avenue
REHOBOTH BEACH, DE 19971
☐ Lesbian and gay bookshop.

USAB41

The First Page
2219 Wilton Drive
FORT LAUDERDALE, FL
☎ 305 564 9045
☐ Feminist bookshop.

USAB42

Goering's Book Center
1310 W University Avenue
GAINESVILLE, FL
☎ 904 378 0363
☐ Bookshop with women's studies section.

USAB43

Shades of Lavender
1502 Hendricks Avenue
JACKSONVILLE, FL
☎ 904 346 3182
☐ Feminist bookshop.

USAB44

Brigit Books
Suite 5, 3434 4th Street North
ST PETERSBURG, FL 33704
☎ 813 522 5775
☐ Feminist bookshop.

USAB45

Rubyfruit Books
666 4th W Tennessee Street
TALLAHASSEE, FL 32304
☎ 904 222 2627
☐ Alternative bookshop with feminist section.

USAB46

Three Birds Bookstore
1518 7th Avenue
TAMPA, FL 33604
☎ 813 247 7041
☐ Feminist bookshop.

USAB47

**Laughing Goddess Wymyn's Mail Order
Bookstore**
2002 H Hunnewell Street
HONOLULU, HI 96822
☐ Women's mail order bookshop.

USAB48

Jane Addams Book Shop
208 South Neil
CHAMPAIGN, IL
☎ 217 356 2555
☐ Feminist bookshop.

USAB49

Women and Children First
5233 North Clark Street
CHICAGO, IL 60640
☎ 312 769 9299
☐ Feminist bookshop.

USAB50

Platypus Book Shop
606 Dempster
EVANSTOWN, IL 60202
☎ 708 866 8040
☐ Feminist bookshop.

USAB51

One World Books
3262 Edson Road
ROCKFORD, IL 61109
☎ 815 874 7491
☐ Feminist bookshop.

USAB52

Trilogy Books
200 South Grand Avenue E
SPRINGFIELD, IL 62704
☎ 217 744 2522
☐ Feminist bookshop.

USAB53

Horizon Bookstore
517 South Goodwin
URBANA, IL
☎ 217 328 2988
☐ Feminist bookshop.

USAB54

Aquarius Books
116 North Grant Street
BLOOMINGTON, IN 47401
☎ 812 336 0988
☐ Feminist bookshop.

USAB55

Dreams and Swords
828 East 64th Street
INDIANAPOLIS, IN 46220
☎ 317 253 9966
☐ Feminist bookshop.

USAB56

SisterLit
108 Duff
AMES, IA 50010
☎ 515 232 5217
☐ Feminist bookshop.

USAB57

Women's Works Bookstore and Art Gallery
1506 Harrison
DAVENPORT, IA 52803
☎ 309 326 4518
☐ Feminist bookshop.

USAB58

Kindred Spirits
426 Houston
MANHATTAN, KS 66502
☎ 913 539 6137
☐ Feminist bookshop.

USAB59

Haveley-Cooke Bookstores
Shelbyville Road Plaza
LOUISVILLE, KY
☎ 502 893 0133
☐ Bookshop with women's studies section.

USAB60

Mystic Moon
5509 Magazine Street
NEW ORLEANS, LA 70115
☎ 504 891 4266
☐ Feminist bookshop.

USAB61

The 31st Street Bookshop
425 East 31st Street
BALTIMORE, MD
☎ 301 243 3131
☐ Feminist bookshop.

USAB62

Crone's Harvest
761 Centre Street
Jamaica Plain
BOSTON, MA
☎ 617 983 9530
☐ Feminist bookshop.

USAB63

New Words Bookstore
186 Hampshire Street
CAMBRIDGE, MA 02139
☎ 617 876 5310
☐ Feminist bookshop.

USAB64

World Eye Bookshop
518 Washington Street
GLOUCESTER, MA 01301
☎ 617 772 0844
☐ Alternative bookshop with women's studies section.

USAB65

Radzukina's
714 North Broadway
HAVERHILL, MA 01832
☎ 508 521 1333
☐ Feminist bookshop.

USAB66

Lunaria
90 King Street
NORTHAMPTON, MA 01060
☎ 413 586 7851
☐ Feminist bookshop.

USAB67

The Crystal Works
301 North Street
OAK BLUFFS, MA
☎ 617 442 5532
☐ Alternative bookshop with feminist section.

USAB68

Womancrafts
376 Commercial Street
PROVINCETOWN, MA 02657
☎ 508 487 2501
□ Women's bookshop, music and crafts.

USAB69

Pandora
226 West Lovell Street
KALAMAZOO, MI 49007
☎ 616 388 5656
□ Feminist bookshop.

USAB70

Golden Thread Booksellers
915 State Street
NEW HAVEN, MI 06511
☎ 203 777 7807
□ Feminist bookshop.

USAB71

Amazon Bookstore
1612 Harmon Place
MINNEAPOLIS, MN 55403
☎ 612 338 6560
□ Feminist bookshop.

USAB72

Southern Wild Sisters
250 Cowan Road
GULFPORT, MS 39507
☎ 896 6453
□ Feminist bookshop.

USAB73

Phoenix Books
6 West 39th Street
KANSAS CITY, MO 64111
☎ 816 931 5794
□ Lesbian and gay bookshop with women's studies section.

USAB74

Left Bank Books
399 North Euclid
ST LOUIS, MO
☎ 314 367 6731
□ Feminist bookshop.

USAB75

Common Ground
200 West Centre Street
MANCHESTER, NH 06040
☎ 203 649 9380
□ Women's bookshop.

USAB76

Pandora Book Peddlers
68 West Pallisade Avenue
ENGLEWOOD, NJ 07631
☎ 201 894 5404
□ Feminist bookshop.

USAB77

Full Circle Books
2205 Silver SE
ALBUQUERQUE, NM
☎ 505 266 0022
□ Feminist bookshop.

USAB78

Boulevard Bookshop
15 Central Avenue
ALBANY, NY 12210
☎ 518 436 8848
□ Feminist bookshop.

USAB79

Emma
168 Elmwood
BUFFALO, NY
☎ 716 885 2285
□ Women's bookshop.

USAB80

Smedley's Bookshop
307 West State Street
ITHACA, NY
☎ 607 273 2325
□ Feminist bookshop.

USAB81

Alternatives Corner Bookstore and Women's Community Center
675 Woodfield Road
West Hempstead
LONG ISLAND, NY 11552
☎ 516 483 2050
□ Feminist bookshop and information centre.

USAB82

Black Books Plus
702 Amsterdam Avenue
MANHATTAN, NY
☎ 212 749 9632
□ Black studies bookshop with feminist section.

USAB83

Judith's Room
681 Washington Street
MANHATTAN, NY 10014

☎ 212 727 7330
☐ Lesbian feminist bookshop.

USAB84

Three Lives and Company
354 West 10th Street
MANHATTAN, NY
☎ 212 741 2069
☐ Alternative bookshop with women's section.

USAB85

Dorrwar Bookstore
107 1/2 Hope Street
Providence
RHODE ISLAND, NY
☎ 401 521 3230
☐ Feminist bookshop.

USAB86

Silkwood Books
633 Monroe Avenue
ROCHESTER, NY 14607
☎ 716 473 8110
☐ Feminist bookshop.

USAB87

Wild Seeds Bookstore
704 University Avenue
ROCHESTER, NY 14607
☎ 716 244 9310
☐ Feminist bookshop.

USAB88

My Sister's Words
304 North McBridge Street
SYRACUSE, NY
☎ 315 428 0227
☐ Feminist bookshop.

USAB89

Malaprop's
61 Haywood Street
ASHEVILLE, NC 28801
☎ 704 254 6734
☐ Alternative bookshop with feminist section.

USAB90

Ladyslipper
PO Box 3130
DURHAM, NC 27705
☐ Supplier of women's music. Mail order available.

USAB91

Southern Sisters
411 Morris Street
DURHAM, NC 27701

☎ 919 682 0739
☐ Feminist bookshop.

USAB92

White Rabbit Books
1833 Spring Garden
GREENSBORO, NC
☎ 919 272 7604
☐ Alternative bookshop with feminist section.

USAB93

Cricket's
2824 North Boulevard
RALEIGH, NC
☎ 919 790 0765
☐ Alternative bookshop with feminist section.

USAB94

The Crazy Ladies Bookstore
4039 Hamilton Avenue
CINCINNATI, OH 45223
☎ 513 541 4198
☐ Feminist bookshop.

USAB95

Tomorrow's World
4471 Signal Road
COLUMBIANA, OH
☎ 216 482 2482
☐ Feminist bookshop.

USAB96

Fan the Flames Feminist Bookstore
65 South 4th Street
COLUMBUS, OH 43215
☎ 614 228 0565
☐ Feminist bookshop.

USAB97

Iris Books
1100 North Main Street
DAYTON, OH 45405
☎ 513 228 1534
☐ Feminist bookshop.

USAB98

Herland Sister Resources
2312 NW 39th Street
OKLAHOMA CITY, OK 73112
☎ 405 521 9696
☐ Feminist bookshop.

USAB99

Mother Kali's Books and Records
2001 Franklin Boulevard
EUGENE, OR 97403

☎ 503 343 4864
☐ Feminist book and record shop.

USAB100

Book Gallery
19 West Mechanic Street
NEW HOPE, PA 18938
☎ 215 862 5110
☐ Feminist bookshop.

USAB101

Giovanni's Room
345 South 12th Street
PHILADELPHIA, PA 19107
☎ 215 923 2960
☐ Gay, lesbian and feminist bookshop.

USAB102

Wooden Shoe Books and Records
112 South 20th Street
PHILADELPHIA, PA
☎ 215 569 2477
☐ Alternative bookshop with women's studies section.

USAB103

Gertrude Stein Memorial Bookstore
1003 East Carson Street
PITTSBURGH, PA
☎ 412 431 9666
☐ Feminist bookshop.

USAB104

Woman Vision Books
PO Box 87
SPRINGFIELD, PA 19064
☎ 215 622 2492
☐ Feminist mail order book service.

USAB105

Meristem
930 South Cooper Street
MEMPHIS, TN 38104
☐ Feminist bookshop.

USAB106

The Book Oasis for Women
5604 Meadowcrest Lane
NASHVILLE, TN 37209
☐ Women's bookshop.

USAB107

Charis Books & More
419 Moreland Avenue NE
ATLANTA, TX 30307
☎ 404 542 0304
☐ Feminist bookshop.

USAB108

Book Woman
324 East 6th Street
AUSTIN, TX 78701
☎ 512 472 2785
☐ Feminist bookshop.

USAB109

Celebration
108 West 43rd Street
AUSTIN, TX 78751
☎ 512 453 6207
☐ Alternative bookshop with women's studies section.

USAB110

Liberty Books
1014B North Lamar
AUSTIN, TX
☎ 512 495 9737
☐ Feminist bookshop.

USAB111

Ellie's Garden
2812 34th Street
LUBBOCK, TX 79410
☎ 806 796 0880
☐ Feminist bookshop.

USAB112

A Woman's Place
1615 Foothill Drive
SALT LAKE CITY, UT 84108
☎ 801 583 6431
☐ Feminist bookshop.

USAB113

Everyone's Books
71 Elliot Street
BRATTLEBORO, VT 05301
☎ 802 254 8160
☐ Alternative bookshop with feminist section.

USAB114

Womanstuff
7306 Maple Place
ANNANDALE, VA 22003
☎ 703 256 8383
☐ Feminist bookshop.

USAB115

Out of the Dark
530 Randolph Road
NEWPORT NEWS, VA 23601
☎ 804 596 6220
☐ Feminist bookshop.

USAB116

Bailey/Coy
408 Broadway East
SEATTLE, WA 98102
☎ 206 322 8842
☐ Alternative bookshop with women's studies section.

USAB117

Red and Black Books
432 15th Avenue East
SEATTLE, WA 98112
☎ 206 322 7323
☐ Alternative bookshop with women's studies section.

USAB118

Imprints Bookstore
917 North 2nd Street
TACOMA, WA 98403
☎ 509 383 6322
☐ Feminist bookshop.

USAB119

A Room of Ones's Own
317 West Johnson Street
MADISON, WI 53703
☎ 608 257 7888
☐ Feminist bookshop.

USAB120

People's Bookstore
458 West Gilman Street
MILWAUKEE, WI 53701
☎ 414 251 0576
☐ Alternative bookshop with women's studies section.

USAB121

Grand Books
970 West Broadway
JACKSON, WY 83001
☎ 733 1687
☐ Alternative bookshop with women's studies section.

Libraries, Archives, Resource Centres and Information

USAL1

Archives and Special Collections on Women in Medicine
Medical College of Pennsylvania
3300 Henry Avenue
PHILADELPHIA, PA 19129
☐ Special collections include Black Women's Physicians Project, nineteenth-century textbook collection and college and hospital records of women physicians.

USAL2

Boston Women's Health Collective
47 Nichols Avenue
WATERTOWN, ME 02172
☐ Information service and public reference library.

USAL3

California State University Sacramento Women's Resource Centre
6000 'J' Street
SACRAMENTO, CA 95819
☎ 916 278 7388
☐ Support groups and information service.

USAL4

The Community Feminist Library
304 Stiven House
708 South Mathews
URBANA, IL
☎ 217 333 2990
☐ Feminist library.

USAL5

Connexxus Women's Centre
1017 North Lane Cienega Boulevard
West Hollywood
LOS ANGELES, CA
☎ 213 652 3894
☐ Referrals and information centre.

USAL6

International Centre for Research on Women
Suite 501
1717 Massachusetts Avenue NW
WASHINGTON, DC 20036
☐ Provides services to development agencies to assist evaluation of projects that encourage women's participation. Library.

USAL7

June L. Mazer Collection
3271 North Raymond Avenue
ALTADENA 91001, CA
☎ 818 791 4561
☐ Lesbian archives.

USAL8

Lesbian Herstory Archives
Lesbian Herstory Educational Foundation
PO Box 1258
NEW YORK CITY, NY 10016
☐ Past and present records of lesbian lives.

USAL9

National Archives for Black Women's History
1318 Vermont Avenue
WASHINGTON, DC 20005
☐ Special collections, material on black women's studies and the records of the National Council of Negro Women.

USAL10

National Museum of Women in the Arts
801 13th Street NW
WASHINGTON, DC
☎ 202 783 5000
☐ Museum of women in the arts.

USAL11

National Women's Hall of Fame
76 Fall Street
SENECA FALLS, NY 13148
☎ 315 568 2936
☐ Women's museum and archive.

USAL12

National Women's History Project
Box 3716
SANTA ROSA, CA 95402
☐ Provides consultation, information and referral services.

USAL13

New Alexandria Lesbian Library
Box 402
FLORENCE, MA 01060
☐ Lesbian books, periodicals, videos, etc. Research assistance.

USAL14

Peoples Translation Service
4228 Telegraph Avenue
OAKLAND, CA 94609
☐ Aims to unite the global women's movement. Provides library, research and documentation services.

USAL15

Schlesinger Library
Radcliffe College
10 Garden Street
CAMBRIDGE, ME 02138
☎ 617 495 8647
☐ The history of women in America.

USAL16

Sophia Smith Collection
Smith College Library
NORTHAMPTON, ME
☐ Contemporary and historical collection.

USAL17

Women in International Development
202 International Centre
Michigan State University
EAST LANSING, MI 48824
☐ Library, consultancy services, research and speakers. Disseminates work dealing with the lives of women in Third World countries.

USAL18

Women and International Development
Research and Information Centre
University of Minnesota
MINNEAPOLIS, MN
☐ Information on women and development.

USAL19

Women's Action Alliance
370 Lexington Avenue
NEW YORK CITY, NY 10017
☐ Information and resource centre for women and women's groups.

USAL20

Women's Bureau
Office of the Secretary
US Department of Labor
200 Constitution Avenue NW
WASHINGTON, DC 20210
☐ Government agency producing publications on women's work and related issues.

USAL21

Women's International Resource Exchange
Room 570
475 Riverside Drive
NEW YORK CITY, NY 10115
☐ Distribution and evaluation centre for materials on women in the Third World and Third World women in the USA.

USAL22

Women's Library
PO Box 3220
632 West Dickson Street
FAYETTEVILLE, AR 72702
☐ Women's library available by appointment.

USAL23

The Women's Project
2224 Main Street
LITTLE ROCK, AR 72206
☐ Lending library and community-based projects.

Women's Organisations

USAO1

African American Women in Defense of Ourselves
Suite 199
317 South Division Street
ANN ARBOR, MI 48104
☐ Organisation opposed to the election of Clarence Thomas as Associate Justice of the US Supreme Court.

USAO2

Alliance Against Women's Oppression
The Women's Building
3543 18th Street
Box 1
SAN FRANCISCO, CA 94110
☐ Socialist feminist organisation which focuses on women's issues from an anti-imperialist, anti-racist perspective.

USAO3

Alliance of Women in Architecture
PO Box 5136
FDR Station
NEW YORK, NY 10022
☐ Professional association of women architects.

USAO4

American Association of University Women
2401 Virginia Avenue NW
WASHINGTON, DC 20037
☎ 202 728 7603
☐ National federation of university women.

USAO5

American Medical Women's Association
465 Grand Street
NEW YORK, NY 10002
☐ Supports and promotes women doctors and medical students.

USAO6

Association for Women in Development
PO Box 66133
WASHINGTON, DC 20035
☐ Networks between scholars, development workers and policy-makers, and aims to increase women's participation in development.

USAO7

Association for Women in Psychology
Graduate Center Room 609
33 West 42nd Street
NEW YORK CITY, NY 10036
☐ Campaigning for equal opportunities for feminist academics in psychology.

USAO8

Association of Women in Science
Suite 303
3401 Virginia Avenue NW
WASHINGTON, DC 20037
☐ Campaigns to improve the employment and educational opportunities for women in all scientific areas. Also publishes resource materials.

USAO9

Boston Women's Health Book Collective
47 Nichols Avenue
WATERTOWN, ME 02172
☐ Aims to improve health care for women and to assist women to make informed choices about health care. Publishes wide-selling books on women's health care.

USAO10

Catalyst
250 Park Avenue South
NEW YORK CITY, NY 10003
☐ Provides documentation for women and work, and also offers careers advice to women and campaigns to improve the status of women in the workplace.

USAO11

Center for the American Woman
Eagleton Institute of Politics
Rutgers University
NEW BRUNSWICK, NJ 08901
☎ 201 828 2210
☐ Distributes and develops information about women in politics and public life.

USAO12

Center for Women and Religion
Graduate Theological Union
2400 Ridge Road
BERKELEY, CA 94709
☐ Campaigns for equality and justice in and through religion.

USAO13

Center for Women Policy Studies
Suite 508
2000 P St NW
WASHINGTON, DC 20036
☎ 202 872 1770
☐ Conducts policy research and campaigns for change in the legal, political and social status of women.

USAO14

Committee on Women in Asian Countries
　　Association for Asian Studies
　　University of Minnesota
　　MINNEAPOLIS, MN 55455
☐ Promotes research on women and networks for women in Asian studies.

USAO15

Desert Women's Association
　　PO Box 718
　　Cathedral City
　　PALM SPRINGS, CA 92235
☐ Campaigning group on women's issues.

USAO16

Feminist Futures International Network
(See International section)

USAO17

International Black Women's Congress
(See International section)

USAO18

International Council of African Women
(See International section)

USAO19

International Council on Women's Health Issues
(See International section)

USAO20

International Federation of Women Lawyers
(See International section)

USAO21

International Women's Rights Action Watch
(See International section)

USAO22

International Women's Writing Guild
(See International section)

USAO23

Lucy Stone League
　　Box 4K, 303 Lexington Avenue
　　NEW YORK CITY, NY 10016
☐ Feminist organisation which supports research and libraries on the status of women.

USAO24

National Association of Women Lawyers
　　7th Floor, 750 North Lake Shore Drive
　　CHICAGO, IL 60611
☐ Association for women working in the legal profession.

USAO25

National Coalition Against Domestic Violence
　　Suite 305
　　2401 Virginia Avenue NW
　　WASHINGTON, DC 20037
☐ Radical umbrella group for women's shelters in the USA. Also has individual members.

USAO26

National Council for Research on Women (NCRW)
　　5th Floor, Sara Delano Roosevelt Memorial House
　　47–49 East 65th Street
　　NEW YORK CITY, NY 10021
☐ A feminist network between research centres which also produces collaborative research.

USAO27

National Council of Women of the USA
　　777 United Nations Plaza
　　NEW YORK, NY 10017
☐ Umbrella organisation.

USAO28

National Institute for Women of Colour
　　Suite 104
　　1400 20th Street NW
　　WASHINGTON, DC 20036
☐ Promotes educational and economic equality for women of colour.

USAO29

National Organisation for Women (NOW)
　　Suite 800
　　1401 New York Avenue NW
　　WASHINGTON, DC 20005
☎　202 347 2279
☐ Campaigns on a wide range of political and social issues.

USAO30

National Women's Health Network
　　224 7th Street SE
　　WASHINGTON, DC 20003
☎　202 543 9222
☐ Feminist network and campaigning group of organisations and individuals concerned with women's health.

USAO31

National Women's Party
　　Sewall-Belmont House
　　144 Constitution Avenue NE
　　WASHINGTON, DC 20002
☐ Campaigns and lobbies on equal rights for women.

USAO32

National Women's Studies Association
University of Maryland
COLLEGE PARK, MD 20742–1325
☎ 301 405 5573
☐ National network for women's studies.

USAO33

Organization for Research on Women and Communication
c/o Department of Speech Communication
Humboldt State University
ARCATA, CA 95521
☐ Network for women researching gender and communication.

USAO34

Project on Equal Education Rights
9th Floor
1413 K Street NW
WASHINGTON, DC 20005
☐ Feminist organisation working for educational equality in schools.

USAO35

Self-Employed Women's Association India (Video SEWA)
Village Video Network Secretariat
c/o Martha Stewart Communications
147 West 22nd Street
NEW YORK CITY, NY 10011
☎ 212 255 2718
☐ Video co-operative providing media training as a tool for political organising for women's rights.

USAO36

Society of Women Engineers
354 East 47th Street
NEW YORK, NY 10017
☐ Organisation for professional women engineers.

USAO37

Sociologists for Women in Society
830 Sprowl Road
BRYN MAWR, PA 19010
☐ National organisation of student and academic sociologists concerned with anti-discrimination.

USAO38

United Nations Development Fund for Women
(See International section)

USAO39

US–Japan Women's Centre
926 Bautista Court
PALO ALTO, CA 94303
☎ 415 857 9049

USAO40

University of Southern Maine Women's Forum
94 Bedford Street
PORTLAND, ME 04103
☎ 503 780 4085
☐ Feminist group with a variety of political and social activities.

USAO41

Wai'anae Women's Support Group
Women's Studies Program
University of Hawaii
HONOLULU, HI
☐ International networking.

USAO42

Women and Food Information Network
24 Peabody Terrace #1403
CAMBRIDGE, MA 02138
☐ Researchers interested in women's role in world food production.

USAO43

Women in the Arts Foundation
Room 200
325 Spring Street
NEW YORK CITY, NY 10013
☐ Women in the arts organisation.

USAO44

Women Library Workers
c/o Women's Resource Centre
Room 100 T–9
University of California
BERKELEY, CA 94720
☐ Professional association of women library workers.

USAO45

Women's Caucus for Art
Moore College of Art
20th and the Parkway
PHILADELPHIA, PA 19103
☐ Promotes equality of opportunity within the arts and has groups throughout the country.

USAO46

Women's History Network
Box 3716
SANTA ROSA, CA 95402

☐ Networking between groups and individuals concerned with women's history in the USA.

USAO47
Women's Institute for Freedom of the Press
    3306 Ross Place NW
    WASHINGTON, DC 20008
☐ Network for women working in the media. Organises conferences and research.

USAO48
Women's International League for Peace and Freedom
    1213 Race Street
    PHILADELPHIA, PA 19107
☎   215 563 7110
☐ US umbrella group of worldwide organisations working for peace and disarmament.

USAO49
Women's International Network
    187 Grant Street
    LEXINGTON, MA 02173
☐ Feminist worldwide networking organisation.

USAO50
Women's International Public Health Network
    7100 Oak Forest Lane
    BETHESDA, MD 20817
☐ Worldwide network for women working in public health.

USAO51
Women's Law Project
    Suite 1012
    112 South 16th Street
    PHILADELPHIA, PA 19102
☐ Supports women in court with cases concerning women's rights.

USAO52
Women's Legal Defense Fund
    Suite 400
    2000 P Street NW
    WASHINGTON, DC 20036
☐ Provides advocacy and legal action for women, especially in areas of employment and family law.

Uruguay

Women's Organisations

URUO1
Group for the Study of Women in Uruguay
    Juan Pamillier 1174
    MONTEVIDEO

☐ Organisation studying women in Uruguay.

Venezuela

Women's Organisations

VENO1
The Bad Life
    Res. La Colina
    Apt. 13, Avda. La Colina
    Las Acacias
    CARACAS 104
☐ Campaigns for change in women's position, produces a magazine and runs debates, conferences and workshops.

VENO2
Maracaibo Feminist League (LIFEM)
    Apartado 30
    MARACAIBO
☎   061 75833
☐ Feminist campaigning group.

VENO3
Movimientode Mujeres de Merida
    Apartado 0101
    Residencias Domingo Salazar
    Santa Ana
    MERIDA
☐ Merida women's group.

Zimbabwe

Libraries, Archives, Resource Centres and Information

ZIML1
Zimbabwe Women's Resource Centre and Network
    Suite 203, Stemar House
    Speke Avenue/Kaguvi Street
    HARARE
☐ Library and information centre. Networking and campaigning group for women in development and gender issues.

Women's Organisations

ZIMO1
Federation of African Media Women
    c/o Zimbabwe Inter-Africa News Agency
    PO Box 8166
    Causeway
    HARARE

☐ Monitors women in the media and provides training for women in media skills.

ZIMO2

Women's Action Group
PO Box 135
HARARE
☐ Women's campaigning group

ZIMO3

Zimbabwean Women in Contemporary Culture Trust
1 Shillingford Close
Ballantyne Park
PO Chisipite
HARARE

International

INT1

African Training and Research Centre for Women
UN Economic Commission for Africa
PO Box 3001
ADDIS ABABA
Ethiopia
☐ Conducts research and training, and promotes women in development.

INT2

African Women Link
PO Box 50795
NAIROBI
Kenya
☐ Networks between individuals, organisations and agencies working in development in Africa.

INT3

Arab Women's Solidarity Association
25 Murad Street
GIZA
Egypt
☐ Promotes the status of Arab women.

INT4

Asian and Pacific Centre for Women and Development
c/o APCD PO Box 2224
KUALA LUMPUR
Malaysia
☐ Encourages research and training.

INT5

Asian Women's Institute
c/o Association of Kinnaird College for Women
LAHORE 3
Pakistan
☐ Networking for equal opportunities and improving women's status in Asia. Carries out research and courses in women's studies.

INT6

Associated Countrywomen of the World
50 Warwick Square
LONDON SW1V 2AJ
England
☐ Worldwide membership working for training and development for women.

INT7

Association of African Women for Research and Development
BP 3304
DAKAR
Senegal
☎ 23 02 11
☐ Network of African women researchers and development workers.

INT8

Caribbean Association for Feminist Research and Action
PO Bag 442
Tunapuna Post Office
TUNAPUNA
Trinidad and Tobago
☐ Communication network between feminist organisations and individual members. Conducts research.

INT9

Caribbean Women's Association
PO Box 49
BASSETERRE
St Kitts
☐ Represents women's organisations in 13 Caribbean countries.

INT10

Centre for Research on European Women
38 rue Stevin
1040 BRUSSELS
Belgium
☎ 02 230 51 58
☐ Research and consultancy services to international organisations.

INT11

Change
> PO Box 824
> LONDON SE24 9JS
> England
☎ 071 277 6187
☐ Researches and publishes reports on the condition and status of women worldwide.

INT12

Committee for Asian Women
> CCA–URA, 57 Peking Road
> 5/f KOWLOON
> Hong Kong
☐ Co-ordinates endeavours throughout Asia to improve women's working conditions.

INT13

Commonwealth Secretariat – Women and Development Programme
> Marlborough House
> Pall Mall
> LONDON SW1Y 5HX
> England
☎ 071 839 3411
☐ Promotes the interests of women in the Commonwealth through education, research and training.

INT14

Co-ordinator for Nordic Women's Studies
> Solveig Berman
> Åbo Akademi University
> Institute for Women's Studies
> 20500 ÅBO
> Finland
☎ 21 654 813

INT15

DAWN, Development Alternatives with Women for a New Era
> Rua Paulino Fernandez 32
> Botofogo
> 22270 RIO DE JANEIRO
> Brazil
☎ 021 246 1830
☐ International organisation supporting women's Third World development projects.

INT16

ENDA Third World
> BP 3370
> DAKAR
> Senegal
☎ 21 60 27
☐ International organisation with affiliates in India, Morocco, Mauritius, Zimbabwe, Dominican Republic

and Colombia. Works with grassroots groups concerned with women's issues and income-generating projects.

INT17

European Association Against Sexual Harassment at Work
> 71 rue St Jaques
> 75005 PARIS
> France
☎ 46 28 74 08
☐ Campaigns against violence to women at work.

INT18

European Network of Women
> 38 rue Stevin
> 1040 BRUSSELS
> Belgium
☎ 02 230 51 58
☐ Pressure group monitoring the impact of EC legislation on women.

INT19

European Network of Women's Studies
> Ministry of Education and Science
> Postbus 25000
> 2700 LZ ZOETERMEER
> The Netherlands
☎ 079 53 38 85/079 53 37 70
☐ A network for scientific and technical co-operation. Supports research in women's studies and provides postgraduate training.

INT20

European Women in Mathematics
> National Heart and Lung Institute
> Dovehouse Street
> LONDON SW3 6LY
> England
☐ European network of women in mathematics.

INT21

European Women's Lobby
> 1a Place Quetelet
> 1030 BRUSSELS
> Belgium
☎ 02 217 9020
☐ Women's lobbying group for the European Parliament. Promotes women into decision-making posts.

INT22

Federation of African Media Women
> c/o Zimbabwe Inter-Africa News Agency
> PO Box 8166
> Cuaseway
> HARARE
> Zimbabwe

☐ Monitors women in the media and provides training for women in media skills.

INT23

Feminist Futures International Network
Institute for Women and the Future
PO Box 1081
NORTHAMPTON, ME 01061
USA

☐ Network for women in diverse concerns about the environment.

INT24

Institute for Women's Studies in the Arab World
Beirut University College
PO Box 13
5053 BEIRUT
Lebanon
☎ 811968

☐ Research and resource centre.

INT25

International Alliance of Women
President's Office
PO Box 355
VALETTA
Malta

☐ Organisation with worldwide affiliated groups working for improvement in women's equal rights status.

INT26

International Association of Women in Radio and Television
43 Gainsborough Street
SUDBURY CO10 6EU
England

☐ Holds conferences and networks between women. Index of women willing to work in Third World broadcasting projects.

INT27

International Black Women's Congress
Suite 200
1081 Bergen Street
NEWARK, NJ 07112
USA

☐ Organisation for support and socio-economic development for women of African descent. Organises regional and international workshops and conferences.

INT28

International Centre for Research on Women
Suite 501
1717 Massachusetts Avenue NW
WASHINGTON, DC 20036
USA

☐ Provides services to development agencies to assist evaluation of projects that encourage women's participation. Conducts research and runs education programmes in the USA and abroad. Library.

INT29

International Committee for Prostitutes' Rights
Postbus 725
1000 AS AMSTERDAM
The Netherlands

☐ Worldwide campaign for rights of prostitutes.

INT30

International Council of African Women
PO Box 55076
WASHINGTON, DC 20011
USA

☐ Network of African women working with women of colour internationally.

INT31

International Council of Women
13 rue Caumartin
75009 PARIS
France
☎ 47 42 19 40

☐ Central organisation for women's councils in 75 countries. Conducts research and brings together women's voluntary organisations. Books, literature and reports.

INT32

International Council on Women's Health Issues
c/o The College of Nursing
University of S Florida
Box 22
12901 Bruce D. Downs Boulevard
TAMPA, FL 33612
USA

☐ Information and network for health care professionals interested in health care for women worldwide.

INT33

International Federation of University Women
37 Quai Wilson
GENEVA 1201
Switzerland
☎ 022 31 23 80

☐ Promotes friendship and understanding among university women in 51 national federations. Conducts research, organises conferences and has small scholarship fund.

INT34

International Federation of Women Lawyers
186 Fifth Avenue
NEW YORK CITY, NY 10010
USA
☐ Individual and affiliated members in 70 countries. Promotes the principles of the United Nations and the welfare of women and children.

INT35

International Information and Archives Centre for the Women's Movement
Keizersgracht 10
1015 CN AMSTERDAM
The Netherlands
☎ 020 624 42 68
☐ Large collection of books, archival material, periodicals and photographs on the women's movement. Quarterly review of newly catalogued books.

INT36

International Lesbian Information Service
COC. Rosenstraat 8
1016 NX AMSTERDAM
The Netherlands
☐ Lesbian international network.

INT37

International Network of Women in the Arts
KIK. Niels Henningsengade 8
2nd Floor
1153 COPENHAGEN
Denmark
☐ Worldwide network of women working in the arts.

INT38

International Organisation for Women in Mathematics Education
Ontario Institute for Studies in Education
252 Bloor Street West
Toronto
ONTARIO M5S 1V6
Canada
☐ Aims to further research into gender and mathematics, and increase the participation of girls in mathematics. Worldwide membership.

INT39

International Union of Women Architects
14 rue Durmont d'Urville
75116 PARIS
France
☐ Professional association of women architects.

INT40

International Women's Rights Action Watch
Humphrey Institute of Public Affairs
301 19th Avenue South
University of Minnesota
MINNEAPOLIS, MN 55455
USA
☎ 612 625 2505
☐ Monitors women's rights worldwide.

INT41

International Women's Writing Guild
PO Box 810
Gracie Station
NEW YORK CITY, NY 10028
USA
☐ Supportive network for women writers.

INT42

Isis International
Via San Saba 5
00153 ROME
Italy
Isis International
Casilla 2067
Correo Central
SANTIAGO
Chile
Isis International
85–A East Maya Street
Philamlife Homes
1104 QUEZON CITY
Philippines
☎ 632 993292
☐ Aims to eliminate sex discrimination and to improve women's social, economic and political position. Worldwide information and communication services with offices in Italy, the Philippines and Chile.

INT43

Isis Women's International Cross-Cultural Exchange (ISIS–WICCE)
3 chemin des Campanules
GENEVA 1219
Switzerland
☎ 022 796 44 37
☐ An international women's resource centre. Extensive network with annual cultural exchanges around changing themes.

INT44

MATCH International Centre
205–200 Elgin Street
Ottawa
ONTARIO K2P 1L5
Canada
☐ Funds women's projects in Third World countries, and supports women's groups to organise supportive links with Third World women.

INT45

Medical Women's International Association
Weihburggasse 10–12
1010 VIENNA
Austria
☐ International affiliated and individual members. Aims to unite medical women worldwide.

INT46

Mediterranean Women's Studies Institute (KEGME)
192BL. Alexandras
11545 ATHENS
Greece
☎ 3615660
☐ Information and documentation centre. Researches and teaches the position of Mediterranean women.

INT47

Pacific and Asian Women's Forum
4 Bhagwandas Road
NEW DELHI 110001
India
☐ Network of women activists in Asia and the Pacific. Provides research and consultancy services.

INT48

Pacific Women's Resource Bureau
South Pacific Commission
PO Box D5
NOUMEA
New Caledonia
☐ Resources and information for women in the South Pacific.

INT49

Regional Information Network on Arab Women
Social Research Centre
American University of Cairo
PO Box 2511
113 Sharia Kasr-el-Aini
CAIRO
Egypt
☐ Information centre.

INT50

Reseau Femmes et Developpement
15–21 rue de l'Ecole de Médecine
75005 PARIS
France
☐ Women's and development organisations network in France and the Third World.

INT51

Third World Movement Against the Exploitation of Women
PO Box 1434
2800 MANILA
Philippines
☐ Network for women's organisations and individuals. Data bank on women's resources.

INT52

United Nations Branch for the Advancement of Women
Centre for Social Development and Humanitarian Affairs
Room E–1283, Vienna International Centre
PO Box 500
1400 VIENNA
Austria
☐ Worldwide publications and information.

INT53

United Nations Development Fund for Women
304 East 45th Street
11th Floor
NEW YORK CITY, NY 10017
USA
☐ Aims to ensure that women are included in and benefit from development.

INT54

United Nations International Research and Training Institute for the Advancement of Women (INSTRAW)
Calle Cesar Nicolas Penson 102 A
Apartado Postal 21747
SANTO DOMINGO
Dominican Republic
INSTRAW
PO Box 52–4121
MIAMI, FL 33152
USA
INSTRAW
Room DC1–1106
United Nations
NEW YORK CITY, NY 10017
USA
☎ 212 963 5684
☐ Research and evaluation on women's participation in development.

INT55

University Women of Europe
71 Waalsdorperweg
2597 HR THE HAGUE
The Netherlands
☐ Campaigns to improve women's education and status. Aids development of affiliated societies in European countries.

INT56

Womankind
122 Whitechapel Street
LONDON E1 7PT
England
☎ 071 247 9431
☐ Development agency which finances and supports women's enterprises in the Third World.

INT57

Women in International Development
202 International Centre
Michigan State University
EAST LANSING, MI 48824
USA
☐ Disseminates work dealing with the lives of women in Third World countries. Library, consultancy, research and speakers.

INT58

Women of the World – Office for Inter-cultural Education and Encounter
Warendorferstrasse 6
5000 COLOGNE 91
Germany
☎ 0221 896977
☐ Worldwide women's networking with emphasis on links with Third World women.

INT59

Women's Global Network on Reproductive Rights
Nieuwe Zijds
Voorburgwal 32
1012 RZ AMSTERDAM
The Netherlands
☐ International network of organisations working to secure women's control over their own fertility.

INT60

Women's Information Service of the Commission of the European Communities
200 rue de la Loi
1049 BRUSSELS
Belgium
☎ 02 235 28 60
☐ Information service about women in the European Community.

INT61

Women's International Democratic Federation
Unter den Linden 13
1080 BERLIN
Germany
☐ Eastern European women's federation, uniting women in Eastern Europe and the Third World.

INT62

Women's International League for Peace and Freedom
1 rue de Varembe
CP 28
GENEVA 1211
Switzerland
☐ Central organisation for worldwide movement of affiliated organisations and individuals. Aims to bring women together to achieve peace and disarmament.

INT63

Women's International Network
187 Grant Street
LEXINGTON, MA 02173
USA
☐ Worldwide women's communication network supporting development and equality. Speakers and research and consultancy services.

INT64

Women's International Resource Centre
173 Archway Road
LONDON N6 5BL
England
☐ Resource and information centre with worldwide links with women's groups.

INT65

Women's International Resource Exchange
475 Riverside Drive
Room 570
NEW YORK CITY, NY 10115
USA
☐ Distribution and evaluation centre for materials on women in the Third World and Third World women in the USA.

INT66

Women's International Studies Europe (WISE)
Institute for England and Amsterdam
Johann Wolfgang Goethe-Universitat
Kettenhofweg 130
6000 FRANKFURT AM MAIN 60
Germany
WISE
University of Utrecht
Heidelberglaan 2
3584 CS UTRECHT

☎   030 531881
☐ Women's studies exchange network.

INT67

Women's Research and Documentation Unit
University of Ibadan
Institute of African Studies
IBADAN
Nigeria
☐ Documentation centre. National and international network and focus for women's studies.

INT68

World Association of Women Journalists and Writers
3945 Boulevard St Martin Quest
Chomedey
Laval
QUEBEC H7T 1B7
Canada
☐ World network of women journalists.

4 | *Publications: Journals, Magazines, Dictionaries and Handbooks*

Introduction

It has been astonishing and very exciting to discover that one of my strongest beliefs about the second wave of feminism has been confounded, namely that only white, middle-class women have had the time, financial resources and inclination to engage with it. My researches have uncovered an enormous amount of women-centred journals and magazines (periodicals) currently existing in over 80 countries throughout the world. These have been created by women with very differing cultures, ideologies and relationships, engaging in economic activities in many different ways, who nevertheless find common ground in their beliefs that women should be prioritised and given a voice, recognition and validity, through publications devoted to issues which are relevant to women.

There are some journals and magazines which I have labelled 'not only for women', indicating they are intended for both sexes. Most of these are intended for lesbians and gay men who, in North America in particular, have found it appropriate, powerful and financially viable to unite to obtain recognition, basic civil rights and equal opportunities.

I make no apology for the fact that at least two-thirds of the listings are from the USA. All information about women-centred/feminist/women's studies periodicals is good news. Because most of the information obtained comes from one country, this does not invalidate my findings. Rather, what is needed is more information from other countries, not less from the USA. Please write with news about the many journals and magazines that have been omitted, and they will be included in the next edition of *WISH*.

I would like to apologise publicly for the amount of disturbance I caused in the Feminist and Fawcett libraries in London as I grunted and rumbled around with endless boxes of periodicals, like a pig hunting for truffles – in particular to the woman who received a nasty bump on the head from a box I dropped from a top shelf directly above where she was sitting. I am sorry for the annoyance and any bruises caused. A man would have taken me to court for damage to his person and my carelessness; the woman, however, only smiled – rather wanly, it is true. What it is to be a woman.

The way I have distinguished between journals and magazines is by cover. To my way of thinking, a journal almost always has a hard-backed cover, while a magazine's cover is flimsy, and a journal usually, but not always, is smaller in page size than a magazine. Hence the difference between, say, *Everywoman* (a magazine) and *Feminist Review* (a journal). The difficulty comes when a magazine, according to my methods of classification, describes itself as a journal – *Manushi*, for instance. Then some magazines are in fact newspapers, such as the wonderful and vital *Off Our Backs*. Not to have included *OOB* would have been insane. And some periodicals which call themselves newsletters are in fact magazines ... Probably I should have compiled a list of periodicals without distinction which would have done away with the confusion, but my brief was to distinguish between journals and magazines.

Very sadly I have not been allowed the space, and have not had the time, to include listings of the very many thousands of vitally important newsletters that are currently being circulated. Newsletters are probably the most important of all women-centred publications. They indicate the need for a voice and the ideas of women who feel strongly enough to commit a great deal of energy, time and sometimes money they can ill afford to produce small documents to share their thoughts with other women. I hope very much that a worldwide listing of newsletters will be made in the future.

How to use this section

Each periodical is listed in alphabetical order within its country of origin. The address follows and every effort has been made to include a telephone number. The telephone numbers are listed according to area and local codes only; country codes have been omitted. I have given prices, but please note that these tend to rise very rapidly and that by the time this book is published there may be a number of periodicals which cost more than stated. It is always best to check first by writing or phoning before sending off a cheque.

I have listed the date when first published wherever possible, and the number of issues of each publication published each year. Also, I have attempted to place each entry into categories (for example, radical feminism, socialism, philosophy, equal opportunities, civil rights), and have included, where possible, some short notes about the publication, what it contains and its focus.

There is a small section listing dictionaries and a larger listing of handbooks, which comprises a selection of classic texts, bibliographies and up-to-date directories. Every effort has been taken to ensure easy access to publications. Thus, where the publisher has merged with another publisher since publication of the handbook, I have listed the most recent address.

I hope you find the information provided exciting, valuable and worthwhile searching for.

Acknowledgements

I have received a lot of help from many women all over the world, and want to thank them all. I would like to acknowledge the following for their special contributions to this compilation: Janette Norton, Rebecca Norton and Linda Shult. I also want to mention Frances Austin, Solveig Bergman, Sarah Carter, Gail Chester, Ann Deutsch, Monica Sjöö, Debbie Perez, Valsa Verghese and Hiroko Yamamoto. There are also three men whom I would like to thank very much: Bradley Brown, David Doughan and Angus Norton.

The following organisations have been particularly helpful: KVINFO in Denmark, IIAV in the Netherlands and Isis-WICCE in Switzerland.

I looked at an enormous number of publications and would like to acknowledge the following which I found particularly helpful when engaged in my research: *Canadian Feminist Periodicals/Periodiques Feministes du Canada* (1988); *Directory of Alternative & Radical Publications* (1991–2 edition); *Directory of Periodicals: Feminist, lesbian and gay magazines, newspapers and letters* (1992); *Feminist Collections: A quarterly of women's studies resources* (No. 4, Vol. 13, summer 1992); *Feminist Periodicals 1855–1984: An annotated critical bibliography of British, Irish, Commonwealth and international titles*, by David Doughan and Denise Sanchez; *The International Guide to Lesbian and Feminist Periodicals: A current listing of contents* (No. 2, Vol. 12, summer 1992); *Ms* (July/August 1992); *The Radical Bookseller Directory* (1992), edited by Fergus Nicol; *RFD/DRF* (Nos 1/2, Vol. 20, 1992); *Ulrich's International Periodicals Directory* (1991–2 and 1992–3 editions); *WLW Journal* (No. 14, Vol. 4, summer 1991); and *Women's Studies: A guide to information sources*, by Sarah Carter and Maureen Ritchie (1990).

Loulou Brown
London
May 1993

Journals

Australia

AUSJO1

Arena: A Marxist journal of criticism and discussion (Socialism)
Arena Publications Association
PO Box 18
NORTH CARLTON, Vic. 3054
☎ 03 489 9244
Subscriptions: AUS$28.00
Pub. frequency: quarterly
☐ First published 1963. Analyses of the media, popular culture, technological change, nuclear politics, feminist theory, the world economic crisis and regional politics.

AUSJO2

Australian Feminist Studies
(Social sciences/Methodology)
Research Centre for Women's Studies
University of Adelaide
PO Box 498
ADELAIDE, SA 5001
☎ 08 228 5267
Contact: Susan Margarey
Price: AUS$19.95
Subscriptions: AUS$43.00
Pub. frequency: half-yearly
☐ First published 1979. Academic articles, book reviews, discussion papers. Themes in 'the fields of feminist research and women's studies courses'. Some issues are devoted to special topics.

AUSJO3

Australian Woman's Book Review (Media/Literature)
34 Godfrey Avenue
ST KILDA EAST, Vic. 3183
Price: AUS$3.99
Subscriptions: AUS$10.00
☐ A review of women's books. Each issue contains at least one feature as well as reviews.

AUSJO4

Hecate: A woman's interdisciplinary journal
(Socialism)
PO Box 99
St Lucia
BRISBANE, Qld 4067
☎ 07 377 4401
Contact: Carole Ferrier
Price: AUS$6.00
Subscriptions: AUS$15.00
Pub. frequency: half-yearly
☐ First published 1975. The journal includes creative writing, illustrations, reviews and historical and critical articles. It is 'interested in contributions which employ a feminist, Marxist, or other radical methodology'.

AUSJO5

Journal of Australian Lesbian Feminist Studies (Lesbian/Culture)
Lesbian Studies and Research Group
PO Box 364
GLEBE, NSW 2037
Price: AUS$8.00
Subscriptions: AUS$16.00
Pub. frequency: half-yearly
☐ First published 1991. 'This journal is here because we felt the lack of a forum for developing lesbian feminist theory.' Articles about the politics and cultures of lesbianism. Book reviews.

AUSJO6

Lilith: A feminist history journal (History)
PO Box 154
Fitzroy
MELBOURNE, Vic. 3065
☐ Historical articles and reviews with a feminist focus.

AUSJO7

Women and Work (Paid work)
Dept of Employment and Industrial Relations
Australian Government Publication Service
Department GPO
PO Box 84
CANBERRA, ACT 2601
Price: free
Pub. frequency: quarterly
☐ First published 1977.

Austria

AUJO1

Frauensolidarität (Civil rights/Literature)
Weygrasse 5
1030 VIENNA
Price: s0.40
Subscriptions: s160.00
Pub. frequency: quarterly
☐ Focuses on women in Third World countries and feminist literature.

AUJO2

l'Homme: Zeitschrift für feministische Geschichtswissenschaft (General)
Bohlau Verlag Ges.
Sachesenplatz 4–6
1201 VIENNA
Contact: Eva Barilich

Subscriptions: DM56.00
Pub. frequency: three per annum
☐ First published 1990. Articles.

Belgium

BELJO1

Femmes d'Europe/Women of Europe   (Equal opportunities/Civil rights)
>   Commission of European Communities
>   200 rue de la Loi
>   1049 BRUSSELS
☎   02 235 97 72
Price: free
Pub. frequency: six per annum
☐ First published 1977. Commissioned by the European Community. Articles on women's rights, civil rights, equal opportunities and women in developing countries. The text is in French.

BELJO2

Open Door International for the Emancipation of the Woman Worker   (Equal opportunities/Civil rights)
>   Open Door International
>   16 rue Americain
>   1050 BRUSSELS
Price: free
Pub. frequency: irregular
☐ First published 1929.

BELJO3

Supplements of Women of Europe
(International/General)
>   Commission of European Communities
>   Directorate General of Information
>   200 rue de la Loi
>   1049 BRUSSELS
☎   02 239 94 11
Price: free
Pub. frequency: irregular
☐ First published 1977. Contains news and information about activities and women in European countries. Published in twelve languages. Specific topics as well as general information.

BELJO4

Université des Femmes   (Education)
>   1a Place Quetelet
>   1030 BRUSSELS
☎   02 219 61 07
☐ A women's studies journal.

Canada

CANJO1

Amazons d'Hier, Lesbiennes d'Aujourd'hui
(Lesbian/Politics)
>   PO Box 1721
>   Station Place du Parc
>   Montreal
>   QUEBEC H2W 2R7
☎   514 849 3061
Contact: Louise Turcotte
Pub. frequency: three per annum.
☐ First published 1982. Published in French only. A national and international journal for lesbians.

CANJO2

Annual Report/Report Annuel/Canadian Advisory Council on Women   (General)
>   110 O'Connor Street
>   9th Floor
>   PO Box 1541
>   Station 'B' Ottawa
>   ONTARIO K1P 5R5
☎   613 992 4975
Price: free
Pub. frequency: annual
☐ First published 1973. Provides an analysis of women's issues. The English and French editions are contained in one issue.

CANJO3

Atlantis: A women's studies journal/Revue d'études sur la femme   (General)
>   Mount Saint Vincent University
>   166 Bedford Highway
>   Halifax
>   NOVA SCOTIA B3M 2J6
☎   902 443 4450
Contact: Susan Clark
Price: CAN$10.00
Subscriptions: CAN$20.00
Pub. frequency: half-yearly
☐ First published 1975. Text in English and French. Articles, book reviews, poetry, photography, illustrations. Special issues. 'An interdisciplinary journal devoted to critical and creative writing on . . . women.'

CANJO4

Canadian Journal of Feminist Ethics
(Philosophy)
>   Department of English
>   Concordia University
>   1455 de Maisonneuve Bd W
>   Montreal
>   QUEBEC H3G 1M8
☎   514 931 8992
Contact: Kathleen Martindale

☐ First published 1986. A journal for the academic, political and feminist community about feminist ethics. In English only.

CANJO5

Canadian Journal of Women and the Law/Revue Femmes et Droit   (Law)
National Association of Women and the Law
575 King Edward Avenue
Ottawa
ONTARIO K1N 6N5
☎ 613 238 1545
Contact: Elizabeth Sheehy
Subscriptions: CAN$42.80
Pub. frequency: half-yearly
☐ First published 1985. Bilingual journal. To 'establish a feminist forum for publication of discussion and debate of issues that concern women and law'. The text is in both French and English. The focus is on criminal activity.

CANJO6

Canadian Woman Studies/Les Cahiers de la Femme   (Education/General)
212 Founders College
York University
4700 Keele Street
Downsview
ONTARIO M3J 1P3
☎ 416 736 5356
Contact: Elizabeth Brady
Price: CAN$9.56
Subscriptions: CAN$32.10
Pub. frequency: quarterly
☐ First published 1978. Current issues in women's studies, advocacy, action and theory. Articles, book, art and film reviews and creative writing. The text is in both English and French.

CANJO7

CRIAW Papers/ICREF   (Education/General)
Suite 408
151 Slater Street
Ottawa
ONTARIO K1P 5H3
☎ 613 563 0681
Price: varies
Pub. frequency: irregular
☐ First published 1981. Original research papers and review articles from various disciplines are published which advance the knowledge and understanding of women's experience.

CANJO8

Diva: A quarterly journal of South Asian women   (Development)
346 Coxwell Avenue
Toronto
ONTARIO M4L 3B7

☎ 416 778 6945
Contact: Fauzia Rafig
Pub. frequency: quarterly
☐ 'To provide a platform where issues could be discussed to enable women within South Asia to struggle from outside their own countries.'

CANJO9

Feminist Perspectives/Perspectives Féministes
(Culture/Social sciences)
CRIAW/ICREF
Suite 408
151 Slater Street
Ottawa
ONTARIO K1P 5H3
☎ 613 563 0681
Price: CAN$3.00
Pub. frequency: irregular
☐ First published 1985. The text is in both English and French.

CANJO10

Healthsharing: A Canadian women's health quarterly   (Health)
Women Healthsharing Inc.
14 Skey Lane
Toronto
ONTARIO M6J 3S4
☎ 416 532 0812
Price: CAN$12.00
Subscriptions: CAN$24.00
Pub. frequency: quarterly
☐ First published 1979. Critical, feminist analysis of women's health issues. A national magazine, published in English only.

CANJO11

Ontario Advisory Council on Women's Issues Annual Report   (Equal opportunities/Civil rights)
Ontario Advisory Council on Women's Issues
880 Bay Street
5th Floor
Toronto
ONTARIO M7A 1N3
☎ 416 326 1840
Price: free
Pub. frequency: annual
☐ First published 1974.

CANJO12

Recherches Féministes   (Education/Social sciences)
GREMF
3e Etage
2336 Chemin Ste-Foy
Université Laval
QUEBEC G1K 7P4

☎ 418 656 5418
Subscriptions: CAN$22.00
Pub. frequency: half-yearly
□ First published 1991. Interdisciplinary journal publishing original research for the Groupe de Recherche Multidisciplinaire Féministe (GREMF) of the Laval University. Mainly empirical but also theoretical. Articles are in French with summaries in English and French.

CANJO13

Room of One's Own: A feminist journal of literature and criticism   (Literature)
Growing Room Collective
PO Box 46160
Station G
Vancouver
BRITISH COLUMBIA V6R 4G5
☎ 604 327 1423
Contact: Jean Wilson
Price: CAN$5.00
Subscriptions: CAN$15.00
Pub. frequency: quarterly
□ First published 1975. Original prose and poetry is published. Also book reviews. In English only. Published nationally.

CANJO14

Tessera   (Creative writing/Literature)
350 Stong College, Dept of English
York University
4700 Keele Street
North York, Downsview
ONTARIO M3J 1P3
Contact: Barbara Godard
Subscriptions: CAN$18.00
Pub. frequency: half-yearly
□ First published 1983. Publishes 'theoretical and experimental writing of Quebecoise and English-Canadian feminist writers', to sustain 'a dialogue for women across Canada interested in feminist literary theory.'

CANJO15

Woman Artists' Monographs   (Arts)
Gallerie Publications
2901 Panorama Drive
North Vancouver
BRITISH COLUMBIA V7G 2A4
Price: CAN$5.00
Subscriptions: CAN$12.00
Pub. frequency: bi-monthly

CANJO16

Women's Education/Education des Femmes
(Education)
Canadian Congress for Learning Opportunities for Women
47 Main Street
Toronto
ONTARIO M4E 2V6
☎ 416 699 1909
Contact: Christina Starr
Subscriptions: CAN$18.19
Pub. frequency: quarterly
□ First published 1982. Focuses on women's access to education with a feminist analysis of education and learning. The text is in English and French. 'To facilitate exchange and dialogue between learners and practitioners.'

Denmark

DENJO1

Kvinder, Kon Og Forskning
(Sex and gender/Education)
Centre for Women's Studies
University of Copenhagen
Njalsgade 106
2300 COPENHAGEN
☎ 31 54 22 11
Contact: Kirsten Hansen
Price: Dkr100
Subscriptions: Dkr250
Pub. frequency: quarterly
□ First published 1992. An interdisciplinary, scholarly journal published in Danish with summaries in English.

Finland

FINJO1

Naistutkimus – Kvinnoforskning
(Education/General)
Department of Finnish
University of Helsinki
PO Box 3
Fabianinkatu 33
00014 HELSINKI
☎ 90 191 2370
Contact: Auli Hakulinen
Price: Fmk35
Subscriptions: Fmk140
Pub. frequency: quarterly
□ First published 1988. Published in both Finnish and Swedish, this multi-disciplinary women's studies journal has articles and essays which concentrate mainly on social science and arts subjects. Book reviews.

France

FRJO1

Bulletin Mensuel du Service de Documentation Secrétariat d'Etat (Civil rights/International)
    Droits des Femmes
    31 rue le Peletier
    75009 PARIS
☎ 47 70 41 58

FRJO2

Cahiers du CEDREF (Education/General)
    UFR Sciences Sociales
    Couloir 24–34
    2 étage
    2 Place Jussieu
    75005 PARIS
□ A women's studies journal.

FRJO3

Diplomées
    Association Française des Femmes
    4 rue de Chevreuse
    75006 PARIS
Subscriptions: FF90
Pub. frequency: quarterly
□ First published 1952.

FRJO4

Etudes Féministes: Association Nationale des Etudes Féministes (International/General)
    Association Loi 1901
    9 bis rue de Valence
    75005 PARIS
Subscriptions: FF150.00
□ First published 1987. Information about events worldwide. Lists of conferences and meetings. Book reviews and articles about the status of ANEF.

FRJO5

Expression: Revue culturelle féminine internationale (Literature/Culture)
    Editions Expression/Communication
    1 Avenue de Chatou
    92561 REUIL-MALMAISON
Pub. frequency: annual
□ First published 1964. The text is in English, French and German.

FRJO6

Femmes en Littérature (Literature)
    Editions Klincksieck
    11 rue de Lille
    75005 PARIS
Price: varies
Pub. frequency: irregular
□ First published 1976.

Germany

GERJO1

Ariadne: Almanach des Archivs der Deutschen Frauenbewegung (General)
    Archiv der Deutschen Frauenbewegung
    Sommerweg 1B
    3500 KASSEL
☎ 0561 55600
Subscriptions: DM16.00
Pub. frequency: half-yearly
□ First published 1985. Journal of the Archives of the German Women's Movement Library and Centre for the Study of the First German Women's Movement. Articles are on one specific theme per issue, e.g. women and money, suffrage.

GERJO2

Clio: eine feministische Zeitschrift zur gesundheitlichen Selbsthilfe
(Reproductive rights/Health)
    Frauen des Feministischen Frauen
    Gesundheits Zentrums
    Bambergerstrasse 51
    1000 BERLIN 30
☎ 030 213 95 97
Price: DM6.00
Subscriptions: DM24.00
Pub. frequency: monthly
□ First published 1976. Women's health, diseases, feminist critiques of medical care, self-help, reproductive technologies. Book reviews, articles, photos and illustrations.

GERJO3

Eule, Die (Philosophy/Social sciences)
    Arbeitsgruppe für Anti-psychoanalyse
    Heide Heinz
    Augustrasse 123
    5600 WUPPERTAL 1
Price: DM1.00
Pub. frequency: annual
□ First published 1978. Articles about feminist perspectives on psychoanalysis and philosophy. Illustrated.

GERJO4

Feminist, Der: Beiträge zur Theorie und Praxis (Methodology)
    Forderkreis zum Aufbau
    der Feministischen Partei
    Christrosenweg 5
    8000 MUNICH 70
Price: DM8.50
Pub. frequency: irregular

☐ First published 1976. Reports on the theory and practice of feminism. Criticism of Christianity and theology.

GERJO5

Feministische Studien   (Education)
Deutscher Studien Verlag
Postfach 100154
6940 WEINHEIM
Price: DM4.00
Subscriptions: DM36.00
Pub. frequency: monthly
☐ First published 1982. Academic, women's studies journal. Special subjects in most issues.

GERJO6

Frauen-Informationsblatt   (Education)
Freie Universität Berlin
Zentralein Richtung für
Förderung Frauenstudien
Königin-Luise-Strasse 34
1000 BERLIN 33
Pub. frequency: annual
☐ First published 1988. Information about women's studies courses, conferences and research projects. Book reviews.

GERJO7

FrauenPress   (Education/General)
Informationsdienst Journalistinnenbüro
5000 COLOGNE
☐ A women's studies journal.

GERJO8

Hamburgerfrauenzeitung   (General)
Postfach 201603
2000 HAMBURG 20
Price: DM5.00
Subscriptions: DM20.00
Pub. frequency: quarterly
☐ Articles on culture, literary women, arts and events pertaining to Hamburg.

GERJO9

Kofra, Arbeitschrift für Feminismus und Arbeit   (Education/General)
Hrsg. Kommunikationszentrum für Frauen
8000 MUNICH
☐ A women's studies journal.

GERJO10

Philosophin, Die: Forum für feministische Theorie und Philosophie (Philosophy)
Edition Diskord
Schwarzlocher Str. 104/b
7400 TUBINGEN
☎   07071 40102

Contact: Ursula Konnertz
Subscriptions: DM25.00
Pub. frequency: half-yearly
☐ First published 1990.

GERJO11

Women of the Whole World
(International/Civil rights)
Women's International Democratic Federation
Unter den Linden 13
1080 BERLIN
Subscriptions: US$5.00
Pub. frequency: six per annum
☐ First published 1951. Information about women's social, legal and economic position worldwide. 'For equality, development, peace, national independence.'

Ghana

GHAJO1

Ghana National Council on Women and Development Annual Report
(Equal opportunities/Development)
National Council on Women and Development
PO Box M53
ACCRA
☎   21 229119
Pub. frequency: annual
☐ First published 1976. Reports on activities of the Council at all levels as it works to ensure the integration of women in Ghanaian society during the development of the country.

Great Britain and Northern Ireland

GBJO1

Affilia: Journal of women and social work
(Social sciences)
Sage Publications
6 Bonhill Street
LONDON EC2A 4PU
☎   071 374 0645
Subscriptions: £26.00
Pub. frequency: quarterly
☐ First published 1986. Social work from a feminist perspective. 'Committed to the discussion and development of feminist values, theories and knowledge as they relate to social work research, education and practice.'

GBJO2

The European Journal of Women's Studies
(Education/General)
Sage Publications
6 Bonhill Street
LONDON EC2A 4PU

☎ 071 374 0645
Subscriptions: £15
Pub. frequency: half-yearly
☐ First published 1994. An interdisciplinary journal, academic 'placed firmly within a European context'.

GBJO3

Feminism & Psychology: An international journal (Social sciences/International)
　　　Sage Publications
　　　6 Bonhill Street
　　　LONDON EC2A 4PU
☎ 071 374 0645
Contact: Sue Wilkinson
Subscriptions: £21.00
Pub. frequency: three per annum
☐ First published 1991. Fosters the development of feminist theory and practice in psychology. 'Represents the concerns of women in a wide range of contexts across the academic applied "divide".'

GBJO4

Feminist Legal Studies (Law)
　　　Deborah Charles Publications
　　　173 Mather Avenue
　　　LIVERPOOL L18 6JZ
☎ 051 729 0371
Contact: Belinda Meteyard
Subscriptions: £14.00 (students £8.00)
☐ First published 1993. The first legal studies journal to be published in Great Britain, it has 'an international scope and distribution' and seeks particularly to provide multi- or cross-disciplinary approaches.

GBJO5

Feminist Praxis (Social sciences/Methodology)
　　　University of Manchester
　　　Department of Sociology
　　　MANCHESTER M13 9PL
☎ 061 275 2496
Price: £4.00
Pub. frequency: bi-monthly
☐ First published 1984. Feminist research within the social sciences. There is a concentration on epistemological issues and their relationship to praxis.

GBJO6

Feminist Review (Socialism/Sex and gender)
　　　11 Carleton Gardens
　　　Brecknock Road
　　　LONDON N19 5AQ
☎ 071 583 9855
Price: £8.99
Subscriptions: £21.00
Pub. frequency: three per annum
☐ First published 1979. Academic articles on contemporary feminist issues 'informed by an awareness

of changing political issues'. About six articles per issue. Book reviews. Ideas and articles welcomed.

GBJO7

Feminist Theology (Religion)
　　　Sheffield Academic Press
　　　343 Fulwood Road
　　　SHEFFIELD S10 3BP
☎ 0742 670044
Price: £4.00
Subscriptions: £12.00
Pub. frequency: three per annum
☐ First published 1992. 'The journal of the Britain and Ireland School of Feminist Theology.' Aims to give a voice to the women of Britain and Ireland in matters of theology and religion.

GBJO8

Gender and Education
(Sex and gender/Education)
　　　Carfax Publishing Co.
　　　PO Box 25
　　　ABINGDON OX14 3UE
☎ 0235 555335
Contact: Lynda Measor
Subscriptions: £39.00
Pub. frequency: three per annum
☐ First published 1989. Covers all aspects of education in relation to gender. Aids the distribution and exchange of feminist research and ideas in the multidisciplinary international arena. Ideas and articles welcomed.

GBJO9

Gender & History (Sex and gender/History)
　　　Basil Blackwell
　　　108 Cowley Road
　　　OXFORD OX4 1JF
☎ 0865 791100
Contact: Leonore Davidoff
Subscriptions: £69.00
Pub. frequency: three per annum
☐ First published 1989. Covers all historical periods. Special topics, methodological issues, source materials. 'Founded as a response to the recent upsurge of interest in historical questions about femininity and masculinity.'

GBJO10

Gender & Society (Social sciences/
Sex and gender)
　　　Sage Publications
　　　6 Bonhill Street
　　　LONDON EC2A 4PU
☎ 071 374 0645
Subscriptions: £28.00
Pub. frequency: quarterly

☐ First published 1987. 'Official journal of sociologists for women in society.' Gender is seen as a 'primary social category' and as 'a basic principle of the social order'. Emphasis on theory and research.

GBJO11

Gender, Place and Culture: A journal of feminist geography   (Social sciences/Sex and gender)
    Carfax Publishing Co.
    PO Box 25
    ABINGDON OX14 3UE
☎ 0235 555335
Contact: Liz Bondi
Subscriptions: £26.00
Pub. frequency: half-yearly
☐ First published 1994. The journal will provide 'academic articles in geography and related disciplines concerned with gender issues.'

GBJO12

History Workshop: A journal of socialist and feminist historians   (History/Socialism)
    Journals Subscription Department
    Oxford University Press
    Walton Street
    OXFORD OX2 6DP
☎ 0865 56767
Price: £19.00
Subscriptions: £32.00
Pub. frequency: half-yearly
☐ First published 1976. Run by a women's collective. Contains articles on history as viewed from the left. Reports from history workshop conferences. 'It is . . . interested in the visual and literary representation of the past.'

GBJO13

Journal of Feminist Studies in Religion
(Religion)
    T. & T. Clark Ltd
    59 George Street
    EDINBURGH EH2 2LQ
☎ 031 225 4703
Contact: Judith Plaiskow
Price: £11.95
Subscriptions: £16.95
Pub. frequency: half-yearly
☐ First published 1985. Articles, letters, reports and comments. Articles on religion from a feminist perspective. 'The editors are committed to rigorous thinking . . . in the service of the transformation of religious studies.'

GBJO14

Journal of Gender Studies   (Sex and gender/ Social sciences)
    University of Humberside
    Inglemire Avenue
    HULL HU6 7LU
☎ 0482 440550
Contact: Lucy Vulliamy
Subscriptions: £6.00
Pub. frequency: half-yearly
☐ First published 1991. 'An interdisciplinary journal which publishes articles relating to gender from a feminist perspective within a wide range of subject areas covering the social and natural sciences and popular culture.'

GBJO15

Journal of Social and Personal Relationships
(Social sciences/Sex and gender)
    Sage Publications
    6 Bonhill Street
    LONDON EC2A 4PU
☎ 071 374 0645
Subscriptions: £30.00
Pub. frequency: quarterly
☐ First published 1984. Not only for women. Multi-disciplinary examination of personal relationships.

GBJO16

Midwifery Matters
    62 Greetby Hill
    ORMSKIRK L39 2DT
☎ 0695 572776
Contact: Sandra Arthur
Subscriptions: £22.00
Pub. frequency: quarterly
☐ The journal of the Association of Radical Midwives. Contains articles, book and film reviews, letters, events and a noticeboard. Illustrations and photographs.

GBJO17

Psychology of Women Quarterly
(Social sciences/Sex and gender)
    Cambridge University Press
    Edinburgh Building
    Shaftesbury Road
    CAMBRIDGE CB2 2RU
☎ 0223 312393
Contact: Judith Worell
Subscriptions: £29.00
Pub. frequency: quarterly
☐ First published 1976. Aims to 'encourage and develop a body of feminist research'. Book and film reviews. Empirical studies, review articles and theoretical articles to establish a greater understanding of women's issues.

GBJO18

Radical Philosophy: A journal of socialist and feminist philosophy (Philosophy/Socialism)
North View
Dundry Lane
Dundry
BRISTOL BS16 2JD
☎ 0272 642986
Contact: Jean Grimshaw
Price: £2.95
Subscriptions: £8.50
Pub. frequency: three per annum
☐ First published 1972. Not only for women. Reviews, news, articles, interviews and book reviews.

GBJO19

Reproductive and Genetic Engineering (Reproductive rights)
School of Applied Social Studies
University of Bradford
BRADFORD BD7 1DP
Subscriptions: £25.00
Pub. frequency: three per annum
☐ First published 1988. Designed 'to facilitate the development of feminist, multidisciplinary, and international analyses on the new reproductive technologies and genetic engineering and their impact on women.'

GBJO20

WAF: Women Against Fundamentalism (Religion/Civil rights)
PO Box 2706
LONDON WC1 3XX
☎ 071 272 6563
Price: £2.00
Subscriptions: £6.00
Pub. frequency: quarterly
☐ First published 1992. Articles about women's struggles worldwide for civil rights and an end to oppression. Also brief news items about fundamentalist campaigns.

GBJO21

Woman Engineer, The (Equal opportunities/Sciences)
PO Box 665
LONDON SW20 8RU
☎ 081 947 5686
Subscriptions: £18.00
Pub. frequency: six per annum
☐ First published 1919. Articles of technical and career interest to women employed as engineers and scientists. News and features.

GBJO22

Women: A cultural review (Arts/Culture)
Journals Subscription Department
Oxford University Press
Walton Street
OXFORD OX2 6DP
☎ 0865 56767
Contact: Isabel Armstrong
Price: £16.00
Subscriptions: £42.00
Pub. frequency: three per annum
☐ First published 1990. Explores the representation of women in the arts and culture. Articles covering feminist theory and present-day debates on sex and gender. Subjects covered include television, sculpture and poetry.

GBJO23

Women in Management Review (Paid work)
MCB University Press
62 Toller Lane
BRADFORD BD8 9BY
☎ 0274 499821
Price: £37.95
Subscriptions: £259.95
Pub. frequency: seven per annum
☐ First published 1985. For personnel and human research managers. Covers discrimination, equal opportunities and childcare. Abstracts from articles about women in management. Published in association with the Equal Opportunities Commission.

GBJO24

Women's History Review (History/International)
Triangle Journals Ltd
PO Box 65
WALLINGFORD OX10 0YG
☎ 0491 838013
Contact: June Purvis
Subscriptions: £30.00
Pub. frequency: three per annum
☐ First published 1992. International history journal to publish 'scholarly articles in the rapidly expanding field of women's history'. Emphasis on nineteenth and twentieth centuries. Ideas and articles welcomed.

GBJO25

Women's Studies (Education/Social sciences)
Gordon & Breach Science Publishers
PO Box 90
READING RG1 8JL
☎ 0734 560080
Contact: Fiona Cairns
Subscriptions: £106.00 (universities)
Pub. frequency: quarterly

☐ First published 1972. Scholarly journal. Articles and criticism about women in literature, history, art, sociology, law, political science, economics, anthropology and the arts.

GBJO26

Women's Studies International Forum
(International/Education)
> Pergamon Press
> Headington Hill Hall
> OXFORD OX3 0BW
☎ 0865 794141
Price: £21.00
Subscriptions: £39.00
Pub. frequency: six per annum
☐ First published 1978. An international academic journal with contributors from all over the world. There is a section called Feminist Forum which contains notes and announcements. Ideas and contributions welcomed.

GBJO27

Women's Writing: The early modern period
(Literature/History)
> Triangle Journals Ltd
> PO Box 65
> WALLINGFORD OX10 0YG
☎ 0491 838013
Contact: Marie Mulvey Roberts
Subscriptions: £30.00
Pub. frequency: three per annum
☐ First published 1994. 'Will focus upon women's writing before 1830. . . . The aim . . . is to open up a forum for dialogue, discussion and debate.'

GBJO28

Writing Women   (Creative writing/Literature)
> Unit 14, Hawthorne House
> Forth Banks
> NEWCASTLE UPON TYNE NE1 3SG
Price: £2.00
Subscriptions: £6.50
Pub. frequency: three per annum
☐ Contains poems, fiction and articles.

India

INDJO1

Association of Medical Women in India Journal   (Sciences)
> Association of Medical Women in India
> IMA Building
> 16 Haji Ali Park
> Keshavrao Khudye Marg
> BOMBAY 400034
Subscriptions: Rs15.00

Pub. frequency: bi-monthly
☐ First published 1920. The text is in English.

INDJO2

Samua Shakti: A journal of women's studies
(Education/General)
> Centre for Women's Development Studies
> B-43 Panchsheel Enclave
> NEW DELHI 110017
Pub. frequency: irregular
☐ First published 1983. Publishes research articles on a variety of topics, with the main focus on women in India.

Italy

ITJO1

Giornale dei CAF, Il   (Education/General)
> Comitati Associazioni Femminile
> Corso Vinzaglio 14
> 10121 TURIN
☐ A women's studies journal.

ITJO2

Leggere Donna   (Culture/General)
> Centro Documentazione Donna
> Contrada della Rosa 14
> 44100 FERRARE
Pub. frequency: bi-monthly

ITJO3

Minerva   (Education/General)
> Edizione Club delle Donne
> Piazza Ippolito Nievo 5
> 00153 ROME
☐ A women's studies journal.

ITJO4

Nuova Donnawomanfemme   (Education/General)
> Studi Internazionali sulla Donna
> Via S. Benedetto in Arenula 4–12
> 00186 ROME
☐ A women's studies journal.

ITJO5

Quotidiano Donna   (Education/General)
> Centro Studi e Documentazione
> Femminista (Pampeo Magno)
> Casa della Donna
> Via del Governo Vecchio 39
> 00100 ROME
☐ A women's studies journal.

ITJO6

Storia Donna   (Education/General)
   Centro Studi 'Storia Donna'
   Collegio Universitario Castiglioni Brugnatelli
   Via S. Marino 18
   PADUA
☐ A women's studies journal.

Lebanon

LEBJO1

al-raida   (General)
   Institute for Women's Studies in the Arab
   World (IWSAW)
   Beirut University College
   PO Box 13-5053
   5053 BEIRUT
☎ 1 811968
Subscriptions: LL6000
Pub. frequency: quarterly
☐ First published 1976. English-language journal
publishing current information on Arab women in the
Middle East. The journal of the Institute for Women's
Studies in the Arab World. Research, articles, profiles
and book reviews.

Malaysia

MALJO1

**Asian and Pacific Women's Resource and Action
Series**   (Development/General)
   Asian and Pacific Development Centre
   PO Box 12224
   50770 KUALA LUMPUR
☎ 03 254 8088
Contact: Noeleen Heyzerc
Price: free
Pub. frequency: irregular
☐ First published 1989. Text is in English. A forum for
women's experiences and thoughts on issues critical to
women's health, the environment, work and law from a
Third World perspective.

MALJO2

Malaysian Journal of Reproductive Health
(Reproductive rights/Health)
   National Population and Development Board
   PO Box 10416
   Jalan Raja Laut
   50712 KUALA LUMPUR
☎ 03 293 7555
Subscriptions: M$50.00
Pub. frequency: half-yearly

☐ First published 1983. The text is in English.
Discusses various aspects of women's health, and
reproduction issues are also covered.

Netherlands

NETJO1

**Jaarboek voor Vrouwengeschiedenis/Women's
History Yearbook**   (History)
   Parkstraat 16
   3581 PJ UTRECHT
Contact: Mirjam de Baar
Pub. frequency: annual

NETJO2

**Tijdschrift voor Vrouenstudies/Journal of
Women's Studies**   (Education/General)
   Spinthuisstraat 2
   6511 TT NIJMEGEN
☐ First published 1980.

NETJO3

Vakblad Vrouweninformatie   (Media/Literature)
   International Informatiecentrum en Archief voor
   de Vrouwen
   Keizersgracht 10
   1015 CN AMSTERDAM
☎ 020 624 4268
Pub. frequency: three per annum
☐ Dutch professional journal with news and developments on all aspects of women's information in the
field of archives, libraries and documentation.

NETJO4

Vrouwenstudies   (Education/General)
   Studium Generale
   Gen. Foulkesweg 1
   6703 BG WAGENINGEN
Price: fl2.50
Pub. frequency: quarterly

New Zealand

NZJO1

NZ Women's Studies Journal
(Education/General)
   New Zealand Women's Studies Association
   PO Box 5067
   AUCKLAND
Price: NZ$16
Subscriptions: NZ$27
Pub. frequency: half-yearly

□ First published 1985. Articles and book reviews. A scholarly journal.

Norway

NORJO1

NORA: Nordic journal of women's studies (Education/General)
        Scandinavian University Press
        PO Box 2959 Toyen
        0608 OSLO
☎   22 67 76 00
Contact: Torill Steinfeld
Subscriptions: Nkr195
Pub. frequency: half-yearly
□ First published 1993. 'A channel for high-quality women's research from all disciplines.' The emphasis is on showing a Nordic profile in women's research, but the journal is international in scope.

NORJO2

Nytt om Kvinneforskning   (Education/General)
        Secretariat for Women and Research
        NAVF
        Sandakerveien 99
        0483 OSLO
☎   22 15 70 12
Contact: Tove Beate Pedersen
Price: Nkr50
Subscriptions: Nkr200
Pub. frequency: six per annum
□ First published 1977. Produced by the Norweigian Research Council for Science and Humanities, Secretariat for Women and Research. Every other number is devoted to special subjects.

Pakistan

PAKJO1

Alam-e-Niswan
        Pakistan Association for Women's Studies
        C-12, Staff Town
        University of Karachi
        KARACHI 75270
☎   471828
Pub. frequency: bi-annual
□ First published 1993. Interdisciplinary. Articles on curricula, courses and teaching strategies related to women's studies. Conceptual and analytical papers on issues related to women's status and role.

Portugal

PORJO1

Noticias Comissão para a Igualdade e Direitos das mulheres (journal)   (General)
        Coleccao Informar as Mulheres
        Avenida República 32-2° Esq.
        1093 LISBON
☎   01 797 6081
Pub. frequency: irregular
□ First published 1979. Women's issues, such as marriage, divorce, separation, children, widowhood, adoption and the menopause.

South Africa

SAJO1

Agenda: A journal about women and gender (Sex and gender/General)
        PO Box 37432
        Overport
        DURBAN 4067
☎   031 305 4074
Subscriptions: R32
Pub. frequency: quarterly
□ First published 1987. Discusses and debates all aspects of women's lives. Aims to be free of race, class and gender oppression. Produced by a collective. News, features, profiles, book reviews and poetry.

SAJO2

Sash   (Black women/politics)
        5 Long Street
        MOWBRAY 7700
☎   021 685 3513
Subscriptions: R20.00
Pub. frequency: three per annum
□ Official journal of the Black Sash. Articles, book reviews and letters.

South Korea

SKJO1

Journal of Asian Women
(Social sciences/Sciences)
        Research Centre for Asian Women
        Sookinyung
        Women's University
        SEOUL
□ First published 1960. Academic sociological journal; also includes scientific articles. Abstracts in English.

SKJO2

Women's Studies Forum   (General)
   Korean Women's Development Institute
   PO Box 2267
   SEOUL
☎   02 356 0070

Spain

SPJO1

Duoda: Revista d'Estudis Feministes
(Education/General)
   Centre d'investigacio historica d'la dona
   Universitat de Barcelona
   C-Brus 61
   08006 BARCELONA
☎   93 200 4567
Subscriptions: Pta2000
Pub. frequency: Yearly
□ A women's studies journal. Articles and poetry. Each issue is usually on one topic only, e.g. power, sex, gender, fundamentalism. The languages are Catalan and Castilian.

SPJO2

Poder y Libertad   (General)
   Partido Feminista de Espana
   Vindicacion Feminista de Espana
   Vindicacion Feminista Publicationes
   C-Magdalena 21-1-A
   28012 MADRID
☎   91 369 4488
Price: Pta1200
Subscriptions: Pta4000
Pub. frequency: three per annum
□ First published 1976. Single-topic issues, e.g. women and Islam, women and power. The language is Castilian.

Sudan

SUDJO1

Ahfad Journal, The: Women and change
(Development/General)
   Ahfad University for Women
   PO Box 167
   OMDURMAN
☎   53363
Contact: Amna E. Badri
Price: US$10.00
Subscriptions: US$20.00
Pub. frequency: half-yearly
□ First published 1984. Covers issues affecting women, families and children in developing countries and the role of women in national development. In English. Research, reports, historical and critical analysis, book reviews.

Sweden

SWEJO1

Kvinnovetenskaplig tidskrift
(Education/General)
   Kungsgatan 95
   90331 UMEA
☎   90 13 55 90
Contact: Gerd Lindgren
Price: Skr50
Subscriptions: Skr190
Pub. frequency: quarterly
□ First published 1980. Articles and letters. An interdisciplinary journal which presents theory, debate and information within women's studies. The major articles have English summaries.

Switzerland

SWIJO1

Alma Mater ist Weiblich, Die/Al'Alma Mater ou Feminin   (Politics/Culture)
   Les femmes à l'Uni. de Fribourg
   Universität Fribourg
   Misericorde
   1700 FRIBOURG
☎   037 21 93 62
□ The text is in French, German and Italian. Articles, interviews and photos.

SWIJO2

Brundtland Bulletin: Towards sustainable development   (International/General)
   The Centre for our Common Future
   Palais Wilson
   52 rue des Paquis
   1201 GENEVA
☎   022 732 7117
Pub. frequency: quarterly
□ Not only for women. The journal lists organisations concerned with development.

SWIJO3

Femmes (Suisse)   (General)
   Case Postale 1345
   Carouge
   1227 GENEVA
☎   021 903 26 06
Price: SF5.60
Subscriptions: SF55.00
Pub. frequency: ten per annum

☐ First published 1912. Articles on politics, abortion issues, the professions and book reviews.

SWIJO4

Frauenfragen/Questions au feminin/Problemi al femminile (Education/Social sciences)
Bundesamt für Kultur
Eigerplatz 5
3000 BERN 6
☎ 031 619 27576
Pub. frequency: three per annum
☐ The text is in French, German and Italian. Academic. Articles on education, careers and politics. Book reviews. Campaigns for equal rights in Switzerland.

SWIJO5

Isis International Bulletin (International/General)
Case Postale 301
Carouge
1227 GENEVA
☎ 022 43 40 22
Price: US$3.00
Subscriptions: US$15.00
Pub. frequency: quarterly
☐ First published 1976. The text is in English. It 'reproduces theoretical and practical information and documentation from women's groups and the women's movement around the world'. Each issue is about one special theme.

SWIJO6

Women in a Changing World
(Religion/Civil rights)
World Council of Churches
150 route de Ferney
PO Box 2100
1211 GENEVA 2
☎ 022 791 6111
Pub. frequency: half-yearly
☐ First published 1974. The text is in English. Published by the World Council of Churches. Scholarly articles on women and religion and civil rights for women in the Christian Church.

SWIJO7

Women's Information Updates (General)
Isis-WICCE
3 chemin des Campanules
Aire
1219 GENEVA 2
☎ 022 796 4437
Contact: Valse Verghese
Subscriptions: SF20.00
Pub. frequency: half-yearly
☐ First published 1976. Lists books and documents at the Centre and has lists of resources, information about new groups, activities and campaigns.

SWIJO8

Women's World/Monde des Femmes
(International/General)
Isis-WICCE
3 chemin des Campanules
Aire
1219 GENEVA 2
☎ 022 796 4437
Contact: Valse Verghese
Price: SF10.00
Subscriptions: SF20.00
Pub. frequency: half-yearly
☐ First published 1976. There are English and French editions. Articles on the themes of Isis exchange programmes, including case studies and information about other groups and resources. Theory, case studies and resources.

United States of America

USAJO1

4LW Journal: News–views–reviews for women and libraries (Education/General)
Women Library Workers
McFarland and Co.
PO Box 611
JEFFERSON, NC 28640
☎ 919 246 4460
Contact: Audrey Eaglen
Price: $4.00
Subscriptions: $18.00
Pub. frequency: quarterly
☐ First published 1975. Articles, conference reports, news and reviews.

USAJO2

Ache: A journal for black lesbians
(Black women/Lesbian)
PO Box 6071
ALBANY, CA 94706
☎ 510 849 2819
Pub. frequency: bi-monthly
☐ By black lesbians for the benefit of all black women. Committed to open and critical discussion about issues affecting black lesbian lives.

USAJO3

Affinity (Lesbian/Religion)
Gay and Lesbian Mormons
Box 1868
LOS ANGELES, CA 90078
☎ 213 255 7251
Subscriptions: $20.00
Pub. frequency: monthly

☐ First published 1977. Not specifically feminist. Publication in support of lesbian and gay Mormons. Focuses on the education of authorities and lay members regarding homosexuality.

USAJO4

Angels: Women Working in Film and Video   (Arts/Media)
> PO Box 11916
> MILWAUKEE, WI 53211

Subscriptions: $15.00
Pub. frequency: quarterly
☐ First published 1991. Interviews with women film-makers; reports from film festivals, works in progress and new works in distribution.

USAJO5

Anima: The journal of human experience (Spirituality/Religion)
> Anima Publications
> 1053 Wilson Avenue
> Chambersburg
> PENNSYLVANIA, PA 17201

☎   717 267 0087
Price: $9.95
Pub. frequency: half-yearly
☐ First published 1975. Feminism and women's religious experiences are central themes of the journal. Articles, poetry, illustrations.

USAJO6

Belles Lettres: A review of books by women (Literature)
> 615 Anderson Court
> Department 05
> SATELLITE BEACH, FL 32937

Contact: Janet P. Mullaney
Price: $5.00
Subscriptions: $20.00
Pub. frequency: quarterly
☐ First published 1985. Founded to preserve, promote and celebrate women's writing, both academic and popular. Interviews, rediscoveries and retrospectives. 'Our purpose is to promote and celebrate writing by women.'

USAJO7

Berkeley Women's Law Journal
(Law/Social sciences)
> Journals Division
> University of California Press
> 2120 Berkeley Way
> BERKELEY, CA 94720

☎   415 642 4191
Price: $17.00
Pub. frequency: annual

☐ First published 1986. Explores racial, cultural and socio-economic issues concerning women and the law. 'A forum from which to give voice to the complex and varying perspectives affecting the legal concerns of women.'

USAJO8

Calyx: A journal of art and literature by women   (Arts/Literature)
> PO Box B
> CORVALLIS, OR 97339-0539

☎   503 753 9384
Contact: Margarita Donnelly
Price: $8.00
Subscriptions: $18.00
Pub. frequency: three per annum
☐ First published 1976. Painting, poems, prose and reviews. Submissions welcomed. 'Committed to publishing work by women of color, working-class women, lesbians, and politically active women.'

USAJO9

Camera Obscura: A journal of feminism and film theory   (Media/Methodology)
> Journals Division
> Johns Hopkins University Press
> Suite 275
> 701 West 40th Street
> BALTIMORE, MD 21211

☎   410 516 6987
Contact: Constance Penley
Subscriptions: $18.50
Pub. frequency: three per annum
☐ First published 1976. Sets out current feminist perspectives on the national and international film scene. Many issues are either double or triple.

USAJO10

Columbia Journal of Gender and Law   (Sex and gender/Law)
> 435 West 116th Street
> NEW YORK, NY 10027-7297

Contact: Heidi L. Mortensen
Price: $10.00
Pub. frequency: annual
☐ First published 1991. 'Was founded to publish legal and interdisciplinary writings on feminism and gender issues and to expand feminist jurisprudence.'

USAJO11

Common Lives – Lesbian Lives
(Lesbian/Politics)
> PO Box 1553
> IOWA CITY, IA 52244

Price: $4.50
Subscriptions: $15.00
Pub. frequency: quarterly

□ First published 1981. Documents activities and ideas of lesbians by providing a forum for developing and clarifying lesbian-defined social and political relationships. A forum for previously unpublished lesbian writing.

USAJO12

Contributions in Women's Studies (Education/General)
> Greenwood Press
> 88 Post Road West
> PO Box 5007
> WESTPOINT, CT 06881-5007
> ☎ 203 226 3571

Price: varies
Pub. frequency: irregular
□ First published 1978.

USAJO13

Cornerstone (Ann Arbor) (Education/Paid work)
> Center for the Education of Women
> University of Michigan
> 330 East Liberty Street
> ANN ARBOR, MI 48104-2289

Price: free
Pub. frequency: irregular
□ First published 1965. For women in higher education. Studies the role of women in society with an emphasis on education and careers.

USAJO14

Critical Theory (Language/Methodology)
> John Benjamins Publishing Co.
> 821 Bethleham Pike
> PHILADELPHIA, PA 19118
> ☎ 215 836 1200

Pub. frequency: irregular
□ First published 1985. Not only for women. Focuses on an interdisciplinary approach to language discourse and ideology.

USAJO15

Differences: A journal of feminist cultural studies (Culture/Sex and gender)
> Journals Division
> Indiana University Press
> 601 North Morton Street
> BLOOMINGTON, IN 47404
> ☎ 812 855 9449

Contact: Naomi Schor
Price: $10.00
Subscriptions: $28.00
Pub. frequency: three per annum
□ First published 1989. Focuses on how concepts and categories of difference, especially gender, operate within a culture. A forum of exchange between cultural studies and feminism.

USAJO16

Edith Wharton Review (Literature/Lesbian)
> Edith Wharton Society
> Department of English
> Long Island University
> BROOKLYN, NY 11201
> ☎ 718 403 1050

Price: $10.00
Pub. frequency: annual
□ First published 1984.

USAJO17

Emily Dickinson Journal, The (Literature)
> University Press of Colorado
> PO Box 849
> NIWOT, CO 80544

□ First published 1992. All about Emily Dickinson.

USAJO18

Evergreen Chronicles: A journal of gay and lesbian writers (Lesbian/Literature)
> Box 8939
> MINNEAPOLIS, MN 55408-8939
> ☎ 612 824 6261

Subscriptions: $12.00
Pub. frequency: quarterly
□ First published 1985. Not only for women. Sets out the work of lesbian and gay literary and visual artists.

USAJO19

Feminist Collections: A quarterly of women's studies resources (Literature/Media)
> University of Wisconsin System
> 430 Memorial Library
> 728 State Street
> MADISON, WI 53706
> ☎ 608 263 5754

Contact: Linda Shult
Price: $2.75
Subscriptions: $6.50
Pub. frequency: quarterly
□ First published 1980. Reviews of resources, new reference works, new periodicals, special issues and news and information. Feminist publishing, bookselling and distribution, and feminist librarianship. Mostly N. American.

USAJO20

Feminist Issues (Social sciences/Politics)
> Transaction Periodicals Consortium
> Department 8010
> Rutgers State University
> NEW BRUNSWICK, NJ 08903
> ☎ 201 932 2280

Contact: Mary Jo Lakeland
Price: $9.00

Subscriptions: $15.00
Pub. frequency: half-yearly
☐ First published 1980. Feminist social and political analysis with an emphasis on an international exchange of ideas. Explores core feminist ideas.

USAJO21

Feminist Periodicals: A current listing of contents (Education/Media)
> University of Wisconsin System
> 430 Memorial Library
> 728 State Street
> MADISON, WI 53706
☎ 608 263 5754
Contact: Linda Shult
Subscriptions: $23.00
Pub. frequency: quarterly
☐ First published 1981. Reproduction of contents pages of more than 100 feminist periodicals, and a thorough listing of their focus within women's studies.

USAJO22

Feminist Studies (Education/General)
> Women's Studies Program
> University of Maryland
> COLLEGE PARK, MD 20742
☎ 301 405 6881
Contact: Claire G. Moses
Price: $10.00
Subscriptions: $25.00
Pub. frequency: three per annum
☐ First published 1972. Contains a mixture of scholarly research and personal/creative writing. Essays, art subjects, book reviews, poetry, fiction, history, politics and literature. 'A forum for feminist analysis.'

USAJO23

Feminist Studies (American University Studies, Series 27) (Sex and gender/General)
> Peter Lang Publishing Inc.
> 4th Floor
> 62 West 45th Street
> NEW YORK, NY 10036
☎ 212 302 6740
Pub. frequency: irregular
☐ First published 1990.

USAJO24

Frontiers: A journal of women studies (Education/General)
> Women's Studies Program
> Mesa Vista Hall 2142
> University of New Mexico
> ALBUQUERQUE, NM 87131
☎ 303 492 3205
Contact: Louise Lamphere
Price: $8.00

Subscriptions: $20.00
Pub. frequency: three per annum
☐ First published 1975. Aims 'to find a balance between academic and popular views on issues common to women'. Articles, reviews, creative writing, poetry, fiction, art, photography and mini biographies.

USAJO25

Genders: Art, literature, film, history (Sex and gender/Education)
> University of Texas Press
> PO Box 7819
> AUSTIN, TX 78713
☎ 512 471 7233
Contact: Ann Kebbey
Price: $9.00
Subscriptions: $24.00
Pub. frequency: three per annum
☐ First published 1988. Focuses on sexuality and gender. Articles on art, literature, film and history. Also social, political, racial and economic issues.

USAJO26

Harvard Women's Law Journal (Law/Social sciences)
> Publications Center
> Harvard University Law School
> Hastings Hall
> CAMBRIDGE, MA 02138
☎ 617 495 3726
Contact: Marie Arnold
Price: $15
Pub. frequency: annual
☐ First published 1978. Aims to develop a feminist jurisprudence which explores both the impact of the law on women and the impact of women on the law. Legal issues related to women are clarified. National distribution.

USAJO27

Hawaii State Commission on the Status of Women Annual Report
> State Commission on the Status of Women
> 335 Merchant Street
> Room 253
> HONOLULU, HL 96813
☎ 808 548 4199
Pub. frequency: annual

USAJO28

Health Care for Women International (Health/International)
> Hemisphere Publishing Corporation
> Taylor & Francis Group
> Suite 101
> 1900 Frost Road
> PHILADELPHIA, PA 19007-1598

☎ 215 785 5800
Contact: Phyllis N. Stern
Subscriptions: $41.00
Pub. frequency: quarterly
☐ First published 1980. 'An interdisciplinary approach to health care and related topics that concern women.' Subjects covered are health care, psychology, sociology, anthropology and the nursing profession.

USAJO29

Hypatia: A journal of feminist philosophy (Philosophy)
    Journals Division
    Indiana University Press
    601 North Morton Street
    BLOOMINGTON, IN 47404
☎ 812 855 9449
Contact: Linda L. McAlister
Price: $3.00
Subscriptions: $12.00
Pub. frequency: quarterly
☐ First published 1986. Feminist philosophy and its history. Research into, and reclaiming of, women philosophers. Created by members of the Society of Women in Philosophy.

USAJO30

ILWC Journal (Arts)
    Abilene Christian University
    PO Box 8274
    ABILENE, TX 79699
Contact: Sally Reid
☐ The journal of the International League of Women Composers.

USAJO31

Initiatives: Journal of NAWE (Education)
    National Association for Women's Education
    Suite 210
    1325 18th Street NW
    WASHINGTON, DC 20036-6511
☎ 202 659 9330
Contact: Patricia A. Farrant
Price: $13.00
Subscriptions: $40.00
Pub. frequency: quarterly
☐ First published 1938. Provides professional support for women educators. Articles on administration, counselling and individual development.

USAJO32

Iowa Woman (Creative writing/General)
    Iowa Woman Endeavors
    PO Box 680
    IOWA CITY, IO 52244
☎ 319 987 2879
Contact: Marianne Abel

Subscriptions: $15.00
Pub. frequency: quarterly
☐ First published 1980. Fiction, poetry, essays, interviews, reviews and art by women. 'Non-fiction includes interviews, articles and essays on international living, reports of the activities of women ... and book reviews.'

USAJO33

IRIS: A journal about women (General)
    Women's Center
    PO Box 323, HSC
    University of Virginia
    CHARLOTTESVILLE, VA 22903
☎ 804 924 4500
Contact: Kristen S. Rembold
Price: $5.00
Subscriptions: $15.00
Pub. frequency: half-yearly
☐ First published 1980. Includes features, fiction, poetry, book reviews, art and news focusing on women's issues, as well as information about international affairs.

USAJO34

Issues in Reproductive and Genetic Engineering (Reproductive rights)
    Pergamon Press Inc.
    Journals Division
    Maxwell House
    Fairview Park
    ELMSFORD, NY 10523
☎ 914 592 7700
Subscriptions: $30.00
Pub. frequency: three per annum
☐ First published 1988. Articles on the development of feminist multidisciplinary global analysis of reproductive technologies and their impact on women.

USAJO35

Ithaca Women's Anthology (Creative writing/Literature)
    Box 582
    ITHACA, NY 14850
Price: $3.80
Pub. frequency: annual
☐ First published 1976.

USAJO36

Journal of Feminist Family Therapy (Health/Social sciences)
    Haworth Press Inc.
    10 Alice Street
    BINGHAMTON, NY 13904
☎ 607 722 2493
Contact: Lois Braverman
Subscriptions: $24.00
Pub. frequency: quarterly

☐ First published 1989. Analyses family therapy and practice with a feminist perspective. Explores the possibility of a feminist therapy. 'Articles include those of a theoretical nature as well as . . . empirical research.'

USAJO37

Journal of Gay and Lesbian Psychotherapy (Lesbian/Social sciences)
    Haworth Press Inc.
    10 Alice Street
    BINGHAMTON, NY 13904
☎   607 722 2493
Subscriptions: $24.00
Pub. frequency: quarterly
☐ First published 1988. Not only for women. A forum for discussion of issues relating to the use of psychotherapy for lesbian, gay and bisexual clients.

USAJO38

Journal of Homosexuality (Lesbian/Social sciences)
    Haworth Press Inc.
    10 Alice Street
    BINGHAMTON, NY 13904
☎   607 722 2493
Subscriptions: $40.00
Pub. frequency: quarterly
☐ First published 1974. Not only for women. Theoretical, empirical and historical research on homosexuality, heterosexuality, sexual identity, sex roles and the sexual relationships of men and women.

USAJO39

Journal of Psychology and Human Sexuality (Social sciences/Sex and gender)
    Haworth Press Inc.
    10 Alice Street
    BINGHAMTON, NY 13904
☎   607 722 2493
Subscriptions: $24.00
Pub. frequency: quarterly
☐ First published 1988. Not only for women. Publishes articles and reviews about human sexuality.

USAJO40

Journal of Reprints of Documents Affecting Women (General)
    Today Publications & News Service
    621 National Press Building
    WASHINGTON, DC 20045
☎   202 628 6663
Subscriptions: $40.00
Pub. frequency: quarterly
☐ First published 1975.

USAJO41

Journal of Sexual Liberty (Lesbian/Politics)
    Committee to Preserve our Sexual and Civil Liberties
    PO Box 1592
    SAN FRANCISCO, CA 94101-1592
Subscriptions: $10.00
Pub. frequency: monthly
☐ First published 1985. Not only for women. Summary of recent happenings in the field of sex and civil liberties.

USAJO42

Journal of Women and Aging (Older women/Social sciences)
    Haworth Press Inc.
    10 Alice Street
    BINGHAMTON, NY 13904
☎   607 722 2493
Contact: J. Dianne Garner
Subscriptions: $38.00
Pub. frequency: quarterly
☐ First published 1989. For professionals who want to meet the social, psychological and health-care needs of the older woman.

USAJO43

Journal of Women and Religion (Religion)
    Center for Women and Religion
    Graduate Theological Union
    2400 Ridge Road
    BERKELEY, CA 94709
☎   415 649 2490
Contact: Jane E. Vennard
Price: $3.50
Subscriptions: $20.00 (plus mailings)
Pub. frequency: annual
☐ First published 1981. Focuses on sexism against women within theological circles. 'We have covered areas such as women and power, women and peace.'

USAJO44

Journal of Women's History (History/International)
    Journals Division
    Indiana University Press
    601 North Morton Street
    BLOOMINGTON, IN 47404
☎   812 855 9449
Contact: Christie Farnham
Price: $11.75
Subscriptions: $25.00
Pub. frequency: three per annum
☐ First published 1989. 'Helps specialists in women's history keep up to date and provides material valuable to those outside the field who want to integrate women into Third World, Western Civilization, and US history.'

USAJO45

Kalliope: A journal of women's art
(Arts/Literature)
> 50 Florida Community College
> Kalliope Writers' Collective
> 3939 Roosevelt Boulevard
> JACKSONVILLE, FL 32205-3056
☎ 904 387 8211
Contact: Mary Sue Koeppel
Price: $4.00
Subscriptions: $10.50
Pub. frequency: three per annum
☐ First published 1979. For women in the arts. Provides a means by which women artists may share their work, ideas and opinions. Poetry, short stories and illustrations. Consideration for young/emerging artists and writers.

USAJO46

La Bella Figura (Literature/Lesbian)
> PO Box 411223
> SAN FRANCISCO, CA 94141-1223
Pub. frequency: quarterly
☐ Aimed at Italian American women, especially lesbians.

USAJO47

Lambda Book Report (Lesbian/Literature)
> Lambda Rising Inc.
> 1625 Connecticut Avenue NW
> WASHINGTON, DC 20009-1013
☎ 202 462 7924
Contact: Rose Fennell
Price: $3.95
Subscriptions: $19.95
Pub. frequency: bi-monthly
☐ First published 1987. Not only for women. Reviews contemporary lesbian and gay literature.

USAJO48

Lambda Update (Civil rights/Law)
> Lambda Legal Defense & Education Fund
> 666 Broadway
> NEW YORK, NY 10012-2317
☎ 212 995 8585
Subscriptions: $40.00
Pub. frequency: quarterly
☐ First published 1983. Not only for women. Covers litigation to counter discrimination against lesbians and gays. Cases and articles on the state of lesbian and gay legal and civil rights.

USAJO49

Law & Women Series (Law)
> Today Publications & News Service
> 621 National Press Building
> WASHINGTON, DC 20045

☎ 202 638 0348
Price: $2.00
Pub. frequency: irregular
☐ First published 1972.

USAJO50

Legacy (Amherst): A journal of nineteenth-century women writers (Literature)
> Journals Department
> Penn State Press
> Suite C, Barbara Building
> 820 N University Drive, University Park
> PHILADELPHIA, PA 16802
Contact: Martha Ackmann
Price: $9.00
Subscriptions: $17.50
Pub. frequency: half-yearly
☐ First published 1984. Focuses on pre-nineteenth-century, nineteenth-century and early twentieth-century women writers.

USAJO51

Lesbian Ethics (Lesbian/Philosophy)
> PO Box 4723
> ALBUQUERQUE, NM 87196
Contact: Jeanette Silveira
Price: $6.00
Subscriptions: $14.00 for three issues
Pub. frequency: half-yearly
☐ First published 1984. Radical lesbian ethics and philosophy, 'with a focus on how lesbians behave with each other'.

USAJO52

Letras Femeninas (Literature)
> Asociation de Literaria Femenina Hispania
> Department of Modern Languages
> University of Nebraska
> LINCOLN, NE 68588-0315
☎ 402 472 3710
Subscriptions: $20.00
Pub. frequency: half-yearly
☐ First published 1974. The text is in English, Portuguese and Spanish.

USAJO53

Male–Female Roles: Opposing viewpoints sources
(Social sciences/Sex and gender)
> Greenhaven Press
> PO Box 289009
> SAN DIEGO, CA 92198-0009
☎ 619 485 7424
Price: $10.95
Pub. frequency: annual

☐ First published 1988. Focuses on issues centred around gender roles, women and work, marriage and family issues.

USAJO54

Media Report to Women (Media)
Communication Research Associates
10606 Mantz Road
SILVER SPRING, MD 20903-1228
☎ 301 445 3230
Contact: Sheila J. Gibbons
Price: $10.00
Subscriptions: $30.00
Pub. frequency: bi-monthly
☐ First published 1972. The journal reflects what women are thinking about and doing to change the media. Actions, ideas and research are listed.

USAJO55

Melpomene Journal: A journal for women's health research (Health)
Melpomene Institute for Women's Health Research
1010 University Avenue W
SAINT PAUL, MN 55104-4706
Contact: Judy Remington
Subscriptions: $32.00
Pub. frequency: three per annum
☐ First published 1981. Research articles, scientific bibliographies, personal profiles, news and updates.

USAJO56

Moving Out: A feminist literary and arts journal (Arts/Literature)
PO Box 21249
DETROIT, MI 48221
Price: $6.00
Pub. frequency: annual
☐ First published 1970. Focuses on feminist aesthetics in art and literature.

USAJO57

National Women's Health Network (Health)
1325 G Street NW
WASHINGTON, DC 20005
Pub. frequency: quarterly

USAJO58

National Women's Health Report (Health)
National Women's Health Resource Center
Suite 352
2440 M Street NW
WASHINGTON, DC 200037
☎ 202 293 6045
Subscriptions: $21.00
Pub. frequency: quarterly

☐ First published 1984. Provides clinical, educational and research information.

USAJO59

National Women's Studies Association Journal (General/Education)
English Department
University of New Hampshire
DURHAM, NH 03824
☎ 603 862 3976
Contact: P. Schweickart (ed.)
Subscriptions: $24.00
Pub. frequency: three per annum
☐ First published 1989. Interdisciplinary multicultural feminist research. Reflects 'two decades of feminist scholarship emerging from and supporting the women's movement'. Links feminist theory with teaching and activism.

USAJO60

New Books on Feminism (Literature/Media)
University of Wisconsin System
430 Memorial Library
728 State Street
MADISON, WI 53706
☎ 608 263 5754
Pub. frequency: half-yearly
☐ A bibliography indexed by subject.

USAJO61

Nichibei Josei/US–Japan Women's Journal (Sex and gender)
US–Japan Women's Center
926 Boutista Court
PALO ALTO, CA 94303
☎ 415 857 9049
Subscriptions: $50.00 (for two years)
Pub. frequency: irregular
☐ Aims to provide information about Japanese women to those who live in the USA. Also to enlarge the basis of information available in Japan on feminist theory.

USAJO62

NWS Action (Education/General)
National Women's Studies Association
University of Maryland
COLLEGE PARK, MD 20742-1325
☎ 301 404 5573
Pub. frequency: quarterly
☐ First published 1988. Women's studies articles for those interested in feminist education.

USAJO63

NWSA Journal (Education/Methodology)
National Women's Studies Association
Ablex Publishing Corp
355 Chestnut Street
NORWOOD, NJ 07648
☎ 201 767 8450
Contact: P. Schweickart
Subscriptions: $39.50
Pub. frequency: quarterly
☐ First published 1988. Feminist research is linked with teaching and activism. 'We particularly encourage articles by and about women of color, research analyzing class issues, scholarship examining non-Western cultures.'

USAJO64

On Campus with Women (Education)
Association of American Colleges
Project on the Status and Education of Women
1818 R Street NW
WASHINGTON, DC 20009
☎ 202 387 1300
Subscriptions: $20.00
Pub. frequency: quarterly
☐ First published 1971. Focuses on how women are changing higher education, and examines both research and practice.

USAJO65

On the Issues: The progressive women's quarterly (General/Health)
Choices Women's Medical Center
77–97 Queen's Boulevard
FOREST HILLS, NY 11374
☎ 718 275 6020
Contact: Beverly Lowy
Price: $2.95
Subscriptions: $9.50
Pub. frequency: quarterly
☐ First published 1983. Feminist topics. Anti-racist, anti-sexist and anti-speciesist. Covers politics, health, social reform, animal rights, ecology and global humanism.

USAJO66

PCSW Annual Report (Permanent Commission on the Status of Women) (Equal Opportunities/Civil rights)
90 Washington Street
HARTFORD, CT 06106
☎ 203 566 5702
Price: free
Pub. frequency: annual
☐ First published 1973.

USAJO67

Phoebe (Aesthetics/Methodology)
c/o Women's Studies Program
State University of New York
ONEONTA, NY 13820-4015
Subscriptions: $25.00
Pub. frequency: half-yearly
☐ First published 1989. The subtitle is 'an interdisciplinary journal of feminist scholarship, theory and aesthetics'. Each issue includes feminist theory, articles, fiction, poetry, photos of women's art and book reviews.

USAJO68

Sage: A scholarly journal on black women (Black women)
Sage Women's Education Press
PO Box 42741
ATLANTA, GA 30311-0741
☎ 404 223 7528
Contact: Patricia Bell-Scott
Subscriptions: $15.00
Pub. frequency: half-yearly
☐ First published 1984. Publishes articles on special themes. Reviews, interviews, resource lists and letters. Provides an interdisciplinary forum, promoting feminist scholarship and laying out new knowledge about black women.

USAJO69

Signs: Journal of women in culture and society (Social sciences/Methodology)
University of Chicago Press
Journals Division
5720 South Woodlawn Avenue
CHICAGO, IL 60637
☎ 312 753 3347
Contact: Barbara Laslett
Price: $7.75
Subscriptions: $31.00
Pub. frequency: quarterly
☐ First published 1975. Scholarly articles. International news but mostly news from USA. Focuses on theories and methodologies from a number of disciplines. Provides links between feminist theory and practice.

USAJO70

Sinister Wisdom (Lesbian/Arts)
PO Box 3252
BERKELEY, CA 94703
Contact: Elana Dykewomon
Price: $5.00
Subscriptions: $17.00
Pub. frequency: quarterly

☐ First published 1976. 'A journal for the lesbian imagination in the arts and politics.' Poetry, stories, illustrations, book reviews. Often a special theme for each issue. Ideas and contributions welcomed.

USAJO71

Socialist Review (Socialism)
    Center for Social Research and Education
    2940 16th Street
    SAN FRANCISCO, CA 94103
☏   415 255 2296
Price: $7.00
Subscriptions: $29.00
Pub. frequency: quarterly
☐ Strong feminist emphasis. Radical politics and political economy.

USAJO72

Studies in Gender and Culture (Sex and gender/Culture)
    Gordon & Breach Science Publishers
    270 Eighth Avenue
    NEW YORK, NY 10011
☏ 212 206 8900
Pub. frequency: half-yearly
☐ First published 1988.

USAJO73

Studies in Women and Religion (Religion)
    Edwin Mellen Press
    240 Portage Road
    PO Box 450
    LEWISTON, NY 14092
☏   716 754 8566
Subscriptions: $39.95
Pub. frequency: irregular
☐ First published 1979.

USAJO74

Texas Journal of Women and the Law (Law)
    School of Law Publication
    University of Texas at Austin
    727 East 26th Street
    AUSTIN, TX 78705-3299

USAJO75

Trivia: A journal of ideas (Radical feminism/Lesbian)
    PO Box 606
    NORTH AMHERST, MA 01059
☏ 413 367 2254
Contact: Erin Rice
Price: $5.00
Subscriptions: $14.00 (for 3 issues)
Pub. frequency: half-yearly

☐ First published 1982. Interviews, theory and experimental prose. Where 'women's ideas can assume their original power and significance'. Ideas and contributions welcomed. Predominantly but not exclusively lesbian.

USAJO76

Tulsa Studies in Women's Literature (Literature)
    University of Tulsa
    600 South College Avenue
    TULSA, OK 74104
☏ 918 631 2503
Contact: Holly Laird
Price: $7.00
Subscriptions: $12.00
Pub. frequency: half-yearly
☐ First published 1982. An academic journal. Articles, notes and queries relating to women's literature from all periods and places, including literature in a foreign language. The criticism is feminist in perspective.

USAJO77

Turn of the Century Women (History/Literature)
    Department of English
    Georgetown University
    WASHINGTON, DC 20057
☏ 202 625 4949
Subscriptions: $15.00
Pub. frequency: half-yearly
☐ First published 1984. Academic journal focusing on the lives of British and American women between 1880 and 1920.

USAJO78

WCPS Quarterly (Politics)
    Women's Caucus for Political Science
    343 Codfish Falls
    STORRS, CT 06268-1425
Subscriptions: $25.00
Pub. frequency: quarterly
☐ First published 1982. The journal of the Women's Caucus for Political Science. Information about events, networking and possible jobs.

USAJO79

Wisconsin Women's Law Journal (Law)
    University of Wisconsin-Madison
    Law School
    975 Bascom Mall
    MADISON, WI 53706
☏ 608 262 8294
Contact: Michelle Beeman
Price: $8.00
Pub. frequency: annual
☐ First published 1985. 'Exploration of legal issues relating to women . . . Traditional law review articles are welcome and we encourage practitioner-oriented pieces as well.'

USAJO80

Wise Woman, The: A national journal of feminist issues (Spirituality/General)
    2441 Cordova Street
    OAKLAND, CA 94602
☎ 415 536 3174
Contact: Anne Forfreedom
Price: $4.00
Subscriptions: $15.00
Pub. frequency: quarterly
☐ First published 1980. Focuses on goddess lore and witchcraft. History, news, art, poetry, interviews and research into witch-hunts, women's heritage and women today.

USAJO81

Woman's Art Journal (Arts)
    Woman's Art Inc.
    1711 Harris Road
    LAVERLOCK, PA 19118-1208
☎ 215 233 0639
Contact: Elsa Honig Fine
Price: $7.00
Subscriptions: $14.00
Pub. frequency: half-yearly
☐ First published 1980. Focuses on women in all areas of the visual arts. The subjects covered range from art in ancient times to present-day images. 'We are interested in a re-interpretation of art history.'

USAJO82

Women & Criminal Justice (Civil rights/Social sciences)
    Haworth Press Inc.
    10 Alice Street
    BINGHAMTON, NY 13904
☎ 607 722 2493
Contact: Clarice Feinman
Subscriptions: $24.00
Pub. frequency: half-yearly
☐ First published 1989. Interdisciplinary scholarly research dealing with all areas of women and criminal justice. 'Cross-cultural, historic, and gender studies, women and the law, women in crime and punishment literature . . .'

USAJO83

Women & Health (Health/Social sciences)
    Haworth Press Inc.
    10 Alice Street
    BINGHAMTON, NY 13904-1508
☎ 607 722 2493
Contact: Jeanne M. Stellman
Subscriptions: $36.00
Pub. frequency: quarterly

☐ First published 1976. For all women, consumers as well as providers of health care. Articles, research, bibliographies, book reviews and news. 'A multi-disciplinary journal of women's health issues.'

USAJO84

Women and International Development (International/Development)
    Michigan State University
    Westview Press
    5500 Central Avenue
    BOULDER, CO 80301
☎ 303 444 3541
Price: $25.00
Pub. frequency: annual
☐ First published 1989.

USAJO85

Women and Language (Language/Social sciences)
    George Mason University
    Communication Department
    4400 University Drive
    FAIRFAX, VA 22030
☎ 703 764 6127
Contact: Anita Taylor
Price: $5.00
Subscriptions: $10.00
Pub. frequency: half-yearly
☐ First published 1975. News, research in progress, reviews and short articles related to women, communication and language. 'Identifies courses, conferences, and other events relevant to the study of language and gender.'

USAJO86

Women & Literature (Literature)
    Holmes & Meier Publishers
    30 Irving Place
    NEW YORK, NY 10003
☎ 212 245 4100
Price: varies
Pub. frequency: irregular
☐ First published 1974. Each issue focuses on a specific theme in literary or artistic criticism. The subtitle is 'a journal of women writers and the literary treatment of women'.

USAJO87

Women and Minorities in Science and Engineering (Equal opportunities/Sciences)
    National Science Foundation
    1800 G Street NW
    Room L 602
    WASHINGTON, DC 20550
☎ 202 634 4634

Pub. frequency: half-yearly
□ First published 1982.

USAJO88

Women & Performance: A journal of feminist theory (Arts/Media)
Women & Performance Project
6th Floor
721 Broadway
NEW YORK, NY 10003
☎ 212 998 1625
Contact: Judy Burns
Subscriptions: $14.00
Pub. frequency: half-yearly
□ First published 1983. Devoted to the study of theatre, dance, film, music, video and ritual and performance art. There are discussions of feminist aesthetics, photo essays, interviews, historical material, reviews and scripts.

USAJO89

Women & Politics (Social sciences/Politics)
Haworth Press Inc.
10 Alice Street
BINGHAMTON, NY 13904
☎ 607 722 2493
Contact: Rita Mae Kelly
Subscriptions: $32.00
Pub. frequency: quarterly
□ First published 1980. Aims to unite women's studies with political science, sociology and psychology. Articles and book reviews. Special issues each issue. Academic.

USAJO90

Women & Therapy: A feminist quarterly of research and opinion (Health/Social sciences)
Haworth Press Inc.
10 Alice Street
BINGHAMTON, NY 13904-1580
☎ 607 722 2493
Contact: Ellen Cole
Subscriptions: $36.00
Pub. frequency: quarterly
□ First published 1982. Feminist in orientation, the journal explores multidimensional relationships between women and therapy. Descriptive, theoretical, clinical and empirical perspectives.

USAJO91

Women and Work (Washington): News from the Department of Labor (Paid work)
US Department of Labor
Room S-1032
Office of Information and Public Affairs
Third St and Con. Ave. NW
WASHINGTON, DC 20210
☎ 202 523 7323
Price: free
Pub. frequency: monthly
□ First published 1972.

USAJO92

Women in Culture and Society (Culture/Social sciences)
University of Chicago Press
5801 S Ellis Avenue
CHICAGO, IL 60637
☎ 312 702 7899
Price: varies
Pub. frequency: irregular
□ First published 1984.

USAJO93

Women Lawyers Journal (Law)
National Association of Women Lawyers
750 N Lake Shore Drive
CHICAGO, IL 60611
☎ 312 988 6186
Subscriptions: $16.00
Pub. frequency: quarterly
□ First published 1911.

USAJO94

Women's Health Issues (Health/social sciences)
Jacobs Institute of Women's Health
Elsevier Science Publishing Co.
655 Avenue of Americas
NEW YORK, NY 10010
☎ 212 989 5800
Subscriptions: $78.00
Pub. frequency: quarterly
□ First published 1991. Not only for women. For all who are engaged in women's health issues: social scientists, policy-makers and others concerned with developments affecting women's health care.

USAJO95

Womenwise (Health)
New Hampshire Federation of Feminist Health Centers
Concord Feminist Health Center
38 South Main Street
CONCORD, NH 03301
☎ 603 225 2739
Subscriptions: $10.00
Pub. frequency: quarterly
□ First published 1978. A feminist perspective on women's health issues.

USAJO96

Women's Review of Books, The
(Literature/Media)
Center for Research on Women
Wellesley College
828 Washington Street
WELLESLEY, MA 02181-8255
☎ 617 283 2087
Contact: Linda Gardiner
Price: $2.00
Subscriptions: $17.00
Pub. frequency: monthly
☐ First published 1983. 'In-depth discussion and critique of the latest in writing by and about women in the USA and around the world.' 'A monitor of the currents in contemporary feminism.' An academic journal.

USAJO97

Women's Studies (Champaign)
(Education/General)
University of Illinois Press
54E Gregory Drive
CHAMPAIGN, IL 61820
☎ 217 333 0950
Pub. frequency: irregular

USAJO98

Women's Studies (Lewiston) (Education)
Edwin Mellen Press
240 Portage Road
PO Box 450
LEWISTON, NY 14092
☎ 716 754 8566
Subscriptions: $39.95
Pub. frequency: irregular
☐ First published 1988.

USAJO99

Women's Studies (New York) (Education)
Gordon & Breach Science Publishers
270 Eighth Avenue
NEW YORK, NY 10011
☎ 212 206 8900
Subscriptions: $85.00
Pub. frequency: quarterly
☐ First published 1972.

USAJO100

Women's Studies in Communication
(Education)
Organisation for Research on Women and Communication
Dept of Communication
University of Oklahoma
NORMAN, OK 73019
☎ 405 325 3111

Contact: Sandra L. Ragan (ed.)
Price: $5.00
Subscriptions: $15.00
Pub. frequency: half-yearly
☐ First published 1977. 'To publish material related to gender and communication deriving from any perspective, including interpersonal communication, small group communication, organizational communication, the mass media.'

USAJO101

Women's Studies Quarterly (Education)
Feminist Press at City University of New York
311 East 94th Street
NEW YORK, NY 10128-5603
☎ 212 360 5790
Contact: Nancy Porter
Subscriptions: $25.00
Pub. frequency: half-yearly
☐ First published 1972. Every other issue is devoted to one particular theme, e.g. mothering, peace, war, sexuality, race, culture, art, history and violence. Feminist theory is connected to teaching and politics.

USAJO102

Women's Work: A journal of voices and visions (Culture/Sex and gender)
554 Broadway West
MONTESANO, WA 98563
Price: $1.50
Subscriptions: $9.00
☐ The journal explores culture, gender and mythology. There are essays, reviews, fiction and poetry.

USAJO103

Womyn's Press (Creative writing/Literature)
Womyn's Press Collective
PO Box 562
EUGENE, OR 97440
☎ 503 343 4311
Subscriptions: $7.00
Pub. frequency: bi-monthly
☐ First published 1970. Articles, stories, reviews, poetry and news. Free to women prisoners. Distributed in Eugene and Portland. Free to women living in Eugene.

USAJO104

Working Papers on Women in International Development (International/Development)
Michigan State University
Office of Women in International Development
202 International Center
EAST LANSING, MI 48824-1035
☎ 517 353 5040
Pub. frequency: irregular
☐ First published 1981.

USAJO105

Writing About Women: Feminist literary studies   (Literature/Social sciences)
> Peter Lang Publishing
> 62 West 45th Street
> 4th Floor
> NEW YORK, NY 10036
☎   212 302 6740
Pub. frequency: irregular
☐ A feminist focus on women authors which explores social, psychological, political, economic and historical insights, using an interdisciplinary approach.

USAJO106

Yale Journal of Law and Feminism   (Law)
> 401A Yale Station
> NEW HAVEN, CT 06520
Price: $8.00
Subscriptions: $16.00
Pub. frequency: half-yearly
☐ First published 1987. Bridges the gap between theory and practice, law and policy. Ideas and articles welcomed. 'A forum for the analysis of women, society and the law.' Includes articles, fiction, criticism and poetry.

Magazines

Albania

ALBMA1

Shqiptarja ere (General)
 Union des Femmes d'Albanie
 TIRANA
Subscriptions: US$7.40
Pub. frequency: monthly

Algeria

ALGMA1

Djeza'iriyyah, Al (Culture)
 Union National des Femmes Algeriennes
 Villa Joly
 24 av. Franklin Roosevelt
 ALGIERS
Pub. frequency: monthly
☐ First published 1970. The text is in Arabic and French. Illustrated.

Argentina

ARMA1

Feminaria (Methodology/Literature)
 Casilla de Correo 402
 1000 BUENOS AIRES
☎ 568 3029
Contact: Lea Fletcher
Subscriptions: US$20.00
Pub. frequency: annual
☐ First published 1988. Literary theory and criticism. Interviews and notes about women and their activities. Prose and poetry written by women. Illustrations.

ARMA2

Mujeres (Argentina) (General)
 Sarmiento 2210
 1 Piso
 BUENOS AIRES
Contact: Ana Maria Giacosa
Pub. frequency: monthly
☐ First published 1981.

Australia

AUSMA1

Disabled Women International
(Disability/International)
 12 Ravenswood Avenue
 RANDWICK, NSW 2031
Contact: Joan Hume

AUSMA2

Ink WEL (General)
 Women's Electoral Lobby ACT
 3 Lobelia Street
 O'Connor
 CANBERRA, ACT 2601
Subscriptions: AUS$45
Pub. frequency: bi-monthly
☐ First published 1978. Discussion of many issues from a feminist perspective.

AUSMA3

Lesbian and Gay Counselling News (Lesbian)
 Gay/Lesbian Counselling Service NSW
 PO Box 5074
 SYDNEY, NSW 2001
☎ 02 552 1691
Price: AUS$30.00
Pub. frequency: annual
☐ First published 1980.

AUSMA4

Lesbian Network (Lesbian)
 PO Box 215
 ROZELLE, NSW 2039
☎ 02 660 1565
Price: AUS$5.00
Subscriptions: AUS$24.00
Pub. frequency: quarterly
☐ First published 1983. 'Working to promote a strong and positive lesbian-centred lesbian community.' 'For womin-identified wimmin only.' Features, stories, reviews, poetry, news, an extensive notice board and lesbian listings.

AUSMA5

Lesbian Network Australia Wide (Lesbian)
 PO Box 215
 ROZELLE, NSW 2039
Subscriptions: AUS$13–$18 (suggested)
Pub. frequency: quarterly
☐ By, for and about lesbians.

AUSMA6

Lesbians On the Loose   (Lesbian)
   PO Box 798
   NEWTOWN, NSW 2042
☎   02 660 2981
Pub. frequency: monthly
☐ Distributed in Sydney, Canberra, Newcastle, Gosford, Wollongong, Blue Mountains and Perth.

AUSMA7

Out Loud   (Arts/Lesbian)
   PO Box 535
   ELTHAM, Vic. 3095
☐ First published 1992. Music and culture with a lesbian emphasis.

AUSMA8

Refractory Girl   (General)
   PO Box 648
   GLEBE, NSW 2037
☎   02 557 1955
Subscriptions: AUS$20.00
Pub. frequency: quarterly
☐ Articles, letters, illustrations and photos.

AUSMA9

Right to Choose: A woman's health action magazine   (Reproductive rights/Health)
   Woman's Abortion Action Campaign
   PO Box E233
   ST JAMES, NSW 2000
Subscriptions: AUS$8.00
Pub. frequency: quarterly
☐ First published 1972.

AUSMA10

Scarlet Letter
   Council for Single Mothers and Children
   PO Box 1399 M
   MELBOURNE, Vic. 3001
☎   091 261 6581
Subscriptions: AUS$15.00
Pub. frequency: bi-monthly
☐ First published 1969.

AUSMA11

Scarlet Woman: Socialist feminist magazine (Socialism)
   Scarlet Women Collective
   PO Box A222
   SYDNEY SOUTH, NSW 2000
Subscriptions: AUS$6.00
Pub. frequency: half-yearly

☐ First published 1975. Concerning the family and aboriginal women as seen from a feminist perspective.

AUSMA12

Westside Observer   (Lesbian)
   PO Box 152
   MAYLANDS, WA 6051
☐ Not only for women. A lesbian and gay magazine.

AUSMA13

Wimminews   (General)
   3 Lobelia Street
   O'Connor
   CANBERRA, ACT 2601
☐ A feminist magazine about women in Australia.

AUSMA14

Woman and Earth   (General)
   PO Box 4528
   MELBOURNE, Vic. 3001
Pub. frequency: half-yearly
☐ First published 1992. The text is in English and Russian. Feminist theory, bilingual letters page, book reviews and poetry.

AUSMA15

Womanspeak   (General)
   PO Box 103
   Spit Junction
   SYDNEY, NSW 2088
Subscriptions: AUS$10.00
Pub. frequency: quarterly
☐ First published 1974. Information on women's involvement in film, arts, fiction, theatre, work, domesticity, politics and feminist activism. Covers issues such as child care, rape, pornography, prostitution and law reform.

AUSMA16

Women and Media: Report from Australia (Media)
   Women's Health Centre
   PO Box 665
   SPRING HILL, Qld 4044
☐ 'Many stereotypes about women are perpetuated in the Australian media ... One effort to counter this is the formation of a national media watch organisation.' – Hence Women and Media.

Austria

AUMA1

Anschläge: Feministisches Magazin für Politik, Arbeit und Kultur (Politics/Culture)
Postfach 172
1080 VIENNA
□ First published 1982.

AUMA2

AUF: Eine Frauenzeitschrift (General)
Postfach 817
1011 VIENNA
Price: s38
Subscriptions: s170
Pub. frequency: quarterly
□ First published 1974. Focuses on feminist theory. Articles, photos, news and book reviews.

AUMA3

Blickwechsel: Eine schwullesbische Zeitschrift für Jede (General)
Postfach 385
4010 LINZ
Pub. frequency: monthly
□ First published 1990.

AUMA4

Lesbenrundbrief (Lesbian)
Hosi Lesbengruppe Novaragasse 40
1020 VIENNA
Price: s30
Pub. frequency: irregular
□ First published 1982.

AUMA5

Stimme der Frau (Politics)
Bund Demokratischer Frauen Ost.
Hochstadtplatz 3
1206 VIENNA
Pub. frequency: monthly

AUMA6

Women 2000 (Equal opportunities/Civil rights)
Division for the Advancement of Women
Centre for Social Development
Vienna International Centre
1400 VIENNA
Pub. frequency: bi-monthly
□ 'Published to promote the goals of the Nairobi Forward-looking strategies for the advancement of women.' Each issue tends to focus on one particular theme. Statistics, articles and conferences.

Bangladesh

BANMA1

Begum (General)
66 Loyal Street
DHAKA 1
☎ 2 233789
Pub. frequency: weekly
□ The text is in Bengali.

Barbados

BARMA1

Woman's Voice (Equal opportunities/Civil rights)
National Organization of Women
Import Productions
BRIDGETOWN
Barbados
Subscriptions: US$12.00
Pub. frequency: monthly
□ First published 1977.

BARMA2

Women Speak! (Development)
WAND – Extra Mural Department
University of West Indies
Pinelands
ST MICHAEL
Pub. frequency: three per annum
□ First published 1979. A Caribbean women's magazine, with an emphasis on women's history and culture.

Belgium

BELMA1

Chronique Féministe (Education)
Université des Femmes
1a Place Quetelet
1030 BRUSSELS
☎ 02 219 61 07
Price: BF150.00
Subscriptions: BF500.00
Pub. frequency: quarterly
□ Articles, book reviews and listings. Mainly for students. Recent issues have concentrated on women in the military and family violence.

BELMA2

Echos du Cota (Development)
18 rue de la Sablonniere
1000 BRUSSELS
☎ 02 218 18 96
Subscriptions: BF300.00
Pub. frequency: quarterly

□ First published 1979. The text is in French. Focuses on technical solutions to problems in developing countries. Information, studies and research and technical advice.

BELMA3

Homo-en Lesbiennekraut (Lesbian)
Federatie Werkgroepen Homofilie
Danbruggestraat 204
2008 ANTWERP
☎ 03 233 25 02
Subscriptions: BF500.00
Pub. frequency: monthly
□ First published 1975. Not only for women. The text is in Flemish.

BELMA4

ILGA Bulletin (Lesbian)
International Lesbian and Gay Association
81 rue Marche-au-charbon
1000 BRUSSELS
☎ 02 502 2471
Contact: Antenne Rose
Subscriptions: BF45.00
Pub. frequency: bi-monthly
□ First published 1981. Not only for women. The text is in English and French. International lesbian and gay news.

BELMA5

Iris Bulletin (Equal opportunities/Civil rights)
Equal Opportunities Unit
Commission of the European Communities
200 rue de la Loi
1049 BRUSSELS
☎ 02 236 58 62
Contact: Margarida Pinto
Pub. frequency: quarterly

BELMA6

Lesbianaires, Les: Revue de presse (Lesbian)
BP 2024
BRUSSELS 1
Contact: Isabel Dargent
□ The magazine of the Centre de Documentation et de Recherches sur le Lesbianisme Radical.

BELMA7

Mouvement des Femmes (Politics)
Actuelles Association
14 rue des Deux Points
1040 BRUSSELS
☎ 02 583 47 73
Contact: Jacqueline Rassant
Price: BF40.00
Pub. frequency: monthly
□ Listings, news and views.

BELMA8

Schoppenvrouw (General)
Generaal Drubbelstraat 43
2600 BERCHEN
☎ 03 218 81 57
Contact: Kitty Roggenann
Price: BF60.00
Subscriptions: BF300.00
Pub. frequency: six per annum
□ Illustrated.

Bolivia

BOLMA1

De Textos (Social sciences)
Centro de Investigaciones Sociales
Casilla 6931
Correo Central
LA PAZ
Price: varies
Pub. frequency: irregular
□ First published 1985.

BOLMA2

Escoba (Culture)
Centro de Informationes y Desarrollo Mujer
Casilla 3961
LA PAZ
Pub. frequency: quarterly
□ First published 1986.

BOLMA3

Estudios de Promocion Femenina (Culture)
Centro de Investigaciones Sociales
Casilla 6931
Correo Central
LA PAZ
Pub. frequency: irregular
□ First published 1978.

BOLMA4

Monografias de Promocion Femenina (General)
Centro de Investigaciones Sociales
Casilla 6931
Correo Central
LA PAZ
Price: varies
Pub. frequency: irregular
□ First published 1985.

Brazil

BRAMA1

Dawn Informs   (Development/General)
IUPERJ
Rue Pauline Femareles 32
22270 RIO DE JANEIRO
Pub. frequency: quarterly
☐ The text is in English. Focuses on organisations and research groups related to women's issues.

BRAMA2

Folha de Eva   (Civil rights/General)
Group of Alternative Communication
Rua Belisano Tavora
647302 RIO DE JANEIRO

BRAMA3

Libertacao   (General)
Caixa Postal 18
SAO SEBASTIAO
Subscriptions: cz1,000,000
Pub. frequency: quarterly
☐ A women-centred magazine.

Cameroon

CAMMA1

Femmes e Sante   (Development/Health)
Secrétariat Général de L'IPD
BP 4056
DOUALA
Price: free
Pub. frequency: quarterly
☐ Focuses on women's health and women and children.

Canada

CANMA1

A Friend Indeed/Une Véritable Amie   (Older women/Health)
PO Box 515
Place du Parc Station
Montreal
QUEBEC H2W 2P1
☎   514 843 5730
Subscriptions: CAN$30.00
Pub. frequency: ten per annum
☐ First published 1984. Information, support and exchange for women in menopause and/or mid-life. The text is in English or French.

CANMA2

Action Now/A L'Action   (Equal opportunities/Civil rights)
National Action Committee on the Status of Women
Suite 505
344 Bloor Street West
Toronto
ONTARIO M5S 3A7
☎   416 922 3246
Pub. frequency: eight per annum
☐ Published to encourage action in response to legislative issues of concern to the National Action Committee on the Status of Women.

CANMA3

Angels   (Lesbian)
Lavender Publishing
Society of British Columbia
1170 Bute Street
Vancouver
BRITISH COLUMBIA V6E 1Z7
☎   604 688 0265
Subscriptions: CAN$24.00
Pub. frequency: monthly
☐ First published 1983. Not only for women. A community magazine offering lesbian and gay perspectives on contemporary events, politics, arts and entertainment. Distributed in western Canada.

CANMA4

Aquelarre: Latin American women's magazine (Development)
PO Box 65535
Station F
Vancouver
BRITISH COLUMBIA V5N 5K6
Pub. frequency: quarterly
☐ The text is in English and Spanish. The magazine links Latin American women to Latinas in Canada. It focuses on feminism, particularly arts and culture, in Latin America and the Caribbean.

CANMA5

At the Crossroads: A journal for women artists of African descent   (Arts/Literature)
PO Box 317
Station P
Toronto
ONTARIO M5S 2S8
Price: CAN$8.00
Subscriptions: CAN$14.00
Pub. frequency: half-yearly
☐ First published 1992. 'Documentation of Black Canadian women's art.' Profiles of artists, newsnotes, announcements, reports on events and book reviews. There is also fiction, poetry and reproductions of artwork.

CANMA6

Autre Parole, La   (Religion)
PO Box 393
Succursale
Montreal
QUEBEC H2L 4K3
☎   514 332 0635
Contact: Rita Hazel
☐ For women interested in feminism and Christianity and who want to be the instrument of change for a better and more just society. Published in French only.

CANMA7

B. C. Voice   (Environment/General)
British Columbia Voice of Women
PO Box 586
Keremeos
BRITISH COLUMBIA V0X 1N0
Price: CAN$6.00
Pub. frequency: quarterly
☐ First published 1963. Main subjects covered are world peace and the environment.

CANMA8

Body Politic, The   (Lesbian)
PO Box 7289
Station A
Toronto
ONTARIO M5W 1X9
☎   416 364 6320
Pub. frequency: monthly
☐ Not only for women. A lesbian and gay magazine distributed throughout Canada.

CANMA9

Cayenne: A socialist feminist bulletin
(Socialism/Development)
Cayenne Collective
394 Euclid Avenue
Suite 308
Toronto
ONTARIO M6G 2S9
☎   416 324 8766
Pub. frequency: three per annum
☐ First published 1984. The text is in English. The focus is on Third World politics.

CANMA10

Common Ground: The news and views of PEI women   (General)
PO Box 233
Charlottetown
PRINCE EDWARD ISLAND C1A 7K4
☎   902 368 5040
Contact: Anne McCallum
Price: CAN$2.75

Subscriptions: CAN$12.50
Pub. frequency: bi-monthly
☐ First published 1982. The focus is on women's issues as they affect PEI women. 'It strives to present positive and varied images of women and to support the network of Islanders promoting women's equality.'

CANMA11

Communiqu'Elles   (General)
3585 St-Urbain Street
Montreal
QUEBEC H2X 2N6
☎   514 844 1761
Subscriptions: CAN$14.00
Pub. frequency: bi-monthly
☐ First published 1978. There are both French and English versions of this magazine.

CANMA12

Diversity: The Lesbian Rag   (Lesbian)
PO Box 66106
Station F
Vancouver
BRITISH COLUMBIA V5N 5L4
☎   604 254 8458
Pub. frequency: monthly
☐ First published 1988. 'For lesbians and friends.'

CANMA13

Feminist Action/Action Féministe   (Politics/Law)
National Action Committee on the Status of Women
57 Mobile Drive
Toronto
ONTARIO M4A 1H5
☎   416 759 5252
Subscriptions: CAN$25.00
Pub. frequency: seven per annum
☐ The magazine reports on the status of women and policies which might threaten women's rights.

CANMA14

Femmes d'Action: Revue d'information
(Politics/Culture)
Fédération Nationale Femmes Canadiennes Françaises
325 rue Dalhousie
Porte 525
Ottawa
ONTARIO
K1N 9Z9
☎   613 232 5791
Subscriptions: CAN$12.00
Pub. frequency: six per annum
☐ First published 1971. Published in French only. Focuses on the opinions of French women living within a minority culture.

CANMA15

Femmes d'ici (Education/Politics)
>   Association Féminine d'Education et d'Action
>   Sociale
>   5999 rue de Marseille
>   Montreal
>   QUEBEC H1N 1K6

☎ 514 251 1636
Pub. frequency: annual
☐ First published 1977. News of the Association. Biographies of well-known feminists. Reports of congresses and committee activities.

CANMA16

Femzine (Lesbian/Politics)
>   2 Bloor Street West
>   Suite 100
>   PO Box 120
>   Toronto
>   ONTARIO M4W 3EZ

☐ Hard-hitting political feminist magazine with elements of spirituality.

CANMA17

Fine Balances/Juste Equilibre (Law/Politics)
>   Canadian Advisory Council on Women
>   110 O'Connor Street
>   9th Floor, PO Box 1541
>   Station B, Ottawa
>   ONTARIO K1P 5R5

☎ 613 992 4975
Price: free
Pub. frequency: annual
☐ First published 1986.

CANMA18

Fireweed: A feminist quarterly (General)
>   Fireweed Inc.
>   PO Box 279
>   Station B
>   Toronto
>   ONTARIO M5T 2W2

☎ 416 323 9512
Price: CAN$4.00
Subscriptions: CAN$18.00
Pub. frequency: quarterly
☐ First published 1978. Book and film reviews, fiction, essays and poetry. Illustrated. A forum for feminist discussion and thought. A national magazine, published in English only.

CANMA19

Focus on Women (General)
>   Campbell Communications Inc.
>   1218 Langley Street
>   3rd Floor
>   Victoria
>   BRITISH COLUMBIA V8W 1W2

☎ 604 388 7231
Subscriptions: CAN$20.00
Pub. frequency: monthly
☐ First published 1988.

CANMA20

Galerie (Arts)
>   2901 Panorama Drive
>   North Vancouver
>   BRITISH COLUMBIA V7G 2A4

Pub. frequency: quarterly
☐ First published 1988. The magazine has photographs of works by women artists and essays of art criticism.

CANMA21

Gazette des Femmes, La (Literature/Arts)
>   Conseil du Statut de la Femme
>   8 rue Cook
>   3e Etage, Bureau 300
>   QUEBEC G1R 5J7

☎ 418 643 4326
Price: free
Pub. frequency: six per annum
☐ First published 1979. Book and film reviews as well as articles. The text is in French only. 'La Direction des Communications du Conseil du Status de la Femme.'

CANMA22

Hecate's Loom (Spirituality)
>   PO Box 5206
>   Station B
>   Victoria
>   BRITISH COLUMBIA V8R 6N4

CANMA23

Herizons (General)
>   PO Box 128
>   Winnipeg
>   MANITOBA R3C 2G1

☐ First published 1992.

CANMA24

Herspectives (Reproductive rights/Environment)
>   PO Box 2047
>   Squamish
>   BRITISH COLUMBIA V0N 3G0

Price: CAN$6.00
Subscriptions: CAN$22.00
Pub. frequency: quarterly

☐ First published 1989. Focuses on reproductive freedom, feminization of poverty and 'peaceful co-existence with all living things'. Gives women 'full expression in whatever voice and manner they choose'.

CANMA25

Images (General)
PO Box 736
Nelson
BRITISH COLUMBIA V1L 5R4
☎ 604 352 9916
☐ First published 1972. For women in British Columbia, published in English only.

CANMA26

Just Wages (Paid work/Civil rights)
Women's Resource Centre
101–2245 West Broadway
Vancouver
BRITISH COLUMBIA V6K 2E4
Subscriptions: CAN$10.00
Pub. frequency: quarterly
☐ First published 1991. A magazine giving information about equal pay and wage discrimination.

CANMA27

Kick It Over (Politics/Environment)
PO Box 5811
Station A
Toronto
ONTARIO M5W 1P2
Price: CAN$2.50
Subscriptions: CAN$9.00
Pub. frequency: quarterly
☐ First published 1981. Looks at political and personal issues from a feminist perspective. Focuses on methods of social change and radical ecology.

CANMA28

Kinesis: News about women that's not in the dailies (General)
Vancouver Status of Women
Suite 301
1720 Grant Street
Vancouver
BRITISH COLUMBIA V5L 2Y6
☎ 604 255 5499
Subscriptions: CAN$20.00
Pub. frequency: ten per annum
☐ First published 1972. News, politics and debates about current feminist theories. Features, international reports and resources. Free to prisoners.

CANMA29

L'Une à L'Autre (Health)
PO Box 249
Succ. E
Montreal
QUEBEC H2T 3A7
Pub. frequency: three per annum
☐ First published 1983. Focuses on maternity issues and women's health.

CANMA30

Match News (Development)
Match International Centre
1102–200 Elgin Street
Ottawa
ONTARIO K2P 1L5
☎ 613 238 1312
Subscriptions: CAN$25.00
Pub. frequency: quarterly
☐ First published 1976.

CANMA31

Maternal Health News
(Reproductive rights/Health)
Box 46563
Station G
Vancouver
BRITISH COLUMBIA V6R 4G8
☎ 604 438 5365
Contact: Sue Gregory
Pub. frequency: quarterly
☐ First published 1976. International. Childbirth, midwifery and maternal rights and issues. In English only.

CANMA32

Matriart: A Canadian feminist art journal (Arts)
Women's Art Resource Centre
Suite 309
394 Euclid Avenue
Toronto
ONTARIO M6G 2S9
☎ 416 324 8910
Contact: Linda Abrahams
Pub. frequency: quarterly
☐ First published 1990. 'Canada's only national magazine devoted specially to women artists and cultural production.' Articles, artists' profiles, exhibition reviews and listings of current and forthcoming events.

CANMA33

Newsmagazine by Alberta Women, The (General)
Apartment 808
10126–100 Street
Edmonton
ALBERTA T5J 0P1
☎ 403 429 3570

Pub. frequency: six per annum
☐ First published 1985. A national magazine for the community of women. News, features and reviews. Published in the English language only.

CANMA34

Northern Women's Journal   (General)
184 Camelot Street
Thunder Bay
ONTARIO P7A 4A9
☎   807 345 7802
Contact: Carolyn Greenwood
☐ First published 1973.

CANMA35

Optimist, The   (General)
Apartment 206
302 Steele Street
Whitehorse
YUKON Y1A 2C5
☎   403 667 4637
Pub. frequency: quarterly
☐ First published 1973. A periodical for Yukon women with specific items of national interest. Published in English only.

CANMA36

Pandora   (General)
PO Box 8418
Station A
Halifax
NOVA SCOTIA B3K 5M1
☎   902 454 4977
Contact: Debbie Mathers
Subscriptions: CAN$15.00
Pub. frequency: quarterly
☐ First published 1986. For Nova Scotia women. Relates women's experiences about women. Published in English only.

CANMA37

Parole Métèque, La   (Culture)
5005 chemin de la Côte St Catherine
Bureau 12
Montreal
QUEBEC H3W 1M5
☎   514 737 2666
Contact: Ghila Benesty Sroka
☐ First published 1987. Written in French in collaboration with immigrant and Quebecoise women to promote feminist culture.

CANMA38

Promin   (Civil rights/General)
Ukrainian Women's Association of Canada
612 24th Street East
Saskatoon
SASKATCHEWAN S7K 0L1
☎   306 244 1188
Subscriptions: CAN$17.00
Pub. frequency: monthly
☐ First published 1960. The text is in English and Ukrainian.

CANMA39

Revue Treize, La   (Lesbian/International)
PO Box 771
Succursale C
Montreal
QUEBEC H2T 3A7
Pub. frequency: bi-monthly
☐ First published 1984. A national and international magazine for lesbians.

CANMA40

Rites: For lesbian and gay liberation   (Lesbian/Civil rights)
PO Box 65
Station F
Toronto
ONTARIO M4Y 2L4
☎   416 964 7577
Subscriptions: CAN$20
Pub. frequency: ten per annum
☐ First published 1984. Not only for women. News and analysis of lesbian and gay liberation from a feminist and anti-racist perspective.

CANMA41

Socialist Challenge   (Socialism)
PO Box 12082
Edmonton
ALBERTA T5J 3C2
Subscriptions: CAN$5.00
Pub. frequency: six per annum
☐ First published 1980. News about socialist feminist action in Canada. Reports on conventions and up-to-date information about protests.

CANMA42

Songs of the Dayshift Foreman: Journal of a rainforest witch   (Spirituality)
PO Box 71
Kananaskis
ALBERTA T0L 2H0
Subscriptions: CAN$10.00 (suggested)
Pub. frequency: eight per annum
☐ Focuses on rural witchcraft in the rainforest of the Cordillera between Alaska and California.

CANMA43

Spartacist Canada (Politics)
Trotskyist League of Canada
Spartacist Canada Publishing Association
PO Box 6867
Station A, Toronto
ONTARIO M5W 1X6
☎ 416 593 4138
Price: CAN$2.00
Pub. frequency: quarterly
☐ First published 1975.

CANMA44

Tapestry (General)
PO Box 1242
Vernon
BRITISH COLUMBIA V1T 6N6
☎ 604 542 7531
Contact: Sherri Taber
Pub. frequency: quarterly
☐ First published 1981. A national magazine for the women's community with a focus on urban and rural scenes. In English only.

CANMA45

Tiger Lily (General)
PO Box 756
Stratford
ONTARIO N5A 4A7
☎ 519 271 7045
☐ First published 1986. A national magazine for women covering international women's issues.

CANMA46

Tightwire (Civil rights/International)
PO Box 15
Kingston
ONTARIO K7L 4W7
☎ 613 545 8492
Pub. frequency: quarterly
☐ First published 1968. An international magazine for women in prison to help networking. Published in the English language only.

CANMA47

Vie En Rose, La (General)
3963 St-Denis
Montreal
QUEBEC H2W 2M4
Pub. frequency: monthly
☐ The magazine is produced in a French edition only.

CANMA48

Vox Benedictina (Religion)
Peregrina Publishing Co.
409 Garrison Crescent
Saskatoon
SASKATCHEWAN S7H 2Z9
Pub. frequency: quarterly
☐ 'To make available through translations and articles the rich heritage of feminine monastic spirituality from the period of the early church to the present.'

CANMA49

WaterLily (General)
WaterLily Collective
PO Box 367
Station C
St John's
NEWFOUNDLAND A1C 5J9
Subscriptions: CAN$10.00
Pub. frequency: quarterly
☐ Publishes interviews, reports, reviews and articles on many various subjects, e.g. women and AIDS, women and tobacco, women and the law, women and reproductive technologies.

CANMA50

Womanist, The (General)
Catalyst Research and Communications
Suite 201
541 Sussex Drive
OTTAWA K1N 6Z6
☎ 613 233 2621
Contact: Joan Riggs
Price: free (CAN$10 for mailing)
Pub. frequency: Irregular
☐ First published 1988.

CANMA51

Women & Business (Paid work)
Alder Arthur & Associates
Suite 202
540 Mt Pleasant Road
Toronto
ONTARIO M4S 2M7
☎ 416 482 2878
Subscription: CAN$26.00
Pub. frequency: monthly
☐ First published 1984.

CANMA52

Women & Environments (Environment/Social sciences)
Weed Foundation
736 Bathurst Street
Toronto
ONTARIO M5S 2R4
☎ 416 516 2379

Contact: Kim Pearson
Price: CAN$4.00
Subscriptions: CAN$20.00
Pub. frequency: quarterly
☐ First published 1976. Women's relationship to urban, social and natural environments is examined in detail. Among subjects covered are: planning, architecture, design, housing, urban sociology and geography.

CANMA53

Women in the Labour Force/Les Femmes dans la Population Active   (Paid work)
Canada Women's Bureau
Labour Canada
Ottawa
ONTARIO K1A 0J1
☎   819 994 0543
Price: free
Pub. frequency: irregular
☐ First published 1964.

CANMA54

Zhinochyi Svit/Woman's World   (General)
Ukrainian Women's Organization
937 Main Street
Winnipeg
MANITOBA R2W 3P2
☎   204 943 8230
Subscriptions: CAN$25.00
Pub. frequency: monthly
☐ First published 1950.

Chile

CHIMA1

Bolentina, La   (General)
Coordinadora Organizaciones Mujeres
Bulnes 78
SANTIAGO
☎   2 928 58
☐ First published 1989.

CHIMA2

Mujer/fempress: Unidad de Communication Alternativa de la Mujer   (General)
Casilla 16-637
SANTIAGO 9
☎   2 232 2557
Subscriptions: Esc5000
Pub. frequency: monthly
☐ First published 1981. Published in most countries in South America and contains articles and letters from women throughout the sub-continent. Documents major trends but sets out differences within each country.

CHIMA3

Nueva Mujer   (General)
Barros Arana
Casilla 1225
CONCEPCION 333
☐ Focus on feminist issues. Photographs.

CHIMA4

Revista   (General)
Isis International
Casilla 2067
Correo Central 1
SANTIAGO
☎   2 441 50
Pub. frequency: quarterly
☐ First published 1984. Co-ordinated by Isis.

CHIMA5

Women's Health Journal   (Development/Health)
Latin American and Caribbean Women's Health
Isis International
Casilla 2067
Correo Central 1
SANTIAGO
☎   2 441 50
Pub. frequency: quarterly
☐ First published 1987. General news and updates, conference reports, campaigns. Areas focused on are: AIDS, teenage pregnancy, population policies and contraception and abortion.

China

CHMA1

Funu   (General)
Funu Zazhishe
25 Heping Dajie Erduan
Shenyang
LIANNING 110002
Subscriptions: US$35.90
Pub. frequency: monthly
☐ 'Funu' means 'women' in Chinese.

CHMA2

Funu Gongzuo   (General)
Zhonghua Quanguo
Funu Lianhehui No. 50
Dengshikou
BEIJING 100730
☎   554931
Pub. frequency: monthly
☐ 'Funu gongzuo' means 'women's affairs' in Chinese.

CHMA3

Funu Shenghuo (General)
Funu Shenghuo Zazhishe 15
Jinshui Lu
Zhengzhou
HENAN 450003
Price: Y80
Pub. frequency: monthly

CHMA4

Funu Zhi You (General)
Heilongjiang Sheng F. Lianhehui 11
Ashihe Jie
Nangang-gu
Harbin
HEILONGJIANG 150001
☎ 34059
Pub. frequency: monthly
□ 'Funu zhi you' means 'women's friend' in Chinese.

CHMA5

Nei Menggu Funu (Development)
Nei Menggu Zizhiqu Funu Lianhehui
9 Zhongshan Donglu
Huhhot
NEI MENGGU 010020
☎ 662584
Pub. frequency: monthly
□ First published 1992. The text is in Mongolian. A magazine for 'Inner Mongolian women'.

CHMA6

Nuzi Shijie (General)
Hebei Sheng Funu Lianhehui
244 Nanma Lu
Shijiazhuang
HEBEI 050051
☎ 27871
Pub. frequency: monthly
□ 'Nuzi shijie' means 'woman's world' in Chinese.

CHMA7

Shidai Jiemei (General)
Jilin Sheng Fung Lianhehui
49 Stlain Street
Changchun
JILIN 130051
☎ 802316
Pub. frequency: monthly

CHMA8

Xiandai Funu (General)
Xiandai Funu Zazhishe
213 Minjiaqiao
Lanzhou
GANSU 730000
☎ 465667

Pub. frequency: monthly
□ 'Xiandai funu' means 'modern women' in Chinese.

CHMA9

Xingfu (General)
Wuhan Shi Funu Lianhehui
22 Haomengling Lu
Hankou
Wuhan
HUBEI 430010
☎ 512071
Pub. frequency: bi-monthly
□ The magazine of the Wuhan Municipal Women's Association. 'Xingfu' means 'happiness' in Chinese.

CHMA10

Yanbian Funu (General)
Yanbian Funu Lianhehui
1 Youyi Lu
Guangming Jie
Yanji
JILIN 133000
☎ 518494
Pub. frequency: monthly
□ The text is in Korean. A magazine for Yanbian women.

CHMA11

Zhiyin (General)
Hubei Sheng Funu
Lianhehui Shengwei Dayuan
Shuiguo Hu
Wuhan
HUBEI 430071
☎ 711030
Subscriptions: US$35.90
Pub. frequency: monthly
□ First published 1985. 'Zhiyin' means 'bosom friend' in Chinese.

CHMA12

Zhongguo Funu (Politics/Civil rights)
Zhongguo Funu Zazhishe 24A
Shijia Hulong
BEIJING 100010
☎ 5126980
Subscriptions: Y13.20
Pub. frequency: monthly
□ First published 1956. Focuses on developments and setbacks regarding women's economic and political rights, in work, childcare, healthcare and marriage, and in women's role in Chinese culture. The title means 'Women of China'.

CHMA13

Zhongwai Funu Wenzhai   (General)
 Neimenggu Zizhiqu Funu Lianhehui 9
 Zhongshan Donglu
 Huhhot
 NEIMENGGU 010020
Pub. frequency: monthly

Croatia

CROMA1

Zena   (General)
 Savjet za Pitanja Drustvenog
 Polozaja Zene Pk SSRNH
 Vlaska 70a–111
 41000 ZAGREB
Subscriptions: US$18.00
Pub. frequency: bi-monthly
☐ First published 1943.

Cuba

CUBMA1

Mujeres   (General)
 Federacion de Mujeres Cubanas
 Editora de la Mujer
 Galiano 264
 Residencia Neptuno
 Apartado 2545
 HAVANA
☎   7 61 5919
Subscriptions: US$27.00
Pub. frequency: monthly
☐ First published 1959.

Czech Republic

CZMA1

No (Slovak Women's Union)
(Equal opportunities/Civil rights)
 Zivena
 Nalepkova 15
 81264 BRATISLAVA
☎   07 330420
Price: Kcs145.60
Pub. frequency: weekly
☐ First published 1951.

Denmark

DENMA1

Dialogue   (Development)
 KULU Women and Development
 Landgreven 7
 3 Left
 1301 COPENHAGEN
Pub. frequency: quarterly
☐ The text is in English. Articles, illustrations and photographs.

DENMA2

DKKF-nyt Risskov: Dansk Katolsk Kvinde-Forbund   (General)
 Elbnekvej 16
 8240 RISSKOV
Subscriptions: Dr30
Pub. frequency: bi-monthly
☐ First published 1981. Illustrated.

DENMA3

Hvidlogs Pressen: Et Blad for Lesbiske
(Lesbian)
 c/o Kvindehuset
 Gothersgade 37
 1153 COPENHAGEN K

DENMA4

Konkylien   (General)
 Soemandskoneforeningen af 1976
 Sandbjergvej 7
 3660 STENLOSE
Contact: Jette Haugaard
Subscriptions: Dkr80
Pub. frequency: ten per annum
☐ First published 1977.

DENMA5

Kvinder, Kvinder   (Lesbian)
 Lesbisk Bevaegelse
 Kvindehuset
 Gothersgade 37
 1153 COPENHAGEN K
Pub. frequency: annual
☐ First published 1972. Illustrated.

DENMA6

Kvindestudier Ved AUC Aalborg   (General)
 Aalborg Universitetscenter
 Institut for Samfundsudvikling og planagning
 Aalborg Universitetsflg.
 AALBORG
Price: Dkr132
Pub. frequency: annual
☐ First published 1982.

DENMA7

Nyt Forum for Kvindeforskning (General)
Nyhavn 22
1051 COPENHAGEN K
☎ 13 50 88
Contact: Susanne Possing
Pub. frequency: three per annum
☐ First published 1981. A forum for women. Every other issue is devoted to special subjects. Illustrated and with photos.

DENMA8

Pan Bladet (Lesbian/Culture)
175 Aktiesel Skabet Pan
Knabrostraede 3
PO Box 1023
1007 COPENHAGEN K
☎ 13 19 48
Subscriptions: Dkr175
Pub. frequency: ten per annum
☐ First published 1954. Not only for women. National and international discussions about homosexuality. Interviews, civil rights, culture and health.

Dominican Republic

DOMMA1

Ambar (Socialism/Language)
CE-Mujer
Apartado Postal 21880
SANTA DOMINGO
☎ 686 3388
Pub. frequency: monthly
☐ Articles, book reviews, notice board and photos.

DOMMA2

Instraw News (Development/Civil rights)
Apartado Postal 21747
SANTA DOMINGO
☎ 685 2111
Price: free
Pub. frequency: half-yearly
☐ First published 1980. A magazine for the UN International Research–Training Institute for the Advancement of Women. In-house and regional news. Women's rights, women in the labour force and network building.

DOMMA3

Quehaceres (General)
CIPAF
Apartado Postal 1744
Apartment 358
Del Ensanche Quisqueya
SANTA DOMINGO
☎ 563 5263

Contact: Luis F. Thomen
Pub. frequency: monthly
☐ First published 1980. Magazine of Investigacion Para la Action Femenina (CIPAF). The focus is on feminist issues. Illustrations.

Ecuador

ECUMA1

Abeja, La (General)
Los Rios 2238
GANDARA
☎ 230 844
☐ A magazine which helps to promote the rights of women through action.

ECUMA2

Hogar: La revista de la familia Ecuatoriana (General)
Editores Nacionales
Aguivre 730
PO Box 1239
GUAYAQUIL
Subscriptions: $50.00
Pub. frequency: monthly
☐ First published 1964.

ECUMA3

Mujer, La (General)
Instituto des Estudios Familia–Centro Inf. y Apoyo Mujer
Pinto 145 y 6 Diciembre
QUITO
Pub. frequency: half-yearly
☐ Magazine of the IEF–CIAM.

Fiji

FIJMA1

Balance (Equal opportunities/Civil rights)
Fiji Women's Rights Movement
PO Box 14194
SUVA
☎ 313 156
Subscriptions: US$5.00
Pub. frequency: quarterly

FIJMA2

Fiji Women (General)
George Rubine Ltd
PO Box 12511
SUVA
☎ 313 944
Pub. frequency: monthly
☐ The text is in English.

FIJMA3

Newsclipping Pawornet/Women Workers
(General)
Pacific Regional YWCA Office
PO Box 3940
SAMABULA
☎ 304 961
Pub. frequency: quarterly
☐ There are separate French and English issues.

Finland

FINMA1

Uusi Nainen   (General)
Democratic League of Finnish Women
Palmikot ry
Vilhonkatu 16C27
00100 HELSINKI 10
Subscriptions: Fmk230
Pub. frequency: monthly
☐ First published 1946.

France

FRMA1

Bulletin: Association Nationale des Etudes Féministes   (Politics/Literature)
34 rue du Professeur Martin
Association Loi 1901
31500 TOULOUSE
Subscriptions: FF150.00
☐ Articles, literary information, conferences and book reviews.

FRMA2

Cahiers du Féminisme   (Socialism/International)
14 rue de Nanteuil
75015 PARIS
☎ 45 32 06 23
Subscriptions: FF35.00
Pub. frequency: monthly
☐ First published 1976. Articles, news and comment.

FRMA3

Droits des Femmes   (Civil rights/General)
31 rue le Peletier
75009 PARIS

FRMA4

Femme Nouvelle   (Arts)
Association Française et Internationale d'Art et de Creation
23 rue des Volontaires
75015 PARIS

Pub. frequency: monthly
☐ First published 1976.

FRMA5

Lesbia Magazine: Revue lesbienne d'expression, d'information, d'opinion   (Lesbian/Civil rights)
BP 35
75521 PARIS 11
☎ 43 48 49 54
Price: FF22.00
Subscriptions: FF250.00
Pub. frequency: monthly
☐ First published 1982. Focuses on lesbian civil rights both in France and elsewhere.

FRMA6

Mémoire des Femmes   (Literature)
Editions Syros
6 rue Montmartre
75001 PARIS
Price: varies
Pub. frequency: irregular
☐ First published 1978.

FRMA7

Nouvelles Questions Féministes   (General)
IRESCO
59–61 rue Pouchet
75049 PARIS 17
☎ 40 25 11 91
Contact: Christine Delphy
Subscriptions: FF260.00
Pub. frequency: three per annum
☐ First published 1982. The oldest French feminist periodical. It frequently has double issues on special topics.

FRMA8

Paris Féministe: bulletin d'information et de liaison   (General)
Maison des Femmes de Paris
8 Cité Prost
75011 PARIS
☎ 43 48 24 91
Pub. frequency: monthly
☐ For feminists living in and around Paris.

FRMA9

Revue Internationale de Solidarité   (General)
BP 23
34790 GRABELS
☎ 67 45 24 47
☐ Concerned with women living under Muslim laws.

Gambia

GAMMA1

AWA   (Development/General)
   The Gambia National Women's Bureau
   No.1 Marina Parade
   BANJUL
Contact: Marina Darboe

Germany

GERMA1

AB 40: Zeitschrift von, für, über Frauen
(General)
   Jakob-Klar-Strasse 1
   8000 MUNICH 40
Contact: Dr Greta Tullmann
□ A magazine by, for and about women.

GERMA2

ALFA-Rundbrief   (Reproductive rights/Health)
   Aktion Lebensrecht
   Fuer Alle
   Bornheimer Strasse 90
   5300 BONN 1
☎ 0228 656481
Subscriptions: DM20.00
Pub. frequency: quarterly
□ First published 1985. Information about new fertility techniques and abortions. Bioethics and ethical questions related to abortions are discussed in detail.

GERMA3

Andere, Die: Frauen-reden und Gegenreden
(General)
   'die andere'
   Mauerber 31
   8900 AUGSBURG

GERMA4

Blatt Gold   (Lesbian/Travel)
   Potsdamer Strasse 139
   1000 BERLIN 30
☎ 030 215 6628
Pub. frequency: monthly
□ Lesbian travel. Lists bars and entertainment.

GERMA5

Dorn Rosa: Demokratische Lesben und Schwulenzeitung   (Lesbian)
   Verlag 'Frühlingserwachen'
   Schiffbeker Hohe 39k
   2000 HAMBURG 74
□ First published 1986.

GERMA6

Emma: LeserInnen-Service   (General)
   Postfach 810640
   7000 STUTTGART 80
Price: DM6.00
Subscriptions: DM32.40
Pub. frequency: monthly
□ Illustrations and photographs.

GERMA7

Emma: Das Magazin von Frauen für Frauen
(Radical feminism/Culture)
   Frauenverlag GmbH
   Kolpingplatz 1a
   5000 COLOGNE 1
☎ 0221 210282
Price: DM6.00
Subscriptions: DM72.00
Pub. frequency: monthly
□ First published 1976. Nationwide circulation. Also distributed in Austria, the Netherlands and Switzerland. Feminist news, features, arts reviews and international news. Also cartoons, book reviews, sport and film news.

GERMA8

Frankfurter Frauenblatt   (General)
   Am Industriehof 7–9
   6000 FRANKFURT AM MAIN 60

GERMA9

Frau Anders   (General)
   Redaktion
   Engleplatz 10
   6900 JENA

GERMA10

Frau om Unserer Zeit: Materialien zur Freiheitlich Sozialen Politik   (Socialism)
   Ernst Knoth GmbH
   Postfach 226
   4520 MELLE 1
☎ 05422 2895
Subscriptions: DM18.00
Pub. frequency: quarterly
□ First published 1971.

GERMA11

Frau und Musik: Info Archivnachrichten   (Arts)
   Int. Arbeitskreis Frau und Musik
   Vogesort 8e
   3000 HANOVER 91
Contact: Adelheid Klammt

GERMA12

Frauen in der Literaturwissenschaft (Literature)
Literaturwissenschaftliches Seminar
Universität Hamburg
Von-Melle-Park 6
2000 HAMBURG 13
Contact: Kerstin Wilhemls

GERMA13

Frauen und Film (Media/Culture)
Stroemfeld-Roter Stern
Postfach 180 147
Holzhausenstrasse 4
6000 FRANKFURT AM MAIN 1
☎ 069 599999
Subscriptions: DM30.00
Pub. frequency: half-yearly
☐ First published 1974.

GERMA14

Frauenrundbrief (General)
Die Grünen Baden-Württemberg
Forststrasse 93
7000 STUTTGART 1
Contact: Ulrike Thomas
Pub. frequency: monthly
☐ First published 1990.

GERMA15

Frauenzeitung, Die: FrauenInfoSudwest
(General)
Hohlgasse 7
7570 BADEN-BADEN
Contact: Ulrike Droll

GERMA16

Frei-Räume
FOPA
Adlerstrasse 81
4600 DORTMUND
☐ FOPA is the Feministische Organisation von
Planerinnen und Architektinnen – the feminist org-
anisation for architecture and planning.

GERMA17

**Freida: Die Zeitung von Frauen für Frauen aus
der Wetterau** (General)
Frauenzentrumsverein Friedberg
Usagasse 8
6360 FRIEDBERG/H

GERMA18

Gruppe L74 (Lesbian)
UKZ
Postfach 310609
1000 BERLIN 31

GERMA19

**Hypatia: Zeitschrift des Netzwerkes historisch
Arbeitender** (History)
Frauenbuchversand
Postfach 5266
6200 WIESBADEN

GERMA20

IAF – Information (General)
Interessengemeinschaft der mit Aus. Ver.
Frauen eV
Mainzer Landstrasse 147
6000 FRANKFURT AM MAIN 1
Subscriptions: DM17.00
Pub. frequency: quarterly
☐ First published 1975.

GERMA21

IFPA (Initiative Frauen-Presse-Agentur)
(General)
Büro der FI
Kirschallee 6
5300 BONN

GERMA22

**Ihrsinn: Eine radikalfeministische
Lesbenzeitschrift** (Radical feminism/Lesbian)
c/o Frauenbuchladen Amazonas
Schmidtstrasse 12
4630 BOCHUM

GERMA23

Informationen für die Frau (General)
Deutscher Frauenrat
Simrockstrasse 5
5300 BONN 1
☎ 0228 223008
Subscriptions: D34.00
Pub. frequency: monthly
☐ First published 1952. Periodical of the National
Council of German Women's Organisations dealing
with political topics of concern to women.

GERMA24

**Koryphae: Medium von Frauen aus
Naturwissenschaft und Technik** (General)
Cloppenburger Strasse 35
2900 OLDENBURG

GERMA25

Krampfader (Politics)
Aradia Frauenbuchladen
Reginastrasse 14
3500 KASSEL

Price: DM4.00
Subscriptions: DM20.00
Pub. frequency: quarterly

GERMA26

Lesbenstich: Das Lesbenmagazin für den aufrechten Gang (Lesbian/General)
Lesbenstich-Presse-Verlag
PO Box 360549
1000 BERLIN 36
Subscriptions: DM20.00
Pub. frequency: quarterly
☐ First published 1980. For all German-speaking lesbians.

GERMA27

Liesebuch: Rezensionen, Essays, Portraits, Glossen, Informationen (Literature)
Emmeringer Strasse 9
8000 MUNICH 60
Contact: Hinrike Gronewold
Pub. frequency: quarterly
☐ First published 1990. A review of women's literature. Articles, interviews with women and listings.

GERMA28

Lilit: Zeitschrift für Religionswissenschaft Institut (Religion)
Reutlinger Strasse 2
7400 TUBINGEN

GERMA29

Monatliche, Die: Frauen-abhängige Zeitung für Thuringen (General)
FIT – Fraueninitiative Thuringen
Thomas-Muntzer-Strasse 20
5020 ERFURT
☐ First published 1992.

GERMA30

Python: Die innovative Lesbenzeitung (Lesbian)
Krugstrasse 15
8500 NUREMBERG
Contact: Petra-Lucia Graf

GERMA31

Rosa Flieder: Die Schule Zeitschrift (Lesbian)
Verein Rosa Flieder eV
Bleichstrasse 25
PO Box 910480
8500 NUREMBERG 91
☎ 0911 267779
Subscriptions: DM36.00
Pub. frequency: bi-monthly
☐ First published 1979.

GERMA32

Schlangenbrut: Streitschrift für feministisch und religiös (Religion/Spirituality)
Schlangenbrut
Postfach 7467
4400 MUNSTER
Price: DM6.00
Subscriptions: DM24.00
Pub. frequency: quarterly
☐ For feminists interested in religion. Christianity with regard to women, magic and astrology.

GERMA33

Sozialwissenschaftliche Forschung und Praxis (Socialism)
Herwarthstrasse 22
5000 COLOGNE

GERMA34

Spinnboden Texte (General)
Burgdorfstrasse 1
1000 BERLIN 65
Contact: Melitta Blagi

GERMA35

Stechpalme: Die Erlanger Frauenzeitung für Nordbayern (General)
Zeitungsgruppe im Frauenzentrum
Frauenzentrum eV
Gerberei 4
8520 ERLANGEN

GERMA36

Streit: Feministische Rechtszeitschrift (General)
Frauen streiten für ihr Recht eV
Stegstrasse 34
6000 FRANKFURT 70
Contact: Renate Blumler
Pub. frequency: quarterly
☐ First published 1983.

GERMA37

Tarantel: Frauenzeitung aus Bielefeld (General)
Tarantel Kollektiv
Am Zwinger 16
4800 BIELEFELD

GERMA38

Terre des Femmes (General)
Postfach 2531
7400 TUBINGEN
Contact: Christa Stolle

GERMA39

UKZ-Zeitschrift von und für Lesben   (Lesbian)
Gruppe L74
Postfach 310609
1000 BERLIN 31
Subscriptions: DM60.00
Pub. frequency: bi-monthly
□ First published 1975.

GERMA40

Unerhört!: Eine Zeitung von Frauen für Frauen über Frauen   (General)
Frauenreferat
Universitätsstrasse 2
8900 AUGSBURG

GERMA41

Unter Uns: Zeitschrift für Frauen und Madchen   (Disability)
Deutsche Blindenstudienanstalt
Postfach 1160
3550 MARBURG
☎   06421 606100
Subscriptions: DM85.00
Pub. frequency: monthly

GERMA42

Virginia: Frauenbuchkritik   (Literature)
Postfach 5266
6200 WIESBADEN
Contact: Anke Schafer
Pub. frequency: monthly
□ First published 1987. Book reviews.

GERMA43

Wir Frauen   (Politics)
Demokratische Fraueninitiative
Rochusstrasse 43
4000 DUSSELDORF 1
☎   0211 4912078
Subscriptions: DM16
Pub. frequency: quarterly
□ First published 1982.

GERMA44

Women's International Democratic Federation Magazine   (General)
WIDF
Postfach 940
Dresdener Strasse 43
1020 BERLIN
☎   27 550 28
□ To exchange information on women's lives. To defend women's rights at work. To work for peace and disarmament.

GERMA45

Y (Ypsilon): Zeitschrift aus Frauensicht
(General)
'die andere' Basis Druck Verlags
Postfach 148
1058 BERLIN

GERMA46

Zaunreiterin: Eine Zeitschrift von Frauen für Frauen   (General)
Tschaikowskistrasse 5
7010 LEIPZIG

GERMA47

Zif Bulletin   (General)
Zentrum Interdisziplinare Frauen
Humboldt Universität Berlin
Unter den Linden 6
R. 3070
1086 BERLIN
Contact: Gabriele Jahnert

GERMA48

Zweiwochendienst Frauen und Politik   (Politics/ Civil rights)
Gesellschaft für Chancengleichheit
Siebengebirgsallee 61
5000 COLOGNE
Contact: Marion Luhring
Subscriptions: DM84.00
Pub. frequency: monthly
□ First published 1987. Focuses on women in politics and suggests how to better women's chances in education and business.

Great Britain and Northern Ireland

GBMA1

Akina Mama wa Afrika/African Woman   (Black women/Development)
London Women's Centre
Wesley House
4 Wild Court
LONDON WC2B 5AU
□ First published 1988. Articles on women's development and political issues in Africa.

GBMA2

Arachne: A journal of matriarchal studies
(Spirituality)
Arachne Collective
c/o 14 Hill Crest
SEVENOAKS TN13 3HN
Pub. frequency: irregular

□ First published 1984. Focuses 'on female aspects of divinity'. Articles on aspects of the goddess and information on archaeological and mythical findings.

GBMA3

Bad Attitude (England) (Radical feminism/Lesbian)
121 Railton Road
LONDON SE24 0PH
☎ 071 978 9057
Price: £1
Subscriptions: £5.00
Pub. frequency: bi-monthly
□ First published 1993. A magazine covering a wide range of feminist issues. 'Dedicated to the overthrow of civilisation as we know it.'

GBMA4

Bitch (General)
Bitch Publications Ltd
43 Church Row
HOVE
BN3 2BE
☎ 0273 747755
Price: £1.20
Pub. frequency: monthly
□ First published 1992. Ironic comment on news/events. Take-off of traditional women's magazines. Cartoons and photographs.

GBMA5

Breaking Chains (Reproductive rights/Law)
Abortion Law Reform Association
88 Islington High Street
LONDON N1
Subscriptions: £8.50
Pub. frequency: quarterly

GBMA6

Candice (General)
New Horizons Publishing
PO Box 2037
LONDON W12 8JS
Subscriptions: £9.90
Pub. frequency: six per annum
□ First published 1992. Issues covered include health, arts, book reviews, fashion, travel and music. Illustrations and photographs.

GBMA7

Chrysalis: Women and religion (Religion)
Movement for the Ordination of Women
Napier Hall
Hide Place
Vincent Street
LONDON SW1P 4NJ
Pub. frequency: three per annum

□ News and articles about the ordination of women in England. The magazine for the Movement of the Ordination of Women.

GBMA8

CIA (Lesbian/General)
Nottingham Community Arts
39 Gregory Boulevard
Hyson Green
NOTTINGHAM NG7 6BE
Price: 90p
Pub. frequency: monthly
□ First published 1992. Comic strips, anti-racist, letters, notice board.

GBMA9

Daskhat (Literature/General)
90 Dunstable Road
LUTON LU1 1EH
Contact: Seema Jena
Price: £3.00
Subscriptions: £5.00
Pub. frequency: half-yearly
□ First published 1992. The UK's first South Asian literature magazine. Stories, poetry, book reviews and critical essays. Ideas and contributions welcomed.

GBMA10

Everywoman: The current affairs magazine for women (Politics/General)
Everywoman Publishing Ltd
34 Islington Green
LONDON N1 8DU
☎ 071 359 5496
Contact: Barbara Rogers
Price: £1.65
Subscriptions: £19.80
Pub. frequency: monthly
□ First published 1985. Current affairs for women. Covers food, health, green issues and politics. Also articles on international issues. Book, theatre and film reviews. Comprehensive notice board.

GBMA11

Explorations in Feminism (Social sciences/Sex and gender)
Women's Research & Resources Centre
Explorations in Feminism
c/o Silver Moon Bookshop
68 Charing Cross Road
LONDON WC2H 0BB
Pub. frequency: irregular
□ First published 1981.

GBMA12

Feminist Arts News (FAN) (Arts/Politics)
    Unit 26
    30-38 Dock Street
    LEEDS LS10 1JF
☎ 0532 429964
Price: £2.25
Subscriptions: £9.00
Pub. frequency: quarterly
☐ First published 1989. Radical arts magazine. Cultural politics in a critical framework. Illustrated. Poetry, film, art. Each issue focuses on one particular theme.

GBMA13

From the Flames (Spirituality)
    42 Mapperley Road
    NOTTINGHAM NG3 5AS
Price: £1.50
Subscriptions: £4–20 (sliding scale)
Pub. frequency: quarterly
☐ First published 1991. 'A quarterly journal of radical feminist spirituality, magic and the goddess.' Articles from readers welcomed. Poetry and illustrations. Lists of contacts, coming events and network listings.

GBMA14

Gay and Lesbian Humanist
    Gay and Lesbian Humanist Association
    34 Spring Lane
    KENILWORTH CV8 2HB
☎ 0926 58450
Price: 80p
Subscriptions: £6.00
Pub. frequency: quarterly
☐ Not only for women. News, features, book reviews and readers' letters. Also photos and cartoons.

GBMA15

Gay Scotland: For lesbians, gays and bisexuals (Lesbian)
    58A Broughton Street
    EDINBURGH EH1 3SA
☎ 031 557 2625
Price: £1.50
Subscriptions: £18.00
Pub. frequency: monthly
☐ First published 1981. Not only for women. Lesbian, gay and bisexual news and entertainment.

GBMA16

Gay's the Word Review (Lesbian/Literature)
    Gay's the Word
    66 Marchmont Street
    LONDON WC1N 1AB
☎ 071 278 7654
Price: 50p
Subscriptions: £4.50
Pub. frequency: irregular

☐ First published 1981. Not only for women. Reviews new feminist and gay literature.

GBMA17

Girl Frenzy (Lesbian)
    BM Senior
    LONDON WC1N 3XX
Price: £1.50
Pub. frequency: irregular
☐ First published 1992. Comic strips, film and book reviews.

GBMA18

Girls' Own and Artemis (Lesbian)
    BM Princess
    LONDON WC1N 3XX
Contact: Jenny Falconer
Price: £1.00
Subscriptions: £10.00
☐ First published 1993. 'A national magazine for lesbians, bisexual women and all women who prefer women.' Contact service provided.

GBMA19

Harpies & Quines (General)
    PO Box 543
    GLASGOW G20 9BN
☎ 041 353 1550
Price: £1.50
Pub. frequency: bi-monthly
☐ First published 1992. A new feminist magazine from Scotland.

GBMA20

Just Women
    Sky Cottage
    Buckland St Mary
    Chard
    SOMERSET TA20 3ZR
☎ 0823 254310
Price: £1.00
Subscriptions: £5.80
Pub. frequency: quarterly
☐ First published 1988. 'The magazine for women in the South West.' Features, fiction, poems and topics of current interest.

GBMA21

Medical Woman (Sciences/Health)
    Medical Women's Federation
    Tavistock House North
    Tavistock Square
    LONDON WC1H 9HX
☎ 071 387 7765
Contact: Lyn Perry
Subscriptions: £20.00 (suggested)
☐ Articles, medical news and activities. Items of interest to women doctors and patients. The magazine of the Medical Women's Federation.

GBMA22

Noticeboard   (Politics)
  300 Group
  36–37 Charterhouse Square
  LONDON EC1M 6EA
☎ 071 600 2390
Contact: Clare Pettitt
Price: free
Pub. frequency: quarterly
☐ Articles written by MPs, interviews and features.

GBMA23

Pandora's Jar   (Spirituality)
  'Blaenberem'
  Mynyddcerrig
  LLANELLI SA15 5BL
Price: £1.50
Subscriptions: £3.50
Pub. frequency: three per annum
☐ First published 1991. 'A radical journal of Earth-centred Pagan spirituality and politics ... Dedicated to "Greening the Earth Anew".' Political and spiritual radical ecological politics.

GBMA24

Shebang: The dyke active ingredient   (Lesbian)
  77 City Garden Row
  LONDON N1 8EZ
☎ 071 608 2566
Price: free
☐ First published 1992. Articles, news, current events and photos.

GBMA25

Society of Women Artists Publication   (Arts)
  Society of Women Artists
  Orchard House
  Adam and Eve Mews
  167–169 Kensington High Street
  LONDON W8 6SH
Price: £1.00
Pub. frequency: annual

GBMA26

Trouble and Strife: A radical feminist journal   (Radical feminism/Lesbian)
  PO Box 8
  DISS IP22 3XG
Subscriptions: £7.50
Pub. frequency: three per annum
☐ First published 1983. Interviews with radical feminists, book reviews, articles, news and notice board. Illustrated. 'To record the history of the current wave of feminism worldwide.'

GBMA27

Widening Horizons   (Paid work/International)
  International Federation of Business and Professional Women
  Studio 16, Cloisters House
  Cloisters Business Centre
  8 Battersea Park
  LONDON SW8 4BG
☎ 071 738 8323
Subscriptions: £3.75
Pub. frequency: half-yearly
☐ First published 1931. News about the International Federation of Business and Professional Women as well as information about intergovernmental organizations.

GBMA28

Womankind (Worldwide)   (Development/International)
  122 Whitechapel High Street
  LONDON E1 7PT
☎ 071 247 9431
Subscriptions: £10.00
Pub. frequency: half-yearly
☐ First published 1989. To raise funds for women's self-help initiatives in developing countries.

GBMA29

Women Against Fundamentalism   (Religion)
  PO Box 2706
  LONDON WC1N 3XX
☎ 081 571 9595
Price: £1.20
Subscriptions: £6.00
Pub. frequency: quarterly
☐ Affiliated to the Women Against Fundamentalism organisation. Examines and analyses the question of women and fundamentalism in all religions from a number of perspectives.

GBMA30

Women and Computing   (Technology/Paid work)
  London Women's Centre
  Wesley House
  4 Wild Court
  LONDON WC2 5AU
☎ 071 430 0655
Price: £2.00
Subscriptions: £8.00
Pub. frequency: quarterly
☐ Produced by a feminist collective, the magazine provides information on women's jobs in information technology. Researches into VDU hazards and comments on women's technology initiatives worldwide.

GBMA31

Women in Europe (General)
Commission of European Communities
8 Storey's Gate
LONDON SW1P 3AT
☎ 071 973 1992
Pub. frequency: eight per annum
☐ First published 1985. A British focus on news and views about women in the European community.

GBMA32

Women's Art Magazine (Arts)
Women Artists Slide Library
Fulham Palace
Bishops Avenue
LONDON SW6 6EA
☎ 071 731 7618
Contact: Genevieve Fox
Price: £2.50
Subscriptions: £15.00
Pub. frequency: bi-monthly
☐ First published 1985. Covers the work of women artists. Documents individual works. Listings. In-depth articles. Exhibition news. Book reviews. Theoretical pieces on art history and criticism. Ideas welcomed.

GBMA33

Women's Choice: A magazine of reproductive rights (Reproductive rights)
National Abortion Campaign
The Print House
18 Ashwin Street
LONDON E8 3DL
☎ 071 923 4976
Price: £1.00
Subscriptions: £5.50
Pub. frequency: quarterly
☐ First published 1992. Articles on all issues related to reproductive rights. Produced by the National Abortion Campaign.

GBMA34

Women's News (General/International)
185 Donegal Street
BELFAST BT1 2FJ
Subscriptions: £10.00
Pub. frequency: 11 issues per year
☐ News about the women's movement in Ireland and worldwide. Creative writing, events, listing and illustrations.

GBMA35

Wood and Water (Spirituality)
77 Parliament Hill
LONDON NW3 2TH
Contact: Daniel Cohen
Price: £1.00

Subscriptions: £4.00
Pub. frequency: quarterly
☐ Not only for women, but Goddess-centred and feminist influenced. A mixed collective. Articles, poems, book reviews and a list of other pagan magazines. Material from readers welcomed.

Greece

GREMA1

'Gay' Magazine (Lesbian/General)
One Steit Street
ATHENS 10055
☎ 1 321 7413
☐ Not only for women.

Hong Kong

HKMA1

Women's News Digest (General)
Association for the Advancement of Feminism
444–446 Nathan Road
87 KOWLOON
☐ The magazine of the Association for the Advancement of Feminism. Advocates 'social changes which will bring about a society with equality for both sexes'.

Iceland

ICEMA1

Husfreyjan (Civil rights)
Kvenfelagasamband Islands
Hallveigarstoedum
Tungotu 14
REYKJAVIK
Subscriptions: kr1500
Pub. frequency: quarterly
☐ First published 1949.

India

INDMA1

Chetna News (Development/General)
Centre of Health Education, Training and Nutritional Awareness
Third Floor
Drive-in-Cinema Building
Thaltej Takra, Ahmedabad
GUJARAT 380054
☎ 490 378 496325
☐ The focus is on women and development and feminist issues.

INDMA2

Highland Booknews: Book review magazine
(Literature)
> Women's Alliance for Publishing
> Cheeroth Building
> Kodimatha
> KOTTAYAM 686039

Price: Rs20
Pub. frequency: quarterly
☐ First published 1990. The text is in English and Malayalam.

INDMA3

Kaluvabala: Women's fortnightly   (General)
> Andhra Patrika
> 12–14–21 Mallikarjuna Rao
> Gandinagar
> VIJAYAWADA 520003
☎   61247
Pub. frequency: fortnightly

INDMA4

Manushi: A journal about women and society   (General)
> Manushi Trust
> C/202 Lajpat Nagar 1
> NEW DELHI 110024
☎   11 6833022
Contact: Madhu Kishwar
Price: Rs7
Subscriptions: Rs42
Pub. frequency: bi-monthly
☐ First published 1979. About women and society. The Hindi title means 'woman'. Produced in English and Hindi. Articles on all aspects of women's life in India. Also distributed outside India. News, reviews, features and letters.

INDMA5

Vanita Jyoti
> Labbipel
> VIJAYAWALA 520 010
☎   866 474 532
Subscriptions: Rs54
Pub. frequency: monthly
☐ First published 1978. Focuses on women's problems. Interviews professional and world-famous women.

Indonesia

INMA1

Drong/Bret (International Bulletin of KalyanimitraFoundation)   (Development/General)
> JL Raya Bogor KM 20/30
> JAKARTA 13510
☎   21 809 2603

☐ The text is in English. Focuses on social issues related to women. Illustrated.

INMA2

Kowani News   (Development)
> Kongres Wanita Indonesia
> Jl. Imam Bonjol 58
> JAKARTA
☎   21 364 921
Pub. frequency: three per annum
☐ First published 1986. There are both English and Indonesian editions. The publication of the Indonesian Women's Congress.

Iran

IRAMA1

Mahjubah: The magazine for Muslim women   (General)
> PO Box 14155–3987
> TEHRAN

Ireland

IREMA1

OUT Monthly   (International/General)
> Top Floor
> Dublin Resource Centre
> 6 Crow Street
> DUBLIN 2
☎   01 771974
Price: I£1.20
Subscriptions: I£17.50
Pub. frequency: monthly
☐ International news relating to lesbian issues. In-depth interviews, safe-sex information, reviews. Free classified ads.

IREMA2

Women's Clubs Magazine   (General)
> Irish Federation of Women's Clubs
> Maxwell Publicity
> 49 Wainsfort Park
> DUBLIN 6
☎   01 904168
Price: I£1.50
Pub. frequency: quarterly
☐ First published 1971.

Israel

ISRMA1

Isha L'isha/Woman to Woman   (General)
   Isha L'isha Haif Feminist Centre
   PO Box 3610
   HAIFA
Pub. frequency: bi-monthly
☐ First published 1973. The text is in Arabic, English and Hebrew.

ISRMA2

Naamat: Magazine for women in work, society and family   (Paid work/Civil rights)
   Histadrut
   93 Arlozorov Street
   TEL AVIV 62098
☎   03 431111
Subscriptions: IS55
Pub. frequency: ten per annum
☐ First published 1934. Focuses on women's roles in work and society. Also concentrates on women's status and legal rights.

ISRMA3

Networking for Women   (General)
   PO Box 3171
   JERUSALEM 91031
Pub. frequency: quarterly
☐ A quarterly publication of the Israel Women's Network. Focuses on political, legal and gender issues.

ISRMA4

Noga   (General)
   PO Box 21376
   TEL AVIV 61213
☎   03 227663
Subscriptions: IS16
Pub. frequency: three per annum
☐ Published by an Israeli women's collective, the text is in Hebrew. News, features, feminist theory, arts and book reviews. Information and research on women from an international viewpoint.

ISRMA5

Yidion   (General)
   Israel Women's Network
   PO Box 3171
   JERUSALEM 91031
☎   02 690358
Subscriptions: US$15.00
Pub. frequency: quarterly

Italy

ITMA1

Bollettina Del Cli: Collegamento fra le lesbiche Italiane   (Lesbian)
   CLI
   Via S. Fran. de Sales 1A
   00165 ROME
☐ First published 1981.

ITMA2

Clio Notizie
   Franco Angeli Editore
   Viale Monza 106
   PO Box 17175
   20100 MILAN
☎   02 2895762
Pub. frequency: three per annum
Subscriptions: L38,000
☐ Information about work for women.

ITMA3

Emergenze   (General)
   Via Santa Maria dell'Anima 30
   00186 ROME
☎   06 68332
Price: L3,000
Subscriptions: L20,000
Pub. frequency: half-yearly
☐ Articles and illustrations.

ITMA4

Lapis: Percorsi della reflessione femminile (General)
   Gruppo Editoriale Faenza Editrice
   Via Pierde Crescenzi 44
   48018 FAENZA RA
☎   0546 663488
Subscriptions: L35,000
Pub. frequency: quarterly
☐ First published 1990.

ITMA5

Mediterranea – L'observatorio delle donne (General)
   Editrice Pellegrini
   Via Roma 74
   Casella Postale 158
   87100 COSENZA
Subscriptions: L40,000

ITMA6

Memoria: Rivista di storia delle donne (Culture/Politics)
   Rosenberg & Sellier
   Via Andrea Doria 14
   10123 TURIN

☎ 011 5613907
Subscriptions: L44,000
Pub. frequency: three per annum
☐ First published 1981. The emphasis is on the culture of feminism. Focuses on women's oppression through marriage, patriarchy, dress and motherhood.

ITMA7

Noi Donne: Mensile dell'udi (General)
    Cooperativa Libera Stampa
    Via della Trinita
    dei Pellegrini 12
    00186 ROME
☎ 06 6864562
Subscriptions: L40,000
Pub. frequency: monthly
☐ First published 1944.

ITMA8

Quarto Mondo (General)
    Fronte Italiano di Liberazione Fem.
    Piazza Apostoli 49
    00187 ROME
Pub. frequency: monthly
☐ First published 1971.

ITMA9

Reti – Pratiche e Saperi di Donne (General)
    Editori Riunti
    Via Serchio 9–11
    00198 ROME
☎ 06 866383
Subscriptions: L41,000
Pub. frequency: bi-monthly
☐ First published 1987.

ITMA10

Via Dogana: Circolo Cooperativo delle donne 'Sibilla Aleramo' (General)
    Libreria delle donne
    Via Dogana 2
    20123 MILAN
☐ First published 1991.

ITMA11

Women in Action (Italy) (International/General)
    Isis International
    Santa Maria dell'Anima 30
    00186 ROME
☎ 06 5746479
Subscriptions: US$20.00
Pub. frequency: quarterly

☐ The text is in either English or Spanish. News and information about groups, conferences, events and resources. Keeps up to date with the Women's Liberation Movement worldwide.

Ivory Coast

IVMA1

CIFAD: Bulletin d'Information (Development/General)
    BP 5147
    ABIDJAN 01
☎ 22 93 84
☐ Magazine for the Comité Internationale des Femmes Africaines pour le Developpement. Focuses on women and health issues.

Jamaica

JAMMA1

Sistren (Development/General)
    Sistren Theatre Collective
    20 Kensington Crescent
    KINGSTON 5
☎ 929 2457
Subscriptions: J$12.00
☐ Focuses on feminism in the Caribbean: women and survival strategies, child sex abuse, women in prison, civil rights, housing difficulties, women and the media, and women and health.

Japan

JAPMA1

Fujin Koron (General)
    Chuokoron-sha
    No. 2–8–7 Kyobashi
    Chuo-ku
    TOKYO
Subscriptions: Yen8950
Pub. frequency: monthly
☐ First published 1916. The title means 'women's public opinion'.

JAPMA2

Inter Act (General)
    3–12–3–607 AOBA Shinamotocho
    Mishinagun
    OSAKA 618
Subscriptions: Yen500
Pub. frequency: monthly
☐ The emphasis is feminist. The text is in both English and Japanese.

JAPMA3

Japanese Women (General)
Fusae Ichikawa Memorial Association
21–11 Yoyogi 2–chome
Shibuya-ku
TOKYO 151
☎ 03 3370 0238
Subscriptions: Yen330
Pub. frequency: half-yearly
☐ The text is in English. Issued by the Women's Suffrage Centre, a public service corporation covering politics, education and research on improving the status of women. It documents surveys.

JAPMA4

Nihon Fujin Kagakusha No Kai Nyusu (Sciences)
29 2 203 Koenji Kita 4-Chome
Suginami-ku
TOKYO 166
Pub. frequency: irregular
☐ First published 1958. The periodical covers news of the Association of Japanese Women Scientists.

JAPMA5

Women and Health (Japan) (Health)
Women's Centre Osaka
1 3 23 Gamo Joto-ku
OSAKA 536
☎ 06 933 7001
Subscriptions: Yen2000
Pub. frequency: quarterly
☐ First published 1991. Information about Japanese women's health.

Kenya

KENMA1

HIC Women and Shelter Network (Development/International)
Mazingira
PO Box 14564
NAIROBI
Price: free
Pub. frequency: annual
☐ Mainly relating to African women who are for the most part connected to the Network. Also international news, Network meetings, congresses and articles about women's experiences.

KENMA2

WWB Africa (General)
Women's World Banking/Africa
Bima House
8th Floor
PO Box 55919
NAIROBI
Pub. frequency: quarterly
☐ First published 1986. Articles on women's organisations in Africa, training, the World Bank, and women and the African economy.

Malaysia

MALMA1

Issues in Women and Development (Development/General)
Asian and Pacific Development Centre
Pesiaran Duta
PO Box 12224
50770 KUALA LUMPUR
☎ 03 254 8088
Pub. frequency: half-yearly
☐ First published 1989. Aims to provide a forum through which the needs, interests and situations of women in the region can be widely articulated. Also aims to promote stronger networking and sharing of resources.

MALMA2

Resource Update (Development/General)
Women's Development Collective
43C Jalan SS 6/12
47301 Petaling Jaya
SELANGOR

Mauritius

MAUMA1

Mariemou: Revue de la jeune fille et de la femme Mauritaniennes (General)
BP 47
NOUAKCHOTT
Pub. frequency: quarterly
☐ First published 1969. Editions in Arabic and French.

Mexico

MEXMA1

Companeras (General)
Mujeres para el Dialogo
Apartado 19-493
MIXCOAC 03910
☐ A magazine about topical feminist issues. Illustrated.

MEXMA2

Fem   (Culture/General)
  Difusion Cultural Feminista AC
  Avenida Universidad 1855
  PIS04 Col. Oxtopulco
  CP 04310
  ☎   550 73 06
Subscriptions: $60.00
Pub. frequency: monthly
☐ First published 1976. Each issue has a definite theme, particularly relating to women in Mexico and South America generally.

Namibia

NAMMA1

Sister   (Development/General)
  Sister Collective
  PO Box 60100
  WATUTURA 9000
Subscriptions: R10
Pub. frequency: quarterly
☐ First published 1989. 'A news journal for and about women.' Focuses on women and development issues: sex education, women and health, women and the environment, and family planning.

NAMMA2

Women's Voice   (Development/General)
  Namibian Women's Voice
  PO Box 7256
  9000 Katutura
  11 PA de Wet Street
  WINDHOEK
  ☎   061 215418
Pub. frequency: quarterly
☐ First published 1988. The text is in both English and Africaans.

Netherlands

NETMA1

Briljantine: Driemaandelijks tijdschrift
(General)
  Damstraat 19
  3513 BP UTRECHT
Pub. frequency: quarterly
☐ First published 1990.

NETMA2

Feministisch Maandbiad Opzij   (General)
  PO Box 1311
  1000 BH AMSTERDAM
  ☎   020 551 85 25
Pub. frequency: quarterly

NETMA3

Furore: Feministisch Maandblad   (General)
  PO Box 1994
  1000 BZ AMSTERDAM
  ☎   020 627 50 35
Pub. frequency: monthly
☐ First published 1983. Independent feminist magazine.

NETMA4

Lesbisch Informatieboekje   (Lesbian/General)
  Nederlandse Veren. tot Intergratie van
  Homoseksualiteit coc
  Rozenstraat 8
  1016 NX AMSTERDAM
  ☎   020 623 11 92
Price: fl6.75
Pub. frequency: annual
☐ First published 1983.

NETMA5

Lust & Gratie: lesbisch cultureel universeel tijdschrift   (Lesbian/Culture)
  PO Box 18199
  1001 ZB AMSTERDAM
  ☎   020 662 261
Subscriptions: fl54.00
Pub. frequency: quarterly
☐ First published 1983. Contains essays, prose, poetry, illustrations and photographs. The focus is on culture. Illustrated with photos.

NETMA6

Ma'dam   (Lesbian)
  Rozenstraat 14
  1016 NX AMSTERDAM
Pub. frequency: monthly

NETMA7

Man to Man Guide: gay–lesbian guide to Holland   (Lesbian/Travel)
  City Map Produkties
  PO Box 10419
  1001 EK AMSTERDAM
  ☎   020 626 07 02
Price: fl9.50
Pub. frequency: annual
☐ First published 1975. Not only for women. The text is in Dutch, English, French, German and Italian.

NETMA8

Nemesis   (Politics)
  Samson H. D. Tjeenk Willink
  PO Box 316
  2400 AH ALPHEN A/D RIJN
  ☎   017 209 32 70
☐ Focuses on women on the right in politics.

NETMA9

SEK: Lesbisch en homoblad (Lesbian)
> Rozenstraat 8
> 1016 NX AMSTERDAM
☎ 020 623 11 92
Subscriptions: fl27.00
Pub. frequency: monthly
☐ First published 1971. Not only for women.

NETMA10

Surplus: Tweemaandelijks tijdschrift over literatuur van vrouwen (Literature)
> Surplus Foundation
> Postbus 16572
> 1001 RB AMSTERDAM
☎ 020 620 77 67
Subscriptions: fl25.00
Pub. frequency: bi-monthly
☐ First published 1987. Women's review of books.

NETMA11

Vrouw en Kunst (General)
> Rulmte
> PO 14851
> 1001 IJ AMSTERDAM
☎ 020 626 65 89

NETMA12

WEP International News (Equal opportunities/ Civil rights)
> Mathenesserlaan 177
> PO Box 25096
> 3000 HB ROTTERDAM
☎ 010 436 01 66
Price: fl15.00
Subscriptions: fl23.95
Pub. frequency: half-yearly
☐ The text is in English. Civil rights and women's conferences.

NETMA13

WISE Women's News (Education/General)
> Women's International Studies Europe (WISE)
> Heidelberglaan 2
> 3584 CS UTRECHT
☎ 030 53 18 81
Subscriptions: Ecu15
☐ News, comment, lists of names and addresses, and short articles. The text is in both French and English.

New Caledonia

NCMA1

Women's News (New Caledonia)
(Development/General)
> South Pacific Commission
> BP D5
> NOUMEA
☎ 687 26 20 00
Pub. frequency: quarterly
☐ First published 1982. The publication of the Pacific Women's Resource Bureau with regional and international action-oriented information relating to special concerns of Pacific region women. News of conferences and workshops. The text is in English and French.

New Zealand

NZMA1

Broadsheet (Radical feminism/General)
> WomanFile
> PO Box 56147
> 228 Dominion Road
> AUCKLAND 3
☎ 09 608 535
Price: NZ$4.50
Subscriptions: NZ$35.00
Pub. frequency: ten per annum
☐ First published 1972. Feminist magazine covering a wide range of issues in the form of articles and news items. Strives to incorporate the views of indigenous women and to be anti-racist. Focus is on New Zealand.

NZMA2

RGC: Race Gender Class (Sex and gender)
> The Co-ordinating Collective
> Race Gender Class
> PO Box 1372
> OTAUTAHI (CHRISTCHURCH)
Price: NZ$5.00
Subscriptions: NZ$14.00
Pub. frequency: irregular
☐ Articles, book reviews, photos.

Nicaragua

NICMA1

Somos (General)
> Association de Mujeres Nicaraguenses
> 'Luisa Amanda Espinoza'
> Apartado Postal A-238
> MANAGUA
☎ 02 71661
Pub. frequency: three per annum
☐ First published 1982.

Nigeria

NIGMA1

WORDOC (General)
    Women's Research and Documentation Centre
    Institute of African Studies
    University of Ibadan
    IBADAN
Pub. frequency: half-yearly
☐ Information about conferences and activities.

North Korea

NKMA1

Women of Korea (Development/General)
    Korean Democratic Women's Union
    Central Committee
    PYONGYANG
Pub. frequency: bi-monthly
☐ Text in English. Illustrated.

Pakistan

PAKMA1

Asian Women (Development/General)
    The Asian Women's Institute
    International Office
    Association of Kinnaird Colonial Women
    LAHORE 3
Pub. frequency: three per annum

PAKMA2

Subha (Development/General)
    1 Bath Island Road
    KARACHI 75530
☎ 021 573079
☐ The focus is on women and development: educational awareness, women and health, and civil rights.

Papua New Guinea

PNGMA1

Nius Blong Meri (Development/General)
    Dept of Home Affairs and Youth
    PO Box 7354
    BOROKO NCD
☐ Articles on literacy, violence against women, and women's health issues.

Paraguay

PARMA1

Centro de Documentacion y Estudios
Informativo Mujer (Development)
    Pai Perez 737
    ASUNCION
Subscriptions: US$35.00
Pub. frequency: monthly
☐ First published 1989.

PARMA2

Informativo Mujer (Development/General)
    Pai Perez 737
    Casilla Postal 2558
    ASUNCION
☎ 021 23591
Subscriptions: PP35,000
Pub. frequency: monthly
☐ First published 1988. Diaries of women's events. Articles on abortion and prostitution.

PARMA3

Microfona, La (General)
    Farina Casilla de Correo 2558
    ASUNCION
☐ First published 1990.

PARMA4

Puerta, La (General)
    Centro de Estudios Humanitarios
    Azara 3267
    ASUNCION
Subscriptions: US$10.00
Pub. frequency: quarterly
☐ First published 1990.

Peru

PERMA1

Cendoc Mujer (Development/General)
    Centre de Doc. Sobre la Mujer
    Avenida La Mar 170
    LIMA 18

PERMA2

Chacarera: Boletin de la Red Rural (General)
    (Flora tristan centro de la mujer peruana)
    Parque Hernan Velarde 42
    LIMA 1

PERMA3

Mujer Sociedad (General)
    Avenida Nicholas de Pierola 677
    LIMA 1

☎ 014 246627
☐ Focuses on feminist issues. Illustrated with photographs.

PERMA4

Serie Mujer (General)
Asociacion Amauta
Apartado Postal 982
CUSCO
Pub. frequency: monthly
☐ First published 1982.

PERMA5

Viva: Revista feminista (Development/General)
Centro de la Mujer Peruana
'Flora Tristan'
Parque Hernan Velarde 42
LIMA 1
☎ 014 240839
Subscriptions: US$30.00
Pub. frequency: quarterly
☐ First published 1984. Feminist magazine with articles on the activities of the Peruvian women's movement.

Philippines

PHIMA1

Asian Womenews (Development/General)
Asian Women's Human Rights Council
PO Box 190
MANILA 1099
☎ 2 721 8883
☐ First published 1991. Human rights from the perspective of Asian women.

PHIMA2

Balikatanews (Development)
Balikatan sa Kaunlaran
Malvar Wing
Philippine Women's University
Taft Avenue
MANILA
☎ 2 58 7175
Pub. frequency: irregular
☐ First published 1979. The text is in English.

PHIMA3

Flights (Development/Civil rights)
PO Box 110
Dilinan
QUEZON CITY
☎ 97 28 60

☐ A publication of the Women's Resource and Research Centre. Articles related specifically to women in the Philippines: US military bases, child prostitution, tourism and women's workshops.

PHIMA4

Gabriela Women's Update
(Development/Environment)
Public Information Department
PO Box 4386
MANILA 1800
Subscriptions: P20.00
Pub. frequency: quarterly
☐ News about the Gabriela National Women's Coalition in the Philippines. The issues focused on are development, environment and violence against women. The text is in English.

PHIMA5

GROOTS (Grassroots Organizations Operating Together for Sisterhood) (Development/General)
c/o Pilipina
PO Box 208
DAVAO CITY 8000
Pub. frequency: quarterly

PHIMA6

Igorota: The alternative women's magazine in the Cordilhera (Development/General)
Igorota Foundation Inc.
PO Box 251
BAGUIO CITY 2600
Subscriptions: P50.00
Pub. frequency: quarterly
☐ Focuses on economics, development, children, spirituality, feminist theology and women as healers.

PHIMA7

ISIS International Women's Book Series
(International/Literature)
Isis International
85-A East Maya Street
Philamlife Homes
QUEZON CITY 1100
Contact: Marilee Karl
Subscriptions: US$20.00
Pub. frequency: bi-monthly
☐ First published 1984. Concentrates on issues women are trying to change. The text is in English and Spanish. Articles, editorials, conference reports and resource guides.

PHIMA8

Laya (General)
35 Scout Delgado Street
QUEZON CITY
Pub. frequency: quarterly

☐ First published 1992. Published by a women's Filipino collective. The text is in English and Tagalog.

PHIMA9

Mare (Development/General)
National Commission on Women
1145 J. P. Laurel
San Miguel
MANILA
☎ 2 721 5266
Pub. frequency: quarterly
☐ A magazine of the National Commission on the Role of Filipino Women. Articles on arts, women in shelter, new initiatives for women, and women in non-traditional trades.

PHIMA10

NFE – WID Exchange – Asia Newsletter (General)
University of the Philippines at Los Banos
College of Agriculture
Dept of Agricultural Education
LAGUNA 3720
Pub. frequency: three per annum
☐ First published 1981.

PHIMA11

Women in Action (International/Civil rights)
Isis International
85-A East Maya Street
PO Box 1837
QUEZON CITY 1100
Subscriptions: US$20.00
Pub. frequency: quarterly
☐ For women around the world. The main issues are civil rights and health. The text is in English.

PHIMA12

Womenews (Philippines) (Development/General)
Women Studies and Resource Centre
Room 207
Santos Building
Malvar Ext.
DAVAO CITY 8000
Subscriptions: US$12.00
☐ First published 1984. Focuses on women and family relations, women activists as single parents, marriage, children in wars, the political future for women and the economy.

Portugal

PORMA1

Cadernos Condicão Feminina (General)
Comissão da Condicão Feminina
Avenue da Republica 32-1
1093 LISBON

Price: varies
Pub. frequency: irregular
☐ First published 1975.

PORMA2

Mulheres (General)
Alameda St
Antonio dos Capuchos 6B
1100 LISBON
☎ 01 670193
Price: Es150.00
Subscriptions: Es1500.00
Pub. frequency: monthly
☐ Illustrations.

PORMA3

Noticias (General)
Comissão da Condicão Feminina
Avenida da Republica 32-1
1093 LISBON
☎ 01 7976081

Romania

ROMMA1

Dolgozo No (General)
National Women's Council
Street Nopoca 16
CHUJ-NAPOCA
Pub. frequency: monthly
☐ First published 1945. The text is in Hungarian.

ROMMA2

Femeia: Revista Social Politica si Culturala (Culture/Politics)
Editura Scinteia
Piata Presei Libere 1
71341 BUCHAREST
Price: 36 lei
Pub. frequency: monthly
☐ First published 1948. Books and film reviews. Illustrated.

Russia

RUSMA1

Sibirskii Variant (Lesbian)
Barnaul'skaya Assotsiatsiya Gomosekvalistov i Lesbiyanok
Abonementnyi Yashcick 73
656099 BARNAUL 99
☎ 24 88 32
Pub. frequency: annual
☐ First published 1991. Not only for women. A magazine for lesbians and gay men.

RUSMA2

Sovetskaya Zhenshchina/Soviet Woman
(General)
    Kuznetsky Most 22
    103764 MOSCOW
☎ 095 221 0781
Pub. frequency: monthly
☐ First published 1945. Focuses on social and political issues and the arts. There are special reports on current events and health issues. There is also news from international women's organisations.

RUSMA3

Zhenshchina: vek xx (General)
    Komitet Sovetskikh Zhentshckin TASS
    Tverskoi Bul'var 10-12
    103009 MOSCOW
Price: Rub1
Pub. frequency: monthly
☐ First published 1991.

RUSMA4

Zhenshchiny Mira (General)
    Mezhdunarodnaya Demokraticheskaya
    Federatsiya Zhenshchin
    MOSCOW
Subscriptions: Rub5.20
Pub. frequency: quarterly
☐ First published 1958.

Senegal

SENMA1

Bulletin de Liaison de l'APAC (General)
    Association Professionel Africaines Communical
    BP 4234
    DAKAR
Pub. frequency: quarterly
☐ Focuses on women and AIDS, family planning, women and the UN, environment, women and the economy, health, politics and the media.

SENMA2

Echo (Black women/General)
    AA Word
    BP 3304
    DAKAR
Subscriptions: US$10.00
Pub. frequency: quarterly
☐ The text is in both English and French. Concerned with black feminism in Africa.

SENMA3

FIPPU (Civil rights/General)
    Yewwu Yewwi pour la Liberation des femmes
    DAKAR
Subscriptions: FF120.00
Pub. frequency: quarterly
☐ First publshed 1987. Focuses on civil rights for women.

SENMA4

Satis (Development/General)
    BP 2664
    DAKAR
☎ 221 217595
Pub. frequency: quarterly
☐ First published 1991. Focuses on women in unions, abortion, teenage pregnancy and civil rights.

South Africa

SAMA1

Speak (South Africa) (General)
    PO Box 45213
    Mayfair 2018
    JOHANNESBURG 200
Subscriptions: US$20.00
☐ A feminist magazine focusing on peace, literacy, disabled women and health issues, among others. 'Puts women's liberation on the agenda of the South African liberation struggle.'

South Korea

SKMA1

Korean Women Today (Development/General)
    PO Box 2267
    SEOUL
☎ 02 356 0070
☐ Focuses on the current status of women in Korea. Articles on sex discrimination and reviews of Korean feminist literature.

SKMA2

Women/Yeo Sung (General)
    Korean National Council of Women
    40-427 3ka Hangangro
    Yongsanku
    SEOUL
Price: free
Pub. frequency: monthly
☐ First published 1964. The text is in English and Korean.

Spain

SPMA1

Amaranta: Revista de la asamblea feminista de Madrid (General)
Asamblea Feminista de Madrid
C-Barquillo 44-2-IZQ
28004 MADRID
☎ 91 319 3689
Subscriptions: Pta1200
Pub. frequency: quarterly
☐ A feminist magazine with an international section. The language is Castilian.

SPMA2

Caja de Pandora (General)
Colectivo de Mujeres de Filosofia y Letras
C-Pizarro Cenjor 4-3
GRANADA
☎ 958 243564
Contact: Eva Texido Aranegui

SPMA3

8 de Marzo: Comunidad autonoma de Madrid (Civil rights)
Direction General de la Mujer
C-Conde Penalver 63-1
28006 MADRID
☎ 91 580 2063
Price: free
Pub. frequency: quarterly
☐ A local government publication. The language is Castilian.

SPMA4

Emakunde (General)
Instituto Vasco de la Mujer
C-Manuel Iradier 36
01005 VITORIA
☎ 945 132613
Price: free
Pub. frequency: quarterly
☐ A government publication. The languages are Basque (Vasco) and Castilian.

SPMA5

La festa de la palabra silenciado (Literature)
Feministas Independiente Gallegas
C-Rigueiro 15-5
36211 VIGO
☎ 986 417582
Contact: Maria Jose Queizan
Subscriptions: Pta1400
Pub. frequency: annual
☐ Articles and poetry. Except for the poetry, everything is written in Gallego.

SPMA6

Mujer: Trabajadora (Paid work/Civil rights)
Area de la Mujer de la Confederacion General de Trabajo
C-Sagunto 15
28010 MADRID
☎ 91 447 5769
Price: Pta200
Pub. frequency: quarterly
☐ A trade union magazine. Covers women and work issues, sexual politics and special events. The language is Castilian.

SPMA7

Mujeres, mulleres, dones, emakumeak (General)
Instituto de la Mujer
Ministerio de Asuntos Sociales
C-Almagro 36
28010 MADRID
☎ 91 347 8000
Price: free
Pub. frequency: three times per year.
☐ A state publication. Articles, interviews, news, book reviews and information on a wide range of issues about, and of interest to, women. The language is Castilian.

SPMA8

SAL: Revista de MLIM (General)
Movimiento para la Liberacion e Igualdad de las Mujeres
C-Campomanes 8-2-C
28013 MADRID
☎ 91 559 5134
Subscriptions: Pta 1000
Pub. frequency: quarterly
☐ The language is Castilian.

Sri Lanka

SLMA1

Voice of Women: A Sri Lankan journal for woman's liberation (Development/General)
Voice of Women
125 Kirula Road
COLOMBO 5
Subscriptions: Rs35
Pub. frequency: quarterly
☐ First published 1980. Focuses on women in development.

Sudan

SUDMA1

Women (Development/General)
Scientific Association for Women Studies
PO Box 167
OMDURMAN
☐ The focus is on women and development, and feminist issues.

Sweden

SWEMA1

Hertha: Tidskrift for den Svenska kvinnorrorelsen (General)
Fredrika-Bremer-Forbundet
Hornsgatan 52
11721 STOCKHOLM
Pub. frequency: bi-monthly
☐ First published 1914.

SWEMA2

Kvinnobulletinen (General)
Grupp 8
Snickarbacken 10
11139 STOCKHOLM
☎ 08 10 76 26
Subscriptions: Skr130
Pub. frequency: quarterly
☐ First published 1971.

SWEMA3

Micaela (Equal opportunities/Civil rights)
PO Box 4121
10263 STOCKHOLM
Price: Skr10
Subscriptions: Skr80
☐ The text is in Spanish. The journal of the Association of Latin American Women in Sweden.

SWEMA4

Morgonbris (General)
Sveriges Socialdemokratiska Kvinnofürbund
PO Box 11545
10061 STOCKHOLM
☎ 08 44 95 80
Subscriptions: Skr50
Pub. frequency: eight per annum
☐ First published 1904. Explores all aspects of the Women's Liberation Movement.

Switzerland

SWIMA1

BOA (General)
BOA–Infostelle
Freyastrasse 20
8004 ZURICH

SWIMA2

Come Out: Blatt für Sexuelle Variation, Politik und Kultur (Lesbian)
Arcados Verlag
Rheingasse 69
4002 BASLE
☎ 061 681 31 32
Subscriptions: SF30.00
Pub. frequency: monthly
☐ First published 1984. Not only for women. A regional forum for the social and political problems facing lesbians and gays. The text is in German.

SWIMA3

Donnavanti – Giornale dell'organizzazione per i Diritti della Donna (General)
Casella Postale 3178–6900
LUGANO
☎ 091 52 60 00
Subscriptions: SF20.00
☐ Illustrated.

SWIMA4

Ella: Das Lesben-Forum (Lesbian)
Frauenzeitschrift Ella
Postfach 323
4016 BASLE
Pub. frequency: monthly
☐ First published 1991.

SWIMA5

Emanzipation: Die feministische Zeitung für kritische Frauen (Civil rights/Paid work)
Postfach 168
3000 BERN 22
☎ 031 41 42 31
Price: SF4.50
Subscriptions: SF42.00
Pub. frequency: ten per annum
☐ First published 1974. The text is in German only. The focus is on working women. Recent articles have been about sexual harassment, careers and financial politics.

SWIMA6

FAMA: Feministisch-theologische Zeitschrift
(Religion)
> Verein FAMA
> Hebelstrasse 97
> 4056 BASLE

Contact: Doris Strahm
☐ First published 1985.

SWIMA7

Femmes au Travail/Women at Work   (Paid work)
> 8 Rampe du Pont-Rouge
> 1213 Petit-Lancy
> GENEVA

☎   022 93 22 33
Pub. frequency: monthly
☐ The text is in French. Illustrated.

SWIMA8

Frau Ohne Herz: Eine Zeitschrift für Frauen und andere Lesben   (Lesbian)
> Mattengasse 27
> 8005 ZURICH

Price: SF20.00
Pub. frequency: half-yearly
☐ First published 1975.

SWIMA9

Frauezitig Fraz.   (General)
> Postfach 648
> 8025 ZURICH

☎   01 242 73 71
Price: SF6.00
Subscriptions: SF20.00
Pub. frequency: quarterly
☐ First published 1982. The text is in German. The main focus is on women in Switzerland, but there are also articles on feminism throughout the world and comparisons of different cultures.

SWIMA10

Mosquito   (General/Development)
> Postfach 5218
> 3001 BERN

Price: SF6.00
Subscriptions: SF48.00
Pub. frequency: ten per annum
☐ The text is in German. Focuses on women's issues in Switzerland and the Third World: health, civil rights and equal opportunities.

SWIMA11

Passerelle: Journal d'association des meres monoparentales
> ARM–ANCF
> 27 rue Lamartine
> 1203 GENEVA

☎   022 44 11 11
Subscriptions: SF15.00
Pub. frequency: half-yearly
☐ First published 1986. Focuses on single-parent families and mothers alone. Also health issues and art.

SWIMA12

Pax et Libertas   (International)
> Women's International League for Peace and Freedom
> 1 rue de Varembe
> 1211 GENEVA 20

☐ Women and the United Nations. Articles on disarmament. Letters.

SWIMA13

Rote Heft, Das: Die Frau in Leben und Arbeit   (General)
> Zentralsekretariat SPS
> Pavillonweg 3
> 3001 BERN

☎   031 42 55 33
Subscriptions: SF50.00

SWIMA14

Schritte Ins Offene: Okumenische Zeitschrift
(General)
> Badenerstrasse 69
> 8026 ZURICH

☐ First published 1970.

Taiwan

TAIMA1

Female Workers in Taiwan   (Law/Civil rights)
> Grassroots Women Workers Centre
> 4th Floor
> 208 Chien Kag Road
> TAIPEI 10577

Contact: Yvonne Lin Mei-jung
☐ First published 1991. Comments on relevant new laws, labour organisation participation and issues related to multinational corporations.

Tanzania

TANMA1

Sauti ya Siti/Woman's Voice
(Development/General)
> Tanzania Media Women's Association
> PO Box 6143
> DAR ES SALAAM

☎   051 41905

Subscriptions: Sh600
Pub. frequency: quarterly
□ First published 1988. There are both Swahili and English editions. Focuses on literacy, politics, sexual harassment, violence, discrimination, culture, food, refugees and children's welfare.

Thailand

THAMA1

Anjaree   (General)
PO Box 322
Rajadamnern
BANGKOK 10200

THAMA2

Voices of Thai Women   (Development/General)
PO Box 47
BANGKOK 10700
☎ 02 433 5149
Subscriptions: US$5.00
Pub. frequency: half-yearly
□ First published 1989. Focuses on sexual violence, women in distress, civil rights and prostitution.

THAMA3

WINAP: Women's Information Network for Asia and the Pacific   (Development/General)
Social Development Division ESCAP
United Nations Building
Rajadamnern Avenue
BANGKOK 10200
Pub. frequency: half-yearly
□ First published 1987. Focuses on women and development.

THAMA4

Women's Studies News   (Development/General)
Women's Studies Centre
Faculty of Social Science
Chiangmai University
CHIANGMAI 50002
□ News and views about the position of women in Thailand.

Togo

TOGMA1

Tev Fema   (General)
Ministry of Social and Women's Affairs
19 Ave Nouvelle Marche
BP 1247
LOME
☎ 21 37 18

Pub. frequency: monthly
□ First published 1977. The text is in Kabiye.

Trinidad and Tobago

TTMA1

Cafra News/Novedades Cafra
(Development/General)
Caribbean Association for Feminist Research and Action
PO Box 442
TUNAPUNA
☎ 663 8670
Contact: Rowena Kalloo
Subscriptions: US$25.00
Pub. frequency: quarterly
□ First published 1987. Poems, written accounts of conversations, letters and notices of meetings. Also information about organisations. Aims to break down language barriers in the region and stimulate women's creativity.

Uganda

UGAMA1

ACFODE   (Development/General)
Action for Development
3rd Floor, Spear House
Jinja Road
PO Box 16729
KAMPALA
☎ 041 245 936
□ Focuses on women and development and civil rights issues.

UGAMA2

Arise   (Development/General)
ACFODE
3rd Floor, Spear House
Jinja Road
PO Box 16729
KAMPALA
☎ 041 245 936
□ First published 1990. Subjects include health, projects, education and leisure. There is also a lot of information about specific issues provided in each issue as well as interviews and a letters column.

UGAMA3

Uganda Association of University Women Bulletin   (Development/General)
c/o Makerere University Library
PO Box 7062
KAMPALA
Price: US$5.00

Pub. frequency: annual
☐ First published 1987. Articles by and about women. Reports from committees and research projects. Also listings.

United Arab Emirates

UAEMA1

Fajr al-Jadid/New Dawn (General)
Jam'iyyat al-Nisa'iyyah
Umm al-Quwain Women's Society
PO Box 43
UMM AL-QUWAIN
☎ 06 666455
Pub. frequency: monthly
☐ First published 1973. Covers activities of the Umm al-Quwain Women's Society and the state of the women's movement in the UAE, together with women's health issues. The title means 'New Dawn'.

UAEMA2

Sawt Al-Mar'ah/Woman's Voice (General)
Jam'iyyat al-Ittihad al-Nisa'iyyah
Al Lajnah al-Thiquafiyyah
PO Box 142
SHARJAH
☎ 06 22646
Pub. frequency: monthly
☐ First published 1976. The magazine covers women's issues throughout the UAE.

UAEMA3

Zahrat al-Khalij (General)
Al-Ittihad Press
PO Box 3342
ABU DHABI
☎ 02 451600
Pub. frequency: weekly
☐ Focuses on issues of interest to women throughout the Arab world.

United States of America

USAMA1

13th Moon: a feminist literary magazine
(Creative writing/Literature)
Department of English
SUNY at Albany
1400 Washington Avenue
ALBANY, NY 12222
☎ 518 442 4181
Contact: Judith E. Johnson
Price: $8.00
Subscriptions: $13.00
Pub. frequency: half-yearly

☐ First published 1973. Publishes literary work by women, in particular feminist and working-class lesbian literature. Poetry, fiction and critical articles. There are also translations of works other than in English.

USAMA2

Advocate (Los Angeles 1967) (Lesbian)
Liberation Publications Inc.
PO Box 4371
LOS ANGELES
CA 90078-4371
Subscriptions: $50.00
Pub. frequency: fortnightly
☐ First published 1967. Not only for women. National magazine for lesbians and gays.

USAMA3

Against the Current (Socialism)
7012 Michigan Avenue
DETROIT, MI 48210
☎ 313 841 0161
Subscriptions: $15.00
Pub. frequency: bi-monthly
☐ First published 1979. Not only for women. Discussions of movements for social and political change. Commentary from socialist and feminist viewpoints. Emphasis on labour.

USAMA4

Alaska Women (General)
HCR 64
Box 453
SEWARD, AK 99664
☎ 907 288 3168
Contact: G. R. Gardner (ed.)
Subscriptions: $30.00
Pub. frequency: quarterly
☐ First published 1990. Poetry, articles, art, photos, cartoons, interviews, criticism and reviews.

USAMA5

Albuquerque WOMAN (Paid work/General)
PO Box 6133
ALBUQUERQUE, NM 87197
☎ 505 247 9195
Pub. frequency: bi-monthly
☐ Targeted mainly towards business and professional women in the Albuquerque area. News, networking information and profiles.

USAMA6

Alert (Paid work)
Suite 500
2001 S St NW
WASHINGTON, DC 20009-1125
☎ 202 328 1415
Pub. frequency: bi-monthly

☐ First published 1980. The magazine for the Federation of Organizations for Professional Women. Aims to influence policy and enhance the status of professional women.

USAMA7

Amazon Times (Lesbian/General)
> PO Box 135
> OWINGS MILLS, MD 21117-0135

Pub. frequency: quarterly
☐ A national magazine covering all topics of interest to lesbians.

USAMA8

American Woman (General)
> GCR Publishing Group Inc.
> 1700 Broadway
> NEW YORK, NY 10019

Price: $7.99
☐ First published 1990. Relationships, careers and changing lifestyles.

USAMA9

Amethyst: a journal for lesbians and gay men (Lesbian/Arts)
> Southeastern Arts Media and Education Project
> PO Box 54719
> ATLANTA, GA 30308

Price: $5.00
Subscriptions: $12.00
☐ Not only for women.

USAMA10

At the Crossroads (Spirituality/General)
> PO Box 112
> ST. PAUL, AZ 72760

☐ First published 1992. Essays, articles, book reviews, theory, research and first-person narratives. The magazine uses 'the tools and perspectives of feminism, spirituality and "new paradigm" science to explore reality'.

USAMA11

Athena (Abuse)
> Athena Press (Westlake Village)
> Suite 110
> 31220 La Baya Drive
> WESTLAKE VILLAGE, CA 91362
> ☎ 805 379 3185

Price: $3.00
Pub. frequency: half-yearly
☐ First published 1983. Essays, fiction, poetry by and about battered women and children. Campaigning for victory over domestic violence.

USAMA12

Atlanta NOW News (Equal opportunities/ Civil rights)
> National Organization for Women
> Altanta Chapter
> PO Box 8556
> Civic Center Station
> ATLANTA, GA 30306-0556
> ☎ 404 523 1227

Subscriptions: $15.00
Pub. frequency: monthly
☐ First published 1973.

USAMA13

Aurora (Madison) (Literature)
> Society for the Furtherance and Study of Fantasy and SF Inc.
> PO Box 1624
> MADISON, WI 53701-1624

Subscriptions: $10.00 for 3 issues
Pub. frequency: irregular
☐ Feminist science fiction.

USAMA14

AWIS Magazine (Science)
> Association for Women in Science
> Suite 820
> 1522 K St NW
> WASHINGTON DC 20005
> ☎ 202 408 0742

Pub. frequency: bi-monthly
☐ First published 1971. Concerned with policies and status of women in science.

USAMA15

Backlash Times (Radical feminism/Politics)
> Feminists Fighting Pornography
> PO Box 6731
> Yorkville Station
> NEW YORK, NY 10128
> ☎ 212 410 5182

Subscriptions: $20.00
Pub. frequency: half-yearly
☐ First published 1983. Data on pornography provided by feminists fighting pornography.

USAMA16

Bad Attitude (Lesbian/General)
> Bad Attitude Inc.
> Box 110
> CAMBRIDGE, MA 02139
> ☎ 617 426 4469

Subscriptions: $24.00
Pub. frequency: six per annum
☐ First published 1984. Art, fiction, non-fiction and poetry for lesbians.

USAMA17

Bad Haircut (General)
    3115 SW Roxbury Street
    SEATTLE, WA 98126-4151
Price: $14.00
Pub. frequency: irregular
□ First published 1987. Not only for women. Covers progressive political causes: environmental, feminist, peace, anti-nuclear and human rights issues.

USAMA18

Beltane Papers, The (Spirituality/Religion)
    PO Box 8
    CLEAR LAKE, WA 98235

USAMA19

Best of Health (Black women/Health)
    Box 40–1232
    BROOKLYN, NY 11240-1232
☎ 718 756 2245
Subscriptions: $14.00
Pub. frequency: quarterly
□ First published 1987. A magazine for Afro-American women about health issues.

USAMA20

Better Homes & Dykes (Lesbian)
    Iowa City Lesbian Alliance
    130 N Madison
    IOWA CITY, IA 55240
Price: $2.00
Pub. frequency: irregular

USAMA21

BG Magazine (Lesbian/Black women)
    PO Box 1511
    NEW YORK, NY 10276
☎ 212 629 1887
Pub. frequency: bi-monthly
□ Not only for women. For black lesbians and gay men. Distributed nationally.

USAMA22

Black Women's Voice (Black women)
    National Council of Negro Women
    1211 Connecticut Ave NW
    702 WASHINGTON, DC 20036-2701
Pub. frequency: quarterly

USAMA23

Blk (Lesbian/General)
    Blk Publishing Co.
    PO Box 83912
    LOS ANGELES, CA 90083-0912
☎ 213 410 0808
Subscriptions: $18.00
Pub. frequency: monthly
□ First published 1988. Not only for women. A national news magazine for black lesbians and gay men. News, stories, listings, cartoons and resources.

USAMA24

Boston Woman (General)
    PO Box 1260
    BROOKLINE
    MA 02146-0010
☎ 617 783 8000
Pub. frequency: monthly
□ Focuses on Boston women in business, politics, the professions, creative arts and the community.

USAMA25

Bridges: A journal for Jewish feminists and our friends (Religion)
    PO Box 18437
    SEATTLE WA 98118
☎ 206 721 5008
Subscriptions: $15 (suggested)
Pub. frequency: half-yearly
□ First published 1990. 'A commitment that combines the traditional Jewish values of justice and repair of the world with insights honed by the feminist, lesbian and gay movements.' Free to women prisoners and nursing homes.

USAMA26

Broomstick (Older women)
    Apartment 3
    3543 18th St
    SAN FRANCISCO, CA 94110
☎ 415 552 7460
Contact: Mickey Spencer
Price: $5.00
Subscriptions: $15.00 (suggested)
Pub. frequency: quarterly
□ First published 1978. By, for and about older women. Facts about the menopause. Tries to combat the stereotyping of older women. Writing by older women: poems, stories, articles, news and notice board. Networking.

USAMA27

California Women (Equal opportunities/Civil rights)
    Commission on the Status of Women
    Suite 400
    1303 J Street
    SACRAMENTO, CA 95814
☎ 916 445 3173
Price: free
Pub. frequency: quarterly
□ First published 1978.

USAMA28

Career Woman Magazine   (Paid work/Education)
Equal Opportunity Publications
44 Broadway
Greenlawn
NEW YORK, NY 11740
☎   516 261 8899
Subscriptions: $13.00
Pub. frequency: three per annum
☐ First published 1973. A career magazine for college graduates looking for their first job.

USAMA29

Caribbean Heat Magazine   (Lesbian)
106 de Diego Avenue
PO Box 78
SANTURCE, PR 00907
☎   809 726 1807
Pub. frequency: monthly
☐ Not only for women. A magazine for lesbians and gay men which focuses on Puerto Rico, the Virgin Islands and the Caribbean.

USAMA30

Cassandra   (Radical feminism/Health)
Cassandra Radical Feminist
Nurses Network
Box 181039
CLEVELAND HTS, OH 44118
Subscriptions: $35.00
Pub. frequency: three per annum
☐ First published 1982. Radical feminist nurses' news magazine.

USAMA31

Cauldron   (Lesbian)
PO Box 349
CULVER CITY, CA 90232-0349

USAMA32

Center Stage (New York)   (Lesbian)
Lesbian and Gay Community Services Center
208 West 13th Street
NEW YORK, NY 10011
☎   212 620 7310
Subscriptions: $25.00
Pub. frequency: monthly
☐ First published 1987.

USAMA33

Christopher Street   (Lesbian)
PO Box 1475 ⸱
Church Street Station
NEW YORK, NY 10008
☎   212 627 2120
Pub. frequency: monthly

☐ Not only for women. A magazine for lesbians and gay men. Distributed nationally.

USAMA34

Circle Network News   (Spirituality)
PO Box 219
MOUNT HOREB, WI 53572
Price: $3.00
Pub. frequency: quarterly
☐ Witchcraft, paganism and magic.

USAMA35

Class Magazine   (Black women/Development)
R. E. John-Sandy Communications
8th Floor
900 Broadway
NEW YORK, NY 10003
☎   212 677 3055
Subscriptions: $15.00
Pub. frequency: monthly
☐ First published 1979. Global black perspective on women of the Third World.

USAMA36

Clear Beginnings   (Creative writing)
Women's Writers Workshops
5533 38th Avenue NE
SEATTLE, WA 98105-2203
Contact: P. Fender
Price: $3.00
Pub. frequency: three per annum
☐ First published 1981.

USAMA37

Colorado Woman News   (General)
Suite 205
1900 Wazee Street
DENVER, CO 80202
☎   303 296 3447
Pub. frequency: monthly
☐ For all women living in Colorado. A feminist perspective on women's health and news. Also discusses feminist trends. Notice board.

USAMA38

Common Ground   (General)
1115 Orchard Park Road
WEST SENECA, NY 14224
Subscriptions: $16.00
Pub. frequency: ten per annum

USAMA39

Conditions   (Lesbian/Literature)
PO Box 159046
Van Brunt Station
BROOKLYN, NY 11215-9046
☎   718 258 4102

□ First published 1971. Lesbian creative writing. Book reviews.

USAMA40

Connexions: An international women's quarterly
(International/General)
    People's Translation Service
    4228 Telegraph Avenue
    OAKLAND, CA 94609
☎   415 654 6725
Price: $4.00
Subscriptions: $15.00
Pub. frequency: quarterly
□ First published 1981. International women's quarterly, reprinting articles from international women's magazines and journals and alternative presses. Each issue concentrates on one particular theme.

USAMA41

Contemporary Women Writers of Spain
(Literature)
    4th Floor
    62 West 45th Street
    NEW YORK, NY 10036
☎   212 302 6740
Pub. frequency: irregular

USAMA42

Convergence/Convergencia
(Language/Literature)
    International Council for Adult Education
    University Microfilm International
    300 North Zeeb Road
    ANN ARBOR, MI 48016
Price: $7.20
Subscriptions: $25.20
□ The text is in Spanish and English.

USAMA43

Creative Woman, The   (Creative writing/Arts)
    Governors State University
    University Park
    ILLINOIS, IL 60466
☎   708 534 5000
Subscriptions: $12.00
Pub. frequency: three per annum
□ First published 1977. Articles, poetry verse, essays, photographs relating to women's endeavours, book reviews and original graphics.

USAMA44

Crone Chronicles, The
(Older women/Spirituality)
    Crones
    PO Box 81
    KELLY, WY 83011
Price: $3.00

Subscriptions: $12.00
Pub. frequency: quarterly
□ First published 1989. A 'grassroots networking journal intended to activate the archetype of the Crone within contemporary western culture'. There are features on the menopause, mothers and croning ceremonies.

USAMA45

Cruise Entertainment Magazine   (Lesbian)
    Tony Rome Enterprises Inc.
    19136 Woodward North
    DETROIT, MI 48203
☎   313 369 1900
Subscriptions: $60.00
Pub. frequency: weekly
□ First published 1979. Not only for women. Information on lesbian–gay activities in the Michigan–Ohio states of the USA.

USAMA46

CWAO News (Coalition of Women's Art Organizations)   (Arts/Law)
    123 E Beutel Road
    PORT WASHINGTON, WI 53074
☎   414 284 4458
Subscriptions: $10.00
Pub. frequency: monthly
□ First published 1982. Provides information on pending legislation concerning the arts and also provides a network with women's groups.

USAMA47

Daughters of Sarah   (Religion/Sex and gender)
    3801 N Keeler
    CHICAGO, IL 60641-6790
☎   312 736 3399
Contact: Reta Halteman Finger
Subscriptions: $18.00
Pub. frequency: quarterly
□ First published 1974. A Christian feminist magazine. Sets out issues of interest to women in the church. Biblical interpretation of poverty, racism, divorce, and sexuality. Also personal stories.

USAMA48

Defiance: (General)
    112 Park Avenue
    STROUDSBURG, PA 18360
Pub. frequency: quarterly
□ Non-fiction, fiction, art, poetry, cartoons and photographs.

USAMA49

Deneuve (Lesbian/General)
FRS Enterprises
Apartment 15
2336 Market Street
SAN FRANCISCO, CA 94114
☎ 415 863 6538
Price: $4.00
Subscriptions: $22.00
Pub. frequency: bi-monthly
☐ First published 1991. Covers a wide variety of topics for the national lesbian community, e.g. news, politics, sports, arts, entertainment and trends. It includes fiction, poetry and profiles.

USAMA50

Dimensions (Lesbian)
PO Box 856
LUBBOCK, TX 79408
☎ 806 797 9647
Pub. frequency: monthly
☐ A lesbian magazine distributed in Louisiana, New Mexico, Oklahoma and Texas.

USAMA51

Dinah (Lesbian)
Lesbian Activist Bureau Inc.
PO Box 1485
CINCINNATI
OH 45201
Subscriptions: $10
Pub. frequency: quarterly
☐ First published 1976.

USAMA52

Disability Rag, The (Disability/Law)
PO Box 145
LOUISVILLE, KY 40201
☎ 502 459 5343
Pub. frequency: bi-monthly
☐ Updates on legislation. Articles, poems, book excerpts and a letters column. Ideas and articles welcome.

USAMA53

Diseased Pariah News (Health)
PO Box 31431
SAN FRANCISCO, CA 94131
Pub. frequency: monthly
☐ Not only for women. News, features and humour about HIV and AIDS.

USAMA54

Dyke Diannic Wicca Separatist Amazon Magick (Lesbian/Spirituality)
Box 486
BERKELEY, CA 94701-0486

Price: $3.00
Pub. frequency: irregular

USAMA55

Dyke Review (Lesbian)
Apartment 456
584 Castro
SAN FRANCISCO, CA 94114
Pub. frequency: quarterly

USAMA56

Dykes, Disability & Stuff (Lesbian/Health)
PO Box 8773
MADISON, WI 53714
Pub. frequency: quarterly
☐ A lesbian magazine which focuses on health issues as well as radical disability politics.

USAMA57

Earth's Daughters: A feminist arts periodical (Arts/Literature)
Box 41
Central Park Station
BUFFALO, NY 14215
☎ 716 837 7778
Subscriptions: $14.00
Pub. frequency: three per annum
☐ First published 1971. A literary arts magazine with a feminist perspective which publishes poetry, fiction and artwork.

USAMA58

Emerge! (Lesbian/Religion)
Kentner Scott
PO Box 581
KENTFIELD
CA 94914-0581
☎ 415 485 1881
Subscriptions: $20
Pub. frequency: bi-monthly
☐ First published 1986. Not only for women. A Christian science publication supporting lesbians and gays. Articles, poems and writings about spiritual healing.

USAMA59

Entrepreneurial Women (Paid work)
Entrepreneur Inc.
2392 Morse Avenue
IRVINE, CA 92714
☎ 714 261 2325
Subscriptions: $16.95
Pub. frequency: monthly
☐ First published 1989. Information for women on running or starting up a business.

USAMA60

Equal Means: Women organizing economic solutions (Equal opportunities/Civil rights)
    PO Bóx M
    Suite 3
    2512 Ninth Street
    BERKELEY, CA 94710-9902
☎   510 549 9931
Price: $6.00
Subscriptions: $24.00
Pub. frequency: quarterly
☐ First published 1991. A publication for the MS Foundation for Women. It covers the 'strategies women are developing around economic justice, economic development, and empowerment ... multicultural international links'.

USAMA61

Equal Rights (Law/Civil rights)
    National Women's Party
    144 Constitution Avenue NE
    WASHINGTON, DC 20002
☎   202 546 1210
Subscriptions: $15.00
Pub. frequency: quarterly
☐ First published 1930.

USAMA62

Equality NOW! (Equal opportunities/Civil rights)
    National Organization for Women
    Madison Chapter
    Box 2512
    MADISON, WI 53701
☎   608 255 3911
Subscriptions: $5.00
Pub. frequency: monthly
☐ First published 1972.

USAMA63

Essence (New York): The magazine for today's Black woman (Black women)
    Essence Communications Inc.
    6th Floor
    1500 Broadway
    NEW YORK, NY 10036
☎   212 642 0600
Subscriptions: $16.00
Pub. frequency: monthly
☐ First published 1970. Focuses on the advancement and lifestyle trends of African American women. Looks at public affairs, education and entertainment in relation to the black community.

USAMA64

Esto No Tiene Nombre (Lesbian)
    4700 NW 7 Street
    Apartment 463
    MIAMI, FL 33126
☎   305 541 6097
Pub. frequency: quarterly
☐ For Latina lesbians. Published in Spanish, Spanglish and English.

USAMA65

Etcetera (Lesbian)
    PO Box 8916
    ATLANTA, GA 30306
☎   404 525 3821
Pub. frequency: weekly
☐ Not only for women. A magazine for lesbians and gay men.

USAMA66

Executive Female (Paid work)
    National Association of Female Executives
    127 West 24th Street
    NEW YORK, NY 10011
☎   212 645 0770
Subscriptions: $29.00
Pub. frequency: bi-monthly
☐ First published 1978. Details career and financial management topics and work-related issues for women.

USAMA67

Feminisms (Education/General)
    Center for Women's Studies
    Ohio State University
    207 Dulles Hall
    230 West 17th Avenue
    COLUMBUS, OH 43210
Contact: Cecilia C. Kavanaugh
Price: $1.50
Subscriptions: $8.00
Pub. frequency: bi-monthly
☐ First published 1988. 'To celebrate the varieties of feminist expression.' Articles, essays and creative writing, including poetry and book reviews. The magazine of the Center for Women's Studies.

USAMA68

Feminist Bookstore News (Literature/Media)
    Suite 6
    456 14th Street
    PO Box 882554
    SAN FRANCISCO, CA 94188-2554
☎   415 626 1556
Contact: Carol Seajay
Subscriptions: $60.00
Pub. frequency: bi-monthly

□ First published 1976. Reviews of over 250 books from all over the world, and news from the feminist book world. Also news about women's bookstores and feminist publishers worldwide. National distribution.

USAMA69

Feminist Broadcast Quarterly of Oregon, The (General)
PO Box 19946
PORTLAND, OR 97280
☎ 503 220 6413
Pub. frequency: quarterly
□ First published 1992. A multicultural and multiracial magazine 'so that we may explore our commonalities and seek solutions together'. Specifically for women who live in Oregon.

USAMA70

Feminist Network News (General)
4471 Signal Road
COLUMBIANA, OH 44408

USAMA71

Feminist Renaissance (General)
Feminist Renaissance Publishing
191 Grand Street
No 10
NEW YORK
NY 10013
Contact: Joan Boccafola
Subscriptions: $10.00
Pub. frequency: bi-monthly

USAMA72

Feminist Teacher (Education)
442 Ballantine Hall
Indiana University
BLOOMINGTON, IN 47405
☎ 812 855 5597
Price: $6.00
Subscriptions: $12.00
Pub. frequency: three per annum
□ First published 1984. For teachers in traditional and non-traditional settings. Fights sexism, racism and homophobia. Articles, news, resource lists and bibliographies. A forum for new ideas in the classroom.

USAMA73

Feminist Voices (General)
PO Box 853
MADISON, WI 53701-0853
☎ 608 251 1845
Subscriptions: $12.00
Pub. frequency: ten per annum

□ First published 1987. The magazine 'exists to provide an open forum so that women can speak; that our voices will be heard. Our goal is to bridge the diversity of feminist thought.' Distributed nationally.

USAMA74

Feminists for Animal Rights
PO Box 10017
North Berkeley Station
BERKELEY, CA 94709

USAMA75

FEW's News and Views (Paid work/Law)
Federally Employed Women Inc.
Suite 425
1400 Eye Street NW
WASHINGTON, DC 20005
☎ 202 898 0994
Subscriptions: $12.00
Pub. frequency: bi-monthly
□ First published 1969.

USAMA76

Fighting Woman News (Sport)
6741 Tung Avenue West
THEODORE, AL 36582
☎ 205 653 0549
Pub. frequency: quarterly
□ Feminist martial arts.

USAMA77

Fighting Woman News (New York) (Sport)
PO Box 1459
Grand Central Station
NEW YORK, NY 10163
Subscriptions: $10.00
Pub. frequency: quarterly
□ Feminist martial arts.

USAMA78

Fighting Women News (Sport/Health)
114382 Cronridge Drive
OWINGS MILLS, MD 21117
Subscriptions: $10.00
Pub. frequency: quarterly
□ First published 1975. For women in the martial arts, self-defence and combative sports.

USAMA79

Free Focus (Literature)
Wagner Press
224 82nd Street
BROOKLYN, NY 11209
☎ 718 680 3899
Contact: Patricia D. Coscia
Subscriptions: $5.00
Pub. frequency: half-yearly

☐ First published 1985. The magazine of the Woman's Literary Guild. Reviews literature by women.

USAMA80

Freedom Socialist Voice of Revolutionary Feminism (Socialism/Lesbian)
 Freedom Socialist Party
 5018 Rainier Avenue S
 SEATTLE, WA 98118-1927
☎ 206 722 2453
Contact: Andrea Bauer
Subscriptions: $5.00
Pub. frequency: quarterly
☐ First published 1966.

USAMA81

From the State Capitals: Women and the law (Law/Politics)
 Wakeman-Walworth Inc.
 300 N Washington Street
 ALEXANDRIA, VA 22314
☎ 703 549 8606
Subscriptions: $65.00
Pub. frequency: monthly
☐ First published 1984. Information on a wide range of legislative and regulatory subjects relating to women.

USAMA82

Gay Book (Lesbian/General)
 Rainbow Ventures Inc.
 Suite 632
 584 Castro
 SAN FRANCISCO, CA 94114
☎ 415 928 1859
Subscriptions: $9.95
Pub. frequency: half-yearly
☐ First published 1981. Not only for women. Resource guide for lesbians and gays with information about clubs, organisations and AIDS. It includes women's business listings.

USAMA83

Gay Chicago (Lesbian)
 3121 North Broadway
 CHICAGO, IL 60657
☎ 312 327 7271
Pub. frequency: weekly
☐ Not only for women. A weekly magazine for lesbians and gay men living in and around Chicago.

USAMA84

Gay Community News (Boston) (Lesbian/Arts)
 Bromfield Street Educational Foundation
 Suite 87
 62 Berkeley Street
 BOSTON, MA 02116-6215
☎ 617 426 4469

Subscriptions: $39.00
Pub. frequency: weekly
☐ First published 1973. Not only for women. National weekly for lesbians and gays. Includes book, theatre and film reviews. Illustrated. Free to prisoners. Distributed nationally.

USAMA85

Gay People's Chronicle: (Lesbian/General)
 KWIR Publications
 Box 5426
 CLEVELAND, OH 44101
☎ 216 621 5280
Price: varies
Pub. frequency: monthly
☐ First published 1984. Not only for women. Provides information on international issues to Cleveland's lesbian and gay communities.

USAMA86

Gay Vote (Lesbian/Politics)
 Harvey Milk Lesbian and Gay Democrats Club
 Box 14368
 SAN FRANCISCO, CA 94114
☎ 415 773 9545
Subscriptions: $30.00
Pub. frequency: monthly
☐ First published 1978. Not only for women.

USAMA87

Gay Writes (Lesbian/Politics)
 Gay & Lesbian Democrats of America
 114 15th Street NE
 WASHINGTON, DC 20002
☎ 202 543 0298
Subscriptions: $25.00
Pub. frequency: quarterly
☐ First published 1985. Not only for women.

USAMA88

Gaypaper (Lesbian/General)
 Gay & Lesbian Community Center Baltimore
 Box 22575
 BALTIMORE, MD 21203
Subscriptions: $25.00
Pub. frequency: bi-monthly
☐ First published 1979. Not only for women.

USAMA89

GBF (Gay Black Female) (Lesbian/Black women)
 1680 North Vine Street
 Apartment 1211
 LOS ANGELES, CA 90028
☎ 213 467 7952
Pub. frequency: bi-monthly
☐ For black lesbians. Distributed in and around Los Angeles.

USAMA90

Giovanni's Room: Gay and feminist literature
(Lesbian/Literature)
345 South 12th Street
PHILADELPHIA, PA 19107
☎ 215 923 2960
Subscriptions: $2.00
Pub. frequency: half-yearly
☐ First published 1977. Not only for women. Promotes lesbian and gay literature.

USAMA91

GLC Voice News and Opinion for Gays, Lesbians and Civilized Others (Lesbian/Civil rights)
GLC Media
Suite 206
1624 Harmon Place
MINNEAPOLIS, MN 55403-1916
☎ 612 339 2072
Subscriptions: $25.00
Pub. frequency: monthly
☐ First published 1979. Not only for women. Concentrates on civil rights for lesbians and gays.

USAMA92

GLIB News (Lesbian)
Old South Haven Presbyterian Church
PO Box 203
BROOKHAVEN, NY 11719
☎ 516 286 3178
Subscriptions: $10.00
Pub. frequency: bi-monthly
☐ First published 1981. Not only for women. Provides information for gays and lesbians who live in Brookhaven, Long Island. Events, programmes and news.

USAMA93

Golden Threads (Lesbian/Older women)
PO Box 3177
BURLINGTON, VT 05401-0031
☐ For lesbians over 50 who want to network.

USAMA94

Grapevine (Seaside) (Lesbian/Travel)
828 W Kansas Avenue
CHICKASHA, OK 73018-3342
Contact: L. J. Allen (ed.)
Pub. frequency: quarterly
☐ Not only for women. Travel for lesbians and gays.

USAMA95

Guide Magazine (Seattle) (Lesbian/General)
One in Ten Publishing Co.
PO Box 23070
SEATTLE, WA 98102
☎ 206 323 7374
Subscriptions: $15.95
Pub. frequency: monthly
☐ First published 1986. Not only for women. 'Interpretive essays examining personalities.' Also humour, poetry, stories, politics, science, religion, current events and art 'as they relate to gay life'.

USAMA96

Hag Rag: Intergalactic Lesbian Feminist Press (Radical feminism/Lesbian)
PO Box 93243
MILWAUKEE, WI 53203
☎ 414 372 3330
Contact: Justice Fire
Price: $3.00
Subscriptions: $10.00 (suggested)
Pub. frequency: bi-monthly
☐ First published 1986. Reviews of books, theatre, film and music, and analysis of topics affecting lesbian lives: ethics, sexuality, radical lesbian feminism, and class and race consciousness. Ideas and contributions welcomed.

USAMA97

HANOW Herald (Civil rights)
National Organization for Women
PO Box 66351
HOUSTON, TX 77266
☎ 713 668 9008
Price: $3.00
Pub. frequency: monthly
☐ First published 1970.

USAMA98

Harvest (Spirituality)
PO Box 378
SOUTHBOROUGH, MA 01772
Price: $2.00
Subscriptions: $5.00
Pub. frequency: eight per annum
☐ Not only for women. A neo-pagan magazine. News and articles of interest to the pagan and wiccan community. Networking, reviews, rituals, songs, poetry and recipes. Ideas and contributions welcome.

USAMA99

Headway (Sport)
Women's Sport Foundation
Suite 728
342 Madison Avenue
NEW YORK, NY 10173
☎ 212 972 9170
Pub. frequency: quarterly
☐ First published 1985. Aims to cover all areas of women's sports with an emphasis on issues which affect women's participation in sports.

USAMA100

Heresies: A feminist publication on art and politics   (Arts/Politics)
    Heresies Collective Inc.
    PO Box 1306
    Canal Street Station
    NEW YORK, NY 10013
☎   212 227 2108
Price: $6.25
Subscriptions: $23.00
Pub. frequency: half-yearly
☐ First published 1977. Edited by a collective. Examines art and politics from a feminist perspective. The magazine features experimental writing, essays, poetry, fiction, interviews, illustrations and photographs.

USAMA101

HERS   (Reproductive rights/Sciences)
    HERS Foundation
    422 Bryn Mawr Avenue
    Bala Cynwyd
    PHILADELPHIA, PA 19004
☎   215 667 7757
Subscriptions: $20.00
Pub. frequency: quarterly
☐ First published 1982. Articles related to hysterectomies, discussing the consequences and possible alternatives.

USAMA102

Hikane: The capable woman   (Disability/Lesbian)
    PO Box 841
    GREAT BARRINGTON, MA 01230
☎   413 528 3844
Price: $4.00
Subscriptions: $14 (suggested)
Pub. frequency: quarterly
☐ 'Disabled wimmin's magazine for lesbians and our wimmin friends.' Stories, poetry, drawings, essays, networking, reviews, letters. Ideas and contributions welcomed.

USAMA103

Hot Flash   (Older women/Health)
    National Action Forum for Midlife and Older Women
    PO Box 816
    STONYBROOK, NY 11790-0609
Subscriptions: $25.00
Pub. frequency: quarterly
☐ First published 1981. For women going through the menopause and all older women.

USAMA104

Hot Wire: A journal of women's music and culture   (Arts/Culture)
    Empty Closet Enterprises
    5210 North Wayne
    CHICAGO, IL 60640
☎   312 769 9009
Contact: Toni Armstrong Jr
Price: $6.00
Subscriptions: $17.00
Pub. frequency: three per annum
☐ First published 1984. Mainly concerned with women in the music business. Focuses on lesbian feminist music and culture. Includes interviews, festival coverage, articles, essays and concert photographs.

USAMA105

Human Sexuality: Opposing viewpoints sources   (Lesbian/Sex and gender)
    Greenhaven Press Inc.
    PO Box 289009
    SAN DIEGO, CA 92198-0009
☎   619 485 7424
Pub. frequency: annual
☐ First published 1985. Not only for women.

USAMA106

Hurricane Alice: A feminist quarterly (Creative writing/General)
    207 Lind Hall
    207 Church Street SE
    MINNEAPOLIS, MN 55455
☎   612 625 1834
Contact: Martha Roth
Price: $3.00
Subscriptions: $12.00
Pub. frequency: quarterly
☐ First published 1983. Feminist prose, poetry and illustrations. 'The mission ... [is] to evolve a new prose form that integrates personal voice and personal experience into critical reviews of our arts and culture.'

USAMA107

Ikon   (Culture/Politics)
    PO Box 1355
    Stuyvesant Station
    NEW YORK, NY 10009
Contact: Susan Sherman
Price: $6.00
Subscriptions: $12.00
Pub. frequency: half-yearly
☐ First published 1982. Shows 'the experience of third world women, lesbians, Jewish and working women, women in all our diversity'.

USAMA108

Images (Lesbian/Religion)
  PO Box 436
  Planetarium Station
  NEW YORK, NY 10024
Pub. frequency: quarterly
□ For Catholic lesbians.

USAMA109

In Step (Lesbian)
  225 South 2nd Street
  MILWAUKEE, WI 53204
☎ 414 278 7840
Pub. frequency: monthly
□ Not only for women. A magazine for lesbians and gay men distributed statewide.

USAMA110

In View (Education)
  Whittle Communications LP
  Corporate Communications
  505 Market Street
  KNOXVILLE, IN 37902
☎ 615 595 5300
Pub. frequency: bi-monthly
□ First published 1989. For women in college/ university. Focuses on an individual's emotional life, family relationships, friends, careers, sexuality and health.

USAMA111

Indigenous Woman (Equal opportunities/Civil rights)
  Indigenous Women's Network
  PO Box 174
  LAKE ELMO, MN 55042
Price: $4.00
Subscriptions: $15.00
Pub. frequency: half-yearly
□ First published 1992. A magazine for indigenous women of north America. Illustrations, photos, fiction, poetry and articles on issues relevant to indigenous women.

USAMA112

Inn Places (Year) (Lesbian/Travel)
  Ferrari Publications Inc.
  PO Box 37887
  PHOENIX, AZ 85069
☎ 602 863 2408
Subscriptions: $14.95
Pub. frequency: annual
□ First published 1988. Not only for women. A bed and breakfast guide. Lists accommodation for lesbian and gays worldwide.

USAMA113

Inner Woman (Spirituality)
  PO Box 51186
  SEATTLE, WA 98115
Price: $1.00
Subscriptions: $7.50
Pub. frequency: quarterly
□ Explores women's spirituality. Ideas and contributions welcomed.

USAMA114

Inter-American Commission of Women
Noticiero (General)
  Inter-American Commission of Women
  Organization of American States
  1889 F Street NW
  WASHINGTON, DC 20006
☎ 703 941 1617
Pub. frequency: irregular
□ First published 1951. Published in both English and Spanish editions.

USAMA115

Island Lesbians Magazine (Lesbian)
  PO Box 1371
  HONOLULU, HI 96807
□ A magazine for lesbians which is distributed locally.

USAMA116

Kahawai: Journal of women and Zen
(Spirituality)
  Diamond Sangha
  2119 Kaloa Way
  HONOLULU, HI 96822
☎ 808 946 0666
□ The focus is on feminism and Zen Buddhism.

USAMA117

KAM: A journal of traditional Wicca
(Spirituality)
  Keepers of the Ancient Mysteries
  PO Box 2513
  KENSINGTON, MD 20891
Subscriptions: $5.00
Pub. frequency: half-yearly
□ First published 1976.

USAMA118

Kinheart Connection (Lesbian/Education)
  2214 Ridge Avenue
  EVANSTON
  IL 60201
☎ 708 491 1103
Pub. frequency: quarterly
□ First published 1992. News, listings and articles.

USAMA119

Kuumba   (Black women/Lesbian)
    Blk Publishing Company
    Box 83912
    LOS ANGELES, CA 90083-0912
☎ 213 410 0808
Subscriptions: $7.50
Pub. frequency: half-yearly
☐ First published 1991. Not only for women. Poetry magazine for black lesbians and gays.

USAMA120

Labyrinth   (General)
    4722 Baltimore Avenue
    PHILADELPHIA, PA 19143
☎ 215 724 6181
Subscriptions: $15.00
Pub. frequency: monthly
☐ First published 1983. Antiracist. For women in Philadelphia and nearby. Speaks for women excluded from traditional media. Covers a wide range of feminist issues. Debates on abortion, film reviews and creative writing.

USAMA121

Lavendar Life: A monthly magazine for your gay reading enjoyment   (Lesbian/Literature)
    215 Cleveland Avenue
    ENDICOTT, NY 13760
Subscriptions: $15.00
Pub. frequency: monthly
☐ Not only for women. Fiction and music reviews and classified ads.

USAMA122

Lavender Morning   (Lesbian)
    Box 729
    KALAMAZOO, MI 49005
Subscriptions: $12.50
Pub. frequency: monthly
☐ First published 1980.

USAMA123

Lavender Prairie News   (Lesbian)
    PO Box 2096
    Station A
    CHAMPAIGN, IL 61820
Subscriptions: $10.00
Pub. frequency: monthly
☐ First published 1976. For lesbians living in central Illinois.

USAMA124

Lesbian Center News   (Lesbian)
    Ambitious Amazons
    Elsie Publishing Institute
    PO Box 811
    EAST LANSING, MI 48826
☎ 517 371 5257
Subscriptions: $4.00
Pub. frequency: bi-monthly
☐ First published 1975.

USAMA125

Lesbian Connection: For, by and about lesbians   (Lesbian/General)
    Helen Diner Memorial Women's Center
    Ambitious Amazons
    Elsie Publishing Institute
    PO Box 811
    EAST LANSING, MI 48826
☎ 517 371 5257
Price: $3.00
Subscriptions: $18.00 (suggested)
Pub. frequency: bi-monthly
☐ First published 1974. Extensive listings, news, reviews and letters. Distributed internationally.

USAMA126

Lesbian Contradiction: A journal of irreverent feminism   (Lesbian)
    584 Castro Street
    Apartment 263
    SAN FRANCISCO, CA 94114
Contact: Jan Adams
Price: $1.50
Subscriptions: $6.00
Pub. frequency: quarterly
☐ First published 1982. Commentary, analysis, reviews and illustrations by and for women. 'Woman only' rather than 'lesbian only'. Non-lesbian women are welcome to submit work. Free for women prisoners.

USAMA127

Lesbian Feminist   (Lesbian/General)
    Lesbian Feminist Liberation
    2170 Broadway
    No. 2243
    NEW YORK, NY 10024-6642
Price: $3.00
Pub. frequency: monthly

USAMA128

Lesbian News   (Lesbian)
    7985 Santa Monica Boulevard
    Suite 109–13 West
    HOLLYWOOD, CA 90046
☎ 213 658 0258
Contact: Deborah Bergman

Subscriptions: $15.00
Pub. frequency: monthly
☐ First published 1974. Information and ideas from the lesbian community in southern California. News, articles, reviews and ads.

USAMA129

Lesbian–Gay Law Notes   (Lesbian/Civil rights)
Bar Association for Human Rights
PO Box 1899
Grand Central Station
NEW YORK, NY 10163
☎ 212 302 5100
Subscriptions: $25.00
Pub. frequency: monthly
☐ First published 1980. Not only for women. Contains a summary of legal developments in lesbian and gay rights and AIDS.

USAMA130

Lesbians Rising   (Lesbian)
Hunter College
Room 245
695 Park Avenue
NEW YORK, NY 10027
Pub. frequency: half-yearly

USAMA131

Lilith: The independent Jewish women's magazine   (Religion/General)
Suite 2432
250 West 57th Street
NEW YORK, NY 10107
☎ 212 757 0818
Contact: Susan W. Schneider
Price: $5.00
Subscriptions: $24.00
Pub. frequency: quarterly
☐ First published 1976. Publishes fiction, poetry, drama. Articles on issues, personalities and developments in feminist theory. 'Lilith is named for the legendary predecessor of Eve who insisted on equality with Adam.'

USAMA132

Listen Real Loud: News of women's liberation worldwide   (International/General)
American Friends Service Committee
Nationwide Women's Program
1501 Cherry Street
PHILADELPHIA, PA 19102
☎ 215 241 7051
Contact: Sarlee Hamilton
Price: $2.50
Subscriptions: $10 to $20 (suggested)
Pub. frequency: quarterly

☐ First published 1979. A publication of the Woman's Program of the American Friends Service Committee. Against discrimination and anti-war. Promotes communication and debate among regional and national staff.

USAMA133

Literary Xpress   (Black women)
PO Box 438583
CHICAGO, IL 60643
Pub. frequency: quarterly
☐ By and about black women. Distributed in and around Chicago.

USAMA134

Maize: A lesbian country magazine   (Lesbian)
PO Box 130
SERAFINA, NM 87569
Pub. frequency: quarterly
☐ About rural lesbian experience. A forum for the exchange of skills and strategies for economic survival and for building up a community.

USAMA135

Mama Bears News and Notes   (Lesbian)
Mama Bears Bookstore Coffeehouse
6536 Telegraph Avenue
OAKLAND, CA 94609
☎ 415 428 9684
Subscriptions: $6.00
Pub. frequency: bi-monthly
☐ First published 1983. A lesbian feminist perspective in articles. Also listings.

USAMA136

Mamaroots: Truine Spiritual Forum (Spirituality)
Asungi Productions
Suite 108
3661 North Campbell
TUCSON, AZ 85719

USAMA137

Math Science Network Broadcast   (Equal opportunities/Sciences)
Math Science Network
2727 College Avenue
BERKELEY, CA 94705
☎ 415 841 6285
Subscriptions: $25.00
Pub. frequency: quarterly
☐ First published 1978. Seeks to enhance the participation and advancement of women involved with mathematics, science and technology.

USAMA138

Matrix Women's Magazine   (General)
   Apartment 14
   108 Locust Street
   SANTA CRUZ, CA 95060
Pub. frequency: monthly
☐ For women who live in the California central coast and Bay area. Articles, news, art, poetry and reviews by and about women.

USAMA139

Media Reporter   (Lesbian/Media)
   Gay and Lesbian Press Association
   PO Box 8185
   UNIVERSAL CITY, CA 91608-0185
☎   818 902 1476
Price: free
Pub. frequency: quarterly
☐ First published 1981. Not only for women. Information for and about the gay media and articles related to those who work with it.

USAMA140

Midwifery Today   (Reproductive rights/Health)
   PO Box 2672
   EUGENE, OR 97402
Pub. frequency: quarterly

USAMA141

MINERVA's Bulletin Board
   1101 South Arlington Bridge Road
   ARLINGTON, VA 22202
Subscriptions: $20.00
Pub. frequency: quarterly
☐ 'The news Magazine on Women and the Military.' The near combat activities of women involved in combat are questioned. Issues regarding women in the military are analysed in brief.

USAMA142

MINERVA: Quarterly report on women and the military
   Apartment 210
   1101 South Arlington Bridge Road
   ARLINGTON, VA 22202
☎   703 892 4388
Contact: Linda Grant De Pauw
Subscriptions: $40.00
Pub. frequency: quarterly
☐ First published 1983. Articles related to service women, military wives and women veterans. Book, play and film reviews. 'The editorial policy emphasizes diversity rather than consensus.'

USAMA143

Minnesota Women's Press   (General)
   771 Raymond Avenue
   ST PAUL, MN 55114
☎   612 646 3968
Pub. frequency: fortnightly
☐ Reflects both the diversity and common experiences of women. Its motto is: 'A Woman's Place Is in the News.'

USAMA144

MOM Magazine: Mothers and others for midwives   (Reproductive rights)
   PO Box 1068
   SUGARLOAF, CA 92386
☎   714 585 4175
Subscriptions: $12.00
Pub. frequency: quarterly
☐ First published 1984. Focuses on women's choices in health care. There is information about alternative birth and parenting practices.

USAMA145

Mom's Apple Pie   (Lesbian/Civil rights)
   Lesbian Mothers National Defense Fund
   PO Box 21567
   SEATTLE, WA 98111
☎   206 325 2643
Subscriptions: $5.00
Pub. frequency: quarterly
☐ First published 1974. For and about lesbian mothers. Distributed nationally.

USAMA146

Mooncircles   (Spirituality)
   Circles of Exchange
   Suite 333
   9594 First Avenue NE
   SEATTLE, WA 98115
☎   206 654 9610
Subscriptions: $11.00
Pub. frequency: eight per annum
☐ First published 1985.

USAMA147

More Light Update   (Lesbian/Religion)
   PO Box 38
   NEW BRUNSWICK, NJ 08903-0038
☎   201 846 1510
Subscriptions: $10.00
Pub. frequency: monthly
☐ First published 1980. Not only for women. Focuses on the concerns of lesbians and gays in the Presbyterian church.

USAMA148

Mothering (Health/Culture)
PO Box 532
MOUNT MORRIS, IL 61054
Subscriptions: $22.00
Pub. frequency: quarterly

USAMA149

Mountain Laurel (Lesbian/General)
65 South Morgan Drive
BEVERLEY SPRINGS, WV 25411-9578
☎ 304 258 5079
□ Women-only magazine. National circulation. Net-working, news, events, book and music reviews, recipes and health issues.

USAMA150

Ms Magazine, The World of Women
(General/International)
Lang Communications
230 Park Avenue
7th Floor
NEW YORK, NY 10169-0014
☎ 212 551 9500
Contact: Robin Morgan
Subscriptions: $45.00
Pub. frequency: bi-monthly
□ First published 1970. Now free of ads. International news about women. Articles about feminist issues and concerns. Fiction and poetry. Ideas welcomed. Distributed internationally.

USAMA151

National Businesswoman (Paid work/Civil rights)
National Federation of Business and
Professional Women's Clubs
2012 Massachusetts Avenue NW
WASHINGTON, DC 20036
☎ 202 293 1100
Subscriptions: $10.00
Pub. frequency: quarterly
□ First published 1919. Focuses on items of interest to the working woman: economic equality, care for dependants, reproductive freedom and professional women.

USAMA152

National Gay and Lesbian Task Force
(Lesbian/Politics)
Task Force Reports
1734 14th Street NW
WASHINGTON, DC 20009-4309
☎ 202 332 6483
Subscriptions: $30.00
Pub. frequency: quarterly

□ First published 1973. Not only for women. A national publication covering lesbian and gay issues, including AIDS and violence against homosexuals.

USAMA153

National NOW Times (Equal opportunities/Civil rights)
National Organization for Women
Suite 700
1000 16th Street NW
WASHINGTON, DC 20036-5705
☎ 202 347 2279
Subscriptions: $35.00
Pub. frequency: bi-monthly
□ First published 1968.

USAMA154

National Order of Women Legislators News & Views (Law)
Sheeham Associates
Suite 1200
727 15th Street NW
WASHINGTON, DC 20005
☎ 202 347 0044
Subscriptions: $25.00
Pub. frequency: quarterly
□ Reports on women in public affairs.

USAMA155

National Women's Studies Action
(General/Education)
National Women's Studies Association
University of Maryland
COLLEGE PARK, MD 20742-1325
☎ 301 404 5573
Pub. frequency: quarterly
□ First published 1988. Articles on all women's studies subjects with an emphasis on education.

USAMA156

NCJW Journal (Religion)
National Council of Jewish Women
53 West 23rd Street
NEW YORK, NY 10010
☎ 212 645 4048
Price: $2.00
Pub. frequency: quarterly
□ First published 1978.

USAMA157

Network (Lesbian)
PO Box 10372
NEW BRUNSWICK, NJ 08906
☎ 908 873 0266
Pub. frequency: monthly
□ Not only for women. A magazine distributed through-out the state of New Jersey for lesbians and gay men.

USAMA158

Network (New York): An alliance and network (Creative writing/Literature)
International Women's Writing Guild
PO Box 810
Gracie Station
NEW YORK, NY 10028
Subscriptions: $35.00
Pub. frequency; bi-monthly
☐ First published 1980. News by and of women writers.

USAMA159

Network News (Black women/Civil rights)
National Institute for Women of Color
Suite 702
1301 20th Street NW
WASHINGTON, DC 20036
☐ To promote economic and educational equality of opportunity for women of colour.

USAMA160

Network News (Older Women) (Older women)
AARP
1909 K Street NW
WASHINGTON, DC 20049
☐ For older women, particularly pensioners. The emphasis is on civil rights.

USAMA161

Network: The IWWG Magazine (Creative writing/Literature)
Cultural Council Foundation
625 Broadway
NEW YORK, NY 10012
☐ First published 1980. Magazine of the International Women's Writing Guild – a network for the empowerment of women through writing.

USAMA162

Networker: Justice for women and families (Equal opportunities/Civil rights)
Interfaith Impact for Justice & Peace
110 Maryland Avenue NE
WASHINGTON, DC 20002
☎ 202 543 2800
Price: varies
Pub. frequency: half-yearly

USAMA163

New Cleveland Woman Journal (Paid work/Law)
104 East Bridge Street
BEREA, OH 44017
☎ 216 243 3740
Subscriptions: $17.00
Pub. frequency: monthly

☐ First published 1983. Offers advice to women living in the Cleveland area on legal, business, financial, health and fitness matters. Also provides information on stress management.

USAMA164

New Directions for Women (General)
108 West Palisade Avenue
ENGLEWOOD, NJ 07631-3000
☎ 201 568 0226
Contact: Phyllis Kriegel
Price: $2.00
Subscriptions: $12.00
Pub. frequency: bi-monthly
☐ First published 1972. Investigative reporting, interviews, social commentary and reviews. Covers legislation, health, education, books, arts, theory, child care and international news. Free to prisoners. International distribution.

USAMA165

New England Community Guide for Gay Males and Lesbians (Lesbian)
M. Kennedy Publishing
Suite 283
105 Charles Street
BOSTON, MA 02114
☎ 617 723 5130
Price: $5.95
Pub. frequency: annual
☐ First published 1980. Not only for women.

USAMA166

New Jersey Woman Magazine (General)
27 McDermott Place
BERGENFIELD, NJ 07621
☎ 201 384 0201
Pub. frequency: eight per annum
☐ For women living in New Jersey. Emphasises women's accomplishments.

USAMA167

New York (City) Commission on the Status of Women Status Report (Equal opportunities/Civil rights)
Commission on the Status of Women
52 Chambers Street
Room 209
NEW YORK, NY 10007
☎ 212 788 2738
Price: free
Pub. frequency: irregular
☐ First published 1977. News and lists of publications on issues to do with women's roles and activities. Listings of conferences and workshops of interest to women.

USAMA168

News of the Gay Lesbian Community
(Lesbian/General)
Arkansas Gay and Lesbian Rights
PO Box 2897
FAYETTEVILLE, AK 72701
☎ 501 521 4509
☐ Not only for women.

USAMA169

News on Women in Government (Politics)
Center for Women in Development
SUNY Albany
Draper Hall 310
1400 Washington Avenue
ALBANY, NY 12222
☎ 518 442 3900
Pub. frequency: half-yearly
☐ First published 1978.

USAMA170

NOW News (Boston) (Equal opportunities/
Civil rights)
National Organization for Women
Suite 700
1000-16th Street NW
WASHINGTON, DC 20036
☎ 202 331 0066
Pub. frequency: monthly
☐ First published 1973.

USAMA171

NOW San Diego News (Equal opportunities/
Civil rights)
National Organization for Women
San Diego County Chapter
PO Box 80292
SAN DIEGO, CA 92138
☎ 619 237 1824
Subscriptions: $20.00
Pub. frequency: monthly
☐ First published 1971.

USAMA172

Nuestra Voz (Literature)
Peter Lang Publishing
4th Floor
62 West 45th Street
NEW YORK, NY 10036
☎ 212 302 6740
Pub. frequency: irregular
☐ Focuses on women writers in Spain and Latin
America.

USAMA173

Octava (Spirituality/Religion)
PO Box 8
CLEAR LAKE, WA 98235

USAMA174

Of a Like Mind (Spirituality/International)
PO Box 6021
MADISON, WI 53716
Pub. frequency: quarterly
☐ International news. Articles, reviews, illustrations
and networking of spiritual women. Distributed inter-
nationally.

USAMA175

Off Our Backs: A woman's news journal
(General)
2nd Floor
2423 18th Street NW
WASHINGTON, DC 20009-2003
☎ 202 234 8072
Price: $2.00
Subscriptions: $19.00
Pub. frequency: monthly
☐ First published 1970. International news. Conference
coverage. Comprehensive information about feminist
controversies. Reviews of books, films, theatres, music.
Contributions welcome. Free to prisoners.

USAMA176

On Our Backs (Lesbian/Sex and gender)
526 Castro Street
SAN FRANCISCO, CA 94114
☎ 415 861 4723
Subscriptions: $34.95
Pub. frequency: bi-monthly
☐ First published 1984. Focuses on sex.

USAMA177

**Organizing Against Pornography News
Update**
Suite 109
310 38th Street E
MINNEAPOLIS, MN 55409
☎ 612 822 1476
Subscriptions: $20.00
Pub. frequency: bi-monthly
☐ First published 1984. News about the pornography
industry and actions which challenge it.

USAMA178

**Other Black Women: An international magazine
for women** (Black women/Lesbian)
72–15 41 Avenue
Station D 43
JACKSON HEIGHTS, NY 11372
Subscriptions: $9.95

Pub. frequency: quarterly
☐ First published ·1981.

USAMA179

Our Special: Magazine devoted to matters of interest to blind women (Disability)
National Braille Press Inc.
88 St Stephen Street
BOSTON, MA 02115
☎ 617 266 6100
Price: free
Pub. frequency: monthly
☐ First published 1930.

USAMA180

Our Stories (Lesbian/History)
Gay & Lesbian Historical Society of Northern California
PO Box 424280
SAN FRANCISCO, CA 94142
Subscriptions: $20.00
Pub. frequency: quarterly
☐ First published 1985. Not only for women. The publication covers the history of lesbians, gays and other sexual minorities in northern California.

USAMA181

Our World: The international gay travel magazine (Travel/Lesbian)
Suite 251
1104 North Nova Road
DAYTONA BEACH, FL 32117
☎ 904 441 5367
☐ Not only for women, but useful for lesbians travelling around USA.

USAMA182

OUT (Lesbian)
Out Publishing Inc.
Suite 804
594 Broadway
NEW YORK, NY 10012
☎ 212 334 9119
Contact: Eva Leonard
Subscriptions: $11.95
Pub. frequency: quarterly
☐ First published 1992. Not only for women. General interest magazine for lesbians and gays.

USAMA183

Out-Look: National lesbian and gay quarterly (Lesbian/Culture)
Out-Look Foundation
540 Castro Street
SAN FRANCISCO, CA 94114-2512
☎ 415 626 7929
Subscriptions: $21.00

Pub. frequency: quarterly
☐ First published 1988. Not only for women. A cultural and political forum for lesbians and gays.

USAMA184

Outdoor Woman (Travel)
Gentian Mountain Inc.
PO Box 834
NYACK, NY 10960
☎ 914 358 1257
Subscriptions: $22.50
Pub. frequency: ten per annum
☐ First published 1990.

USAMA185

Outing Travelogue (Lesbian/Travel)
PO Box 4513
PORTSMOUTH, NH 03802
Pub. frequency: monthly
☐ Not only for women. A travelogue for lesbians and gays.

USAMA186

Outlines: The voice of the gay and lesbian community (Lesbian)
Lambda Publications
3059 N Southport
CHICAGO, IL 60657
☎ 312 871 7610
Subscriptions: $30.00
Pub. frequency: monthly
☐ First published 1987. Not only for women. Articles, news and entertainments listings for lesbians and gays in and around Chicago.

USAMA187

Ozark Feminist Review (General)
PO Box 1662
FAYETTEVILLE, AZ 72702
Subscriptions: $15.00
Pub. frequency: monthly
☐ First published 1991.

USAMA188

Patlar (Lesbian)
PO Box 1413
WEST SACRAMENTO, CA 95691
Pub. frequency: monthly
☐ Not only for women. A gay magazine for lesbians and gays distributed nationally.

USAMA189

Peace & Freedom (Civil rights/Politics)
Women's International League for Peace and Freedom
1213 Race Street
PHILADELPHIA, PA 19107-1691

☎ 215 563 7110
Contact: Roberta Spivek
Subscriptions: $10.00
Pub. frequency: bi-monthly
☐ First published 1970. 'Articles and news notes covering the international women's peace and justice movement. Emphasis on racism, disarmament, and US global intervention.' Distributed nationally.

USAMA190

Peacelines (Politics)
    Women Strike for Peace
    Suite 1500
    1930 Chestnut Street
    PHILADELPHIA, PA 19103
☎ 215 563 2269
Subscriptions: $10.00
Pub. frequency: bi-monthly

USAMA191

Pen Woman, The (Arts/Literature)
    National League of American Pen Women
    Pen Arts Building
    1300 17th Street NW
    WASHINGTON, DC 20036
☎ 202 785 1997
Subscriptions: $7.00
Pub. frequency: ten per annum
☐ First published 1922. News about members, art and music. Letters. Poetry, music composition, illustrations and interviews.

USAMA192

Perceptions (Literature)
    1530 Phillips
    MISSOULA, MT 59802
☎ 406 543 5875
Pub. frequency: three per annum
☐ A magazine devoted to the development of women writers.

USAMA193

Places of Interest to Women: USA and worldwide (Lesbian/Travel)
    Ferrari Publications Inc.
    PO Box 37887
    PHOENIX, AZ 85069
☎ 602 863 2408
Price: $10
Pub. frequency: annual
☐ First published 1992. International lesbian travel guide.

USAMA194

Plainswoman (Creative writing/Literature)
    PO Box 8027
    GRAND FORKS, ND 58202

☎ 701 781 4234
Contact: Elizabeth Hampsten
Subscriptions: $15.00
Pub. frequency: ten per annum
☐ First published 1977. Publishes 'articles, essays, fiction, poetry, reviews, graphics for and about women in the Plains region, focusing especially, but not exclusively, on lives of rural women'.

USAMA195

Primavera (Chicago) (Creative writing/Arts)
    PO Box 37–7547
    CHICAGO, IL 60637-7547
☎ 312 324 5920
Price: $7.00
Pub. frequency: annual
☐ First published 1975. The magazine publishes fiction, poetry, illustrations and photos that reflect the experiences of women.

USAMA196

Prooman (Paid work/Social sciences)
    MatriMedia
    PO Box 6957
    PORTLAND, OR 97228
☎ 503 452 0121
Pub. frequency: bi-monthly
☐ Focused primarily on professional and managerial women. Covers social and political issues from a feminist perspective.

USAMA197

Prototype Magazine (Lesbian)
    PO Box 4851
    ROCK ISLAND, IL 61201
☎ 309 788 0625
Pub. frequency: monthly
☐ Not only for women. A magazine for lesbians and gay men distributed in Iowa in Davenport and Bettendorf, and in Illinois in Rock Island and Moline.

USAMA198

Radcliffe Quarterly (General)
    Radcliffe College Alumnae Assocation
    10 Garden Street
    CAMBRIDGE, MA 02138
☎ 617 495 8608
Price: free
Pub. frequency: quarterly
☐ First published 1916. Covers issues of interest to academic women.

USAMA199

Radiance: The magazine for large women
    PO Box 30246
    OAKLAND, CA 94604

☎ 510 482 0680
Contact: Alice Ansfield
Subscriptions: $15.00
Pub. frequency: quarterly
☐ First published 1984. 'Focusses on self-esteem and acceptance of women of all sizes of large.' For all ages, lifestyles and ethnic groups, emphasizing positive health and well-being. Health, media, fashion and politics.

USAMA200

Rainbow City Express   (Spirituality)
   Rainbow City
   PO Box 8447
   BERKELEY, CA 94707
Price: $6.00
Subscriptions: $24.00
Pub. frequency: quarterly
☐ 'Kundalini arousal, archetypal activity, true encounters with the Great Mother, and other controversial/social issues.' Illustrations. 'Challenging, unique, lively, participatory.'

USAMA201

Response to the Victimization of Women and Children   (Abuse/Law)
   Guildford Publications
   72 Spring Street
   4th Floor
   NEW YORK
   NY 10012
☎ 212 966 6708
Subscriptions: $27.50
Pub. frequency: quarterly
☐ First published 1976. Addresses wife and child abuse, child sexual assault, sexual abuse, abuse of older women, pornography, sexual harassment and international human rights.

USAMA202

Richmond Lesbian Feminist Flyer   (Lesbian)
   Richmond Lesbian Feminists
   PO Box 7216
   RICHMOND, VA 23221
Subscriptions: $10.00
Pub. frequency: monthly
☐ First published 1973.

USAMA203

Room: A woman's literary journal   (Literature)
   PO Box 40610
   SAN FRANCISCO, CA 94110
Price: $3.50
Pub. frequency: annual
☐ First published 1975.

USAMA204

Sacred Cycles   (Spirituality)
   Golden Dolphin Publications
   29636 Orinda Road
   SAN JUAN CAPISTRANO, CA 92675
☎ 714 364 3487
Price: $3.00
Subscriptions: $26.00
Pub. frequency: monthly
☐ Devoted to honouring the divine feminine. Astrology, meditations and ceremonies.

USAMA205

SageWoman Magazine   (Spirituality/Religion)
   PO Box 641
   POINT ARENA, CA 95468
☎ 707 882 2052
Contact: Lunaea Weatherstone
Price: $6.00
Subscriptions: $18.00
Pub. frequency: quarterly
☐ First published 1986. Celebrates the Goddess in every woman.

USAMA206

San Diego Woman Magazine   (Equal opportunities/Paid work)
   4186 Sorento Valley Boulevard
   Suite M
   SAN DIEGO, CA 92121
☎ 619 452 2900
Pub. frequency: monthly
☐ Articles and information for women living in the San Diego area and information important for professional and personal growth.

USAMA207

San Francisco Bay Times   (Lesbian)
   Bay Times Coming Up!
   288 7th Street
   SAN FRANCISCO, CA 94103-4004
☎ 415 626 8121
Subscriptions: $32.00
Pub. frequency: monthly
☐ First published 1979. Not only for women. Lists events for lesbians and gays in the Bay area around San Francisco.

USAMA208

SFNOW Times   (Equal opportunities/Civil rights)
   National Organization for Women
   San Francisco Chapter
   PO Box 1267
   SAN FRANCISCO, CA 94101
☎ 415 861 8880

Subscriptions: $4.50
Pub. frequency: monthly
☐ First published 1971.

USAMA209

Short Fiction by Women   (Creative writing/ Literature)
   PO Box 1276
   Stuyvesant Station
   NEW YORK, NY 10009
☎   212 255 0276
Subscriptions: $18.00
Pub. frequency: three per annum
☐ First published 1991. The magazine publishes short stories and excerpts from novels from both new and established writers.

USAMA210

Sing Heavenly Muse!: Women's poetry and prose   (Creative writing/Literature)
   PO Box 132320
   MINNEAPOLIS, MN 55414
☎   612 626 1826
Subscriptions: $19.00
Pub. frequency: half-yearly
☐ First published 1978. Founded to publish women's poetry and prose, and to foster the work of women poets, fiction writers and artists.

USAMA211

SingleMOTHER
   Just Me & You Kid Publishing
   PO Box 68
   MIDLAND, NC 28107
Pub. frequency: bi-monthly
☐ Practical information, news and support for single mothers. Its motto is 'A Support Group in Your Hands'.

USAMA212

Sisters United   (Lesbian)
   Women Prints Enterprises
   118 W Sparks Street
   GALENA, KS 66739
Subscriptions: $7.00
Pub. frequency: quarterly
☐ First published 1979.

USAMA213

Sistersong: Women across cultures   (Creative writing/Arts)
   PO Box 7045
   PITTSBURGH, PA 15213
Pub. frequency: three per annum
☐ First published 1992. Artwork by women artists, poetry, fiction, essays and women's journal entries.

USAMA214

Sobering Thoughts   (Health/International)
   Women for Sobriety
   QUAKERTOWN, PA 18951
Subscriptions: $18.00
Pub. frequency: monthly
☐ First published 1976. For women who are recovering alcoholics. Autobiographical pieces, poetry and news of self-help groups worldwide.

USAMA215

Social Anarchism: A journal of practice & theory   (Politics)
   2743 Maryland Avenue
   BALTIMORE, MD 21218
☎   301 243 6987
Subscriptions: $14.00
Pub. frequency: half-yearly
☐ First published 1980. Not only for women. Anarchism, feminism, ecology and the community. Articles, reviews and illustrations.

USAMA216

Sojourner: The women's forum   (General)
   42 Seaverns Avenue
   JAMAICA PLAIN, MA 02130
☎   617 524 0415
Contact: Karen Kahn
Price: $2.00
Subscriptions: $19.00
Pub. frequency: monthly
☐ First published 1975. Politics, culture, opinion, articles, arts reviews, creative writing and news. 'Our editorial policy is to consider for publication anything that is not racist, sexist or homophobic in content.'

USAMA217

Sophia Circle   (Radical feminism)
   8319 Fulham Court
   RICHMOND, VA 23227-1712
☎   804 266 7400
Pub. frequency: half-yearly
☐ First published 1978. Advocates abolishing patriarchy.

USAMA218

Successful Woman in Business   (Paid Work)
   American Society of Professional and Executive Women
   1429 Walnut Street
   Philadelphia Road
   PHILADELPHIA, PA 19102
☎   215 536 4415
Subscriptions: $42.00
Pub. frequency: bi-monthly
☐ First published 1979. Ideas and practical strategies for women who want to achieve career, monetary and management goals.

USAMA219

TBP's Octavia: A news-journal of women's spirituality and theology   (Spirituality/Religion)
New Moon Collective
PO Box 8
CLEAR LAKE, WA 98235
Subscriptions: $10.00
Pub. frequency: eight per annum
□ First published 1984.

USAMA220

Teen Voices
Women Express
PO Box 6009
JFK
BOSTON, MA 02114
Pub. frequency: monthly
□ By, for and about teenage and young adult women. Focused on the Boston area, but the magazine covers topics of universal concern.

USAMA221

Telewoman   (Lesbian/Literature)
Telewoman Inc.
PO Box 2306
PLEASANT HILL, CA 94523
Subscriptions: $20.00
Pub. frequency: monthly
□ First published 1979.

USAMA222

Tenpercent   (Lesbian)
University of California
112 Kerchhoff Hall
LOS ANGELES, CA 90024
Subscriptions: $20.00
Pub. frequency: six per annum
□ Not only for women. For lesbians and gays.

USAMA223

Thesmophoria: Voice of the new women's religion   (Spirituality/Religion)
Susan B. Anthony Coven No. 1
5856 College Avenue
PO Box 213
OAKLAND, CA 94618
☎   415 444 7724
Subscriptions: $10.00
Pub. frequency: eight per annum
□ First published 1979.

USAMA224

Thing   (Lesbian/Black women)
2151 West Division
CHICAGO, IL 60622-3056
☎   312 276 0398
Pub. frequency: monthly

□ Not only for women. Features news and focuses on art for black lesbians and gays. National distribution.

USAMA225

Third World Woman's Gay-zette
(Development/Lesbian)
Salsa-soul Sisters
41–11 Parsons Boulevard
FLUSHING, NY 11355
Contact: Candice Boyce
Pub. frequency: monthly
□ First published 1976.

USAMA226

This Month in Mississippi   (Lesbian)
Mississippi Gay–Lesbian Alliance
PO Box 8342
JACKSON, MS 39284
☎   601 371 1318
Subscriptions: $15.00
Pub. frequency: monthly
□ First published 1973. Not only for women.

USAMA227

Together (Los Angeles)   (General)
University of California
112 Kerchhoff Hall
LOS ANGELES, CA 90024
Subscriptions: $18.00
Pub. frequency: six per annum
□ Explores issues from a feminist perspective.

USAMA228

Trade Trax   (Paid Work)
Tradeswomen Inc.
PO Box 40664
SAN FRANCISCO, CA 94140
☎   415 821 7334
Pub. frequency: monthly
□ First published 1983.

USAMA229

Tradeswoman Magazine   (Paid work)
PO Box 40664
SAN FRANCISCO, CA 94140
☎   415 821 7334
Subscriptions: $35.00
Pub. frequency: quarterly
□ First published 1981. A national publication by and for women in non-traditional blue-collar jobs. News, articles and interviews.

USAMA230

Tribune, The: A woman and development quarterly (International/Development)
International Women's Tribune Center
777 United Nations Plaza
NEW YORK, NY 10017
☎ 212 687 8633
Price: $3.00
Subscriptions: $12.00
Pub. frequency: quarterly
☐ First published 1976. There are editions in English, French and Spanish. Main areas covered are: women and organising; science and technology; communications and networking; community and economic development.

USAMA231

Trikone: Gay and lesbian South Asians (Lesbian)
PO Box 21354
SAN JOSE, CA 95151
☎ 408 270 8776
Subscriptions: $10.00
Pub. frequency: quarterly
☐ First published 1986. Not only for women. Focuses on lesbian and gay South Asians. International distribution.

USAMA232

Two Eagles (Lesbian/Development)
PO Box 10229
MINNEAPOLIS, MN 55455
Pub. frequency: quarterly
☐ Not only for women. By and for native American lesbians and gays.

USAMA233

Uncoverings: Research papers (Arts)
American Quilt Study Group
Suite 400
660 Mission Street
SAN FRANCISCO, CA 94105-4007
☎ 415 495 0163
Subscriptions: $18.00
Pub. frequency: annual
☐ First published 1981. Looks at the history of quiltmaking and textiles. Also a more general research into women's arts.

USAMA234

Valley Women's Voice: A chronicle of feminist thought and action (Culture)
University of Massachusetts
321 Student Union
AMHERST, MA 01003
☎ 413 545 2536
Subscriptions: $15.00

Pub. frequency: monthly
☐ First published 1979. The bulk of the magazine is concerned with analysing feminist culture, but news, illustrations and poetry are also included.

USAMA235

Venus Rising (General)
PO Box 21405
SANTA BARBARA, CA 93121
Pub. frequency: monthly

USAMA236

Visibilities (Lesbian)
Visibility Press
PO Box 1169
OLNEY, MD 20830-1169
☎ 212 473 4635
Subscriptions: $18.00
Pub. frequency: bi-monthly
☐ First published 1987. Creates a positive image for lesbians.

USAMA237

Visions (Arts/Media)
BF/VF
1126 Boylston Street
BOSTON, MA 02215
Pub. frequency: monthly
☐ The magazine focuses on film, video and performance arts with an emphasis on women and multiculturalism.

USAMA238

Voice of Guatemalan Women (Development)
Women for Guatemala
National Coordinating Office
PO Box 232
GAITHERSBURG, MD 20884-0232
☎ 913 243 1013
Subscriptions: $10.00
Pub. frequency: irregular
☐ First published 1984. Information about Guatemalan women and children.

USAMA239

Voice of Working Women (Paid work)
New Jersey Federation of Business
& Professional Women
37 Elm Street
WESTFIELD, NJ 07090
☎ 201 233 0110
Pub. frequency: quarterly
☐ First published 1962.

USAMA240

Voices From the Attic (Literature/Education)
Women's Studies Research Center
University of Wisconsin
209 N Brooks Street
MADISON, WI 53715
☎ 608 263 2053
Pub. frequency: half-yearly

USAMA241

WAND Bulletin (Politics)
Women's Action for Nuclear Disarmament
Box B
ARLINGTON, MA 02174-0001
☎ 617 643 6740
Subscriptions $35.00
Pub. frequency: quarterly
☐ First published 1982. Aims to educate women in political action to enable them to work towards eliminating weapons of mass destruction, and to redirect military spending to help women and environmental needs.

USAMA242

Washington Equal Times (Equal opportunities/ Civil rights)
National Organization for Women
Washington DC Metropolitan Chapters
PO Box 7279
WASHINGTON, DC 20044
☎ 202 331 0066
Subscriptions: $10.00
Pub. frequency: monthly
☐ First published 1969.

USAMA243

Washington Woman News (General)
PO Box 1458
TACOMA, WA 98401
Pub. frequency: bi-monthly
☐ A magazine for women distributed in the Seattle–Tacoma region.

USAMA244

Wavelength (Lesbian/International)
3030 South Bradford
SEATTLE, WA 98108
☐ First published 1988.

USAMA245

Welfare Mothers' Voice
4504 North 47 Street
MILWAUKEE, WI 53218
☎ 414 444 0220
Pub. frequency: quarterly

☐ The text is in English and Spanish. Articles, poetry, herbal cures, tips for mothers and news.

USAMA246

WID Bulletin (Equal opportunities/International)
Office of Women in International Development
Michigan State University
202 International Center
EAST LANSING, MI 48824-1035
☎ 517 353 5040
Subscriptions: $9.00
Pub. frequency: three per annum

USAMA247

WID Forum (International/Development)
Office of Women in International Development
Michigan State University
202 International Center
EAST LANSING, MI 48824-1035
☎ 517 353 5040
Pub. frequency: irregular
☐ First published 1984.

USAMA248

WIN News: All the news that is fit to print by, for and about women (General/International)
Women's International Network
187 Grant Street
LEXINGTON, MA 02173
☎ 617 862 9431
Contact: Fran P. Hosken
Price: $5.00
Subscriptions: $30.00
Pub. frequency: quarterly
☐ First published 1975. Focuses on the status of women and women's rights throughout the world. Each issue concentrates on about six major women-related areas, such as women's rights, the environment and violence.

USAMA249

Wishing Well, The (Lesbian/General)
PO Box 713090
SANTEE, CA 92072-3090
☎ 900 903 3343
Price: $5.00
Pub. frequency: bi-monthly
☐ First published 1974. Provides contacts for lesbians. Letters, poetry, resources and reviews.

USAMA250

Woman Activist: An action bulletin for women's rights (Equal opportunities/Civil rights)
2310 Barbour Road
FALLS CHURCH, VA 22043
☎ 703 573 8716

Subscriptions: $17.00
Pub. frequency: ten per annum
☐ First published 1971. 'From the courthouse to the White House.'

USAMA251

Woman Engineer (US) (Equal opportunities/ Sciences)
    Equal Opportunity Publications
    44 Broadway
    GREENHAM, NY 11740
☎   516 261 8899
Subscriptions: $17.00
Pub. frequency: quarterly
☐ First published 1980. Career magazine for women engineers.

USAMA252

Woman in History (History)
    Monument Press
    PO Box 160361
    LAS COLINAS, TX 75016-9198
Price: varies
Pub. frequency: irregular
☐ First published 1980.

USAMA253

Woman of Mystery (General)
    Wom'n
    PO Box 1616
    Canal Street Station
    NEW YORK, NY 10013
Subscriptions: $30.00
Pub. frequency: monthly
☐ First published 1986.

USAMA254

Woman of Power: A magazine of feminism, spirituality and politics (Spirituality/Politics)
    PO Box 2785
    Department 1
    ORLEANS, MA 02653
☎   508 240 7877
Contact: Char McKee
Price: $8.00
Subscriptions: $26.00
Pub. frequency: quarterly
☐ First published 1984. Feminism, spirituality and politics. Aims to empower women, to explore in each issue a central theme relevant to women's spirituality. Interviews, articles, fiction, poetry, photography.

USAMA255

Woman Poet (Creative writing/Literature)
    Women-in-Literature
    PO Box 60550
    RENO, NV 89506

☎   702 972 1671
Subscriptions: $12.95
Pub. frequency: irregular
☐ First published 1980.

USAMA256

Womanews (General)
    Women's Focus
    PO Box 220
    Village Station
    NEW YORK, NY 10014
☎   212 989 7963
Subscriptions: $15.00
Pub. frequency: monthly
☐ First published 1979. Free to prisoners.

USAMA257

Womanwise (Health)
    Federation of Feminist Health Centers
    Concord Feminist
    CONCORD, NH 03301
☎   603 225 2739
Subscriptions: $10.00
Pub. frequency: quarterly
☐ First published 1978. Women's health issues with a feminist perspective.

USAMA258

Women and Recovery (Health)
    PO Box 161775
    Suite 97
    CUPERTINO, CA 93016
Pub. frequency: monthly
☐ A magazine for women who are recovering alcoholics.

USAMA259

Women and Revolution (Politics)
    Spartacist Publishing Co.
    PO Box 1377
    NEW YORK, NY 10116
☎   212 732 7861
Price: $1.00
Subscriptions: $3.00
Pub. frequency: three per annum
☐ First published 1971. Communist journal of the Women's Commission of the Spartacist League. Each issue contains many articles supplemented with photos.

USAMA260

Women Artists News (Arts)
    Midmarch Associates
    PO Box 3304
    Grand Central Station
    NEW YORK, NY 10163
☎   212 666 6990
Contact: Cynthia Navaretta
Price: $3.00

Subscriptions: $12.00
Pub. frequency: quarterly
☐ First published 1975. For and by women in the arts. Articles, criticism, reviews and a nationwide almanac of exhibitions, conferences, performances and career opportunities by and for women artists.

USAMA261

Women Arts News (Arts)
  Midmarch Arts Press
  PO Box 3304
  Grand Central Station
  NEW YORK, NY 10163
☎ 212 666 6990
Subscriptions: $12.00
Pub. frequency: quarterly
☐ First published 1975. For and by women in the arts. Articles, exhibitions, reviews, lists of events and exhibitions in poetry, pottery, quilting and tapestry.

USAMA262

Women in Business (Paid work)
  American Business Women's Association
  9100 Ward Parkway
  PO Box 8728
  KANSAS CITY, MO 64114-0728
☎ 816 361 6621
Subscriptions: $12.00
Pub. frequency: six per annum
☐ First published 1949.

USAMA263

Women in Libraries (Media)
  American Library Association
  Feminist Task Force
  50 East Huron Street
  CHICAGO, IL 60611
☎ 312 944 6780
Subscriptions: $5.00
Pub. frequency: six per annum
☐ First published 1971. The magazine of the American Library Association's Feminist Task Force. It contains items of interest and discussion of issues of concern to women library workers.

USAMA264

Women in the Arts (Arts)
  Women in the Arts Foundation Inc.
  1175 York Avenue No. 2G
  NEW YORK, NY 10021
☎ 212 751 1915
Contact: R. Crown
Subscriptions: $9.00
Pub. frequency: bi-monthly
☐ First published 1971.

USAMA265

Women Outdoors (Sport/Travel)
  55 Talbot Avenue
  MEDFORD, MA 02155
Subscriptions: $20.00
Pub. frequency: quarterly
☐ First published 1980.

USAMA266

Women Strike for Peace: Legislative alert (Civil rights)
  105 Second Street NE
  WASHINGTON, DC 20002
☎ 202 543 2600
Subscriptions: $25.00
Pub. frequency: ten per annum
☐ An update on peace and human rights issues.

USAMA267

Women Unlimited (General)
  603 Sumner Avenue
  SPRINGFIELD, MA 01108
☎ 413 733 1231
Contact: Alice Stelzer
Subscriptions: $10.50
Pub. frequency: bi-monthly
☐ First published 1989. For women who live in northern Connecticut and the Pioneer Valley of Massachusetts.

USAMA268

Women with Wheels (Technology)
  1718A Northfield Square
  NORTHFIELD, IL 60093
☎ 708 501 3519
Contact: Susan Frisselled
Subscriptions: $15.00
Pub. frequency: quarterly
☐ First published 1989. By and for women and their automobiles.

USAMA269

Women Writers of Italy (Literature)
  Peter Lang Publishing Inc.
  4th Floor
  62 West 45th Street
  NEW YORK, NY 10036
☎ 212 302 6740
Price: varies
Pub. frequency: irregular
☐ Focuses on Italian women writers. Includes translations, essays and Italian feminist criticism.

USAMA270

Women's Caucus for Art National Update   (Arts)
Women's Caucus for Art
Moore College of Art
20th and the Parkway
PHILADELPHIA, PA 19103
☎ 215 854 0922
Pub. frequency: quarterly
☐ First published 1978. For women in the visual arts.
Short articles.

USAMA271

Women's History Network News   (History)
National Women's History Project
7738 Bell Road
WINDSOR, CA 95492
☎ 707 838 6000
Subscriptions: $25.00
Pub. frequency: quarterly
☐ First published 1983.

USAMA272

Women's Journal-Advocate   (Law)
PO Box 81226
LINCOLN, NE 68501
☎ 402 476 7348
☐ Distributed locally.

USAMA273

Women's Network: National newsletter for women   (General)
2137 Quimby Avenue
Bronx
NEW YORK, NY 10473
☎ 212 597 7091
Price: free
Pub. frequency: half-yearly
☐ First published 1977.

USAMA274

Women's News (US)   (Paid work/General)
33 Halstead Avenue
PO Box 829
HARRISON, NY 10528
☎ 914 835 5400
Pub. frequency: monthly
☐ For women in business in the state of New York.
Covers business, money, health, education, art, law,
politics and careers. It endorses political candidates.

USAMA275

Women's Political Times   (Politics)
National Women's Political Caucus
Suite 750
1275 K Street NW
WASHINGTON, DC 20005
☎ 202 989 1100

Subscriptions: $20.00
Pub. frequency: quarterly
☐ First published 1971.

USAMA276

Women's Record, The   (Paid work/General)
55 Northern Boulevard
GREENVALE, NY 11548
☎ 516 625 3033
Pub. frequency: monthly
☐ Focuses on Long Island women's achievements,
resources, business, finance, medical and health news.
Also looks at national women's interests which are
brought into local focus.

USAMA277

Women's Research Network News   (Education/ International)
National Council for Research on Women
Sara Delano Roosevelt Memorial Hall
47–49 East 65th Street
NEW YORK, NY 10021
Contact: Debra L. Schultz
Subscriptions: $35.00
Pub. frequency: quarterly
☐ First published 1988. 'To disseminate news about
and promote the visibility of research, policy, and
educational resources of women in the US and
internationally.'

USAMA278

Women's Rights Law Reporter   (Civil rights/Law)
c/o Rutgers Law School
15 Washington Street
NEWARK, NJ 07102
☎ 201 648 5320
Contact: Lynn E. Miller
Price: $6.00
Subscriptions: $20.00
Pub. frequency: quarterly
☐ First published 1971. Focuses on areas of the
law affecting women's rights and sex discrimination.
Articles, comment, reviews and bibliographies. There
is an extensive section devoted to book reviews.

USAMA279

Women's Rights to Women Leaders   (Equal opportunities/Civil rights)
DC Commission for Women
Women's Program Managers Committee
Room 354,
2000 14th Street
WASHINGTON, DC 20009
☎ 202 939 8083
Price: free
Pub. frequency: quarterly
☐ First published 1982.

USAMA280

Women's Sports and Fitness (Sport/Travel)
Suite 421
11919 14th Street
BOULDER, CO 80302
☎ 303 440 5111
Subscriptions: $19.90
Pub. frequency: half-yearly
☐ First published 1974. How-to articles, mini biographies, articles on travel and controversial issues related to women's sports are aired.

USAMA281

Women's Times (General)
Suite 14
930 West Washington Street
SAN DIEGO, CA 92103
☎ 619 294 9918
Pub. frequency: monthly
☐ For women living in San Diego County.

USAMA282

Women's Traveller (Travel)
Damron Company Inc.
PO Box 42-2458
SAN FRANCISCO, CA 94142-2458
☎ 415 255 0404
Price: $12.00
Pub. frequency: annual
☐ First published 1989. A travel guide for women. Information about accommodation.

USAMA283

Womenews (General)
Commission for Women
209 Finance Building
PO Box 1326
HARRISBURG, PA 17120-0018
☎ 717 787 8128
Price: free
Pub. frequency: quarterly
☐ First published 1975.

USAMA284

Womyn's Words (Lesbian/General)
Women's Energy Bank
PO Box 15524
ST PETERSBURG, FL 33733-5524
☎ 813 823 5353
Pub. frequency: monthly
☐ Lesbian news magazine with an emphasis on local events. Distributed in Clearwater, St Petersburg, Sarasota and Tampa.

USAMA285

Woodswomen News (Travel/Philosophy)
25 West Diamond Lake Road
MINNEAPOLIS, MN 55419
☎ 612 822 3809
Pub. frequency: quarterly
☐ For women interested in outdoor life. Philosophy, how-to features, and accounts of personal adventures. Also information about tours around the USA and other countries.

USAMA286

Words of Women (General)
Hartford Women's Center
350 Farmington Avenue
HARTFORD, CT 06105-4402

USAMA287

Working Women (Paid work)
Lang Communications
230 Park Avenue
NEW YORK, NY 10169
☎ 212 309 9800
Subscriptions: $9.97
Pub. frequency: monthly
☐ First published 1976.

USAMA288

WREE – View of Women (Equal opportunities/ Civil rights)
Women for Racial and Economic Equality
Room 606
198 Broadway
NEW YORK, NY 10038
☎ 212 385 1103
Subscriptions: $6.00
Pub. frequency: quarterly
☐ First published 1976. Focuses on racism and women's economic security and equality.

USAMA289

Writing for Our Lives (Creative writing/ Literature)
Running Deer Press
647 North Santa Cruz Avenue
LOS GATOS, CA 95030
☎ 408 354 8604
Price: £3.60
Subscriptions: £7.00
Pub. frequency: half-yearly
☐ Poems, fiction, stories, letters and autobiography.

USAMA290

Young Gay–Lesbian Life   (Lesbian)
ONE IN TEN Publishing Co.
PO Box 23070
SEATTLE, WA 98102
☎   206 323 7374
Subscriptions: $15.95
Pub. frequency: monthly
□ First published 1990. Not only for women. Looks at parents and all issues related to young lesbians and gays.

USAMA291

Z Magazine: (General)
Institute of Social and Cultural Communication
150 West Canton
BOSTON, MA 02118
☎   617 236 5878
Subscriptions: $25.00
Pub. frequency: monthly
□ First published 1988. Focuses on feminism, US politics, ecology, economics, political activism and foreign news.

USAMA292

Zontian   (General)
Zonta International
557 West Randolph Street
CHICAGO, IL 60661-2206
☎   312 930 5848
Subscriptions: $7.00
Pub. frequency: quarterly
□ First published 1923. The text is in English with summaries in French, German, Japanese and Spanish.

Uruguay

URUMA1

Cacerola, La: Grupo de Estudios Sobre la Condicion de la Mujer   (Development)
Miguel del Corro 1474
Casilla de Correos
MONTEVIDEO 11200
☎   2 41 64 15
Price: URG$500
Pub. frequency: irregular
□ First published 1984.

URUMA2

Cotidiano Mujer   (General)
Colectivo Editorial Mujer
Jackson 1270
MONTEVIDEO
□ First published 1990.

Venezuela

VENMA1

Tejiendro – Nuestra Red Venezuela (Development/General)
Todas Juntas
Apartado 4240
San José de Avila
CARACAS 1010–A
□ Current events related to Venezuela and women. Articles concerned with indigenous women.

VENMA2

Todas Juntas   (Development/General)
Apartado 4240
San José de Avila
CARACAS 1010–A
☎   02 813885
Pub. frequency: bi-monthly
□ Focuses on women and civil rights, and violence against women. Illustrated.

Vietnam

VIEMA1

Phu Nu Viet-Nam/Women of Vietnam (Development/General)
Vietnam Women's Union
39 Hang Chuoi Street
HANOI
☎   53143
Subscriptions: US$8.00
Pub. frequency: quarterly
□ First published 1973. There are editions in both English and French.

Zaire

ZAIMA1

BEA Magazine de la Femme   (General)
2 avenue Masimanimba BP
113380 KINSHASA I
Pub. frequency: fortnightly

Zambia

ZAMMA1

VOW: Voice of Women   (Black women/ Civil rights)
African National Congress of South Africa
Women's Liberation Movement
PO Box 31791
LUSAKA
Subscriptions: US$10.00
Pub. frequency: bi-monthly

☐ First published 1974. The text is in English. Focuses on anti-apartheid and human rights movements.

Zimbabwe

ZIMMA1

AWC News (General)
     64 Cnr Selous Avenue/Seventh Street
     PO Box UA 339
     HARARE
Price: 50 cents
Pub. frequency: quarterly
☐ Magazine of the Association of Women's Clubs.

ZIMMA2

Mahogany: Africa's magazine for women
(General)
     Munn Publishing Ltd
     PO Box UA 589
     Union Avenue
     HARARE
☎   04 700475
Subscriptions: Z$4.50
Pub. frequency: bi-monthly
☐ The text is in English.

ZIMMA3

Speak Out/Taurai/Khulumani (Civil
rights/General)
     Women's Action Group
     PO Box 135
     Ivory House, 5th Floor
     95 Robert Mugabe Road
     HARARE
☎   04 702986
Pub. frequency: quarterly
☐ The text is in English and local languages. The magazine covers AIDS, employment, rape, child sexual abuse and statutory and customary laws affecting women. It also focuses on the law to make it accessible.

ZIMMA4

Zimbabwe Women's Resource Centre &
Network New Bulletin (Development/General)
     Suite 203
     Stemar House
     Speke Avenue/Kguri Street
     HARARE
Subscriptions: Z$100
☐ First published 1990. Articles on women and development. News of national and local events.

Dictionaries

Canada

CAND1

Canadian Feminist Thesaurus
(Language/Literature)
　　OISE
　　252 Bloor Street West
　　Toronto
　　ONTARIO
　　M5S 1V5
Price: CAN$55.00
☐ First published 1991. Bilingual feminist thesaurus featuring over 6,000 items.

Great Britain and Northern Ireland

GBD1

Dictionary of Feminist Theory, The
(General/International)
　　Harvester Wheatsheaf
　　Campus 400
　　Maylands Avenue
　　HEMEL HEMPSTEAD
　　HP2 7EZ
Price: £9.95
☐ First published 1989. 'A broad, cross-cultural and international account of contemporary feminist thought.' The author is Maggie Humm.

GBD2

Macmillan Dictionary of Women's Biography, The (General)
　　Macmillan Publishers
　　4 Little Essex Street
　　LONDON WC2R 3LF
☐ Compiled by Jennifer Uglow. The second edition was published in 1989 and contains over 1,700 entries.

GBD3

Sexwords (Language)
　　Penguin Books
　　Bath Road
　　HARMONDSWORTH UB7 0DA
☐ By Jane Mills. First published 1993.

GBD4

Womanwords: A dictionary of words about women (Language)
　　Longman
　　Longman House
　　Burnt Mill
　　HARLOW CM20 2JE

☎　0279 42671
☐ By Jane Mills. First published 1989.

Netherlands

NETD1

Vrouwenthesaurus (General)
　　International Informatiecentrum en Archief voor de Vrouwen
　　Keizersgracht 10
　　1015 CN AMSTERDAM
☎　020 624 42 68
☐ First published 1992. A Dutch thesaurus on the position of women and women's studies. Designed to be used as a uniform indexing system by the women's information services in the Netherlands. There are 2,200 terms.

United States of America

USAD1

Amazons, Bluestockings, and Crones: A woman's companion to words and ideas
(Language)
　　HarperCollins Publishers
　　10 East 53rd Street
　　NEW YORK, NY 10022
☎　212 207 7000
☐ Originally published as *A Feminist Dictionary* by Pandora/Unwin Hyman in 1985.

USAD2

Nonsexist Wordfinder, The: A dictionary of gender-free usage (Language)
　　Oryx Press
　　PHOENIX, AZ
☐ First published 1977. Compiled by Rosalie Maggio. Guidelines for non-sexist writing and selected readings from other publications on language, gender and sexism.

USAD3

On Equal Terms: A thesaurus for nonsexist indexing and cataloging (Language)
　　Neal-Schuman
　　NEW YORK, NY
☐ First published 1977. Compiled by Joan K. Marshall.

USAD4

Webster's First New Intergalactic Wickedary of the English Language (Language/Literature)
　　Beacon Press
　　25 Beacon Street
　　BOSTON MA 02108

☎ 617 742 2110
☐ First published 1987. Written by Mary Daly.

USAD5

Woman's Dictionary of Symbols and Sacred Objects, The (Spirituality)
> Harper & Row
> c/o HarperCollins Publishers
> 10 East 53rd Street
> NEW YORK, NY 10022

☐ First published 1988. Compiled by Barbara Walker. The author aims to give women 'time-honoured female symbols' and to reclaim many symbols 'which evolved from very different contexts in the pre-patriarchal past'.

USAD6

Womb With Views: A contradictionary of the English language (Language)
> Mother Courage Press
> 1533 Illinois Street
> RACINE, WI 53405

☐ Written by Kate Musgrave. Illustrated.

USAD7

Women's Thesaurus, A (Language/Literature)
> HarperCollins Publishers
> 10 East 53rd Street
> NEW YORK, NY 10022

☎ 212 207 7000
☐ First published 1987. The subtitle is: 'an index of language used to describe and locate information by and about women'. A non-sexist terminology for information on all aspects of women to be retrieved. By Mary Ellen S. Capek.

USAD8

Words and Women: New language in new times (Language)
> Anchor Press/Doubleday
> c/o Bantam Doubleday Dell
> 666 Fifth Avenue
> NEW YORK, NY 0103

☎ 212 765 6500
☐ First published 1976. Written by Casey Miller and Kate Swift. This book has recently been updated (in 1991) with the new title *Updated Words & Women: New language in new times*.

Handbooks (including Directories and Bibliographies)

Australia

AUSHA1

Directory of Women in Business Professions and Management (Paid work)
    56 Rose Street
    MELBOURNE, Vic. 3143
☎   03 822 4396
Price: AUS$15.95
Pub. frequency: annual
☐ First published 1987. Biographical information on career women.

AUSHA2

Directory of Women's Studies in Australian Universities
    Women's Research Centre
    University of Western Sydney
    Napean
    PO Box 10
    KINGSWOOD, NSW 2747
☐ First published 1992.

AUSHA3

Facts on Women at Work in Australia (Paid work)
    Australian Government Publishing House
    GPO Box 84
    CANBERRA, ACT 2600
Price: AUS$1.90
Pub. frequency: annual
☐ First published 1979. Government publication.

AUSHA4

Women and Appropriate Technologies: A bibliography (Technology)
    Noyce Publishing
    PO Box 2222T
    MELBOURNE, Vic. 3001
☐ First published 1988.

Belgium

BELHA1

GRACE – Report (Education/General)
    c/o GRIF
    29 rue Blanche
    1050 BRUSSELS
☎   02 583 84 87

☐ First published 1992. Phase 1 of the Women's Studies in the European Community Databank Project Report.

BELHA2

Les Cahiers du Grif/GRACE
(Education/General)
    29 rue Blanche
    1050 BRUSSELS
☎   02 538 84 87
☐ First published 1974. Feminist reviews and European women's studies databank (GRACE).

Canada

CANHA1

Canadian Feminist Periodical Index 1972–1985
(Literature)
    OISE
    252 Bloor Street West
    Toronto
    ONTARIO M5S 1V5
Price: CAN$85.00
☐ First published 1991. Indexes fifteen English and French Canadian feminist periodicals published between 1972 and 1985. Contains over 14,000 records and provides access by subject, author and title.

CANHA2

Canadian Women in History: A chronology
(History)
    OISE
    252 Bloor Street West
    Toronto
    ONTARIO M5S 1V5
Price: CAN$25.00
☐ Written by Moira Armour and Pat Staton. Significant historical details relevant to Canadian women's studies.

CANHA3

Canadian Women's Directory (General)
    Communiqu'Elles
    3585 St Urbain Street
    Montreal
    QUEBEC H2X 2N6
☎   514 844 1761
Price: CAN$10.95
Pub. frequency: annual
☐ Lists over 3,000 women's organisations in every region of Canada.

CANHA4

Canadian Women's Periodical Index
(Literature/General)
> 11019–90 Avenue
> University of Alberta
> Edmonton
> ALBERTA T6G 2E1
☎ 403 492 3093
Subscriptions: CAN$30.00
Pub. frequency: three per annum
☐ First published 1984. The text is in English and French.

CANHA5

Directory of Women in Canada Specializing in Global Issues, A (General/ International)
> The Women's Directory Project
> Council for International Co-operation
> CRIAW
> Suite 408, 151 Slater Street
> ONTARIO K1P 5H3
☐ Profiles of women of distinction, statistics, resources and national advisory and editorial committees.

CANHA6

Feminism and Education: A Canadian perspective (Education/General)
> Publications Committee
> Centre for WS in Education
> OISE, 252 Bloor St West
> Toronto
> ONTARIO M5S 1V5
☎ 416 923 6641

CANHA7

Making a World of Difference
(General/International)
> Women's Directory Project
> Canadian Council for International Co-operation
> CRIAW
> Suite 408, 151 Slater Street
> OTTAWA K1P 5H3
☐ A directory of women in Canada which specialises in global issues.

CANHA8

Montreal Women's Directory/Annuaire des Femmes de Montreal (General)
> Eds. Communiqu'Elles
> 3585 St Urbain Street
> Montreal
> QUEBEC H2X 2N6
☎ 514 844 1761

Price: CAN$19.95
Pub. frequency: annual
☐ First published 1973. A directory of services, groups and resources for women living in and around Montreal.

CANHA9

RFR/DRF: Resources for feminist research/doc. sur la recherche féministe
(Education/International)
> Ontario Institute for Studies in Education
> 252 Bloor Street West
> Toronto
> ONTARIO M5S 1V6
☎ 416 923 6641
Subscriptions: CAN$26.75
Pub. frequency: quarterly
☐ First published 1979. A women's studies reference source. International information: research in progress, new publications, conferences and lists of organisations. Book reviews, bibliographies and periodicals guide.

Chile

CHIHA1

Isis International Women's Data Base (General)
> Isis International
> Casilla 2067
> Correo Central 2067
> SANTIAGO
☐ First published 1988. This is a printed publication containing bibliographic citations with abstracts and has five indexes: thematic, individual author, geographic area, conferences and a list of over 500 periodicals.

Finland

FINHA1

Research on Women from Finland
> Council for Equality
> Box 267
> 00171 HELSINKI
☎ 0 160 5705
Contact: Liisa Husu
☐ First published 1993. Written in English, the handbook lists articles and books (published in non-Nordic languages) written by Finnish women.

France

FRHA1

Archives, Recherches et Cultures Lesbiennes Bulletin (Lesbian)
> BP 362
> 75526 PARIS 11

☎   48 05 25 89
Subscriptions: FF100.00 (for two years)
Pub. frequency: half-yearly
☐ First published 1984.

FRHA2

Bulletin du CRIF   (General)
CRIF
1 rue Fosses-St-Jacques
75005 PARIS
Pub. frequency: quarterly
☐ A 'current awareness' bulletin which reproduces the contents pages of a worldwide range of feminist periodicals.

Germany

GERHA1

Changing Role of Women in Society, The (General)
Akademie-Verlag
BERLIN
☐ By Werner Richter, Liisa Husu and Arnaud Marks. Second edition 1989. Lists over 700 research projects under 14 subject headings.

GERHA2

Frauen Informations Blatt   (Education/General)
Zentraleinrichtung zur Förderung
Frauenstudien/Frauenfors
Königin-Luise-Strasse 34
1000 BERLIN 33
☎   030 838 6254
Pub. frequency: annual
☐ Lists conferences, book reviews and (mostly German) meetings.

GERHA3

Frauenfrage in Deutschland, Die: Bibliographie (Education/Literature)
KG Saur Verlag KG
Ortlerstrasse 8
Postfach 701620
8000 MUNICH 70
☎   089 769020
Price: varies
Pub. frequency: irregular
☐ First published 1951. Lists women's studies titles written in German and those in other languages related to women in Germany.

Great Britain and Northern Ireland

GBHA1

Annotated Bibliography of Feminist Criticism, An   (General)
Harvester Press
c/o Harvester Wheatsheaf
Campus 400
Maylands Avenue
HEMEL HEMPSTEAD HP2 7EZ
☎   0442 881900
☐ First published 1987. Written by Maggie Humm.

GBHA2

Bloomsbury Guide to Women's Literature (Literature)
Bloomsbury Publishing
2 Soho Square
LONDON W1V 5DE
☎   071 494 2111
Price: £25.00
☐ First published 1992. Edited by Claire Buck.

GBHA3

Contemporary Feminist Thought   (Methodology/Philosophy)
George Allen & Unwin
c/o HarperCollins Ltd
77–85 Fulham Palace Road
LONDON W6 8JB
☎   081 741 7070
☐ First published 1984. Written by H. Eisenstein.

GBHA4

Everywoman Directory, The: Women's businesses, networks and campaigns   (General)
Everywoman Publishing Ltd
34 Islington Green
LONDON N1 8DU
☎   071 359 5496
Contact: Barbara Rogers
Pub. frequency: annual
☐ 'The Handbook of the Women's Movement.' Lists names and addresses of businesses owned and run by women. Compiled by Barbara Rogers and Chris George.

GBHA5

Feminism, Culture and Politics   (Socialism/Culture)
Lawrence & Wishart
144A Old South Lambeth Road
LONDON SW8 1XX
☎   071 820 9281
☐ First published 1982. Edited by R. Brunt.

GBHA6

Feminist Periodicals 1855–1984: An annotated bibliography (Literature/General)
    Harvester Press
    c/o Harvester Wheatsheaf
    Campus 400
    Maylands Avenue
    HEMEL HEMPSTEAD HP2 7EZ
☎ 0442 881900
☐ First published 1987. Compiled by David Doughan and Denise Sanchez. The subtitle is 'An annotated bibliography of British, Irish, Commonwealth and international titles', and the focus is on British journals and magazines.

GBHA7

Feminist Theory (Methodology/Education)
    Harvester Press
    c/o Harvester Wheatsheaf
    Campus 400
    Maylands Avenue
    HEMEL HEMPSTEAD HP2 7EZ
☎ 0442 881900
☐ First published 1982. Edited by N. O. Keohane and others.

GBHA8

Framing Feminism (Methodology/Philosophy)
    Routledge & Kegan Paul
    c/o Routledge
    11 New Fetter Lane
    LONDON EC4P 4EE
☎ 071 583 9855
☐ First published 1987. Edited by R. Parker and G. Pollock.

GBHA9

French Feminist Thought
(Methodology/Philosophy)
    Basil Blackwell
    c/o Blackwell Publishers
    108 Cowley Road
    OXFORD OX4 1JF
☎ 0865 791100
☐ First published 1987. Edited by T. Moi.

GBHA10

Gaia's Guide (Lesbian/International)
    11 Worthington Street
    LONDON WC1
Price: £9.50
Pub. frequency: annual
☐ First published 1973. An international guidebook for lesbians. It lists bars, clubs, publications, centres, switchboards and bookstores.

GBHA11

Half the Earth: Women's experience of travel worldwide (Travel)
    Pandora Press
    c/o HarperCollins Ltd
    77–85 Fulham Palace Road
    LONDON W6 8JB
☐ First published 1976. By Miranda Davies and others. Countries are listed, including contacts, accommodation and other travel notes listed under each country.

GBHA12

Handbook for Women Travellers (Travel)
    Piatkus Books
    5 Windmill Street
    LONDON W1P 1HF
☐ First published 1987. By Maggie Moss and Gemma Moss. Information about all aspects of travelling, particularly in the Third World.

GBHA13

Knowledge Explosion, The: Generations of feminist scholarship (Education/General)
    Harvester Wheatsheaf
    Campus 400
    Maylands Avenue
    HEMEL HEMPSTEAD HP2 7EZ
☎ 0442 881900
☐ First published outside of North America 1993. Edited by Cheris Kramarae and Dale Spender. See also USAHA32.

GBHA14

Out on the Shelves: Lesbian books into libraries (Lesbian)
    AAL Publishing
    NEWCASTLE-UNDER-LYME
☐ First published 1989. Written by Jane Allen and others. Based on the idea that 'everybody should be able to read about their own lives in books supplied by libraries'.

GBHA15

Oxford Guide to British Women Writers, The (Literature)
    Oxford University Press
    Walton Street
    OXFORD OX2 6DP
☎ 0865 56767
☐ By Joanne Shaltock. First published 1993. Over 400 entries 'from Aphra Behn to Jeanette Winterson.'

GBHA16

Papers on Patriarchy (General)
    Women's Publishing Collective
    LEWES
☐ First published 1976.

GBHA17

Radical Bookseller Directory, The
(Literature/Media)
    265 Seven Sisters Road
    LONDON N4 2DE
Contact: Fergus Nicol
Pub. frequency: annual
□ Not only for women. Has a list of British feminist periodicals.

GBHA18

Sexual Meanings: The cultural construction of gender and sexuality (Sex and gender/Social sciences)
    Cambridge University Press
    The Edinburgh Building
    Shaftesbury Road
    CAMBRIDGE CB2 2RU
☎ 0223 312393
□ First published 1981. Edited by S. Ortner and H. Whitehead.

GBHA19

Studies on Women Abstracts (General)
    Carfax Publishing Co.
    PO Box 25
    ABINGDON, OX14 3UE
☎ 0235 555335
Contact: Jane Purvis
Subscriptions: £68.00
Pub. frequency: bi-monthly
□ First published 1983. An international abstracting service for librarians and teachers, students and researchers of women's studies subjects. Theoretical and empirical materials are covered. Free inspection copy on request.

GBHA20

Theories of Women's Studies
(Education/General)
    Routledge & Kegan Paul
    c/o Routledge
    11 New Fetter Lane
    LONDON EC4P 4EE
☎ 071 583 9855
□ First published 1983. Edited by G. Bowles and Renate Duelli Klein.

GBHA21

What is Feminism? (General)
    Blackwell Publishers
    108 Cowley Road
    OXFORD OX4 1JF
☎ 0865 791100
□ First published 1986. Edited by J. Mitchell and Ann Oakley.

GBHA22

Women 1870–1928: A select guide to printed and archival sources in the UK (General)
    Mansell Publishing Ltd
    c/o Cassell
    Villiers House
    41–47 Strand
    LONDON WC2N 5JE
☎ 071 839 4900
□ First published 1980.

GBHA23

Women and Society (Social sciences)
    Virago Press
    Centro House
    20–23 Mandela Street
    LONDON NW1 0HQ
☎ 071 383 5150
□ First published 1981. Edited by the Cambridge Women's Studies Group.

GBHA24

Women Going Places (Lesbian/Travel)
    The Business Factory
    15a Norfolk Place
    LONDON W2 1QJ
☎ 071 706 2434
Pub. frequency: annual
□ International lesbian/women's travel guide.

GBHA25

Women in British Humanities Index
(Education/Literature)
    Bowker-Saur Ltd
    59–60 Grosvenor Street
    LONDON W1X 9DA
☎ 071 493 5841
Subscriptions: £35.00
Pub. frequency: quarterly
□ First published 1989. Selected reports from the British Humanities Index of specific interest to those studying women's studies.

GBHA26

Women in Developing Countries: A select annotated bibliography (Development)
    Institute of Development Studies
    University of Sussex
    BRIGHTON
□ First published 1988. Written by Janet Townsend. A selection of 524 items, organised by country and grouped by continent.

GBHA27

Women's Movements of the World   (General)
> Longman
> Longman House
> Burnt Mill
> HARLOW CM20 2JE
☎ 0279 426721
☐ First published 1988.

GBHA28

Women's Rights: A practical guide   (Civil rights)
> Penguin Books
> Bath Road
> HARMONDSWORTH UB7 0DA
☐ By Anna Coote and Tess Gill. Third edition 1981. A guide to women's rights in the UK, arranged in sections.

GBHA29

Women's Studies (British Library Occasional Papers no. 12)   (Education/General)
> British Library
> Great Russell Street
> LONDON WC1B 3DG
☐ First published 1989. Compiled by Albertine Gaur and Penelope Tuson. Papers produced for a Colloquium of Resources for Women's Studies held on 4 April 1989.

GBHA30

Women's Studies: A bibliography of dissertations 1870–1982   (Education/General)
> Blackwell Publishers
> 108 Cowley Road
> OXFORD OX4 1JF
☎ 0865 791100
☐ First published 1985.

GBHA31

Women's Studies: A guide to information sources   (Education/International)
> Mansell Publishing Ltd
> c/o Cassell
> Villiers House
> 41–47 Strand
> LONDON WC2N 5JE
☎ 071 839 4900
☐ First published 1990, 'for all those people engaged in teaching and research, and all those students who choose to write essays and dissertations on the subject of women'. The authors are Sarah Carter and Maureen Ritchie.

Japan

JAPHA1

Joseigaku Nenpou   (Education/International)
> 10–28 Youzei
> Momoyama-cho
> Fushimi-ku
> KYOTO 612
☎ 075 601 0685
Contact: Ogino Miho
Price: Yen1000
Pub. frequency: annual
☐ First published 1979. Annual report of Women's Studies Society. International coverage of current events in women's studies with an emphasis on women in Japan.

JAPHA2

Joseishigaku   (History)
> Kagoshima University of Economics
> 8850 Shimohukumoto-cho
> KAGOSHIMA 891 01
☎ 0992 65 5112
Contact: Dr Noguchi Minoru
Price: Yen1000
Pub. frequency: annual
☐ First published 1991. The annals of women's history. Sets out the history of women in Japan and China in articles, essays and book reviews. Also included are conference reports and academic trends. English abstracts.

Netherlands

NETHA1

All'erta   (Education/General)
> International Informatiecentrum en Archief voor de Vrouwen
> Keizersgracht 10
> 1015 CN AMSTERDAM
☎ 020 624 42 68
Pub. frequency: quarterly
☐ References in current and recently completed Dutch women's studies research.

NETHA2

Best Guide to Amsterdam and the Benelux (Lesbian/Travel)
> Eden Cross
> PO Box 12731
> 1100 AS AMSTERDAM
☎ 020 699 15 83
☐ First published 1986. Not only for women. A tourist guide to Amsterdam, the Netherlands and some cities in Belgium for lesbians and gays. English text. Summaries in English, French and German. City maps.

NETHA3

GIDS (General)
> International Informatiecentrum en Archief voor
> de Vrouwen
> Keizersgracht 10
> 1015 CN AMSTERDAM
> ☎ 020 624 42 68

☐ First published 1992. A guide to women's archives, libraries and documentation centres in the Netherlands. From the International Information Centre and Archives for the Women's Movement.

NETHA4

Lesbisch Archivaria (Lesbian)
> Anna Blaman House
> Zuidvliet 118
> PO Box 4062
> 8901 EB LEEUWARDEN
> ☎ 058 12 18 29

Pub. frequency: irregular
☐ First published 1982.

NETHA5

Lover: Literatuuroverzicht voor de vrouwenbeweging (Literature)
> International Informatiecentrum en Archief voor
> de Vrouwen
> Keizersgracht 10
> 1015 CN AMSTERDAM
> ☎ 020 624 42 68

Subscriptions: fl28.50
Pub. frequency: quarterly
☐ First published 1974. A literary review. Articles on current themes. Reviews of national and international periodicals. Annotated bibliography of recent Dutch, French, German and English publications. Summaries in English.

NETHA6

Overzicht van de Archieven (General)
> International Informatiecentrum en Archief voor
> de Vrouwen
> Keizersgracht 10
> 1015 CN AMSTERDAM
> ☎ 020 624 42 68

☐ First published 1991. A survey of the archives in the International Information Centre and Archives for the Women's Movement in Amsterdam. It details 100 archives, describes 88 women and lists 127 unpublished documents.

Norway

NORHA1

Women's Research Literature from Norway
(Literature)
> Secretariat for Women and Research
> The Research Council of Norway
> Sandakerveien 99
> 0483 OSLO
> ☎ 22 15 70 12

Contact: Tove Beate Pedersen
☐ First published 1992. Written in English, the handbook lists papers and books written by Norwegian women.

Portugal

PORHA1

Portugal. Comissão Para a Igualdade e Direitos das Mulheres (General)
> Informacão Bibliografica
> Avenida da Republica 32–1
> 1093 LISBON
> ☎ 01 797 6081

Pub. frequency: bi-monthly
☐ First published 1976.

Sweden

SWEHA1

Ny Litteratur om Kvinnor: En bibliografi
(Literature)
> Göteborg University Library
> Kvinnohist. Samlingarna
> Centralbiblioteket
> PO Box 5096
> 40222 GOTHENBURG

Subscriptions: Skr170
Pub. frequency: quarterly
☐ First published 1980. A bibliography of new literature about women. The text is in both Swedish and English.

Switzerland

SWIHA1

International Women and Health Resource Guide (Health/Education)
> Isis-Wicce
> 3 chemin des Campanules
> 1219 Aire
> GENEVA
> ☎ 022 796 4437

Contact: Valse Verghese

☐ First published 1980. An annotated guide to materials and resources.

SWIHA2

Women in Development: A resource guide for organisation and 'action   (International/Third world)
> Isis Women's International Information
> Intermediate Technology Publishers
> 3 chemin des Campanules
> 1219 Aire
> GENEVA
> ☎ 022 796 4437

☐ First published 1983. The handbook focuses on multinationals, rural development, health, education, communication, migration and tourism as seen from a feminist perspective.

United States of America

USAHA1

A Different Light Review: A catalog of gay and lesbian literature   (Lesbian/Literature)
> A Different Light Bookstores
> 548 Hudson Street
> NEW YORK, NY 10014
> ☎ 212 989 4850

Price: free
Pub. frequency: three per annum
☐ First published 1979. Not only for women. A review of lesbian and gay literature and descriptions of newly published titles.

USAHA2

Age Discrimination   (Law/Older women)
> Shepard's – McGraw-Hill Inc.
> Box 35300
> COLORADO SPRINGS, CO 80935–3530
> ☎ 800 525 2474

☐ Not only for women. 4 volumes. Annotations of more than 3,200 cases and hundreds of statutory and regulatory provisions.

USAHA3

Battered Women's Directory   (Abuse/Civil rights)
> 2702 Fairlawn Road
> DURHAM, NC 27705–2774

Contact: Terry Mehlman
Price: $12.00
Pub. frequency: irregular
☐ First published 1975.

USAHA4

Bibliographies and Indexes in Women's Studies   (Education/General)
> Greenwood Press Inc.
> 88 Post Road West
> PO Box 5007
> WESTPORT, CT 06881–5007
> ☎ 203 226 3571

Price: varies
Pub. frequency: irregular
☐ First published 1984.

USAHA5

Bibliography of Bibliographies, A
(Education/General)
> G. K. Hall
> BOSTON, MA

☐ Second edition 1987. Compiled by Patricia K. Ballou. There are 906 entries with name, title and subject indexes.

USAHA6

Black Lesbians: An annotated bibliography
(Black women/Lesbian)
> Naiad Press
> TALLAHASSEE, FL

☐ First published 1981. Written by J. R. Roberts.

USAHA7

Building Women's Studies Collections: A resource guide   (Education/General)
> Choice Publications
> MIDDLETOWN, CT

☐ First published 1987. Compiled by Joan Ariel. The guide gathers together lists of feminist publishers, publishers with women's studies lists, working papers and reports, bookstores, databases and many other resources.

USAHA8

Canadian Feminist Periodicals: A directory
(Literature)
> Women's Studies Librarian
> 430 Memorial Library
> 728 State Street
> MADISON, WI 53760
> ☎ 608 263 5754

Contact: Linda Shult
☐ First published 1986. Compiled by Eleanor Wachtel.

USAHA9

Community Yellow Pages   (Lesbian)
> 2305 Canyon Drive
> LOS ANGELES, CA 90068-2411
> ☎ 213 469 4454

Price: free
Pub. frequency: annual

☐ First published 1982. Not only for women. Directory of organisations, business and professional services owned, operated and staffed by lesbians and gays which welcome lesbians and gays.

USAHA10

Contributions in Women's Studies
(Education/General)
    Greenwood Press Inc.
    88 Post Road West
    Box 5007
    WESTPORT, CT 06881-9990
☎   203 226 3571
Price: varies
Pub. frequency: irregular
☐ First published 1978.

USAHA11

Damron Road Atlas   (Lesbian/Travel)
    PO Box 42-2458
    SAN FRANCISCO, CA 94142-2458
☎   415 255 0404
Price: $12.00
☐ First published 1989. Not only for women. Atlas for lesbians and gays highlighting lesbian and gay locations and tourist attractions.

USAHA12

Directory of Homosexual Organizations and Publications   (Lesbian/General)
    Homosexual Information Center
    115 Monroe Street
    BOSSIER CITY, LA 71111
☎   318 742 4709
Price: $6.00
Pub. frequency: irregular
☐ Not only for women. Guide to 'the homosexual movement in the US'. Access to sources and services.

USAHA13

Directory of Women Historians   (History)
    American Historical Association
    WASHINGTON, DC
☐ First published 1975. Compiled by Joyce Allen Justice. A list of women historians, giving details of their positions, special interests and publications. A supplement was issued in 1976.

USAHA14

Directory of Women in Environment
(Environment)
    World Wide Network
    Suite 903
    1331 H Street NW
    WASHINGTON, DC 20005
Price: $17.50
Pub. frequency: annual

☐ First published 1989. Lists almost 1,000 women in over 95 countries working in related fields. The publication is intended to encourage global networking.

USAHA15

Directory of Women's Media   (Media)
    Women's Institute for Freedom of Press
    3306 Ross Place NW
    WASHINGTON, DC 20008
Pub. frequency: annual
☐ First published 1972. Includes a list of women's periodicals around the world as well as lists of presses, publishers, news services, media organisations and bookstores.

USAHA16

DWM: A Directory of Women's Media   (Media)
    National Council for Research on Women
    47–49 East 65th Street
    NEW YORK, NY 10021
Price: $30.00
☐ First published 1992. Compiled by Dawn Henry.

USAHA17

Encyclopedia of Feminism   (General)
    Facts on File Publications
    460 Park Avenue South
    NEW YORK, NY 10016
☐ First published 1986. Compiled by Lisa Tuttle. A survey of the feminist movement mainly in the UK and USA.

USAHA18

Feminism and Philosophy   (Philosophy)
    Littlefield, Adams
    TOTOWA, NJ
☐ First published 1977. Edited by M. Vetterling-Braggin.

USAHA19

Feminist Criticism   (General)
    Pantheon Books
    Random House
    201 East 50th Street
    NEW YORK, NY 10022
☎   212 572 2600
☐ First published 1985. Edited by E. Showalter.

USAHA20

Feminist Research Methods: An annotated bibliography   (General)
    Greenwood Press Inc.
    88 Post Road West
    Box 5007
    WESTPORT, CT 06881-9990
Price: $45.00

☐ First published 1991. Written by Connie Miller with Corinna Treitel.

USAHA21

Feminist Spirituality and the Feminine Divine (Spirituality)
    Crossing Press
    TRUEMANSBURY, NY
☐ First published 1986. Compiled by Anne Carson. Over 700 entries with annotations.

USAHA22

Gayellow Pages (Lesbian/General)
    Renaissance House
    Box 292
    Village Station
    NEW YORK, NY 10014
☎   212 674 0120
Price: $12.00
Pub. frequency: annual
☐ First published 1973. Not only for women. Lists businesses, bars, entertainments and resources.

USAHA23

Goddesses and Wise Women (Spirituality)
    Crossing Press
    FREEDOM, CA
☐ First published 1992. Compiled by Anne Carson. The subtitle is 'The literature of feminist spirituality 1980–1992 – an annotated bibliography'.

USAHA24

Guide to Women's Art Organizations: Directory for the arts (Arts)
    Midmarch Arts Press
    300 Riverside Drive
    NEW YORK, NY 10025
☎   212 666 6990
Price: $8.50
Pub. frequency: irregular
☐ First published 1979.

USAHA25

Higher Education Opportunities for Minorities and Women (Education/Politics)
    US Department of Education
    WASHINGTON, DC 20202
Price: free
☐ Annotated selections.

USAHA26

International Directory of Gay and Lesbian Periodicals (Literature/General)
    Oryx Press
    PHOENIX, AZ

☐ First published 1987. Not only for women. Compiled by Robert H. Malinowsky. There is a subject/geographic index enabling all lesbian journals to be easily identified and also all feminist ones. There are 1924 lesbian and gay periodicals included.

USAHA27

International Guide to Lesbian and Feminist Periodicals (Lesbian/General)
    Tsunami
    PO Box 42282
    TUCSON, AZ 85733
Price: $7.00

USAHA28

International Women's Writing Guild Yearbook (Literature)
    International Women's Writing Guild
    Box 810
    Gracie Station
    NEW YORK, NY 10028
Price: $20
Pub. frequency: annual
☐ First published 1976.

USAHA29

Introduction to Library Research in Women's Studies (Education/General)
    Westview Press
    5500 Central Avenue
    BOULDER, CO 80301
☐ First published 1985. Written by Susan Searing. Part 1 is a guide to using a library. Part 2 is a description of reference works.

USAHA30

Journal of Women's History Guide to Periodical Literature (History)
    Journals Division
    Indiana University Press
    10th and Morton Streets
    BLOOMINGTON, IN 47405
☎   812 855 9449
Price: UK £30.00
☐ First published 1992. More than 5,000 historical articles drawn from over 750 journals. All are extensively cross-referenced.

USAHA31

Key International Guide (Lesbian/Travel)
    House of Leehei
    PO Box 330406
    Coconut Grove
    FLORIDA, FL 33233
Price: $8.95
Pub. frequency: annual

□ First published 1984. Not only for women. Contains a worldwide listing of travel accommodations of interest to lesbians and gays.

USAHA32

Knowledge Explosion, The: Generations of feminist scholarship   (Education/General)
Pergamon Press
ELMSFORD, NY
□ First published 1992. Edited by Cheris Kramarae and Dale Spender.

USAHA33

Lesbian Studies Present and Future   (Lesbian)
Feminist Press
OLD WESTBURY, NY
□ First published 1982. Written by Margaret Cruik-shank. It covers the academic world, schools, research and documentation.

USAHA34

Lesbianism: An annotated bibliography   (Lesbian)
Scarecrow
METHUEN, NJ
□ First published 1988. Written by Dolores J. Maggiore. An annotated bibliography and guide to the literature 1976–86. There are some 350 publications and organisations listed, and it is primarily for social workers.

USAHA35

Madison Gay Lesbian Resource Center Directory   (Lesbian)
Madison Gay Lesbian Resource Center
PO Box 1722
MADISON, WI 53701
Price: free
Pub. frequency: annual
□ First published 1988. Not only for women.

USAHA36

Michigan Feminist Studies   (General)
234 West Engineering Building
ANN ARBOR, MI 48109-1090
Price: $7.00

USAHA37

NAACOG's Women's Health Nursing Scan   (Health)
Nursecom Inc.
1211 Locust Street
PHILADELPHIA, PA 19107
☎ 215 545 7222
Subscriptions: $35.00
Pub. frequency: bi-monthly
□ First published 1987. Abstracts from multidisciplinary literature on topics in women's health nursing.

USAHA38

National Directory of Women-Owned Business Firms   (Paid work)
Business Research Services
Suite 202
2 East 22nd Street
LOMBARD, IL 60148
☎ 312 495 8787
Price: $195.00
Pub. frequency: annual
□ First published 1986. Lists 25,000 women-owned firms in the USA.

USAHA39

Nature of Women, The: An encyclopaedia and guide to the literature   (General)
Edgepress
INVERNESS, CA
□ First published 1980. Compiled by Mary Anne Warren. An alphabetical list of authors and topics. It includes bibliographical references.

USAHA40

New Books on Women & Feminism   (Literature)
University of Wisconsin System
430 Memorial Library
728 State Street
MADISON, WI 53706
☎ 608 263 5754
Contact: Susan Searing
Subscriptions: $23.00
Pub. frequency: half-yearly
□ First published 1979. A subject-arranged, indexed bibliography of new titles in women's studies, listing books and periodicals.

USAHA41

New Feminist Scholarship: A checklist of bibliographies   (Education/General)
Feminist Press
OLD WESTBURY, NY
□ First published 1979. Written by Jane Williamson. Contains nearly 400 entries. Mostly US or Canadian publications.

USAHA42

New Reference Works in Women's Studies (Literature)
Women's Studies Librarian
430 Memorial Library
728 State Street
MADISON, WI 53706
☎ 608 263 5754
Contact: Linda Shult
Pub. frequency: annual
□ Compiled by Susan Searing.

USAHA43

Northwest Gay Guide: Directory of gay–lesbian businesses (Lesbian)
One in Ten Publishing Co.
PO Box 23070
SEATTLE, WA 98102
☎ 206 323 7374
Pub. frequency: annual
☐ Not only for women.

USAHA44

Odysseus: An accommodation and travel guide for the gay community (Lesbian/Travel)
Odysseus Enterprises
PO Box 1548
PORT WASHINGTON, NY 11050
☎ 516 944 5330
Price: $18.00
Pub. frequency: annual
☐ First published 1985. Not only for women. An international accommodation and travel guide for lesbians and gays. There is information about hotels, bed and breakfast accommodation and resorts all over the world.

USAHA45

Our Bodies, Ourselves (Health)
Simon & Schuster
1230 Avenue of Americas
NEW YORK, NY 10020
☎ 212 698 7000
☐ First published 1971. Compiled by the Boston Women's Health Collective. There have been many subsequent editions since this handbook was first published.

USAHA46

Performing Woman: A national directory of professional women musicians (Arts)
J. D. Dinneen
21910 Grand View Avenue
HAYWARD, CA 94542
Price: $5.00
Pub. frequency: annual
☐ First published 1978.

USAHA47

Politics of Women's Spirituality, The
(Spirituality)
Anchor Press
c/o Bantam Doubleday
666 Fifth Avenue
NEW YORK, NY 10103
☎ 212 765 6500
☐ First published 1982. Written by C. Spretnak. The subtitle is 'Essays on the rise of spiritual power within the feminist movement'.

USAHA48

Radical Feminism   (Radical feminism)
Quadrangle Books
NEW YORK, NY
☐ First published 1973. Edited by A. Koedt.

USAHA49

Sage Yearbooks in Women's Policy Studies
(General)
Sage Publications Inc.
2455 Teller Road
NEWBURY PARK, CA 91320
☎ 805 499 0721
Price: $17.95
Pub. frequency: annual
☐ First published 1976.

USAHA50

Selected Bibliography of Homosexuality
(Lesbian)
Homosexual Information Center
115 Monroe Street
BOSSIER CITY, LA 71111
☎ 318 742 4709
Price: 50 cents
Pub. frequency: irregular

USAHA51

Sisterhood is Powerful   (General)
Vintage Books
c/o Random House
201 East 50th Street
NEW YORK, NY 10022
☎ 212 572 2600
☐ First published 1970. Edited by Robin Morgan.

USAHA52

Statistical Record of Women Worldwide   (Equal opportunities/International)
Gale Research Inc.
PO Box 33477
DETROIT, MI 48332-5477
☐ Surveys the status of women around the world. Some 800 detailed statistical tables from hundreds of published and unpublished US and international sources.

USAHA53

Wisconsin Women Writers of Adult Fiction and Poetry 1962–1982   (Literature)
Women's Studies Librarian
430 Memorial Library
728 State Street
MADISON, WI 53706
☐ Written by Maureen Welch.

USAHA54

Woman's Encyclopedia of Myths and Secrets, The (Spirituality)
Harper & Row
c/o HarperCollins
10 East 53rd Street
NEW YORK, NY 10022
☎ 212 207 700
☐ First published 1983. Written by Barbara Walker.

USAHA55

Womanspirit Rising (Spirituality)
Harper & Row
c/o HarperCollins
10 East 53rd Street
NEW YORK, NY 10022
☎ 212 207 7000
☐ First published 1979. Edited by Carol Christ and Judith Plaskow.

USAHA56

Women: A world survey (General)
World Priorities
PO Box 25104
WASHINGTON, DC 20007
☎ 202 965 1661
Price: $6.00
Pub. frequency: irregular
☐ First published 1985. By Ruth Leger Sivard. Provides statistical and factual information on the situation of women today.

USAHA57

Women and Information Technology: A selective bibliography (Technology)
Women's Studies Librarian
430 Memorial Library
728 State Street
MADISON, WI 53706
☎ 608 263 5754
Contact: Linda Shult
☐ First published 1984. Compiled by Linda Shult.

USAHA58

Women and International Development Annual (International/Third world)
Westview Press
5500 Central Avenue
BOULDER, CO 80301
☎ 303 444 3541
Subscriptions: $25.00
Pub. frequency: annual
☐ First published 1989.

USAHA59

Women and Philosophy: Toward a theory of liberation (Philosophy)
G. P. Putnam
c/o Putnam Publishing
200 Madison Avenue
NEW YORK, NY 10016
☎ 212 951 8400
☐ First published 1976. Edited by C. C. Gould.

USAHA60

Women and Power: A bibliography of feminist writings (Literature/General)
Women's Studies Librarian
430 Memorial Library
728 State Street
MADISON, WI 53706
☎ 608 263 5754
Contact: Susan Searing
☐ First published 1983. Compiled by Susan Searing.

USAHA61

Women and Science: Issues and resources (Sciences)
Women Studies Librarian
430 Memorial Library
728 State Street
MADISON, WI 53706
☐ Originally compiled by Susan Searing. Phyllis Holman Weisbard revised the sixth edition.

USAHA62

Women and Work (Newbury Park) (Paid work)
Sage Publications
2455 Teller Road
NEWBURY PARK, CA 91320
☎ 805 499 0721
Price: $36.00
Pub. frequency: annual
☐ First published 1985.

USAHA63

Women and World Literature (Literature)
Women's Studies Librarian
430 Memorial Library
728 State Street
MADISON, WI 53706
☎ 608 263 5754
Contact: Linda Shult
☐ First published 1992. Compiled by Carolyn J. Kruse. The subtitle is 'A bibliography of anthologies of women's literature in translation'.

USAHA64

Women, Culture and Society (Social sciences)
Stanford University Press
STANFORD, CA 94305-2235

☎ 415 723 9598
☐ First published 1974. Edited by M. Rosaldo and L. Lamphere.

USAHA65

Women, Households and Change (General)
United Nations Publications
Sales Section Room
DC2-0853, Dept 798
NEW YORK, NY 10017
☎ 212 963 8302
Price: $45.00

USAHA66

Women in Broadcast Technology Directory (Media)
2435 Spaulding Street
BERKELEY, CA 94703
☎ 415 540 8640
Price: $15.00
Pub. frequency: annual
☐ First published 1984.

USAHA67

Women in Decision-Making (General)
United Nations Publications
Sales Section Room
DC2-0853, Dept 798
NEW YORK, NY 10017
☎ 212 963 8302
Price: see below
☐ There are three separate publications, on Sweden, Costa Rica and Greece, costing $27, $12 and $10, respectively.

USAHA68

Women in LC's Terms (Language)
Oryx Press
PHOENIX, AZ
☐ First published 1988. Compiled by Ruth Dickstein, Victoria A. Mills and Ellen J. Waite. Lists all the headings and cross references (over 3,500) which relate to women.

USAHA69

Women in Politics and Decision-Making (Politics)
United Nations Publications
Sales Section Room
DC2-0853, Dept 798
NEW YORK, NY 10017
☎ 212 963 8302
☐ First published 1992.

USAHA70

Women of Mathematics: A bibliographic sourcebook (Sciences)
Greenwood
NEW YORK, NY
☐ First published 1987. Essays on 43 mathematicians, excluding anyone born after 1925. Each entry has a biographical section, a description of the author's work and a bibliography.

USAHA71

Women, Race and Ethnicity: A bibliography (General)
University of Wisconsin System
430 Memorial Library
728 State Street
MADISON, WI 53706
☎ 608 263 5754
Contact: Linda Shult
Price: $7.00
☐ First published 1992. Includes over 2,400 annotated entries classified under 28 disciplines and topics. The work supersedes a preliminary version published in 1988.

USAHA72

Women Studies Abstracts (Education/General)
Rush Publishing Co.
PO Box 1
RUSH, NY 14543
☎ 716 624 4418
Contact: Sara Stauffer Whaley
Subscriptions: $56.00
Pub. frequency: quarterly
☐ First published 1972. Listings and abstracts from articles from women's studies publications.

USAHA73

Women-Identified Women (Radical feminism/Lesbian)
Mayfield
PALO ALTO, CA
☐ First published 1984. Edited by T. Darty and S. Potter.

USAHA74

Women's Computer Literacy Handbook, The (Technology)
New American Library
NEW YORK, NY
☐ First published 1985. Written by Deborah L. Brecher.

USAHA75

Women's History Resource Catalog (History)
National Women's History Project
7738 Bell Road
WINDSOR, CA 95492

☎   707 838 6000
Pub. frequency: annual
☐ A multicultural women's history resource.

USAHA76

Women's Music Plus: Directory of resources
(Arts/Culture)
Empty Closet Enterprises
5210 North Wayne
CHICAGO, IL 60640
☎   312 769 9009
Price: $10.00
Pub. frequency: annual
☐ First published 1977. The handbook provides contact information for women's music and culture. There are free listings, contacts and venues for performers.

USAHA77

Women's Organizations & Leaders Directory
(General)
Today Publications & News Services
621 National Press Building
WASHINGTON, DC 20045
☎   202 638 0348
Price: $65.00
Pub. frequency: annual
☐ First published 1973.

USAHA78

Women's Organizations: A national directory
(General)
Garrett Park Press
PO Box 1901B
GARRETT PARK, MD 20896
☎   301 946 2553
Price: $25.00
Pub. frequency: irregular
☐ First published 1986.

USAHA79

Women's Organizations: A New York City directory   (Paid work/Law)
Commission on the Status of Women
Room 209
52 Chambers Street
NEW YORK, NY 10007
☎   212 788 2738
Price: $6.95
Pub. frequency: irregular
☐ First published 1982. Annotated listing of nearly 500 women's business, professional and advocacy groups in New York City.

USAHA80

Women's Sphere, The: Rare and antiquarian books on women and gender   (Sex and gender)
Second Life Books' Catalogue No. 85
Second Life Books
55 Quarry Road
LANESBOROUGH, MA 01237
☐ First published 1992. Contains 920 listings.

USAHA81

Women's Studies: A recommended core bibliography 1980–1985
Libraries Unlimited
PO Box 263
LITTLETON, CO 80160-0263
☐ First published 1987. By Catherine R. Loeb, Susan E. Searing and Esther F. Stineman. Abstracts on over 100 texts. Also lists a few periodicals.

USAHA82

Women's Studies in Western Europe: A resource guide   (Education/General)
Association of College and Research Libraries
American Library Association
CHICAGO, IL
☐ First published 1986. In three sections: women's publishing, a survey of women's studies activities in western Europe, and an account of the Fawcett Library in London. By Stephen Lehmann and Eva Sartori.

USAHA83

Women's Studies in Wisconsin: Who's who & where   (Education/General)
University of Wisconsin
430 Memorial Library
728 State Street
MADISON, WI 53706
☎   608 253 5754
Contact: Linda Shult
☐ 'A biographical directory of librarians, faculties, students, and community representatives involved in women's studies in Wisconsin.'

USAHA84

Women's Studies Index (year)
(Education/General)
G. H. Hall & Co.
70 Lincoln Street
BOSTON, MA 02111
☎   617 423 3990
Price: $125.00
Pub. frequency: annual
☐ First published 1990. Articles are indexed covering a broad range of topics both in and relevant to the field of women's studies in over 100 journals ranging from popular magazines to scholarly journals.

USAHA85

Women's Yellow Pages   (General)
   PO Box 66093
   LOS ANGELES, CA 90066
☎   213 398 5761
Price: $5.95
Pub. frequency: annual
□ First published 1977.

USAHA86

Women's Yellow Pages Arizona   (General)
   Directories Ltd
   PO Box 15828
   PHOENIX, AZ 85060-5828
☎   602 230 8668
Price: $6.95
Pub. frequency: annual
□ First published 1975. A directory of women's businesses, services and professions.

USAHA87

Womensource: Women's books – women's presses   (Literature/Media)
   625 Heather Drive
   DAYTON, OH 45001

USAHA88

Words to the Wise   (Language/Literature)
   Firebrand Books
   ITHACA, NY
□ First published 1987. Written by Andrea Fleck Clardy. Lists of North American presses and periodicals. Aimed to help women to get their writing published.

USAHA89

World's Women 1970–1990: Trends and statistics   (General)
   United Nations Publications
   Sales Section Room
   DC2-0853, Dept 798
   NEW YORK, NY 10017
☎   212 963 8302
Price: $19.95

USAHA90

Yearbook of Women's Studies
(Education/General)
   Edwin Mellen Press
   240 Portage Road
   PO Box 450
   LEWISTON, NY 14902
☎   800 753 2788
Price: $19.15
Pub. frequency: annual

Form for new Handbook entries

If you would like your women's studies resource to be considered for inclusion in the next edition of this Handbook, please complete the form below and return it, or a photocopy, to: The Editor (WISH), Harvester Wheatsheaf, Campus 400, Maylands Avenue, Hemel Hempstead, Herts, HP2 7EZ.

1. Category: women's studies course   _____
   women's studies centre   _____
   training course   _____
   women's organisation   _____
   library or archive   _____
   journal   _____
   magazine   _____
   handbook   _____

2. Full name/title of resource:

_____

3. Contact address (including postcode):

_____

_____

_____

4. Full name of person to contact:

_____

5. Contact telephone number (including dialling code):

_____

6. Brief description* (no more than 50 words) of the resource your institution/organisation/company provides and its relevance to women's studies. Longer entries may be cut at the editor's discretion.

_____

_____

_____

I declare that the above information is correct and I authorise its inclusion in the next edition of WISH. I understand the entry is free.

_____   _____

Signature   Date

_____

Position

If you would like to order a copy of the Handbook, please put a tick in the box and we will send you a pro-forma invoice once a price has been set.

Harvester Wheatsheaf gives permission for the above form to be photocopied.

*For women's studies courses/centres include course title and qualification awarded; for training courses include course title; for journals or magazines include price per issue, subscription rate and publishing frequency.